We see the bright colors of the farmer's market, and smell the fresh vegetables. We hear the banter of carefree classmates. We feel the comfortable family relationships in an affluent family, and a child's confusion as those family bonds fray in the terror of a police state.

Helen Szablya gives us a front-row seat on a drama that still plays out today; the eternal hunger of individuals for freedom. We saw it play out again twenty years ago in Eastern Europe and we're seeing it play out again in the Middle East today. We can understand it better, and how to respond to it, if we read Helen Szablya's vivid recollections from inside the drama."

*Sheilah Kast, a journalist who covered the collapse of Soviet communism and is now host of "Maryland Morning" on WYPR, and her husband, State (MD) Sen. Jim Rosapepe, former U.S. ambassador to Romania (1998-2001), are co-authors of* Dracula Is Dead: How Romanians Survived Communism, Ended It, and Emerged Since 1989 as the New Italy

"Ms. Szablya's dramatic account of her younger years is an exceptionally touching one that moves you from the tense and fearful challenges of living in communist controlled Hungary to the relief and realization of her determined quest for freedom. One may never again take their freedoms for granted once they have read Consul General Szablya's inspiring story."

*Brad Owen, Lt. Governor of Washington State*

"The author is one of the unfortunate people who grew up in Hungary during WWII and the following years. During that time Hungary was invaded by two totalitarian countries: Nazi Germany and the communist Soviet Union. Partly through her and her family's experiences Helen Szablya vividly illustrates the inhumane treatment of people during fascist and communist rule; similar in many respects: military aggression, elimination of opponents, and hatred for selected groups of people. The author escaped to freedom after the failed Hungarian Revolution of 1956, when the brutal Soviet forces defeated the uprising. In the United States she found the freedom and democracy that she yearned for so much while living under totalitarian rules."

*Csaba Téglás, renowned architect, is the author of* Budapest Exit, A Memoire of Fascism, Communism, and Freedom

"A teenager's memories of the days in Stalin's red paradise describing her family's experiences during Hungary's holocaust after WWII"

*Béla Lipták, Professor Emeritus, Yale University, Chief co-author of the 16 points of the Hungarian Uprising of 1956, author of* A Testament of Revolution, *Editor of the* Engineers' Handbook, *and innumerable technical publications*

# MY ONLY CHOICE:
## *Hungary*
## *1942 – 1956*

*Helen, the author, and younger sisters Marie and Elisabeth, 1948*

# MY ONLY CHOICE:

## Hungary
## 1942 – 1956

To Alex our trusted friend

Helen Szablya

March 10, 2013.

Helen M. Szablya

My Only Choice: *Hungary 1942 – 1956*

ISBN: 978-1479210206

LCCN 2012924251
CreateSpace Independent Publishing Platform
North Charleston, SC

First Edition

～

## Also by Helen M. Szablya

In English:

> *The Fall of the Red Star* (first prizes from Washington Press Association and
> National Federation of Press Women)
> *Hungary Remembered* (an oral history drama) George Washington Honor
> Medal from the Freedoms Foundation and Gold Medal Hungarian
> Congress, Árpád Academy, Cleveland, Major Grant Washington
> Commission for the Humanities

Translation and collaborator for the English version:

> Ernest Töttösy's book *Téboly* Hungarian into English: *Mind Twisters*

In Hungarian:

> *A vörös csillag lehull* (grant by Ministry of Hungarian Heritage, Hungary)
> *56-os cserkészcsapat*
> *Emlékezünk* (an oral history drama as above)

～

Printed in the United States of America

*To the love of my life, my husband John;*
*And to God's great gifts to us,*
*The four generations of our family*

# *Foreword*

The greatest value a personal memoir of historic events provides is its instant credibility and context of reality. Helen Szablya's compelling family saga, *My Only Choice*, does exactly that. Through her family story she paints a vividly detailed picture about the daily lives and struggles of Hungarian citizens in the period between World War II and the Hungarian Revolution in 1956. For me, a fellow Hungarian American, discovering this book was truly a pleasure. Through Helen's writing some of the incredible stories told by my own parents suddenly came alive. But one certainly doesn't have to be Hungarian to appreciate this book; Helen's story will amaze and touch the imagination of all readers.

*My Only Choice* is infused with the special poignancy of a child's observations. Recently, Hungarian Foreign Minister János Martonyi introduced his own recollections of 1956, by saying: "I was twelve-and-a-half years old in 1956 – a kid who knew nothing and everything." Helen Szablya, too, was forced by history to know nothing and everything at an even younger age.

In the book she depicts the daily life of the well-to-do and highly principled Bartha-Kovács family and their wide circle of friends. As we observe their actions even under the most difficult circumstances, we see evidence of their patriotism, courage, family solidarity and deep faith. Throughout the years it is exactly these characteristics that enable them to survive the war and its brutal aftermath, the Soviet take-over of Hungary in 1948, the next eight years of communist dictatorship and the crushed hope of the 1956 Revolution and Freedom Fight.

Through the eyes of the nine-year-old Helen we gain insight into the fear and devastation caused by Russian and German troops in the 51 day-long siege of Budapest in 1944. We observe the superhuman efforts made by Helen's parents not only to assure their own family's survival, but to also provide safe shelter and food to many others, including Hungarian Jewish families, amidst the wide-spread hunger and deprivation of the post-war period.

Along with her personal recollections Helen Szablya also provides essential background information for readers unfamiliar with Hungarian history. This is especially useful in explaining how Hungary's Soviet "liberators" who first pretended to support political pluralism gradually showed their true intentions when they fixed the 1948 elections to assure communist rule. Thus, Hungary's fate was sealed. Thereafter, for eight years the Soviet dictatorship ruled with an iron fist as it nationalized all private property, arrested, tried and executed many Hungarians, attempted to destroy churches and turn education into indoctrination, infiltrated Hungarian society by creating a vast system of spies, forced the reorganization of an agrarian society into an industrial one, and introduced the system of "domestic deportation" of families considered "enemies of the people."

Because the Bartha-Kovács family certainly belonged to that category, they learned to deal with poverty and hunger and to protect each other against the increasingly harsh realities of life under Soviet rule.

But the Soviet system, as all dictatorships, contained the seeds of its own destruction. The death of Stalin in 1953 brought short-lived improvements in Hungary with the introduction of "communism with a human face." But soon thereafter, Moscow reasserted total control, causing grave dissatisfaction in Hungary and several neighboring Soviet-ruled countries.

The final chapters of *My Only Choice* describe Hungarian hopes for freedom and independence and the eventual tragic defeat of the 1956 Revolution. Although many fine books have been written about this subject, through her day-by-day description of dramatic events Helen Szablya does a masterful job of communicating the incredible excitement, the euphoric desire for freedom that Hungarians felt in those fateful twelve days, between October 23 and November 4, 1956. As she describes the hopes and eventual tragic defeat of the Revolution and her family's desperate attempts to escape to Austria, Helen Szablya tells a truly compelling story of universal significance.

Edith K. Lauer
*Chair Emerita, Hungarian American Coalition*
*Witness to the Hungarian Revolution*

# *Preface*

"It happened to me!" are the most powerful words in the human language. *My Only Choice* is the story of what happened to me! It is the pursuit of freedom as lived through my coming of age journey – a seven-year-old little girl who becomes a woman and mother in Hungary, 1942–1956.

Often I begin my lectures by asking: "What do you think Anne Franck would look like today?" Then I proceed to tell them that she would look and sound somewhat like me and, if she had lived in Hungary, whether she was Jewish or not, she would have been persecuted by the Communists, as she had been by the Nazis; two terrifying regimes in a row.

The history of the Victims of Communism is just as important as the history of Victims of the Holocaust. We have to work to ensure that neither extreme Left nor extreme Right should ever come to rule again. The only fit way for human beings to live is in freedom and democracy. We may criticize the construct of our government, but it is still the best there is on this earth. Let us cherish and defend it, lest we should be forced to re-live the lives of the less fortunate.

What better way to do this than learning from the experiences of those who can say: "I lived it. It happened to me!"

# Acknowledgments

There are so many people I need to thank and I do not want to leave out anyone. First of all I thank God for giving us these experiences and letting us live through them, so we can tell others about it. I thank all those who lived the story with me. My wonderful late husband John, (John F. Szablya, PhD., P.E.) who taught me, this sixteen-year-old, how to live a happy life, and was my equal and loving partner all through our 54-year honeymoon. Our love for each other helped us through every challenge coming our way.

I want to thank every one of my children with all the work they put into this book. Not one of them escaped editing and proofreading, but the heroes were my husband John, whose memories are incorporated in this book, Helen A. Szablya, Alexandra Szablya-Ramdin, Rita Pool and Niki McKay, my daughters and Kate Fowles Szablya, my daughter-in-law.

Thanks go to Edith Lauer, Founder and Chair Emerita of the Hungarian American Coalition, who wrote the excellent Foreword, and the Hungarian American Coalition's Board along with President Max Teleki for publicizing my book.

I am thankful to The American Hungarian Federation, Ferenc Koszorús Jr. and Bryan Dawson for offering my books through their website, and for having made me a featured member for a former book.

Thanks to Julia Bika (Nyugati Hírlevél) and the American Hungarian Journal in Los Angeles for publicizing my books.

The Hungarian American Association of Washington and the Seattle-Pécs Sister City Association are both a delight to work with. I look forward to their launching of the book for local Hungarians.

Thanks to all those who wrote pre-publication reviews: Dr. Géza Jeszenszky, former Minister of Foreign Affairs in Hungary, also Hungarian Ambassador to the USA and now to Oslo; Anne Applebaum, columnist for the *Washington Post*, author of *Gulag: A History*, and several other books; Charles Fenyvesi, former staff writer for the Washington Post, author of several books and plays; Sheilah Kast, journalist and author, host of "Maryland Morning" on WYPR, and her husband, State (MD) Sen. Jim Rosapepe, former U.S. ambassador to Romania (1998-2001) and author; Csaba Téglás, renowned architect and author of *Budapest Exit*; Béla Lipták P.E., chief co-author of the 16 points during the 1956 Uprising, Prof. Emeritus of Yale University, author of *A Testament to Revolution* and innumerable technical books and articles; Annette Lantos-Tilleman-Dick, daughter of Congressman Tom Lantos; and Brad Owen, Lt. Governor of Washington state, a great lover of Hungary.

I want to thank the Authors' Guild, especially Anita Fore, Director of Legal Services and Tibor Purger, Washington Bureau Chief of Duna TV and Director of Integrated Information Systems at Rutgers University, for giving me invaluable advice on publishing. Roz Noonan, author of many books was a great help, as was Paul Olchváry, Editor-In-Chief of New Europe Books.

I owe deep gratitude to the Spokane Writers' Club, a critique group that helped me from the first minute, especially the late Neta Lohnes Frazier who read and edited my book twice from beginning to end at an early stage.

Jennifer McCord and Sheryl Stebbins went through the entire book as well and helped with the website. I thank Molly Bullard and the Authors' Guild for establishing my website: www.helenmszablya.com

My heartfelt gratitude goes to Ann Marra who designed the book and Leann Rayfuse who did the copyediting.

# Introduction

To my dear friends, whose lives appear in this book: everything in the book is true. Thank you for living the book with me. However, to be historically more precise, I would like to tell you that your names have been changed in order to protect the innocent, as I started writing this autobiography in 1977. I also merged several similar characters into one character to make the story clearer, more understandable. May you enjoy reliving our lives by reading this book as much as I enjoyed writing it!

To my readers who are too young to remember any of these historical events: may you receive some insight into what it was like to live, feel, and survive when we were young.

Happy reading to All!

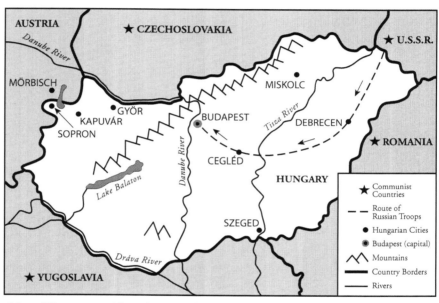

*Map of Hungary, 1956, with points of interest for the story.*

1

Budapest, Hungary, January 26, 1949

*Early Morning*

Thumps of heavy boots echoed through the staircase as the secret policeman pushed Mother down the stairs. She kept turning back. Her eyes searched mine. Our eyes locked and I felt her plea in my heart, "You will take care of them, won't you?" As her last desperate look reached me my whole being answered, "You can trust me!" I thought I saw her body relax as she suddenly changed her pace and hurried beside the thumping boots.

The police car door closed behind her. I stood dumbfounded for a minute, while my two sisters tugged at my sleeves. Tears were running down their cheeks and they hid their faces as they saw our mother for what might be the last time. Would I ever see her again?

"Will she come back, Helen? Will she?"

My fourteen-year-old heart throbbed in my throat. There was only one answer I could give them, "Of course she will come back!"

I turned around and made a quick decision. Mother had entrusted me with their lives. I was not going to let her down. I looked into Marie's dark brown eyes, into her round face that still had baby fat despite her teenaged features and at Elisabeth, the little one, with her wondering blue eyes. She did not understand anything. They *had* to go to school, it occurred to me. Today they would learn about the "liberation of the people" that we were going through. Right now we were being "liberated" from our mother. I clenched my fists and ground my teeth in helpless rage. "They should not, they cannot, notice that I too...." I did not want to finish the sentence, not even in my thoughts. I knew if I did, I too would break down. Right now I could not afford to let that happen.

I heard Grandfather shuffling toward the staircase. I swirled around and gave a little shove to my sisters; I had to overtake him before he reached the door in his long underwear and flowing nightgown, his usual attire at this hour of the day.

"Come on, girls," I urged, "we have to comb your hair or you'll be late for school."

19

Grandfather reached the door at the same time we did. "What day is it? I can't figure out what day it is!" he demanded as if it mattered! I looked at him; I did not know myself what day it was. The girls and I had to go to school, so it must be a weekday. I thought again of Mother's eyes and their pleading, "You *will* take care of them?"... I looked at Grandfather and I knew I had to figure out myself what day it was. I had to know, in order to get back to reality. What did we do yesterday? I noticed that he wore no slippers. He must have heard the noise as the policemen were coming in, the doorbell, and it probably did not make any sense to him. He was looking for the meaning of what he heard by trying to find out what day it was.

Then I remembered something I could hang onto, my history assignment, due today.

"It is Wednesday, Grandfather, it is Wednesday! Your friend will be coming around lunchtime."

"Oh yes, yes, so he will," he muttered and started back toward his room.

He stopped, caught by some thought.

"Where is Baba? Didn't I hear her talking to a man? Who was he? Did she leave? Where is my daughter?"

"She did leave with the man, but she will soon be back. He wants to ask her a few questions about Father," I gently urged him back into his bedroom.

"Water, water! Please give me some water!" Grandmother cried from their room, where she lay heavily drugged.

To satisfy her plea, Grandfather headed towards the bathroom. He moved slowly supported by a cane, which he had used ever since he had broken his hip.

Grandmother opened her eyes. "Don't be so slow!" The usual clarity of understanding and her characteristic good heart had disappeared from her eyes in the last couple of days. The stupor of morphine took over; she had had cancer surgery only a few days before.

Grandfather was on his way back from the bathroom. I was combing Elisabeth's hair.

"What day is it?" he demanded again. "And where did my daughter go? She cannot go out with a strange man. Who was he?"

"Marie," I called to my sister, "run down to the janitor and ask her to please come up and stay with our grandparents. Hurry or we'll be late."

Usually she would not accept orders from me, but today she was too frightened to disobey.

"It is Wednesday, Grandfather," Elisabeth smiled at him and grabbed the water glass from his hand. She ran over to Grandmother and handed it to her. At least she tried but she noticed that Grandmother's eyes wandered and that she was not quite herself. She pulled the glass away and set it on the nightstand. Then she ran back and hid her face in my skirt.

"What's the matter with her, Helen? What's the matter? She was always so loving, so sweet. I want to hug her and kiss her and…" Tears came streaming down her soft, little face. She had idolized Grandmother from the day she could recognize her.

Grandfather reached the old-fashioned, inlaid, lemon-wood bed that had seen so many years of marriage. He put his arm under Grandmother's sweaty, gray hair, tangled and short, and poured some water into her mouth, between the dry lips that soaked up the moisture. It seemed as if a spark of gratitude appeared in her eyes and then disappeared in the blankness of not understanding, not knowing.

I dragged Elisabeth with me into another room. Grandmother would not have her to see her that way. I caressed her soft hair and whispered so that nobody should hear what I said, "Grandmother is very sick, we must pray for her. Also for Mother, for Father, who escaped; we must pray for us all." I had to stop because unshed tears choked my throat.

The round figure of the janitor stood in the doorway. She was a good woman. She was also generously paid to remain loyal. I often thought that she would be loyal anyway, but it was better not to take any chances. It was a good feeling that I could count on her.

"What happened?" she asked.

"Today at 7 o'clock the secret police came to get Mother. They wanted to know something I don't know what, they promised to bring her back."

Both of us knew that from these words the only thing that meant something were the words "the secret police took her." She looked at me, alarm in the blue eyes under the dyed-blond, curly permanent. Neither of us said anything. I squeezed her pudgy hands and she returned the squeeze.

"Run along, I'll go down to see my husband and I'll be back right away."

I appreciated her promise, especially since her husband was paralyzed from the waist down. Thank God for the elevator. To run the stairs between floors, carrying that considerable weight of hers would have been unthinkable.

"Helen, where is Baba?" Grandfather demanded again.

"She went with the man, Grandfather. She will be back before I come home from school."

Grandmother was throwing herself around in bed. I went to her.

My Lord, I thought, help her to relax. She must have felt the situation. She sat up with a start.

"Where is my daughter? Why is she never around? Cursed be everyone. You let an old woman die without helping her. You must help me. You'll see. She'll not even be home when I die. Must I go alone?"

Nobody had ever heard Grandmother curse until these last couple of days when the morphine-stupor took over.

"Will she ever come back?" Grandmother's words tore at my soul. Would I ever see my mother again! I screamed inside. Yet, I had things to do. I beckoned the girls.

"You'll have to leave now or you'll be late for school."

I closed the door behind them and the one leading to my grandparents' bedroom. Then I dialed the number of our lawyer.

"Mother was taken by the secret police," I told him. "Yes, this morning... I should wait?!? What kind of advice is that? Can't you do anything? You must help me... You must. You are a good friend. My grandmother is very ill. Grandfather keeps asking 'what day is today?' My sisters are no more than babies, and I am only fourteen. What am I to do? What *can* I do?"

Not even our best lawyer could help.

I knew I must get to school. No one must suspect anything. They mustn't think things like maybe I was "out-of-line," a "reactionary," or a "subversive."

If only I could talk with my old teachers. But they were gone. The schools had been nationalized and our teachers, taken somewhere.

"The ruling class has to be revenged, punished, the 'insects' will have to be exterminated so that we can have a rewarding, beautiful future. If society is happy, all its members 'by necessity' are also happy. The words of today's history assignment echoed in my ears as silently I began to cry. Tear after tear after tear...

My mother, she was so beautiful and nice and kind to everybody. And she was innocent; I knew she was. Thoughts kept flying back and forth in my mind as I searched for the meaning of life, as I tried to find some coherence in what was happening. But nothing made sense.

I remembered the years since the war had broken out. The suffering of all our friends, relatives, and ourselves did not cease for a day. Then this morning, when the policeman kicked at our door, brutally pushed us around, and finally took our Mother. Only a week had passed since Father had escaped.

I sobbed quietly while in the back of my mind pictures appeared from the past and I began to relive my life as I remembered it, searching for an answer.

2

My memories took me back seven years to a dramatic night in September of 1942. A thunderous blast pierced the air. Clinking of broken glass and a sharp whistling sound, one I had never heard before, woke me from deep sleep.

"What was that?" Mother cried.

"A bomb!?" Father's voice sounded doubtful.

Grandmother's "Oh my God!" came from the floor below, and I heard Grandfather's heavy steps on the carpeted stairs.

That instant my governess, Elsie, shot by me and out onto the terrace, where we suddenly all stood, mesmerized.

A screeching whistle supplied the "background music," a triumphant call of a bird of prey diving for its victim.

And the birds of war came flying, the sounds of propeller engines and repeated explosions made it clear that World War II, that had started a few years earlier, had now broken loose in our town of Budapest, the capital city of Hungary.

"To the cellar!"

"Lights out!"

Father scooped me up in his arms and ran down the stairs. I struggled to free myself; I needed to go to the bathroom.

The huge menacing head of a man created by the voice of the sirens, whistling sounds, and detonations appeared behind my closed eyes, his features swallowed up in the fog of incomprehension.

I had to go to the bathroom...dark stairs...that deadly menace, the head of that man...he told me without words that I could die, any minute... yet, I had no fear of death. Only seven years old then, I felt incapable of dying. Everyone else might fade away in this curious holocaust, but I knew I was still going to be there when it was over.

"Oh my God!" The maids crossed themselves as they ran from window to window to open them. The house was completely dark, only the peeping sound of the tiny, hand-operated flashlights, the "peeper" a new invention of necessity, could be heard.

The stairs creaked now as Father ran with me, and I knew that we had reached the uncarpeted bottom of the stairs that led to the make-shift air-raid shelter in the servants' quarters.

A shrill whistle! Then a blast! We were now in the basement, two stories of reinforced concrete above us. I heard the peeping of the light as someone pulled down the dark shades in the cook's room. The "peeper" gave barely enough light to silhouette the people, yet I felt the fright, the burning eyes of every grown-up in the room even though some of them had their backs turned towards me.

The head of the threatening man disappeared with the last sound of the siren. We were all in the relative safety of the basement.

"I have to go to the bathroom!" I screamed in anguish, and somebody held a basin under me. I don't know who it was, but I felt thankful to be relieved.

"I am thirsty!" my sister Marie cried out. She clung to Mother. "Take that dog out of here!"

"There is no dog here!" I heard myself say in a sleepy voice, as I used to repeat automatically, every time she awakened with the same nightmare ever since she was a baby.

"Yes, there is." Her voice was swallowed up by a loud detonation, and she dug her head into Mother's shoulder. "I am afraid," she sobbed.

Elisabeth, the little two-year-old, slept cuddled on Grandmother's soft, large breasts. She was safe; her sweet dreams could not be disturbed by anything. She even smiled in her slumber.

The chauffeur practically fell in the door as he tore in from the outside where he and the governess had been watching the infernal fireworks from our mountaintop rose garden.

He cried, "It's coming close! We'd better lie down!"

Lie down? We scarcely had room to stand.

Grandmother prayed: "Our Father, who art in Heaven..."

That burning within me returned. I had to go to the bathroom again.

"The dog!"

"There is no dog," Mother smoothed Marie's unruly hair. Her tears were smeared all over her tiny face; she was so slender, so fragile.

"I have to go to the bathroom!" I yelled.

"She's very nervous," Father explained as he helped me again.

I felt ashamed; I was already seven, yet unable to control myself. I knew it was fright and worry that caused it. But to go to the bathroom in front of all these people? Some of them men? Usually I would not even do it in front of my father.

The murmuring increased. "Our Father..." Grandmother started praying for the third time.

The roar of the guns filled the sky. I knew those furious sounds outside brought death, but I still had no fear in me. I had heard that Heaven followed death and in a way I longed for it. Heaven was beautiful.

But until then, I felt the nervousness in the trembling prayers, in the strong, loving hug of my father, the concern and fear in the face of Mother, in Grandmother's stoic nature that now seemed helpless, in Grandfather's wordless worry, in everybody's sudden silent wonder or intermittent, flustered talk.

The shade was moved by someone. Through the tiny hole I saw a shining light, a fire burning, search lights criss-crossing the sky, things falling and flying. It lasted only a few seconds and the shade was back in place again.

"Lord, have mercy on us."

"It's happened! The war is here!"

"What business do we have being in this war?"

"Do we need that?"

"Business??? It is more a question of how we can avoid being a part of it."

"I never thought it would come to that. After a couple of years of nothing."

"War was declared, but who cared? *We* were not involved. Some men, maybe, but the population of the backland? Why?"

"Bombing!??"

I heard the words but I could not distinguish who spoke them. I knew that we expected war otherwise we would not have arranged air-raid shelters in the basements. We prepared when we rehearsed for air raids at school: "When we hear the voice of the siren…" Just the thought of the words made that menacing face reappear. "We have to go to the cellar." Some of us had permission to leave for home if somebody picked us up when the first warning siren blew. Funny, I never had seen the face of that man when it was only a rehearsal at school. Yes, we were prepared, yet we never really believed it would happen. And it was happening. I buried my face in Father's arms. Even in my fright I noticed how good he smelled. His face was freshly shaven. They must have just gone to bed.

The sounds slowly became less cutting, the detonations faded into the distance. The prayers died down. The "All-Clear" sounded, the air raid was over.

～

The morning sunshine poured into the spacious room I shared with my sisters. The first thing that came to my mind was: "No school yet today!" I ran out onto the terrace in anticipation of a day filled with fun and excitement when I suddenly remembered the frightened voices of yesterday as we realized that the air raid was not a test this time.

Today everything seemed to be in place from the yellow gravel of the upper garden to the pink circle of phlox, Grandmother's pride and joy, farther down. The gardener waived at me from the rock garden that encircled the lower part of the driveway. His son was busily mowing the lawn with a hand lawnmower, a novelty in those days in Hungary. A machine to cut grass, even if it had to be pushed by hand, was something of a marvel.

I watched as Mother kissed Father goodbye on the serpentine driveway which lead up to the wrought-iron gate entrance beyond the rose garden, the silver firs, the phlox, and the rock garden. Our yard continued way beyond our home that looked more like a palace in its dimensions than a house. Grandfather had given it to Mother on her birthday one year for a summer home, but also as an investment. The swimming pool and tennis court saw many guests and the fruit trees bore a heavy burden each year. Our vegetable garden was not much to speak of, but Father liked to putter in it with us for a rare relaxation. He enjoyed the fresh taste of the tomatoes, green peppers, green onions, and parsley. As a child he had lived in the country and he always liked to remember his childhood. I wished he had more time to tell us about it.

Right now Father settled into his Fiat and honked at me when he noticed my small figure on the terrace. He liked to drive and preferred to take his own car, while the chauffeur remained there with another car to drive Mother or my grandparents to town whenever they wanted to run some errand or visit friends. I imagined that as usual Mother would be going to have her hair done. I also wanted to have my hair done and Mother promised that while it was growing she would let me have a permanent. I was looking forward to that day. I couldn't wait to become part of the adult world that seemed to be all fun and no work.

When Father's car sped away, Grandfather made his daily round of smelling the roses. His delicate sense of fragrances was the basis of our family fortune. He manufactured his own line of cosmetics, perfumes, and soaps. Our family owned and operated a chain of drugstores. All of the grocery stores and drugstores in the country sold our products, made to perfection by him alone. Now that Father had taken over the business empire, Grandfather had more time to enjoy his hobbies. Every day he would go out and sniff the delicate flowers. He especially enjoyed the exquisite scent of his two hundred selected rose bushes. Their golden pink, deep velvety red, dark maroon, snow white, French pink, and peachy orange glowed in the sunshine. No menacing face here! I felt ashamed I ever made up that monster. Now there was nothing threatening or awful about life, only beauty.

As if to prove my statement, Mother looked up with her young smile, her face mirroring the color of the roses. She looked like one of the flowers herself in her rose-colored silk negligee.

I lifted my head and looked beyond Mother's smiling face. The city rose in its glittering beauty from the morning mist of autumn. I was proud of my home town, Budapest, the "pearl of the Danube." I looked towards our winter home, on the other side of the river.

We had two houses in the city, one in Pest that we used in the winter, the other in the hills of Buda. They were similar in design and equal in conveniences, though the winter one was built according to the specifications of Grandfather, while he bought the other one already built. In both homes, the main floor was occupied by my grandparents, the second floor by us. In each there was a daylight ground floor for the servants' quarters. In our hillside (summer) home, the kitchen was also on that floor. On each floor we had spacious bedrooms and rooms to entertain guests decorated throughout with treasures of art, original paintings, sculptures, oriental rugs, antique china, crystal, bronze, and sterling silver. I noticed all these things for one reason, we were to be very careful with them and we were not allowed to roughhouse around the precious doo-dads.

My eyes drank in the beauty of the panoramic view from the terrace and wandered to places I wanted to see. The ice skating rink should be there in the distance, about a mile beyond the St. Stephen basilica. I could see the steeples and the cupola well, but the rest disappeared in the misty morning. My school. It hid behind the National Museum if I tried to find it from here. Our winter home should not be too far from there, the bridges I could see clearly, the Elisabeth Bridge, the Chain Bridge, farther down the Margaret Bridge and Margaret Island. That was a fun place with its swimming pools, the ponds with their water lilies and the tennis courts, the Grand Hotel.

"Helen, get dressed!" Elsie, my governess, was after me. "You will catch a cold in your nightgown." I felt a little cold breeze but the sunshine made up for it and I did not care. How could I? I was alive and the nightmare was gone. As a matter of fact I was convinced that it had been a dream. It could not have really happened, or the sun would not shine as it did today and the cocoa would not smell so tantalizing, the rolls would not be so fresh and hard, and...

"Last night's air raid failed to accomplish its purpose," the radio news report stated. "None of the industrial zones were hit by the Soviet planes. Most bombs fell helter-skelter. The first victims, two children, were killed instantly in their beds. The next bomb fell on a church and completely destroyed it."

An iron fist closed around my throat. "They were killed in their beds." How awful! They hadn't known about the air raid. For them, death had come so suddenly that the threatening "siren-man" of my cloudy imagination hadn't had time to warn them.

# 3

Life returned to normal after a few more air raids. The first day of school arrived sooner than I wished. My two friends, Magdi and Martha, who lived next door, and I piled into the Chrysler limousine to be driven to school by the chauffeur. Grandfather joined us as usual. He went to the factory every day to conjure up some new perfume or to the flagship store to sit and watch the business from his desk on the gallery.

Grandmother also came to town. She went to church, to attend to her duties there and to run errands with the car, while Grandfather amused himself with his business.

We could hardly wait to get to school in our crisp, new uniforms; pleated navy skirts, light blue blouses, and navy ties. Brown shoes and socks finished our weekday look. Our hair was smoothed down, not a curl was allowed under the navy blue French berets with the shiny "S" on the front to indicate the name of our school, the Convent of the Sacred Heart "Sophianum," which we affectionately nicknamed "Sophie."

"Who will be your teacher this year?" Magdi asked while her red cheeks became even redder with excitement. Her dark brown hair hung in two nice braids. She was a year older than me and I used to think that she was the most beautiful girl in the world. I envied her complexion and the fact that she did not have to have dinner at 7 o'clock, not until 8. Whenever I asked about changing our bed time, the answer was always, "When you will be her age." I was old enough now to know that this would never happen. I never would be her age. Although I was envious, I admired her and I was grateful that she and Martha accepted me into their graces the first day we met. Since then, we rode together to school.

"We'll know who our teacher is when we get there." Martha was much quieter; her pale, blond hair hung straight and her brown eyes looked calm.

The chauffeur started the car. I was glad that we used the Chrysler on the first day of school. There weren't many of that kind of automobile in Hungary; everybody recognized its musical horn which reminded me of a church organ.

"Dreamy!" Magdi exclaimed. She stretched her neck towards the fan that started blowing fresh air in her face, rippling a few loose strands of hair around it.

That instant the chauffeur switched on the radio and even Martha gave a startled "Oh-h-h!" to express her surprise. "It's just like a boat," she whispered and gave herself completely to the pleasure of the smooth ride down the driveway and out the gates toward the city, sparkling in the morning sunshine even through the September mist.

Since the war broke out, Grandmother reminded us every day as the full view of the city came closer and closer, "Look at this sight and etch it well into your memories. Who knows, tomorrow this may not be here at all." As always, it went in one ear and out the other. Life was too beautiful and too exhilarating.

"How much is five times five?" Grandfather started to drill us as he always did on our way to school.

"But Grandfather, it is only the first day of school! That is not fair!" I objected. Yet I did not want him to think that I did not know so I quickly added, "Twenty-five. But it still isn't fair."

He laughed heartily but went on asking the times tables as we breezed down the mountain of beautiful gardens and villas, along the tracks of the cog-wheel railway. Chestnut trees were laden with their soft-thorned, wild fruit; an orgy of autumn colors lined our way on both sides.

We drove past the old church in the district called Krisztinaváros. Then the tunnel swallowed us with its perpetually hungry, dark, open mouth. From there the road led straight onto the Chain Bridge, its two stone lions guarding it from invisible enemies. Unlit light bulbs followed the chain design of the bridge. I had heard my parents describe it so often that I thought I remembered seeing the bridge in the glory of all its lights, though since the beginning of the war the lights did not work anymore.

"Do you know, girls," Grandfather interrupted my thoughts, "that the tunnel was built to provide a place where the Chain Bridge could be stored during a rainstorm?"

We burst into laughter at the familiar joke but Grandfather went right ahead and made us calculate how much longer the bridge was than the tunnel. Now, that was too much for my knowledge, but the two other girls, being one year older than me, went along with his reasoning.

"Look at this site well," said Grandmother again, "See the beauty of our two-chamber Parliament. Do you know, girls that we have had the same kind of constitution as the British since 1222 even though all the other European countries had a different governmental structure?"

"I don't think they really understand that," Grandfather chuckled as Grandmother tried to teach us history.

He was right. I did not quite grasp the meaning of what she said but I know I tried to remember it just because I loved her and it seemed so important to her.

The Parliament with its stony lace silhouette etched against the blue sky in the morning sunshine was indeed beautiful. The car silently glided by apartment houses in the most elegant part of downtown, then we passed the National Museum and turned near the fountain on Calvin Square. Another turn led us straight to the gates of our school. The heavy glass and wood door opened automatically when Aunt Ida, the gatekeeper, noticed us.

"Laudetur Jesus Christus," we greeted Mother Rossini at the door. She did not speak Hungarian at all; the greeting was in Latin. We felt very grown up for knowing how to say that.

"In aeternum, amen," came her answer. "Hurry, hurry, then later you can tell me about your summer. The bell will ring in a minute," she added in German.

As if to prove her statement, a sister came by with her hand bell, shaking it to enhance the sound of the electric bell which was rung upstairs for the high school students. We were not allowed on the upper floors, our domain was the second floor. We took the stairs by twos to reach our hallway then started to run and slide past the auditorium and the gymnasium, then through a door to our classrooms. Sliding was strictly forbidden, yet the freshly waxed long hallways were so inviting that all over the world students or alumnae of our school could recognize each other by the sure sign: sliding along a corridor upon any given opportunity. The pleasure was even greater because it was forbidden.

When we got to the classrooms we had to part. Magdi and Martha were third-graders.

My teacher was Aunt Esther; she always taught second grade. Her bulky figure was as steady as her good-humored nature. She loved and understood the little ones. Living in the convent, on the same floor where our classroom was, she had no other worries. Her life belonged to her students; her attention was undivided. Everyone loved her. I was happy that she was still there with her white hair, smiling brown eyes and her round, dimpled face.

Our desks were the same, only my classmates were bigger, stronger, and tanned.

"What were you up to during the summer?" Aunt Esther asked the class.

"We went to Lake Balaton!" half of us volunteered.

"One at a time, girls, one at a time!"

"I went to my aunt's wedding and I was a flower girl!" I proudly proclaimed when it was my turn. "My sisters and I, we all had long, pink dresses and matching hats made from tulle and we rode in a carriage, just like in the olden days. My new uncle is an officer, and he had a sword. It was all so exciting."

"Where was that, Helen?" the teacher asked. "It is not so often one gets to ride in a carriage anymore in Budapest."

"The wedding was in Cegléd. That is where my father comes from. My grandparents live there and that is where my aunt got married. They rented the carriage especially for the wedding. It was so exciting!"

Maria was also eager to tell about her adventures. "We went to Lake Balaton. We even sailed in a sailboat and then the storm came and I was scared to death that we would turn over, but in the last minute we made it to the shore before it started raining."

"The Balaton is a big lake; 50 miles long and about two and one-half miles wide, but very shallow." Aunt Esther used the opportunity to teach us about geography. "It is one of the largest lakes in Europe. It has great storms and forecasting them is almost impossible. The weather changes there very rapidly and when the wind comes, so do the whitecaps, because the lake is so shallow."

"I know, we had to walk way out into the lake to be able to swim," said Maria.

Again Aunt Esther picked up the thread of conversation. "You must have been on the Somogy side of the lake. Have any of you been on the other side?"

Eva raised her hand, "We stayed in Tihany and there the lake was thirty feet deep right at the shore."

"On the Zala side the lake is much deeper but Tihany is the only place where it is that deep because Tihany is at the end of a peninsula. Otherwise, the Zala side is excellent for swimming."

Everybody said something except Betty. She never talked. She was with us last year also and finally it became a game with all of us to make her talk. She did not open her mouth, ever. Not even to answer the teacher's questions. She had to take a private exam at the end of the school year. Nobody could understand why. Both her parents taught at our school and her three brothers and sisters talked and played like everybody else. She smiled, but she never answered any question directed at her.

After recess we had catechism class. Today's lesson was about Abraham and his son, Isaac.

"God chose the Jewish people out of all mankind as His special people. From Abraham's family a Savior will be born to free us all from sin."

The Jewish people, the Jews, where did I hear somebody talk about them? I racked my brain to try to remember. Yesterday, when a lady came to our house she was talking to my mother about a Jewish man in Germany, someone beat him to death or something like that. What was it exactly? Why did they switch subjects so quickly when they noticed that I was around?

Then I remembered a scribble on a wall in town: "Dirty Jews" and a swastika beside it. What did the swastika have to do with all that? I saw newsreels at the movie before *Snow White and the Seven Dwarfs* started and I remembered seeing the swastika on people's arms. They wore armbands and Hitler was talking, yelling, screaming, yet everybody seemed so happy. They chanted and clapped and they gave him flowers at the end.

Now I heard that the Jews were God's chosen people. What did all of this mean?

The bell rang again. Recess, we ran out to the corridor and played our favorite game "Lion." A girl held on to the pipes of the steam heating and caught whoever was close enough. Then there were two of them and they tried to catch everybody else, who, of course, teased them and came as close to their reach as possible without getting caught. The "lion" became longer with every new captive and we shrieked in delight. Everything was forgotten. The problems of class and life disappeared into our happy childhood.

Last period was French. When school was out, the class marched to the bottom of the stairs in two neat rows. Mother Pongrác, our homeroom supervisor, had a funny little instrument in her hand with which she made the tiniest clap every time we were ready to make the next move on our way to the entrance hall; all we had to do was obey her signals and a minute later we were in the arms of our parents, or whoever came to pick us up.

Today it was Grandmother who came with the chauffeur to get us. We drove to the Market Hall. I loved to go shopping with her. As we entered the enormous building the smell of fresh food—vegetables, fruits, meats, fish, poultry, and home-made sauerkraut—permeated our nostrils until it took over every square inch of our bodies.

First, we went to the poultry section. Naked carcasses of ducks and geese lay beautifully prepared, cleaned to the last feather. Grandmother only shopped at choice stands. They knew her and gave her the best they had; she was not easy to satisfy. She also knew what she was talking about and the vendors appreciated that. Many rich women had no idea about cooking or keeping house. Grandmother wanted us to learn all the tricks. "You have to know," she would say, "you cannot supervise something if you have no idea what they are doing." So we all had to listen and learn while she was showing us how. She also taught Mother when she was a young girl but since we lived together Mother seldom had to go shopping for the kitchen. She took care of the rest of the house and of the entertainment for business purposes. She was young and beautiful and I loved her as much as I loved Grandmother. It would have been a hard choice should I ever have had to choose between them. I felt so lucky! The yellow skin of the ducks made me think of them when they were already roasted with red cabbage and potatoes. The force-fed animals' huge livers made my mouth water.

Grandmother picked two ducks and paid.

"How is the family?" she asked the blond woman in the white apron whose weight showed that she liked to sample her own merchandise.

"Thank you for asking, they are doing well. My daughter had the measles last week, but she is doing much better." The woman smiled, happy that somebody cared.

"Who is taking care of her when you are here?" Grandmother went on while the chauffeur took the package to the car.

"My mother lives next door to us. She is truly a blessing on days like these," the woman answered while she quickly turned around to yell at a little boy, "Don't touch that, you little good-for-nothing!" The boy ran away as fast as he could. "These little nincompoops would ruin my whole business! Touching the merchandise!" she pouted.

We went on to the next stand where we bought red cabbage. I liked the smell of sauerkraut which became so strong here that it even made me sneeze sometimes. I always felt like taking a big bite of the whole heads of cabbages that decorated the barrels filled to the brim with sauerkraut. This vendor was an old lady, thin, her nose like an eagle's beak, always screaming at the other vendors, customers, passersby, her flimsy gray hair flying around her head:

"Come and look at my beautiful merchandise! Have you seen the like of it? And how is your son? Is he up and around yet? Oh, I am sad to hear that! Get out of here, you little...I am sorry, what did you ask? The red cabbage, the freshest in the Market Hall! It was picked this morning." She went on and on, non-stop, in a voice that made everyone think she was quarreling when she was only having fun, enjoying such a nice day.

"Potatoes? Did you say potatoes? I have the prettiest potatoes in town!" Continuing her monologue she produced a bag of first-class potatoes. They looked as if every one of them had been washed and dried by hand. Everybody seemed to have saved the best of everything for Grandmother.

"Now, let's get back to the car," Grandmother said, and I hurried beside her. She was big, tall, and heavy. I felt secure whenever she was near. I knew that she would never let us get into trouble; she would protect us in the face of anything. I held her strong, warm hand and squeezed it.

"Thanks for bringing me along," I beamed a smile at her and skipped to the car.

This time after we glided through the tunnel in our dream-car, we stopped at August's, the famous confectionery, in Krisztinaváros.

Dark coolness greeted us after the sparkling afternoon outside. Heavy velvet curtains kept out the sunshine. At the small tables old ladies and young couples were eating heaps of whipping cream, pastry, and cakes. The ultimate desires of any child could be fulfilled here. Castles of butter frosting and parfait, mignons (French pastries), and tea cakes were piled high behind the glass counters.

"What should we buy?" Grandmother asked and let me help choose the pastries. The one with the red cross of candied cherries on it with marzipan below and also the one that had a mound of chocolate cream adorned with hazelnuts then buried in thin chocolate glaze.

"We must get the one with the glazed maronies, Grandmother, that is Mother's favorite." We piled the little tray full and then another one also. Finally she bought me salty tea cakes which I really liked, with caraway seed and cheese.

By the time the car reached the gates of our villa it was 3 o'clock.

"We'll have a late lunch today, but it was worth it!" I said and hugged Grandmother as we got out from the car under the shadow of the chestnut tree, where Marie and Elisabeth were playing.

The girls instantly snatched Grandmother from me and did not leave her alone until she hugged them and promised them a surprise. I already knew about the surprise, the cakes we had bought, and that made me feel very important.

I left the girls and Grandmother and I ran up the stairs into the living room: "Mother, Mother, guess what we brought from town?"

Mother looked a bit flustered and she changed her worried look into a smile to greet me. She was talking with a lady who was crying and tried to stop her tears when she saw me enter.

Again that curious happening. Was it always like that ever since I was born but I only started to notice it because now I was getting older, or did it just start happening? Wasn't I allowed to hear any adult conversation?

"Mother dear, darling, is there something wrong? What is the matter?" I asked, bewildered.

"Oh, nothing, nothing…" Mother seemed embarrassed but she went on in a steady voice. "This lady's name is Mrs. Heinz. She is from Germany. The bombs fell there also and now they have nowhere to go. They'll come and stay with us until they can find a solution."

Mrs. Heinz had collected herself by that time. The explanation was simple but I thought that it was not quite what the real problem was. I sensed something strange in the air.

I ran to greet Elsie, my governess, in German. She was a great friend. I hugged her then whispered in her ear, "Elsie, is Mrs. Heinz Jewish?" She shoved me at arm's length and looked me straight in the eye, "Now why would you ask a question like that? How should I know?"

"I don't know," I muttered while I unbuttoned the skirt and the blouse of my uniform to get into more comfortable clothes.

"Lunch is ready!" Grandmother's voice announced and the two of us sat down to enjoy the big meal of the day. The others had already eaten. Usually they would have waited for Grandmother but today we were extra late.

The dumbwaiter's bell admonished the maid; food arrived from the basement kitchen. She brought in the soup and bread, Muscatel wine with the meal, Grandmother's favorite. I did not like wine, but Grandmother, as was her custom, poured me half a glass and prodded.

"Drink your wine, it's good for you!"

After soup we had meat, vegetables, potatoes, dill pickles, and finally, dessert. Today the food tasted good. I was rarely hungry. Normally the soup itself supplied me with enough calories. Hungarian soups can be very filling.

Through the windows I could see my sisters with Elsie in the sandbox. Mariska, the children's maid, was helping them build a sand castle. Marie wore long white tights and white gloves. She was prone to bladder infections and had bad eczema. The fact that she was completely dressed in burning sunshine, all the way down to her white gloves, bothered our neighbors more than it bothered her. I overheard the maids talking about them. Neighboring servants spread the gossip that we made her play in gloves because we were so finicky. I was unhappy only because I could never play in wet sand, make a good mud pie, or the like, if I was with her.

"Grandmother!" I turned to her as she was finishing her lunch. "Tell me, are Jews good or bad? I am confused. At school we learned that they were the chosen people. Was Jesus Jewish? He came from the family of Abraham, didn't He? We learned about Abraham and Isaac today."

"Yes, they were the chosen people. Among them there are good and bad people, like among all people there are good and bad ones. Just because somebody is Jewish, or German, or Hungarian, or Catholic, it makes no difference."

I tried to understand the answer but it did not satisfy me. "Why do people write on walls 'Dirty Jews'? Does it have something to do with the swastika, that sign I saw on armbands at the movie?"

"Like I explained to you, there are good and bad people and some of the bad ones wrote those signs. As to the swastika, it is the sign of the national-socialist party of the German nation. Their leader is Adolf Hitler, whom you have seen in the movies. Now run along and do your homework."

I shook my head because it was still not clear to me what this was all about. I started up the stairs but suddenly I slowed down. I heard voices from the upstairs living room. Elsie said, "She asked me today about the Jews, whether Mrs. Heinz is Jewish."

"How can we tell her the truth?" Mother answered with a question.

"She cannot talk about things she does not know but she could easily betray us if we told her that Mrs. Heinz was Jewish, that she and her family want to escape the atrocities of the concentration camps. Rumors are going around about concentration camps, whatever they are. Yet you know as well as I do that we are on the side of Hitler in this war and we cannot openly express our opinions even if what I heard this afternoon was true. If we tell her..." My mother did not sound quite coherent, yet Elsie seemed to understand what she said.

Elsie was a great fan of Hitler's, at least I thought so. I had a German alphabet book from which I had learned to write in German that summer. Every time I saw Hitler's picture there I felt uneasy: a uniform with an armband in a school book, where I usually saw only pictures of perfect families. He was supposed to be the loving Father of all Germany, as a matter of fact, all German-speaking people wherever they lived as far as I understood. Whenever I asked her about him, she said that it was true.

When Austria was overrun by the Germans, she had to go to the embassy and all Austrians were declared German citizens. She often told me that she would like to become a Hungarian citizen and that she wanted to get married. Marriage would have made her a citizen instantly. All this came back to me while I was listening to these two women, who were so close to my heart, talk about me. Did Elsie playact also? And Mother, and Grandmother? And everybody? Why were they afraid of ME? What harm could I possibly do to them? By asking questions? Maybe of the wrong people? At the wrong time?

I had never eavesdropped before but I wanted to hear everything they said now. My whole life seemed to depend upon it. Why would two such loving people, so important in my life, lie to me? But as I recalled their words I noticed that they never did lie; they were simply evasive.

Mother continued, "We don't exactly know what is happening in Germany. However, diplomat friends of ours said that something went wrong. Jews are harassed to death, they disappear. Hitler's book, *Mein Kampf*, clearly states that they have to be eliminated. Yet, almost none of them believe it can be done. Mrs. Heinz and her family are moving to Hungary as there is no chance for them to move anywhere else because of the war. They will be relatively safer here than in Germany. Many of her friends are already in deep trouble." Mother swallowed her words as I burst into the room.

"Oh, Mother, Mother, Elsie! I overheard you! Please, please tell me everything. Always, you can trust me. I won't utter a word to anybody. The little ones, I'll keep it a secret from them. But you can rely on me." My voice broke into sobs as I finally began to understand. I hugged them and cried both in sorrow for what I had heard and even more in happiness that I had the explanation, that the secret uneasiness between us had been dissolved.

4

Two years passed. It was spring 1944, and I was a big fourth grader. Many things had changed, but I still had dinner at seven and I had to go to bed with my sisters at eight. We now stayed in our winter residence in the middle of downtown Budapest, facing the trees and budding flowers of a park. There stood the lovely building of the Károlyi Palace. From my windows I could see the mountains of Buda, especially Mount Gellért with its "Citadella," an old round castle. I gazed at it often in the setting sun, while I dreamed of how life would be when I finally reached the age that never seemed to come.

"You can wear an evening gown when you are sixteen to the Opera, the theater, for dinner parties and balls." I knew what the Opera was like because I went there quite often with Grandmother. She took us to every ballet, children's performance, folk opera, anything she thought we might be interested in. The magic "golden horseshoe" of the balcony and the red velvet curtain of the enormous stage embraced the audience. We had a box of our own, binoculars, big ribbons in our hair, and our dresses were all ruffles and frills. It definitely represented a glance at our future, of how beautiful it would be!

Today was a grand day. The flowing music of the huge organ still rang in my ears. The church, only a block from us, was the University Church of the downtown Budapest Seminary. Five churches were within easy walking distance from where we lived; one more beautiful than the next. We had gone to the noon Mass because a friend of ours played the organ. He was Director of Music and taught the seminarians, directed their choir. Right now he was downstairs with my parents, grandparents, uncle, and aunt.

The phone rang. The maid answered it, and then called out to us:

"Children, it's time to eat!"

I threw my hooded velvet cape around my head and shoulders and ran down the stairs. The staircase was not heated in this house. During the days of war-time rationing, it would have been cold at any rate.

Hungary always has been rich in food. Although we had rationing, it was not as severe as in other countries and food could always be bought from peasants who brought it straight up to one's door. We also had a farm. Not big, just enough to feed our household which consisted of approximately sixteen people on any given day, even though our family numbered only seven. The cook, governess, chauffeur, maids, laundress, seamstress, and anybody else who happened to be by and seemed hungry ate with us as a matter of course.

By the time I skipped into the dining room, my tastebuds were awakened by the tantalizing smell of roast chicken and soup, almost everybody was assembled, only my sisters came after me, following close. We took our places at the end of the table and waited silently for grace.

Then the clinking of heavy silver spoons against the delicate china drowned out all my thoughts about evening gowns. I was a hungry child again who enjoyed every bit of the food she was eating. I took big bites of the white bread. Fran, our cook, made it herself. Since the beginning of the rationing we had to bake our own bread. Whoever was "self-supporting" (had access to food in any other way) did not get ration cards. As a consequence I loved bakery bread and often exchanged mine with people who were "lucky enough" to have the dark bread coming from the baker. Needless to say, they were more than eager to exchange.

The phone rang in the middle of dinner. Although it was not her custom, Grandmother answered it. I could not understand why. She did not speak much. "Is that so?" "Thank you." She sat down again and continued eating. The adults were discussing politics and I let myself drift back into my own thoughts. Then all of a sudden Father's voice was especially loud and I listened, "…Berchtesgaden." I turned to Elsie, "Berchtesgaden?"

"Yes," she said, "It seems that Governor Horthy was invited to go to Berchtesgaden to the Führer's summer place. They are having talks there."

"Is that good or bad?" I asked, not really caring, only curious if it had any special significance.

Everybody was finishing up with dessert and Grandmother looked around, "That telephone call. Yes, Governor Horthy was held back at Berchtesgaden. The Germans are invading the country. Do you know what that means?"

Everybody started talking at once.

"It means…" Faces turned white, Elsie got a red rash on her face and on her hands as she always did when she became nervous.

"What are we going to do?" Mother asked, verbalizing my thoughts.

"Elsie, what does this mean?" I turned to her again, because she was sitting closest and children were not supposed to be heard all the way down the long, long table.

She looked at me, opened her mouth, then closed it again. "It means… It means… Good Lord, if any of us would know what it means!? They will keep him there, he will come back. What can he do if he does come back? What it means..." thoughts must have raced through her head that seemed to make her dizzy. "We are being invaded by the Germans, who are our allies. Invaded by allies. Is the Governor being taken prisoner, or is he negotiating?"

Father's voice thundered. "They called him away so that we should not resist a complete takeover of Hungary." Then his voice trailed off, "By our allies..." With puzzlement on his face he looked around and met the same confusion in everybody's eyes.

Mother turned on the radio. Music. She turned to the other station. Also music. She ran to the window, there was only sunshine. Yet she knew as well as everybody else in the room that the news was true. Grandmother's sources never lied.

Mother turned back, "What are we going to do? What will happen to our Jewish friends?"

The quiet, happy atmosphere of a Sunday afternoon with a contented stomach was gone. Even though we had no confirmation through the radio of the betrayal of Hungary, we knew that this was no rumor.

"Attention, attention, this is Radio Budapest One! Our Governor, Miklós Horthy, was cordially welcomed by The Führer. He is negotiating about the details of the housing of the German Army whose presence is appreciated by the Hungarian people to aid us in our fight against the enemy."

So it was true. I sat on the floor in front of the radio set. The head of my secret "siren-man" seemed to speak the words. I saw him again. He was made of nebulous clouds and he turned and churned and ... I felt his grip in my stomach as suddenly, without ringing the bell, somebody burst in. How could that have happened? Our gate downstairs was always locked.

The intruder was sobbing. "I'm scared! What'll happen to us? Godmother!" She turned to Grandmother. "Can you do something?" Grandmother took the young girl into her arms.

That is Eva, I recognized her. She was the daughter of the landlord from the apartment house right behind us. Grandmother became her godmother when the whole family was baptized. Were they also Jewish? I suddenly remembered the door in the ancient city wall that divided the two back yards from each other. She must have come through that. That's why we heard no doorbell.

It was quite dark on the floor where I sat, still staring at the radio. Music was playing again. I noticed that somebody had switched on the lamp. I got up slowly and went to the window. Nobody paid any attention to me. They heatedly discussed what to do.

Outside the sun was setting, throwing its blood-red rays into the glowing gold of the afternoon sky. Blood, war, the siren-man were taking over the golden contentedness of the leisurely afternoon. As I watched the sun go down I felt myself step out from the little girl's body and become, or at least start to become, that "grown-up" I always longed to be. I felt a strange peace inside of me. In my dreams, there were no longer any evening gowns, opera, or balls. It did not matter when we went to bed. I knew that from then on whatever came I would have to face it as an adult. I stood there drinking in the beauty of nature. My sadness was slowly drowned out by an overwhelming joy. Whatever comes, God will accompany me on my way towards youth, towards life. It was completely dark outside now and the others were still discussing ways to act. My sisters had gone upstairs. No one stopped me as I sat down among the adults and I no longer felt out of place. I too wanted to help.

Days passed and our back entrance became popular as the persecution of our Jewish friends and their protectors began to intensify.

It was April 4, 1944, when the sirens suddenly began to shriek. I covered my ears while we all ran for the air-raid shelter. Since 1942, the bombings had stopped. The Allies realized that Hungary was not a real enemy. Yet, now that we were occupied by the Germans, they had to bomb supply lines, war factories. This was to be expected.

A detonation shook the house.

"It must have been right next to us!" I whispered as I huddled closer to Mother. Grandmother sat with my two sisters in her arms. She started praying loudly and everybody joined in. I had my doll in my arms. I felt ashamed that I should think of something so superfluous when I should have thought only of survival, yet I was only nine years old, and she was my favorite doll. Marie and Elisabeth shook as all the inhabitants of the house filed in one by one.

"This time we'll really get it!"

"These are American bombers!"

"Don't worry, they know their business!"

I looked up and saw with astonishment that Uncle Karl had said these last words. He was in the cellar with us. He talked from experience, he was an officer. He had just returned from Germany, where American bombing was much more extensive.

"The Americans have more accurate maps of our country than we do. I saw the scarf of one of the airplane pilots who was shot down. The map was printed on it. When Americans bomb they go for their target and practically annihilate it. Experts call it 'saturation bombing'."

"What does that mean?" Mother turned to him.

He was pleased that he could explain and divert our attention from the constant whistling of bombs.

"The pilots draw a square on the map. All bombs should fall within that square and wipe out the target. They then turn around and leave. The Soviets on the other hand drop their bombs wherever they feel like dropping them. Do you remember the air raids of 1942? They bombed churches, rural areas, what have you."

Indeed it seemed that the bombs were not falling too close, the noise came from the southern part of the city, where on Csepel Island many factories were located. The free port of the Danube was also situated there. It was a strategic location.

Then I heard anti-aircraft guns and a whistling sound. That must be our house. I did not know then that if I already heard the whistle, the bullet or bomb would not hit me, it had passed. I looked around. Everybody was lying on the floor. Cruel blows sounded on the door.

"I'm coming," I heard Father's voice. I did not even know he was home. When did he come? It was strictly forbidden to be in the streets during an air raid. I then saw that he had his helmet on. I remembered he was a member of Civil Defense and therefore he could go out during bombings.

A group of SS soldiers burst in through the door and surrounded him.

"Why did you signal them?" they screamed at Father.

"Why did…who… what?" he did not understand.

"Put out the light, right now. That's an order." It was no longer necessary to put out the light. Other soldiers pushed their way onto the first floor and, to our greatest surprise, they found the lights on and the blinds open in one of the rooms.

"We don't need to ask any more questions!" one declared triumphantly, "They put on the light in order to signal the planes. They destroyed a school!" He turned to Father who was quite pale by then.

"Collaborating with the enemy. That calls for instant death. Don't you know about martial law?" the triumphant one declared.

"But the light was out!" I screamed. "I know, I turned it off!" The soldier spat.

"You should have known," he was still talking to Father, "that you must turn off the main switch, you should have known." The soldier grabbed Father's arm and swore at him.

"I am telling you that nobody switched on those lights. If they did go on … maybe it was the blast of a bomb that put the lights on." Father said as he regained his confidence.

"He did not do it," Mother interjected.

"I was here all the time. You can see that I am an officer," Uncle explained in fluent German. That dampened the soldiers' fighting spirit a bit but they were adamant. Father and Mother must go with them. There is martial law. Only the judge can decide. If they were guilty: instant death.

I began to sob and I clung to them both. Marie and Elisabeth hung onto them and we screamed, "You can't take them from us!" "We won't let you!"

"Let go of them!" The bombs kept falling as the soldiers tore my parents away from us and forced them between their shining guns towards the door.

"I'm going with them," Uncle Karl announced and he too took his gun.

Grandmother's lap was now big enough for all three of us. We prayed aloud and everybody in the cellar added their own supplication for the safe return of our parents.

~

"We must get you out of town!" I heard Father's voice and leapt out of bed. Thank God he was home and unharmed. At least his voice was the same as always.

"You must get out of town! I want you to go with the children. As soon as possible. It is quite enough for me to stay. There is no reason why you should be in any trouble, when we can afford to go away," Father continued.

I heard Mother sob.

"Where should we go?" I wondered. "Why does Mother cry?"

"How did you do it? How did you get out?" I asked while I kissed and hugged Father and Mother. "Marie, Elisabeth! They're home, they're home!"

We twirled and danced around the two and slowly Mother's tears dried up.

"We are going to a wonderful place," she announced. "It is called Mátrafüred, in northern Hungary. A beautiful resort, mountains, and forests, little houses."

"Can we swim?"

"Go on hikes?"

"Are there any animals there?"

Our excitement was contagious and Mother seemed to forget what bothered her. While the others were busy with Mother, I pulled Father aside and asked him again.

"How *did* you get out?"

"The judge used to be one of our employees and when he saw whom they had brought in he assured the soldiers of our good will and acted as character reference on our behalf. Yet, I think that you and Mother together with your grandparents should move to Mátrafüred. Beautiful surroundings, no bombs, and, we hope, fewer Germans, too."

"Thank God that you are home. It was so terrible when they took you. What did those horrible men want from you?" I wiggled my face against Father's and took a deep breath from his cologne. He always smelled so good and fresh. His face was always smooth, but today he had had no time to shave and the stubble pricked my overly sensitive skin.

"Apparently our lights went on after the big explosion. It must have been the blast that activated a switch and right after that a bomb fell on the high school nearby. There was nobody in the building. It must have been a falling plane unloading the bombs as there were hardly any other bombs reported in residential districts. Csepel is in a pretty bad shape, though. Uncle Karl was right in what he said, the Americans do terribly destructive but relatively 'clean' work. It seems as if they wanted to spare human lives."

"But, you did not put on the lights, did you?"

"No. I did not."

"They still could have killed you for it?"

"Yes. This is martial law. If the judge had not been an old acquaintance, I would no longer be here."

I could not understand. Why did these gruff soldiers have the power to take innocent people out of their homes never to return them to their children? Who were they? Who gave them the power? Who sent them? Was it the smiling Führer who accepted flowers from children in my alphabet book?

The next day we went to school for the last time. It was a breezy, sunny, April day. Grandmother came with us to school and again, as always, she reminded us to take in all the sights, marvel at their beauty because, who knows, maybe tomorrow. Somehow by now that tomorrow started to make sense. I looked and tried to etch every detail into my memory. We'll be leaving for Mátrafüred tomorrow. What would we find when we came back, if we came back?

~

Mátrafüred turned out to be an earthly paradise. We moved into our tiny "villa." Two rooms, a bathroom, and a kitchen. Grandfather lived in the "penzio" (a small boarding house) next door. Grandmother, Mother, and the two girls slept in one room, in the other one Elsie and I. This second room also served as the living-dining room for the whole family. Here began a life for me that was filled with mystery and adventure, because this is where I started listening to the voice of the world.

During the day I was a happy child. Maybe the happiest days of my childhood passed on the fields and in the forests of Mátrafüred. In its old, big swimming pool I finally learned to swim well and jump into the water, green with algae and impossible to see through, even on the days when they changed it. I waded in the clear ice cold creek that ran down from the mountains, on the winding trail leading to the "Little Maria," the statue of Our Lady in the shrine of the green woods. Every day we would trot to the grocery store with Grandmother on our way to church. We would buy fresh lettuce and radishes. Then, as summer progressed we would change to the freshest vegetables of the season. Milk was brought to our house and we used it in every way, making our own cottage cheese, buttermilk, yogurt, sour cream, and whipping cream. We ate these fresh delicacies with relish. We would sometimes visit the confectionery. The confectioner made only two kinds of goodies because of the war and rationing. A yummy, fluffy cream between crispy pastry sheets and another one made with poppy seeds and whipped egg whites. They were both mouthwatering. It was hard to make up one's mind when it came to choosing between them. The souvenir shop also had its special interests. On our way home from the swimming pool we would often stop there and admire the merchandise making secret choices, hoping somebody would discover them.

But the real adventure opened up for me when the other children were sent to bed while I was allowed to stay up. The radio was turned on and we all listened. Grandfather also joined us for these secret sessions.

As we were preparing the room, making it secure against outside ears, I thought of a lecture I heard on the radio during the day. A professor of economics was talking about the Jews. He explained how they always managed to make money from other people's sweat. "When you saw two people digging and one supervising them, you did not even have to look. The one supervising was the Jew among them. He received all the money and paid out only half, or even less, to the two who did the work. This is how their economy worked. Always!" I was appalled. Could that be true? I didn't remember any of our Jewish friends acting that way. But this was a professor. Wasn't he supposed to know what he was talking about?

After having listened all day to the German-influenced stations and hearing how we were "retreating as planned," how we never had any losses, only gains, while trainload after trainload of cripples and wounded arrived back from the front, it was strange and exciting to hear in Hungarian:

"This is Radio Moscow..." and all of a sudden the news was turned inside out. The "retreating as planned" turned into a glorious victory for the Soviet troops, the trainloads of wounded, cripples, and dead became a reality, the number of the prisoners of war "Missing in action" tripled, at least. Truth... which one was the truth? This radio told about suffering Jews, the evils happening in Germany. Evil committed by German troops and our own?

In the daytime I heard that our enemies were trying to kill children. They allegedly threw dolls and fountain pens from airplanes that had tiny time-bombs in them. I even saw the posters depicting a little girl, she was crying and her hand was torn off, bleeding.

Radio Moscow was signing off, "Death to the German conquerors!"

The head of the siren-man seemed to say these words.

Maybe these people, ending the broadcast with a curse would be able to do such atrocities as the Germans claimed they did, like taking children away from their parents. Just how did they do it? I thought I'd rather die than be separated from them. I also felt that if this should ever happen I would take care of my sisters; I would be their mother. I started to shiver and curled up underneath my blanket on the narrow sofa where I slept.

Music followed and then came the news from the BBC. The voice sounded so peaceful. The statistics of casualties were somewhere in between those I heard on the two other radios. It spoke of evils but also of hope, of looking ahead toward the end of this holocaust, when there would be freedom. Freedom!? What does it feel like to be free??? Does it mean that one can talk, say anything to anybody? One does not have to cover up, to hide in the air-raid shelters? Does it mean no more suffering because one is Jewish, or Christian, or whatever?

It was 11 o'clock, the news, with the commentators talking into the night and darkness hoping that someone, behind the front lines, on the other side of the war would be listening.

I heard, with relief, when the English radio signed off with its usual, "Good night to our Hungarian listeners!" A good wish instead of a curse. It seemed that someone somewhere did care.

It was during one of those sessions of listening to the broadcasts of the British Broadcasting Corporation that I first heard about D-day and the wonderful heroism of the British people and their Allies. How could they mobilize all those small boats to transport the troops over! How did they do the impossible! What driving force conquered their fear and filled them with courage! While admiration and awe filled my heart I suddenly realized that our troops were fighting against these heroic human beings. Why did they have to fight against them? Why were we in this war at all?

I asked Grandmother who was to me the source of all knowledge, especially political knowledge, in those days.

"We did not want to enter this war, Helen. The Germans needed Hungary as a neutral ground to cross over to the Soviet Union. They forced us to enter the war on their side by bombing one of our cities with airplanes that had the emblem of the Soviet Union painted on them. We were attacked; we had to defend ourselves. However, our Prime Minister, Count Teleki, committed suicide in protest or he was killed by the Germans, because he protested, we'll never know which. When he had heard of Count Teleki's death, Winston Churchill, the British Prime Minister, declared, that an empty chair should be reserved for Count Teleki at the time the peace treaties are signed to honor the fact that Britain recognized his valiant protest against Hungary's entering the war on Hitler's side. We really had no choice. Had we resisted, the Germans would have simply occupied the country and treated us like an enemy. Many people were saved by the fact that Germany was our ally, especially Jewish people. Until now, most of them were not dragged away to Germany as were a great number of the Jews from Holland, Belgium, all thirteen countries occupied by Hitler's 'Blitzkrieg'."

"What is 'Blitzkrieg,' Grandmother?"

"'Blitzkrieg' means a war as quick as lightning. If a nation does not declare war on another, it is possible to catch them unaware and occupy the whole country before they realize what has happened. This is how Hitler occupied most of Europe."

"Did he occupy Italy also?" I asked.

"No. Italy joined Germany of its own free will, Mussolini's Fascist Party rules there, as you know. Everybody speculated on the question of whether Mussolini was going to join the Allies or the Germans just before they entered the war. I remember someone asking right after he heard that Italy was at war: 'On whose side?' The two countries, Germany and Italy, seemed to have so many conflicts even though they both were extreme rightist countries, that it looked impossible from the outside that the two could reconcile their differences and fight on the same side in the war. Yet, when the chips were down, ideologies were what really counted. Fascism and Nazism are variations on the same theme. One is as bad as the other."

We had many similar conversations with Grandmother while she was busy knitting socks for soldiers. She taught me how to knit also. I enjoyed doing as the grown-ups did and helping our "poor boys suffering on the front," as most people referred to them.

There was another great segment of the population that suffered just as much. Those whose apartments were bombed, or who were running from the enemy, the first refugees of the war to reach Hungarian soil. We did not see them in Mátrafüred but the papers wrote about the casualties and the needs of those who were bombed-out. In the security of our mountain abode we wanted to do something for these people. We also knew that any day we might join their ranks. Bombs fell where they wanted. They did not discriminate.

～

An explosion! I jumped out of bed. It can't be! What could it be, here in Mátrafüred? Who would want to bomb a few little houses in the woods with old ladies and children?

"Out! Out into the forest! Under the trees!" Mother was pulling me out of bed, Elisabeth in her arms, Marie clinging to Grandmother's hand. Elsie and the maid were opening the door and we all ran as fast as we could while the infernal noise of the explosions chased us farther and farther into the woods. Branches tore at our nightgowns. Then we were lying on our stomachs, huddling close to the ground. In these small houses there were no air-raid shelters. No sirens in a resort town.

"What was this?" Grandmother wondered as we lay there still. Nobody knew the answer, of course. Everything was still, only the stars blinked in the sky. Was there more to come? Marie started to cry. I wanted to explain to her that it does not help to cry, nothing will change as a result of crying, but I could not open my mouth. What if a bomb falls right on us? We were out in the open with nothing to protect us, except the trees. It was better than being either in the house, or outside without cover, but I could not help shaking and, as I noticed with great astonishment, crying.

A half an hour passed and no more bombs fell.

"Do you think we should go back?" Mother asked Grandmother.

"I think it would be safe to try," she whispered and we started out, tripping and falling in the dark night through the forest, without a flashlight, or street lights, to guide us. Will it start again? Are "they" gone?

❧

The next day we found out from the newspapers that the local narrow gage train carrying people to the next city was spotted by an overly eager pilot and he dropped his remaining bombs on this small toy of a train, missing all six shots. The bombs fell in the field and did not harm anybody. The only victims were an old couple, who tried to find refuge among the vineyards using a flashlight along the line. The flashlight was noticed immediately and the plane blew a machine gun volley at them. They died instantly, not even knowing what hit them.

# 5

Father usually visited us on weekends, whenever he could get away. To leave the capital city every citizen needed to carry with him his whole genealogy proving that not even his grandparents were Jewish.

This time Father was upset and excited when he arrived.

"When we reached Hatvan (a city 40 miles from Budapest), an eerie light appeared on the sky in the rearview mirror. I looked back and thought I saw northern lights. The thought passed as soon as it came. I remembered that I was in Hungary; too far south to see northern lights. I stopped the car and stepped out. The lights came from the direction of Budapest. Even from this distance it seemed that the city was going up in flames."

"Did you find out what it was?" Mother asked, worry filling her eyes.

"Budapest was burning. What, or how? I must call our manager right now. Maybe he knows more."

The connection was bad and the operator did not sound promising.

"There was a big bomb attack on the city and I don't know when I will be able to reach the number you want to call."

We kept on trying but it was not until the next day in the afternoon that Father could get a hold of our manager. Everything was in good order. The attack was a big one but it did less damage than could have been expected from the sight of the spectacular fire. That was one thing to be thankful about. Yet, I could not help but think of the possibilities if Father had still been, in the city, in that fire…he was constantly in danger of bombs, the Germans. I did not even dare to think of how much else.

Before Father left I gave him the biggest hug ever. I did not want to let go of him. Maybe I'd never see him again; Grandmother's "tomorrow" was applied to people now. I had to drink in every moment of his stay; the hide-and-go-seek, the cops and robbers we played that beautiful, relaxing Sunday afternoon, because who knew? I might never see him again. One after another, black news from the front killed off all hope for families of friends. It was the death of a son, father, brother—No! something screamed inside of me.

Radio Moscow was talking about more and more victories for the Soviets, while I joined the hopes of *my* family and friends that the British would get to Hungary first. Personally I preferred to have someone wish me good night than to curse the Germans as a lullaby. Then there were the rumors of children being "taken" from their parents by the Soviets. Would they tear us out of their arms? Would they take them to prison? I read a story about the GPU, the Soviet Secret Police, that sent shivers up and down my spine. A little boy was so loyal to the state that he denounced his parents because they did something that the communists would not approve. The parents were dragged away to a concentration camp and killed. The little boy was held in great esteem. They even built him a statue. I did not want to get into the arms of the Soviets and find out first-hand. I wished for the peaceful voice of the BBC. They must be better than either the Germans, or the Communists. But what could I do?

I was not the only one busy with this question. Every night the whole family sat together and discussed possibilities.

"We'll have to go somewhere from here! We are closer to the Soviets and they'll definitely reach us first," said Grandmother.

"But we do not like the bombs either," Mother said. "It is not safe to stay in the capital anymore."

"At least we would be home." Grandmother was all for returning to Budapest.

"What if we would move towards the West? Into another small place?" Grandfather suggested. "There is a toothbrush factory in Magyaróvár. I have close friends there. Maybe we could settle there for a few months in order to escape the bombs and be farther from the Soviets."

The idea sounded good and the next weekend when Father was home he agreed to try and find us a place on the other side of the country.

Elsie knew Magyaróvár well. A small town close to the Austrian border, it was her first place of employment. She had been the governess to Tommy, the son of the local pharmacist.

She had told me many things about Tommy and I could hardly wait to meet him. I always pictured myself a university student sneaking out to dates with this boy, though I only saw pictures of him. He was five years older than I was. Just the right age in Hungary in those days. By the time I would be old enough to get married he would be ready to support me, having just finished university. There was no doubt about it, of course, that he would be a pharmacist like his father.

Then she talked about the city, "It is a beautiful city. We could go out into the fields, maybe. Pick wild flowers. I could visit my parents or they could come and see me." Elsie fantasized, then realized the impossibility of it all. "There is war. My parents live in Vienna. We cannot travel. I don't know what got into me. I think I just get overly excited when I think about going back there." The red dots appeared again on her face and hands. She blushed. "Come, I'll help you make a nice hairdo," she tried to distract me now. She did not want to talk about it any more.

The day came when we finally had to leave our beloved Mátrafüred. We packed up all our things in the business truck, two of our cars came down to the country to move us back. There were seven of us and European cars were not made for many people, my grandparents each weighing over 225 pounds.

When we arrived back in Budapest we drove straight to our summer house. It stood there in its usual splendid beauty. The maids, the cook, the gardener and his family seemed overjoyed to see us.

As soon as we arrived, though, the sirens sounded. It was the first warning. "Danger of an air raid!" The second warning could call a minute later, an hour later, or maybe not at all. The first warning meant that planes were heading towards the capital and everybody should hurry to the place where they planned to stay for the air raid. The second warning meant that everybody had to be at an air-raid shelter. Nobody was allowed on the streets any longer. The sound of the siren that meant either the end of the first or the second warning was different. However, most people had a radio close by all day. When enemy planes crossed the Hungarian border the radio would stop playing and a code language would indicate which way the planes were going. Little maps with flags were available and one could follow their paths and see when to run for shelter.

"Into the cars! Quick!" Father urged us to jump. It was dark outside and not even a tiny light was to be seen. I remembered the old couple around Mátrafüred and started praying.

"Where are we going?" Mother asked as the two cars glided down silently along our driveway towards the huge iron gates. The tiny "peeper" flashlight, designed especially for air raids, was the only one we could use. Its light was so insignificant that I could not figure out why the gardener, George, thought it would help the driver if he ran in front of the car with that minuscule beam.

"George, jump into the car!" Father ordered him to stop that nonsense. He complied without objections. I thought he felt a little ashamed at being so childish in his panic.

"Where are we going?" Now Grandmother was wondering from the back seat of the Chrysler. We used this car during the war for special occasions or emergencies only. This time we had too many people to transport.

"Where?" we all echoed the question.

"You'll see." Father expertly drove the car, while the chauffeur followed us in the other with the rest of the household crammed into the Fiat limousine.

We drove up the steep hill of Diana Street and I felt again, with amazement, the ease with which the Chrysler took the hill while the other cars always groaned and grunted when they reached the middle of this incline. We reached the center of Svábhegy, the hill we lived on, then swerved to the left and down and turned into a driveway.

"Quick! Go inside that hole in the hill." Inside the hill?! I could not believe my eyes. Inside the hill there was a long corridor with cave-like rooms opening on both sides. The air-raid shelter, hewn of rock, was jam-packed. They led us to the end of the corridor because the rooms were full. The chauffeur opened up folding chairs for Grandmother and Grandfather. We crowded around them. Mother sat on the dirt floor in her silk dress. The corridor continued in a long dark shaft that dropped another 60 feet into the side of the mountain.

More people crowded in from all over Svábhegy.

"What is this place?" Marie asked with eyes wide open.

"Why are we here? We have a cellar," I exclaimed,

Elisabeth, only four years old, did not seem to care as long as she could sit on Grandmother's lap. Her baby blue eyes kept closing until she finally fell asleep.

"This is a rock shelter," Father explained. "It was dug while you were in Mátrafüred—if there is enough warning before an air raid, we and half the hill, whoever lives close enough, tries to make it over here. There is very little chance that the whole mountain should cave in, especially because it was dug in pure rock."

"Who built this?" I was amazed at the amount of work it must have been to hew out all the rock in order to accommodate hundreds of people.

"The Germans ordered it and Uncle Joseph, our agent, you remember him, honey, don't you? He also worked here." Father answered my question. "It was an especially difficult job."

It was on the tip of my tongue to ask the question why Uncle Joseph would have worked on such a project, when his job was not that of an architect but to sell perfume, but it dawned on me that Uncle Joseph was Jewish. The realization came like being hit with a sledgehammer, the Germans had made our Jewish friends build that rock shelter.

Father's voice died down to a whisper as he continued, "He was happy with his job as this kept him in Hungary for a long time." By now I learned to understand double-talk. Did that mean that Jews were taken from Hungary? Since when?

I recalled the grayish, big-bodied, gentle old man and tried to picture him with a wheelbarrow, feeling blessed for being able to haul rocks. Where did they take the Jews? To a concentration camp? What was a concentration camp?

I heard a scream. A woman collapsed. Father and the chauffeur lifted her and took her outside.

"Some able-bodied young people should go downstairs into the lower shaft," a soldier declared and right away volunteers started to lower themselves on the steep slide, with the help of the rails fastened to the side walls. I don't think that any of us could have made it down but the ones who could would also be more secure.

The air started to become very stuffy. By now so many people were pushing their way into the shelter that, sitting close to the floor as we did, it became hard to breathe. I stood up. My head felt a little cooler. Father returned and told us about the world outside.

"Géza (the chauffeur) stayed outside with Elsie. Many soldiers are standing outside because of the stuffy air. They are watching the 'fireworks.' The rockets nicknamed 'Stalin candles' light up a whole section of the city so the pilots can see their targets. Falling bombs can clearly be seen in these lights. When an airplane is hit, it falls to its fiery grave within seconds and explodes. It looks like a shooting star."

His words were interrupted by a great shove. Somebody nearly fell down the shaft. Commotion and sounds from the front warned, "They are coming this way!" Everybody who was watching wanted to come inside now.

We were all praying hard. The minutes passed as slowly as hours would. Would it never end?

Finally, I felt some cool air breeze through the corridor and a sigh of relief ran like a wave across the human sea standing tensely in the stuffy air.

"The air raid is over!"

We groped our way to the cars and slid back in complete silence through unpopulated streets.

When we arrived at our house, it was still standing, nothing had changed.

For a while now I had been noticing that Jews had been wearing yellow stars. Or white ones. I asked Elsie about this. The answer was simple. Those who were not "all Jewish" were allowed to wear a white star to show that they were part Christian.

"You know what?" Elsie asked. "I heard that some young people in defiance have decided that they too were going to wear the star if Jewish people had to wear it."

"Can I wear one, too?" I asked her, intrigued by the idea. I felt excitement every time when I heard of adventure, or "resistance." I did not quite know what it meant, but it sounded heroic.

"Unfortunately, they were discovered and they were ordered to stop it. Only Jews were allowed to wear a yellow star from then on."

I felt disappointed. I wanted to do something but felt helpless.

As we were getting ready to move to Magyaróvár again (with the same foreboding thought of "maybe ..."), I saw Mother talking with a young man.

He was good looking. I thought he said he was an engineer. I heard his agreeable voice now, "I'm going out tomorrow again. I'm getting married, for the 24th time," he said. "You can find someone else for me by the end of the week."

I thought people only got married once but I learned by now not to ask any questions while somebody was there.

When he was gone, I could not resist any longer to learn the answer. "What did he mean, Mother, getting married 24 times?"

"The wives of Christians are not considered to be Jewish. He has wives in every city. Lately he got married every week to save a friend."

"B..b..but won't they catch him?" I worried for the brave man.

"If they do, he'll hang. If they don't he has saved many of his friends." Mother looked deep into my eyes. She was beautiful. I could not think of anything else when I looked at her. She had helped many a friend with her beauty. If she asked for something, few officials could say no to her charm. Now her look was very serious. As if in answer to my thoughts Mother said, "I know you are good at keeping secrets. In the afternoon, you can come with Father and me and we'll go visit Uncle Paul."

"A secret? Uncle Paul? Is he also Jewish?"

"Yes and no. He is a good Catholic but he is considered Jewish."

"Why? Why?"

"His Grandmother became a Christian only after her marriage. This is the law today."

The afternoon sun shone golden on the highway and reflected from the turrets of tanks and military equipment being hauled towards the front, which was now on Hungarian soil. I realized that we must be going towards the West, because the German tanks faced us as we drove into the sunset.

I felt excited to be part of the adult world. I was looking forward to meeting Uncle Paul again. I had not seen him for ages. He was a diplomat and his duties often called him out of the country. Where can he be now? The gray ribbon of the Danube disappeared into the mountains as we drove through little villages. Geese scurried helter-skelter out of the path of our car, little boys chased them with long supple branches cut from nearby bushes. Dogs barked at us. We turned from the highway and proceeded on dirt roads. Dust enveloped the car; children looked wide-eyed at us as we passed on roads seldom frequented by cars. A roadside crucifix appeared from the dust cloud. The weather-beaten tin roof about it shone like the star of Bethlehem. The car bumped into holes and swallowed the miles. Its rhythmic swing soon lulled me to sleep.

I opened my eyes and saw Father's blue-gray eyes above me. He laughed at me, "You sleepyhead! Here we are! Jump out of the car and let's go!"

I had no idea where we were. A huge building, something like a palace or monastery loomed above us. And here was Uncle Paul! I recognized him immediately. Only he did not look like himself somehow. I looked again. Of course! He had never worn a habit before. What? Habit? He was no priest, or monk, to the best of my knowledge?! Had he become a priest?

He smiled and hugged me as usual. His embrace was the same and I gave him a good squeeze in spite of my surprise. Soon other monks gathered around us and I could hardly believe my eyes.

"Uncle George?" I asked bewildered. "Did you become a priest also? Uncle John? Uncle Jim? Gabriel? All of you?"

"It is nice to be a monk at times like ours," Uncle Paul explained with a twinkle in his eye. I remembered, 'He is a good Catholic, but his Grandmother was Jewish.' I then realized that all these other people I saw were our friends who also thought that it would be a good idea to become a monk, eh?... not a priest, for the time being.

"The bishop took good care of us," Uncle Paul whispered. "When he heard that I was in trouble he offered this solution. Jews cannot be seen if they hide behind a habit. Besides, who cares about a poor monk? Even if I had to go out into the city, I could pull my hood over my face."

"But, how did the others get here? Uncle...," I asked.

"Shhh! Not uncles, brothers," Mother corrected me.

We walked around the beautifully maintained park. Uncle Paul caressed the roses with his pudgy hands. "I like to take care of them. Being a monk agrees quite well with my taste. You know that I never had a great desire to marry."

"Where is your mother, your sister?" Mother asked.

"They are safe at a convent. I'll never be able to repay what the Church has done for us," Uncle Paul said while he looked at his watch. "I think you better head home now. We shouldn't attract any attention or we might be discovered. It was so good of you to visit. The Lord only knows when I'll see you again."

Again Grandmother's "tomorrow." I bumped into it now every day, many times, not only from Grandmother but from everybody. I hoped and prayed that the siren-man's head should never look like Uncle Paul's, that he should not disappear, like so many others, in the churning, turning fog of uncertainty.

～

A few days later our things that were considered most important were packed and we started out in cars against the stream of tanks and cannons that were rolling toward Budapest with a thunderous roar. Again we drove head on into their constant flow toward the front. Our goal: Magyaróvár, where the kindly toothbrush manufacturer had reserved two apartments for us; one for my grandparents, one for my parents and the children. As usual, Father stayed behind again to take care of the business.

Magyaróvár was a medium-sized town close to the Austrian border, about a four- to five-hour drive from Budapest under normal conditions. Only God knew how long it would take us now.

Our car slowed down. I looked out the window. Only a few days ago I saw omnipresent geese running out of the car's way and now, what was it that made us stop? I gazed at an unbelievable sight. People marched on the road, or rather just pulled one leg after another. Their eyes were blank. A man pushed a wheelbarrow with a cupboard in it. He let the sweat run down his forehead and directed his glassy eyes towards the ground a long way ahead of himself as if he would stake out the next few yards he had to cover. I wondered how long he would be able to continue walking. An old man leaned on his wife. He could hardly drag his feet.

"Grandmother, where are they going? Who are they?" I asked.

"I don't want to see that," Marie screamed and stamped her feet.

Elisabeth did not say anything. She just looked with her big blue eyes.

"They are leaving Budapest, maybe even the country. They are going toward the West, toward Austria and Germany. They want to escape from the bombs, just like we do. They also want to escape the Soviets," Grandmother answered, while she put her hands over Marie's eyes. She was a nervous child and occasionally she would throw up for days on end. If that happened she could not keep down anything and usually ended up in the hospital, where they fed her intravenously. We could not afford to lose time now. If she did not want to see it then she better not look at all.

"Mother," Elisabeth pulled Mother's sleeve, "Look, look at that little girl, she has a dolly. She is so dirty and sad. Why?"

"Because she has no home. She does not know where she'll sleep tonight or what she'll eat," Mother answered.

"But she has a mother, doesn't she?" Elisabeth asked again.

"Yes, dear, she has, but her mother doesn't know what to do or where to go either. All they know is that they have to go on until they find a place where they would want to stay, where they can stay because someone will help them."

"Do you know where to go, Mother?" Elisabeth lifted her eyes at Mother. Her blond curls danced around her head as she hoped for the answer she wanted to hear.

"Yes, dear. Today I know where we are going," Mother answered, while she ran her fingers through the soft baby hair.

I noticed when she said "today" she knew where we were going. Grandmother looked at her and asked, "Is that why we left our home in Budapest? Is this the kind of life you want for your children? What does your husband want? We too should go onto the highways and wander with the children like that? How much longer can we go on with the car? Should we too carry our belongings and roam around in the world? Where are these people going to stop?" Grandmother blurted out her worries. I remembered the time when she chose to go home from Mátrafüred.

"At home we'll be safe," she would say. "People know us. We can make it at home."

Home must mean very much to her, I thought.

Mother turned her head away and did not answer for a while. "I love Budapest. I think that my homeland will always love me and give me whatever I need," she finally said and her voice trembled. "Only the children...we should not leave them in danger."

"Is it going to be better for them in Magyaróvár? We hardly know anybody there. Do you intend to go on?" Grandmother went on with her reasoning.

"I don't know," Mother's voice trembled. "But I am grateful that we know where we are going. I wish we had some place in the car to help at least one of these people."

We were riding in the Fiat and with the chauffeur there were seven of us. The other car was a truck. Elsie, another chauffeur, and the maid rode in that one. We proceeded very slowly. We were surrounded by a sea of refugees, carting all of their earthly belongings. A young mother sat on a stone beside the road and nursed her baby. The last rays of the sun surrounded her and her smile, reflected from her baby's face, flowed like a halo amidst the human misery surrounding her.

"A contemporary Madonna?" Mother mused, as she pointed her out to us. "She looks just like Mary could have looked on their long escape to Egypt. How many times did she feed her little Son on the wayside?"

Darkness crept slowly over the car and over the sea of people and covered them up. We no longer saw their worn faces, torn clothes, their miserable plight which we were unable to alleviate.

～

I woke up in a spacious room, on a bed that smelled of fresh linen. The sun shone through the big windows. Marie, Elisabeth, and Elsie were all sound asleep. I dashed to the window, I wanted to see where I was, where I was going to spend the coming months. Who knew how long we would be able to stay in our new place? Yet, as long as I was here, I wanted to take advantage of every minute.

Outside I saw a park. Apartment houses were scattered in it, as if a playful giant had lifted a handful and tossed them at random. Flowers of the late autumn and yellowing trees provided color. I saw people walking on the trails between the buildings. They seemed completely unaware of the war. Other roads, that were obviously made for cars because they were much wider, laced their way through the park.

"So this is Magyaróvár," I thought.

Outside our door I heard whispering and the unmistakable voices of people preparing breakfast. Are there others in the apartment? I wondered.

I smelled coffee. I could hardly wait for the day to begin. I went over to Elsie's bed and gently kissed her. She opened half an eye and muttered, "Who is it?"

"It's me. Helen. When are we going to get dressed? I want to go out. I want to meet Tommy." Today the dream of my life would come true. Elsie promised that she'd take me to see Tommy.

"What time is it? It was so late last night when we arrived. Don't wake up the others. Why don't you wait a little? Maybe you could read if you cannot sleep," Elsie muttered. She was reluctant to face the world.

Read? I felt very disappointed but I did not want to bother Elsie because I liked her and she was always so nice to me.

I pulled out a book from my bag and also my knitting. Which one should I do first? I started reading but my hands did not feel right. Then I started knitting but that too was boring all by itself. "Why couldn't I try and do both at once?" The question haunted me. Indeed, why not?

At first the book did not want to stay open, then I dropped a needle and my knitting started to unravel. Yet, by the time my family woke up I had mastered the feat, I managed to do two of my favorite things, to read and to knit, at the same time.

The sounds of the organ always made me feel at home. If I closed my eyes I was back in the University Church in the middle of Budapest, in its shady coolness, under its shining marble colonnade. However, today I did not feel like closing my eyes. On the contrary, I kept them wide open to observe every detail of the church in Magyaróvár. I quickly discovered what I was looking for. Tommy was there. Elsie had pointed him out to me in the crowd that assembled for Sunday Mass in this provincial looking, heavily gold-painted, clay-statued church. He was about to go to communion. He must be fifteen, I thought, I looked him over from head to toe. His small head was perched on a tall, slim body. His face was not good looking, yet interesting with its dark tanned skin, brown eyes, brown hair, and a very different-looking nose. His Adam's apple protruded on his disproportionately long neck. What can he be like? What will he think of me? I never thought much about my own looks. So often have I heard that looks are not important, only tidiness, cleanliness. "What matters is inside a person," I learned to ignore my looks. In turn, I was often scolded that I did not pay attention to what I considered "superficialities." Yet, I know that first impressions counted. I knew that from experience. Everybody always picked Marie for looks, or my soft little baby sister, while I was told that knowledge was much more important. I tried hard to imagine what I looked like. My hair was in braids. I supposed most boys would have a desire to pull them. That was the common experience of people with braids, I mean girls. I was told that I had brown eyes; some people liked my eyes very much. Mother told me about comments men made about my eyes. They claimed my eyes spoke. I was not aware of that. I thought I was plump, at least I weighed much more than Marie, but she was younger and she was practically skin and bones. When I looked in the mirror I saw a girl, probably typical for her age. I was average size in my class. I thought sometimes that my nose was too big. Or did my nose grow before I did? My hands and feet were enormous. Is that part of growing up? My feet were the same size as Mother's. It was my turn to go to communion and all of a sudden I felt ashamed. How could I let myself be so distracted during Mass? I tried hard to concentrate on Jesus who was going to come into my heart. Since the war broke out I had this inexplicable desire every time I went to communion to die while walking back towards my pew. Wouldn't it be wonderful to go straight to Heaven?

Today somehow I did not want to die. I was curious what Tommy would be like after Mass.

～

The sun shone beautifully as Elsie introduced Tommy and me. His father and mother, the town pharmacists, suggested that we take a walk through the park and the city to get to know our new neighborhood better. Tommy, a little awkward with his big hands and feet, stiff-backed as if he'd swallowed a stick, proved to be very friendly.

"I have heard much about you from Elsie. She always wrote to me about your house, your sisters, and friends. I could hardly wait to meet you." He talked to me as a gentleman would talk to a lady.

Of course, I thought, Elsie had done a good job bringing him up.

"Come, I'll show you our store and house." He pulled me inside a very neat-looking pharmacy. "Do you like books?" he asked while he pulled me up the stairs to his room. It was just as Elsie had described it, the walls lined with books, a desk, a single window to the garden. He showed me everything. He talked about chemistry. He made me forget about being a girl and thinking of him as a boy, as somebody of the opposite sex. We were on common ground.

"You know what, you are fun to be with," I declared.

He looked embarrassed for a minute, then, he laughed. "You, too. I don't even notice that you are a girl. As a rule I don't like girls a lot. They giggle too much."

"Is it true that you want to come to Budapest when you go to college?" I asked all of a sudden. I wanted to make sure that we'd meet again when we were older. Then it occurred to me that we were talking about a "tomorrow" which might never come, that we did not even know if we would be alive by then, let alone be in Budapest.

"I plan to," he answered seriously, "I am going to be a pharmacist and for that I would have to study there. I'll look you up if I get there."

"I'll be waiting," I promised. Even though we talked seriously the idea seemed so absurd that we both burst into laughter and chased each other back to the park. It felt good to be young and to recognize the fact that boys could be fun, too.

He did not even pull my braids.

❧

The Industrial Park where we stayed was a few miles from downtown. We ate every day at our Grandparents' apartment. There was more space there. They lived with a lady, whose husband was an officer, away in the war.

We lived in the apartment of a lady doctor, whose husband was also away with the Medical Corps. Three families lived in our apartment and there was only one kitchen and one bathroom. The third family had arrived recently. They were refugees from Transylvania, a doctor and his family.

Mother went to Budapest with Father for a week. Two days later at lunch time, one o'clock, my sister and I started for the other house, where the meals were served. We skipped and chased each other on our way to the other house. The sun shone but its rays were no longer warm. Yellow and brown leaves covered the green of the lawn, hard red berries adorned some of the trees. The maroon and red of ornamental bushes enhanced the evergreen of the pines. It was October 15, 1944.

We burst into the room only to be shushed by Grandfather and by the frightened look on Grandmother's face.

"What's the matter?" I asked as I felt all my blood run down into my legs. "Is there something wrong with Mother and Father?"

"No," Grandmother answered. "The Governor has just been on the air. He declared Hungary an open country. He wants the Soviets to march across the land toward Germany in order to escape the destruction of a siege. A whole division of our Army has already capitulated. They laid down their arms."

"I wish your parents were here now and not in Budapest," Grandfather sighed.

I looked at him with surprise. I had never heard him worry about anybody; that was Grandmother's department. The danger seemed even greater to me now because he had voiced his concern. What if the dreaded "tomorrow" was here for us now and it would be Mother and Father whom we would never see again? No "what ifs!" something inside of me commanded and drowned out even the possibility of panic. Marie and Elisabeth were already crying. The radio was on, nothing but music. The fatal words were said and we now had to endure the music because any minute a new development might follow. The food was on the table but nobody seemed interested.

"Elsie, you must immediately go back home," I heard Grandmother's voice. "As a citizen of the former Austria you are considered to be a German and I hate to think of what the Soviets will do to any German found in Hungary."

"I heard that they kill Germans on sight," Grandfather went on. "If you are at home, everybody is German. They will not kill every resident in Vienna. Here..."

Elsie broke out in a loud sob. I grabbed her around the neck as if I would never want to let go of her. Her face and hands broke out in a rash. My sisters both clung to her too. Marie stamped her feet, "She cannot leave us, her home is with us," she screamed.

"Your home is in my heart, always," I whispered in her ear and she squeezed me so hard I could not breathe for a minute. "But you know you must go, I don't want you shot. We'll meet again, I know it." I kissed her tear-soaked face and knew that this time "tomorrow" was a reality for at least one person I loved more than anything in the world. I loved her as much as I loved Mother and Grandmother and I too was crying an unending river of tears.

# 6

Leaden clouds sat heavily over the houses, the colors of the autumn faded into their ominous gray. Elsie had packed her bags and left. Our call had not gotten through to Budapest yet. The radio was on; no news, only music. Horrible, sweet, lulling music.

To kill time I was watching a bird. He ruffled his feathers. This is how I felt, too. I wanted to scream at the whole world. Why did Elsie have to go away? Why couldn't our stupid chauffeur marry her instead of driving her to the border? According to Hungarian law she then would become, instantaneously, a Hungarian citizen. What were they doing now? Were they saying good-bye somewhere? I imagined her with red rash all over, her eyes swollen from crying all afternoon. Would we ever see her again? I hoped that we would, that in only a short time we would have her back with us, where she belonged.

My fingers drummed a tune on the windowsill. "Und das heißt, Erika…" I caught myself humming the German march, the radio changed from its sleepy-time music to that German march. At a time when we were expecting the Soviets to march across the country? "Lili Marleen," another march, what is this?

The phone rang.

"Finally," Grandfather picked up the phone. "Are you all right? What is happening over there? They did? Can you make it? Don't do anything that would endanger your lives. We'll see you then as soon as you can make it." He turned to us after he put down the receiver. "Your parents will leave town as soon as possible and try to come back here. At least we'll be together. There are rumors that the Germans have taken over the radio tower at Lakihegy and they are sending reinforcements toward the capital."

"Grandfather, Grandfather," I turned to him and cried. "Listen to the radio! The rumors must be true! If they weren't, who would play German marches?"

Everybody listened as one march was played after another. Still, no news.

We wept ourselves to sleep that night without Mother, without Elsie. Grandmother came over to our house to sleep.

Morning came and went and the afternoon also. Much of the food was left untouched.

61

Finally we had news. The Germans had taken over the country. We were now doomed to fight the war to the bitter end.

We had no idea what the highway was like between Budapest and our present home, Magyaróvár. Our parents said they would arrive as soon as they could. The last word we heard was yesterday. We could only hope that our silently uttered prayers would be answered. Time passed so slowly, it seemed forever until Elisabeth screamed, "I can see the car!"

"Where? Where?" Marie and I flew to the window. Grandmother ran outside to be the first to greet them.

They were tired and their eyes betrayed the fact that they had not slept all night. The car was covered with dust.

"The devil take that car! We had 32 flat tires," exclaimed Father to cover up his embarrassment over the tears that welled up in his eyes as he returned our hugs. "What roads!"

"The highway is completely occupied by German war equipment: tanks, cannons, anti-aircraft guns, troops, horses, trucks, what have you..." continued Mother. Her clothes were wrinkled, her hair all messed up, I had never seen her like this. Yet, her smile beamed at us. "We are together again! That is all that matters."

"Where is Elsie?" Father looked around.

"I sent her home," Grandmother answered. "I was afraid for her safety, being a German citizen and all." She looked puzzled now whether she had done the right thing.

"Thank God! I certainly would not want to be the cause of her death," Father said with relief.

"Is it that bad?" I asked. "Tell us all!"

"Let's go in first, we want something to eat." Father used this as an excuse to get us all inside before he would say anything more.

"I don't think we should talk out there. It's no longer safe. Even the walls have ears!" he repeated the well-known Hungarian proverb.

His suit was oily and muddy. They had no luggage with them.

"How did you get out?" I could hardly wait for them to start talking but I noticed that Marie and Elisabeth were still in the room. I tugged at Mother's sleeve. "Is it all right for them to stay?" I asked and looked in their direction.

"Marie, please, fetch the maid, we want something to eat!" Grandmother called her in answer to my question. By the time Father and Mother washed up and sat down to eat the two little ones were happily playing in the other apartment. Their problems were over; our parents were home, safe and sound.

Father finally started to talk, "Yesterday, when we started out we barely drove to the edge of town when we met head-on with what seemed like the whole German army. By that time the radio played German marches. We were stopped instantaneously and turned back by them," Father said.

"They said there was no way that we could get through," Mother continued. "We turned around and thought immediately of that SS officer who helped us with the soap rations."

"The SS helped?" I asked with astonishment. That was the first time I heard anything like that.

"For money!" Father brushed the comment aside, then went on, "We had to find him. Believe me, it was not easy. These opportunists, who are in it for the money, are hard to find when you need them, when times become difficult. Finally, we found him in a bar. He was drinking. Luckily he was not too far gone yet, when we found him, and he understood our plight. He wrote us a piece of paper that we travel on official German business and we had to drive to Magyaróvár. Now we had a right to come here. But how?!?"

"There was no highway. Every vehicle in every lane was coming in the opposite direction. Even the stream of refugees stopped. There was nowhere to go now. A friend of ours, a traffic policeman, agreed to accompany us. He had a gun. When the Germans stopped us they disarmed him. We all had to go to the police station and he had to throw his rifle and his revolver on a big pile of arms that were taken from the Hungarian police. They certainly did not trust Hungarians with guns yesterday."

"We had our friend with us and the paper worked wonders, but there still was no room for us on the road. Our friend, the policeman, knew every blade of grass between here and Budapest. His knowledge came in handy for all of us. We left the highway and followed dirt roads all 150 miles, though, I should say it was more than 250 by the time we arrived here."

"And it felt like 500. It took us all night and nearly a day," Mother added.

"In the first half hour we had a flat tire. We did not have a spare so we had to fix it with our questionable glue and the air pump. We took turns pumping. I bet we'll all feel our muscles tomorrow. In fifteen minutes, we had another flat. This time another tire. Then another and again another, then the first one again. Every time it took us quite a while to find a house with water. Then we had to find the hole in the tire, fix it, then, start up again. This happened thirty-two times. At the very end in one of the outer tires I discovered a rusty nail that could have caused at least some of our flats by puncturing the inner tube again and again. Still that did not explain the flats on the other wheels. I guess war-time tires and third-class dirt roads don't mix very well."

"Thank God that we had our friend with us. He was quite an expert with tires. It was impossible to get another tire anywhere. We were lucky to have had the tools with us so we could fix the torn ones. We thought we'd never make it back to you. I prayed and prayed," Mother said.

"I'll never forget this trip as long as I live," Father concluded.

<br>

"Helen, come quick, we have fresh bread! Come!" Christine, the daughter of the refugee doctor who lived in the next room, ran in and pulled me with her. I went over to their room frequently. Since we had picked up our report cards in April from my old school we did not go to any kind of school. Christine who studied to become a teacher decided that she would teach me and my sisters whatever she could.

Her eyes glowed with excitement. The bread in her hand was piping hot. I never had bread that fresh. Grandmother was afraid that it would cause stomach ache. Today I wanted to risk it, the aroma of bread was tantalizing.

"Look what else I have," she said while she opened a jar of golden honey.

I did not like honey as a rule but this looked so mouth-watering that I could hardly wait. I wolfed down the bread and honey then, asked for more. I'd never tasted anything so good in my life!

"Oh, Christine, thank you! How did you know I would love it so much?"

Her eyes shone. "I just knew you would. It's something nobody can resist."

Her mother and father watched our excitement.

The three families lived practically on top of each other. Yet, instead of feeling cramped, closeness gave us a feeling of security. I had always wanted to go camping but Grandmother never let me. Now I imagined that we were camping with friends. Our everyday experiences, the sharing of what we had, filled our days with fun.

Then, out of the blue, there it was again. The siren-man would not want us to enjoy or be content for too long. His voice screeched away our peace. We had to run for shelter. As soon as the screaming sound stopped clawing at us we heard the voice of thunder. Only it could not have been thunder. It was not that time of the year and it did not stop. We listened closely from the safety of the cellar with the door open. The thunder went on and on. No bombs, only thunder.

Christine's father finally decided to go out and investigate.

"Hundreds of planes are going above us," he reported back in a few minutes. "It's an unbelievable sight! The sky is colored dark by them and their noise is something to hear!"

"Yet they throw no bombs?!" Christine could not believe her ears.

"No! No bombs, no shots!" her father answered.

"Yet, Helen," he turned to me, "I think you should never knit during an air raid. Should they throw a bomb the air pressure alone can cause you to poke yourself in the eye with the needles and that just wouldn't be worth it. I see many emergencies at the hospital."

"So do I," our landlady joined in the conversation. The cellar was not divided, everybody from the apartment house shared the same room. "Last night they brought in a little boy. A lady panicked during the air raid and grabbed her clothes, hangers and all, while she ran to the shelter. One of the hangers got hold of the little boy right near his eye and he was dragged by the hysterical woman a few steps before she knew what happened and stopped. I could barely save the boy's eye. It is very important never to panic no matter what."

I reluctantly put away my knitting. When moments of great tension came during an air raid, everybody prayed; but when nothing happened there was nothing to do either.

Again, Christine came to the rescue. "Come, girls, I'll teach you a game." We rallied around her and learned game after game as the hours wore on and on and on. Finally, the air raid was over. We were starved by then and quickly ran to Grandmother's house to eat. We barely made it back when the siren sounded again.

From then on every one of our days was spent like that. We had to hurry over for breakfast so we would be able to get back for the air raid, then lunch, then another air raid. After we had learned from the British broadcasts what these air raids were all about they did not trouble us anymore. They became a way of life. Allied bombers were making their way to Germany, then back after the attack. They never dropped a bomb but their constant thunder, that sounded no more than a hum after a while, accompanied the rhythm of our lives.

Father was back in the capital. The road there and back was an easy four- to five-hour drive if one did not attempt to drive those miles exactly on the day of the German occupation of Hungary. We had no plans to move on and we did not know where to go. Finally, Grandmother's idea of going back to our own home to spend the war there seemed more and more attractive.

Father and Mother talked and talked into the night whenever he could make it to Magyaróvár. The number of refugees grew and there was no place that could accept them. It was decided that we would move back to our summer house on the mountain, a residential district, not to the downtown house. It was supposed to be safer.

I saw Tommy only a few times and now it was good-bye again. I hoped that he would make it to Budapest for college. It was fun while it lasted. When we saw them last his mother wore a white star. A white star meant that one of her ancestors was Jewish. The human palm-sized, star-shaped patch danced in my mind all day. "She, too?" I could hardly believe it.

They were very religious and good people, well-liked by everybody. Now she too was in danger, even if the danger was less immediate than it was for those who wore a yellow star.

# 7

When we arrived in Budapest on a dreary November day we knew that it could not be long before the enemy, unfortunately the Soviets and not the British we hoped and prayed for, would occupy the capital.

There were fewer air raids here than in Magyaróvár but the ones we had did not lack bombs. I missed Elsie more than ever. We now lived in our summer home. This was the place where we used to spend the whole day together. In the summer when there was no school she would teach us arts and crafts or we would go for walks in search of wild flowers on a nearby field. Sometimes we would venture all the way to the middle of the mountain, where the shops were. We would buy postcards at the tobacco shop. Both Elsie and I were ardent collectors of fancy postcards. She also collected stamps. On our way she would tell the three of us stories about her childhood. Ski trips, excursions in the Alps. "What does she do now?" I often wondered. We got no letters from her.

One day I overheard Grandmother say, "I wish this thing would be over with. I wish the Soviets were already here then at least we would know what would happen to us. They cannot be as bad as they seem. After all, they are only human."

At the same time, a young woman, who came every day to teach us math, history, literature, all the subjects we would have learned at school, seemed very enthusiastic, "We are going to win. You'll see. All the young Hungarians fighting not so far from here know that we have our faith and trust in them and they are not going to let us down. They know that they are the only obstacle between the enemy and their families."

And she went on and on.

Then, one evening, I saw a light come and go on the horizon very, very far away.

"Look, Mother! Look, what is that?" I pointed in the direction. "And there it is again and again!"

Mother's face turned pale. "It must be, it must be cannon fire! But that close?"

Marie and Elisabeth ran to the window, "Where? Where?" The three of us were so excited we could barely contain ourselves.

"Real cannon fire? You mean it?" I was overwhelmed.

"Is it very close?" Marie worried.

"Grandmother, Grandmother," I yelled into the telephone-intercom. "We can see the cannon fires! Come up and see for yourself!"

Then I ran to the "hotline" that connected with the kitchen in the basement.

"Everybody! We can see the cannon fires! The enemy is shooting!" I yelled at the top of my lungs.

Grandmother arrived in the elevator to look for herself.

"Yes, those are cannons, in the distance. Thank God, they cannot reach us yet. It will take a while. We can see them because it's dark and we are so far above them." She was very quiet. "They must be at least thirty miles from here. Let's turn on the radio."

The radio did not announce anything. A maid was stuffing the ceramic stove with wood and coke. We sat on the floor with my sisters and made Christmas decorations for the tree. It never even occurred to us that maybe we would have no tree this year. There was just no Christmas without a Christmas tree!

Will the enemy really take us away from our parents? the thought haunted me. I remembered again the stories about the GPU, the security police in Soviet Russia, about the constant fright people lived in. I wanted to talk about it but I did not dare talk to Marie because I was afraid I would make her nervous and trigger another of her attacks. Elisabeth would not understand. I let my ten-year-old imagination run rampant. I thought of ways to take care of my sisters if I should be left alone with them. What would we take with us if we should have to go? I wore a maroon knitted dress with embroidered flowers on it. I liked it very much. I wanted to wear that dress if we were taken because then I would have it. It was practically new and a good dress. It would last for a while. I started to collect my little "survival package" and saw to it nothing should be thrown out that we would be able to use later if we needed it. Even a broken shoelace could be of some use. My thoughts ran wild in the playroom as I glued and cut, then glued again, working on the decorations.

"Listen," Marie whispered and shook my arm. "What's the matter with you? I have tried to talk to you many times now. Look!" She pointed at Elisabeth who had fallen asleep on the floor in the middle of the Christmas ornaments.

I woke as from a dream and looked around, where was everybody? We were alone on the floor. I smiled at the sight of the beautiful child asleep, then lifted her quietly and put her on her bed. She didn't wake up.

"Let's clean up!" I lead Marie back to the pile of gaily colored papers. The radio played a song that had become very popular, in Hungary in the last year, "The world is but one day…our life is but an only kiss…"

"Come, Helen," Mother said, "today you can come with me to town. I have some shopping to do.

I was ready in minutes. These days it happened seldom that any of us could go to town; Budapest had air raids every day.

The car rolled down the hill as usual, people moved about on the streets as soon as we passed the villa district, where houses were far from each other. Everything was the same except…I looked to the right and to the left. There were houses in shambles and ruins. People passed them and did not even look. It was an everyday sight. One house was totally demolished in the front but the wall that was standing had a crucifix still hanging on it. It must have hung over somebody's bed. Right beside it on a fragment of the floor, a remainder from the whole room stood a closet, untouched. It made me think of people who were killed by that bomb, or maybe they were in the air-raid shelter and had to come up to find their home destroyed. Did they have children? I wanted to know all about them.

"Look, Mother! The crucifix is still hanging on that wall. Do you think the people had time to escape?"

"I don't know, dear," she answered with a sigh and smoothed back my hair, "they could have. At the same time, yesterday a friend told me that both of her parents died during an air raid. They just sat down to their evening meal when a bomb fell on the dining room. They did not even know what hit them."

Again that "siren-man" of mine! He had no time to warn them. His face resembled an elderly couple now, their features blurred together with thousands of other faces like theirs.

The car weaved its way through the streets. I saw many German uniforms, very few people with yellow stars. Suddenly we were again surrounded by people streaming in one direction. I remembered that aimless crowd from before. They looked ahead with empty eyes and dragged their feet as they pushed ahead in the lead-colored snowy sludge. Snowflakes drifted through the air only to be transformed into slush when they reached the ground. I thought they were just like these people who had left their homes healthy and strong with a definite purpose, trusting there was a chance for them somewhere to start anew. They were transformed into these leaden figures of misery. They were not beggars; they did not ask for anything. They silently moved towards the West only to be shot by machine guns or die of starvation or exhaustion. Their destination? Few knew where they wanted to go. Away from the enemy!

"Mother!" I turned to her. "Why are there so few people with the yellow star on the streets? Did they change the regulations about them?"

"No, Helen, the Germans put them in ghettoes, or they took them to Germany. We have no idea, only rumors as to what happens with them there."

"Mother!" I huddled up close to her in the car. "What will the enemy do? Will they really take us from you? How can they?"

"These are some of the rumors," Mother said quietly, "but I don't think that this will happen. At least I decided that this could only happen over my dead body. Don't worry, Helen. Remember that no matter where we are, God is with us and if He is with us, there is nothing to fear." She stroked my hair.

"I said that we are going shopping," she continued. "We will, but first we'll have a meeting with the Swedish Embassy. We are going to arrange for a Swedish Children's Home in our house. Sweden is neutral. If we have their flag on the house the enemy may treat us better. Your father has worked out the details with them. Today the first family is going to arrive. She is an old grandmother with two little half orphans. Both the parents were our employees. The man left his wife and she hung herself.

"She did?!?" I shuddered. "Why would she do a thing like that? With two young children to bring up? Isn't that a great sin?"

"Yes, it is," Mother answered. "However, I think she must have been mentally ill or she could not have gone through with it."

"How old are her children?" I asked.

"They are the same age as Marie and Elisabeth," came the answer. "They'll stay on the first floor. Then Margit, a former maid of ours, and her illegitimate child will come to live with us also. Another good friend will come with her boys and spend the siege with us if they can get to our house before the enemy does. They too want to take advantage of the Swedish flag."

"What is an illegitimate child?" I inquired.

"If someone has a baby before she has a husband."

"How can that be?" I wondered.

"Every baby has a father. If a woman and a man live together they can have a baby even if they are not married. When you were very little Margit was a beautiful young girl. She used to take you for a walk. Then, one day you met a policeman. He started to talk to you and you answered him. Soon he was talking to her. She fell in love with him. He used to come and pick her up to go to church. After a few months it turned out that they did not go to church at all. They went and slept together. Margit was pregnant.

"What is 'pregnant'?" I asked.

"Pregnant is when someone expects a baby," Mother answered.

"So Margit had a baby," I said.

"Yes, honey. Sex is beautiful and it has its place in our lives, but not before we are married. We should keep ourselves for our one true love, for our husbands. You should not even kiss a man until he has asked you to marry him. I only kissed your father and Grandmother only kissed Grandfather."

"Is it bad to have an illegitimate child?" I wanted to know everything.

"It is very bad," Mother answered, "It's bad for the mother and for the child. The only one who does not get into trouble is the father. I went and talked to that policeman myself. He simply stated that he had another six children by six different women. 'Should I marry them all?' he asked."

"How could he do that?" I was appalled by his wickedness. I sat quietly thinking about the many new things I had heard while the automobile wound its way through the city's streets. Every now and then a house was missing from the perfect row, like teeth in old ladies' smiles. Ruins pointed towards the leaden sky like crooked fingers. I thought of the bomb-stricken families for whom we raised money in Mátrafüred during the summer. Where are those people now? What are they doing? Where do they live? Are some of them part of the stream of refugees walking towards Germany? Questions came to my mind, then were immediately crowded out again by other, more important issues.

We reached the Elisabeth Bridge. Its slim, lacy design, its golden color always reminded me of a delicate lady. Her sole arch stretched over the Danube, her piers leaned against the two shores. "The longest single span in Europe," I heard the words echo in my ears as we passed through the bridge. Every ten feet or so stood a tiny wooden house guarded by a soldier. I caught myself praying very hard. Just like I did every time we crossed any bridge since that memorable day...

～

Tremendous explosions shook the air and we all ran out into the garden.

"What is it?" asked the maid.

"What is it?" answered Grandmother.

We could see the entire city from our vantage point. A dust cloud rose from the direction of the Margaret Bridge, a strategic public transportation link between Buda and Pest and the only access to beautiful Margaret Island in the middle of the Danube. As the trembling air settled the dust, we could see the two arms of the graceful bridge helplessly fallen into the gray water; a mother's arm groping for her lost, drowning children.

We found out later that the ammunition, piled up in the tiny wooden houses, for a future strategic explosion of the Bridge during the anticipated siege exploded prematurely. People, traveling on the bridge from one side of the town to the other, rode to their watery graves in streetcars, buses, automobiles. The pedestrians were luckiest. Many of them escaped. Young men jumped into the water and pulled out people one after the other. They made as many trips back into the whirling water as their strength would allow. They dove as long as they saw survivors struggling in the waves. A friend of ours from Mátrafüred, an old Greek gentleman, I could still see his ruddy face and snow-white hair, also died in that mishap. He must have felt that his end would come by an explosion because he was so much afraid of bombs; this was why he lived in Mátrafüred. He met his fate nevertheless on the Bridge, while on a short trip to the capital.

Many people waited in vain for their loved ones to return home that day.

Their "tomorrow" came while crossing the bridge. Was it an accident? Sabotage? Guerrilla warfare? We never found out.

I looked at the last one of these unpredictable "time-bombs" on our bridge as we passed it and shuddered.

Men and women on the Pest side of the Danube reminded me of a busy ant colony as they hurried along the streets. They bought up everything edible, everything usable in preparation for the siege. The gray German uniforms among the khaki colored ones of the Hungarian soldiers did not let us forget that the war, the siege, would be enforced to the last.

The car rolled past the centuries-old Downtown Church. It had seen many enemies, even the long forgotten Turkish times when this church was made into a mosque for 150 years. Now another occupation awaited the thick old walls. Both Mother and Grandmother were married in this church. This is where I, too, wanted to get married.

The car now passed the millinery shop where Mother used to buy her hats. We stopped in the Petőfi Sándor Street, in front of our business' main store and offices.

Despite the war, the store was filled with customers although there was little merchandise left. We entered through the main door. To the right hand was the place for soaps, toothpaste, perfumes, and toiletries that glittered under the lights, on the left what used to be cameras, liqueurs, novelties. Then through an archway we arrived at what used to be a fairyland of toys. This was my favorite place. I looked at the remainder of the dolls, the many war toys, trains, stuffed animals that should have inspired people for Christmas shopping. I loved to play with toy soldiers. Our whole life, all I ever heard about, was connected with the war; our future depended on its outcome. My ability to survive was the most important aspect of being. I played often with miniature lead soldiers in the sandbox in Mátrafüred. Yet, now, when the shooting drew so very close I was not quite sure that I really wanted to acquire firsthand experience of life on the front. I dreamed of becoming a woman soldier, whenever I heard about heroic American and English ladies who joined the Armed Forces. Naturally, in my mind they were angelic and they fought everything that was evil. My soldiers were always knights in shining armor, they never got killed or wounded; they were always victorious and gentlemanly. In my imagination there were only soldiers like the ones I had seen first, at the beginning of the war. They were the first ones to leave, on flower-covered trains, singing, waving with a promise on their lips; "We'll come back victorious!" I intentionally wiped out of my memory the pictures I had seen later in newsreels, when the same trains came back not as gloriously as was expected but rather broken and war-beaten, filled with wounded young men. These newsreels were always short, the longer sections showed our victories and the losses of the enemy. Our troops always marched ahead with flowers on their helmets. Why did they end up in our own backyard then, fighting so close that in good weather we could see the cannon fire? I did not want to ask the question but I knew like everybody else did that it could not last much longer.

"It is insane to go on with that war," I heard someone whisper into Mother's ear.

"My son was home yesterday from the front," she continued. "He went back today—he took the streetcar."

"Are they that close?" Mother could hardly believe her ears.

"Yes, my dear," the old lady went on. "I can't see why we couldn't just stop fighting and let them march across Budapest."

"I think I know why," Mother looked meaningfully towards the door, where two German soldiers just entered.

"Yes," the old lady whispered then continued in a loud voice, "I hope that you'll have a nice Christmas. Wish me luck to find something to buy." She squeezed Mother's hand and disappeared into the crowd.

Father seemed very busy in his glass cubicle in the middle of the store from where he could oversee the whole business. "We managed to get more soap. I am so happy when we can supply our customers for another day and then again another."

He took off his white lab coat and slipped on his jacket. "Let's go to the Embassy," he said.

A fat, blond woman greeted us with a smile at the Swedish Embassy. Everything was settled. We received the flags and the directions, the regulations for the Swedish Children's Home we were about to establish. It didn't take very long before we were back in the store. Father stayed but Mother and I went to our downtown winter home.

"I'll show you a few places now," Mother said to me very seriously, "that you should never talk about to anybody. They are hiding places. We have things already hidden in them. Who knows what they'll be good for in the future. If necessary..." she didn't finish the sentence.

She held me by the hand and led me up the stairs, then into the attic.

"Are we above the elevator now?" I asked.

"We'll be there in a minute. I want you to know these places because… because…," again she left the words hanging in the air, unfinished. I kissed her hand vehemently and pressed it to my chest. She hugged me.

We stepped over the big wheels of the elevator and—there it was. Mother opened the wall. In a small space behind it were jewelry, gold pieces, documents, salt, and food.

"Why salt, Mother? Why food?" I wondered.

"Because there will be no food, and salt will be priceless during and after a siege. It may save our lives and that of many others. Now, not a word about this. This alone is enough for us to start our business anew, as many people had to do after the First World War."

"Why didn't you hide money, Mother? Wouldn't that be the most logical thing to do?" I asked.

"After the First World War money was not worth anything. After the Revolution in Russia, aristocrats starved with bags of diamonds in their hands. Nobody would give them bread for diamonds. There was none. Your father and I tried to save a little of everything in the 'hole' as I call our hiding place. I felt that I had to show you this, just in case." Again she did not say it, but it was implied, just as in Grandmother's "tomorrow." Death loomed over everything, over the whole town, busily preparing for Christmas, desperately trying to forget that the enemy is only an earshot away. Again, I had to think of the hit song, "The world is but one day…our life is but an only kiss…"

"Now, let's go down to the cellar," said Mother while she cautiously stepped over the wheels of the elevator and helped me across, too. The house was empty except for a housekeeper-cook, a fortyish, militant woman, the kind cartoonists draw with turned-up sleeves and a menacing rolling pin in their hands. We passed the second floor, then the first, the shiny doorknobs, the immaculately clean hallways, and down the stairs to the main floor. In the servants' quarters we met Pista, a trusted employee.

"Hi!" I greeted him. "You live here now?"

"Yes, he does," Mother answered for him. "Pista, would you please come with us and help me get into the 'hole'?"

"Another 'hole'?" I asked Mother.

"Yes, another one. Pista is the only one besides your father, grandparents, and you who knows every little square inch in this house. We asked him to move over here when his house was struck by a bomb," Mother explained.

Pista came with us as a matter of course. He helped my parents to set up these "holes," as Mother called them.

It was dark in the cellar but Pista brought a flashlight and in no time at all we stood at the door or rather bricks that led to the mysterious place. I knew the general direction we were going but I was not sure that I would find the place if I were alone.

As if in answer to my thought, Mother said, "You know the empty rooms of our former laboratory on the main floor?"

I nodded.

"We are right underneath those now," she continued.

Then she lifted the bricks with the help of Pista and a much bigger "hole" than the one in the attic opened up in the weak beam of the flashlight. Here, Mother and Father even hid clothes and bed linens. Pictures, very beautiful ones, sterling silver sets, and food again.

I did not need to ask now, I already knew why.

"Thank you for showing me; I will not betray you, ever." I embraced Mother and held her very close. She gave a signal to Pista, who started right away to put the bricks back in place,

"Thank you, Pista," we both shook hands with him.

"Now we are going 'fun-shopping'," Mother's eyes glowed with excitement. "We'll buy toys for your sisters. What should we buy for Father? He seems to have everything and he does not smoke," Mother seemed puzzled. She acted as if nothing had happened, while I was still in a daze from all the new things I had seen.

Agnes, the housekeeper-cook, poured an unending litany of gossip over our snack in the kitchen.

"You know the landlord next door?" she blabbered.

"Eva's father?" I asked then turned to Mother. "She was the one who ran over to ask Grandmother if she could help them, wasn't she?"

"Well, they were taken, the whole family," Agnes went on as Mother nodded her "yes" to my question. I couldn't help thinking that "tomorrow" had become yesterday for them, too.

Agnes' gossip was endless, "I heard they were taken to Germany, at least that is what the janitor said. Where he gets his information, I really don't know. I would like to see the whole war over with! I hate this suspense! Why couldn't the enemy come quicker and save many people from being taken?" She did not take a breath while she talked. Every part of her tall figure expressed her story.

"Do you think the Soviets will be better?" Mother asked her with a worried frown. Whenever she did that I wanted to smooth those frown wrinkles away. I couldn't stand looking at them on her smooth skin.

"Who knows? At least there would be no bombs. The Germans say many bad things about the Soviets, but I say that they are only people, only human, like us. What could they do to us? My son was here yesterday to visit from the front. What a handsome soldier he is! He said the same thing. He said there is no use to fight any more. They'll get us one way or another. Why do we have to kill so many people in the process?" She put a plate in front of Pista and heaped food onto it.

Pista dug his fork in the food as if it were the first he had seen in weeks but his sturdy figure belied this assumption.

"Don't you think, Agnes, that the Germans are human also? Yet how much wrong have they done to all of us," Mother said quietly.

Agnes looked at her and for once she did not know what to answer.

"Agnes and Pista," Mother started, "when we are not around, take care of this house as if it was your own. I don't know what will happen in the near future but in your able hands I know everything will be as safe as is humanly possible." Mother folded her napkin and stood up. Her eyes as well as the eyes of the other two were full of tears. I was embarrassed. Finally, I hugged Agnes and shook Pista's hand.

I felt relief when we were outside the delicately carved wooden door with its cut glass inlays. The key turned in the lock. The house was closed from the outside world. For how long? Only God knew.

Playful snowflakes fell and I stuck out my tongue to feel their fresh ice-cold softness melting in my mouth.

"When are we going to ice skate?" I asked Mother. As soon as I said it I knew it was nonsense because… "Did they open the ice skating rink in Városliget at all this year?" I went on.

"No, they didn't. Not this year," Mother answered. "I bet the snowflakes made you remember the days when I picked you up at school and we went ice skating. Wasn't it fun?"

"Oh, yes, Mother, I can hardly wait to go skating again! Maybe next year! If we can we will go, won't we, won't we?"

"Of course we will. You'll see. We'll dance again on the ice and I'll call our dancing partners. Do you remember Uncle Tihamér, the one with the red hair? I can't imagine how he always had time to come with us!" Mother remembered.

"I can imagine. I know why," I looked at Mother with admiration, "because you are so beautiful and nice and kind to everybody. That is why they all want to be with you, they all come when you call." I squeezed her hand and skipped along the sidewalk in the floating ballet of the snowflakes. Just the perfect weather for Christmas shopping! We wove our way through the sea of shoppers along the two main streets. We had a store on each of them, and two more on the street that was perpendicular. We stopped at one of our shops, "I have to get toys for all the 'Swedish' children, also," Mother counted them on her fingers. There were eight of them altogether, ranging from eight months to fourteen years old; all extra-special, hand-picked children.

Those "Swedish" children none of whom spoke a word of Swedish but about to be protected by the good will of the Swedish Red Cross, became my brothers and sisters from that day on. They belonged to the family, together with their families, who also moved in with us.

By the time we arrived back at our summer home, where we decided to weather the siege, one of the families Mother talked about had already arrived. Grandmother was busy settling them.

Mrs. Rosta who came with her two grandchildren was a perfect grandmother figure. She was short and round with white hair flying around her benevolent face. The two girls, eight and five years old, were quiet and looked around with wide eyes. It didn't occur to me then but they had probably never before seen a house like ours before. They curtsied very politely to my mother and Mrs. Rosta made an attempt to kiss Mother's out-stretched hand.

Juli, the older girl, wore glasses. I always wanted to have glasses because Elsie wore glasses when she read and I thought they made a person look very smart. Juli had dark brown eyes and she looked cross-eyed. The little one was a delicate beauty with huge blue eyes and blond, curly locks.

While I shyly approached them I could not escape the thought, How could their mother leave them, how could she take her life, when she had such lovely children?!?

It was hard to think of something to talk about. They were obviously awestruck, and I felt like a circus attraction the way they looked at me.

"Come, I'll show you some toys," I ushered them into the playroom. If possible their eyes grew even bigger when they saw our doll houses. We had two exquisite structures, one was two stories high, the other had a lazy susan-like inside and we could turn the rooms around in a circle. Marie and Elisabeth brought out dolls and games. Soon Juli and Ili, the two new sisters, became part of the family.

As I was crawling into the bathtub later that night I noticed something unusual. If I poked my breast with even a finger, it hurt. There was something firm in it, yet soft as a pillow. The nipples stood up and while I bathed I noticed hair on my body in different places where I had never seen it before. Until now, my body looked like that of my sisters and now it started to become like Mother's. I felt happy and proud, even though it hurt a bit, yet, this little hurt reminded me of the fact that I was growing up.

# 8

"Hey, you know what? Our other grandparents are coming for Christmas!" I shouted as I burst into the room. "They just called from Auntie's house. Auntie, Uncle, their baby, and Grandma and Grandpa are going to come and stay with us, until all this will be over!" I grabbed Elisabeth and waltzed around the room with her.

"Is the little baby coming, too?" Marie could not hide her happiness. She was in love with babies, any and all, especially this one, our only first cousin so far.

"Yes, yes, yes!" I assured her while twirling around in happiness. Juli and Ili joined in too, although they did not even know them.

Margit and her son, Joe, had arrived the day after Mrs. Rosta came with her two grandchildren. It was very easy to play with the two girls but Joe just could not put up with all the female company. He was a true boy, mischievous to his last bone. Margit's features showed her former beauty that was crowded out only by her extreme weight gain since she was no longer a young girl. The two of them had a room in the basement and Joe spent quite a bit of his time in the yard or in the kitchen. He found the company of adults more fascinating than the company of girls.

"Come, everybody, let's prepare the rooms for Grandma and Grandpa!" Mother called us and we skipped across the living room to the room that used to be Elsie's. Another room right next to it and a sun porch looked down onto the tennis court and the grassy hillside that led up to it.

Father's parents lived in Cegléd, forty miles from Budapest. My tiny grandmother (she was only four feet, nine inches, so we all called her Little Grandma) was someone who rarely came even for a visit. She liked to stay in her own house and nowhere else in the world. Grandfather stood six feet, three inches tall and weighed at least 230 pounds. The most unlikely couple. I loved them dearly and I cherished the memory of every minute I spent in their house, where my father grew up.

We brought in the best of everything: pillows, featherbeds, blankets. We put up our old crib for baby Imi and changed the bed linen for his parents. My uncle, who was an officer, was home because he had been wounded at the front. They lived downtown close to our usual winter home and only a half hour's drive from where we stayed now. They arrived very soon after we fixed their beds.

"Imi! Oh, how beautiful you have become since I last saw you!" Marie could not take her eyes off the baby, while I hugged my Little Grandma. I was the one who knew her best. Every year I had my own little vacation at her place.

"How is everything at your house in Cegléd?" I asked her.

She sighed and tears started rolling down her face as she answered, "How should I know? The enemy took our home already. We came up here to be together. My house is important, but my children and grandchildren," by now she was sobbing, "are much more important to me."

I hugged and squeezed her vehemently. "Don't cry, Grandma! Don't cry! I am so happy that you are with us! Everything is better if we are together at least!" I repeated the often-heard sentence myself now. I didn't know if it would help, I just knew that this was the thing to say.

"We heard so many horrible things," she sobbed, "in one of the villages they supposedly killed every tenth man because they found a hidden German soldier. There was fright in her eyes as she looked at me, "I shouldn't say things like that to you, after all..." She hugged me again. I noticed with consternation that I was nearly her size.

"Come now, Mother, calm down," Auntie embraced her shoulders. "Look at Marie and Imi. Isn't he cute? She is so happy with him."

I had to look in the same direction and I realized that Imi had grown into a remarkably lovely eight-month-old, cooing, smiling, explaining with all his might. That could not help but cheer up Grandma, her attention turned entirely to her grandchildren now.

"You have grown so much, all three of you! Helen, you are nearly as tall as I am! Marie, you surely enjoy babies, don't you? You'll make a good little mother some day. Elisabeth! Come here, little one. I don't even dare to say 'little one' anymore! How old are you? Oh my, oh my, how time flies! And who are these little girls?"

"They are Juli and Ili. They live downstairs, in Grandfather's study. And Margit, you know, who used to be our maid, lives here with her son, Joe, also." I tried to introduce everyone at once.

Father arrived home with many parcels, and the maids brought up the suitcases for Grandma to unpack. Grandpa's huge frame appeared in the door right after Father came in.

"The traffic is unbelievable! Most people from Buda want to go over to Pest to spend the siege, while the ones in Pest are trying to get to the other side of the Danube. All bridges are loaded with panic-stricken people. Only God knows where it will be best but I am sure happy that we are all together," Father reported. "Today we ran out of soap. I could not secure enough anymore, the demand is overwhelming. But it's not only soap, everything is bought up with a dizzying speed. As soon as merchandise comes in one door it immediately goes out the other. I brought home a truckloadful of baby cereal that we are selling at the store. It will be fine food if we run out of everything else."

Grandmother had just arrived from downstairs, "Our chickens are happily laying eggs in the chicken coop beside the garage."

Little Grandma turned to her. "You have chickens now? I never knew you could keep chickens in the capital?"

"Of course we never could and we never did," answered Grandmother who towered above Little Grandma like the steeple beside a small village church, "it is only in preparation for the siege that I acquired about thirty of them. They are live food, after all."

Little Grandma seemed pleased with the idea. By the time the intercom phone from the kitchen announced that supper was ready, everybody was settled comfortably. We were thankful that no air raid interrupted our work.

By now air raids became so much a part of everybody's life that even though they held the same dangers as they did before and sometimes even fiercer ones, nobody made a big deal out of them.

The first time I heard in school that one of my classmates was killed in an air raid I walked around in a daze for days. Her face still appeared in front of me. She was a refugee from Poland. Her name was Christa. She wore gold-rimmed glasses. Her thin face and blue eyes spoke of early maturity. She had to live fast; she died when she was but ten years old. Maybe she too, had experienced the feeling of her growing breasts, the first pangs of sexuality I struggled through during the endless nights.

It happened more and more often that I woke up in the middle of a dream, or I could not go back to sleep after an air raid because I felt my body on fire. I knew it was sinful. At least it had something to do with the sixth commandment as far as I could interpret from what I heard grownups say. Yet, it was something wonderful that yearned to be fulfilled. I threw myself around in bed and tried not to let go of myself and become enveloped completely into that overwhelming, beautiful desire. For what? I felt it was a desire for everything, to create, to help everybody, to build new life, to become.

In those days, morning came slowly, stealing darkness away with its gray fingers. My sisters slept like logs.

Three days before Christmas, Mother took me downtown again. We went past the Déli Pályaudvar (Southern Railroad Station). Ambulances swarmed around the building that did not look like a building at all anymore. It looked more like a skeleton of an extinct, prehistoric animal. Among its ribs dirty ghostlike figures moved and cleaned the remains of the repeated air raids.

"Who are they?" I asked Mother.

"They are Jews, ordered to work on projects that are military in nature but they are behind the lines, to prevent them from getting into contact with the enemy," Mother answered.

Our car passed a conglomerate of railroad cars that were pressed together like an accordion by a giant player, then thrown away, as if in boredom. A staircase hung in the air, leading nowhere.

"Where are they taking those people?" I noticed that stretcher after stretcher disappeared into the skeleton of the former railroad station, as if the monster would feed on human lives.

"They are probably evacuating them," Mother sighed. "The whole town, everything is being 'evacuated' by the Germans." Her voice sounded sarcastic when she said the word "evacuated."

I repeated the word, "Evacuated?"

"Yes," Mother said, "evacuated." She sounded the same again. "Just yesterday a good friend of ours had his factory 'evacuated' by the Germans. They even took the towel bars off the wall and loaded everything on trucks. He could not say a word."

"Where do they go?" I asked.

"They go to Germany. Why? Don't ask me. The Allies are breaking through to the Germans from the other side. All they can gain is to be captured on the road. Their homes will be occupied by others by the time they'll be back. At least that is how we see it," Mother answered.

"Do they think that they can win the war? Still?" I could hardly believe my ears.

"Yes, there are idealists who think we still could win."

"Is that why they go out onto the highways and try to escape from the enemy's advance? Is that why they keep running?" I asked again.

"Some are convinced. Others are panicky. Most everybody is, in this holocaust." Mother looked around. "See all these people how they hurry from here to there? It is not easy to sit still and wait. Everybody's nerves are jittery. We must constantly do something in order to keep our minds off the war but it is very difficult to think."

We crossed the bridge again. I prayed hard all the way across but in the meantime I let my eyes drink in the wonder and the beauty of the still intact Elisabeth Bridge, the majestic outlines of the Parliament, the beauty of those buildings that were still standing. "Tomorrow" may wipe them out completely.

We arrived at our destination. We were in the middle of downtown, in front of the Franciscan Church. I heard a big bang as we stepped into the pharmacy to collect a huge package of medicines we were going to keep in stock for the siege. Another big bang followed. They sounded far away, they were not bombs. There was no air raid. What was it then? I looked around and saw jittery old ladies make the sign of the cross. The pharmacist said quietly, "Cannonfire, approximately 15 to 20 kilometers away."

Mother's face became pale.

"I think we better hurry home. Who knows how long the bridges will still be there? God bless you." We hurried out of the store with our enormous bundle.

In front of the church I whispered, "Jesus, help us!" we stopped by the store, Father assured us that he would come as soon as he could.

For some reason I kept thinking about the Christmas tree. Would we have one this year? Would we have one at all?

Our Christmas tree was always delivered by little baby Jesus and his angels, always on the 24th of December, in the evening. Naturally I knew that it was my parents who had prepared it but I had to pretend because of my sisters. Yet, I did not want to ask Mother. She had enough on her mind. This year I had to hope for a miracle.

~

December 24 was a gray winter day. When I woke up I felt a lump in my throat from sheer excitement. Will the little Jesus come on His birthday? My sisters were still asleep; I could hear their rhythmic breathing. The cannons' thunders from the not-too-far distance struck resonance with the heartbeat I felt in my throat. I tiptoed out of the room and down the staircase on the red carpet to the downstairs dining room, where we planned to celebrate Christmas Eve. If the little Jesus was going to come the room would be locked.

I peeked through the door of the lounge. The door was closed. That still did not mean it was locked. I ran across the lounge to the door and tried the handle. The door did not budge. Joy leapt through me, we are going to have a Christmas! I scampered back to bed and I was happy that no one had noticed me.

~

In the afternoon, at about 6 o'clock, right after Father had come back from the store, silver bells announced the arrival of the angels. The wide glass doors with their fine muslin curtains opened without visual interference of human powers. A flood of lights and sparkles chased away the darkness of winter from the rooms around it. There was no war now. Even the cannons stopped their infernal music. The Savior was born for us in the middle of man-made human misery, on the doorstep of a siege, the end of which may find none of us alive. It was all forgotten now. Even if we would have had to die that instant, we were in the process of celebrating the fact that centuries ago our lives were made worthwhile by the arrival of an Infant who had changed the world.

The children stood in awe, the adults frequently wiped their tears as we sang the age-old carol: "Angels from Heaven came down to you, shepherds…" The magic of Christmas held us all spellbound. The whole household, twenty-two people in all, gathered in the dining room to celebrate and cry the tears of the persecuted and the homeless under the roof which belonged to every one of us now. I imagined that we lived in a medieval castle that withstood the siege of the enemy forever. A curious peace embraced those who thought of their loved ones far away, of their homes they had left to be with their children and grandchildren, who escaped to the relative safety of our "castle," bearing the flag of Sweden.

There were presents for everybody under the Christmas tree. They spoke of the love we felt towards each other.

My favorite present was a red leather purse with a golden buckle on it. It came from Grandpa, the one who had just arrived from Cegléd. His store there sold purses, suitcases, harnesses, saddles, everything made from leather. I loved to sit there and watch his men work. He left his store now, his life savings, his house— everything he held dear in his life. Yet, he did not forget to bring me this last present. I started crying while I opened the little package and smelled the leather, felt the silk lining, and ran my fingers down its dainty seams. Through my tears I could hardly see the beautiful books I received. I was glad to get books any day, but now with all the air raids, they were doubly precious. An amber necklace came from my godfather. He was an army officer also, as most everybody was whom I knew, but he too remembered me. No matter what the conditions were, his present was always under the tree as long as I could remember.

I was proud to have received adult gifts, not toys like the ones Marie, Elisabeth, Juli, Ili, and Joe received. They were much more like the gifts of someone like the gardener's daughter. She was fourteen years old and I looked up to her. I liked to play with her but she seldom had time. She always had to help her widowed mother. Our gardener had died from tuberculosis, the son got married, and more and more of the burden fell on the two women left in the gardener's place. The son and his wife came to help often. They were with us today also. They planned on spending the siege with us and taking advantage of the Swedish flag, if there was any advantage to it. This nobody knew yet. It was hard to know anything. There were many rumors, yet… what could be believed?

I was so involved in admiring everyone's presents that it came as a cruel awakening when the cannonfire started again, much stronger than it had ever been before. I heard Father's voice, "I think we'd better get our things together and move to the cellar before it's too late."

Grandmother blew out the candles on the tree. Christmas was over; war was back again.

The presents were cleared away in no time at all. I ran to my giant Grandpa and stood on my tiptoes. He still had to bend down to accept my kiss.

"Oh thank you, thank you, Grandpa," I rubbed my face against his scratchy chin (no matter how clean-shaven he was, his chin always scratched me a little) and took a deep breath from his manly cigar smell. He was the only one in our family who smoked and I liked his peculiar smell which I associated with carefree summers at his house.

Then I grabbed my treasures and headed toward the cellar. As I passed the phone, it rang. Grandmother answered it, then she summoned Father and said in a low voice, "The city is surrounded by the Soviets. Our next door neighbor just called, you know, the one who is director of all public transportation. He gets reports and promised to let us know of every move as long as the phone is working. Under Pest, on the southern side, the Soviet army troops met with troops coming from the other side of the Danube, near Csepel. Another arm of the Soviets advanced to the new St. John Hospital right beneath our hill. They were stopped there but the ring is complete.

I heard their conversation because I was nearby and already the first sentence curdled my blood. I could not move an inch. I had to listen.

"I think we better sleep in the cellar," Father sad aloud. Then he whispered to me, "Don't tell anyone what you heard. There is no need to frighten everybody. Whenever they get here, they'll be here. We are in God's hands."

I remembered what Grandmother always told me when I was little,

"The Lord is with me, I will not be afraid; what can men do to me?" The move to the cellar began. Somehow everybody sensed that this time our stay would be longer than mere hours.

～

The morning of the 25th was cold and gray, yet several of us, including Little Grandma and I, decided that we would try to go up the hill to Mass. Grandmother's source reported that the army was still in the same position, there was not much shooting, even the cannonfire seemed to have died down in the morning. It was a steep 15 to 20 minute walk to church in the brisk

December cold; but the choice that faced us, to spend the time idly in the cellar, made it infinitely more attractive. We set out on foot walking in the middle of the road. Soon we met neighbors who whispered, "The city is surrounded. I just talked to a man whose truck was turned back last night at the edge of the city because the guards claimed that the enemy had completely surrounded us."

"Surrounded? Is that so?" We pretended not to have heard it already. I felt frightful excitement all over. What did it mean?

"Should we go on?" I asked Grandma.

"I think we should. God will protect us, we are going to church. Besides, Leningrad was besieged for 900 days. Do you want to spend it all in the cellar? Just in case..." She smiled and we doubled our speed.

We cut across the frosty field. Patches of dirty snow lay on the hopelessly gray ground and frozen mud. It was quite a delight to go past the roadside crucifix, from its tin roof icicles hung and shone through the gray landscape. As I looked through them they turned the world into a black and white kaleidoscope. Reality lost its weekday attire and was clothed into the characters of fairytales. The road was slippery. We found a nice stick and Grandma steadied herself with that. I didn't mind slipping; I was a good skater and hardly ever lost my balance. I guess as one got older one became more aware of danger and therefore more susceptible to fall victim of it.

The church was filled with whispering people. Everybody seemed to have heard the news and I too could talk about it now because I had heard it on the street. The whispers were loaded with fear, worry, and excitement. Nobody knew what to expect, yet there was also a desire for liberation of war, of the Germans. Could all the propaganda we had heard be true? The Soviets were only human...

The candles burned on the altar but the church was in near darkness. Nobody wanted to attract attention. We prayed for just peace in the world on the birthday of the Prince of Peace.

I remembered the wedding of one of my aunts in this church, just a few weeks back. She married a Swedish gentleman who was going to protect her. She wore a brown dress with a beautiful lilac flower. Mother said it was an orchid. I had never seen one like that before. The wedding was sad. The bride was the daughter of a very rich auto-body manufacturer, a beauty queen. Everybody expected a different marriage, a different husband for her. Yet, under the circumstances she made the best bargain, or this is how it seemed at the time. "What are they doing today? How is their Christmas?" I wondered. According to what we had heard they were still under German occupation. Their house was on Kissvábhegy. This was the headquarters for air defense in Budapest. "Are they still alive?" I asked myself.

Then it was communion time. Jesus came into our hearts on His birthday. I begged Him to keep us alive. As soon as I uttered the words I remembered how, not so long ago, I would have felt happy to die right after communion. What happened? Was death such a close reality that from this distance it did not seem desirable anymore?

Mass ended with the national anthem. "God bless the Hungarians" our cry tore the words straight from our hearts. "Our suffering nation had atoned already for the sins of past and future." The last bars sounded strong amidst the strengthening cannonfire. Nobody said it but everybody knew it: we would not be together in this church any more before the siege was over.

"The Mass is ended, go…Ite, missa est!"

# 9

I no longer knew or cared what the weather was like. Sometimes I went out into the kitchen and saw through its door-sized windows that it was dark and gray outside. According to our friend next door, the Soviets had already occupied the church; they were on their way down the hill. Two houses from us Germans held a great big villa, like ours. Two summers before a successful Hungarian movie, Fever of Love, was filmed in that house and in ours. Now, that other house was about to be shot to pieces. Any house that was occupied by soldiers faced that fate unless they surrendered. And surrender was out.

Two frightened-faced, young soldiers banged on the kitchen window. Our kitchen and the servants' quarters were in the downstairs of the house. The kitchen window was fixed in a manner that it could also be used as a door, then five steps led down to the enormous kitchen. Since we lived in the cellar, the whole household ate at the kitchen table, which could comfortably accommodate at once all twenty-two inhabitants of our "castle."

"Wir sind hungrig!" the two boys pleaded. One of them looked much like Tommy. The cook, a big, kind woman, looked at Father, who nodded approval. They were let in. "Es ist kalt." They rubbed their freezing hands. Their cheeks were fallen in. They had no resemblance to the young people of newsreels, Hitler Jugend, the blond, smiling, marching, singing troops. They had no flowers around their necks. The cook poured hot soup in two big bowls and cut a generous portion of sausage for each to eat with their bread.

I listened carefully as they started to talk. "I am so tired. I wish I could go home," the one that looked like Tommy said.

"Where is your home?" Father asked. I did not even dare to come close. I looked from the corner of the kitchen as he answered. "Bayern" (Bavaria). Then he continued to wolf down the food.

"How old are you?" Father inquired.

"I'm sixteen, my friend is seventeen. We were drafted three months ago straight from high school," he answered.

"Straight from school? Did you volunteer?" Father pursued the issue.

86

"Volunteer? Are you kidding?" the boy's eyes opened as wide as a saucer.

"They took you from school?" Father did not know about anybody in Hungary taken without volunteering at that age.

"They let the 14-year-olds volunteer but not the ones our age," he laughed at the idea. Apparently the warm food made him feel at home.

"I volunteered," the other one started to talk suddenly. "Two years ago. I still believed something could be done. I don't know why I did it. I forgot the reason while fighting in the dirty muddy fields, the houses that were shot to smithereens, my buddies who had died in my arms, the ones I could not even give that comfort. I was wounded but when I recovered they sent me back to the front lines…" his voice trailed off.

"We should be out there now," the image-of-Tommy remembered when he heard the mention of the "front lines."

"Where is the front now?" asked Father.

Both of them looked at him surprised. "You mean to say you don't know that we are on the front? This is the front. What did you think it would be like? On today's front we don't know whom we shoot, we don't see the enemy, we only feel them. Their fire shatters us and ours shatters them. We fight the invisible."

We were all silent for some time. Finally, Father broke the silence,

"We knew the front was close, but we didn't know it was that close. Can we do anything else for you?"

"Thank you for letting us rest awhile. We must go." They climbed back up the stairs and gave a last longing glance at the friendly fire in the big wood stove, where the kind cook was baking one of her huge breads.

Father called after them, "Come back later, we'll have fresh bread."

"We'll be back." Their eyes, sparkled as they waved good-bye.

I loved the smell of the bread and tried to stay in the kitchen as much as I could. Something was always happening there, I liked to sit beside the cook and talk about just anything that came to my mind. It was boring in the ironing room, where we had arranged our air-raid shelter. It had an emergency exit through a man-sized window reinforced with bricks and sandbags. Strong beams supported the ceiling that was made of reinforced concrete, like the rest of the two-story house that stood above the air raid shelter ironing room. The shelter was only one door away from the kitchen. Beside it there was an enormous food storage area and a toilet, right across from it, the laundry room. Both rooms had iron stoves for heat. The maids' rooms had windows toward the garden, the view of the city. The hall that led there opened from the kitchen on the other side, on the side where we sat with the cook and watched the bread bake.

"I wonder what my Mother and Father are doing?" the cook said.

"I never heard you talk about them before," I answered. "Where do they live?"

"I never talked about them because I saw them at least once a week. They live right below the hill, in Fö utca," she said.

"I have a beautiful young sister, too. She is seventeen, do you want to see her picture?"

"Yes, I want to see her," it was hard for me to imagine that the big, kind cook who was forty years old had a little sister, seventeen.

She hurried into her room and brought back the picture of an angelic looking young girl. Her hair was pulled back into a knot, but some locks loosely curled around her neck and forehead. "Isn't she beautiful?" she asked proudly,

I thought she looked very beautiful and I said so. Then Grandmother noticed that I was not in the shelter.

"You get back there," she pointed towards the door.

"Yes, Grandmother," I dragged my feet. Just what was the matter? I didn't want to understand what difference it could possibly make… then a big blast shook the windows.

Grandmother grabbed me and pushed me through the door and into the shelter. "Now you stay in here!" she scolded.

I couldn't really get mad at her because she only wanted to save me, yet…

~

December 27. More rumors came through the phone. The Soviets were only two streets away from us now. We heard that they had found a record player in one of the houses, then they started to make music. They needed dancers, they took all the young girls they could find to their party. They were drinking, and then they ended up raping the girls.

"What is rape?" I asked Mother.

"Rape is when they take a girl and live with her against her will," she answered. "You know that we spoke several times about keeping yourself innocent and pure for your marriage. How many times did I tell you that you were not supposed to kiss anybody before you were engaged to him? Do you remember, Helen? These Soviets take advantage of the purity and innocence of young girls. I heard of a father, who killed his daughters, because the Soviets wanted to take them, then, he committed suicide with the same pistol. It is a very grave problem, indeed."

"I am going to take precautions," Father said while he hid our gramophone and records. Then he went into the food storage and one after the other our priceless reserve of liquors and wines were poured down the sink. I watched motionless as the dark golden cognacs, the brown-orange rums, imported liqueurs, the famous Hungarian apricot brandy by the gallon were poured down the drain. Then came Grandfather's wines, the ones he was so proud of. He had a great cellar both here and in our winter house and stored bottles by the thousands of his favorite wines under his own label. Now all of these had to go. It seemed to me a form of suicide. I couldn't move away from the spot where I stood. Then all of a sudden everything became dark. The lights went out in the whole house.

"Quick, let's fill up everything with water!" I heard Grandmother's voice. "I'm sure water will be the next thing to go. During the First World War there was no water either." She ran to the nearest tap and held a bucket under it. Mother ran upstairs to fill the bathtubs. Father decided to fill the tub on the second floor. The maids and I helped Grandmother by handing her pot after pot.

The gardener's widow, Mrs. Varga, and her family came over. "I don't dare to stay at my house any longer," she said. "Somehow it felt more secure when more were together. Her son, János, was looking for Father. He said he found two bleeding Germans in the garden and he knew Father was a medical doctor.

"Where are they?" Father was back from the second floor, "Show me the way."

They left through the back door. When they came back Father's face was as white as the wall, "They are dead. They are the two young boys who never came back last night. They were only a few steps from safety when something hit them." He turned his face away from us and went out of the kitchen.

The phone rang upstairs. I heard Father's voice, then he yelled downstairs, "The Soviets are on the street right above us, in the street of our neighbor who kept calling. This was his last call." Father came back. As soon as he closed the door behind him the water stopped running.

There was a long and dark silence after we all scrambled into the air-raid shelter, interrupted only by occasional machine gun fire and the usual sound of the cannons. The heavy artillery fire was going back and forth above us at this point. No close detonations. Then all of a sudden a new, hitherto unknown noise, the butts of guns thumping on our door and the iron bars of the kitchen windows simultaneously. Father and the cook ran out to open the window before they broke it. Two menacing soldiers burst into the air-raid shelter. We cried in loud prayer and screamed the word, "Magyarski! Magyarski!" at their long litany of curses. They looked around in disgust. The word did not mean anything to them. Our intention was to let them know that we were Hungarians. We tried to achieve this by putting the suffix "ski" to our Hungarian word for our nationality. Although they did not understand what we meant, they saw that all they found in our house was hysterical women and children, except for Father. They did not see János, the gardener's son, whom we hid behind the children. For the time being they were satisfied with Father's company. He tried to show them the Swedish flag in the kitchen. He also spoke a few words of Russian. Before the siege Mother and Father had learned some Russian to be able to talk with them if it ever became necessary.

Now his knowledge proved useful, as they would not respond in either German, French, or English let alone Hungarian. The only language was Russian. One of them had a sore arm. Blood was seeping through his heavy coat. Father motioned him to the table and pointed to his wound. He just signaled with his hand that it was not important. Then Father took out his bag that had a few medical instruments in it. The soldier's eyes lit up. He threw off his coat, Father looked at the wound. The other soldier stepped to the Swedish flag. He started to explain something but when he saw that he got nowhere with his explanation he became angrier and angrier. Finally, he stepped to our First Aid kit and pointed to the Red Cross emblem on it.

Father was finished with the wound and could give all his attention to the irate soldier now. He slowly understood while the soldier pulled the Red Cross emblem and the Swedish flag together that the soldier was trying to tell him to put out a Red Cross flag, indicating that medical help could be found at our house.

"Choroshy doctor," the other soldier said, gratefully observing his arm. Then he muttered some words about the fact that there were no doctors around.

"No doctors and we are in the front line?" Father could not believe his ears. The two soldiers kept repeating the sentence trying to express that they meant every word of what they said.

For the next six weeks, while the front lines were one block from our house, Father and our kitchen became the First Aid Station for wounded soldiers.

# 10

Days and nights flowed into one. Nobody measured time any more. We had no watches. The first Soviet soldiers yelled, "Tshasy! Tshasy!" and that was the end of all watches. We lost a few to their insistence to possess all time pieces, the rest were hidden. We didn't need to know the time anyway. We ate when we had something to eat, we slept when we could. In the air-raid shelter we had two bunk-beds and one single bed. Grandmother and Grandfather slept on one of the lower bunks. In the upper bunk, we hid Mother behind the three of us. Whenever we were not there to cover her, we piled pillows and featherbeds in front of her. She was the most beautiful among the young women; she had to be hidden all the time. The room was completely dark. We saved the candles for emergencies. In the corner of the room we had an "uncandle" (a small wick swimming in oil) as the sole source of light. I liked to spend time in the upper bunk and try to make out the letters one by one in my new books. I did not get far, yet I had the illusion that I was reading. I enjoyed the story and if I could not read any longer I made up my own tales. The other bunk belonged to Aunt, Uncle, Imi, Little Grandma, Mrs. Rosta and her grandchildren. We widened the single bed with a makeshift bench-like structure. Grandpa, Father, and Margit with her son, Joe, lay on that crosswise. Father stayed right next to the door. Anybody who came in had to fall over him. The gardener's son and wife slept on top of a big case between the bunk-bed and the emergency exit-window. His sister, Ica, made her bed on three upholstered chairs in front of the case. Everybody else put big featherbeds on the floor and slept there. When we all settled down for however many hours of sleep we could get in a row, nobody could move in the room. It was packed solid, twenty-two people in a room fifteen by twenty feet. It was more comfortable, whenever we decided that it was daytime, because then everybody was sitting up and some of the people went to the kitchen, or moved into other rooms of the downstairs. The cook spent most of her time in the kitchen. She wanted to find out about her parents. She became so obsessed with the idea she went completely berserk. She yelled at everybody, threw temper tantrums, and slobbered all over any Soviet soldier who entered the house.

Everybody tried to restrain her from becoming a victim of her own behavior.

"Look, Betty, the soldiers will misunderstand what you are doing. They'll think that you want to go to bed with them," Grandmother warned her but nothing helped.

One day a captain took her. Then she decided that the captain was a nice man. She took her stuff and moved out into the room where the captain stayed.

The Red Cross emblem helped indeed. The Soviets, knowing that Father would be the first to see them if anything happened to them, became very tame every time he was around. Very often he wasn't though. He established a hospital next door, in an empty house. Our kitchen was only an emergency station.

The very first day when they came, the Soviets completely expropriated the kitchen. We were very hungry by night, yet they decided not to let us enter their "headquarters."

"We must eat," Grandmother decided. "Let's see what we can find. We have a stove right here in the room."

"We have flour and fat in the food storage," said Mother, "we can make soup."

Grandmother edged her way out of the room which was quite a feat considering her size. She pulled out her enormous bunch of keys and we were in business. We found the wooden spoon that we used to boil the linen in the laundry. It was too big for the job but since there wasn't anything else it had to do.

"We need water," Mrs. Rosta said very matter-of-factly.

"Water," Father said pondering the chances. "The kitchen is closed. The next well is pretty far from here. I better go upstairs and see what I can find."

While we waited for the water I felt that I was awfully thirsty. How come I did not think about it before we realized that we were without water? The few minutes that passed seemed like hours. Father appeared with a bucket of fresh water,

"From the hot water tank, upstairs. Fresh, clean water. We have everything now, let's start the soup."

In no time at all the room filled with the tantalizing smell of the simplest soup on the Hungarian menu, one that everybody usually hated passionately. Yet, at this moment, it was the most tempting food anyone could have imagined. We ate our fill and gave thanks to the Lord for having given us our daily bread.

～

The New Year came and went. Nobody paid any attention to it. We had very little water, but we got back the use of our kitchen.

An earth-shattering commotion threw two drunken soldiers into the room. They stood with feet apart looking into the eyes of every female among us. The young ones were hidden, only the children and the older ones were in plain sight. One of them finally rested his eyes on Ica, the 14-year-old. "Tac, tac" he kept repeating and showed with a sweeping motion that he wanted her to come and finish a cleaning detail. "No!" we screamed at the top of our lungs. "Tac, tac" he became more and more excited. He then said, "granat," meaning a hand grenade and that he would use it on us. Grandmother talked to him, "Look, she is only a child, you wouldn't want her." The soldier did not want to be convinced. He kept saying, "Tac, tac, granat," and his face turned red. At this instant, the door flew open and our friend Peter walked in. Captain Peter, whom Father rescued from a malaria attack with quinine he could not get from anywhere else, surveyed the situation and understood without words. He spit on the ground then hit the other guy on the shoulder, "That's only a child. Phui on you! You wouldn't want her!" The other spat in disgust when he saw that an officer was trying to talk him out of a rape he wasn't convinced he desired anyway. He left without saying a further word.

Ica was shaking all over. Her mother was crying; I had the chills.

Captain Peter came back. He had a box of rolls with him. "Here, I brought you something to eat." He grabbed one of the rolls and bit into it. We understood that he did this to show that the rolls were not poisoned. He was a kind man, we appreciated his presence. He protected us from the war-crazy, woman-hungry, drunken slobs. Now he wanted to make up for the agony we suffered. He stroked Ica's hair.

"If anything like that happens and I am not around, tell the soldiers that I will be back in no time, I only went out to check something." He wanted to prepare us for the coming experiences. His words were comforting even though we had no idea how we would be understood by common soldiers. Captain Peter spoke some high school French.

We didn't have to wait long for the foretold experiences. They rolled around with every coming hour.

A yelling, pistol swaying Soviet soldier stumbled in the darkness demanding that we give him all our guns. We only stared at his wild angry demand. "Guns?" It was pretty obvious that we had no guns. He found a small jewelry box with imitation jewelry. He poked around in its contents with the pistol. Was it loaded?

"You crazy kid," Grandmother said in Hungarian, "are you looking for guns in the jewelry box?" He was rummaging around on the beams. This was where I had hidden my box camera. I held my breath. If he discovered it he would surely take it. After watches, cameras were the soldier's favorite objects of prey. We had already learned the first basic principle of the Soviets.

"Whatever is yours is also mine, communal, but whatever is mine is taboo for you." He turned and stormed out.

Three soldiers demanded help to peel potatoes another night-like day. They mimicked and played all the possible interpretations in pantomime.

"Oh, you mean peel potatoes?" Grandmother asked. "O.K. here we go." Grandmother and Little Grandma, the gardener's widow, Mrs. Rosta, a whole army of nice old ladies turned fairyland witches through the darkness and dirt of two weeks with additional wrinkles painted with soot from matches, marched with the three soldiers who nearly cried with disgust. They looked around, there was nobody old enough to help them besides the ones they took. Everybody else was conveniently hidden, even Ica. We children glared at them with big empty eyes. They let out a curse and slammed the door.

Once again we were saved.

"Come!" Father led me by the hand to the kitchen, another day. "I want to introduce you to this nice young doctor!"

The doctor looked very young, he was blond with laughing blue eyes. He shook my hand and asked Father how old I was. I said I was nine. We decided to say nine whenever anybody asked to make me younger. Even I was afraid of rape. We talked with hands and feet when an excited soldier ran in and tugged at Father's sleeve, "Come, doctor, come, emergency!"

"Here is your own doctor!" Father laughed. "Why do you need me?"

The soldier spat then looked the doctor straight in the eye, "Our doctor! Ha! He is no doctor at all. One-two semesters, then out to the front!" his voice became sincerely admiring when he said, "Hungarian doctor old professor!"

Father looked at the Soviet doctor. He good-heartedly laughed at the other one, "He is right."

I looked at Father and noticed that he looked like an "old professor" indeed. I never thought of him as a wise old man. Yet, he had not shaved since Christmas. His beard was completely gray, though his hair was still the blondish brown I had always known. He looked definitely ancient beside the young Soviet "doctor."

I encountered another Soviet doctor a few days later. She was a real doctor, she had finished medical school. She had the hugest breasts I had ever seen on a woman. I did not know then but it was fashionable among Soviet women to wear thick padding, something like falsies, to emphasize their femininity. She didn't stay very long. If Father could take care of that part of the front there was no reason for her to stay.

The young one became a good friend of my Father. He was the only one who had seen Mother at all. We made up Mother for the performance. She put on a black sweater and a black scarf, then we painted wrinkles around her mouth with the burnt matches.

"She has T.B.," Father said in a sad tone to the young doctor.

We all knew that this one word would keep the Soviets out of the shelter. There was no real cure for T.B. yet, especially not on the front. "Diphtheria" was another word that would make them run for their lives. Slowly we learned the tricks of survival.

But what were we going to do for water? Grandfather speculated that we could use mouthwash which we had in great quantities and we also found some hidden rum. The adults were swallowing that.

Grandpa volunteered to try and reach the well that lay about thirty minutes walk from our house up the hill. Some of the older ladies volunteered to go with him. The young ones had to stay hidden because they could have been taken by the enemy. Joe, Margit's son, wanted to go but he was voted out. He was too young to get killed, only eight years old. The shooting went on as usual. The volunteers decided to take the wagon we children used to have so much fun with. They sneaked out the back door and through the garden above us. The less time they spent on the street the better off they were.

When they did not return for hours we all became frantic, especially Little Grandma. "Where can he be? He must be shot somewhere. I must go out and find him."

"You can't. I'll go and see what happened." Father had a little breather between cases and he spent the rest of his time outside anyway, so he decided to investigate.

"I'll go with you," said Little Grandma.

He knew that she would not stay so he said, "All right, you can come. Maybe you'll be able to do some good. If they captured him you can cry a little for the guards."

An hour passed, then another one. Finally we heard their footsteps. They sounded vigorous and almost happy.

"Those dumb Soviets captured us," said Grandpa. "They took us to the commandant. We would still be there maybe as spy-suspects or who knows what, if you hadn't come, Son," he turned to Father.

As soon as they saw that they had captured the doctor's father and relatives they let them go," said Little Grandma and looked at Father with such pride that she grew a few feet just with that look alone.

"Luckily we were already on our way back with the water. We brought a good barrel-full on the wagon," said Grandfather.

Water! That crystal-clear, thirst-quenching wonder of nature. I never thought I'd be so happy to taste water!

Grandpa was the hero of the day along with the two old ladies who went with him, Mrs. Rosta and the gardener's widow, Mrs. Varga.

95

Little Grandma was full of tales about her doctor son. She was so proud of him. Why, he could save anyone because he was a doctor.

"You know," she told me later on that day, "when your father was only three years old he would come to me and tell me about his dreams, his plans for the future. I was sick at the time and every day the doctor would come to our house. He came in a beautiful carriage drawn by four horses. Lovely horses they were, too. Little Louis, your father, would stand at the gate and stare at the horses. He loved the old doctor but if possible, he loved the horses and the carriage even more. Well, one of those days, when the doctor was gone, he came and told me, 'Mother, I want to become a doctor, like Dr. Gombos. I must have the same kind of carriage with those beautiful horses. You'll see, I'll become a doctor.' I decided then and there that he had to become one. I knew that I was going to do everything in my power to help him to live out his dream. He made it. He became a doctor." Grandma's eyes glittered through her horn rimmed glasses.

I felt so proud of my father, too. I continued the story without saying it out aloud. Then he married Mother and because her brother had died the same year they got engaged, Mother was the sole heiress of the fortune, of all the stores. Father just finished as an internist, and there his dream stopped. He knew he had to take over the business from Grandfather some day. It was not an accepted custom in Hungary for women to lead business empires and Mother was not cut out to do that anyway. No paid manager could be trusted with an operation like ours. Father's medical knowledge was put in mothballs. His only contact with the reality of his former world was through periodicals which he read avidly whenever he had the time. Otherwise he was completely involved with his business until he became the "old professor doctor" of the Second World War. Indeed he was admirable. He had an innate talent to soothe and cure people, not only their bodies but also their souls, to hide his own worries and fears from them. He could only be himself when he was at home.

That must have been the reason, Mother often said, that the only place he really got angry was at home. I had seen him a few times when he was mad. His anger came suddenly and often, it seemed, without reason. I was afraid of him most of the time, because I never knew when he would blow up, yet I desperately desired his presence, his serious attention. I would have done anything to make him notice me. I did not know at the time how much he tried and how much he loved me because his ways of showing it took him out of the home so much.

I watched him in the cellar, night after night, when he returned from his long, mysterious trips. He lay on his back and between his hands he held the rosary. He prayed until he fell asleep. Before long there would be another knock on the door. Somebody would need him again. Neighbors, soldiers…

In a few days, everybody knew that they could come to him for advice, for help. They could rely on him. He even talked with the Soviets. He very seldom told us anything of what was happening outside. He was too tired.

One evening we ran out of water again. Grandmother and Little Grandma had exhausted all our resources, when Father said,

"Give me a bucket! Have you been outside today, at least in the kitchen, anybody? Did you look out the window?"

We looked confused. What did that have to do with water?

He did not say a word, just went outside and returned in a few moments. The bucket was full of fresh-fallen snow.

"Snow! Snow!" The children jumped up and down and grabbed handfuls out of the bucket.

"No!" Father stopped us. "Not so fast! Put it all back. We have to cook it first for ten minutes before we can drink it. But it is water! We have abundant water from now on straight from Heaven! But I don't want to see anybody put it in his mouth before it is boiled. You obviously did not go outside in the last couple of weeks. There are dead bodies, dead horses, and dirt in the snow. It would be very dangerous to drink it, or even eat it like we usually bite into the snow for fun."

It didn't take me very long to find out that snow tasted like water but it sure did not quench thirst.

"Why do I feel like I'm still thirsty?" I asked everybody.

Grandfather, who was a pharmacist, had the answer, "Because there are no minerals in snow and with the cooking they would come out of the water anyway, even if there had been any to start with. But, Helen," he stroked my hair, "it is still better than getting typhoid."

I didn't know much about typhoid, but I had heard that many people died of it during the First World War, in Russian prison camps. I didn't say anything but later I felt that I would even risk death to have a good, satisfying drink.

We cooked with snow and we washed in snow. Ourselves, our clothes. After washing, our clothes had a different grayish dirt color than they had had before.

Then came the day when a long, drilling noise echoed through the whole house. It sounded like a giant tool trying to tear the structure to pieces. It could have lasted seconds or hours; to us it seemed like eternity. We just knew that the house would collapse on us as soon as the sound ended, or maybe before? We screamed the Our Father. It was a minute similar to the one when the first Soviets came in and we were trying to convince them that we were Hungarians. We were now trying to convince God that we belonged with Him, in case our lives in this world ended.

Then it stopped… and we stopped… there was deadly silence. Then nothing. Absolutely nothing happened. We were too terrified to move.

Father finally said, "I'm going out to look!"

"No!" Mother clung to him hysterically. I had never seen her like that before. Whatever Father decided she stood by him. What had the tension of these recent weeks done to her? I saw my beautiful Mother transformed into a hysterical old mask, clinging to the last thread that bound her to life outside this dark room, outside her lair behind the featherbed. What if he died? I started crying at the thought. It would mean the end of all of us. I wasn't the only one who cried.

Father must have thought something similar because he stroked her hair and stayed. "I can ask the soldiers later."

However, when nothing happened in the next hour or so we relaxed.

Captain Peter came in from outside and reported. "Your house is really well-built! A cannonball tried to drill its way between the two floors right where the lamp fixture was and still is, defying all laws of physics. The cannonball simply fell back. I could not believe my eyes. It's a miracle!"

So that's what it was! That drilling sound.

"No wonder they are shooting our way. There are five cannons in our own yard," said Father.

"What, five cannons, right here? How come we don't get more of this then?" Grandmother inquired.

"Because the Soviets are up here, shooting down onto the city, onto the Royal Castle, while the Germans stand one street below us. Far below. You know how steep Óra Street is. They are on the bottom of that. You are plain lucky," laughed Captain Peter.

"Lucky!" we had a different word for luck but we did not think that Captain Peter knew much about Providence so we skipped the issue.

～

Apparently, Captain Peter had to leave for a few days because he certainly wasn't around when another grenade-swaying young officer made his entrance among the usual confusion and declared, "Here front! You must leave the house!"

Great solution. He wanted us to leave the house because there was war outside.

Grandmother had a better idea and conveyed it to him.

"Why should we go outside into the war?" She motioned to him to follow her. Then she mimicked that he should put all of us right beside the wall and go "Puff, puff, puff!" Shoot the bunch of us. Much more ingenious, quicker done, etc. She also told him her opinion in beautiful Hungarian using some words I had never heard before. It was now the soldier's turn to become confused. He looked at the elderly woman whom he respected in a way as everybody accepted Grandmother to be the wife of Father. Mother did not show her face ever.

"Wait!" he pantomimed, said something in Russian then disappeared.

We waited. In the meantime Father came back and Grandmother told him about the problem.

"I think they want us out of the house because they think that we hid something. Maybe drink, maybe Germans, whatever. It certainly does not make sense to go out just because there is war. It is worse outside than in here." Father speculated. He decided to find the soldier. All of a sudden I felt that everything would turn out all right. The matter was in competent hands.

In school we had learned about Ilona Zrinyi. She was a heroine who lived in the seventeenth century. She defended a castle against the Turks for several years, after her husband was taken by them. I thought Grandmother resembled her more and more every day. I thought she was awfully brave. I even told her so.

"Grandmother, you are like Ilona Zrinyi!" She smiled at the idea but I knew she was happy to be admired.

I remembered the day when she first "accepted" Father as her "husband." She came into the shelter and said to Little Grandma, "Hi, Mother-in-law!"

Little Grandma was not pleased with the idea at all, "Just what do you mean by that? I am a year younger than you are!"

Grandmother started laughing, "Your son just declared to a soldier that I was his wife!"

Now it was Little Grandma who burst out laughing. The situation seemed somewhat comical, especially when they looked at each other. They resembled scarecrows. They both looked as undesirable as they possibly could. We heard that nobody was safe from the soldier's rage. Therefore, even the old ladies and children made themselves look as bad as was humanly possible.

They both wore elegant dustrags on their heads, huge aprons tied around their waists with string, their hair stood in all directions, their clothes were a uniform gray from dust, snowy washes, ashes, whatever they had come into contact with in the past couple of weeks.

It felt good to find something to laugh at and forget everything for an instant. Then it was all over again, like a soap bubble that brings joy for a few seconds then disappears as fast as it came into being.

The Soviet soldier returned. He grabbed Grandmother's hand and said, "One house, two house. You go there, spend a few days, then you come back." While he said this, he pretended that he was walking, showed on his fingers the number of houses, pretended to go to sleep a few times, and called Grandmother "Babushka."

# 11

The shelter turned into a beehive. Everybody was busy preparing a bundle to take to our new "home." What we took would be ours to keep. What was it that we needed most? I had kept my treasures all together ever since that day when we first saw the cannonfire. Now I added other pieces of clothing and food. They let us return as many times and as often as we wanted to walk between the two houses, only one block away from the front. Needless to say, only Father, Grandfather, Grandpa, and the old ladies were allowed to risk it at all. We had to be very selective in our choices.

"Look," said Father, "it won't be forever. The Soviets will have to leave some day. They'll let us come back. I'm sure all they want is to search through the whole house undisturbed. They cannot haul away everything. Something will remain when all will be over. Let's just take food and clothing. I'll do something to make them let us come back soon. That other house has no air-raid shelter. The owners did not live in it this winter. We'll have to stay upstairs. At least we'll have a roof above our heads. We'll be able to make a fire. It's awfully cold out there. Don't go out, anybody, until I tell you that it's all right. The Germans are still only one block away. We'll have to wait for the opportune moment. Thank God that most shots don't reach us, as Captain Peter told us. I wish he were here now."

"Tomorrow" loomed once more. Would anything ever be the same again? A strong explosion shook the house. Our screaming prayers besieged God anew. Had our day come?

After the explosion there was no sound for a long time. Father ventured up the stairs to see what had happened. When he came back he reported that a cannonball had come in through the wall of the upstairs bathroom, turned, and exited through the next wall.

Was it sheer "luck" again that we were still alive and well?

The young officer came back and urged us to get moving. "The gun fire has stopped for a while, it is the right time," he explained to Father, emphasizing his words through vehement body language.

Father accompanied the young women across. It was decided that if he was on hand he could always explain to the rape-hungry soldiers that these innocent-looking ladies were carriers of the dreaded T.B. or diphtheria. Then came the old ladies; leading and carrying the children. Ica and I were on our own. We followed very close to the Grandmothers. Suddenly Ica grabbed my arm, "Listen! Did you hear that whistle? That was a bullet!"

We started running in the ankle-deep snow through the yard, toward our destination. We reached the house before anybody else did and burst right in. That lone whistle had scared us out of our wits.

I had not been in this neighbor's villa for quite a while. The change was drastic. In the living room there was hay scattered on the hardwood floor. The piano was thrown out onto the snow. It was obvious that the room was used as a barn. Apparently the horses didn't like the piano in their bedroom. In the next room, the one that had huge French doors toward the garden, I saw several beds. A warm wave swept through my heart when I realized that it was our own bedlinen that was piled up high. Father must have brought it over before our arrival.

"This will be our home for a few days!" Father said. "I can't imagine why the windows are not broken yet."

We settled far from the windows. Now that we were above ground the shooting was much more audible. The cannons thundered back and forth. Thank God that it was above us. As Captain Peter had said, we were out of reach for most of them, being right in the middle between the lines of hostile cannons.

Up here we could clearly distinguish the different shots: the thunder of the cannons, the staccato explosions of the hand grenades, the popping sound of the machine guns, occasional whistles of bullets. All were accompanied by loud prayers that turned into screaming every time the sounds came especially close.

Hour after hour passed and we made our beds for the evening. We cooked something edible in the kitchen with snow, dried vegetables, whatever could be found and ate it. The prayers died down. We got used to the new kind of "music." We were all in God's hand.

Night came and with it the usual darkness. We felt at home in the dark. We did not see the foreign walls, the unusual pieces of furniture, only each others' faces and even then very dimly in the light of the "uncandle." There were no bunkbeds here. I tried to get as close to the light as I could, I had a special project for that night.

One of the treasures I had brought with me was the prayer book I had received for First Communion. I opened the golden buckle of its ivory cover with the little Jesus on it. I looked for a song that I had discovered a few days before. It was in Latin and it was always sung when the Blessed Sacrament was put out for adoration. I admired the adults who knew the words. Now I decided that the best thing for me to do was to learn the song right then and there, in the middle of the battle, under the as yet unbroken windows. I did not know the meaning of the words, I could only guess, but I wanted to do it. I sat beside Grandmother and asked her to translate.

"Tantum ergo Sacramentum veneremur cernui," was the first line.

"Down in adoration falling, this great Sacrament we hail," Grandmother said.

"Now, how did you do that? How did you translate it in verse?"

"Sometimes we sing it in Hungarian," she said, "I am just telling you the words of the Hungarian version."

We translated the whole song, line by line Grandmother and I. It was wonderful to sit in her embrace and listen to the music of her voice which even drowned out the thunder of the cannons.

I learned the whole song and fell asleep in the security of her arms repeating the last sentence.

I dreamt that I was running in a field blooming with flowers of the spring, when a great thunder woke me up. It was followed by the clinking of broken glass and screams, one of the windows had broken. At least no one was hurt. It was wise to move the beds to the back of the room. The two Grandfathers got busy nailing a board in place of the window because now the gusty wind blew snow and cold into the room. The iron potbellied stove was already cold. Mrs. Varga tried to make a fire without success. The wood was wet. Her son found a broken drawer in the kitchen. It was dry. He quickly cut it up and stuffed it into the stove. Small tongues of fire caught on to the dry wood and soon it started crackling in the little dwarf of a stove that had been pulled into the room by some soldiers. The big fireplace would have been no use during the war. It took out more heat than it generated.

Light came in through the remaining windows and colored the sky a very light gray. I had forgotten what things looked like in the light.

Father came in with a big bundle. "I brought meat."

"Where did you get it?" Grandmother inquired.

"A horse was dying outside and we slaughtered it," said Father. "A butcher lives a bit farther down our street. We divided it among the people we could reach."

A horse? I saw Grandmother and Little Grandma jump into action.

"We'll make paprikás! I remember during the First World War we did not even notice the horsemeat's characteristic sweet taste when we cooked it with paprika!"

"I'll go over to the other house and get some!" volunteered Father.

I could hardly believe my ears. Grandmother, who only bought the best of everything, talked about horsemeat as a delicacy. And Little Grandma!

Her food was well-known all over the county! What delicious meals she cooked always! Now she was eager to cook this meat! I would never have thought I would want to taste a horse! Yet, now I could hardly wait to dig my teeth into it.

"Can I help?"

"Of course!" both Grandmothers answered at once.

When the other children saw me in the kitchen they all wanted to help. The stew was ready to be cooked in no time at all. Little Grandma kneaded dough for dumplings. We all took turns to punch and pinch, to peel and stir. Where can Father be for so long? Isn't he ever going to get back with the paprika? Was there something wrong?

But no nothing was wrong, I heard the firm steps close to the kitchen door.

"Those darn Soviets! They found one of our 'holes'!"

"Which one?" asked Grandmother.

"The one that opened from the wall of the elevator shaft," answered Father. They made scrambled eggs from 100 eggs they found hidden there. They invited me to feast with them. After the royal lunch we had entertainment. They used the elevator as a shooting gallery. Even I had to give a shot at the mirror. What fun to see the splinters fly! They were in a mighty good mood. They wanted to have alcohol but all they could find was some perfume oil I brought home once. As it smelled like perfume they drank that hoping that it contained alcohol. They drank it from our best teacups. I hope they won't get sick and then blame everything on us. That's all we need. The doctor poisoned them! That's what they'll say! Anyway, here is the paprika. I grabbed that from the kitchen."

"Too bad about the 'hole'," said Grandmother, "but the main thing is that we are alive and together."

"Thanks for the paprika," said Little Grandma. "We started to worry about you."

We heard voices outside. We couldn't understand them because they were in Russian. Then all of a sudden we recognized the shouting. It was Captain Peter.

"He is back! He is back!" Marie, Elisabeth, Juli, Ili, and I broke into an Indian war dance. "We are saved! Captain Peter is back! He'll get us back into our house."

The door flew open and under the directions of Captain Peter the piano was pushed, pulled, and dragged back into the house by four Soviet soldiers.

Captain Peter had a big grin on his face. "War or no war, we'll have no such things as pianos in the snow. These men better learn some culture."

"You must stay with us and have some of the stew," Grandmother told him in French.

His eyes lit up, especially when Father pulled out a bottle of wine from his coat, "Look what else I found when I went over to our home."

He opened the bottle and poured a glass for Captain Peter. He sat down with us on one of the beds and savored the fine wine.

"Budapest must have been a beautiful city. It is such a pity to shoot the marvelous buildings to bits and pieces. I'd love to be with my family instead of having to fight my way through country after country, destroying everything that comes into my way."

The wine colored his cheeks rosy. "I've had enough of these Russians," he exclaimed.

"Enough of these Russians? What are you, then?" asked Grandmother.

"I'm Ukrainian. To be a Ukrainian is to hate Russians. It's the same old story as it is with the Irish and the British. Except they already have their independence, while we…. We are required to celebrate the anniversary of the day, hundreds of years ago, when our country was annexed by Russia."

"You mean these soldiers here are not all Russians?" asked Father.

"No. They are not. The four guys who helped me with the piano are all from the Ukraine. Others are from Latvia, Lithuania, Armenia, Uzbekhistan, from everywhere in the Soviet Union, which is made up of sixteen different republics. The biggest of them is the Russian Soviet Socialist Republic; Russians are the rulers. We all learn Russian in the schools. We can all speak it. But to be called Russians is as much an insult to us as it would be for an Irishman to be called English."

"You speak French, you seem to know much about history. Does every captain get as good an education as you did?" asked Grandmother.

Captain Peter blushed, "No. I taught history at the university before I was drafted. As a history professor I had access to many books that nobody in the USSR is allowed to see. I have my own ideas. Sometimes I wish I didn't. They are hard to conceal and they make me dissatisfied. I feel helpless and at the mercy of the government that has the power to make me silent forever."

Suddenly he stopped talking and looked around. When he saw that only the usual crowd was there, no Soviet soldier within earshot, he relaxed. He also knew that only a few of us understood French.

He got up and walked over to the piano. He ran his fingers down the keys. He closed his eyes and started to play. The tune of a Chopin waltz emerged under his able hands. The melody flowed over into the other rooms and out into the snow-filled night. I didn't even notice when darkness came. Through the window I could see the stars in the sky. I watched them as long as I could. Soon the blanket would be put over the window again, then the "uncandle" would be lit, and the magic would be over. For a minute the war halted and we gave a salute to the immortal universal beauty of the human soul expressed through the music of a genius, interpreted by a soldier who recognized the soul brothers and sisters among the enemy.

The next morning Captain Peter was back, "Hurry up now! You can get back to your home! It's empty."

On our way back I saw a soldier go after Grandpa. He pushed him to the wall of the neighbor's house.

"Burzhuj! Burzhuj!" he repeated. We knew what that meant. "Burzhuj" was the deadly enemy of the people, a member of the bourgeois class.

All of us stopped and watched. Obviously the soldier saw him as a big, fat man who must have grown fat by exploiting others. We didn't have to be afraid for Grandpa! He had a good head on his shoulders. We heard his voice, "Look at my hands!" he stuck them under the nose of the soldier. His hands were as rough as those of a worker. He had worked with leather all his life. He had big fingers. The soldier looked, then spat in the snow in disappointment, "Ah, robotnik!" he exclaimed. So this one was a worker, too! At this point Father arrived at the scene.

The soldier turned to him.

"We are going to occupy Budapest, then Vienna, then Germany, then England, then America," he counted them on his fingers. "But after that… I'm going home and I'm going to kill Stalin. He lied to us. He said that everybody is exploited here. I opened the suitcase of your maid, she had silk stockings in it. Nobody has silk stockings in the Soviet Union. That man here! Look at his hands! I thought he was a capitalist with that big stomach! He is a worker! Where does he get enough food to become so fat!?!" he spat again and fumed away in disgust.

While we were walking across I heard sirens from far away. In Pest, on the other side of the Danube, they warned people to run for shelter. A few minutes later we saw the airplanes and the falling bombs.

For them occupation had not come yet. For us it was a thing of the past. I remembered when we used to say not so long ago, "they are only human…" How many were saying it right now?

Father embraced me in the garden before we went back to our eternal nights in the shelter.

"I want you to be very careful. Don't take any chances."

"Is there something wrong?" I asked as I looked up and saw his worried face.

"Two streets from here a little girl was raped, eight years old."

I felt as if a dumpling was stuck in my throat. I grabbed his arm and tried to hide in it. He accompanied me down into the shelter.

"You stay here now," he said.

The house was in an uproar when we got back. Nothing was in its original place but apart from the elevator and the "hole" in its shaft, nothing was badly damaged.

"The room where you stayed last night…today a cannonball exploded right in front of the glass window. God keeps a special watch over you." Captain Peter brought us the news the next morning. He didn't say anything about luck this time. Did he believe in Providence also? "The piano is gone," he said, then turned and ran out of the room.

# 12

One lightless day passed after another, interrupted by strange events that appeared from the darkness then disappeared again. It was like watching a very weird, unpredictable mystery-adventure movie. The only disconcerting fact was that we were the actors in the film and there was no script.

I sat there, or lay on the bed with the anticipation that practically anything could happen at any time. Everything was interesting, more exciting than mere existence, yet my whole being tried to ward off the dangers connected with it. When it arrived I no longer panicked. I knew that we were in God's hands. I was always worried but never afraid when disaster struck.

Death became a friend. We looked into her eyes and shook hands with her. "Tomorrow" came for many and because of that it was no longer as menacing as it used to be. If our number came up we had to go. That was all there was to it.

When everything was quiet I used to comb Grandmother's thin, gray hair. She did not mind. She just sat there hour after hour, while we created different hairdos for her. Whenever soldiers waddled, jumped, burst, or tore their way into the shelter we stopped and stared at them with big eyes. Because of Father's warning I hid with the rest of the young women and only listened to what Grandmother was going to tell them this time. She was the spokesperson for the earth-colored shadows who lived in the shelter.

Imi, the baby, cried a lot. He had gotten pneumonia on the way to the neighbor's house. Aunt was afraid for him and held him all the time. Little Grandma was also preoccupied with him. He was very sick but he was a strong little nine-month-old. I was sure that he would pull through his illness. Marie was brokenhearted about Imi and spent much time gazing or cooing at him. Sometimes that would make him laugh and then everybody was relieved. If he laughed he must be on his way to recovery, Father came in often to check on him.

It happened in those days that Father was called to the council three hills away from us. We wouldn't have let him go but a Soviet soldier came and took him, reassuring us again and again that he would also bring him back. We did not think much of his promise and wanted to make sure that all went well. The soldier carried a piece of paper; it definitely came from the district council. At least we knew where to look for Father if he did not show up.

Wonder of wonders! He came back the same day wet to his knees as they had waded through knee-deep snow all the way to reach their destination, then back again. The soldier grinned as we offered him dinner for bringing Father back.

"You know what?" asked Father. "Our relatives from up the hill were there also. All of us were named captains of our districts; two streets each. We were made responsible for cleaning up and burying the dead. There was no reason to be afraid after all."

Mother could not let go of him. She was so happy to have him back in our house.

The next day Father rounded up all the men who were in "his" two streets. The Grandfathers helped him find every able-bodied person who dared to show himself on the streets.

The men listened carefully to what Father told them but they were terrified at the prospect of having to leave their families alone, "We can't just walk out and leave the women! You know what the roving troops will do! We must think of something!"

Father interjected, "We must bury the dead. I have heard that as the snow begins to melt, more and more dead bodies will be found. If we don't do something we'll have typhoid, maybe even cholera. Epidemics come always in the footsteps of major disasters."

The men understood this very well. Then an old man with horn-rimmed glasses and a goatee started to talk, "I was a general when I was younger and I learned about all kinds of methods and signals. All we have to do is equip every house with a device that can make lots of noise. Let's say pots and pans strung up on a strong rope or something like that." He talked slowly, but wisely. "Every house will have its signal. If drunken soldiers or other problems are spotted, the house would give a distress signal and then the neighbors could transmit it until it reaches the work gang or Soviet patrol. I'm sure they would cooperate with us. After all, they organized this whole 'district' or whatever they want to call it. Our whole area is only two streets, the work gang could be anywhere wherever we are needed in no time at all."

"Excellent idea! Is this acceptable to all of us?" Father asked.

The nodding heads seemed to approve. Work could get started.

"The first thing is to bury the dead and to shoot or slaughter all stray horses. Everybody could take home a good chunk of food. That would give us the strength to dig all those graves," said Father matter-of-factly.

Work began that very day. By the time darkness rolled around everybody had a piece of meat from the first slaughtered horse. Father reported that they had found sixteen unburied bodies within the district's two streets.

One of the knocks, a very humble and soft one, did not come from soldiers. Grandmother let in through our kitchen window a shriveled up old lady.

"I heard that you had chickens before all this broke out," she motioned towards the outside.

"Yes, we did," said Grandmother. "We slaughtered them all before the Soviets came. Chickens are no exceptions. Their survival rate during wartime is even worse than that of people. They get eaten."

"I also heard," the little old lady went on undisturbed, "that you had some dry bread you used to feed them. I was wondering if you could spare some of that so I could take some food to my family?" there was an indescribable plight in her eyes.

"Sit down," said Grandmother. "You want to eat those dry bread-crusts we saved for the animals?"

"It is much better than nothing," she whispered. "My grandchildren are hungry."

"Where do you live?" asked Grandmother.

"Down the street. Very close to where the Germans are. This is why I did not dare to come out until now. But now..." her voice broke, "it was a matter of starving or risking to come over."

Grandmother got out her big keychain, "Stay here. I'll be back in no time."

"Is your Father the doctor?" she asked me, while she waited for Grandmother.

"Yes. Do you know him?"

"He told me about you and your family. He is a wonderful man. I saw it with my own eyes when he did surgery on a soldier with a razor blade. He also treats my poor sister. She has water all over in her body. I don't think that she'll survive the war. Why couldn't the good Lord take her before all of this happened?"

Grandmother returned with a big boxful of the baby cereals Father had brought home from the store just before the siege started. She had other things in the box, preserves, one of the chickens that were well-preserved in the cold, outside the house, under a beachbasket. The soldiers missed that hiding place.

The old lady's eyes filled with tears. "How can I ever thank you?"

"Wouldn't you have done the same?" Grandmother asked. "If you run out, send word."

"Or maybe my father can take something to you if he goes there anyway," I added.

"He comes, the Lord bless him. He looks at my poor sister every day."

It was hard to believe that Father went that close to the German lines only in order to comfort two old women. Why was I ever afraid of him?

The next knock on the door was no knock at all. The door swung open and a wild soldier appeared, a pistol in each hand. He was gesticulating wildly and demanded "Germanskys."

"Where are they? Hand them over!"

"Germanskys?" asked Grandmother, "I haven't seen any since Christmas."

The soldier was yelling at the top of his lungs and swung the pistols back and forth.

"Look man, if those pistols are loaded as I am sure they are, stop shaking them. They might go off," said Grandmother, although she knew that it was not much use to argue because they did not understand each other at all.

"Germansky, Germansky!" he insisted.

"Captain is coming back any minute now," said Grandmother and this time she motioned with her hand, repeating the word "Captain" several times.

The soldier stopped swaying the guns: "Captain? Captain?" He grabbed the "uncandle." To do that, he had to put away one of his pistols. He lifted the light and pushed it under everybody's face one after another.

"Germansky nyet, eh?" he quieted down somewhat.

He looked around again and spat out a sentence: "Nye cultura!"

"Now what in the world got into you?" inquired Grandmother. "You realized that we had no Germans, therefore we have no culture?"

"Royal," the soldier said.

Now that we understood. That word meant piano. We had found that out when Captain Peter ordered his soldiers around to bring the piano back in from the snow.

"'Royal' in the laundry room, where we iron? Is that where you keep yours at home?" Grandmother went on with her one-sided inquiry.

The soldier spat on the floor, a custom we had learned to accept by now, then turned and stomped out the door.

Not long after he left two very quiet officer-types came through the kitchen window. They handed a can of something to Mrs. Varga, who happened to be standing there, and motioned to her that they wanted it opened. They did not remove their long officer's coats. They did not say a word. They looked very tired.

Grandmother came out into the kitchen and according to Captain Peter's instructions told the two young men that the Captain would be there shortly. She used sign language to explain herself better. The two officers looked at each other when they heard the word "Captain." They swallowed their soup from the can then jumped up. They did not say a word. They left.

Were they the Germans for whom the Soviet soldier wanted to kill us? They had never uttered one word in Russian, or in any other language for that matter. They had never removed their long, Soviet army overcoats. What did they have underneath?

We knew something wonderful must have happened when Father came home. His face was serene, yet smiling at the same time.

"I must tell you about what just happened to me. Come everybody and listen. You know the gardener's family three houses down? You know that she was expecting a baby? She could deliver any minute now. A few days ago a mad Soviet raped her. She is so close to delivery she shouldn't even have intercourse. I was gravely worried about her. I had no Sulfadiazine left whatsoever. She contracted an infection from that animal; I can't find a better name for the soldier who raped her. I had no idea where to get help. Then I looked to the sky and trusted her to God's mercy. While I wracked my brain for a solution I absent-mindedly wiggled my foot back and forth in the snow. Something scraped the sole of my boots. I looked down. The corner of something orange showed through the snow. I looked more closely. It was a box of Sulfadiazine. I heard that German airplanes dropped containers with medicine and food for their soldiers. It must have fallen out from one of those. I gave the medicine to the woman, then went back to look for the container. I found it in the bushes not so far from the place where I uncovered the first box of medicine. How that box ever got out of the container I'll never know, I can't describe the feeling of gratitude that overcame me."

Maybe he couldn't describe it, but he didn't need to. We all felt it.

A few days later a beautiful little blue-eyed girl was born to the raped woman. The baby was healthy and strong. She need never know what had happened to her mother.

As life comes, life also goes. The poor old lady's sister, who had water all over in her body, had died. Before she died she had a good meal and she knew that people cared for her. There was no priest on this side of the hill, Father buried her himself. A Jewish man, named David, who came out from hiding in the lady's house, made the coffin for her. Until now the lady's water-filled body hid David from the eyes of the Germans. He was hidden in the bed, right under her. He repaid for his life now by accompanying her to her grave together with Father. The little shriveled up old lady cried beside them. Father read the prayers from his old prayer book, blessed the coffin, then, quickly threw the symbolic handful of earth onto it, leaving David to finish the job. He was needed by the living.

From then on David became a constant companion to Father. He found out that Father had not changed clothes since Christmas; he did not have any. All his suits, forty-two to be exact, had been stolen. Soviet soldiers collected civilian clothes, too, besides watches and cameras. We remembered the outbursts of Captain Peter and of the soldier who wanted to kill Stalin. Were there some who did not intend to go home? The two shy, wordless soldiers, who came with the can of soup, who we thought were Germans, were they really? Or were they Russians trying to escape? There was no way to solve the mystery.

The only thing we knew for sure was that Father had only one pair of pants, one jacket, and forty-two vests. We finally found a sport coat and a pair of leisure pants that had decorative cords on them. Probably that is why they were left. David turned out to be a good tailor. In no time at all he fixed up the pants for Father. He had the luxury now of a change of pants when he came in from the snow. He no longer had to dry his clothes while he was still wearing them.

Edith, a little girl from about three houses down, knocked on the kitchen window one day. She had several watches in her hand, some money, and golden chains.

"What in the world do you have there?" asked Mrs. Varga as she let her in.

"Isn't that neat?" she asked and showed off her possessions. "I took them off dead soldiers. They don't need them anymore."

"You take them right back!" Mrs. Varga exclaimed. "What do you think you are doing? Those things belong to the soldiers, dead or alive. Not to you…"

"But Mrs. Varga," she said indignantly. "The Soviets will take them anyway. Why should I leave them there for others?"

My blood froze when I heard her talk. She was only eleven years old. I wouldn't have wanted to touch a dead body for anything. What made that child so cruel? So indifferent? Was it worth risking her life to rob dead soldiers?

She didn't stay long. She didn't feel comfortable with Mrs. Varga staring at her.

# 13

"Look what I brought you!" Father came in with a big jar of plum jam. "I traded it for flour from the lady, two houses down, whose husband owns the Big Circus. It tastes delicious!"

We could hardly wait to have a spoonful. It smelled like cinnamon. It was sweet and brought back memories of Christmas. Grandmother had always made some of our Christmas cakes with this kind of jam. Only it had never tasted as good as this one. Was it because we had not tasted any for a while? Was it the taste of Christmas and the feeling of security that welled up in me when I tasted it? What made it so special?

"Does she have more? Can we have another jar?" All the children loved it.

"I'll see what I can do," laughed Father. "She has quite a few jars but she ran out of flour. We have flour. She just might want some more…"

The day started well. Were we to have other surprises?

The door was slightly open and all of a sudden I could clearly hear the Soviet war cry "Hoorie, hoorie, hoorie!" At least that's what it sounded like. Many voices shouted it in unison. It must have been quite loud to be heard in the abyss of our shelter. Where did it come from?

"What in the world?" Father hurried out but was stopped by the beaming young "doctor" in the kitchen.

"It's all over. We won! The Germans tried to break out of the Royal Castle, their only stronghold! Kaput! They are all dead. The siege is over. I couldn't sleep all night. I knew it would happen soon. We had our information. I was very worried. Rumor had it that troops from Germany would wedge in and join them if they tried to break out. But it's all over!" He hugged and kissed Father, according to the Russian custom, "We have to celebrate!"

I remembered the tired young boys, the Germans, who were fighting to keep the Royal Castle. They must have been like the ones who died in our garden, the one that looked like Tommy. I could not keep my mind off them. They were all dead now. Were they all tired of fighting? Was there even one left that believed in victory? And, even if he believed, was it worth his while?

"So it's all over," said Grandmother. She looked around. Everybody sat stupefied.

"How long have we been here in our dark hole?" someone asked.

"It's been fifty-one days," said Little Grandma.

"And what do we do now?" asked Grandpa. He was always for doing something.

"For one thing, we can leave this cave of ours," suggested Grandfather.

I grabbed Ica's hand and we went out into the kitchen. Then we ventured into the maids' quarters, towards the front of the house. We had avoided that part before because we were afraid of the shooting. The windows there were man-sized. Light streamed in so strongly that I had to cover my eyes at first because they hurt from the sudden exposure.

"Look! Look! Ica! That must be us!" I pointed to the mirror. I had not seen one since Christmas. Our faces looked green, the color of my dress. We had black circles under our eyes. The sudden light brought into the open all the dirt and grime that had been covered for weeks by the darkness of the shelter.

"Is that really me?" Ica looked at her dress and at the one the girl in the mirror wore. She, like me, must have remembered the last image of ourselves we saw before this holocaust started. We burst into sudden laughter because despite everything we were alive and well and the war, at least for the inhabitants of the capital, was over.

"Buda kaput. Buda elesett," were the words screamed at us from a loudspeaker in Russian and Hungarian from somewhere in the distance. Our half of Budapest had fallen to the enemy. The date was February 11th, 1945. Pest, the other half of the capital had already fallen on January 21. Was that a cause to rejoice? Were we supposed to cry? Which one was better, the Germans or the Soviets? Would there be freedom after the signing of the peace treaties? Important questions, yet the most important fact was that for the next few days nobody would shoot. We would be able to look around and start over. We would be alive again, what we did would matter once more.

～

Grandmother reached down and pulled me up by the hand. We were standing on the roof of the three-story house that gave us an additional twenty feet of height. We wanted to see as much of the city as was possible.

I looked down. The city did not resemble a city at all. It was, rather, a huge pile of rubble. Grandmother's "tomorrow" had reached into its tiniest corners. I was glad that she had not been swept away by the wind of history; that we could look at the disaster together.

There was not one bridge left. The spans of all the bridges were frozen into the waves of the Danube. The arteries of the city were cut in two. Was there communication at all between Buda and Pest, the two ancient cities that had become the pride of the Danube in a modern capital city, Budapest?

Before, when I looked down, I could see distinct lines of streets and avenues that connected the squares and hills, bridges and parks. Now, there were no streets or avenues to be seen.

"Where are the streets, Grandmother? I asked her.

She pointed in certain directions as she said, "That used to be Krisztina Boulevard. There is the church of Krisztinaváros: that tower there, if you can make it out. It's the church that is across the street from the confectioner's store. You remember, don't you? We used to buy lots of goodies there on our way home after I picked you up from school. We cannot see the streets because the houses crumbled straight across them and they are covered completely by ruins."

"Everything seems so quiet. No sound comes from that big city. Is everybody dead under the pile of rubble?" I inquired.

"I don't think so. But they, too, like you and me, are just awakening from a long nightmare. They are just feeling their way out of the air-raid shelters. The buses, streetcars, cars, even military vehicles are gone. That's why we hear no noise. Look at the Royal Castle." She pointed.

It was a good thing too that she pointed. I would never have found the Castle otherwise. The brick-skeleton of the once proud dwelling of kings stood there black from the soot of fire. Smoke rose from it as it would from a heathen altar. The Castle, too, had become an offering for the cruel god of war and revenge.

"Did it burn?" I turned to Grandmother.

"It still burns. It has burned for weeks," she said.

"Didn't somebody do something? Why did it have to burn?" I cried. I remembered Grandmother's words, "Look at the Royal Castle. Maybe it is the last time that you'll see it in its beauty." The graceful cupola was gone; the windows stared like empty eyes. The Royal Castle had been "defended" to pieces.

"How could anybody have tried to extinguish the fire?" Grandmother answered. "Do you remember that we didn't even have drinking water? Do you think that they were better off, having been surrounded by the Soviets for the past fifty-one days? Those dead-tired young kids, the old women, starved to death, who, can you tell me, who could have done anything against a fire that could be seen even from here? Your Father told me often and I saw it with my own eyes when it was dark as the flames groped for the sky."

I thought of the beauty inside the palace. I had been there on a field trip with the school. A substantial part of the Castle was preserved as a museum. I remembered the gorgeous pale blue satin curtains with the Anjou lilies embroidered on them in real gold and silver, the velvets, the brocades, the glittering chandeliers. They were all gone through one single blow of history.

115

Yet their value and beauty amounted to nothing when compared to even one human life. How many could be lying there, under the rubble, in the ruins?

Grandmother must have thought the same thing because she suddenly remarked, "I hope that the cold weather will last, for a while. At least until the dead can be buried or we'll have epidemics you've never heard of. I brought you up here because I want you to remember this picture forever. I want to bring up all of the children one by one and show them also. Let's go now!" she helped me down the ladder-like wooden stairs into the attic.

Everybody walked out of the shelter but they took their newly learned caution with them. Even the young women ventured out but dressed as my mother did. She put on her fur coat inside out and tied a string around it. That was the usual way to wear coats in those days. They looked perfectly awful this way and therefore did not wake the desire of any souvenir-hunting soldier.

"Come, Helen, let's gather wood for the stove! Marie, Elisabeth, Juli, Ili! Look, here is a big branch that fell off a tree. Let's break off the little branches! They would be just right for the stove." Mother was smiling again. The cold sunshine kissed roses onto her pale face and her eyes sparkled. We were out of the shelter.

"Juli! Marie!" I called to the bigger ones. "We'll step on the thicker branches and we'll break them by our weight. Come on, let's try." They ran over. We pushed and pulled, then, Mother came to the rescue and gave it a big shove. It broke right where we wanted it.

"Elisabeth, Ili!" called Mother, "You can break the little branches, gather up the twigs and haul them to the kitchen window!"

Mrs. Rosta stood at the window. She smiled at our enthusiasm and gathered up the wood by the armful as it arrived at the window.

The frozen air sparkled in the bright sunshine, snow crystals danced and floated through the sunbeams and broke their light into the colors of the rainbow. I felt like diving into the air and swimming through it as butterflies swim above flower-filled fields in the summer.

I heard Father's voice and ran to the front of the house. As I was running I saw a thing on the ground. I did not know what it was, therefore I did not touch it.

"Father!" I called out, "Come over here, quick, see what this is!"

"This is a cannon shell! It did not explode yet. This must be the one that gave that awful grinding sound during the siege. Remember the one that, according to Captain Peter, could not drill its way through the ceiling?" He looked up. "Do you see the place where it nearly made a hole beside the light?" I looked up. The hole was right there.

"B-b-but... c-c-can't this explode any minute?" I stuttered.

"It could but it's not very likely if it did not do that until now. Anyway, leave it alone. I'll take it away from here. I don't want the children to bump into it."

Father had on his hideous purple mittens. Grandmother had made them especially ugly because she hoped that they would not be taken by the Soviets. They looked atrocious. Father squatted down and lifted the thing carefully. He straightened himself with the cannon shell in his hand and walked ever so slowly down the driveway, then out the gate. I didn't dare to move, not even to whisper. I only thought my prayers after him. I waited for a long time. There was no sound. He must have gotten rid of it by now, I thought he was very brave. He didn't want someone else to blow up. But what if he had been blown to pieces? No "what ifs..." a built-in mechanism reminded me. I turned and ran back to the others.

Mrs. Varga brought out one bucket after another. "Fill them up with snow! We'll have a bath today!"

"A bath! A bath, a bath, we'll have a bath..." the children chanted danced and jumped in the snow.

We wanted to do everything at once. We wanted to make up for the many weeks of darkness and despair.

Father and David began to put up the storm windows which had been taken off when the bombings started and were stored in a safe place, according to the advice of the Civil Defense people. We were happy that we had taken their advice. All the windows that were left in place had been broken.

We went all over the house to explore. We started to clean up. None of the women wanted to clean the toilets. The soldiers apparently were not much used to such conveniences and all the ones upstairs were filthy. No running water either. We filled the bathtubs with snow and Mother, the first one who could master her disgust, cleaned out one of the toilets. It took her a long time but she felt that it was a worthwhile effort. From that moment on nobody protested against any kind of dirty work. If Mother could do it they certainly were not going to hide when it was their turn.

After a few hours of dedicated work, the bathroom was reasonably clean for our first bath since Christmas.

Children were the first ones to be cleaned up. By the evening Mrs. Varga had a good amount of melted snow and some more kettles were waiting in the kitchen, on the stove. We hauled out the baby bathtub that was about five feet long and stood on a frame. The first one in it was Imi. He had recovered fully from his pneumonia and laughed happily at the lukewarm water. He splashed around with his tiny fists and made everyone laugh. Naturally, all the children stood around and admired him. We kept pouring hot water into the tub in order to keep it lukewarm. After the baby came Elisabeth and Ili. Then Marie and Juli. Joe was next and then it was my turn with Ica. She and I had private baths because we were too big to share the bathtub with another person.

That was all for the day. The adults had no turns. The water was black despite the constant adding of hot water. It hadn't been crystal clear to start with. After all, it was melted snow. We first had to fish out pieces of straw and mysterious black things from it before we would go in. Still, it was an unheard-of luxury. I felt myself completely covered by the lukewarm water. I used soap all over my body, I saw again that I had grown more like a woman; even in the cellar, in the darkness of the shelter, the process had not stopped. Nature went on creating something that was beyond my control. My new body was the product of it and I enjoyed being aware of myself.

We went to bed on the first floor for the first time in almost eight weeks. We did not want to go back to the shelter. We avoided it like the plague. Father brought us a suitcase.

"Are we going someplace?" asked Mother.

"No. Not yet. I hope we'll soon go over to Pest… but not just yet. Anyway, joking aside, when you take off your clothes put them into this suitcase. I gave everyone some mothballs for their suitcase or box or whatever."

"What's that for? We'll stink to high heaven," laughed Mother.

"It's still better than lice," said Father. "Today a soldier grabbed my neck and said, 'partisan!' (guerilla) 'Not me,' I protested. Then he started laughing and showed me a louse between his two fingers. 'Not you, him.' We must do something because lice are the carriers of many bad diseases. I figured if we put our clothes into mothballs every night that would kill any lice that might get into them during the day."

From that day on, our clothes went straight into the suitcase every night and we dressed from it every morning. The smell was quite obtrusive, but we quickly got used to it. I thought it was easier to get used to the stink than to boiled water.

We actually had water now. The Waterworks were only a block away and we were allowed to bring water from the reservoir, although it still had to be boiled because a horse had drowned in it. Boiled water or snow; both lacked water's most important quality; neither of them quenched thirst.

We were no longer on the front lines and all our neighbors were busy setting up their lives again. Yet, Soviet soldiers still ran rampant. The city was only a few miles back from the front, and they still believed that all that we owned, including our bodies, was their rightful prey. They still thought of Father as the "old professor" (he still had not shaved his beard) but they no longer needed him as badly as they had before. The knocks on the doors and windows were less frequent, but just as vehement. During these "raids" all the young women disappeared to their hiding places but during the day, they were out working.

One of our main occupations was to trade back furniture. Neighbors three and four streets away came to look for their tables, chairs, cupboards, curtains, even pots and pans. We put all that did not belong to us in one of the rooms on public display.

Grandmother got out her tools and started to sew back together one of our enormous oriental rugs. Apparently a Captain or some other important person needed only a runner for a hallway because about a yard of the carpet had been cut along the pattern.

A few days passed just trying to clean the house of tons of dust. There was joy and laughter whenever we discovered something we thought we had lost forever.

"Look what I found!" Mother lifted a can of pineapple from the mess that she was cleaning. "We had saved that for a special occasion, I think that our survival is special enough! We'll eat it today!"

That was the first time I had ever eaten pineapple. Its tangy taste brought sunshine onto our table that night. Everybody had a spoonful of it.

"This pineapple grows in the eternal summer of an island," explained Mother. "Do you know where Hawaii is?" She showed us in the big Atlas. "It is far from here. Now that the war is over maybe we'll get all these delicacies again. You'll have oranges, bananas, lemons, maybe even grapefruit."

"What is grapefruit?" asked Marie. Although I could answer most of her questions, I did not have the answer to this one. As a matter of fact, it was hard for me to remember when I had last eaten a banana. Oranges and lemons had been scarce during the war. But grapefruit? I wracked my brains in vain.

"It's like a big orange, only it tastes sour and also somewhat bitter."

"Bitter?" that word seemed to turn off Marie completely.

"It is bitter, but it was one of my favorites when we could get it. In England, I always ate that for breakfast," said Mother.

England! I decided then and there that I was going to like grapefruit very much.

"I want to see England!" I told Mother.

"I'll take you as soon as we can go. I love the English language, as you well know. Would you like to start learning it?" she asked.

"Yes. I would very much like that. I am bored with German and French. English sounds so much more exciting."

"Maybe you could go to England to study instead of Switzerland," said Mother thoughtfully. Then she looked around. "It's about time we woke up from our daydreams. Right now it would be nice to figure out how we could get news from the other side of the Danube. Start working again…"

In the evening I overheard her conversation with Father.

"David said that he talked with someone who made it across the icy Danube. Apparently the water is still frozen and one can walk across. There is also a temporary bridge at Csepel Island in the south, but Soviet patrols are standing on both sides of the river. Many men who are taken do not come back. There are rumors that they are taken to Siberia."

Mother shuddered at even the thought of Siberia. There were still Hungarians in Siberia who had not made it back since the First World War. We had talked about that often in the last few weeks.

"David suggested that he and I should try to go to Pest," Father continued. "He thinks that I would have a better chance to make it than most people because I am a doctor. I could always claim that I am on official business, in a hurry to see a captain or something like that. What do you say?"

Mother was naturally worried. What would we do without Father?

They sat there for a while and I didn't hear any sounds, but knowing Father I guessed that it would not be long before he would take off with David.

# 14

Father and the work gang had dug graves for all the dead they had found and had buried them. The few horses still alive had been slaughtered and distributed among the area families for meat. The alarm system worked according to the old general's plans. It was time for Father and David to leave.

The trip to Pest and back took them three days. When they arrived back safe and sound they had so much to tell they didn't know where to begin.

"Our house downtown is in perfect order," Father began. "Downstairs the maid's quarters served as barns but Agnes and Feri did not even let the Soviets set foot in the rooms upstairs. I think Agnes' tongue scared even the 'Rouskies' away. That is what the Soviets are called downtown. I wish they would not identify them as Russians because the Russians themselves suffer as much from the communists as all the other nationalities within the Soviet Union. Soviet is a term that makes the distinction clear. However, I'm afraid that people will call them 'Rouskies' anyway. It's a very catchy name, I must say. You know, people are hardly out of their shelters and graffiti had already appeared on the walls of the ruins: 'Rousky domoy,' 'Russians go home.' But to get back to our house. Miraculously no direct hit. Some plaster fell off the walls, but barely visible. By the time I got there Feri had put up all the storm windows, so it was quite cozy inside."

"Thank God," Mother could not believe her ears.

"How about the stores?" asked Grandmother.

"The main Molnár & Moser store that had two million worth of stock in the cellar burned out completely. Soviet soldiers climbed all over it and 'admired' its contents by the light of torches made of paper napkins. When the 'torch' burnt down to their fingers they threw it onto the floor. Pretty soon they had to run for their lives. All the contents burned and the windows are broken but the store is there." Father looked at Grandfather determinedly. "And that's all that we need to start again. We still have our name that inspires trust." Then he quietly added, "if there is anything in this world that can still inspire trust."

"What happened with our factory?" Grandfather inquired.

"I did not have any time to actually go out and see for myself but I heard from our managers that all the perfume oils are safe. The director of the factory made the soldiers believe that the place where he kept the barrels belonged to his apartment. He, as you well know, is a pharmacist and helped the Soviets with the wounded just as I did here. He befriended the soldiers and even managed to save some soap."

"That will be plenty to begin," Grandfather smiled in anticipation of the work he enjoyed so much. Although Father had taken over the management of the business, Grandfather, with his famous nose, was still the one who mixed perfumes and mouthwashes, toothpastes, soaps, and ointments according to his secret recipes. The formulae were written down and well hidden. While Grandfather was alive and well, nobody was going to take his pleasure away from him. I watched his contented face and hoped that I too would have something as satisfying in my life when I reached his age.

"This is how we started again after the First World War," he murmured.

"Several of the stores are in much better shape," Father continued with his account. "I think we should move to Pest as soon as possible. You know, maybe it wasn't such a bad idea of yours," Father turned to Grandmother, "to come home from Magyaróvár. I see now how important it is to be here on the spot. Our house is untouched as I said; it is also full. Two of our managers live in it, some distant relatives of ours also moved in. All of them thought that we were dead or that we had gone away with the Germans to the West. They were utterly surprised when they recognized me."

"Where are we going to go then if they live in our house?" asked Grandmother.

"Two of them are moving out this week. The Soviets made them leave their homes during the siege but they have permission now to return. We can put up with the rest until they find themselves something better," answered Father.

"But how are we going to cross the Danube? How did you?" I was curious to know.

"We went along the streets and watched out for the Soviets," Father began. "We walked and walked but often our walk was more like a climb. Houses lay across even the widest streets. Earth-colored people rummaged and poked around with sticks in the ruins. They looked like tired raccoons that look for their food in a garbage can."

I didn't exactly know what raccoons were but I did not want to interrupt.

"They lifted their glassy eyes to look at us but did not make a move. We didn't either. We tried to hurry as much as we could. Csepel is very far from here, let me tell you."

"We were awfully tired by the time we reached the vicinity of the pontoon bridge. When we saw the guards we watched at first from afar," David said.

Father took up the story, "I looked for the paper I had received from Captain Peter, stating in Russian that I was a doctor and should be left to go after my business. It also mentioned my invaluable services to the Soviet Army," Father remarked.

"I put on my Red Cross armband and grabbed my case with a huge Red Cross on it," said David. "As we were preparing, we observed a group of soldiers yelling: 'Robotny, robotny, edei-souda, robotny!' ('Work, work, come here, work!') They rounded up a few men and marched them away, towards the railroads. They looked in our direction but we were well hidden. We waited until everything was calm again."

"I whispered to David that he should limp," Father continued the story. "We reached the guard and handed him our documents. He even saluted as we passed by him. The same thing happened at the other side of the bridge."

Mother let out a sigh of relief then asked, "But how are we going to get through? We can't all walk that far! That must be ten miles!"

"I don't want you to walk. There is no way that we could walk over. I procured a truck for us." Father answered.

"A truck?!?" everybody asked at once. "Who has a truck nowadays?"

Father looked as if he felt absolutely glorious.

"A business associate of ours from Czechoslovakia already has a truck. He said he would come and pick us up. He has both a vehicle and an operator's permit. He is coming over next Wednesday to get us. He'll also have papers for us. Until then we'll have to get everything ready. For a while it will not be easy to run back and forth between our two houses."

"How could you do all that in such a short time?" I looked at my father with admiration. He smiled. "Someone up there must be looking out for us."

Finally the day came when the big truck rolled up on the driveway.

A crippled man with reddish blond hair jumped down from the high seat. He wasn't much bigger than I was and limped terribly, but his smile made up for everything. His broken Hungarian sounded like the trumpet of the angels. After all, he heralded our free passage to Pest, to the beginning of our new life after our long dark hibernation.

The long procession started. Bundles and suitcases preceded the people who settled down on top of everything after the truck was loaded full. Only Mrs. Varga and her family would stay behind in the big empty villa. Ica and I stood beside each other. When would we meet again? How long would the two parts of the city be separated? There was no telephone, no mail, nothing. We used to go to school from this hill, yet the parting now seemed so final that we both cried. We kissed each other which turned out to be for the last time, then, I climbed in after my family. Parents, grandparents, Aunt, Uncle,

Imi, Mrs. Rosta and her grandchildren, Margit and Joe, all had tears in their eyes. Even the house looked like a crying giant in the gray weather.

The truck started rolling. Ica and her family disappeared in a last veil of tears as the truck turned out onto the street and we left the wrought iron gate behind us. We were on our way.

The gardener's wife three houses down and her baby daughter waved good-bye as we drove past. Everybody who heard the noise of the truck hurried to the door to see what was going on.

After we turned the corner our slow descent began towards the streets that from the attic had looked like cemeteries for apartment houses. What would it look like close-up?

Suddenly my heart filled with anticipation. We were going to go down into that pile of rubble. I would see what it was like; I would touch its stone-firm reality, walk or climb on its skeletons. I would be part of rebuilding this city! I was part of history!

We passed through the vicinity of Óra út, the bottom of the steep street where the battle front had stood for six weeks. The walls that remained upright looked like the faces of teenage boys spotted with acne. Some were completely torn off the building; roofs sat on top of ruins like crazy hats on tipsy people after a New Year's Eve party. There was no life under these stones. The recent inhabitants had escaped to Germany long before the siege started. The original inhabitants had been dragged away to an unknown fate much earlier. I was happy that we passed by these villas quickly.

Slowly the rows of houses became dense. We had arrived from the mountain in the city of Buda. Side-streets were overflowing with ruins. As it had seemed from the attic view, most were not passable. An occasional pedestrian tried to climb across the rubble to get to the other side. Or maybe they wanted to find something?

We reached a happier region. Here people actually worked. They had shovels and they dug their way through the stones and dust. They waved at us.

"Hey! Where are you going?" A bearded middle-aged man with horn-rimmed glasses swung his shovel above his head in sheer delight to see a truck. He showed his white teeth in a big grin and ran after us for half a block. Then we left him behind also.

The remains of a house appeared on the left side. A young woman and three little children poked around in the sooty mess. She found a bucket and wiped it clean with the sleeves of her coat. Her face looked ashen. She was dressed in the uniform-of-the-day, overcoat turned inside out with a string around her waist, dirty dust rag over her scarecrow-hair. The children were of the same earth-color. I remembered the moment when I had looked into the mirror for the first time after the siege. I knew that I did not offer a much brighter picture. Yet, they seemed miserable, while I was extremely happy. I wanted to embrace and kiss everybody. I felt so very lucky to be alive and well, to be young and to be able to begin life again with a head start.

It was a long ride, even though we had traveled barely a mile and a half so far, because the truck had to find its way through the rubble on the partially cleared streets. We were now past the Southern Railroad Station. Its prehistoric alligator-skeleton seemed to swallow up greedily whatever was left of the city after the siege as its huge mouth loomed empty over the tiny ant-people who moved about within its reach, I was glad we hurried past that also. On every corner burnt-out tanks, cannons, all kinds of artillery, fallen airplanes littered the road to the bridge.

As far as our eyes could see ruins lay along and across the streets and the raccoon-like shadows of the inhabitants searched for remnants of their former life, just as Father had told us.

Soviet patrols marched by. Our truck must have had some special emblem, because it was not stopped by them.

We reached the icy Danube that thundered around the crippled piers and fallen spans of a bridge. If there ever was a way to cross the Danube on foot across its ice-cover, it did not exist anymore!

"Stoy!" We had reached the Soviet checkpoint at the temporary bridge.

"Document!" declared the guard.

The little good-humored man with the reddish-blond hair jumped off the driver's seat again and explained in a flamboyant, crackling dialect whatever it was he said. None of us could understand a word. He pulled a big paper from his pocket; the writing was in Russian.

The Soviets waved us by. We crossed the temporary military bridge.

Another historic moment; we had arrived in Pest. Near the bridge there were hardly any people. It seemed that nobody had survived the war. However, the farther away we got from the dangerous raid-zones of the bridge head, where Hungarians were gathered up to do some "robot" (meaning "work"), the more people appeared on the streets. They were preoccupied with their own business. The streets were much cleaner than in Buda. I remembered that the war was practically over here a good three weeks sooner than for those who lived in Buda. In some of the shop windows I saw people standing around selling their wares.

"Flintstones, saccharin!" the sound came like the hissing of a serpent. At first I did not even understand the words.

"What are they saying?" I turned to Grandmother.

"They are hissing something," Marie said.

"Saccharin, he said something about saccharin," I said,

"And flintstones," Grandmother added, "contraband stuff and valuable these days."

There were many of these peddlers around.

The streets of Pest! How many poems and songs had been written about their charm, their beauty and elegance, their very special flavor that could be felt even when the streets lay there half-dead as they did on that unforgettable day.

"We are home!" Mother exclaimed. "Where else in the world can you feel the pulse of the city, the rhythm of life as you can in our town?" She threw back her head and stretched out her arms. Father kissed her on the lips.

Yes! There definitely was a certain magic about the streets of Pest. No matter how desolate they looked, how wretchedly ruinous the siege had been. I began to recognize the streets as we neared our home. It took us much, much longer than the usual half-hour to get from one house to the other.

The truck turned into our street and I saw Károlyi Park. It was full of graves; little hills with wooden crosses and the Soviet graves with their characteristic small pyramids adorned with the red star. There were some German graves with "iron cross" markers. I saw the big sand hill in the middle beside the huge water reservoir. Both were there in preparation for an eventual fire during the war. Beside them two houses lay as flat as the streets in front of them. Did they burn? Why didn't anybody use the tremendous supply of water and sand that was within arm's reach of the ruins?

I wanted to ask but there was no time left. The door of our house opened and before anybody could say anything Agnes' words showered us with news.

"You are here!" she shrieked. "Am I glad to see you! Was it a great responsibility to keep the Soviets out of this house! I could hardly manage to do it! But I told every single one of them. I told it to them in no uncertain terms, in Hungarian, I know, but then they must have understood me. I told them that they were not allowed upstairs. If they needed to bring in their filthy horses from the street they could keep them downstairs, I said. One of the horses fell into the pool in the park and dragged an awful lot of mud in. Where should I start? Oh my God and Christ in Heaven, isn't it wonderful that you are all here? Feri, come and help them with their things! I prepared beds for all of you. Oh, I did the best I could. You know, everybody thought that you were dead already and people moved in. Well, I could not throw them out. After all, they were, well, you know, your friends, relatives, employees. I let them in, but as soon as they heard that you were back…Oh, why do I talk so much! Are you hungry? Of course, you are! How can I ask such stupid questions?"

"Agnes, Agnes!" Father tried to interrupt her. "We'll listen to everything during dinner, all right?"

"Yes, of course, Dr. Bartha-Kovács. You're right. I'll be as quiet as I can but I am going to burst with all the news. Yes, I'll try…" she led the way for the family and relatives who were going to stay.

Mrs. Rosta and her grandchildren were taken home by the truck. She had her own house on the outskirts of the city and she was anxious to get back to see what was left of her home. Now it was my sisters' turn to cry for their dear friends as they left.

It was hard to imagine life without them but we had more hope to see them soon than the ones who remained in Buda. At least we both were on the same side of the Danube.

Thank God for Agnes' tongue! She saved the situation. "Now come, come, you are not going to cry because they have a nice ride home! They are not going to the end of the world, you know. I talked with Mrs. Rosta, if all is well at home she'll be back next week to help me with the housework."

Margit and Joe went to live with her sister, a former cook of ours who upon retirement became the manager of one of our apartment houses. She was a jolly woman, as wide as she was tall. It was much easier to say good-bye to Joe than to any of the girls and yet I knew that we were going to miss him.

An elderly couple, distant relatives, just then arrived home from their trip to the downtown tents and broken shop-windows in an attempt to find food.

"We could hardly get anything," Uncle John murmured, while he hugged everybody. His wife, Aunt Mary, showed us the content of her straw shopping bag.

"Look. I got some dried parsnips, a quart of molasses, and a few carrots. I guess it'll be stew and cookies for us," she said.

"How do you make stew without meat?" I asked.

Indeed I saw. For the next couple of weeks I not only saw but ate so much of that dried parsnip stuff I did not want to even look at it anymore. However, on our first night home Agnes made soft boiled eggs for us and produced butter from her mysterious resources to spread onto our bread. I had not even heard of eggs since the soldiers had made that omelet of all 100 eggs we had hidden. We would never have eaten them; we stored them to have eggs whenever we needed them in recipes and then only used half of what was prescribed. I remembered that after the eggs were devoured by the soldiers we made "cookies" from flour, paprika, pepper, and water. They were in the shape of chocolate chip cookies but they tasted entirely different.

Today we had real eggs again. Prepared to be eaten. I savored every bite and ate as slowly as possible. I wanted to feel the texture, the smell, the wonder of this unusual food. With dinner we had water from the tap. Real, running, tap water! It was not boiled. I enjoyed its characteristic taste. It quenched my thirst!

That night we went to bed content. Our bodies were tired, excited, and well-fed. And it was fun to think of tomorrow.

# 15

Under and above the ruins one could feel the pulse of the city. Wherever there is life, it must go on and the first, most important thing is to find food. The whole town seemed to be busy doing just that.

After a few days, Grandpa and Little Grandma went back to their home in Cegléd with the aid of our Czechoslovakian friend. With his beautiful, young wife, he quickly became a constant presence in our house.

Father, Grandfather, the two managers who took refuge in our house, and Feri set out to revive our business. Grandfather started production at the factory. The news traveled by word of mouth only but more and more of our old employees showed up and started work. They sold soap and toothpaste from clothes hampers, standing in the broken windows of our burnt-out main store. While Grandfather was manufacturing whatever he could from the leftover raw materials, Father had to acquire more goods and to find food for his employees. Just as Mother had predicted before the siege, most of them preferred food to money when it came to compensation for their work.

The epidemic scare was great. The government ordered mass inoculations; everybody received a "tetra" vaccination that protected against the four most common sicknesses expected: typhoid, diphtheria, tetanus, and spotted fever.

Spring was in the air.

From one day to the next I became ill. I don't know to this day what came over me but I could not eat. Not anything. I felt like throwing up, I had a sore throat, or stomachache, fever, every day brought another symptom. Whenever something new started hurting, Mother gladly latched onto it. "Finally we know what is wrong with you." But when that too had passed, I still felt ill. Dr. Stühmer, our good old pediatrician, diagnosed it as "siege sickness." He said that very many people had it and that there was no explanation for it. I enjoyed being spoiled by the others although I felt guilty for lying around. Yet, I could not get up. I became weaker and weaker with every passing day, because I did not eat. Then one day I had a strange craving for a hard roll with butter. Grandfather volunteered to get me my "impossible dream."

He came back with two rolls and butter. From then on, every day he would bring me the one meal I could even attempt to swallow.

He not only brought me food. Whenever he wanted some rest from his business, he sat by my side and told me interesting stories of his life.

"When I was a very young child, my Mother died of smallpox," he said one day.

"Of smallpox? Do you mean to say that there was smallpox sixty years ago?"

"Yes. Smallpox swept through the country. In our family we had fourteen kids. My mother had just had her last baby, when two of the children came down with the smallpox. She was forbidden to go into their room but she did anyway and nursed them until she got the disease herself. She and seven of my brothers and sisters died at the same time. My father and his mother-in-law, my grandmother, brought up the seven of us who were left. My father had a sawmill on the river Tisza, the second largest river in Hungary, its source is way back in the Carpathian Mountains. Many Slovaks made their living by felling the huge trees. Then they shipped them down the river. Around Szolnok, where my father's mill was, the trees were fished out and worked into boards. I loved to play around in the Tisza, although it was a river of strong currents."

"I thought you didn't know how to swim," I said.

"I don't know the breaststroke. I do the dog-paddle."

"How did you get to Budapest, how come you did not continue with your Father's work?" I asked.

"I did not continue, because I had a fight with my Latin teacher in high school. I wanted out. One way of getting out was to go straight to the university, in those days university started at age sixteen for pharmacists. I said good-bye to my family and left for a brighter future. Could I have known what it involved maybe I would have stayed behind. The pharmacies were open from five o'clock in the morning till ten at night. We, the apprentices, had to go to university and study also, while it was our duty to sleep in the little room adjacent to the pharmacy and take any night calls that would come during the short time when we weren't open. I'll never forget the good old ladies who would knock on the window at five o'clock in the morning for their "Hoffman-drops" that had the reputation of curing heart conditions. They were actually predominantly alcohol. The drops made them feel well and they wouldn't have begun the day without them. Life was hard going but it was beautiful, too. In those days Hungary celebrated her millennium, our one thousandth anniversary. An exhibition to end all exhibitions took place at the edge of the city, in the Városliget."

"Where the big ice skating rink is?" I asked.

"Yes. They built up that whole area in time for the exhibition. The replica of the Castle of Vajdahunyad, the man-made lake that serves as the ice-skating rink today, the fairgrounds behind it, and even the subway that leads out to that part of the city. You know the monument with the statues of the angel of freedom and those of the seven chiefs of the seven Magyar tribes who led us onto this soil in 896?"

"And the statues of our most famous kings and leaders around this monument that embrace the tomb of the unknown soldier?" I quoted my teacher word-by-word.

"Yes, yes. There was an amusement park near the fairgrounds, too." Grandfather added.

"Isn't that the same one where we go at least once a year when we go to visit the Circus?"

"It sure is. Did I have a good time there!" Grandfather reminisced.

"Then your life wasn't all work?" I inquired.

"No," he answered again. "We worked hard and played hard. I'm afraid that is something Grandmother did not quite understand ever. Why I had to go out with my friends so often. There were times when I went out as much as three times a week. Yet, I never missed an hour of work. If I stayed out until the morning I was still there to open business as usual. Without exception."

I knew that in Hungary dinners and friendly gatherings lasted till the morning as a matter of course, and sometimes even went on for days on end. I had heard my parents' friends when they talked about their parties, especially the ones with gypsy music. The guests dozed off while listening to the gypsies, then they woke up and went on partying. In the city, though, partying used to stop in the morning because many of the guests had regular working hours.

"But Grandfather, weren't you sleepy after an all-night binge?" I asked him.

"Not really," he answered, "I found such special pleasure in my work always I could hardly wait to begin in the morning. I also enjoyed good strong coffee."

"I know. Does that help? It tastes so bitter. I don't like it," I said.

Grandfather laughed, "I think you will when you get older. You don't need to even taste it now. Especially with today's coffee prices. You can stick with your chicory and grain coffee with lots of milk and sugar. I bet you like that."

Now it was my turn to laugh. I liked that kind of coffee but I liked hot chocolate even better. Little Grandma always gave me hot chocolate in Cegléd. That thought nearly made me cry. But Grandfather went on with his story and I soon forgot about everything else.

"I had problems with my eyes one year, while I was a freshman at the university. Thinking back now it strikes me as the most important factor in starting my career. I was allowed only half an hour of reading a day for a whole semester. During that time I built up such a strong foundation in chemistry, by memorizing all day what I read in that half hour, that chemistry became part of me. I thought chemistry and I lived chemistry. Maybe that was the secret of my later success in working out the many different products for my new business. That goal was well-hidden from me in those days. I saw my eye problem as an obstacle to my studies. I did not understand what God wanted from me. I was even mad at him. Why did he have to do that to me? But, God works in mysterious ways. I finally finished school and was ready to buy a pharmacy. I already knew your Grandmother."

"What are you saying about me?" Grandmother appeared from nowhere. "No talking behind my back."

"I was talking with Helen about the time when we got married," Grandfather clued her in on our conversation.

"Oh, Helen, you should have seen him then," Grandmother laughed. "He was so very, very thin. My classmates at the cooking school commented on him that he would be quite good-looking if the poor guy didn't have TB. They couldn't imagine that someone could be healthy and be as slim as he was."

Now that was hard to imagine. Grandfather was still close to 230 pounds, despite the inadequate food supplies in the last year.

"I used to be a chain smoker," said Grandfather. "I always forgot my lunch."

"You can say that again," said Grandmother. "Evenings I used to ask you what you had for lunch and you started to wrack your brain: 'Now what was it, what was it? I know, I remember, when I asked the janitor to heat it for me. It must have been soup, or some vegetable. I suppose I must have had meat. I can't recall… Well, I must confess, I don't actually remember having eaten anything…' and then you were very embarrassed."

"This went on until one day a very good friend of mine, Feri Szablya, and I sat together smoking." Grandfather said. "With one flick of his hand he put out his cigarette, a very strong, Egyptian one at that, and said: 'This smoking is not good for us. Why don't we quit, here and now?' Why he thought of it then, why I agreed all of a sudden I'll never know. I just remember that I too put out my cigarette. I never had another smoke in my life until that crazy Soviet soldier stuffed one in my mouth. Remember? I was cutting tobacco for the other men in the kitchen and he felt I was being exploited because I did not smoke. He rolled a cigarette for me from toilet paper and pushed it in my mouth. I could hardly wait for him to get lost so I could quit smoking again. You know, Helen, I used to smoke at least two packs a day and I stopped in an instant."

"I heard that it was difficult to stop smoking," I said.

"Oh, it was, but I felt so much better. I never forgot my lunch again."

"Did you buy the pharmacy before or after you got married?" I wanted to hear the whole story.

"I bought it when we were married. We lived in Óbuda in the same house where the pharmacy was. Both our children were born there. Your uncle, who had died before you were born, got whooping cough when he was only six months old and from then on he was sick very often. He finally died when he was 23 years old. We put his Ph.D. papers on his coffin when we buried him. It was hard for me to lose my only son."

"I wish I might have known him. He looks so kind and understanding in his pictures," I said.

"I think you and he would have understood each other very well. He loved books just like you do. One of his rooms was completely lined with books. He didn't have much fun in his life," Grandfather spoke quietly about him as if he would not want to disturb his eternal rest.

"But let's go on with my story." He obviously did not want to dwell long on a memory that still hurt him. "After the first World War it was much like it is now. Except the Communists had taken over everything right away. For ninety days we had Communist rule. Blood flowed on the streets, human life became very cheap. Nothing was sacred. The populace of Hungary decided then that never, ever, will we have communism again in this country. We tried it and nobody liked it in the least."

"Grandfather," I interrupted, "do you think that there will be communism now? Does Soviet occupation mean that we have to become Communists?"

"Child, I certainly hope it doesn't. You don't know what you are up against if it comes to that. No, I don't even want to think about it. Anyway, after the war I sold the pharmacy and built a five-story apartment house. It was a nice house but I realized that I could not live without pharmacy, or chemistry. I thought hard about business life and I realized that the first thing that anybody will buy is food. The second is cosmetics. And sometimes," he said with a twinkle in his eye, "with ladies, cosmetics come before food. Therefore I decided to go into the drugstore business. A good middle-sized store was up for sale, Molnár & Moser. I bought it. The store had seven employees at the time and it did not have its own line of cosmetics. I had great dreams with that little store and God gave me the talent and endurance that made it possible to realize those great dreams. I became wealthy; my products were sold in every drugstore and grocery store in the country. I had a chain of stores myself."

"How did you feel when you heard that the main store burned, that everything had been ransacked, and that you had to start over? Weren't you mad at those rotten Soviets?" I burst out in indignation. I felt that I wanted to hit them, to take revenge. What right did they have to do that to my Grandfather?

"Hush, child," Grandfather answered. "Naturally, I felt bitterness but at the same time I was aware of God's graces that He lavished on us so abundantly. We were alive and well, together, and we had something left to start over. What your Father told me that day after he had returned from the city spoke of the great gift of 'our daily bread' which we pray for every day in the Our

Father. Every day we only need our daily bread and we had much more left than that. Think of the many who did not receive the special blessings we did."

~

I stood by the window again, and thought about what seemed to be an eternity ago. The year which had gone by since the German occupation had forced me out of the comfortable cocoon of my childhood into becoming an adult, if not in body at least in mind.

The Germans were gone, together with the worries of yesteryear. Were the realities of today any better? Did the red of the setting sun reflect the color of love or did it represent the star of the Soviets?

This hateful emblem appeared on every house, every building, every conceivable thing occupied by them. It was even on the caps of the soldiers. Their "davay-guitars," as we nicknamed their automatic rifles, stood guard on every corner. Tanks and armored cars rolled along the pavement. People in rags were robbed by the soldiers who had to fill themselves with the proceeds of the land.

Churches were jam packed. When there was no place left to turn to, when Man reached the end of his rope, he could only turn one way: he could only lift his face and ask for the solution from his Maker.

The first Mass after this holocaust came to my mind. We went to the University Church, only a block from our house downtown. The songs filled our hearts with memories of days gone by. To go to Church on Sundays was always a matter of course in our family. Yet, we now had missed every Sunday Mass for about three months because of the siege. We did not even notice which day was a Sunday, or when New Year's Day and Epiphany rolled by, while we lived our day-to-day existence in a very special presence of God. Now that we had no way to go to church it seemed that He moved in with us. There were many occasions for swearing and the soldiers' tongues were not tied by our presence. Yet, when death loomed near, everybody's thoughts turned to God instead of against Him. I stood beside Mother on the street when her friend said to her, "When they killed my son I complained against God. I asked him again and again where He was, when they murdered Joey. Then suddenly, in the middle of the night it came to me, He was exactly where He was at the time when His only Son was crucified. Do you know what that means? He took on our fate to be part of our lives forever." When I heard her words of such strong faith I started crying. Would I be able to say the same if my father had been the one who was killed?

~

Our house became a meeting point for many of our friends. Some came for food, some for help, others for a job, or simply to take a bath. Several of our friends continued to visit our bathtub for months. We opened up our hidden treasures in the "holes" and we had the means to keep life going until new supplies arrived. From where? Only God knew.

The once life-filled busy streets were dark and deserted at night. Those unfortunate people who had to go out went in pairs, or groups, if possible. Every now and then a drunken soldier would confront them and ask them at gunpoint to get undressed. At least the first impressions were that they would do it only when they were drunk and that their act would have a sexual connotation...until they started to undress old or unattractive people. More and more we realized that what they were after was not pleasure but civilian clothes.

Soon the unbeatable humor of the people of Budapest made a joke of this misery also: the story was about a policeman, who was told that an undressing (the nickname for that crime) was going on at the corner of Main and Rose streets. "Thank you very much for having warned me," answered the policeman, "I'll avoid the place carefully." There was nothing the local police could do against the glorious Soviet Army as we were supposed to call them.

One night the beautiful wife of our always happy Czechoslovakian friend was shot in the throat by a Soviet soldier. He wanted to take her purse and she would not give it to him because she and her husband had just made a successful business deal. All the proceeds of the deal were in her purse. She survived the ordeal, her youth conquered the disaster, but the menace of the possibility stayed with us.

When Soviet authorities learned about the shooting, the soldier who had committed the crime was shot on the spot by an officer. This was a rare event as the army was not keen to relieve the pressure from the occupied population. Posters, hung by the Communist party, claimed that in a Communist society the greatest value is placed on human life.

Every day children and grown-ups were blown up while trying to clean away the rubble or simply because they were curious and touched something strange. Remains of handgrenades, mines, shells, bombs were hidden everywhere.

Feri came home one day with a huge bandage on his head. The house where he had had lunch collapsed onto him during the meal. He was lucky to escape with a minor injury: a beam fell on his head but he was able to crawl out from under the bricks and dust. His friend died instantly. Feri sat in the kitchen, dazed, his blood soaking through the binding.

People complained about the strangest things. One had lost all her family in the siege, yet the only thing she could think of was that the Soviets had taken all of her black slips. She could not get dressed in mourning because she had no black slip. Her eyes looked somewhere far away. Reality no longer reached her.

Everybody who had survived the siege had a tale to tell.

"They took my husband," a young woman said. "He was only doing his duty. He was an officer and he had to have someone executed who had run away."

"They took mine to Germany because he ran away," another one's plight sounded like the counterpart of the first one.

"Why do the Germans keep fighting? Do they still believe in victory?"

"My daughter was raped by the Soviets. As a result she has VD and she is pregnant. She is only ten."

"My neighbor killed his daughters and then committed suicide when he could no longer protect them from the attack of the rape-hungry soldiers."

"The Germans smashed the head of a Jewish baby against a barn wall while his parents were forced to watch."

"The Germans never raped women; they courted them first and made them fall in love."

A young Jewish neighbor, who was saved in the closet of a friend, was trying in vain to find her husband. Nobody knew what had happened to him. He was called up by the military for work-duty as a Jew the day after their wedding. Sue paid the mailman for delaying the draft-letter by ten days. They had their honeymoon. Now it seemed that those ten days were all they would ever have of their marriage.

"Soviets liked children and fed them. They would have died to protect a child."

"As long as she was under eight."

All day and every day I heard similar remarks.

A new Hungarian government was formed in December 1944, on Hungarian soil. There was an important conference between Roosevelt, Churchill, and Stalin in Yalta in February of 1945, while we were still in the darkness of hibernation in our shelter and cannonballs flew back and forth above our heads. Many important decisions were made, among them the decision for the establishment of the United Nations. We listened to the news on our battery-operated radio, which we had hidden when we were supposed to surrender it to Soviet authorities.

On April 4, 1945, Hungary was liberated from the Germans.

By that time everybody longed for the moment when we would be liberated also from the Soviet troops—the troops we had thought before the siege were "only human…"

*With my sisters, Marie and Elizabeth, at the time when Father had to escape from Hungary, not even a year after our European business trip in 1948. I am in the coat that caused a sensation among visitors of the International Fur Exhibition in Basel, Switzerland. It was a sheepskin coat with the fur inside. The coat was covered with opaque plastic, which was radiant in the lamplight with its golden buttons. It looked like a space suit. It was made and we bought it in Hungary. 1948.*

*Father when he left, 1949.*

*The best photo of my mother, 1940s.*

*Mother, with her father István Bartha in 1933.*

*Mother and Father on their wedding day in the dining room.*
*September 9, 1933.*

*Mother and Father's wedding, 1933.*

*Grandfather's father, János Bartha, a very successful businessman in Szolnok. He had a sawmill on the Tisza. He had fourteen children, seven of them and his wife died in a smallpox epidemic. He brought up the remaining seven with his mother-in-law. 1900.*

*With my mother when I was born. 1934.*

*Mother and Grandmother.*

*Mathilda Kovács – Father's sister and my godmother.*

*Grandpa, Mother (only her face can be seen), Little Grandma holding me, and Father when I was two years old, about six years before the book starts.*

*Grandmother and Little Grandma with me as a two-year-old.*

*Painting of me, age five.*

*Having fun in Cegléd, in the vineyard. Potatoes were planted between the vine stalks and, being harvest time, we were allowed to dig them out. 1940.*

*Vineyard house in Cegléd.*

*My first Communion, May 1941.*

*My Austrian governess, Elsie Krummel with Marie and me before Elizabeth was born.*

*Dance class graduation masquerade party, 1943. On the left in the top row is Alec, my second-cousin. In the middle on the floor sits István (Steve) Kopits, who became the famous USA orthopedic surgeon, featured in Reader's Digest.*

146

*The three Bartha-Kovács girls: Helen, Marie, and Elizabeth. Flower girl dresses we wore to many family weddings and other festive occasions. 1943.*

## ŐSFA

**ÜKSZÜLŐK** (boxes 32–47 / 48–63)

| 32 | 33 | 34 | 35 | 36 | 37 | 38 | 39 | 40 | 41 | 42 | 43 | 44 | 45 | 46 | 47 |
|----|----|----|----|----|----|----|----|----|----|----|----|----|----|----|----|

| 48 | 49 | 50 | 51 | 52 | 53 | 54 | 55 | 56 | 57 | 58 | 59 | 60 | 61 | 62 | 63 |
|----|----|----|----|----|----|----|----|----|----|----|----|----|----|----|----|

**DÉDSZÜLŐK**

| 16 | 17 | 18 | 19 | 20 | 21 | 22 | 23 | 24 | 25 | 26 | 27 | 28 | 29 | 30 | 31 |
|----|----|----|----|----|----|----|----|----|----|----|----|----|----|----|----|

**SZÉPSZÜLŐK**

| 8 | 9 | 10 | 11 | 12 | 13 | 14 | 15 |
|---|---|----|----|----|----|----|----|
| Kovács Lajos | Gondos Mária | Szeleczky János | Szeleczky Rozália | Bartha János | Hötzl Mária Anna | Schmala Károlin | Nuszer Mária |

**NAGYSZÜLŐK**

| 4 | 5 | 6 | 7 |
|---|---|---|---|
| Kovács Lajos | Kovács Lajosné Szeleczky Matild | Bartha Istváné Lajos | Schmala Ilona Magdolna |

**SZÜLŐK**

| 2 | 3 |
|---|---|
| Dr. Bartha Kovács Lajos | Bartha Ilona, Anna, Margit |

**1**

Bartha Kovács Ilona Matild Mária

*Proof of all four grandparents being Aryan. Had to be carried around during Nazi occupation.*

148

*Our summer home as it looks today. "Svábhegy", or as it was later called "Szabadsághegy" Lóránt út 15. Budapest.*

*The house my grandfather built for our family. His lab was on the ground floor until it became too small and our company bought a plant where we manufactured our products, available everywhere, including some foreign countries. I lived there until I was nineteen, my first daughter Helen was born there. Magyar u. 26. Budapest.*

*Cegléd grandfather got this medal in the early 1940s because he organized and raised the funds for building a Guild House for Culture with a movie theater, big auditorium for plays, etc. in the town of Cegléd (70,000 inhabitants).*

*My other grandfather Lajos Kovács's house in Cegléd, after the nationalization.*

149

*Our garden at our summer home on Svábhegy, Lóránt út 15, Budapest.*

*The flagship store of our business Molnár és Moser, Budapest Petőfi Sándor u. 11. It looked like this until 1944. During the siege it burned. Soviet soldiers went through the storage in the basement (merchandise valued at $2 million). As it was dark, they took bundles of paper napkins and lit them to see, then they just threw them down. Soon the entire inventory burned and all the inside of the store. After the siege it was rebuilt to look like this again. Then it was nationalized.*

*Inside one of our branch stores, Neruda.*

*Our employees standing beside the kayaks they built themselves over the winter. This was the Christening of the boats.*

*Our family arrives at the employee boathouse my grandfather bought.*

*This is what the middle of downtown looked like during the siege 1944-45, where our main stores and winter home were located.*

*Széll Kálmán tér Budapest, 1945.*

153

*This is what the Castle District looked like where John and his family lived 1944 – 45.*

*Right after the siege of Budapest 1944/45 December through February.*

*Hungary had the greatest inflation ever, according to Ripley's Believe It or Not! A milpengö was a thousand pengös. 100 million of those...*

*And that was not the highest rate. Then came the b-pengös, which meant a European billion, our trillion pengö, and a 100 million of those... nobody could pronounce the number any more.*

*In the end 1 Forint, the new money which was worth 10 American cents, was worth $6 \times 10^{33}$ meaning 10 followed by 33 zeroes.*

155

*My last picture with braids. 1946.*

*Going to the opera.*

# 16

"Hi, Helen," Magdi flung her arms around my neck in front of the school, "You are alive! So am I." Her dark brown braids flew around her head as she turned and swirled among the girls to greet every one of them before we entered the building. Marti stood beside her, as she always did. She, too, was alive and well. Both of them looked taller and thinner; Magdi's rosy cheeks had paled during the year I had not seen her.

The wood and glass door opened silently with a click. Nothing betrayed the fact that something had changed during the siege; that three stories of the old majestic school building were missing.

Inside the door the hallways were as cleanly scrubbed as ever and the smiles on the faces of the Sisters had not changed either. It had been a year since we had come to pick up our report cards for the last time.

"Whoever completes the last three months of the school year will have graduated this year. You'll have to study very much to accomplish a year's work in ninety days. We have no books. We'll need your full cooperation," Reverend Mother told the students. "We cannot have all twelve classes come to school every day. Instruction will take place in the cellar, in the dining room. Odd grades will come Mondays, Wednesdays, Fridays; the even-numbered grades on the alternate days. I count on you to try your very best."

At the click of Sister's signal, we were guided into the dining room. Our class settled around the assigned table, with the teacher at the head. I could hardly make out what she said because I sat at the other end but I could clearly hear the discussions of 11th grade physics from the table next to ours that completely took my mind off fifth grade geography.

As we had no books our teacher dictated everything she wanted us to remember: the capital of the country, the main mountains, rivers, cities, most important industries, etc. She did not point out borders because she said she didn't know where they would be after the peace treaty. We wrote and wrote as fast as we could whatever we could hear. There was no blackboard.

She looked tired and hungry; so did most of my classmates. Did they think that about me also? I felt a little hungry but we had two meals every day.

Although I hated dried parsnips with a passion, I knew we had to be thankful for whatever we had.

History. To be on the safe side, the teacher talked about olden days. We only discussed history up to the times of Napoleon. The directional policy of history was not yet decided and nobody wanted trouble. Up to Napoleon we sailed on neutral waters.

Next came Physical Education. What were we going to do for physical education in a dining room, where six classes learned together, separately?

The PE teacher blew her whistle. "Make a line and follow me," she commanded the little army of fifth graders. "You stand here, the next one arm's length from you, and the next another arm's length away again. We are going to pass the bricks up to the top floor, which is now the second floor, instead of the fifth floor. We are going to help rebuild the school. Don't throw the bricks lest you hurt someone. Start. One, two, three."

She was the first in line and a Sister stood on the other end. We handed bricks along the human chain for an hour.

I was so proud of being part of the rebuilding process. I was madly in love with school, although when I was asked I always gave the stereotype answer: "I hate school," which was considered to be the "right" one for my peer group. We felt much happier passing the bricks than we did in the semi-darkness of the dining room, listening to geography or literature.

To me school meant that I was back on the ordinary track. I no longer felt that my life was an empty walnut shell on the waves of a rough and stormy sea. School proved to be a safe and sound anchor where I could find rest from life's inevitable problems. I was praised if I did well and punished if I did wrong. There was discipline. I knew where I stood.

"Helen, do you know what the time is?" Maria asked.

"Of course not. I have no watch. Who does? I suppose it must be about halfway between ten o'clock and eleven because we are in third period." I answered.

"Listen," she said as she passed the brick to me. "My uncle felt himself really lucky. Right across the street from him a merchant pulled up the shades from his shop window every day at eight o'clock. So he only needed to look out the window and he knew what the time was. The other day he went down to talk to the merchant and asked him, 'Do you have a watch, or how do you know what the time is?' 'That is rather simple,' answered the merchant, 'Every day when I go out to open my store I look up at your window. If you are standing there I know that it is eight o'clock and it's time to open my store.'"

I laughed so hard I nearly dropped the brick that she had passed to me.

"That's hilarious, that is! I can hardly wait to tell it at home!" I giggled and wiped away my tears with the back of my hands. Nobody dared to display any kind of time piece in those days or it would be immediately taken by a Soviet soldier. How could the Sisters tell time? Maybe they just guessed, or hid their watches under their big black skirts? The bell rang again. Another class came to relieve us.

"You can work some more after school if you want to, but now it's time to go back to your studies," the PE teacher announced and sounded her whistle.

One day workers came to the school gate and asked for help to plant grass on the square in front of the school. I was one of those who was chosen to go out. The seeds were dispersed on the earth. We put on boards over our shoes and held them in place with long wires. We then stamped our feet over the ground to bury the seeds. The spring sunshine embraced us with its warmth. Once more, we became an integral part of making our city beautiful again. In a few months velvety smooth green lawn would smile at us when we looked out the, hopefully completed, windows of our school. This was our country and we were building it for ourselves.

As we were planting, military trucks rolled by with the emblem of the red star on their side, foreshadowing the future we had no way to foretell.

I slept in the dining room where all the people who stayed in our house ate together every night. After I went to bed I always pretended to be asleep, especially because the discussions often became overheated by the emotion of differing views an how to cope with the insurmountable problems of everyday life.

"I must do something to get more merchandise," I heard Father say to Mother one day. "It is a great responsibility to feed this houseful and our employees as well. A few of us merchants decided to try and reach Vienna with a car caravan. We now have a small truck that we use to carry the merchandise to our stores from the factory. I'm going with that auto caravan. Normally the drive should not take us longer than five hours but now it might even take a day."

"How will you get across the border? There are Soviets all along the road," Mother worried.

"I don't know but I'll have to try."

Father tried and he reached Vienna without any significant result. The Austrians had even less than we did. The only thing he acquired from a group of American soldiers was a jar of Nescafé.

Father had a chance to meet with Elsie in Vienna—she was alive and doing reasonably well but she did not promise to return. She was taking care of a retarded girl whose mother clung to Elsie as her only hope for sanity.

159

In Budapest, the stores slowly began to look like stores again despite the shortage of goods. The make-shift tents disappeared from the streets. The windows were patched up with glass, wood, or whatever was available.

Grandpa and little Grandma in Cegléd helped to find food for our employees who preferred food in exchange for their work instead of money. The value of money began to dwindle away. In return for food, our little truck took carloads of merchandise to the farmers.

The land reform took place in March of 1945. We had the right to keep one hundred and fifty acres of our land but we never claimed it. When we first received the news it was already divided up and others were working on it.

I knew it hurt Father that he no longer had land because he liked it so much and he was always proud of it. However, he had no time to dwell on a loss that was mostly sentimental.

He was so busy I hardly saw him. In the evenings, the family discussions became more and more heated.

"We must do something to protect ourselves. If the Communists take over, as I am afraid they will," said Father one night, "it will be the end of us."

"Why do you say that?" Grandmother retorted. "Why should they take over? The Germans came and left and we were happy that we stayed and were here to start again.

Father raised his voice, "Look at the trend in politics. Look how they did it in Russia."

"The United Nations, once they get organized there will be a new spring, a new hope for mankind. People all over the world will be able to choose under what political system they want to live. Hungary will be no exception. What do you want us to do?" Grandmother's voice sounded fiery.

"I don't yet know what," Father quieted down a little, "but we have to expect the worst. Look at the Soviet Union. They've been in this deal since 1917."

"But the Communists will never win here; you know what happened in 1919. The people remember it well. We tried it once. It just can't happen here anymore. This country has had it with communism. The United Nations will make sure that the people, and not the politicians, prevail."

"Hogwash, I still think we should deposit some money in a Swiss bank, while we can," Father blurted.

"What? Take out money from this country, our homeland? You know, Son," Grandfather's voice sounded militant, "it was my generation that made something of Hungarian industry and commerce. We bought only wares 'Made in Hungary,' we manufactured the goods; we devoted our lives to building up our country. I won't let you do that. Not while I'm alive!" I could hear the angry disappointment in Grandfather's voice.

"You said," Father retorted, "that we should never despise the Jews because they have money, we should rather imitate them. This is how you became a millionaire. Many of our Jewish friends take money out of the country. As a matter of fact, they leave the country. They learned their lesson during the German days. They want to build a better future somewhere, anywhere in the world where there is hope for more freedom than here. They go to the West. They know that in Hungary, our class, that of the merchants, of all 'capitalists,' as the Communists call us, will die a slow death. The 'dictatorship of the proletariat' is a bitter revenge on anybody who 'sinned against the people,' whatever it is we have done."

"I'm not afraid," Grandfather said calmly.

"There will be no communism," Grandmother interjected.

"Our employees like us. We have never done anything to deserve their hatred," Mother added.

"It will not depend on our employees," Father continued his frightful oracle. "We have money. The Communists have declared that whoever has money must have stolen it from the people, because in the beginning everything belonged to everybody."

"Where did you hear these things?" Grandmother asked.

"I read them in Soviet novels and newspapers. Look, I picked up a few in town. They reek of propaganda but they depict our future, they show us what we can expect," Father answered.

Grandmother could not believe what she heard. "But what makes you think that the Soviets will have the power to establish a Communist regime in our country? Don't they have to abide by the treaties, by the international agreements? I'm looking forward to a bright future for our country. We are going to have elections pretty soon. You know that Hungary will never go for communism."

"I beg of you, listen to me," Father's voice trembled as he tried to suppress his anger. "It will be too late if we don't act now. The sooner we leave, the better. Why should we rebuild our business here, when we could do it in a much safer place, in another country—America, Canada, South America, even Africa."

Grandfather and Grandmother just shook their heads in disbelief.

"What would become of this country if everybody spoke that way? What if everybody left? If it is so good abroad why do people come back from the West?" asked Grandfather.

Indeed, many people came back and told stories about the miseries of refugee camps, about the bombed cities in Germany, about the starving population all over Europe. Why would it be any better there? I imagined myself in one of those camps. I thought of the bright future of our own country which we were building when we handed bricks to one another, when we planted the grass, when people started their businesses in the shop windows, when they built the first pontoon bridges across to Buda, when they put stone upon stone and laid the bricks, cleared away the rubbish, and planted grass to participate in the rebirth of our capital.

I also thought of the first day when Mariska, one of our former employees, came in from the edge of town. She was looking for work to feed her children. She came often from that day on and cleaned house while she stood on the windowsill and cleaned the windows with newspaper, or when she washed the lingerie she told me many stories. She loved to talk as much as our cook, Agnes, did.

"My father worked for your grandfather from the days when he was still young. He was a messenger boy at your store. There were six of us at home, brothers and sisters. One day he misplaced his salary, or it was stolen, or whatever…he couldn't find it. He was desperate. His whole salary was in this one wallet. Finally he went in to see your grandfather, who, without being suspicious of him gave him another salary right away. There are few men as good as your grandfather. He does not need to be afraid of going to the 'Clearing Committee' to get his clearance. You know, those committees that make you account for your whole life, for anything you ever did, said, or even thought. The employees will bear witness on his side. So will his business associates. As soon as we were old enough, your grandfather gave us work in the store. He was the one who established a school for druggists. I went to that school also after graduating from grade school. It was a three-year course along with practice at the store. Then I worked in your laboratory. One year it was especially cold, I caught a strange sickness. It had to be cured with gold. It was your father who acquired the medicine for me. Oh, those were the good days, when my husband and I were young, married, and we had a room for ourselves and a kitchen. We even had a radio. We had so much fun. Then came this horrible war. During the siege I had a baby girl. I was so happy that she was a girl. I called her Maria. She died, when she was but a day old. She was premature, because I got hit in my lung by a splinter. I'm all right now, I still have my son, but I have lost her. She was so tiny, so sweet."

"Oh, Mariska, I am so sorry," I whispered. I liked to listen to her, even though she talked a mile a minute. She went on and on, "And your grandmother, you know, she is the protecting angel of so many poor you would not even believe it. Her name is actually sold by beggars to other beggars on the Teleki Square. You know, that big market place. Did you know that on that market place nobody wants to accept money anymore? The peasants will exchange their goods for clothing, gold, jewelry, salt, furniture, anything except money."

With the arrival of the warm weather, long trains took desperate people to the country with all their exchangeable possessions in a bundle in search of food. The trains were jam packed. Many of the people traveled on top of box cars, they hung on stairs, were pushed into the train through the windows by friends who hoped to share in the food they might bring back. They went only to find untilled fields, burned down villages, to bump into Soviet soldiers, to be thrown off the trains, robbed of their miserable bundles. Sometimes they had to lug their exchange-articles for long miles on foot, yet if they found somebody who would exchange with them, their efforts paid off—their families had something to eat for a month.

Nobody was allowed to keep dollars, yet the possession of a dollar or of a Napoleon-gold piece meant survival for a family of three or four for a month. Our house was filled to its fullest capacity, yet, after having lived with twenty-two people in one room for fifty-one days during the siege, we felt that we could breathe easily. Compared to others we felt blessed; we had our house and could share it with others. We had enough food to share with others and we were healthy and well, alive and rebuilding the country. The considerable problems of everyday living were dwarfed by the miseries of others.

# 17

We were going to have free elections!

Just as Grandmother predicted. Parties organized. A provisional government was formed by four parties already on the 21st of December, 1944 in a town named Debrecen that was already occupied by the Soviets at the time. Now we would have a chance to approve or disapprove.

Mother and Father's friends went in and out of the house bringing news and carrying other rumors with them. For whom should we vote? The ideas of the Smallholders Party seemed like the ones closest to Western democracy. I listened eagerly to the conversations and to the foreign broadcasts. Only now we did not need to listen in secret. The programs were beamed from the territory that belonged to the Allies. The most important party was the Smallholders Party; then came the Social Democrats, the Peasant Party, and the Communist Party with the backing of the Soviet Union.

School ended in July and we got our report cards. We had muddled through the year despite the many disturbances and inconveniences. The building was being rebuilt, while the boarders slept in the gymnasium and the Sisters on the stage of the old school. Money came from the Motherhouse in Rome and from convents and old pupils all over the world. We helped every minute we could, even outside of PE classes.

Our school was not the only thing that was in the process of rebirth. The whole town experienced the fresh breeze of hope. Nothing but faith could prompt people to lift their half-starved bodies and start the fight to rebuild.

Everybody was hungry. Starvation was written on the faces of old and young alike. Meat was scarce, ingenuity fabricated sausages out of soy beans, crackers from flour, spices, and water; we bought a goat for gold in order to acquire milk. Long lines stood in front of stores that had something, anything, to sell. Father said it was even worse in Vienna. There was nothing to eat there, except the white bread that Americans brought with them. At least there were Americans there; we only had Soviets who were not supplied with C-rations. Their order was to live off the land they had occupied. And they did. Nothing was sacred—be it a patch of vegetable garden, or the last chicken of a widow, they devoured anything they could lay their hands on.

Whoever planted something had a double problem—he had to raise the crop and also to defend it.

Grandfather fell in the street one day and broke his hipbone. He was confined to bed now. We were fortunate because one of the people who lived in our house had just moved out—his house had been rebuilt. Grandfather and Grandmother now had a room of their own. He had to stay in bed for a while and I often sat beside him talking about olden days, his favorite topic. Slowly less and less seemed to interest him about our daily lives and occasionally he forgot that we had just gone through a terrible war. His friends still liked him and came to visit him every Wednesday. They then would sit around, sip wine, and tell stories. All of them were old, most of them pharmacists, rebuilding their lives for the second time, just as they had after World War I.

Grandmother and Grandfather eagerly listened to the foreign broadcasts every day.

Before I knew it I became an avid listener of both the Hungarian and the foreign broadcasts. Politics affected our daily lives, our immediate future, and I was interested. Would we be able to become a free nation? Who would win at the election? Would the United Nations actually have power to enforce all its decisions? The treaties? I watched the forming process of this great organization with great interest. Our personal future depended more on world politics than on anything else. The people of Hungary were already doing their very best to rebuild the country. The progress was enormous.

Germany fell to the Allies and the Soviets on May 8, 1945, but Japan was still fighting. Then something wonderfully awful happened. I first heard on the radio, then I read a detailed description in the Képes Figyelö (one of the illustrated weeklies). On August 6, the first atomic bomb was dropped on Hiroshima. My first reaction was that of glorious victory. The Americans had done it. If they could discover the secret weapon Hitler so desperately wanted, they would bring freedom to all mankind. By then I had seen newsreels of American boys marching. They were the image of health and cleanliness. They sang marches that grabbed my heart and made tears well up in my eyes. Maybe I was sentimental but that clean army of wholesome men was our only hope. And they had done it now, I was so proud of them. I felt that they had finally retorted for Pearl Harbor.

I remembered now that the crying of the newspaper vendors, "Japanese annihilate American fleet," had not stirred much emotion in my six-year-old heart when it happened. After all, preparation for Christmas was much more important to us children. It was years later that I found a stack of newspapers in our attic and, while browsing through them I came across an editorial written the day following Pearl Harbor.

By that time I was more mature and I was appalled by the cruelty of the "Blitzkrieg" theory applied to the Americans by the Japanese. I could not believe my eyes, I read and re-read it again. It went somewhat like this:

The American fleet does not exist anymore. The heroic Japanese airmen made scrap of those boats, whose men would not even get out of bed to defend themselves.

The assessment is clear: "there is nothing that can stop us from victory." With the Axis of Berlin to Rome now extended to Tokyo no power can make a dent on it. It also vindicates those who considered an advance "declaration of war" an unnecessary formality, which gives the enemy time to prepare and make the ensuing war last longer. Not this one.

And for those who still are not firmly behind us, our message is clear: they will perish together with their judeo-capitalistic-demo-liberal Anglo-American friends, starting the line with Churchill and Roosevelt, in a fire even bigger than that of Pearl Harbor. But they will not be heroes.

Our Japanese brethren are!

I remembered the kamikaze pilots, who directed their planes at American ships. Yes, they definitely deserved to be shown strength. I was flabbergasted that they explicitly refused to give up the fight and called to continue on after the first atomic bomb. What did they want? When I read the accounts and saw the pictures taken from the air I could not understand why they would want to go on to fight and expose themselves to the possibility of further air raids.

I did not for one minute think of the many human lives lost. Every air raid had its victims. If it was not caused by one bomb it was caused by many. I was thankful that the war would end and that this one bomb might save the lives of many millions who would have died had the war gone on.

Japan, however, did not stop fighting. As a matter of fact, they vowed to go on with the war till the last Japanese was dead. The Soviet Union now also declared war on them and attacked at Manchuria. On August 9, another bomb was dropped on Nagasaki. Manchuria was taken by the Soviets. Finally the Japanese gave up. On September 2, 1945, Japan fell.

There was peace on earth.

The Papal Nuncio, the Ambassador of the Vatican, who had hidden our Chrysler during the siege, was expelled from the country. The Primate of Hungary, Justinian Serédi, had died during the first days of Soviet occupation. His successor was named immediately by Pope Pius XII, but in those post war days the Vatican had no contact with the Hungarian government, therefore, the message that Joseph Mindszenty, the bishop of Veszprém, was named Archbishop of Esztergom and the Primate of Hungary arrived almost six months later.

"Grandmother, do you know anything about this Bishop Mindszenty?" I asked when I heard the news. I was excited about who Cardinal Serédi's successor would be because the Cardinal had once visited our school and it meant so much to me to see him in person.

"He was the Bishop of Veszprém, as you had just heard. He was ordained bishop in March, 1944, and went to jail for his beliefs and outspoken truthfulness on November 27, 1944. He was famous for hiding Jews, he ordered every convent, monastery, cloister, or religious community to open its doors and hide as many Jews as was possible. He opened the door of his Episcopal mansion to refugees and only kept one room for himself. He is a very saintly and upright, uncompromising man. He comes from a peasant family. Rumor has it that he honors his mother especially. He was freed from prison when the war was over. Anyway he has shown in an admirable way that he has the guts to stand up for his beliefs. That is a most important trait in our times, when we want to build a democracy."

I thought of the Communist slogans appearing on street corners, sides of streetcars, on ruins and walls. I associated them with the Soviet soldiers' presence on every street corner, guarding every public building, staring at us from every vantage point, blotting out our privacy everywhere.

Many families lived under a common roof now, in the same apartment, sharing a bathroom and kitchen if they were lucky enough to have a bathroom at all. Whoever rebuilt his own apartment had the right to use it as he pleased–live in it, share it with friends, or sell it. The problem was to get building materials, manpower and skilled workers–even if one possessed the money. Most people did not. Families lived in rooms that were half or completely bombed, under make-shift roofs. They could not even be sure whether or not the footing would stand up to the burden of their existence or whether it would give way under their weight. The danger of robbery never left them for an instant. There was no way to lock a dwelling that had no door. Bombed-out buildings were taken apart for the building materials but many of the wooden parts had already been burned for warmth during the bitter cold of the winter.

There were pontoon bridges on the Danube now and permanent communication was restored between the two parts of town. To reestablish communication with the countryside, factories worked full blast to reactivate the engines and trains that would transport the fuel and the food to the starving city, although the workers were ill-dressed and hungry.

The market, if we ever went with Grandmother, looked dirty and empty. The same people were there as before, the same once-fat lady grimaced a smile at us. To Grandmother's questions she answered, "We are alive. I can't say much more. Thank God for that, but what now? How are we going to go on?"

She still had something special for Grandmother; she was willing to sell her food. From the looks of it she would not have offered it before even to the little boy who wanted to steal her wares, yet today it was the greatest treasure we could find.

"You were always nice to me. Take this."

Grandmother paid her with bills that would have bought a small house a few years ago. Today she got a skimpy-looking chicken for it.

The scarecrow-like woman, who could not shut up before, sat silently behind her empty stand. "I have nothing," she said sadly. "Today nobody came from the villages. All I can offer you is dried parsnips if you do not have enough of them already."

"Oh, I hope we won't buy any," I prayed silently, while Grandmother bought some anyway.

Later, she told me that she bought it primarily because she knew that the woman needed the money to survive.

"Is it true, Grandmother, that people are selling your name at Teleki Square because they know that you'll help anyone?"

"Who told you that?" Grandmother blushed but she did not answer my question.

〜

"Something indescribably awful happened," Father burst into the room. "Our manager and his wife were killed at the factory."

"What are you talking about? That can't be true?" Mother grabbed his shoulders and shook him, trying to calm him down so he would make sense.

"I don't exactly know what happened. They just called me. That is, his brother just called me, you know, he is our lawyer. Last time, when we had a meeting together, the two brothers kissed when they parted. That was so unlike them, I had never seen two grown men kiss each other after a business meeting. They must have sensed something. Now the uncle and the grandmother are fighting over the kids so I was named legal guardian to straighten out this situation. The children will be coming over... God, what am I going to do? And he was on such good terms with the Soviets. He was the one who saved our soap and perfume oil supply, remember? That's how we could start over. Whom can you trust anymore? How can you trust the Soviets if they kill even their good friends?"

"Let's wait and find out what happened," Mother tried to calm him down, still not able to believe that the news was true.

Children. There were children involved. Then I'd know something also. They'd probably tell what happened. Would they be crying? How old were they? One question chased the other in my bewildered mind.

I had to wait a few days to find out first-hand, but finally the children came. Their uncle brought them. He agreed with the grandmother after all so there was no need for the children to have a legal guardian. They no longer cried when I talked with them. The boy was thirteen years old, just two years older than me, sturdy, dark-haired with thick eye brows that grew together above his dark brown eyes. The little girl, who was eight, had the same coloring. We liked and understood each other from the very beginning. He was very talkative, calm, and collected about their tragic fate.

He didn't need much prodding, the words poured out of him:

"It was like this. We were very friendly with many Soviets. They came to our house ever since the war because father helped them with his medicines. You know, of course, that he was a pharmacist. Anyway this one special Russian, he was a good friend of mine, we played together often. He said he had a brother like me at home. Mother often went to the bakery where they made bread for the soldiers. She mentioned there that she had jewels at home. They may have remembered that, except nobody touched the jewels at our house. I can't understand for the life of me why they did not take the jewels. Nothing, I tell you, nothing was missing except for a few civilian clothes. My father's clothes. They only wanted men's clothing."

"But to start at the beginning; that awful night I woke up to sounds. First somebody banged the door with the butt of a gun and kicked it, too. You know, one knows these sounds from the days of the siege. Curses in Russian, then the door was pushed in. I heard Father's voice and Mother's also. The soldiers talked with them. Then one yelled at them that they had to go to the cellar. I heard shuffling and doors closing then nothing. Then a shot...then as if a sack had fallen down the stairs...a piercing scream... then another shot...then nothing. I pretended to sleep. Somebody leaned over me and beamed a flashlight right into my eyes. I did not open them. Something told me that I, too, would be shot if I gave the slightest sign of being awake. I heard footsteps. They did not open the door to the room where Judy slept. More footsteps and curses. I thought I heard my friend's voice right beside my bed. Through a slit in my eyelids I could see him bend over me.

'He sleeps,' my friend declared.

Then the door banged shut. I listened as if all my being had turned into a huge ear. Many minutes passed and I did not hear anything. Then finally I sneaked out of bed. I crept ever so silently towards the cellar door. I dreaded the moment when I'd have to open it. I did not know what I would find there."

He buried his face into his hands. I felt very embarrassed, yet something made me stroke his unruly dark hair.

"You don't need to continue," I said slowly.

169

"I want to," he answered. "I'll have to live with it all my life. Won't I? Sometimes I wish those soldiers had shot me also. When I opened the door I saw my father lying face down. Blood covered his back as he lay on the stairs. My mother's body covered his as in an embrace. They became one in their death. I had no doubt that they were dead. They looked like rag dolls without the filling; Mother was shot through the head. There was blood everywhere. I went to the phone and dialed my uncle's number. I remember telling him what happened and I remember a silence; then I don't exactly know how I got dressed or how I kept from waking Judy. I did not want her to see them. She was so young. She was still asleep when Grandmother and Uncle arrived with the police."

"Why, why did they do it?" I wailed.

"Why? The Soviet authorities captured some soldiers, among them my friend. All they could find was my father's civilian clothes. Why couldn't they just ask for them? But, I think they wanted to escape, so they wouldn't have to go back to the Soviet Union. Many of them do, you know. They did not want us to know that they were afraid. But why, why did they have to kill my parents for that? Weren't there other ways? Apparently they did not mean to kill them. They claimed that father adjusted his glasses, he was very nearsighted, and the stairs were dark. The soldiers took that as a form of self-defense. They were panicky and afraid themselves. They shot him. Father fell down and Mother screamed. She covered his body with hers in protection. Then they shot her, too. No reason...no reason..."

In my mind, the posters put up by the Communists in the streets, appeared again as they so often did, when I heard stories of this kind: "in the Soviet Union the greatest treasure is human life."

I kept stroking his hair. He was shaking now.

"The authorities said that the soldiers were hanged without trial. Martial law. My friend, too. Why did all this have to happen? Why?" He looked into my face as if searching for an answer.

I just shook my head. I felt my eyes fill with tears that slowly spilled over my eyelids.

"I don't know, I really don't."

# 18

Free elections were held in Hungary in November, 1945. They were supposed to be supervised by the Allied Control Committee which, unfortunately, was itself controlled by the Commander of the Soviet troops in Hungary, General Voroshilov. Only those parties were allowed to take part in the elections that were included in the Provisional Government, formed in Debrecen in December of 1944, under Soviet occupation. There was only one party that was explicitly non-Marxist, the Smallholders Party. This party won the elections with a 57.7% majority, while the Communists received only 17% of the popular vote.

We were overjoyed. Despite the fact that many voters of the middle class were away in prison camps, either as prisoners of war or simply arrested by the police for different, very often fabricated reasons, the Communists could not take over.

"You will see. The Communists cannot bring back their rule to Hungary," Grandmother predicted. "Everybody knows how bad it was."

Father still was not convinced. He looked behind the scenes and shuddered at what he saw.

"In the Soviet Union there are no private businesses, Father retorted, they claim that property is theft. Whatever you take out of your own business, whatever you own, you must have stolen from the people. The land reform has already taken place. What more proof do we need?"

"Some of those lands were awfully big, you know," Grandmother said.

"Yes, but do you see anybody reimbursed for anything? The landowners, if they did not have enough sense to leave the country, are poorer than church mice and even then they are lucky if they could save their skin. Most of them are in prison for the very same crime 'property is theft.' The revenge of the poor over the rich is unleashed and everybody…"

"They won't do that to people like us," Grandmother interrupted. She did not want to hear anything contrary to her idealized picture of the future of Hungary. "You can clearly see it from the elections. The Smallholders Party won. That means…"

"It doesn't mean anything," now it was Father's turn to interrupt. Their voices grew louder with every word. Although many months had passed since the siege, I still slept in the dining room where this conversation took place. I desperately pretended to be asleep because I did not want to become the object of their anger. Yet, I desperately wanted to hear every word.

"Don't you understand," Father went on, "that while the Soviet troops are in the country we can't do anything against their will? All right, so today the Smallholders won, tomorrow they'll execute the leaders, or take them to camps, or whatever… Don't you understand" and Father's fist came down fiercely on the table, "that they let us rebuild this country on our money, our energy, our time, they need us now, but as soon as all that is done they'll no longer need us. They will still want our fortune. They'll take it when they are good and ready."

"I can't believe it. I don't want to believe it."

"A-h-h-h! That's right. What you said just now. You don't want to believe it. Well, open your eyes and look around you. Listen to the people; listen to the foreign broadcasts again. Listen to me, for goodness' sake. I am your son-in-law. It is my family, our family."

Mother looked from one to another and did not understand. She never had had any great desire to know about politics, but she loved our city, Budapest. She had made me fall in love with it also. I thought now of the things that must have come to her mind while listening to this discussion. The quay of the Danube, the flower vendors with their first violets, the busy Váci Street with its many colors, where most of her shopping was done, the fervor with which we started to rebuild that which was ours. Can this be taken away? Can something be taken away that never belonged to one, yet had become an integral part of one's personhood?

"Even if they take everything away, you are still a doctor," she said slowly and deliberately. "You can open a practice."

Father looked at her in astonishment. "Yes, I am still a doctor but what good is a doctor if he is dragged away into a prison camp because of the fact that he happened to 'steal his own property'?"

Was Father astonished because he never thought that Mother might have wanted him to remain a doctor? Did they ever discuss it? Was there a possibility of quitting the business? I certainly did not think so. Already in 1945, at age eleven, I was being brought up to become the future manager. I heard it only too often, "Look at all the businesses that are not managed by someone in the family. In a generation they go into bankruptcy. There is no manager one can really trust. We can't let the control go out of our hands."

Even at this early age I was warned to look out for fortune-hunters. I knew, even then—it seemed to me I had always known—that I would have to scrutinize the motives of every boy who so much as expressed admiration for me. I was worried, how would I be able to do that? How would I know in all certainty that my prince charming was not a villain?

As part of my preparation for the future I was allowed to learn English.

One of the many people who stayed in our house, because they had nowhere to go, was my French teacher whom we had first met in Mátrafüred. She was a refugee from Riga, Latvia, and spoke seven languages. Even though she was older than Mother, I became very good friends with her. Her life was fascinating.

"Please, tell me about the time when you were a little girl," I would beg her in French during our lesson. She was reluctant at first but when she saw my genuine interest she volunteered more and more information.

"You know, I stopped talking a long time ago about my experiences. People are very nice and understanding. They seem interested, yet they can't quite believe what I tell them. 'After all,' they'd say, 'Communists, Soviets, what have you, are only human. What you tell us is out of our experience.' I wonder what those same people think about the Nazis today. Were they too 'only human'? My friends would be polite but I knew that deep down they thought I was biased. Maybe I am, who knows. Is it possible not to be, when one's father is condemned to death? I didn't know of any crime he had committed. Then, by some miracle he was released from prison and escaped from the country the same night. As we learned later his name got mixed up with that of another prisoner. Whatever happened to the other person, only God knows. I hope that the police realized their mistake but I doubt that they would have spared the man.

One man to execute is one man to execute. They had to account for the prisoners. Such a little thing as identity did not disturb them much. Did it bother the Nazis? I was your age at the time and shortly afterwards my mother and I left in a box car. We met Father in Berlin. By the time I was twelve, I had read the classics in four languages. My father was Russian, my mother was German, I had an English nanny, and a French governess. I also spoke Spanish. I started to earn money in my teens in Berlin by translating from Spanish to German. I always loved the magic of words; I liked to play around with them and soon started to write poems and short stories."

"Jeanette," I asked her, "when did you meet your husband?"

"You mean my first husband? He was thirty-two when I was sixteen. We met in Berlin and that is where he married me. I loved him as my father, my provider, my everything—someone that saved me from everyday drudgery for money, from being a miserable refugee. Someone who gave me love and all I needed. I still love him as a friend."

"Where is he now?"

"He is in South America as far as I know. I wrote to him recently. During the war we did not correspond at all."

"You said that he was your first husband? Who was your second?" I urged her on with her story.

"The second one was a Hungarian. I had to divorce him also, although he was the man who taught me the meaning of the word 'falling in love.' Yet, during the war I could not identify with his views. He transported goods for the Nazis. I had to break my relations with him."

"You said that you started writing when you were a teenager."

"Yes, I did. I still write. I do most of my writing in English or Russian. Do you remember the play in 1942 'Aurora Borealis'? It ran in the Comedie Hongroise Theater (Vígszínház). I wrote that."

"You did?" I was flabbergasted. I was speaking to a real author, not only did I speak to her, she was my friend.

This was the lady who first introduced me to the mysteries of the English language. We agreed that we would translate the words I had to study into French or German whichever word was closest to the English one. This way it was easier for me to remember them.

I'll never forget my first English lesson, when she tried to teach me to pronounce the sound "th." There were two ways to do it; even one would have been difficult enough. No clear sounds in English, everything sounded muffled. The whole language struck me as French and German, mixed thoroughly and spoken in pig-Latin. I would have laughed, I guess, if I had not heard the lovely soft music of the words when Mother and Jeanette spoke it together. Mother admired the British and the English language. She often read English poems to me just to show me the melody of the words.

Jeanette spoke about many interesting places in the world. About trips she took in the Alps. She could actually drive a car. There were only a handful of women who could drive cars in Hungary, Mother could drive if she wanted to but she very seldom wanted to. I was determined to get my driver's license as soon as I was allowed to. I wanted to travel to strange places.

Mother told me about foreign countries, her many trips with Father, sometimes on business, sometimes for pleasure. They toured Europe on their honeymoon for three months. They went to the Riviera often during winters before the war broke out and to the World Exhibition in Paris. She told me many stories about England. I felt the desire again to go to an English-speaking country. Most of my friends' older sisters had gone to Switzerland for a year, or longer before the war. If given a chance I wanted to be different from the "crowd." Mother also said that we would go to the Riviera every winter when I was a little older and travel was possible again. Sometimes I wanted to go abroad so badly it hurt. But, there was no prospect of doing so in the foreseeable future. Europe was in shambles and we were occupied by the Soviets.

From September on we were in school again. This time we attended classes on the main floor in the reception rooms and on the first floor. Slowly the upper floors were being finished. My class, grade six, was a big class, we studied in the lounge. A small pot-bellied iron stove supplied all the heat; the ration for the day was a shoebox full of coke (compressed coal). We could often see our breath when a Sister would come in with the shoebox to feed the stove. She invariably received a standing ovation. Getting dressed was quite a task, I wore three sets of warm underwear beneath the spotless uniform. Above it I wore a sweater and a winter coat. Maybe that's why the uniform stayed spotless. Despite our efforts to keep warm, the schools had to close for a prolonged winter vacation that lasted anywhere from six weeks to three months depending on the facilities. For me, it was three months because I had sinus trouble and Grandmother would not hear of letting me go to school to catch another cold. Antibiotics were not known in Hungary at the time. Instead I would walk to church with her every day to Mass. On our way we met many beggars and Grandmother stopped at every one of them.

I especially liked the blind man who had a seeing-eye dog—the dog was plump and sweet. Sometimes I wondered how the dog could be so fat when people went hungry day after day. Rumors had it that all the food was taken by the Soviets for "reparation" of war damages.

Many of the beggars were frightening. They had lost a limb or two during the war and they displayed horrible wounds to arouse the sympathy of passersby. There was a poor woman who was deaf and blind. She was led to her place every morning by somebody in her family and left there, on the street corner, all day. She wore a dark knitted hat over her head. It looked like a stocking and embroidered on it was her handicap. I shuddered every time we put money into her cup. She did not even hear the jingle, or see us put the money down. I felt sorry for her but I knew she would not hear a word I said. She could not speak either.

A few of these beggars made a good living by simply standing at strategic locations. Already in the morning they had a nice pile of money in front of them. They all looked well-fed. Many of them were well dressed. The corners we passed every day with Grandmother were the choicest begging places in town.

Many of our friends still lived in our house. Aunt Lydia, who talked to me first about the dried parsnips right after we had come back to our downtown home, lived alone now. Her husband had been taken by the police. They had asked him to come as a witness, in connection with the work of the Clearing Committees who were busy giving everybody a "Clearance" concerning activities before or during the war. Her husband was accused of calling a worker a Communist in 1933. Therefore he had to go to jail. He was never released from being a "witness," but had no definite sentence. She was not sure where he was kept. Many of our friends were in the same position. At least he knew what he was accused of, many did not. Often it turned out, after a few months of prison-life, that the accusation was unfounded.

I can never forget one young friend. She arrived with her six-month old son in her arms. Her long lashes were bathed in tears as she sobbed to Grandmother, "The Soviets took my husband to do a little work 'robot, robot' and he never came back. I loved him so. We were married for about a year. I was nineteen. A few weeks later I received word from a nearby town to come to the concentration camp there every day and hand in some food through the barbed wire to my sick husband. Guards were lenient and let the food in for those who had spotted fever. I was nursing this little one but my mother traveled to that town and carried the food for three or four days. After that she got word that my husband was dead. They never returned his body. What am I to do?"

Another friend received word that her husband disappeared in Soviet Russia during a cold winter storm. Some of his comrades reported that they saw him sit down to rest for a few minutes. He was a doctor; he should have known better but they said he insisted he would move on in a few seconds. He made them go on; the enemy was at their back. The wife considered a move to the capital but before she made her final decision she opened the Bible and her eyes fell on words that promised return from captivity. She did not dare to move lest her husband should come back and not find her. She stayed in their small home town with her two sons. She had a constant smile on her face; she possessed an incredible faith that she would someday be reunited with her husband. She was convinced that God had given her a sign to stay.

In those days of 1944 to 1946, those were the lucky ones who could and did believe. They were the ones who could hold on and pull through.

Eva, the landlord's daughter from next door, came back one day to visit Grandmother. She was the only one from her family left alive. I wondered when I looked at her smiling face how she could smile after what she had gone through. By now we had seen the pictures of the Nazi torture camps in the illustrated magazines. I was especially appalled by one that pictured a simple table lamp. It would have been a very attractive lamp, except the lampshade was made from human skin. It belonged to one of the prison guards. There was more and more talk about the necessity to call into account those Nazis who did not die via their compulsory suicide. Each of the Nazi dignitaries had a poison ring which they were supposed to empty into their mouths before they were captured, for some of them, the will to live proved overpowering. They now had to face the anger of humankind. The fate of the insignificant little Nazis who were responsible for "only" a few lives was much less drastic, they simply became members of the Communist party. The methods of both parties were the same and so were many of the ideas. They had to change colors, insignia, and directions: from extreme right to extreme left, and voilà—a ready-made Communist. As they had no scruples and were obedient to the new orders they were welcomed by the Communists. The Communist party was the perfect hiding place for them.

In reverse, those who were for true democracy, those who were persecuted by the Nazis, now became the "enemies of the people" as Communists liked to call them.

Uncle Joe, our former agent, came back from wherever his ordeals had taken him and he gave me his usual good-natured hippopotamus-kiss with his huge, always moist, fat lips. I remembered when Father said that he was happy building the rock-shelter during the German times. Whatever his scheme had been, it must have worked for him–he had survived. So did his wife and his beautiful twenty-two-year old daughter. He was always one of those who would make it through anything. It was good to see him again. They invited us over for dinner, I had never eaten kosher food before in my life but I really loved it.

After dinner his daughter showed me her nylon stockings. They were the first ones I had ever seen. She told me,

"It's hard to believe but they don't rip. I have worn this pair for the past six months. You can't compare them with silk stockings. I wash them every evening and in the morning I put them on again."

"They are, oh, so sheer. I have never seen anything as beautiful as that," I exclaimed.

I was just experimenting with synthetic silk stockings myself and that day had been one of those rare occasions when Mother let me put them on. I was still considered a child in certain matters.

A very distressing thing in my life, at age eleven, was that when it came to helping my parents I was considered a grown-up but when it came to privileges, I was not allowed everything adults were permitted to do.

However, some of the things that I enjoyed very much, and that were privileges of age, were almost worth having to help all the time and giving in to my sisters' whims because "you are the oldest." I loved to go to the movies and the theater. Grandmother was an avid theatergoer and she never had a more faithful partner than me.

She loved opera and classical theater pieces as well as the modern ones. We went to the opera at least once every two weeks and in between we went to every theater piece performed in town unless it was quite outrageously

"R" rated. Operettas were our favorites. Hanna Honthy, prima donna, close to Grandmother's age, was still one of the celebrated stars. She, and many of the older actors, among them Tivadar Uray, Hungary's Lawrence Olivier, Grandfather's very good friend, lent many of their own props to theaters and thereby made it possible for the theaters to reopen their doors to the public after the siege.

We usually took the streetcar and the subway to the theater. This was a very unusual experience for me because otherwise we either walked or were driven by the chauffeur. Sometimes we would take a taxi but we practically never traveled by streetcar. I was scared of the streetcars because when I was about six years old I had seen a picture of a big train-derailment in Italy. From then on any kind of vehicle on tracks was always associated with danger for me. What if the streetcar left while only half the family was on board? What if it derailed while we were traveling on it? I prayed silently during every minute of our first trips until the streetcar stopped and we were safely on the sidewalk again. After a few successful rides my worries subsided and I learned to accept public transportation.

The "mini-crime of undressing" still went on in the streets and therefore Grandmother and I always walked in the middle of the road, and only in the sections of the street that were lighted, even if dimly. We did not need to be afraid of cars as there weren't any. All private cars had been taken by either the Germans or the Soviets. Our Chrysler that was hidden in the Nuncio's (Vatican's Ambassador to Hungary) Palace also has been taken by the Soviets along with the other four he tried to safekeep for others. The Soviets emptied his garage while they asked him over for friendly negotiations. A friend later recognized our car in Vienna by its musical horn. It was too late. The Soviet dignitary, who "owned" it, had repainted it by that time. Besides, who would risk his life to testify on behalf of a car?

We learned to be happy with life, with survival, and to wave aside every conceivable material loss with a simple sentence: "They were only things."

The cliché "it's only money" became a reality in our lives. Compared to true values, money meant nothing anymore.

Literally speaking, money did not mean much anymore either. In the early spring of 1946 I saw thousand pengő bills lying around in the mud, later, in the summer million pengő bills joined their ranks.

Jokes about inflation flooded the nation. A cartoon showed a merchant standing beside a bag of sugar with a stop-watch. He said, "In ten minutes the price of a kilo of sugar will reach the ten billion mark."

Those friends of ours who lived on a fixed salary literally ran to the market as soon as they had received their money and exchanged it within the half-hour for goods, for anything. In an hour the money would be worth at least 20% less.

Once again I was listening to Mariska, who faithfully came to clean the windows, floors, wash the lingerie, do odd jobs to earn food for her family. She wailed, "You know, my sister and her husband had saved enough money to move to a little village and buy themselves a house and a carpenter workshop. Then came the war. Their money is not worth anything anymore. Right now they are using the bills for toilet paper. Oh, you just can't imagine what is going on in the world."

She was right. It was hard for me to imagine that somebody would use their life savings for toilet paper; how the dream of a house and workshop, a whole different way of life, could melt along with the value of money.

We had money, even too much money—money by the bagfuls, and we had to get rid of it every day as soon as it came in. If we had kept it till the next day it would have meant the loss of all the profits for that day or worse. The money was taken to the bank from the store every hour and converted into its gold equivalent. The profit had to take care of 150 employees and their families as well as the rebuilding of the stores. We could not afford to lose its value.

In the spring a single newspaper cost as much as 20,000 pengős. In 1939, before the war, a pengő was worth 20 cents in American money and for 5,000 pengős one could buy a nice house and workshop.

People with fixed salaries did not have a chance. Another joke claimed that housewives took shopping bags full of money to the market and what they bought with it would easily fit into their change-purses.

Ingenuity paid off on the black market, opportunists used people to become rich on their misery. Everything was available for the right price.

Artistic talents came to the foreground and old curtains, brocade bedspreads, even American matchboxes and magazines served as raw materials for changeable goods. Everybody "manufactured" something, hand-painted silk scarves, handkerchiefs, and tablecloths brought good prices. Anything that would prove of more durable value than money sold well.

As Grandmother expected, our family had no problems with the "Clearing Committee." The employees stood up for us and the eighty widows who were on our payroll, without ever having worked for the store, tipped the balance in our favor. As a matter of fact, one of the Communists invited Father for a cup of coffee after the session and said, "You know, I was determined to get you. I could not imagine that someone as prominent as you wouldn't have something to hide, that I wouldn't be able to hunt up something that would incriminate you. Congratulations, doctor! As I dug into the history of your fortune I found more and more evidence of all the progressive ideas your father-in-law started and you continued to put to work. The school for druggists is one of a kind. The apartment house for retired druggists, the cottage for druggists in Balaton Lelle, the boat house you are building for your employees on the Shore of the Danube, the company spirit the apprentices have—I could go on and on. I am sorry I was ever against you."

When I heard this from Mother I thought of what Grandmother had said about our employees. Would it depend on them, after all, whether or not we were persecuted?

In those days, I often went to the movies with Mother. She liked American and British films. Every week there was at least one new one and we had to catch up on all the movies we had missed during the war, when there had been only German and Hungarian films available, many of them Nazi propaganda films.

Now we saw *Mrs. Miniver*, *Madame Curie*, *Lady Hamilton*, and *The Titanic*, several times. We saw a war movie about five brothers who had died together on one ship because they went back to save the youngest one. We saw *Yankee Doodle* and Greta Garbo movies, Bing Crosby, Maurice Chevalier, and Fred Astaire.

I admired the American small towns, the scenery, but above all I admired the way of life the films portrayed, the marching young boys, healthy, singing, and *free*. Every time I saw them a patriotic feeling surged up in me and my eyes filled with tears. Why did I feel this way about the Americans? About our "enemies"? Because I had the impression that this honest, kind, good-willed, freedom-loving nation was our only hope to get rid of the Soviets, the Communists. If anyone, they would certainly have the power in the United Nations to make sure that decisions were carried out. They would be the only ones the Soviets would have to listen to because every bit of supply the Soviets owned was either American or something they had taken from the Germans. Even their army boots were "Made in America."

The movies were not the only sources of my information about Americans. More and more people came back from the West where they had escaped from the Soviets, in order to find their families and what was left of their homes. Many of them, like a second cousin of mine, Alex, a seventeen-year-old, came from American-occupied Germany. Their war stories were definitely different from ours.

"When the Americans arrived we were scared, of course. They came like invisible giants. When they fought all you could see, or rather feel or hear, was that you were being shot at. No person in sight. Then the fire would stop. If the Germans did not shoot during the cease-fire a jeep would come forward. If there were no shots, other jeeps would come and the village was occupied.

If the jeep was shot at, it quickly retreated and the heavy artillery went to work again. The Americans repeated this procedure until they could occupy the village. Of course, there were many fronts where this was not possible and they had to go through very heavy fighting but by the time they had reached us even the Germans had lost all interest in war."

"What were the soldiers like after they had occupied the villages?" I asked him. "Did they rape and rob like the Soviets?"

"I should say not. You know that I speak English. They were glad to find someone who could talk with them and we joked and drank Coca-Cola and beer. They gave me food…"

"What is Coca-Cola?" I inquired.

"It's a drink. Nonalcoholic. They seem to like it a lot. I did not mind it but it tastes different. It has the color of vermouth. Many of the soldiers did not go for alcohol. They said they never drank it. Some said it was against their religion…"

"Did soldiers have religion?" I wondered. "It was quite unthinkable of a Soviet soldier to abstain because of religion, to abstain for anything."

"Americans are very, very different from Soviets. Naturally, they come from a different background, a different culture, their upbringing is different. I enjoyed being with American soldiers. They are very good about sharing their food with the refugees, even prisoners of war."

"You mean they have their own food?" I asked in surprise.

"Of course. They have army rations and they have unheardof goodies, like oranges, nylon stockings, you name it, they have it. What did the Soviets do? What did they eat?"

"Our food, naturally," I answered him. "They also raped the girls and women…"

"They did?" Now it was Alex's turn to be surprised. "Americans did not rape the women. They had their own technique for finding themselves 'Fräuleins' (Miss in German). They simply displayed the nylon stockings, oranges, and other good things they possessed on the town square and gave them away to anybody who was willing to keep them company. They had more ladies show up than they could handle, which was just as well because not all of the women wanted male companionship in exchange for the goodies anyway. I was friendly with the Americans, I always had everything I needed and I could take home enough for the family I stayed with. In exchange I offered my services as interpreter. I had a pretty good life. Maybe I should have stayed but I wanted to know about my family, my father and mother, sister and relatives, friends, and our home. On my way home, when I got close … when I was only a few streets away from where I used to live, my heart thumped in my throat because I was so afraid that I would not find our home there as it used to be, only a pile of rubble, smoking ... I don't know why I thought that it would be smoking after all these months, it was just nerves, I guess, that painted this picture of a nightmare. I turned the corner...and...the house was there. It stood, with a few holes in it but erect as always. The garden was looked after. Somebody lived in the house. I started to run in my eagerness to see who was alive...they were all alive! All of my family was there, thank God. I felt that no matter what I had to face in Hungary it was worth coming home because we were together again and being together is one of the great graces and blessings we receive from God."

"You know, Alex, this is what we always said during the war, during the siege, and I think that you are right, although I never tried to be separated from my family. I don't know what it would feel like. Are there times when knowing that your loved one is safe means more than being with him?"

The question remained unanswered but I saw that he was thinking of it also. Next time he came he brought me a bouquet of beautiful lilacs.

# 19

I opened my eyes. For a moment I could not think of where I was. Then the rattling, clinking noise of running horses, people's loud hollering and instructions given through the chaos of children's laughter and merriment reminded me that I had come to Little Grandma's house for a visit.

All I could see were beams of the rising sun, or at least as much of it as came through the slits of the tightly closed shutters.

I remembered the voice of Little Grandma as she softly impressed on me, "You have to sleep in as long as you can, so you will be able to go with us to the market."

"The market!" my heart filled with excitement at the thought. Twice a week and on Sundays, the market people's noisy wheels rolled past my window. While I obeyed Little Grandma and turned over in my bed, tightly shutting my eyes in the half-dark of the room, I anticipated the sights and sounds, the smells and tastes of the market.

I could not sleep, even though, judging from the sun, it could not have been later than 5 a.m., and I knew very well that I would upset anybody whom I would awaken in the house at such an early hour.

The cock crowed outside and soon I could hear the hens stir in the chicken coop.

"The egg-song," I remembered what I had once called the hens' particular sound with which they would announce the production of an egg. A dog barked somewhere.

I imagined the peasants putting out their goods—the many bright-colored fruits, vegetables, and honey-cakes, dolls and ceramics, pots and pans, whistles, noisemakers, toys. I had never really seen them set up the market but now that I was practically grown I could picture the ropes, nails, and hammers.

Yes, I was grown now. I had had my first period not quite a month before. I remembered the first tiny brown flow and my excitement over it. I knew what it was but it was hard to believe that I was old enough to have a baby! I thought of babies as little red wrinkly nuisances but since I'd had my period I guessed that maybe, just maybe, if one had one's own, it would be different. Anyhow, I was glad now to be a woman.

However, in Cegléd, I certainly did not feel like an adult. I felt like what I was, a happy child, going to the market with agile, energetic Little Grandma. Despite the siege she had no gray hair, her little dark brown eyes twinkled with life and she made possible for me everything in her power.

The hammers of the market-preparation reminded me of Grandfather's friend, Uncle Kiss (we called every man Uncle and every woman Aunt, whether they were related or not), who owned a carpenter shop. He built furniture. Was it ever fun to watch his clever hands produce masterpieces out of raw wood! I liked the smell of the fresh wood shavings. Sometimes he even let me "help" with his tools. Today, I dreaded to think what kind of help Marie and I, aged five and seven, had been. He always had a little hammer and nails ready for children who came into his workshop and we were allowed to "work."

I came to Little Grandma's house often by myself. Among all the good things there, I enjoyed one thing especially. My sister was only two years younger than I and I could not remember the time when I was the baby, the one to be cuddled and loved. Here it was that, all over again! Little Grandma seemed to have nothing else to do when I was around but to love me, be with me, enjoy me, and I likewise enjoyed Little Grandma and being the center of attention.

She spoiled me in more ways than one. She was the best cook around and she spared nothing when she cooked for her own family. Food seemed to mean a lot to everybody in Cegléd. Food was the means of communication—the way to express emotions from the love-language of the young, to the consolation of the old.

"You must have some more! Come on, help yourself."

"Wait, I'll give you some more."

"I prepared your favorite food for you."

The family got used to these proddings from our Little Grandma.

Proud boys beamed when they bragged about their girl friends' affection for them. "She made my favorite!" "I helped myself four times to her cake, she made it alone, especially for me!"

The highest form of compliment was to praise the food. "The best meal I ever had." "You outdid yourself today."

I thought of the cozy Sunday afternoons, when Grandfather's cigar smoking friends played cards and sipped the wine from his sandy vineyard.

I was so immersed in my thought-dreams that I did not even hear the door open.

"You sleepyhead! Breakfast is ready." Little Grandma hugged me out of bed and surprised me with my favorite breakfast—marble "kuglof," a kind of angel food cake, with home-made red-sweet strawberry jam and hot chocolate. Yes, everything was just as it had been when I was a little girl. What did it matter that I was eleven years old! Who cared about being lady-like. I licked my fingers so as not to lose even the tiniest drop of the jam and asked Little Grandma, "When are we going to the market? Right now?"

The "little train" whistled in front of the house. It was a commuter train between Cegléd and the surrounding, outlying settlements, such as Grandfather's vineyard. It stopped close to our window and whenever it came I jumped and ran to have a glimpse of the steam locomotive huffing and puffing as people hurried on and off with their enormous baskets of fruit, live chickens, eggs, and all kinds of merchandise. When I looked out the window today I noticed a truck. Several Soviet soldiers were shoveling cucumbers onto it, "Grandma! What are those soldiers doing?"

I could not believe my ears when Little Grandma answered with a bitter swear-word, "The devil should take them! Reparation! They do it every day. Anything they want they grab, take it, and call it reparation. Naturally it is not accounted for. Authorities don't even know what is taken or when and where. I guess it is just one of the curses of the war." I never heard Little Grandma, or any of my family members use words like that before. I put my arms around her and tried to distract her.

"What do you think I should put on today?" She understood and let herself be led to my wardrobe to select the perfect dress for the occasion.

Soon we hurried hand in hand down the main street towards the church, where the market was set up.

We dropped in to say hello to Uncle Kiss who pinched my cheek and teased me, "Are you going to drop over to help me? I've got quite a lot of work! Or are you too old for that, young lady?" He laughed and so did I. Deep down I really would have enjoyed indulging in a little play, but then, what would everybody think? Anyway, even though we both laughed it off, I did not quite dismiss the possibility.

"Look, Grandma, what lovely aprons." The market in Cegléd was our place to get aprons.

"Would you like one?" asked Grandmother.

"Would I?"

She held a red one. It had tiny flowers over it and covered my entire dress. I thought it was adorable.

"This one looks perfect. Let's find one for your mother and sisters also. Here is a huge one. That will fit Grandmother."

Finally, it came to paying. The woman who was selling her handmade aprons counted in her head for quite a while. Finally she said, "One red, two greens, and three blues for the big ones and for the children's aprons one yellow each."

That talk would have sounded strange just a year before but by June of 1946 our bills were colored all the shades of the rainbow in order to be distinguishable. Nobody knew the name of the astronomical numbers printed on them and nobody paid any attention to them anymore.

At the next tent we bought honey-cakes made in the form of hearts and baby-dolls. Again we thought of my sisters and I took one to give my cousin, Imi, who had grown into a talkative two-year-old since the siege.

The woman said to Grandma, "Mrs. Kovács, my husband needs harnesses, why don't we trade merchandise. I would prefer that to money. He'll drop by the store later."

We squeezed through the gossiping, bargaining crowd then stopped again. This stand was filled with the freshest carrots, lettuce, radishes, green onions, all as spotless as if they had been individually washed. We filled our baskets but again, the vendor did not want money for her merchandise. She wanted a purse for her daughter and promised to drop by at Grandfather's store later.

We reached the noisy, whistling, churning section of the market where toys and trinkets were sold. Little Grandma did not ask me. She simply bought one of those birds at the end of a whip that whistle if one twirls it. "Take that for your sisters," she said and she winked. She knew this market-toy was always one of my favorites.

"I need a pot." Little Grandma stopped at a tent that sold pots and pans made from all materials and colors. Most of them were enameled. She picked a fire-engine red six-quart pot. This time she paid again with an assorted color-combination of bills.

The noon bells rang in the church by the time we made our way down the street.

"Let's go in for a minute," Little Grandma suggested. It was cool inside. The 100-degree heat could not enter into the sanctuary with its tall arches. The well-known painted pictures smiled at me as always, the clay statues with their gaudy gold ornaments looked as hideous as ever.

Behind the church was the tall, two-story Building of the Guilds. I was especially proud of that House of Culture, as it was nicknamed by many, because it was my Grandpa who had masterminded it! He was the one who had raised the funds for it while he was President of the Board of Guilds. After it was built he received a gold medal from the Governor. Every day movies were presented in its huge auditorium and occasional theatrical groups performed there, besides the lectures and local performances that took place regularly. This house brought a piece of human enrichment to the 70,000 people who lived in Cegléd.

"Will we be coming to the movies tonight?" I asked Little Grandma.

"Certainly. Why should we miss it?" She winked again. She knew how much I liked movies. "But let's hurry now, your grandpa is waiting in the store. He wants his lunch."

We stopped by the store and walked home with Grandpa along the burning, dusty road. A hot breeze caressed my naked arms and tried to dry the sweat off my brow. Boy, was it hot! Grandpa did not seem bothered by it. When he saw us he said to Misi, his apprentice, "You can have some time off in the afternoon and take Helen to eat ice cream at the confectioner's."

"Wow!" I jumped into Grandfather's arms and hugged him. "You don't really mean that, do you? Oh, I love you, I love you…"

Misi and I were good friends. As an apprentice he lived at Grandpa's house in a room beside the downstairs kitchen. In Cegléd it was customary to have another building in the yard where a summer kitchen was built to keep the heat out of the living quarters during the hot days, as cooking was done on a wood stove. Evenings I went out to watch Misi water the lawn or we would just sit and talk. He was only a few years older than I and I had always enjoyed bicycling with him or our trips to the confectioner's. That was another rare treat that I associated with Cegléd because in Budapest we could seldom eat ice cream cones. Grandmother was afraid of sore throats.

I could hardly wait and naturally, when I wanted to hurry time, the hands of the clock did not seem to budge. Finally, we were on our bikes pedaling towards the confectioner's.

"Chocolate and hazelnut!" I ordered my favorites. Misi bought vanilla and raspberry for himself. Then we went outside, into the sweltering heat where we had left our bikes. We leaned against the wall and started to catch up on each others' news.

"I will soon become a journeyman if I pass my exam."

"That is wonderful, Misi. How old are you now?"

"I am seventeen. That is the usual age to end apprenticeship. Three years. Then I will no longer live at your grandfather's house. I'll have more salary and all …"

"I am sorry that you won't live there anymore, but I am glad for you."

"I will be happy to pass the exam and to get a good salary but I will miss your grandfather. He was always like a father to me. I will not leave his store. I will work for him and some day, maybe, I will buy the store from him if he no longer wants to work. What do you think?"

"Why, I think it is an excellent idea." I thought that this way I would always have him around as a good and trusted friend.

He seemed pleased with himself and with the whole world.

"And how about you? How is life treating you in the big city?" he asked.

"I guess I'm all right. Everything is getting better in the big city. People are rebuilding their apartments and houses. We work a lot on our school. Three stories of the building were bombed down during the siege but it is nearly all repaired. We have to study a lot, but, you know, I like it much better here. Everything seems to be fun when I am in Cegléd. There is time to read and look at the little train and eat ice cream and go to the market. I wish I did not feel so self-conscious about not being a child any more. I would like to go and work at Uncle Kiss' shop like I used to, when I was little."

"You know what?" Misi thought of something as he swallowed the last of his ice cream cone. "Come to your grandfather's shop and I will teach you to sew leather. Really do it, not just pretend like the little kids do."

He did not have to offer twice, I was already on my bike pedaling towards Grandfather's store. Misi let me sit on the little stool with the clamps that held the saddle he worked on. Then he showed me how to push the awl through one side of the leather, then the other. After the hole was made I had to guide a strong needle followed by a reinforced thread through the hole from one side, then do the same thing with another set of needle and thread from the other side. Now I had to pull hard on both needles on both sides. One stitch was done. We spent the afternoon sewing that saddle.

When evening came and Little Grandma tucked me in I remembered the warning about men who would want to marry me for my money. I did not think that Misi ever thought of my money but I wanted to be sure.

"Grandma," I started.

"Yes, Helen…"

"Grandma, if Misi asked me to marry him, would I be allowed to?"

"Why do you ask that question? You are still so young …"

"Well, you know how everybody always warns me to be careful because men will be after my money … Do you think he is honest? Do you think my parents would let me marry anybody as long as he was honest, or would I have to marry someone they chose for me? Would he have to have money, or rank, or something?"

Little Grandma began to understand what it was all about.

"I've known Misi since he was fourteen. I am sure that most people like money but I do not think that he would marry to get somebody's money. I think your parents would let you marry anybody as long as he was honest, but you would have to trust their judgment and cooperate *before* you fall in love. You have to be on the lookout. I am happy that you think of these things, because if one has as much money as your parents it is wise to consider all the possibilities. Yet, I think you have plenty of time to get married, you are only eleven." She laughed as she gave me a final hug.

I felt good about what she had said. Maybe I would be able to marry Misi and settle into Little Grandma's footsteps in this old family home.

~

The next day we went to eat ice cream again. This time Misi mentioned that the confectioner and his family had been confirmed together two weeks before.

"You know, Helen, the Bishop only comes every ten years to this community and the parents missed out about twice so by this time their children were all old enough to get confirmed, it was interesting. I was also confirmed at the same time." He stopped for a minute, then he rambled on... "That reminds me of Cardinal Mindszenty, quite a man! You know, maybe I would be an excellent candidate for the Communist Party but I just don't buy their ideology. I was never rich but I have been treated fairly and I know I can make my way up in society without their help. I wish the Soviets would get out before the Communists pull a fast one on us. The Cardinal fights the Communists, he stands up for what is right. He is for democracy. And so am I. I heard that he was also persecuted by the Nazis, right after he became Bishop."

"Yes, we were told about it in school just the other day," I said, "he was taken to prison by the Nazis. When he was arrested he put on his pontifical vestments and a whole procession followed him to jail, while he blessed the passersby who had grown into a crowd by the time he reached his destination. The next day they arrested the seminarians and priests who took part in the procession to prison. They continued with the theology classes in jail and ten seminarians were ordained while they were captives. The ten had only one candle and one cassock among them but each, including the Bishop, had a separate armed guard standing beside him with a loaded gun."

"Wow! That's guts for you!" Misi exclaimed. "I wonder how long he will be able to resist the Communists."

We did not wonder for long. We had other important things to think about. The swimming pool! We raced on our bikes to the city pool's naturally lukewarm water, where we ducked and played around until I discovered another ice cream vendor.

"Misi, let's have another ice cream," and we indulged in the rare treat for the second time that afternoon.

~

Everything good has to come to an end; I was back in Budapest again where the happiest moments of my life were when I could go to the theater with Grandmother. Although people went hungry, the theaters were always sold out. Theater was a way to escape reality, a way to express, through symbolism or humor, what could not be said out loud, and Hungary was noted for her excellent actors, singers, and dancers. Hungarians were also noted for a curious way of life because of our history of oppression we had learned to smile through our tears, to rejoice even when we were in misery—and our joy was genuine.

Inflation was now out of control. Old clothes and jewels, gold pieces from broken teeth and even pots and pans had more value than the multicolored paper the government constantly rolled off the presses.

War and inflation produced a curious new breed of the nouveau riche who had gotten rich on the black market and whose careers could be compared to that of shooting stars. Occasionally they ended up in prison, more often they escaped and disappeared. Meanwhile, the majority of the country suffered and waited impatiently.

Finally, the government acted. During the month of July the shop windows started to fill up in anticipation of the promised new money, which was named "forint." Everything was made available to the merchants under the condition that they keep their windows well-stocked all the time and only sell merchandise for the new money. That was the strategy to show the population that everything was plentiful, that there was no reason to panic and spend money as soon as it came in the house.

I remembered as we went shopping with Grandmother and I asked her, "Why is everybody still hungry, when the windows are full? Why don't people buy the dresses they want?"

"Because merchandise can only be bought with the new money. Nobody accepts old money anymore."

"But Grandmother, nobody has any forints yet."

"That's exactly why the merchandise stays in the windows," Grandmother laughed.

One day before the new money came out, Grandmother and I wanted to go to the theater but there, too, the prices were already set in forints. There they still had to accept "pengős," the old money, because there was no other way; they could not postpone the performance. When Grandmother heard the price of the ticket converted into the old money she said "I refuse to pay so much for a theater ticket. We will wait until the new money comes in." She laughed, because of course, it was not an outrageous amount in forints, but expressed in the old money the amount sounded absurd.

Next day, on August 1, 1946, the new currency became legal. The "forint" was worth ten cents and was equivalent to 600,000 followed by 30 more zeros, old "pengős." The release of the new money came gradually. People were paid at the end of July with food, as had become usual in the recent past. The first salaries paid in money were handed out only two weeks after the forint came out to prevent people from emptying the stores, and thereby creating another period of instant inflation. In the meantime, the new money was handed out here and there and slowly, very slowly, everybody had a chance to handle the light aluminum coins.

⁓

It was Tuesday evening and as usual, I helped the downstairs maid set the table with the heavy damask tablecloth, the pretty gray-patterned Rosenthal china set and the baroque sterling silver Father had recently bought for Mother. Tuesday evenings were special. Two very good friends of Father's, Uncle Stephen and Uncle Charles, both medical doctors and confirmed bachelors, came to have dinner with us. The war was over and good food was available again. Our cook did her very best on these occasions and I looked forward not only to the delicacies but also to the interesting conversation that centered mostly upon world politics. I myself was quite astonished that I found the topic interesting, but since our lives and lifestyles had become completely dependent on this one subject it occupied my mind more than anything else.

When the table was set, we still had time before dinner and I ran down to the park in front of the house to round up my sisters. The park still bore the traces of the war. Graves were still visible here and there. An enormous sandpile for fire-fighting still towered in the middle of the park, left there from the siege. Several of the surrounding houses burnt down yet the sandpile was there intact. One aspect of sieges was forgotten when the sand was acquired. It would have been impossible to put out the fires without sacrificing human lives. Bombs, shells, machine gun fire was a way of life when the front happened to be next door.

The sandpile served now as a playground for the fantasies of children. They built castles and made mud pies, while we, the older ones, used it as a sort of training ground. Every day we found easier and quicker ways to run down its steep slopes raising a cloud of dust as we came to a sudden halt at the bottom of the hill. I could not resist making a few runs before I called for Marie and Elisabeth. I had hardly opened my mouth, when I noticed a small crowd standing beside the big pool, or rather cistern that served the same purpose during the siege as the sandpile had. It was still filled with water that had become dirty during the years. People said it was filled with ruins, broken guns, stones, branches, and plain filth. Yet nothing could be seen from above because the water was opaque green. Nobody in his right mind would think of swimming in it. But what was that now?

All of a sudden I saw it. Something living. Was it a dog? or…It was a child, a small one at that, it was moving, yes, it must have been a child, about three years old. I saw his playmates, a whole nursery school and two frightened teachers. The child dog-paddled for his life with motions that betrayed that he had never learned to swim. Then as quick as lightning, a young man ran

191

down the sloping sides of the pool and waded in the water to the drowning child. In his left hand he held an open book, with his other he grabbed the little boy and, raising both above his head he ran out of the water as quickly as he had rushed in. He handed the little boy to his teacher and disappeared in the growing crowd. The boy was frightened and sopping wet but all right. I remembered this pool when it had been empty. It was several stories deep and now I had seen with my own eyes that a man of average height could wade in it! What all must have been on the bottom of that pool!

I grabbed Marie and Elisabeth and we raced home. Time had flown while we were busy watching. We burst into the dining room and we all talked at once.

"You should have seen!"

"That little boy nearly drowned."

"That man was brave! He jumped right in after him!"

During dinner Uncle Stephen was the main speaker, as always, "I find it ridiculous that the Communists want to claim credit for the consolidation of Hungary's economy, for the new money. After all, they only had 17% of the vote. But, nobody dares to speak up against them, the Smallholder's Party with 57% of the votes is scared silent, the only one to raise his voice is Cardinal Mindszenty. Although I am a Protestant I think that he is quite a man. His visits at prisons and concentration camps speak of extraordinary courage. He does not ask for permission, he simply goes there and stands at the door. They can hardly reject the Primate of Hungary when he knocks. Unfortunately, our bishops have families and the Communists intimidate them through blackmailing the members of their families."

"I enjoy listening to the Cardinal," said Uncle Charles, "it's amazing how well he disguises his real targets, the Communists, behind examples taken from Hungarian history, a few hundred years back, when the Turks occupied the country. He shows how our faith pulled us through those years. He shows that the most effective defense against atheistic materialism is a deepening of our religious life."

"Even the simplest persons can understand him well," said Father. "In 'Red Csepel,' the hotbed of communism, he is the most popular speaker. He fights the ideological battle against the Marxist by quoting facts."

"Who are the Marxists?" I heard myself ask although I had not meant to interrupt.

"Good question!" said Uncle Stephen. "Karl Marx wrote a book in the past century, called The Capital, in which he discredited the capitalist system and set up a whole new theory, we could even call it a religion, as its theory reaches out and embraces all of the different sciences and tries to give a whole new look at the world, at history, at existence. His followers were called Marxists."

Father took over the explanation, "According to the Soviet novels I read, in the Soviet Union everybody is considered a Marxist who follows Communist principles and the subject taught in school under the heading Marxism-Leninism embraces the works of all Communist leaders."

I understood now why the Cardinal would want to fight Marxists.

Uncle Stephen started talking again, "You know that in most churches Communist agents take down the sermon in shorthand and confront the pastor with it after the Mass is over, don't you?"

Everybody nodded in agreement, while I whispered, "No! Do they really?"

He went on, "One of these agents cried out to a priest during the sermon, which is an unheard of impertinence. He said, 'Say something about the Communists!' to which the priest answered without even thinking it over or getting the least bit perturbed over the interruption, 'We can thank the Communists for the bridges and for the filling of our churches!'"

I laughed so hard I cried. The bridges were indeed in use. Not all of them, but a few, and the churches were full of people who apparently had realized that the only help they could get against the disaster they feared and their present-day miseries was from God.

"But jokes aside," Uncle Stephen continued, "several of the priests have already been arrested on account of their sermons. I am afraid that if the Soviets don't leave the country we'll have no alternative but to turn Communist."

Father looked at Grandmother with reproach. His eyes seemed to say, "I told you so."

Grandmother thought out loud, "But what about the United Nations? What about the peace treaties?"

"Wishful thinking," Uncle Stephen said. "I would like to believe in them, but how can they enforce their decisions? The Soviets can veto anything that comes up in the Security Council."

"But why does our government go along with the Communists' decisions? Why do we let atrocities happen?" I could not understand and I was angry at the injustice of it all.

Father answered, "There are two hundred million Soviets and only ten million Hungarians. They have machine guns, we don't."

"There does not seem to be any hope, and yet…" Grandmother started to talk, "When one thinks of the power our nation shows every time the Cardinal leads a procession, one has to think that we are all for freedom and democracy. Would we be simply swallowed up by the Red Giant? This August 20th on St. Stephen's Day, we had five hundred thousand people marching in the procession and many more watching."

I was so excited that I cut into Grandmother's words but she did not stop me this time, she just smiled at my enthusiasm.

"Oh, you should have been there, Uncle Charles. I saw Uncle Stephen but not you. It was the most exciting event of my life. We all got dressed in traditional Hungarian dresses. You know the kind our ancestors wore when they protested against the Habsburg's reign in the 1830's and 40's? The whole Altar Society of the Downtown Church wore the glittering jewel-studded velvet 'pruszliks' (vests) with the brocade skirts, some of them had real jewels and fur coats that were casually thrown on their shoulders over the bulging sleeves of their dresses. The headdresses were equally decorated."

"You should have seen my dress," Elisabeth interrupted. "Blue velvet pruszlik with gold and pearls and everything..." she was trying to find the words to describe her excitement over the dress that surpassed her imagination, yet now it was hers.

"And we had golden lace aprons, real gold." Marie added.

"Our dresses were white brocade with ruffles on the sleeves." It was Elisabeth's turn again, she looked very wise now with her new glasses.

Uncle Charles smiled at his favorite, the littlest girl, who had grown into quite a young lady by now.

"I wish I could have seen you. Would you put it on for me?"

"You bet!" Elisabeth started running and in a few minutes she arrived back in her glittering Hungarian costume for the admiring Uncle Charles.

In the meantime Grandmother proceeded to describe the procession, "Wherever we went people clapped and shouted. You probably know that each parish walked on foot to the St. Stephen's Basilica in the middle of town, from where the procession was going to start. This way the demonstration, I mean procession, took them to such parts of the city where processions usually did not go. By the time our church group arrived we could not even go close to the Basilica. We started out in lines of four. As we approached the building we received instructions to go in lines of eight, then sixteen, thirty-two, the last command was sixty-four. However, when the organizer saw our group he let us walk in lines of thirty-two so our dresses would be more visible to the applauding crowd. They understood our coded message of freedom and liberty."

"We walked and walked," said Marie, "I thought my legs would break off, but I did not want to quit. Finally someone had to carry Elisabeth. She was really too young for it."

It was funny to hear that from Marie's mouth because I always thought that she herself was too young. Yet, when I looked at my sisters now it struck me that they were growing up.

Uncle Stephen loved to teach us history. He asked Elisabeth now because she was the youngest one, "Do you know what we celebrate on August 20th?"

"The feast of St. Stephen," she answered proudly. Her charming dimples appeared when she beamed at Uncle Stephen.

"Who was he?" came the next question.

This time Marie answered, "The first king of Hungary. He got his crown from the Pope in 1,000 A.D. That was when he was crowned by St. Gellért, the Bishop who brought the crown and came to baptize the Hungarians."

"Good answer, Marie. Do you also know why he wanted the Hungarians to become Christians?"

"Because it is good to be a Christian," Marie quickly said with a little uncertainty in her voice. I came to the rescue.

"That is a good reason but his other objective was to settle the Hungarians. They were a hunting, grazing people until then. He wanted a nation that would be strong and stable among the other countries of Europe. Until then Hungarians were one of the most detested disasters that could ever invade a country. They led wars against the western nations to rob and acquire whatever they needed. The civilized people prayed every day in their litanies 'From the arrows of the Hungarians, save us, Oh Lord.' This had to change unless we wanted to be exterminated by the united forces of Europe. St. Stephen understood that and changed the course of history by the baptism of a nation." I felt very wise and important as I issued this information I had learned at school.

"Yes," said Marie, "and then he had no heir, so before he died, he offered up the crown to the Virgin Mary. According to legend she took the crown from him. That is why we sing about her as Our Lady of Hungary who will keep our nation from all trouble."

"Good girls," Uncle Stephen patted us all on the head. "Then maybe one of you will know if we are still a kingdom?"

"You are funny" Marie laughed. "Of course we are not. We became a republic this year, February 1. We always meet the President of the Republic on our way to school; he takes walks with his wife and smiles at us."

"Very good, very good," said Uncle Stephen. "What else is there on your way to school that is an interesting historical monument?"

"The National Museum," I answered. "That is where the revolution of 1848 broke out on March 15, against the Habsburgs. Our great national holiday."

"It will be a century two years from now," Grandmother mused, "I wonder whether Communists celebrate national holidays or whether we'll be rid of that hideous red star on top of the building by then."

"And the Kossuth Museum in Cegléd, our home town?" wondered Uncle Charles. "I take it you know, girls, that our old professor, your dad's and mine, managed to collect enough memorabilia of the great leader of the 1848 revolution, Louis Kossuth, to fill a little house?"

195

"He was a great leader," added Mother, "he was one of the three famous men who talked in front of the joint session of Congress of the United States, while he was not a head of state."

"Oh, yes," Father said, "and his favorite town was Cegléd, my home town. Remember, Charles, how we used to play around in the swimming pool? And the great 'flood' when we boated around in our cellar in a wash-trough?"

"Your mother was mad when she found out," Uncle Charles laughed. "Remember the Gubody Gardens? The walk where one took girls?"

"I can still hear the serenade the guild members gave my father every year on his namesday. They came with lanterns and a gypsy orchestra."

"It's all over now, I'll never go back to Cegléd," Uncle Charles vowed. "My parents are both dead and I was just notified that they had taken away the fifteen acres of land I had there. Fifteen acres, I don't think I'll be able to ever face those people again."

# 20

"Now remember girls, when you spread the butter on the open-face sandwich, it has to be smoothed to the very edge of the crust. It does not look or taste good if you leave dry spots on the bread," Grandmother told us as we started to make sandwiches for the party on a beautiful sunshiny day in June, 1947.

"Grandmother, why do we have to have these parties?" I inquired.

"You must learn how to behave socially. I know, Helen, that you would spend all your life reading if it depended on you but one must learn the art of conversation, how to address older people, your own peer group, and the maids."

"Aw, I know that," I whined. I really wasn't into making open-face sandwiches that day.

"Then why don't you ever talk with the boys? Whenever I watch you dancing you look utterly bored and make your partner experience the same thing, I'm sure. A lady must be able to talk with people from all walks of life, she must be able to start a conversation and keep it going, to entertain others, and make them feel at ease."

I yawned, "Yes, but what do I tell them? How does one start a conversation? Besides, those 15-16-17-year-old guys all have sweaty palms and their sole interest is sports. They all wear some kind of an insignia..."

"That's a good place to start talking then," answered Grandmother. "You ask him what that insignia stands for and you have a conversation going. He will tell you about himself and that is everybody's favorite topic. Don't you agree?"

"I'd much rather spend the evening with Uncle Stephen or Uncle Charles and listen to their arguments about world politics. At least they make sense. What they say is interesting and stimulating. But those boys ?" I grimaced as I dipped the knife in the butter and reluctantly started to spread it. "It is such a waste to spend all Saturday afternoon making sandwiches for the boys who are going to swallow the whole batch we make in five minutes flat. Sometimes I think they are fasting before they come to our house just to be able to eat faster. Are all boys that hungry, when they are in their teens?"

"Yes, all of them," laughed Grandmother. "Of course, you don't have any brothers. I had two. Yes, they were always very hungry; I remember it well, even today."

We sat in the smoking room on the upstairs floor of our downtown (winter) residence in Budapest as we alternated the boring jobs that were part of the sandwich-making process. We buttered and placed on the breads: sausages and ham sent by Little Grandma from Cegléd, hard boiled eggs, different cheeses, and goose liver (a Hungarian delicacy). Then Marie, who possessed special artistic talents, arranged the pickles, pieces of radishes, green peppers, and beets on top of the open-face sandwiches to make them look as good as they tasted. I especially hated to butter the bread because the butter was as hard as stone, although Grandmother beat it with a wooden spoon. There were no preservatives or salt added to our butter so we could not leave it outside the refrigerator for long or it would have gone rancid. We were among the very few who had a real gas-operated refrigerator—most people had only ice boxes. A horse-drawn carriage sold block ice during the day and when homemakers heard his cry, "Ice! Ice, ice for sale" they would run with their buckets to get some of the precious stuff. Many people did not even bother with that. They went to market every day and bought everything fresh. During the summer everybody canned everything that was available: another job we were looking forward to, yet when it was at hand we got bored with it after the first couple of days. Given the fact that we still fed at least sixteen people a day, Grandmother canned by the hundreds of pounds; but to me, after the first couple of days, it definitely seemed like tons, or wagon loads of the same fruit or vegetable. Like these sandwiches today! If I could at least think with anticipation of this party! Why do I have to dance with a lot of nincompoops? I danced very well. I had gone through dancing school twice, once when I was five, then again when I was ten. It was fun and I was among the best dancers, but again, I preferred dancing with older men, my parents' friends, who knew how to lead, on whose arms I felt like a feather. I did not weigh much more than a feather since the siege and as I looked like a grown-up woman men did not mind dancing with me. I thought of a dreamy man I had danced with. It was a slow waltz… he let go of me and led…I followed and we danced with outstretched arms, not touching, yet our movements flowed into one. I enjoyed it tremendously although I did not even know his name. I guessed at the time that he was about Mother's age, thirty-two. But those young boys … they always stepped on my sandaled feet with their enormous men's shoes. Why did boys have such big feet?

"Helen, what are you dreaming about?" Grandmother's voice brought me back to reality. "Hurry up, Marie doesn't have anything to do."

"She has the easy job! How would she like to spread this hard butter on the fresh French bread, all the way to the crust too!" I murmured but I tried to hurry.

"Leave everything now," ordered Grandmother after a while, "Elisabeth and I will finish the rest. You must get dressed because the guests will be here soon."

I looked at my watch. It was 5:30. We invited everybody for 5 o'clock, which meant that the earliest guests would probably be here around 6:30, but ever since the war more and more people came earlier as if they had forgotten the unwritten rule, "it is not polite to be on time." One should give an hour or two for the hosts to get ready.

Downstairs Mother directed the maids who were setting up for the party. The whole house was once more occupied by our family. All the people who had escaped to our house during the siege had found their way back to their own apartments. Even Uncle and Aunt had their apartment rebuilt. The apartment house they lived in belonged to Marie and me. I had learned that only a few days before, when Father mentioned something to Mother in connection with it. I thought it strange to own an apartment house, or half of one, and not even know about it.

Since only our family now lived in our house I had been given a room of my own. Next door to me Marie and Elisabeth shared a room; then there were the rooms of my grandparents. Father and Mother lived downstairs now. This arrangement came about because my parents had guests, big business-connected parties, at least three times a week. Because of this arrangement we and our grandparents could sleep undisturbed by their noise.

The whole downstairs could be opened up into one big recreational area—the rooms were partially separated by sliding glass doors that were pushed into the brick walls at party-time. The dining room in the middle was the largest room. This is where the dancing took place. A grand piano and an electric record player stood in one of the corners. The enormous dining room table was folded into its smallest possible size to seat twelve and pushed to the end of the room to serve as the buffet table. In another room a mirror-lined baroque bar cabinet, stocked with the best liqueurs and crystal glasses, was set up for the chaperoning parents. Every girl brought at least one of her parents and usually a boy or two. It was the custom to have two boys for every girl to assure a constant change of partners.

I peeked in to see if everything had gone as usual. Mother kissed me, then she looked me over, "Your hair needs to be fixed. Maybe I shouldn't have let you cut it. You can't take as good a care of it as you used to. You had such a beautiful crown of braids!"

"Why, what's wrong with it now? I like it short. It combs much quicker! You know how much trouble it was to wash it and untangle it." I answered quickly. No way was I going to grow it out again.

She did not look satisfied, "Come Helen, I'll help you fix it. Let's go upstairs! What are you going to put on?"

We ran up the stairs; it was much quicker than to wait for the elevator. The sun poured in through the open windows of my room. The lace curtains, the matching lace and the pink ribbons on my copper bed looked as cheery as I began to feel.

"Is Jack going to be here?" I asked Mother, as I suddenly remembered the secret policeman whose looks I had definitely liked. Maybe there would be someone who did not talk exclusively of sports.

"I think you should put on the navy blue taffeta dress," Mother said.

"Why don't you tell me if Jack is going to be here?"

"I think he is. Look, he is much older and he is nothing for you," she continued as she lifted the dress across my hair that definitely did not look very nice now that I had a look in the mirror. I grimaced at myself and deep down I too felt sorry for the beautiful crown I used to fix before guests came. I timed myself once, I could put it up in seven minutes flat although my hair was so long I could sit on it. Still, to have short hair meant I was more like Mother. It was a status symbol and I hated being a child. True, I hoped that it would be easier to take care of short hair, but unfortunately that was not the case. Now I always had to curl it here or there, even though I had a hot permanent in it and I went to the beauty parlor once a week. I liked to sit there, I could read and nobody bothered me. I was thinking about doing just that during the party—to catch an opportune moment and vanish in thin air, come up to my room and read, at least until I'd be discovered.

I think Mother must have guessed what I was thinking,

"Please, don't play tricks on me again I don't want to go hunting for you during the party. Stay there and try to enjoy it. I am doing it for you and your sister. You must learn how to behave socially. You can't do that by simply reading books about it. You must practice!"

"But, Mother, you know how very boring these parties can get for me."

"Maybe it won't be so boring today. You never know when you'll find someone who is interesting to talk to and you'll never find out if you don't start a conversation. Think of Tommy! Remember how well you could talk with him?"

Mother zipped up my dress in the back. A smiling young lady looked back at me from the mirror. The dress had a low-cut neckline surrounded by a thin pink ribbon, tiny sleeves, a tight bodice to enhance my waist and three layers of long ruffles with pink ribbons along the seams all around the dress. Mother helped me slip a pink taffeta ribbon around my head under the locks and tied it into a bow on the side of my head. High heeled black sandals came next, No stockings for tonight, it was warm enough.

Mother twirled me around, "I can't believe that you are only twelve!" I didn't look like myself in the mirror. I thought of the way I had been dressed when I came into the room. I had had on a checkered flannelette dress, its pockets stuffed full with treasures and a handkerchief, with buttons down the front. The metamorphosis that took place in a few minutes was comparable to the well-known frog-prince story.

"Now, try to behave the way you look," Mother advised.

I didn't answer, but I had little hope for a similar metamorphosis inside. I did not have the will to transform myself. Well, maybe, maybe if Jack would show up, I tried to think positively.

"Is Jack coming?" I tried again.

"He is, but I wish that you would not have your eyes on him. He is going to come with a friend," Mother answered.

"A friend? You mean a girlfriend?"

"No, I said a friend."

"Who is the friend? Is it true that Jack works for the police?"

"His friend is a jeweler. Yes, Jack works for the police. He claims that he does it in order to save as many people as possible. As a matter of fact he told us last week that he saved you from being taken to the police."

"Me? What for? I didn't do anything!"

"Remember that church dance? You were one of the hostesses. The Communists decided that they'd run in everybody whose names appeared on the invitation on the grounds that the dance was simply a cover-up for a meeting of the 'conspiracy.'"

"Conspiracy? What conspiracy? I don't even like to go dancing with young people! Why would we have a conspiracy while dancing? I don't understand a word."

"The Communists figure that every church event has to be connected somehow with a 'conspiracy.' Remember the events that started right about the time when the peace treaty was signed in Paris, on February 10?"

"We were very happy that the treaty was signed. Doesn't it mean that the Soviet troops would have to leave in ninety days and we could decide for ourselves?" I asked.

"That is why the Communists want to take over power completely before the Soviets have to leave. They want to be sure. The undermining of the Smallholders' Party started a long time ago. A 56% majority is hard to beat, yet the Communists would have to do better than that in order to oust them from power," said Uncle Stephen, one of the early guests who had suddenly materialized from nowhere. "Don't you remember, Helen, the Communists started to discredit members of the Government and the Parliament months ago. The last and most important member whom they had arrested was Béla Kovács, the Secretary General of the Smallholders' Party. He was arrested in February when the Prime Minister, Ferenc Nagy, and the President of the Republic, Zoltán Tildy, personally advised him to report to the police voluntarily to be questioned on an alleged conspiracy. America tried to intervene but was told by the Soviets to stay out of Hungary's internal affairs."

Yes, now it all came back to me, I remembered the heated discussion about the hated Soviets at our usual Tuesday evening dinners with Uncle Stephen and Uncle Charles.

"But what do I have to do with a conspiracy of the Communists against the Smallholders?" I asked, stupefied.

"Ah, Helen, you have it all wrong. The Communists explain it as a conspiracy of the Smallholders' Party against the Communists and this is where you come in."

"I never was a member of the Smallholders' Party."

"That does not make any difference to them. One of their constant foes is Cardinal Mindszenty and you, as well as I and your parents, are all ardent followers of our leader." Again, Uncle Stephen was calling the Catholic Primate of Hungary "his leader." I noticed but this time I did not question him.

"Wherever Catholics meet, the Communists try to prevent them from expressing their ideas. At dances young people talk and discuss their feelings. They have an opportunity to criticize, to 'conspire,' in their words, against a future Communist government. So, you see, Helen, your mother was right, you could have been questioned by the police because your name was among the hostesses on that invitation. However, I don't really know if Jack simply wants to gain himself some brownie points with your parents or if what he said was really true."

I wanted to listen to Uncle Stephen all night but suddenly the doorbell rang on the ground floor and announced the arrival of the first guests. We went down to greet them.

I hadn't seen Pista for ages. During that time he had become a good looking young man. I did not recognize him, Mother had to tell me, "Remember Pista? You used to meet him when we stayed at Lake Balaton."

"At Lake Balaton?" The faint image of a bespectacled little bookworm appeared in my memory. "Yes, of course, Pista Balogh?" He certainly looked different. He was about six feet tall now, with a wide-grin, elegant gold-rimmed glasses, and a navy blue suit on his slim figure. His blond hair was slicked down, his eyes sparkled. Did he like my looks as well as I did his? Maybe the evening wasn't going to be so boring after all.

When we shook hands I noticed how muscular he was despite his slimness.

"Do you stay in Budapest now?" I asked with a smile.

"Yes. As you well know, all land was taken from landowners who had more than 1,000 acres. There is very little my father could have done in the village after his livelihood was taken away. We received no compensation for our property. We were allowed to keep the house but the upkeep on it wasn't really worth the trouble. An important Communist bought it for his summer home."

He stopped for a minute and I saw that it was hard for him to talk about the loss of a property that had been in his family for hundreds of years.

"Anyway," he swallowed and continued, "we opened an espresso here in Budapest. You know, a kind of fashionable coffeehouse they have on every corner, and that is what my parents are doing now."

I looked at him again and decided that his parents must be pretty good business people, judging by his clothes and his suddenly returned good mood.

"I am so glad you could make it to our party. Do you ever go back to Lake Balaton?"

"I do, but believe me it's not like old times anymore. The Soviets fished with hand-grenades, the darn fools," his face reddened with anger. "After the explosion the fish would float to the top. They then would take out one and leave the rest there, floating…dead. You can sit there now for days and nothing. Maybe a 'keszeg,' or two but only with great luck. I don't even like to talk about it. They littered the whole waterfront with mines, the grenades, and shells. A good friend of mine, a young boy, learned something about explosives from the Germans. You know, I think you even met him. We used to dislike him because he was so rowdy. His parents were divorced."

"You mean Kari?"

"Yes. Remember that he used to go to military school? He was crazy about war. What a talented boy he was, and yet… there was always a certain restlessness in him. In the last days before everything was over the Germans took even fourteen-year-old children. He lied about his age. He was thirteen, but he was in military school and he was well grown. They did not ask for birth certificates from volunteers. They trained him. He knew how to dismantle hand-grenades. After the war he went around disarming them. He knew many things but not enough. He did not know the difference between the makes. Germans and Russians manufacture different ammunition. The timing is different. On one of these attempts to dismantle the hand-grenade he too exploded along with the weapon. It tore off his left arm and both legs. His mother found him but he bled to death on the way to the hospital, on a rickety peasant cart, the only vehicle around. A hitch-hiker got in with them when they were still a few miles from the hospital. The boy's mother said to him that he was welcome to share the cart but she had a very sick boy there. 'He is dead,' screamed the hitch-hiker. His mother looked and found that he was indeed dead."

"How awful! How very, very awful!" I cried.

"He was a bothersome guy, but I wish he had not died, at least not in this way. And his poor mother! She did not have any other children, no husband either. She was quite beside herself. It took her months to recover. She accused herself and her husband for not having given a good home to the child."

"That is hard to judge, especially when one has to live with a trauma like that."

"She buried the boy in the middle of the rose garden. She dug the grave herself. There are few people to be found around the lake in the early spring. Someone made a coffin out of a door."

Magdi, my good old friend, arrived with her brother George and Marti with two other boys. The doorbell rang incessantly now. One of the maids did not even bother to come back up. She stayed downstairs until most of the guests arrived.

The parents gathered in the room next door. Someone changed the record on the gramophone.

George asked me for a dance.

"One-two-three," counted Pista and cut in. George laughed at him and said, "You'll get it for that."

Now George could not cut back in until someone other than Pista had danced with me.

"Did you know that in our parents' days a boy who would ask you back from me would have to fight me in a duel?" Pista laughed at the idea.

"Yes, I did hear about that. Wasn't that stupid, though?"

"I guess it did not make much sense but it definitely kept people from cutting back in and everybody got a chance to dance 'one-two-three' steps with even the most popular girl," said Pista.

"Even today you have to let everybody dance 'one-two-three' steps and I hope you know that! You have to dance with every lady in the room," I flirted with him. I caught myself enjoying the party, and at least for the time being, I was not tempted to run up and read in a hidden corner of the house.

George was dancing with Marie, Marti was being entertained by one of the boys she had brought and in the corner the customary "monkey-island" had already formed. Because of the 1:2 ratio of girls vs. boys there were always leftover boys during the dances who either cut in on the others or gathered in a corner to discuss soccer, the national sport of Hungary; girls; jazz; or politics. I noticed that Jack had arrived with his friend, a puny looking little shrimp, and entered with the parents. "Who needs him anyway," I thought, while I grasped Pista's arm and twirled around the room with him. As I passed by everyone I took inventory, because one of the duties of the hostess was to see to it that every guest was entertained, that everybody enjoyed the party, that there were no 'wallflowers,' that every boy got a chance to dance with every girl. She also had to send relief dancers if a boy got stuck with the same girl for too long.

"Ah, Laci is here!" I said.

"Who is Laci?" Pista asked with a strange overtone. Was he jealous? It flattered me to think that he liked me.

"He is an excellent pianist. I see he is all ready to play."

Laci's hands glided across the piano and produced the craziest, wildest, dancingest jazz.

"I like to dance the swing!" Pista declared and we started in on the wild rhythm. I noticed Jack from the corner of my eye as he poured a drink and handed it to his feminine looking friend. Now why would I be jealous of a friend? What was wrong with me? Besides, finally I was dancing with someone my "own age"—five years older than I, just right according to Hungarian standards. After all, he had to be able to support me by the time we married, which meant that he should have finished university by the time I finished high school.

Except, of course, I was going to finish university also, I knew that. Actually it was Father's dream that I should become a medical doctor. At first I went along with it, but recently I had begun to have serious doubts. Since we went to the Opera so often, I gradually began to fall in love with it and decided that if it were possible I would become an opera singer—a great one, of course. Or a writer. Or maybe both. My family treasured art so much. Yet, I knew Father would have killed my desires even before I ever got to study singing, so I kept silent about them and wove my dreams in the privacy of my own room. Someday, though, I thought I'd be famous... and then, everybody would love me... it would be a cinch. It was so easy for me to do well in school. Why not in life?

"Are you always so quiet?" Pista asked me suddenly.

Oh, my God! I hadn't even noticed. Here, finally, was a boy who was fun to talk with and my usual "party-time-daydreaming" had caught up with me. When I was utterly bored with the parties and there was no way to escape physically, this was my way to express revolt—by simply tuning out everybody, but I had not meant to do it to him. I had to get myself together.

"Oh, Pista, I am sorry. I can confide in you. I don't really like these parties. I'd much rather read, you know me. You probably remember. "

I saw the light of understanding flash across his eyes.

"Yes, I know what you are talking about. I was very shy also, you probably remember. But, to get along in life we must force ourselves."

"Are you forcing yourself?" I asked with a coy smile.

"Your eyes talk," he exclaimed.

Now, he said it, too. Exactly what Mother told me that her friends claimed about my eyes.

"They do?" I asked, plunging into a flirtatious mood.

Just when we had started to dance again there came another boy; I had never met him before. He was one of those whom Marti had brought with her.

He cut in, he was doing his duty; I could see it in his eyes. I decided to be a good girl and act according to Grandmother's instructions.

I reluctantly let go of Pista and looked at him with an expression that said, "send help soon." As I saw him approach the monkey-island I noticed him motion one of the boys towards us—he had understood my silent plea. He, of course, wasn't allowed to cut back in no matter how long the dance lasted. I was condemned to dance with the sweaty-palmed teenager and Pista had to dance with every one of the girls. Following Grandmother's advice, I looked at the lapel of the boy I danced with and, sure enough, he had an insignia.

"What does your button mean?"

"It means that I belong to the Sodality of Mary," he answered quietly.

Thank God it was something different!

"I thought that the Sodality of Mary was for girls. Do they have boys' groups also?"

"They definitely do. Especially nowadays. I go to school to the Piarist Fathers Downtown. We have a great group there. The Communists don't want us to exercise our faith. The more we are for it. Since the persecution of religion, and all that it stands for, every boy wants to join our sodality. We really have to be selective when we choose new members. Some of them want to join only to defy the Communists and to show their solidarity with Cardinal Mindszenty. We must make them understand that we are primarily a religious organization and whatever we do stems from our faith, not from political affiliations."

I could not believe my ears. This was the second boy who made sense today, I completely forgot about Jack and concentrated on his words, "You know, of course, what's been going on in the Smallholders' Party and how the Communists are trying to eliminate all leading forces within that party. A week ago Ferenc Nagy, our prime minister, abdicated because he was accused by the Soviets of having conspired against his own government. He was accused while he was in Zurich. He called the head of the Communist Party,

Matyas Rakosi, long-distance and after they talked he saw no sense in coming home. We now have a new Prime Minister, Lajos Dinnyes. He too is from the Smallholders' Party but if he got in with the blessing of Comrade Rakosi, I don't know how much good he will do us. Everybody, mind you, everybody is accused of this, if you ask me, non-existent 'conspiracy.' My sister, Agi..."

"Oh, Agi is your sister?" I interrupted, of course, now I remembered him too. He was one of those on whom the prince-frog metamorphosis had taken place only half-ways, and although I did not recognize him for who he used to be, he had not climbed out of his cocoon entirely yet. He hadn't looked promising when he'd asked me to dance, but it turned out, as it often did, that "looks aren't everything."

"Yes, Agi's name was on a list of hostesses for a Catholic tea and she was dragged to the security police to be questioned about it."

My blood froze. Jack was right after all. He had burned the invitation before they called me. He was not all bad. Did he receive money from my parents? If he did he must have deserved it. The boy went on. I could not think of his name.

"My parents were out of town. The police took her from school. The principal did not want to let her go but they took her anyway; they had guns. I was notified by the school and I called our lawyer. Three people questioned her at the police station and they were rough with her, but finally they let her go. Under eighteen, they mostly let them go by dinnertime. At least they were supposed to. They brought her back to school in the evening. The principal was still there. She had not dared to leave until she had word that Agi was all right, with our parents away and all that."

"So it was true?" The words slipped out of my mouth.

"Of course it was true," I was happy that he had not noticed my slip.

"I am happy that she's all right now. Have they bothered her since?"

"No, they haven't, but they went through the whole list of names and troubled every one of the families who were involved in that innocent dance. How does one conspire while dancing?" He murmured the last words as if to himself.

That was hard to imagine as we started to jump around to the shrill sounds of a quick swing. That was an American record; I could tell.

Somebody was sent by Pista to cut in to save me, but now Pista was stuck with someone; so after this dance I excused myself and slipped away to the kitchen. Buffet time wasn't far away. Then I dropped into the parents' room where everybody seemed to be in an elevated mood as a result of the fine liqueurs and brandies. I steered close to the place where Jack sat with his friend.

"Hi, Helen, care to dance?" he asked.

"Who is your friend?" I asked him as we started to twirl to the tune of a waltz, played by Grandmother on the piano,

"Alfred?"

"I don't know his name. He came with you."

"Alfred. We live together in an apartment. He is a swell guy," answered Jack. "And how have you been? I think it would do you good if you did not let your name be used on invitations of Catholic dances."

"So it is true that you, I mean... thank you."

His face turned red under the light blond hair, his blue eyes looked straight into mine. His nose was like the beak of an eagle. He was attractive, no doubt about it. I felt grateful for what he had done, yet it bothered me that he should have something to do with the police.

"Do you like your work?"

"You mean being a secret policeman? Right now I can see no other way to help my friends who are dragged to the police day by day. If I am one of 'them' I can at least alleviate some of the suffering."

"So that is true, also?"

"Yes," he was red again with embarrassment.

"What will happen to our country?" I asked.

"The Communists will take over. There is no doubt about that. If we do not work for them we'll be considered 'insects,' as Lenin called them, who will have to be exterminated. That is why I ask you, no more names on invitations. On anything for that matter, that is connected with the church," Jack pleaded.

"Why the church? What does the church have to do with politics?" I asked.

"The church is the only institution that has the power, the strength, the trust of the people, and the courage of the celibate clergy, who are not bound by family, with the leadership of Cardinal Mindszenty, to put up opposition against the complete takeover. At least so far they have been successful. Besides, look at the Soviet Union. One of the first attacks of the Communists when they got into power was against the Church. They annihilated it completely except for a small core which made a compromise with them and which is paid by the government to keep up the semblance of religious freedom. We face the same fate."

"Won't they find out about you?"

"They might, but then again I am very circumspect and at the first sign of trouble I shall leave the country."

I heard Mother's words echo in my ear, "Don't have anything to do with him!"

"What about the United Nations, the United States, can't they do something in order to enforce free, truly free elections and execute the decisions of the

United Nations? After all, they have the 'bomb' and we don't. As a matter of fact, if we go a little further, they have everything. Don't you see that everything the Soviet Army has came either from America or from occupied Germany? I have so much trust in the Americans. Will they too abandon us?"

"I'm afraid so, even though they are our only hope. Nothing happened when America protested against the terrorism exercised in connection with the destruction of the Smallholders' Party…"

Pista cut in at that point.

"What do you think about it?" I asked him.

"About what?" he answered.

"I'm sorry," I laughed. "We were talking about the way Communists treated the Smallholders' Party that the Americans protested, were rejected, and accused of meddling into our foreign affairs. Everything stopped right there. Do you think the United Nations holds any hope? Do you think we have any chance to remain free?"

"I hope and trust as long as I live and I will fight for freedom. The only way is to follow Cardinal Mindszenty's road. Protest what we can, hold out until the last minute, fight for every right we still have and show the free world that we are worthy of freedom, that we want democracy. Otherwise we shall be lost."

I liked hearing that much more than what Jack had said.

"One of the most important battles today is that of religious education. The Communists want to take it away from the schools. They also want their own textbooks in every school. Unfortunately, the leftover leaders of the Smallholders' Party, those who are not in prison yet, went along with that demand. They also agreed to 'purge' all party members who do not favor collaboration between the Communist Party and the other parties. This, of course, means that whatever the Communists desire has to materialize and the other parties have to agree with it. They also decided on a three-year plan for Hungary following the example of the 'Great Soviet Union' and its five-year plan." Pista grimaced when he said "Great Soviet Union" and his voice expressed contempt, which by 1947 had become the usual way to talk about our "Great Liberators."

"One-two-three," and Béla, then, "One-two-three," and Péter, then again, "One-two-three," Roby. I twirled and whirled and enjoyed the evening. It seemed that the boys had decided to make me one of the most popular girls that night. At every party at least two or three girls were honored that way. The boys showed how much they liked them by letting them take only three turns with each boy. As usual we danced and ate, drank wine-punch, played games, and giggled our way through the party to the wee hours of the morning. At five o'clock a.m. Uncle Stephen asked me for a dance, then Father.

I decided to ask Father about Jack. It suddenly occurred to me that he had not danced with anyone, except Mother and me. He had stayed with his friend, Alfred, all the time.

"Father, who is that guy with Jack? Why do they stick together all the time?"

Father just laughed and said, "He likes to be with men. I think he is in love with Alfred."

"What do you mean by that? Alfred is not a woman."

"No, Alfred is a man, but in a way he satisfies Jack's need for a woman. They live together."

"He said they lived in one apartment," I said.

"Yes. But this is more than living together in one apartment. They live together as husband and wife."

"How can they do that?" I asked.

"Some men, or women, are just that way. They prefer to make love with their own sex. They are called homosexuals."

"Is that normal?"

"It's their own business. We just don't comment on them one way or another."

"Is that why Mother said I should have nothing to do with him?"

"Yes. He does not like the company of women but he likes to show up with them here and there because homosexuals don't like to be talked about."

"I understand. If they see him with me or Mother they think that he is courting me," I felt a bit nauseated. Was that the price of getting information from the police?

# 21

By the beginning of August our lives had turned into a frenzied question mark. Although it seemed odd even to me, I sat by the radio every night and listened to the foreign broadcasts. Everything that happened in world politics affected our daily lives. Why, why doesn't the free world, especially the United Nations, do something to ensure world freedom and thereby world peace? By 1947, even a twelve- or thirteen-year-old girl like me knew that peace would be lasting only if it would mean a just and free settlement for everybody. Any kind of revenge would lead to the desire of further retaliation. Yet, all we had experienced since the Soviet troops had come onto Hungarian soil was revenge, punishment, looting in the name of restoration, oppression of every movement, and annihilation of every party that might have led our homeland to independence, to democracy. When would we regain our right to self-determination? Surely it would happen any day now.

The 90 days had passed since the signing of the peace treaty; the date when the Soviet troops should have left Hungary. They lingered on. The "official" reason for their prolonged stay was the supervision of the reparation payments. But we all knew the real reason—they would not leave until they had firmly established Communist rule in Hungary.

There was less than a month left until my thirteenth birthday. It was the beginning of August. The Communists had pushed through a new electoral law on June 25, 1947. They insisted on the reissuance of the list of eligible voters. The Minister of the Interior (code name for the security police) supervised the new registry. Close to a million trustworthy, honest citizens were eliminated from the list. They had no way to protest, but Cardinal Mindszenty and the Bishops of Hungary did it for them—without apparent results. A new party emerged, the Freedom Party, under the leadership of Dezső Sulyok. It seemed for a while that this party would carry 60 to 65% of the votes, because the Smallholders' Party had been ruined through persecution of its leaders and members. Before the elections were called the Communists forced the Freedom Party to dissolve. At first, the leaders had been pressured. When this method did not work the Communists started to arrest innocent members of the party. At this point Dezső Sulyok saw the futility of the resistance, the overwhelming power of the Soviets that stood behind the Communist Party. He gave in.

The Communists proceeded with their next plan. The four government parties (Communist, Social-Democratic, National Peasant, and Smallholders) established the Hungarian Independence Front on July 30, 1947. In the face of the living reality of those days their program sounded beautiful but it was hard to believe in its truthfulness, especially under the auspices of the hammer and sickle. Their program called for religious freedom, the rejection of foreign intervention in Hungary's internal affairs, guaranteed freedom, and the inviolability of private property. What did they mean by "religious freedom?" Which "foreign intervention" would be rejected? The protests of the free world? Freedom would be guaranteed, for whom? For those eliminated from the list of voters? For the prisoners of war? For those who had been taken by the police? Whose private property would be inviolable? The private property of those who had been "liberated" from it like Pista's parents?

One day, as I skipped down the hallway I heard Father's heated voice from the bathroom. He was yelling at Mother, "The Communists will win. They'll take everything from us. The pattern is the same everywhere in the world where they've taken over. Open your eyes!"

"But the guarantees they just gave us," Mother interjected.

"How about the list of voters? Most of our friends were removed from the list!"

"We are still on it," I heard Mother's calm voice.

"We are, now, we are still needed. Can't you see? They need those who have money, who have incentive left, the merchants, yes they still need us because we have to rebuild the country. Why would they want to take it when it is completely in ruins? They need us! Just look at us a year from the time when they decide they don't need us anymore! Why did they stop fighting against the church? They're trying to demonstrate in every possible way how much they appreciate religion. Did you see the postcard of Comrade Rakosi shaking hands with a priest? Can't you understand?" I heard Father's fist come down heavily on the washbasin. It made the glasses in the bathroom clink. I was as quiet as a mouse. I did not dare to move. "They do this to fool the voters. First they eliminate everybody whom they possibly can. Why do all those eliminated belong to the middle class? Why do many of them have religious affiliations? Then they dissolve the Freedom Party. After they call the elections they become great friends with the church. Yes, they even encourage many parties to organize. Yes, many but not one non-Marxist party. The only one we had was forced to disband. Now there are six new ones. Four of them are Christian-oriented. Don't you see? Do they blind even you? They want to divide our vote. By putting Comrade Rakosi on the postcard with the priest they want to demonstrate how well Communists and Christians understand each other. On the other hand, they undermine everything the Church wants to start! Just the other day I heard that the Church wanted to establish a daily newspaper. They were promised the permit and the necessary paper within a week. They did not get either. Why, if they really want to be friends with the Christians? Can you believe that they are sincere in anything?"

They stepped out of the bathroom.

When Father saw me he calmed down and turned to Mother. "Let's go now but I wish that you would look beyond our present-day comfort, the many things we can still afford and do today. Tomorrow it might be different."

"Why?" Mother sighed. "Why would it be different? I'll try, if you want me to but all I can see is that we have everything we need. We have our friends and with your cleverness we always manage to stay out of trouble. There has been more than a decade now of serious political problems. Yet, we are still doing well. It would be so hard to start anew in another country... to have nothing, to leave everything behind. Everything our parents and ancestors left for us, I just can't believe that everything will be that bad. "

"Do you remember when Paul used to kid us, 'Don't ever be afraid as long as you see me. If there is trouble you won't find me anywhere!' Remember?" Father asked.

I suddenly recalled that I had seen Uncle Paul for the last time as a monk, hiding from the Germans.

"Well," continued Father, "He is in Oslo. Right after Prime Minister Ferenc Nagy resigned, he also resigned his post at the Embassy. Don't you remember?"

I stood there after they had gone. I was afraid. What did all this mean? Would we have to lose everything, whether we stayed or left Hungary? Would the Communists take all after we finished rebuilding it? Was Father's pessimism a prophesy or would Mother's hopes materialize? What was Mother's hope, anyway? If we left now, what could we take?

I thought of the parable of the rich boy who came to Jesus and wanted to know what to do to enter Heaven. Jesus told him to keep the commandments. Then, when he asked for more directions Jesus recommended that he distribute all his wealth among the poor. The boy bent his head and walked away. I was often bothered by this parable. Would it be possible for me to get to Heaven at all? I didn't really want to give up what I had, the security of a warm home, and the comforts of our life. Yet, I remembered the days of the siege. We had had nothing then and yet everything had been taken care of in God's mysterious ways.

On August 31, 1947, the elections took place. The results: the four government parties together had received 60% of the vote: Communists 22%, Social Democrats 14%, National Peasant Party 9%, Smallholders' Party

15%. The non-Marxist parties received 40% of the vote. If the Smallholders' Party had been included with these, the proportion of the votes would have remained the same as in the previous election: 55% of the votes for the non-Marxist parties. The Communists named 1947 the "Year of the Turn-About" in honor of their victory over the "reactionary capitalists."

～

Finally, it was my birthday: September 6, 1947. I was thirteen years old and my friends and I celebrated to the swinging music played by Laci on the piano.

It was still warm although the stars already blinked in the sky above the last red streak left by the setting sun. We stayed in our winter home year round now because we had rented our summer home to the French Embassy, in the hope of saving it from confiscation. Comrade Rakosi had expropriated a house nearby and from then on the Communists kept strict control over the surrounding houses. Comrade Rakosi had several homes around the city and nobody ever knew where he stayed. He was afraid for his life. Wherever he went he traveled in three or four identical cars. Only his bodyguards knew which car was to be protected.

Secretly, I was happy that we stayed in the city. I found it much more intriguing since I was allowed alone on the street and there were opportunities to go shopping, to the theater or the movies, to see the boys who were old enough not to spend their summers in resort places as little children would.

This night was simply heavenly!

We went out onto the balcony and Pista told me about the stars. We had studied astronomy in school only the year before in physics, but it sounded so much more interesting when he told me about them with a special starry shine in his eyes. Did I understand at all what he said, or was it only the music of his voice that charmed me?

He put his arm around my waist. I did not dare to move lest the magic disappear. He kissed me on the cheek. Just then I heard Mother's voice: "Helen, Helen, where are you?"

I pressed Pista's hand and answered, "Here, we are out here," while I pulled Pista back inside. "Pista was telling me about the stars. It was so interesting."

Mother just smiled. "You better come in now or you'll catch a cold." She winked at me. "Come, look at your cake."

I blew out the candles on the 12-layer Dobos-cake. The table was bedecked with goodies, open-face sandwiches, which I had not had to make today because it was my birthday, the birthday and other cakes, decorated with apple butter and raisins, butter frosting, and whipped cream.

Again, as always, the young people instantly emptied the table, leaving hardly anything for the parents who had faithfully chaperoned their children at every party. The wine-tea-peach punch, the latest drink for teenage-parties, had been mixed in a huge crystal bowl. Joyful conversation and laughter filled the room. The dance started again. The table was quickly replenished and there was food available all through the night just in case someone needed a refreshment to keep up with the Viennese waltzes and the wild rhythm of jazz.

As we danced along the monkey-island of boys, I heard them discuss the elections. I asked Pista,

"What do you think of the elections?" I wondered whether he would side with my mother or my father.

He became red in the face while he answered, "'List of voters,' indeed! Remember that they issued a new list and left off some of the best people this country had. Not only could they not run for office, they were not even allowed to cast their votes. You know what the Communists did to 'gain' that five percent extra since the last election? Listen! They took Communist Party members around by truckloads. Those who were away from their district of residence were allowed to vote in another district if they had their registration cards with them. The trucks went from village to village and its passengers voted everywhere. I was at Lake Balaton, I saw them do it. A bunch of foreign correspondents trailed the truck and they told me that they had filmed all its voting stops over the day. Then, of course, there were more votes than people and that would not have worked out, except the committees 'corrected' the discrepancies by throwing out the opposition's ballots. The Communists are now in complete control."

"Oh, Pista, do you, too, think that we should leave Hungary and try to make our living elsewhere? Is there no way out? Will we have to become Communists?"

Pista became very serious. He looked me straight in the eye. "No, Helen, I think no such thing. You know the song everybody considers our second national anthem, 'Blessings or curses be your fate / you have to live and die for her, for our country, for Hungary.' He became very solemn when he said that. A tear ran down my cheek. This was a song that few Hungarians could sing without crying.

"Yes. I know," I finally managed to say. "But what good does it do to any one of us to die where our martyrdom will not even be noticed. We can no longer show the world if we die for our principles, for what we believe in. Not since the Nazis introduced the concentration camps and torture chambers."

"Helen, it was not introduced by the Nazis. The Soviets did it first. And it's really beside the point. We will be there, at the time of our deaths. If we have to die, it will matter to us whether we can respect ourselves for our decisions, or live with them if we happen to survive."

"You must be right," I whispered. "Many who came back from death camps, Nazi or Communist alike, said that they were alive today because they had been true to themselves. They never betrayed their faith, their principles. But will we have the strength to do it? What will it take? I am so scared sometimes. Aren't you?"

"Yes, I am scared, often. But I know that if and when the time comes God will give me the strength I need. I have seen the most extraordinary transformations of people under duress during the war. You were younger; they probably did not let you go out so much. But, Helen, when you need that power it is right there. And there is no explanation, none whatsoever, unless you happen to believe in God." His eyes sparkled again.

I thought of the medicine Father had found in the snow to help the raped, pregnant woman before she gave birth to that healthy, blue-eyed baby. Of the woman, who said that when her son was killed God was where He had been when His only Son was crucified. Yes, I too knew about that Power. I gave Pista a little squeeze as we danced along. Somebody cut in.

"Tommy," I gave a sudden cry of surprise, "I haven't seen you since Magyaróvár!"

He just smiled, "I said I would come to Budapest to go to the university and here I am. Now you'll have to put up with me quite often. Your mother can keep secrets well. I came by a few days ago and she suggested that we surprise you."

"I am so happy! You really did come to Budapest! How is your family?"

"Father is all right. We have the pharmacy open as usual. But Mother," his face darkened with sorrow, "she is dead."

"I'm so sorry! What happened?"

"Remember that she wore a white star when you saw us last? She was taken by the Germans in the very last month before the Soviets occupied Magyaróvár. She was in camp there until the last days of the war, when the Germans were going to move the prisoners to Germany. She was a pharmacist. She had always had a poison-ring with her. While the Germans marched the prisoners across the bridge towards the border she took the poison. She wanted to die on Hungarian soil. A few days later the war was over. All the other prisoners who were together with her came back. She was the only one who died."

While he talked we stopped dancing and now we sat on the sofa, facing the open window through which the stars twinkled in from the warm summer night. I stroked his hair; he sat there silently.

"She looks down on us now from that beautiful sky," I said quietly.

Tommy looked at me, "Nobody has said anything as beautiful to me since she died."

# 22

Uncle Joe, our chief buyer, dropped by one gray November Sunday afternoon in 1947. He settled comfortably in an overstuffed armchair near the bar and sipped with great pleasure a demitasse of Grandfather's strong, freshly roasted coffee. Its aroma floated through the house. Although outside it was damp and dark, our home was filled with warmth and soft music.

"I just came from the Franciscan Church," he declared.

"Did you convert?" Mother teased him.

"I did nothing of the sort," he said with indignation. "If I did not do it during the Nazi times, why should I do it now when I can benefit from having been persecuted? I simply went to pay my dues. I put a hundred forint bill into the collection basket."

"Your dues?" I asked with astonishment. "Why would you have to pay dues to the Catholic church?"

"I don't have to," laughed Uncle Joe, "but I want to. They are the only ones who persevere in their protests against the Communists, the only ones who still give us hope for the future. Cardinal Mindszenty is not my leader, I am a Jew; but he is my idol. I wish there were many more like him. He dares to disagree. The least that I can do is to contribute weekly to the cause. Besides, I like the jingle of the bells during Mass," he added with a twinkle.

"You even stayed for Mass?" asked Grandmother.

"Yes, I go regularly, to listen to the sermons. I am shocked by the way the Communists do everything in their power to boycott and sabotage the Marian year that the Cardinal declared on August 15, 1947. Hundreds of thousands, often millions of people try to reach various destinations. The government reduces the number of trains; it uses hoaxed dangers of epidemics in order to quarantine the locations where the services take place. Meetings are disturbed by violence, participants and even the celebrants in processions are sprayed with 'antiseptics.' And all this comes from a government that sent representatives to processions before the elections were held in order to demonstrate their solidarity with the Catholics. I think they are despicable, lowly, good-for-nothings. We were only 'liberated' from the Nazis in order to get into very similar trouble, if you ask me."

This was strange to hear from Uncle Joe. I remembered the time when he had thought himself blessed because he could build a rock-shelter for the Germans; I saw him contentedly sip coffee now and declare that the Communists were as bad as the Nazis. Granted, they had been worse for us but even for him?

"Why do you say that, Uncle Joe?" I asked.

"Because it is true. Just because you see me sit here comfortably today does not mean that I will be able to do that tomorrow. The trend is here. Just like in 1939 when many of the Jews saw what was coming and left the country; many, even more, are leaving today. They have learned their lesson."

I thought of Jeanette, my Russian-refugee-English teacher, and her stories. She had said that she, too, would leave Hungary as soon as she could.

"I have great news for you, Helen," Father said, then he turned to Uncle Joe. "You can tell her now."

"What is it?" my heart began to pound. I could see from Father's smile that it was going to be something good.

"Your father and mother will be going on a business trip to Paris and Switzerland and you'll be going with them…"

Clink! I dropped my glass and it broke into little pieces on the hardwood floor. I leaped onto Uncle Joe's lap and kissed his flabby cheeks. Then I grabbed Father and Mother, Grandmother and Grandfather and kissed everybody in the room.

"I can't believe it! It can't be true!" I chanted as I danced around in circles: "When are we going? How long will we stay?"

"We'll be going in March for about a month; two weeks in Paris and two weeks in Switzerland. We'll be on a business trip but maybe we can look around for a school for you. You are old enough to start your education abroad."

I was so very, very happy. For the first time in my life I would be leaving Hungary to venture into the world I longed to see.

"How about Marie and Elisabeth?" I asked.

"They are still too young," said Grandmother. "Besides, the Hungarian government would not give passports to the whole family, there have to be hostages. It is a wonder that they gave *you* a passport! I guess they know that you would not be deserting us."

"You mean they think that we wouldn't come back?" I asked in astonishment.

"Helen," said Uncle Joe, "very few people receive passports. Almost everybody who gets one stays in the West—they don't bother to come back. Your parents received their passport because the government expects them to make a good deal for Hungary. They have their foreign contacts which means that they can secure valuable merchandise for Hungary that is presently not available."

I listened with only half an ear after I was assured of the fact that we would come back and that we would leave fairly soon. I would see the world…

～

I was still in a daze when we boarded the Arlberg Express in Budapest. The past few weeks seemed like a beautiful dream. We had shopped and had dresses made. We had picked out materials and hats, bought shoes and suitcases, packed and made sure we had everything we needed and much more. We loaded a suitcase with presents, Hungarian food specialties for business friends, and for Hungarian war refugee friends we hoped to meet in Paris and on our way.

Finally, we were settled with our ten suitcases and several handbags. We hung up our coats in the compartment. Mother's winter coat was lined with mink and had a thick otter collar. My coat looked like a spacesuit— quite unreal in those days when nobody could imagine space travel. It was a sheepskin coat, turned inside out, looking like white suede under a cover of see-through opaque plastic. Father had agreed to buy it only with great reluctance, because it was more expensive than anything I had ever worn before. It was one of those rare things that I really wanted and I had begged him for it until he gave in. I just knew I was going to wear it forever. I caressed it with my eyes as I put it on the hanger. The train was warm and as soon as we were moving Father said to me,

"Come, let's have a beer" he opened a thermos bottle and poured some in the top.

"You know I don't like beer," I said as he handed me the cup.

"Just drink a little. This is very good dark beer."

I had only tasted light beer before and I took a swallow. For the first time it tasted good. Was it the taste of beer I liked? Or maybe anything would have tasted good. We were on our way!

The train seemed deserted by the time we reached the Austrian border. There was only one other family on the train, also Hungarians. The two daughters, sixteen and eighteen, were on their way to a Swiss boarding school.

It was the beginning of March, 1948. We passed fields and trees and bushes ready to explode into spring. Buds greeted us here and there while patches of snow melted slowly on the north niches of rolling hills. I hardly noticed the sights that had become so familiar to us in the past few years, the occasional burnt-out tanks and houses in ruins. It took us a few hours to reach the border. We stopped in Győr, the largest city between Vienna and Budapest, thirty miles from the border. We had traveled through this town often when we lived in Magyaróvár.

The border-crossing at Hegyeshalom was uneventful except for my excitement over the fact that for the very first time in my life I had left Hungary.

The dinner in the dining car was exotic, we ate bearpaw steak, with horseradish sauce, the meat was so tender I would never have guessed it to be the meat of such a ferocious animal.

We stopped in Vienna late at night. Through Elsie's stories I thought of this city as a gold-colored dream. What I saw from the window of the express was completely different; it was dark, buildings in ruins, hardly any people on the streets. The station was empty with only a few American, British, French, and Soviet soldiers staring idly at the railroad cars. Then the train sped into the night. Stars blinked through the windows and scattered lights appeared and disappeared in the valley.

Mother and I laughed our way through the evening ritual of getting undressed and brushing our teeth. The sink was ridiculously tiny and the water only flowed as long as somebody pushed the button. Even so I found it miraculous to have water on the train and to be able to wash ourselves.

It took me a while before the unaccustomed rocking of the train lulled-me to sleep. I was too excited—my life was a dream come true.

Shrill sounds woke me when the first dim lights of dawn broke through the slats of the shades.

"But why?"

"Why us?"

"What is wrong?"

Soviet curses and shuffling were the only answers.

"Help!" I heard a young girl scream.

It took me a minute to realize where I was. My dream turned into a nightmare. But what was it all about?

Someone tore at the door of our compartment. Father jumped out of bed. I could see his hand tremble as he asked,

"Yes?"

"Passports! End of the Soviet zone!"

"Help!" came from the other compartment. Then more shuffles and curses.

Father handed the passports to an arm in a Soviet uniform.

"Of course, the bridge on the River Ens," Father muttered and although he was not at ease, he relaxed somewhat. "I was warned of that at home. This is where we cross from the Eastern occupational zone into the Western sector."

The conductor saluted as he returned our passports.

"What is going on next door?" Father asked him, visibly relieved.

"Something seemed to be wrong with the passport of one of the girls and she became hysterical. They took the whole family off the train, what can I do?" he whispered the last sentence.

"What will happen to them?" asked Mother.

"I don't know. If they can settle the question soon they'll be on the next train in two days. If not…"

They will end up in Siberia. My experience with sudden disappearances made me finish the sentence without saying it out loud.

Father got off at the next station and sent a telegram to his business friend in Vienna with the name and description of the people taken off the train. Although it was very early in the morning I could not go back to sleep. This last act of brutality underlined the suddenness of change that I expected, only a few feet from the Soviet zone.

What was I going to see? What would "freedom" be like?

The pink of the rising sun turned gold. The velvety green meadows of the Alps with patches of white and brown cows looked exactly as they had in my books and the colorful calendars we had received from manufacturers we were going to meet on our trip. I had never thought of them as real people, only as an infinite source of calendars and the black and white business letters I sometimes had to translate for Father.

What would they be like?

Too many interesting questions kept me awake. Cities and villages ran past the train. We stopped at the Swiss border. Smiling border guards checked our papers and saluted. By now, every place in the train was occupied, a different language spoken in every compartment. I watched the lazy small town Sunday afternoon outside the window. Our train must have been the great attraction of the surrounding hills. Young girls in colorful dresses and boys in their Sunday best giggled in groups. I wanted to get out and talk with them, but there was no time. The international express halted for only a few minutes.

"Switzerland had never seen war," I remembered suddenly. I saw no soldiers or police officers, the customs people were the only ones in uniform. The people I saw through the window looked well-dressed and well-fed.

Mountains and rivers passed us by.

"Look out on the side of the train, where the water flows," Father reminded me, "it is always more beautiful."

My eyes drank in the sights as long as they could take them, then I fell asleep because I could accept no more of nature's blinding beauty.

The train stopped. We had arrived in Zurich. One of Father's business friends waited for us in the hustle and bustle of the railroad station. He was tall and well-built, his wife about my height and very matter-of-factly dressed. They spoke Hungarian.

The station was so clean I had the impression someone polished it by hand every day. The cab took us through equally clean streets and gleaming shop windows to a hotel that seemed spic and span in its chrome and glass modernness. I was speechless with wonder and did not pay much attention to the adults' talk.

An automatic elevator (no attendant) took us to the second floor. From the window of our room I saw a department store so big I could not believe my eyes—its name was Jelmoli.

"Helen, we are here, we have arrived," Mother hugged me and we danced around the room. I finally woke up from my daydreams.

"It's beautiful! How come everything looks so clean?"

"Because the trains go by electricity. No soot from the locomotives. Central heating does not leave coal deposits on the furniture and people keep it clean. There are no ruins because there was no war here. Now, let me fix your hair."

"Not my hair again! We've hardly arrived."

"I know, but you must always look like a lady on a business trip, that is what I hate so much about them," answered Mother.

If that was the first thing she hated the next thing was certainly to keep the clothes from getting wrinkled. (We had to unload all ten of the suitcases and repack them every second day, or at least every time we moved to another city.)

Finally we were down on the street enjoying sights I had never seen before. It seemed that every second store was a watch and jewelry outlet. The shop windows beamed with understated elegance. One or two pieces were displayed but they were real gems, exquisitely formed, breaking the bright lights into colors of the rainbow.

Jelmoli, the department store I watched from the window, left me dumbfounded. Giant butterflies and baskets of flowers floated from the gallery. The whole store spilled over with spring. I thought I could smell the paper flowers and I looked from one thing to another in a daze. Never, never in my life had I seen that many things in one place! Everything was for sale, at down-to-earth prices. People walked and smiled, stopped and bought things.

There was not one beggar on the streets. I saw workers breaking up the blacktop, their overalls were as clean as those of dolls that had just left the factory. I felt I was walking in a story book, an unreal little part of Europe that, because of the common interest of all participating countries, was left out of the holocaust on either side of its mountain-fortress.

We found a bakery, real Swiss chocolate, butter that did not taste rancid, sweet rolls, and brioches.

"Come, Helen, I'll teach you to eat chocolate," Mother said. "Here, outside. Not in the store. Take a deep breath of the spring air while you bite into that chocolate bar."

It was unbelievable! As I breathed in the smell of the chocolate the taste I experienced was a hundredfold better than I remembered it and the cause lay only partly in the fresh air—this was Swiss chocolate! I had forgotten its taste. All I could remember was war-time Hungarian chocolate and the colored popped wheat we ate for candy. As the chocolate melted in my mouth I imagined that I was now tasting freedom. Yes, I was convinced that freedom must be wonderful if it enabled people to have experiences like these.

I saw bananas in the next store; real, yellow, sweet bananas. I remembered their taste and I remembered thinking of them during the siege, when we had tried pineapple.

"Let's buy bananas," I pointed at them.

"Ok," Mother laughed at my excitement. "Let's eat bananas for lunch and save our money. Maybe we'll find something nice to buy for you."

"Save money on bananas?" this struck me as a surprise.

"Bananas are very cheap and very nutritious," said Mother as we bit into the first one. Its mellow, golden taste brought back memories of when I had been four years old, eating my last banana before the war broke out in Hungary and shipments ceased. I felt the exhilaration of the taste—explosion in the tiniest nerves of my body. We must surely have arrived in Paradise!

Later we looked at fountain pens and matching pencils in leather cases. From the money we saved on our lunch, Mother bought me a set in a green alligator case. When we wanted to pay, Mother noticed that she did not have her purse.

"Oh, my God'" she became quite pale, "Where is my purse? I had my passport in it and all my money"

I was desperate. "We'll never find it!" was my first thought. "I'll run back to the other store, where we bought the bananas, and see." I offered, although I knew it would not be there. I was used to the certainty of stealing. Mother followed closely after me.

I suddenly remembered, "It can't be at the banana place, I paid there, remember? Let's go back to the bakery store!"

We ran faster because now we knew for sure that we would not be able to find the purse.

We burst into the store panting. The lady smiled at us and held out the purse. "You forgot it here when you left, enjoying your chocolate!"

"Thank you very, very much!" we both said at once and Mother tried to give her a five Franc bill.

"But, Madam, I wouldn't take it. It is only natural to return something that does not belong to me."

I began to cry. That was the first time in my life that I had seen someone return a lost item and find it "natural." In this country the proverb, "Finders keepers, losers weepers" did not apply.

We met with this honesty many times in Switzerland. Father forgot his raincoat at a hotel in Zurich and on our way back, three weeks later, he found it hanging on the same hanger. In a small town, when we left the hotel we forgot to take a pair of Mother's pajamas. When the cleaning woman found them shortly after we left, the porter followed us by cab to the railroad station and waved the pajamas at us from afar. "Madam, Madam, you left your pajamas."

Our journey was a kaleidoscope of colorful events—vivid pictures emerged from its constant churn of changes, then broke into pieces through the clattering of the train. The fragments sped by the window only to form a new design at our next stop.

Etched in my memory were pictures of many interesting places, events, and people. We saw every conceivable kind of fur at the Basel World Fur Exhibition; as we passed one booth after another I noticed that Mother owned practically every one of the kinds exhibited. She had ermine and Persian lamb, sheep and foxes of every possible color, mink and otter; even I had a white rabbit cape. There was one shade of mink there that I had never seen before. As we walked farther and farther towards the middle of the fairgrounds I noticed that people kept turning after me. "What did I do now?" I wondered.

"Look," Mother said. "They are trying to figure out your coat. In the whole exhibition there is no coat like yours."

"I can't believe this," I said it out loud now. "I come to a World Exhibition and people watch me?" I felt awkward and self-conscious. Not only in my own home, but even in Switzerland! Was I a perpetual circus attraction?

In Basel I met the owner of the Geigy factory. I was truly unimpressed by him. He was a bachelor and although he was a billionaire, the only thing he was very proud of was his long plaid shawl. To this day I can't imagine why he treasured this possession so much. He was a likable fellow otherwise, thirtyish, brown hair, and blue eyes. He instantly became infatuated with Mother like every man who set eyes on her.

"I am going with you to Paris," he declared. "It's time I went to the Opera again. We don't have an opera in Switzerland. I guess you have noticed already."

"Why not?" I inquired.

"Because an opera costs a lot of money. We built a concert hall and occasionally we have guest troupes from all over the world," he answered.

"But Switzerland seems to have so much money compared to other countries that have operas. Why can't you have one if you want one?" his answer did not satisfy me.

"Oh, we want one, no question about it," he laughed and showed his perfect white teeth, "but we want other things more. We have no opera but we have no beggars either. We have good, quick, and clean trains that will take us to Paris in a night's sleep and we can afford to go to the Opera there. We can afford to buy what we need and to live in peace and quiet. We don't owe money to anybody in the world. As a matter of fact the whole world is eager to deposit money in our secure banks."

That was the first time in my life I heard about priorities, even though the word was not pronounced. "We can't afford it," started to make sense. They chose not to have an opera in order to have something else that meant more to them. This was the second time in Switzerland that I had an experience with money—we saved money on our lunch when we ate the bananas and we bought the pen and pencil set instead. Now I had heard of a country doing the same thing. What did money mean in the life of an average person? Money to me was something I got from Mother's purse, or if she did not happen to have money with her she would take a piece of paper and write on it: 200 Forints, then sign it. The cashier at our store would pay the money to the bearer of the note. Money was definitely no obstacle if one wanted something, or at least not in our lives. Father would mention money sometimes but that was of no special interest to me. It was only natural; he was a man and therefore he was supposed to mutter things about finances. I remembered Mariska, the cleaning woman, talking during the time of inflation. Oh, I knew it was bad not to have money, but, to save it, to budget it, to rank the things by their importance when one bought something? That all sounded strange, yet sensible, despite the fact that inflation taught me a very different lesson: "spend the money while it is worth something." The Swiss did not seem to have this kind of problem. Their currency was stable.

One day we made an excursion by boat on the Thüner See (Lake) then we took the cogwheel railway and finally a chairlift between the Beatenberg and the Niederhorn. We traveled on the tiny chairs above a savage ravine. Rocks and pine trees scared us from below, while from above the warm sunshine and blue skies lured us to the immaculate snowcover on top of the mountain. Every time Mother and I looked down we shuddered.

"Let's get off when we reach the middle station. I am afraid to go on," said Mother. We tried to get off but the man just pushed our chairs onto the next line. "Your ticket is valid to the top," he said, and we floated again above the rocks and snow, this time no more trees, sitting on two tiny chairs with nothing below us.

"There have been no accidents since they've established this 'Sesserli Bahn'," Mother tried to reassure both of us.

I grabbed her hand and said, "If we survived the siege, we'll manage this too!"

At that we had to laugh and our fear evaporated. The view from the top compensated us for all our worries. As far as we could see, snow-covered peaks stretched across the horizon, blue lakes, pine trees, and people skiing in bathing suits. The Alpine sun tanned their skins as brown as their famous chocolate.

I noticed that even in this remote resort there was running water and electricity.

The way down was not half as menacing as it had been coming up. We turned our heads away from the ravines and up onto the snow covers of the nearby peaks that changed slowly from gold to pink in the rays of the setting sun.

Another first I noticed in Switzerland was the absence of maids in private households. We were invited to the home of the head of International Affairs of Geigy S.A., a young couple with a small son, Christopher. While we were there, in order to show us the Swiss way of life, the couple soaked their clothes for the next day, because that was the special day of the month, when the washerwoman was willing to come and the laundry must be ready. They had neither washing machines nor household help! I'd heard about societies without maids—the Soviet Union, or Germany during the war, when "maids" preferred working in factories. However, this was my first experience with live people who did not have maids. Even our maids, when they got married acquired maids of their own; peasant girls who found this a good opportunity to learn about life in the big city and to find a husband among the craftsmen or the soldiers stationed there. They also had an opportunity to make money to buy themselves the necessary linen and other items of their dowry.

The first time that we sat down at a restaurant in Zurich I had the surprise of my life. We ate with Hungarian friends who had escaped before 1939—they were Jewish. Before we started talking I looked around carefully to both sides. I heard Mother's clear, bubbly laughter. Then she said, "Helen, you don't need to do that here. You can talk to your heart's desire. It does not matter who hears you."

I blushed. I forgot...that is, I never remembered a time when I did not have to look around to see if there was anything suspicious before I opened my mouth.

"No need to look around here," Father repeated the words and he too laughed. I was beginning to understand why Father thought that we should leave Hungary; even if we would have to think twice before we decided on what we should spend our money, even if we never went to the Opera again.

We met many Hungarian war-refugees. The Minders, very dear friends of ours, had left when it was still possible. They had dual Swiss-Hungarian citizenship. They simply went home. He was a medical doctor who worked in Zurich. One of his sons had always come to my birthday parties when they lived in Hungary and I loved to go to his because we always had salami there. We seldom had salami at home because it was considered hard to digest. Something forbidden is always much more desirable than what is readily available—naturally I constantly dreamed of salami.

I was looking forward to having a good talk with him about childhood in Zurich. I wore a pink wool dress, hand-embroidered with tiny pink glass-pearls down its long sleeves and around the skirt. The bodice fit tightly to enhance my figure. I was proud of my figure now, since it looked like that of a grown woman.

When the door opened I saw a six-foot hunk of a boy with white-blond short hair, blue eyes, and short pants. We shook hands and that was about the end of our conversation, although he sat beside me and I asked him questions. He answered with a short "yes" or "no" and blushed to the roots of his hair.

His parents were much more talkative and fell from one surprise into another when I took part in their conversation.

"Here in Switzerland children are not allowed to grow up before they are confirmed, around age 16. They cannot wear long pants, no matter how tall they are. It is rather embarrassing for Roby," said his Mother. "They go to school all day. They cannot go to the movies, unless it is a Walt Disney film."

"Sometimes I smuggle him in," Roby's Father said, "to see the newsreel. You know, we have special movies, where they show only the newsreels. He is so tall, I dress him in my clothes and push the hat deep over his head."

I felt sorry that I had not dressed more like a little girl. Maybe he would have talked to me. But how could I have known? And even if I would have… I remembered suddenly that I had not brought any little girl's clothes with me. "On a business trip you have to dress like a lady, always," I remembered Mother's voice on the first day of our trip.

"When do you take extra language classes, piano, art history, if you are in school all the time?" I asked him.

"We are supposed to have everything we need at school," he answered and blushed again.

"Life is built around work and school here, isn't it?" I asked him. "I noticed that work quits for two hours in midday. People go home to have their

227

dinner then they go back and work till seven o'clock. They have their lunch at dinnertime. Don't they? The same as in Hungary. Only we don't close the stores at noon."

"Yes, we come home and go back," he answered with his usual blush.

"What are you allowed to do for fun?" I inquired.

"We go for excursions and play ball, sports." For once he did not blush.

I felt victorious because he finally felt at ease but I definitely did not think that I wanted to spend my childhood in Switzerland. I remembered now the movies and night clubs with their warning signs: children under 18 not permitted. Not once did they ask me for identification, probably because I was a foreigner.

Next time we took a train I saw somebody check in a rifle along with his luggage.

"What is that man doing?" I asked our friend who accompanied us to the station.

"What do you mean?"

"He just checked in his rifle. Or what is it? It must be a rifle."

"Why not?" he wondered.

"A rifle?! If one has a rifle it's because he might need it," I declared.

"Not here," he smiled. "This is probably a young man who goes in for practice."

"What does that mean?" I was suspicious now. In a country where someone checks in a gun nothing was impossible.

"We have no army in Switzerland but every man is trained to defend his country in case of an attack. Everybody has a gun in his house but we do not intend to fight a war with anybody. After the first training there are brush-up practices. The targets are in the mountains. If you watch closely you will see them from the train window," he explained.

I saw them. It was unbelievable. That rugged terrain was where the sharpshooters were trained; the roads to the inland led through mountain passes. If the enemy tried to cross them they would be shot one by one. This country could not be occupied with conventional weapons. It was a good choice for an island of peace in the middle of both World Wars.

Now I knew I had seen the ultimate absurdity a soldier in civilian clothing who was so confident that he would not need his weapon, he checked it in with the rest of his luggage.

We visited several Swiss schools with Mother on one of our side trips and found the two girls who were taken off the train. We were glad that they were alive and healthy but I still felt sorry for them. The boarding school where they stayed seemed very strict, though friendly. Fifteen girls slept in one room. Each had a clay pitcher and bowl to wash in. They were allowed to take a bath twice a week. Discipline was prevalent in every one of their activities. I was happy when we were on our way again, this time to Lugano.

Father stayed in Basel on business but Mother insisted on showing me this exquisite town in Switzerland.

Mountains rose all around the intensely blue lake. Palm trees waved their leaves in the spring breeze of the sunny March day. Tropical and common garden flowers bathed in the lukewarm afternoon. The season had not started yet; there were hardly any tourists.

"This is where you should come for a honeymoon," Mother declared.

"Why? Why here? Didn't you go to the Riviera?"

"I did. But, who knows? Maybe it would be just as well to come here. The Riviera has the sea and the mountains are higher but it is much more expensive. Although the mimosa forests, you know how I love mimosas. They were in bloom… Oh, it was beautiful. Then we went on and toured all of Europe for three months. I don't know though whether it's the best thing to travel much during one's honeymoon. Wouldn't it be nice to stay in one place and just enjoy each other?" Suddenly she looked at me and remembered that I was only thirteen. "But then, you wouldn't know about that yet." She laughed her clear happy laugh again. She always made that same mistake. We were such good friends that she would often ask me, "On my honeymoon, remember?" Then she would laugh just as she did now. "Of course you can't remember, you are my daughter."

It was March 15, 1948. The hundredth anniversary of Hungary's Revolution against the Habsburgs—the day that occupied my mind so often, when I passed the plaque on the National Museum commemorating the event. I remembered thinking, "Would it be celebrated now? Would the red star still spoil the façade of the old museum?" I knew now that the Communists celebrated. In their eyes the 1848 revolution was a progressive one; it helped the cause of the people, the goals of the Communists who could arrive at their destination only through the vehicle of capitalism. In their eyes the purpose of that revolution was to establish capitalism, the breeding ground for communism.

Back in Budapest, I knew, my classmates were all involved in very elaborate drills. Every high school practiced for the exercises which they finally performed in front of the government officials at a huge sports arena: all schools at once, all dressed alike to display the national colors and formations glorifying our "liberators."

For the time being I did not have to think of them, yet it became second nature to me to have them always in the back of my mind, to check my actions against possible consequences. I slowly learned their language, their reasoning, even if it did not make sense.

229

The first stars appeared on the softly lit sky as the sun left the horizon. I sat on the balcony while Mother took a bath and I enjoyed my sudden privacy and the beauty of nature.

The palm trees, the first ones I had ever seen, assured me of the fact that I was free to think, and no one would "hear my thoughts." I was free to let go and be myself; I would not be taken by surprise. I felt completely and totally happy. I had come to think that happiness could not last so I felt that the essence of happiness was the perfection of the minute.

What made me happy? I looked around and saw the black velvet lake surrounded by the crescent of a diamond necklace—the lights along the lakeshore. Some boats made their way to the harbor. The fragrance of the flowers drifted towards the balcony. I felt warm, comfortable, and at peace.

What was most important to me in life? The question was blurred by the intensity of my emotions.

I was overwhelmed by the urge to do something great, to fly above the clouds and give myself to everybody, to help anyone who needed my help, to create something … to create life. Children…a husband…love…they should all be part of it. But it had to be something else also. Something I never seemed to have in my life, despite the many things I owned, or could own. What was it? I thought of myself as first a little child, then a grade school child, finally an adolescent. What was my constant desire? To be able to do as I pleased. And that very thing was what the Communists were taking away, not only from the children but from the adults …I realized that I wanted so desperately to become an adult so that I could do as I pleased. As soon as I realized the emptiness of my hopes, in view of our Communist future, the lights went out inside of me. What was life worth without freedom? I had finally found the word! It was *freedom* I wanted more than anything.

Free will…we had learned so much about it in catechism. But what good was free will when it was up against machine guns? Who had the right to take away our free will if God himself respected it? It was March 15.

I thought of my classmates celebrating our national holiday in the name of communism.

# 23

Paris!... I stood there on the platform still in a daze from having to get up so early in the morning. I felt a bit nauseated, but I was so preoccupied with what I saw that it made me forget the discomfort caused by the sudden stop of the sleeping car's rhythmic movement.

People swarmed like honey bees. They pushed their way from one location to another in bunches, some dropped out from the group and hesitated, others marched on their separate ways with determined faces. Everybody was in a rush to catch trains, subways, and buses. The city was a restless ant colony compared to the peace and quiet of Switzerland.

Uncle Joe's son waited for us at the station. He lived in Paris, his wife was from Southern France. He looked like a typical Frenchman in his indispensable navy blue beret and matching raincoat. After greeting us he said,

"An unbelievable crowd every morning! That's what I thought when I arrived from Hungary, but I got used to it quickly. I am part of them now. Half the city lives in the suburbs; so do I. We commute to work on quick, clean and efficient electric trains. At least two million people arrive at Paris' railroad stations every morning and leave at night."

The shiny aluminum trains glided soundlessly in and out of the station as we pushed our way towards a waiting cab.

I watched speechlessly, while most of the people again seemed to find me a circus attraction in my space-age coat.

If my description of Paris is more a passive than an active one it is because I was there to observe and absorb, as someone who someday would have to head our business empire because I was the oldest and there were no boys in our family.

The magic kaleidoscope of impressions started its dizzy dance and I followed as quickly as I could. My observer-role turned into an active one when Mother became ill for three days and I had to go with Father to interpret at his business meetings with the big French perfume houses: Elisabeth Arden, Lucien Lelong, Roger & Gallet, Lanvin to name a few. From what I had seen, we had achieved the goal of our trip. Our old-time business associates were trusting and eager to renew connections with Hungary.

"We would do business with you anytime," said one of the old gentlemen to me. "Your Grandfather paid the bills even after the war broke out and all debts to enemy countries were canceled. He smuggled out the money because he would not use the opportunity to forego payments."

Often during the business talks, there would be a break and the heads of firms would pull Father aside, "What are the Soviets like? Will they come and occupy us?"

"You bet they will," Father said, "unless you do something about it now. Stand firm in the United Nations. Try to get them out of Hungary and the other Eastern European countries. Now you can still do it without a war. The Soviets don't have anything, only what they receive from the Americans or what they have taken from Germany. They don't have the atomic bomb. The West has the chance now to reorganize a Free World on the basis of self-determination. Don't let it slip between your fingers, I warn you, the Soviets want to 'liberate' the whole world from capitalism and you know what that is going to mean to you."

Most of them were afraid of the Soviet menace, but some voiced an opinion that sounded strange to me,

"Unfortunately, a few million have to suffer in order for other millions to be able to live in freedom and democracy."

I am afraid that our reactions to that opinion showed, although at business meetings one never takes strong political stands—it might ruin the deal.

It was March, 1948. France was recuperating from a long German occupation. As soon as we got settled at the Hotel du Louvre, the maid, who helped us with the unpacking, inquired if we had food with us that we could sell to her. Would we have oranges, chocolate, or anything, just anything, from Switzerland? We gave her what we had, but it certainly seemed peculiar that she would ask hotel guests to sell her food. In a few days, we better understood the situation. It seemed that the food supplies were still low post-war. In the luxury hotel where we stayed the allotment for each guest was four ounces of butter a month, and that too was rancid, as we found out very soon. Our diet consisted mainly of chicken, though Father tried oysters and artichokes and gave me some, too. I liked the artichokes but I did not cherish the idea of swallowing the live, mucousy little creatures Father loved so much. The French sold their bread in long sticks, by the meter. It was fun to watch the delivery boys on their bicycles balancing a load of about twenty loaves.

The streets were crowded with American soldiers and beautiful women. They dressed like the models in fashion magazines with high-heel shoes, longish wide skirts, no shoulder pads, tailored suits, and tight bodices. After the sensible clothing of Switzerland, Paris seemed the more glamorous because of the contrast.

I pointed out some of the ladies to Uncle Joe's son, John. "Aren't they beautiful?"

"Do you want me to quote their prices?" he inquired.

"You mean ….

"Yes, I mean that they are all available for more or less money." I hesitated to believe him, but he lived here. I did not. He was also older. I was still only thirteen.

Life in Paris surpassed all my expectations. Simply to breathe the air and listen to the noises of this metropolis gave me a special feeling. To walk on its characteristic streets with the first flowers of spring in the hands and on the clothes of glamorous-looking women, to watch the diamond glitter of the sun on the windshields of the oncoming cars along the Champs-Élysées, to see the Arc de Triumph and the Eiffel Tower, was not only beautiful it was also free. Every step I took made me think of Mother's favorite quote: "The best things in life are free." While this might sound like a cliché in America she quoted it in English, in Hungary, and I shall never forget it.

On every second pillar we saw a poster advertising the movie "La Vie en Rose," which was "Finally Here" A happy fish floated around in the pink background, blowing bubbles. I soon understood what they meant by "finally." Though the film was released only recently, Edith Piaf, the well-known chanson-singer, "diseuse," as they called them in Paris, had made the song famous much earlier. Even the organ grinders played the tune all day on the street corners. Their little monkeys ran around with the hat collecting money after each song.

Everything cost money in Paris. We had to tip the usher in church to lead us to our pews. We had to tip the attendant at the movies. At the turn of the century waiters at the best restaurants did not get paid at all. They received so much income from tips that the best waiting jobs were up for bids.

I could not understand why everybody was still hungry now that the war was over. Even business people were preoccupied with the thought of when we would have the next meal. We started each meal with a boiling hot consommé. I burned my mouth more times than I care to remember because I did not want to be late for the next dish. My favorite was Pêche Melba, peaches with vanilla ice cream in chocolate sauce.

Elisabeth Arden had a new cosmetic house on the Place Vendôme. A whole house, several stories high, to transform any woman into a beauty queen who entered and could afford it; at age thirteen, I was one of those who entered. "For the experience," Mother said, because it was decided that we would build one of those cosmetic institutes in Budapest when we arrived back home in Hungary, where we were the representatives for Elisabeth Arden.

Mother and I were led into separate small rooms. Without Mother's support, I was now at the mercy of the beautician. She cleansed me until my face felt naked. Then she plucked my eyebrows—it hurt. She did ask me about them, but I honestly did not know what she wanted to do to me. Grandmother did not approve of make-up and not even Mother wore much of it. At least she did not start until she was thirty-two years old and then only because Father liked it.

The beautician gave me some kind of treatment with a mask that hardened on my face, then she shocked both me and my skin with hot and cold towels. She then applied a creamy base foundation, as light as a feather, put lipstick on my lips, and powdered my face ... I looked into the mirror and I could not believe that it was I who looked back.

Mother was similarly transformed and they gave us each a package with all the cosmetics they had used on us. We were royally entertained by the firm on the Montmartre, where all tourists were warned that what they saw was not "scenery." These were real people living their everyday lives. The tiny old houses leaned on each other to support their crumbling walls. There were no curtains on some of the windows and as we walked past we would get a glimpse of old couples sitting around iron stoves, or eating their simple dinners.

There was screaming in one of the streets. I caught sight of two old women with ratty hair as they clawed away at each other. One slapped the other across the face—she fell down onto the cobblestones shouting French obscenities. Passersby just smiled and let them have their "innocent fun." "They are drunk." I heard them say as they moved on. The crooked streets led up to the Basilica of the Sacred Heart. Its dome and towers glowed in their pure white glory. A perfect contrast to the "bohème" quarters of artists who happily lived among the poor old couples and drunks in their cheap sublets or rooms for rent. Painters and artists enjoyed and immortalized Montmartre's little pubs and dancing places, where apache dancers threw their partners across the room only to recover them with a clever twist of their arms and legs. Lovers kissed under every doorpost and under the arches of old buildings. Nothing disturbed their passionate encounters.

The basilica looked upon all that as a wise parent would on their children and their antics. I recalled the story Uncle Joe's son, John, told when he showed us the altar where a picture of the Shroud of Turin was displayed. A young man, an atheist, asked God at this altar to show him that He existed. Nothing happened at the time but ten years later that same young man said his first Mass as a Catholic priest at this altar. He talked about his conversion in his first sermon. He believed it to be the miracle he had asked for.

I loved the story—it was perfect for the setting, for the surroundings.

Soon my attention was diverted. Our "night tour" had just started. From the apache dancers we went on to the Follies Bergère and the Casino de Paris. Everywhere in the audience I saw American soldiers with their girlfriends. Although the French were not overly enthusiastic about foreigners they did not mind their daughters going out with Americans. Neither the Follies Bergère nor the Casino de Paris needed any translation. Father asked me to translate for him but I noticed that by the time he heard my voice he was already laughing. He was laughing so hard I thought he would fall off his chair.

Beautiful girls danced in a row, their figures and legs perfect. They danced the can-can in black dresses lined with pink ruffles that flew above their heads as they kicked up their legs with the precision of a clock. The singing prima donna walked down a long staircase in the midst of the can-can girls and a long train of pink ostrich feathers rolled down after her as she descended.

I was convinced that the productions must have cost millions of dollars. All the chorus girls wore floor length white fur coats with a train as they paraded around the stage. One of their outfits had silver fox trimming. They danced and sang, then came down into the audience and surprised unsuspecting grandfather types by sitting on their laps.

Nudity was displayed tastefully—I saw very elegant strip-tease acts, where the woman would sing a song in period-costume of the days of a great painter, while a picture of the master was displayed in the background. She shed her clothes step by step, then just before she was completely naked the stage went dark. A minute later the lights went on again. She was a part of the picture now, fully naked.

Paris, the turbulent, vivacious leading lady of the world, captured my heart and my imagination. There was beauty and love, spring and riches. But there was a darker side also.

One day we visited good friends who had been part of the flow of refugees leaving Hungary in 1944. The father had been a member of the Parliament. The family, which had four girls, lived in a monastery, where the monks were good enough to give them a room. They said that the abbot was a remarkable man and so kind—he even talked with them. All other Frenchmen considered them "sales étrangers" or "dirty foreigners." They were waiting their turn as D.P.s (displaced persons) to go to Argentina and start a new life. Until then they lived on charity. They shared dinner with us—bread and the worst raspberry jam I had ever tasted. It came out of an unmarked can. Were they right to leave the country? Were we right to stay? Only the future would tell.

"I like him very much," Father said after we had left their place. "He was the only one who congratulated me on the birth of my third daughter. Everybody else felt sorry for me. Girls were not appreciated as much as boys. I'll never forget him for that."

As we walked along a shining avenue from one of the shop entrances a purplish lipstick-smeared mouth grinned at us. The teeth were scarce among the dried-up lips. Above it scarecrow-like gray hair and drunken eyes. The old beggar-woman stretched out her arm and tried to grab my clothes. She smelled of alcohol.

"Hurry," Mother pulled me away from her.

"What is she doing there? What does she want?" I asked.

"Don't look back," Mother warned, "She is drunk; she was probably a whore in her early days and feels that she is still beautiful and desirable when she is under the influence of liquor."

I did not look back, but I knew that I would never be able to forget her grinning, made-up face, the lacquer on her nails that made her look so different from the ordinary beggar women, and her clothes and behavior that made her one of them.

Impressions came and went as fast as I could take them in.

We walked down the Champs-Élysées, one of the best-known streets in the world, in all its springtime vivacity. The city had not quite regained its full splendor according to Mother but to me it was an enchanted fairyland. I had never seen anything so beautiful and exciting. At the end of the avenue I could see the Arc de Triumph and under it the Tomb of the Unknown Soldier. I remembered what this looked like from the Eiffel Tower. The Arc was the meeting point for seven avenues in the form of a star (Étoile) that gained its shine from cars pouring in and out of its center like a constant rhythmical flow of comets. At night the headlights, and during the day the sun, reflected in the windshields of the cars, provided this symphony of lights.

We tried to take a bus but it drove past the bus stop. The conductor waved at us indicating that all seats were taken. That was different! In Hungary, they let people hang from every side of the streetcar until they looked like a bunch of grapes, the same with busses. Here only as many passengers were allowed as could sit, or stand in comfort.

We finally took a cab and crossed the Seine through the bridge of Alexander III, with its golden statues on both sides of the river. That was my favorite bridge of the thirty-three that connected the two sides of Paris. We were on our way to the home of the Hungarian Consul where we met his landlord, his charming wife, and their daughter, Gisèle.

"So you want to come home with us to Hungary," Mother said to her.

"Yes, I would very much like to do that. My brother is working there as a lecturer at the University. His fiancée is a secretary at the Embassy; they plan to get married soon. I would like to visit them," said Gisèle, a twenty-three-year-old, skinny brunette with big, beautiful eyes, and a lovely mouth with a gleaming set of teeth that looked like a toothpaste ad. She smiled all the time. We could not help but like her.

The apartment was small by our standards but we learned that for Paris it was big—two rooms, furnished with dark furniture. Little sunshine came through the windows, maybe because it was afternoon. Gisèle's father owned several of these apartments. He had also been decorated with the Legion of Honor. Before we left he explained to us that it was very important to remember that a subway ticket could be used twice, we should never throw it out after having used it only once. He must have been very thrifty. Maybe this was how he made his fortune.

We did use the subway several times. It was speedy and efficient if you knew where you were going, but to figure that out was something else again! The subways went on different levels and huge maps hung at every station. The trains only stopped for a minute and off they swished. In a way the subway would have been frightening if it had not been for the joviality of the people. They casually kissed at every turn of the wide corridors, laughed, joked, and hurried, lived their lives in front of everybody and thought nothing of it.

Nowhere was this more apparent than in the Latin Quarter, around the university, where students marched along singing and would stop a couple in the middle of the road and would not let them go on until they had kissed.

The atmosphere of the little coffee houses spread on the sidewalks where people discussed politics, art, religion, and life in general, where history was in the making, captured my imagination. I was glad Gisèle was coming with us, then I would be able to come and visit her. She said so. My thoughts ran away with me into a not-so-distant future, when I would be one of the students and would attend the Sorbonne, I knew it was difficult but I liked challenges. I would make it to the Sorbonne…

The Rodin Museum opened a whole new world for me. There, in white marble, I saw love's every dream captured in a flowing movement. The stone, sculpted by a genius, lived, breathed, and kissed in a softly flowing hardness. It was man and woman making love in a most sublime way. "The Thinker," the "Burghers of Calais," "Laucon and His Sons," all immortal beauties of sculpture but I could not take my eyes off the most expressive and at the same time most discreet and lifelike representations of love. "The Kiss," "The Eternal Idol," and many others, some of them studies only half-developed with a mass of raw stone behind them. I was also impressed by "The Cathedral," a pair of hands forming an arch pointing towards Heaven, and the "Hand of God" with the first man and woman taking shape within its all-embracing palm.

The French impressionist paintings were a part of my artistic discoveries. I had studied them in Hungary and had seen many of the Hungarian paintings of this era but the wealth of the impressionist paintings in Paris, the capital of that movement, made me feel like a little child let loose in a candy store.

Mother taught me to love art and shared with me everything she knew about it. We walked among the blurry softly pastel-colored pictures with the mood of a misty afternoon and those that were set in crisp clean air with sharp, clear-cut edges. Some were painted with strong, wide strokes, others made up entirely of dots. All different styles united by the fact that they were created under the impression, the mood of the moment. The very same picture seen by two individuals could be as different as joy and sadness. A famous Hungarian poet wrote in those days, "Some rejoice and some brood, the whole world depends on mood." Mother's favorites were Degas, Manet, Monet, Cézanne, Renoir, Pissarro, Van Gogh, and a very colorful character, Gauguin. He had left his life as a banker and his family to take up residence in Tahiti and become a painter there. I could not understand how he could do that and, although I admired his paintings, I secretly condemned him for what he had done. However, amidst this outpouring of beauty I did not dwell on his personal life for long. I immersed myself entirely in the soft-colored air of the masterpieces, the powder blues and light greens mellowed by earthy dust contrasted by the fresh green of the new spring grass, the pinks of the sunsets and the yellows of cathedrals and peasant huts. Some of the pictures showed wintery landscapes in all the snow-colors of the rainbow. The mood of the master prevailed in the tones and textures of every piece. The people in the pictures stood out, or blended in with the landscape according to the message of the artist.

It was hard to tell which memory was the most beautiful! Was it the cathedral of Notre Dame? The outside light filtered through its rosetta-shaped stained glass windows leaving the church in eternal twilight. One's eyes were drawn naturally to the beauty of these intricate masterpiece-filters, the sources of light in the darkness. The cathedral's delicate, lacy, and gargoyled structure that served as the scenery for the Hunchback of Notre Dame, was the subject for many of the young and old artists, who sat around on the Left Bank and painted away, some to sell their pictures to tourists, some not even thinking of parting with their work.

Everywhere souvenir vendors regarded the tourists as fair prey, including us of course. They sold small mass-manufactured sculptures of every sight in Paris, and little globes of glass with the Eiffel Tower in it. If I turned it over snow fell in the little ball. I was enchanted by it because I had never seen that kind of tourist trap before. Mother bought me one and we bought a few odds and ends for my sisters also. When we asked for the price the woman would not accept French money. She quoted the price of the souvenir in every conceivable type of money except French. Inflation was bad in France and she was not going to let us get away without getting some of our currency.

It was Good Friday when we happened to visit the firm of Lucien Lelong. Although they did not have a fashion show on Good Friday, they staged one just for the two of us. I was fascinated by the models. They told me that all they ate in a day was two hard-boiled eggs, they drank as much tea as they pleased, and were allowed to eat any fruit they liked. Gorgeous dresses and evening gowns, coats, and outfits for every possible occasion were shown.

"Helen, I think you should try on that red coat," Mother said.

"Me!?

"Yes, your coat must be awfully warm for March in this climate. Go ahead, try it!"

I slipped on the coat and it fit me like a glove. It was tightly fitted around the waist and padded around the hips to accentuate the waistline.

"Oh, it's so beautiful! Can I really have it? You mean that? Do you want to buy it?"

We got a good deal on it because it was the one the model used in the displays.

I had a coat from a big French House of Haute Couture! All of this and I was just thirteen years old. I believed that I must be the luckiest girl in the universe. So much happiness. How did I deserve all that? I knew that I did not do anything and I was the more grateful to God for giving it to me. Somewhere deep down I also heard a voice, that of my teacher: "Those who receive more are expected to give more." I tried to be aware day and night of how much I had received and I had the intention to give when the time came.

Finally the day arrived that I had dreaded. We were on the train again in the gray of a Paris morning. The slick aluminum trains glided in and out of the station, the people swarmed like bees, some of them hesitating, others marching ahead with determination. This time I saw everything through a cloud of tears which were running down my cheeks as I listened to the clickety-clack of the accelerating train.

# 24

Gisèle stood by my side as the train pulled into Vienna. Since leaving Paris, we spent every moment looking out the window, talking, discovering new landscapes, and each other.

"It's hard to believe that you are only thirteen," Gisèle said more than once.

Sometimes it was hard for me to believe, too; I had lived through so much, enough for a lifetime. The first time we went through Vienna I saw only glimpses of Elsie's hometown through the windows of the speeding train. This time we got off the train. Again I saw the dreaded Soviets' uniforms and the traditional machine guns on the platform. The realization that we were again under their occupation hit me in the head. It made me remember a scene between Mother and Father that I had witnessed on the train when we were still in Switzerland, on our way home.

Father had begged Mother, "Let us pull the emergency brake! I'll gladly pay the penalty for it! I don't think we should go home!"

"How about our other children, our parents?" Mother asked.

"They can escape by car, I have it all worked out, a friend who serves as a policeman near the border promised me, only please, let's not go back…"

"But our country, all that we have… We have nothing here…We don't know anybody, we would be home there…"

"Everything can be replaced but life itself. I heard that the factories were all nationalized in Hungary while we were away. We are next. You know that."

"I do, and yet, I do not believe it. I can't believe that everything will turn against us. We did not hurt anybody. We have so much going for us."

"Baba," Father called her by that affectionate nickname. "Listen to me. It is not too late to remain here."

Apparently Mother had won because we did not get off the train. Now we were back among the Soviet uniforms.

We got off in Vienna with our luggage, including Gisèle's suitcase, fourteen pieces of luggage in all. The remains of the war struck us with a sharp suddenness as our cab drove to the hotel through rows of houses in ruin. The glass panes of the revolving doors were replaced by thin sheets of wood. The deskclerk informed us that the glass had been shot through the day before by the Soviet patrol. This part of the city was guarded on alternate weeks by one of the Great Powers: the United States, Great Britain, France, and the Soviets. Last night it was the Soviets. He whispered the information and looked over his shoulder before he spoke.

"Keep your door locked at all times," Father warned Gisèle and me.

He did not need to warn us; we held hands all night and even barricaded the door.

❧

Schönbrunn was a famous royal residence right outside Vienna and we wanted to see it. As it turned out it was packed with English-speaking soldiers who lived there. How would we get in?

"Gisèle, would you try? Could you say that you are French and would like to see it? You are one of their allies, France is one of the occupying forces."

"But my English is so bad," Gisèle was embarrassed.

"Never mind, we'll help you if they can't make out what you say."

Gisèle approached the guard at the door with her passport and started to explain in her broken English.

The guard, realizing that she was French, interrupted her and said, "Hurry, hurry, the French group is already on its way with the guide, you can still join them."

We did not wait another second but ran after the group that had just disappeared around the corner. It turned out that the French Ambassador's friends were coming to visit the palace that day and the guard mistook us for part of their company. They did not mind and we were happy to be able to see the treasures of the Austrian Emperor's, (Hungarian king's,) summer castle.

Among the beautiful crystal chandeliers and enormous paintings stood bunk beds. On them lay smiling soldiers, taking their leisurely afternoon siesta, or playing cards. Some of them even tried to talk to us in English.

Our guide, a very knowledgeable old Austrian lady, who spoke both French and English fluently, explained the story of the rooms and the furniture which was pushed out of the way in order to accommodate the soldiers.

Finally we were down in the stables, where the carriages were kept. There were no more soldiers present and the lady felt visibly more at ease. She talked freely about the old days when royalty moved around the spic and span palace instead of jovial soldiers who, no matter how careful they were, at least according to her, desecrated the place by their mere presence.

It was interesting to see the difference between Vienna and Budapest. In Budapest, people dressed in their best clothes, in Vienna they still wore their fur coats inside out, like we did in 1945. Our guide had her coat on that way, tied in the middle with a piece of string. A sure sign that she was still afraid of the crime called "undressing," as we had been in Hungary in 1945.

In Vienna, the rebuilding of the city had not yet started by 1948. In the Opera a small light burned day and night and symbolized their intention to rebuild it, although nobody actually did anything.

There was no food, or hardly any besides the white bread the Americans made available. Clothing was scarce. Uncle Gábor, a good friend of ours who took us around explained, "Did you notice that everybody wears Tyrolean folkcostumes? These are the only clothes, these drab-gray suits with green felt ornaments, that are sold without rations. Other clothes can be bought for rations, obtainable only if one proves that they do not have anything else to wear. Another way of buying clothes is with dollars, but to own dollars is illegal."

"That is a contradiction, isn't it?" I asked.

"It definitely is. Now come with me and I'll show you another contradiction—a place where you can eat, even though there is no food." With that, he led us into a restaurant. People sat around but there was nothing visible to eat. He greeted the owner noisily and walked straight across the restaurant, then out the back door which opened into another place with nicely set tables and contented people eating real food, for dollars. Its quality was not nearly as good as our own food in Hungary, but at least it was edible.

In the evening, we went to an unforgettable show with Marika Rökk. She was a singing, dancing star of Hungarian origin, and she had a complete two-hour show with her company. I saw the best-danced "csárdás," a well-known Hungarian national dance, right there, in Vienna. The twirling, colorful flying ribbons, the red boots kicking in the air, the girls' long braids flapping around reminded me of Cegléd, of the good days at home, and I suddenly felt the same way Mother did. I wanted to go home because something deep down hurt and smiled at the same time. Yes, this was what it meant to be a Hungarian, to be happy and sad at once, to have an unquenchable desire to go back where one could only get hurt. It was the only place on this earth where life was worth living.

When we came out of the theater, the Soviet uniforms woke me up from my dreams of homesickness and patriotism. As we walked along the Kärtnerring, one of the main avenues in Vienna, in our Paris fashions, Gisèle and I a few steps ahead of Mother and Father, a young man tried to pick us up in Hungarian, I had to laugh. I could do it easily with protection right behind me. It seemed that everywhere we had to meet compatriots.

The nightclub after the show was reminiscent of the war. The poor little girl who was the ballerina must have been very young, fifteen at the most, and she looked as if she had borrowed her mother's clothes for the performance.

The only good number was a black couple from America, beautiful people, singing Open the Door, Richard in a most unusual manner, questioning and answering each other, playing with the harmony and melody, twisting the rhythm into different molds.

I saw Elsie for only a moment. The people for whom she worked were deathly afraid that we might take her with us and leave them without anybody to take care of their retarded daughter. We cried and laughed for the short time we were together. We had to enjoy the physical presence of each other. Then it was all over.

We were on our way back to Hungary. Was it the right decision?

As the train approached the capital, I pointed out landmarks to Gisèle. I made an unsuccessful attempt to find a tall mountain in Budapest. On top of it stood a big memorial that was supposed to be the angel of peace. Unfortunately, by the time it was finished the Soviets occupied Hungary, and added the statue of a Soviet soldier which stood right under the angel, guarding it with his "dovoy-guitar" (machine gun)! Anyway, I could not find the mountain no matter how hard I tried. Then I saw the monument and I told Gisèle,

"You see that monument? There was a hill under that when I left. I guess that little mole hill underneath it must be the one. I never realized how tiny a 300-foot "mountain" can be after one comes back from the Alps."

Gisèle laughed and said, "I am sure this is how I'll feel when I go back to Paris and try to find the Montmartre."

We were home. The car waited at the station and Grandmother and my sisters were overwhelmed. We had to tell them all about our trip, until they fell asleep listening, and we ran out of things to say. There was another important and delightful obligation; we had to make Gisèle feel welcome.

Now, that has never been difficult for a Hungarian. All we had to do was notify all our friends that we had a foreign visitor and we had no more problems for the rest of her stay. Invitations poured in one after another, and we ourselves had at least three parties a week at our house—not only for business purposes but also to entertain our new-found friend.

Alec, my second cousin, who was a war refugee in Germany and told me about the American occupation when he returned, showed up more often. I think he must have taken a liking to Gisèle because he claimed he wanted to practice his French. In the meantime, I was Gisèle's constant companion and learned simultaneous translation without realizing it. It was disturbing at first because I had to think about what I was doing, but after a couple of weeks it became second nature to me—I translated everything I heard into French, including the theater plays we attended. Finally, I started to translate to my best friend during class and she whispered, "Hey, I understand what the teacher said." That's when I realized that I no longer had to think in order to translate.

It was one of our usual three-times-a-week dinners, Gisèle and I helped set the table with the embroidered lace-laden tablecloth that covered the table which was opened to its "usual" dinner-size to seat twenty-four people. Then out came the Rosenthal china set that was bought especially for my parents' engagement celebration when they had a sit-down dinner for sixty people. The baroque silver was glittering in the rays of the crystal and bronze chandelier. Members of the government, including the prime minister, were our guests today. One of them did his best to get into the good graces of Gisèle.

The first guests started coming. Paul, Gisèle's brother, was dark and slim with big dark-gray eyes that spoke of compassion. His fiancée, Françoise, had blondish brown hair with blue eyes, was quick, easy-to-please, always smiling. We enjoyed their company. They had arrived before the other guests—they were on time, not like the Hungarians.

One of our guests brought her sister along and introduced her, "This is Marion Mill-Preminger. She has just arrived from America. She was the wife of Otto Preminger and she comes straight from Hollywood. I'm sorry but she can only use the informal 'you.' She has been away for so long she has forgotten the formal one."

I could not take my eyes off this American wonder. Nobody seemed to care that she had forgotten how to speak with the formal "you" which used to be very important. However, we understood that in English there was only one kind of "you." She was tall and her waist was so thin it seemed that I could reach around it with only one hand. Her hair was platinum blonde. She must have noticed my admiration for her because she started to talk to me.

"You would be just right in Hollywood. Your eyebrows are exactly one eye-length apart. That is how they re-make all the starlets and stars once they get into their first make-up session with the beauticians. Then everything about their lives is regulated. They have to walk so many steps a day, do such and such exercises—there is not much freedom in their lives. I know, I was in films."

"You were?" I hardly dared to answer her.

"Yes," She did not seem to be as impressed about Hollywood as I was. "Tell me more," I begged her.

"Hollywood is fascinating, I guess, but there are so many other worthwhile things to do. I've had enough of life there. Here I see that for 150 dollars one can easily live for a month. As a matter of fact, one can live like a millionaire, while at home that was about one quarter of what we paid for our florist bill."

"Florist bill?" I kept wondering what in the world one would do with that many flowers.

"Yes," she skimmed over that.

I kept thinking of the fact that she had actually been the wife of Otto Preminger, the great film director. I felt that I acted stupidly; all my learned lady-likeness seemed to disappear, but she seemed to take a liking to me. Maybe it was because of my childlike adoration of her.

"Look at my purse. See, it is made in the shape of a letter that is addressed to me. It even has stamps on it, embroidered ones. That is the latest fashion in America."

"That is smart," I said. "Is it all right if I make one like that for my sisters and myself?"

"Go ahead!" she laughed. "The sincerest expression of flattery is imitation," she added in English, maybe not expecting me to understand, but I answered her in English and that made us good friends.

We met often after that, next time at the Opera. Gisèle and I loved to go to the Opera and this was a special performance of Lucia di Lammermoor with Mária Gyurkovits, the greatest coloratura soprano in the country, and one of the best in the world. After the performance, she got many offers to go abroad, but she did not want to leave behind her two teenage daughters and her conductor husband, Miklós Forrai.

We drove to the Opera in the chauffeur-driven Mercedes and sat in a box of the golden horseshoe. In the intermission, we walked around in the white marble halls, between the thick pillars and the enormous paintings that covered the walls. The discussions were subdued and those who did not look for subjects of gossip through their opera glasses discussed the music and singers they had just heard. On such trips to the Opera, Gisèle was often invited into the governmental box where complete dinners were served in the back. Or else we would find friends and discuss our plans for the days to come. Were our friends, who sat in the governmental box, going to take away our stores? Would they bring our end? Today Mária Gyurkovits sang the difficult trills, her voluminous tone embraced the whole building yet it sounded light as the song of a bird on a spring morning. In the Opera the bride, misled by her brother, had agreed to marry the rich man he had chosen for her. On her wedding day, after she had pronounced her vows, her love returned. This return was the occasion for one of classical music's masterpieces: the sextet from Lucia di Lammermoor. Then to top it off came the aria during which she went insane in front of the audience while relating the story of how she had stabbed her husband to death on their wedding night.

While Gisèle was enthralled by her sudden social popularity, I got so engulfed in the music that I wished more than ever that my parents were not so rich, that I could become whatever I wanted to be, which of course for the time being, was an opera singer. Whether I would be able to do it did not even occur to me, so strong was the feeling in me that it was impossible even if I had the talent. The lights glistened through the myriads of the glittering crystals of the chandelier. The standing ovation lasted for at least ten minutes. Marion, as Mrs. Preminger wanted me to call her, said that this was the best performance of "Lucia" she had ever seen. She was the one who told me about the foreign contracts offered to the singer.

Another member of the company asked Gisèle, "Do you want to come to Boldog this weekend and see the people in their folk costumes as they go to church?"

"I'd love to." Gisèle could not stop talking to me about the time when this same gentleman was invited to a peasant wedding and took her. There were 500 guests and the event lasted for days. They only stayed a day and a half but when they had left the dancing was still going strong. "It was amazing how much they had to eat and drink at that wedding and only three years after the war, too. They brought one dish after another and the gypsies played. Happy tunes for the dancers and slow ones to eat and drink by. I can't remember the names of the foods but there were different kinds of sausages, smoked ones and blood sausages, liver ones and fresh ones. Then they had cabbage leaves filled with meat and rice and beef, or was it calf, in a red sauce with sour cream… Oh, they were excellent."

"Sounds like veal paprikás and cabbage rolls to me," I said.

"Then they 'sold' the bride. Somebody stood there with a hat and whoever wanted to dance with the bride had to pay. But naturally everybody had to dance with her. They collected thousands of forints that way. I think they needed it too with all the expenses that must have been involved."

"I'll bet."

"You should have seen all the beautiful dresses they wore. The bride's dress was embroidered with flowers erupting with the loudest colors that were tempered by the gold and green of the leaves and the stems, entwined by their own stalks and given over to the imagination of their creator."

"You know, Gisèle, that most of these dresses are designed by the wearer herself, or a member of her family, and that they themselves embroider it during the long winter nights, when they cannot work outside. There is not much else they can do during winters. They cast all their dreams, love, and creativity into these individual beauties."

"It is unbelievable and so beautiful, I wish I could etch it into my memory forever because I don't think any of them would want to part with a dress like that."

246

"No, not these dresses, but we may be able to find something you can take home with you to at least remind you of the beauties you encountered here."

When we went to Boldog—this time I was allowed to go with them—we took a movie camera, loaded with color film. At least Gisèle would be able to show her parents a glimpse of what she had seen.

I had never been to Boldog and when we parked the car and the girls came one by one in the layers and layers of skirts, swinging their hips rhythmically, I had to pinch myself to be convinced that what I saw was not a dream. These were real people in clothes they had made themselves, going to church. Many of them had started to make these dresses when they were only eight years old.

This village had a different pattern of embroidery than the one Gisèle saw at the wedding. Their snow-white stoles wound around them and brought behind their backs had thousands of holes tightly surrounded by stitches. They formed intricate patterns of stylized flowers and butterflies, the starched puffy white sleeves enhanced the dark colored flowery skirts pleated in infinitesimally small pleats. Flower-embroidered ribbons hung from their elaborate headdresses. The heads of the married women were completely covered while the unmarried ones showed their hair in the back. In their folded hands they carried big prayerbooks that contained the hymns they were going to sing after they filed into church, men to the right side pews and women to the left. The men were dressed all in black; they had not a trace of color on their festive clothes.

"Look, Helen, isn't that beautiful?" Gisèle whispered as her movie camera whirred beside me.

Some of the women looked at us and smiled but most of them were busy with one purpose, to reach the church and take their places there before Mass started.

"All this in the twentieth century! I can't believe that this is true," Gisèle exclaimed.

"Well, they don't wear these every day," said our escort. "Weekdays they dress in very sensible clothes. They all work in the fields but when the Lord's Day comes they revert to their age-old tradition. I hope they will keep it up for a long time to come."

"Gisèle, look at these little ones! Aren't they cute?" I screamed as quietly as I could manage. A few little girls appeared in similar, though not as elaborate, clothes. They were still growing, there was no sense in making them clothes that would require extensive work.

The church bell started ringing. It was time to go in. Before we went in I looked back. The road that had been full of color and swinging skirts only a few minutes before was completely empty now. Besides our parked car only a few hens were scratching the dust and some lazy dogs enjoyed the sun of the early summer. Lilac bushes bloomed beside small whitewashed houses. In front of every cottage stood a bench—a place for the head of the house and his wife to sit on Sunday afternoons, or after work on weekdays in the summer, when the sun did not set until late.

Inside the organ started to play; the hymn announced the beginning of the service.

Alec happened to come by every day that spring, even though it was exam time at the university where he studied now to become an engineer. He brought lilacs to Gisèle and always managed to "practice his French" with her one way or another. Sometimes they went to the movies, then to the confectioner's. He was younger than Gisèle but they seemed to enjoy each other's company. Then, suddenly, a young manufacturer became Gisèle's favorite, and he would come every day with his accordion. We had lots of fun with him also, and Alec did not stop coming, except he spent more time with me now, and the next batch of flowers he could find in his mother's garden were for me instead of Gisèle. I did not mind it—I enjoyed being noticed.

We had something to do every day of Gisèle's three month stay and the time for her to leave came quickly. We had a tearful send-off. The next year I was going to spend the summer with her on the Riviera and in Paris, continuing our dream-in-real-life. Life was beautiful and it was going to stay that way.

## 25

Gisele's departure brought an end to our dream world. The gray clouds closed in on me on my way home from school, the early summer air was pregnant with storm. A lone bolt of lightning zigzagged through the sky above the roofs of the drab houses as I crossed the Museum Boulevard to reach our downtown home. Our hillside home in Buda was still rented to the French Embassy. We paid only occasional visits to the house that used to be our summer residence, when we were invited to the military attaches parties, who lived there now.

On that stormy day in June, 1948, I came in through the back door, as we usually did when coming home from school. It was quicker and we did not need to ring the bell for the maid; the back door was open. Nobody knew about its existence as we went through the doorway of an apartment house and then through its cobblestoned backyard to reach a small door through the ancient city wall. When Grandfather built our house he was told that the old city wall was so strong it would have to be dynamited if he ever wanted to get rid of it, besides it was a historic landmark with nice paintings on one side. This door must have been a life saver before and undoubtedly it would be again if time came.

"Is that you, Helen?" Mother asked. "Come here, I want to talk to you." She pulled me out onto the balcony, even though by now big, fat raindrops had started to fall. "I want to talk to you privately. You know what you have always meant to me, I must tell you something."

I listened eagerly. It was not the first time Mother had told me more than my sisters but this time she really seemed distressed. "It's about Grandmother. The doctor said that he wanted to remove her breast. It's probably cancer. Grandmother does not want any of you to know about it but I could not keep it from you."

Mother looked worried; wrinkles appeared in the middle of her alabaster forehead and her eyes mirrored fear.

"Cancer?" I felt my stomach in my throat and my feet take root in the ground. "What are we going to do?"

Mother looked helpless. She dropped her head on my shoulder and shook with sobs for a few seconds then straightened and wiped her eyes.

"We must not cry. She would notice if we did. We should trust in God and in his mercy. She is not old yet. She has so much going for her."

I still could not speak but I held her close. Then it occurred to me that she needed me as a replacement for Grandmother. She came to me because she could not go to Grandmother, at least not with this problem.

"You can count on me. You can tell me anything you wish, always," I whispered. I still did not cry. I seldom did. I remembered that once, when I was five years old, I cut myself. I was hurting but, for the first time, I did not cry. I simply said, "Let's get the iodine." I remembered clearly now that I stopped crying because I realized that it would not hurt less, it would not help me in any way to cry. I was called a hero then, because I did not cry. I remembered Jesus' words of the Sermon on the Mount, "Which one of you can live a few more years by worrying about it?" We had just finished studying it at school. We had to learn the whole sermon word-by-word. Was it for occasions like this? To remember them as long as we lived?

Mother squeezed my hand. I smiled. Our simple ceremony was the beginning of a strong alliance between us.

It was much easier now for her to face the rest of the family!

"Grandmother has to go to the hospital for surgery. We have to pray hard for her but she will be all right."

Marie and Elisabeth snuggled close to Grandmother when they heard the news but they did not hear the menacing opinion of the doctors. They could smile back at Grandmother and honestly believe that there was nothing to fear. Grandmother pretended beautifully.

She was the one who kept everything away from us children, whatever could have frightened us. That task had been difficult during the war but she had done her best. Now she was the first one whom we would see after major surgery. But, by the time we were allowed to see her she was full of smiles and talked about the good time she had at the hospital.

"I could not believe the surgery was over. When I woke up I thought they had not even started yet. You know how much I disliked the idea of general anesthesia. I remember being stuck with a needle for the Evipan and then I woke up in my room. That naughty doctor, I'll never forgive him. 'Look, what he did.' I asked him what these little red dots were on my skin. He said that while I was asleep he fastened a sheet there with a safety pin because it always got in his way."

Grandmother laughed and made us all feel comfortable. Even Mother looked relieved.

Everything seemed all right, when another fear materialized from the blue sky. Our building was finally rebuilt. Time became ripe for the Communists to harvest the fruit of our labor of love.

At school Reverend Mother gathered us all in the auditorium and announced:

"The schools are going to be nationalized beginning at the end of this school year."

When Reverend Mother talked nobody dared to utter a sound as a rule but this time the behavior of a beehive would not describe the chaos that resulted from her words. She could not continue. Everybody was crying, yelling, screaming at once:

"They can't do that to us!"

"They can't take away what we built!"

"We did not do it for 'them'!"

"What about you, Reverend Mother? What is going to happen to our teachers?"

"We will not let 'them' do it."

What indeed? If Cardinal Mindszenty's arguments could not stop them, what could we do? Nobody knew the answer. It was not in our power to tell the Communists how we felt.

I did tell the members of the Government who were invited to our ornate parties, but naturally, that too was in vain. Did they really have the power to do something or were they under the complete control of the Soviets? The frosty palm of fear closed tightly around my throat whenever I thought of this. Were we all, irrevocably, in the power of the enemy? Were Father's predictions going to materialize?

In the meantime, the school year drew close to the end. It was time for the traditional "wandering." Members of the graduating class "wandered" around the building singing age-old student-songs like the well-known "Gaudeamus igitur," always sung in Latin, and the "wandering song" that brought tears to eyes of the most unfeeling people because it reminded them of their own school-days, of growing up, of becoming a citizen in whose hands lay the future of the nation. But this song did not look forward. Instead, it was sad, acquiescing in the fact that we all have to outgrow being carefree students, children. Many other songs were composed by the students, or familiar melodies reworked for the occasion. The girls, in full uniform, with flowers in their hands, would walk from classroom to classroom and sing about the fun times, the problems, the adventures they had in each room.

The seniors always cried as did their parents and teachers who came to see the parade.

This year was different in one big way. Instead of being envious of those graduating we all "wandered" with them in spirit. It was our last year in this school also, at least in its present form. What would it be like next year? Nobody knew but nobody wanted to think about it either.

"Remember when we went to first grade?" Olga beside me asked.

"Mother Olafson was our teacher," I said. "I always wanted to be a nun then because I loved the way she stood in front of the chapel and drew crosses in the air with her hand. It took me a while before I realized that she was conducting the choir."

Olga laughed through her tears.

"Do you remember Mother Gyalus, the little old Mother? She was already old when she taught my aunt, when she went to third grade," I said.

Agnes, who sat next to Olga, reminisced about second grade, "Aunt Esther's second grade was something everybody liked. Remember when she told us about the soapsavers during the war? How she explained the way to save water?"

"That was when we played lion," Mary said, "The way we used to slide down the corridors."

It was everybody's favorite pastime, even today when we thought we could do it unnoticed.

"Do you remember when Mother Jármay, our Reverend Mother, hid and we were supposed to look for her on Playday?"

"We all had to give up finally and she showed up in peasant-girl clothes. We just did not recognize her. She sat there at the door eating a bowl of soup, in plain sight, while we were searching the whole building."

"She is quite a woman," said Olga.

"What will happen to her?"

"Will they be allowed to stay in the building?"

"What does it mean when schools become nationalized?"

"Remember how we passed the bricks while rebuilding the school?"

"Planted the grass on the square?"

"Who has the right to take this from us?"

Questions and memories floated through the air as the seniors passed through our class singing and choking with sobs, as their voices died down at the end of the hall, down the staircase, around the corridors, the gymnasium, the auditorium, in and out of classrooms and study halls, through the chapels, the terrace, and the yard until they reached the entrance door. They touched all the places of their childhood memories. The world that would meet them today was not the one they had expected to face when they first entered this building.

As they looked back from the entrance door a statue of Jesus looked back at them with outstretched arms. It told them without words not to be afraid of anything because wherever their way would lead them He was "the way, the truth, and the life."

~

Then we were all together for the final graduation ceremony. Several hundred girls from first grade to the twelfth all dressed exactly alike, in navy blue pleated skirts and our festive, white blouses with a navy blue necktie. As we sat down on the low benches, in a semi-circle, all at once at the signal of our teacher, our skirts opened up like fans and covered all legs and feet uniformly around the huge auditorium.

We heard Mother Prefect's voice from the back saying the usual words before the prizes were awarded: "The glory is God's alone."

For the last time we were together, celebrating in a bitter-sweet mood.

We held onto every minute as the events raced by during this last hour of togetherness.

Time came to say good-bye. Mother Haraszthy, my favorite teacher, said, "Don't cry," through her pouring tears. "You will see, we'll be back together in a year or so, you'll see…"

Although it was strictly forbidden at other times to kiss in school we all embraced and hugged. Then it was over and the door closed quietly behind the last pleated skirt.

~

We swam, danced, and flirted our way through summer together with the usual crowd, most importantly for me with Alec and Pista. September was here too soon and we were back at our school which had been renamed. instead of the Convent of the Sacred Heart it was called now Mikszáth Kálmán Girls' High School, after a well-known Hungarian writer, mainly because the school was located on the square named after him. Our old teachers were still there, in their usual living quarters, on the other side of the building, but the doors were locked and walls were being built in order to separate us from them.

We met our new principal and the teacher, Miss Julie, who represented the security police inasmuch as her husband was one of them. We learned from our mustachioed little principal who liked to shout at the top of his lungs, that we were to study everything from now on in the one true way, from a Marxist-Leninist point of view. One of our major subjects would be Marxism-Leninism, another political economics, and we would learn biology in the only true interpretation, according to that of the Soviet scientist, Lisenko. With his lecture he put in a few swear words to give momentum to his speech.

After school we visited our old teachers who greeted us with great joy. Mother Haraszthy exclaimed, "When in Berlin Hitler nationalized our school, the graduates and the students did not come back to see us like you do."

We learned many things from the Mothers. First, we were told that some of the graduating seniors entered the novitiate, which then was flown abroad. They were no longer on Hungarian soil, no longer subject to harassment by the government.

"Most Mothers who are still here are Swiss or German citizens," Mother Haraszthy whispered. "Don't talk loudly. We are being watched." She pointed towards the open window.

We had our "Veni Sancte" mass to start school as usual. The only difference was that this time we had to come secretly and Mother Waldeskirchen got up and closed the windows when she noticed that the Communist teachers were taking pictures and watching with binoculars.

The next day at school, after our lesson in Marxism-Leninism, we were outside on the terrace for recess when I, and some other classmates who were elected by the others to be the class leaders, were asked to go to the principal. We were made to help him search the briefcases of the other children to see if they had offensive stuff, like holy pictures, with them. Whenever we found something we thought might "offend" our principal who was great at four-letter words but not so hot for religion, we hid it in our pockets and threw it out onto the corridor for other students to make it disappear before he noticed.

Our class had nothing special to hide but in eleventh grade there was a girl who refused to open her briefcase. The principal threatened to expel her if she did not let them search it. She refused and was expelled. We learned later that she had all the nuns' documents in the briefcase because her parents were trying to get them passports to leave the country.

Then came the interrogations. Miss Julia, the new teacher, her husband, the security policeman, and the principal, who turned out to be an ex-seminarian who turned against the Church, jointly questioned one girl at a time about their parents' activities, about their friends, the nuns, or simply ridiculous topics like what the difference would be between the missions and the pioneer-movement (a Communist youth group). The girl, a seventh grader, who was asked that question said that it was impossible to brush one's teeth with either of them. Not even answers like that discouraged our stern principal. He was out to prove that he would erase all semblance of discipline and encourage everything that would destroy the image of our school.

During Marxism-Leninism class we learned the "necessary and unavoidable" progress of mankind towards communism from the day that the first monkey had picked up a tool and decided to become a man.

Tuesday evenings I had great fun discussing our lessons with Uncle Stephen and Uncle Charles.

"Today we learned, I think it was in history, it is hard to distinguish the classes anymore because we learn the same thing over and over in every subject. Anyway, they said that Lenin's goal was communism but right after the revolution he found it necessary to teach a lesson to the ruling class. He declared the dictatorship of the proletariat. During this period, the country was building socialism. Apparently they are still building it. We were told that socialism is when everybody works as hard as they can and earn as much as he worked for. Then, when the country would reach that stage, socialism, they would start building communism. Communism, they said, was when one worked as hard as he could but received everything he needed regardless of his achievement. Now, if Lenin wanted communism, why didn't he establish that kind of society? After all he changed everything. Why didn't he do what he set out to do?"

"I hope you did not ask this question from your teacher," Uncle Stephen said. "I suppose she is the same teacher you used to have."

"Yes, she only teaches from different books."

"Don't ever embarrass her. She reads what is in the book and tells you that. Besides, the Communists would never let her read up on it now, if she had not done so before. Even if she knew I doubt that she would dare to tell you what I will tell you now. Lenin had recognized, even before the revolution broke out, that idealistic communism, 'everyone according to his talents, to everyone according to his needs,' was a utopia. It required sainthood from people who at the same time had to be convinced that God was nonexistent. I will give you an example. Let's say there is a young brain surgeon who loves his job and keeps at it all day. When he does not operate he reads up on the latest developments. What does he need? A bed to sleep in and nourishment to hold his body together. He is unmarried, he lives for his profession. There is another man, a street-sweeper, who is lazy and claims that he is chronically ill. He works only three to four hours a day, while he has five children and a genuinely sick wife. The children need food, clothing, the wife requires a nurse-maid. How long will it take the young brain surgeon to find out that he is working only to keep these people in money? How long will he accept this when he does not even have the benefit or knowledge of the commandment 'Love thy neighbor?' This is why Lenin released and sanctioned all revenge at first, institutionalizing it under the name of the 'dictatorship of the proletariat.' Even if people had no food in the beginning and not enough of anything, they were occupied by living out their anger against those who had money during the Tsar's regime. Later on that revenge was extended to anybody whom the proletariat disliked, including many of the teachers, doctors, engineers. When the new generation of certain professions grew up the old one was persecuted and annihilated."

"The Soviet Union has not reached the stage of socialism yet," said Uncle Charles. "They claim that socialism is when everybody works according to his talents and gets paid according to his work. But what, may I ask, happened in democratic countries all over the world until now? Didn't we all get paid according to our work? And I am saying that, as someone whose father was a poor shoemaker in Cegléd. Still, I am a doctor and we both, my father and myself, always got paid according to our work if you ask me. Why can't the Soviet Union still not do that? What kind of equality do they have? And why do we have to go through this 'dictatorship of the proletariat' to put something as a goal at the end of our suffering that we already had for decades?" I watched his always white, fine face redden with anger as his voice became louder and louder.

The way Uncle Stephen explained it, Lenin sounded more sensible than what we had learned at school. Lenin was a wise man. He claimed that if there had been only a thousand people in Russia who knew exactly what they wanted to do, had a plan for the country, then communism could not have taken over. Lenin must have known why he re-wrote Marxism and created Marxism-Leninism.

"Helen, don't utter a word of what you have heard," said Grandmother. "You might get us all into trouble. Just recite your lesson as you were taught if you are asked at school."

Just then Father came in and started to eat his supper hurriedly. His movements were jerky. He was always rushed and Mother said that he could not sleep at night even though he took five or six sleeping pills. Whenever a car went by the house during the night he would jump out of bed. Even though we paid police-informers, he was never sure what to expect. The constant threat of nationalization loomed over us.

When Father was around now I tried to become invisible, non-existent. I was afraid that he might burst out in anger at the slightest innocent move or remark.

We still entertained the members of the government and of the diplomatic corps but I no longer asked them questions or informed them about things that bothered me. I felt that they too were helpless in face of a different, much stronger power. I sensed that they were simply trying to save face, to rescue as much of their own hide as they could.

One exception was when I told the representatives of the Geigy Co. that it was not very wise for them to show their patent to the government because it would be stolen. They just smiled at the remarks a child would make then a few days later they sent an apology with Mother. They asked her to tell me that I was right.

The more I feared for the future the more I immersed myself in work. As I was going to take over the business some day if we still owned it then, I began to go to druggist-school twice a week in the afternoon. This was a vocational school, established by Grandfather. A druggist (not a pharmacist) had to study ten years while also working at a drugstore in order to become a master in his profession. He needed to know all the herbs and chemical substances sold in the store. He also had to know how to prepare ointments, perfumes, and the like, and had to study general subjects like language and health.

On other days I studied commercial correspondence in German, French, and English. By that time I knew how to type and I tried my skills at basic shorthand in Hungarian and German.

All of these activities did not keep me away from boys. On weekdays I had great fun studying science with the ones who dropped in for various reasons.

Alec came every day to see if there was something he could help with. Pista dropped by at least two to three times a week and helped me with Latin; he wanted to become a lawyer. Tommy also visited several times a week and we started to have those good times together I always daydreamed about in Magyaróvár.

We all went to "dancing school." That was fun and a welcome relief from everyday drudgery. We could forget school, the Communists, the war, and just swirl around at the tune of the latest hits on the pretense that we were "learning" to dance. The instructor did not even pretend to teach us; we were all good dancers.

Mary, my best friend whom I nicknamed "Bonzi," and I went everywhere together. We became known as the "Siamese twins." We were both very good students and we sat beside each other in school. She was three years older than I was but nobody would have noticed that because she had a puffy baby-face that was a result of her kidney troubles. This was the reason why she was behind in school. I introduced her to boy-girl parties. She confided in me later that she was very hesitant to come to the first one, although she was already seventeen. Her Mother knew how to handle her. She told her, "Naturally you don't have to go if you don't feel like it. I'll buy you some cacti and you can start collecting boxes so that you will prepare well for your life as an old maid."

That made her laugh and she began thinking about what dress to wear for the party.

She and I hurried one cold December day towards the Convent. The frozen earth and the trees glittered with ice as we stopped on every corner to see if somebody followed us. We casually strolled by the Soviet soldiers standing guard at the corner. Other girls came from different directions. We went to visit the nuns often but we hardly ever tried to get the whole school together as we used to. Today was a big holiday: the Feast of the Immaculate Conception. Other years we used to have a procession around the whole building. One year even the then Primate of Hungary, Justinian Serédi, attended our celebration. This year we were going to celebrate in secret. By the time we reached the big back gate of the Convent, our only entrance now, there were a dozen of us. The door had opened slightly and we silently slid in through the crack.

The corridor filled up quickly and we gathered according to classes. We were in full uniform. White veils came out of our pockets and we were given paper lilies to carry on our short procession to the picture of Our Lady where we offered her these lilies as a token of our lives. This procession was always a tear-jerker for parents and maybe some of the seniors regarded it as ridiculous, but this year, when it was no longer allowed, it became a matter of principle. Since religion was against government policy, young people flocked to the churches in great numbers and found their way to the communion rail daily. We met secretly and studied religion together pretending to have parties. We also sang in the choir organized by Mother Haraszthy after school.

Under my feet I saw the famous shining waxed stone of the corridor, blurred through my tears, and I caught myself praying that if we were not able to go to Catholic schools in our days at least our children should have this privilege.

"Mary, I offer you the lily of my heart, keep it and guard it forever."

We sang the hymn that December 8, 1948, as a victory song of those who hope that the good that lives in one's heart will conquer the world.

# 26

On December 26, 1948, Cardinal Mindszenty was arrested. His imprisonment shook the world. It was no longer a secret; the work of the Communist Party within the coalition had been completed. The last voice of opposition was silenced in the Democratic People's Republic. In June, the name of the Party had been changed to the Hungarian Laborer's Party which included the Social Democrats and the National Peasant Party. The former leaders of these two parties were either in concentration camps or they were forced to play along with the 22% Communists who were backed by the entire Soviet Army.

Grandmother's other breast had to be removed and this time she did not recover so quickly. Did her slow healing have something to do with the tension of the calm before the storm?

Then lightning struck although it was the middle of winter; on January 12, 1949, our business was nationalized. Father came home at noon. His face was pale as he said, "They did not even let me bring my briefcase home."

Nobody asked him who "they" were. By then "they" in Hungary meant the oppressors, the Communists, the Government. Everybody else was "we."

He sat down in the armchair and looked straight ahead. Mother put her arms around him. Grandmother did not know what was happening. She was in a daze of morphine after her operation in her bedroom on the second floor. Grandfather was with her. In the last couple of months he had become very forgetful, as if he did not want to remember. He asked several times a day what day it was. He would not recognize old acquaintances. He clearly remembered his childhood, and was as sharp as ever in chemistry but he forgot the most recent events.

Father began to speak, "I did not know what that young hoodlum wanted when he came in with several others of his kind… and just yesterday I talked to a friend of mine in the Government who said that nationalization would not happen for another few months at least. Then he stepped on the airplane and left for the West. I bet we won't see him again! It can't be, I thought when the hoodlum said that he was here to take over my post; I was no longer needed. 'But…' I started. 'No but's about it,' he said, 'I'm here to take over. You owe the bank too much…' I interrupted him, 'I pay the bank regularly,

I never owed any more or less, I don't understand....' He retorted, 'There is nothing to understand. You owe us enough. I take over the business in the name of the Democratic People's Republic. Give me the keys to your car. I'll ride in it from now on."

"He took the car, too?" Mother asked.

"Yes. And he said, 'By the way, from now on I don't want to see you even near the store. Don't come here to buy soap. Your employees are freed from your tyranny. They no longer have to serve you, or even help you if you want to buy something. GO!' So I came home."

Father was completely calm and collected. The worst he had expected for months had passed and yet it was not the worst. We still had each other.

For years, I had anticipated that this would happen and more intensely since I knew Father no longer slept nights and jumped out of bed every time a car passed our window, I expected everything. Except ... the only thing that stuck in my mind now was that a young man, according to Father's description he could not have been more than twenty-eight to thirty years old, took away the car from two old, sick people, my grandparents, who had worked all their lives and made their money in an honest way. "Injustice" the word danced in front of my eyes in burning red letters. I do not know what happened but all of a sudden I found myself screaming and banging the door with both my fists, crying and stamping my feet all at once. Nobody stopped me; Mother and Father sat there calmly and just looked on until I stopped and broke down in quiet sobs.

～

January 19, 1949. Early in the morning Mother woke me up. "Come and say good-bye to Father. He is leaving today for the West. Jack came over and told us that he would be arrested today. The three of us searched the house all night and looked for objectionable items in case the police should come today to do the same. We burned papers and whatever Jack felt advisable to annihilate."

"Why didn't you call me? I would have helped."

"It was too late, there is school today; the fewer people moving around the house, the better. Hurry!"

I ran down the stairs as Mother went over to the girls' room to wake them also.

Father stood in his dark gray winter coat, a light gray hat with a wide band. Just as if he were leaving for work. He put his arms around me and looked into my eyes, "Take good care of your mother and everybody else!"

He wanted me to take care of Mother, I now officially took my ailing Grandmother's place. I was the oldest; fourteen years old. He knew that

Grandfather could no longer understand what was going on. But what did he want me to do? Whatever it was I made a firm decision to do everything in my power to protect them, I said, "Don't you worry! Everything will be all right. You take care of yourself! We will see you soon!"

I don't think he or I believed that statement. There was no fact on which we could have based that assumption. He hugged me with all his might. The two girls arrived, snatched him from me, and clung to him hysterically.

Then Mother whisked him out the door and they were both gone.

When we came home from school there was no news yet, but soon Mother appeared, beaming. "He is on the Orient-express!" She twirled around in happy triumph as she threw down her mink-lined coat with the beaver collar that was so becoming. Even the gleam of her teeth seemed to reflect joy as she told us the adventure-story. As soon as they left here they went over to a friend's house who took Father's passport and bought a ticket at the station. So far so good. Nobody asked him any questions. If there was a warrant out to arrest Father, the railroad did not know about it. Then as soon as the embassies opened, Mother ran over to the French one because we knew practically everybody there from the times when Gisèle visited us. We also had friends at the Swiss Embassy. The most difficult to obtain was the Austrian visa. Everybody had to wait at least two to three months to receive it. Mother had to get all three in three hours. She smiled her way through the two first embassies then tried the Austrian one, but no chance. They would not even listen to her. She ran back to the Swiss Embassy where our friend called the Austrians and the second time as soon as Mother entered she was led to the inside room, where they issued the visa because it was a matter of life and death. She arrived back just in time to see Father off to the train. He was on his way now.

"But when will we see him again? Are we going after him? What are we going to do?" The questions flew at Mother from all sides.

Mother just smiled. She was so happy with their triumph over the Communists she could not think of anything else. She said, "We'll make it! Soon. At the latest in two or three months. Father will send someone to get us. He has a friend at the border who can help us. I don't know yet. The main thing is that he is on that train..." her voice trailed off because she had suddenly realized that this was only the first obstacle. The next one was the border. Would they take him off there? I could see the transformation on her face. "Let us pray for Father. He said he would call from Vienna, if he could, if he arrived there..." her face lost its radiance.

"You must not tell anyone where Father is. We'll simply say that he went to visit his parents in Cegléd to rest up," said Mother later.

Alec arrived just as she pronounced the words. I remembered that we were going to see Hamlet with him; the film starring Lawrence Olivier.

"We can't go to the movies," I started but Mother looked at me and I realized that we had to play along as if nothing had happened. It was not such a bad idea after all. At least the hours would not drag along with the speed of a snail.

Alec was in a good mood. He talked to me about his plans at the university, the details of a machine he was going to design. I let it all flow by me and tried to look interested at the same time. Finally, we reached the movie and in the dark I could silently pray. The train must be on the border by now. Did Father make it?

Soon the magic of Shakespeare distracted my mind from reality. It felt good to be carried away on the rhythmic waves of words, to listen to the Danish Prince's monologue, shudder from the ghost and at the sight of the crazy Ophelia floating down the river on a bed of flowers that surrounded her ethereal body.

Hamlet's question, "To be or not to be" brought me back into reality. He went up to the top of the tower and leaned over the gray stones. Under him the sea stormed against the jagged rocks, sending white pearls of water into the clear air.

I felt that he was talking for me; we too were on top of a tower, looking down into the depths. "There is a way back. There must be one that does not lead to the icy death of the sea or the dagger," I thought.

Hamlet dropped the deadly weapon that fell bumping from rock to rock into the churning water. He returned to life and I knew that I too would choose survival and fight for it as long as there would be breath in me. The future looked glum, I was everybody's fair prey, by birth, in the dictatorship of the proletariat.

When we arrived home Mother greeted us with good news. She did get a phone call that was garbled and not quite understandable, but it was from Vienna. Father made it that far, but there was still the Soviet zone. I remembered the bridge on the Ens, when the guards took off the two young girls on our way to Switzerland. But I also remembered that the airport was in the British zone in Vienna. He could take a plane to Switzerland. Father was safe.

27

My recollections were over. This was the story of my life until today: January 26, 1949. Here I was alone with Grandmother, who was practically unconscious, Grandfather, who forgot even the day of the week, and two little sisters, while the secret policeman shoved Mother down the stairs and I had to go back to school to sing the praises of the Communist Party. What would become of Mother? Who was to help me in my distress? Our best lawyer had just declared that he was powerless. Where should I turn? Sobs shook my entire body although my mind told me that it was no use to cry.

As I remembered past events, the kaleidoscope of my life showed topsy-turvy patterns that did not make sense. Life's broken promises, tyranny and blood, war and lost hopes, wasted lives, and yet…through all of this something always pulled me through. I was alive and healthy. I heard a voice inside me through the chaos. It sounded like Grandmother's. Or was it Mother's? One of my teachers'? Were they all blended into one? It could not have been because it spoke in the first person. "I am with you whenever you need me. I am always your loving Father. There is nothing that you and I together cannot solve."

I recalled our near-escapes, our ability to always solve the problems that came up: the raped pregnant neighbor's "medicine from Heaven," the drilling sound of the shell that did not harm our house, the grenade swaying soldier in the laundry room. I heard the voice again, "There is nothing that you and I together cannot solve." I recalled Grandmother's strength when she had to deal with the Soviets and Father's fearless ways during the siege. Where did they get their power? While these thoughts ran through my mind, the feeling of a perfect and complete freedom filled my whole being. I straightened and wiped my eyes. I realized that there was only one constant relationship in my life: the one between God and myself. All I had to do was to trust in the magic of that moment. I knew that if I did that I was immune from the Communists, from the police, from those who tried to mold my mind to their fanaticism, because I would never again feel alone.

I grabbed my books and kissed my grandparents good-bye.

*John Szablya with parents, on a walk in the Buda hills, 1929.*

*John with parents on a ferry crossing Lake Balaton, 1934.*

264

*John at Lake Balaton in about 1934 playing
with his dog. He was about ten years old—
always very tall.*

*John, age 18, with his parents, when he started the Technical University of
Budapest (Müegyetem), 1942.*

John's aunt, "Tintimama" Ernestine
Lohwag, well know painter who
painted many pictures of John as he was
growing up. They lived together with
John's parents in one beautiful home
designed by John's uncle, "Feripapa"
Ferenc Szablya Frischauf. He became the
Director of the School of Art in Industry.
He was a painter and designer and
remodeled many palaces. There is a room
in Geneva, the room of the Ambassadors
in the house of the League of Nations,
which he designed. Both of them studied
painting in the nineteenth century
Munich school of painting. 1925.

Painting of John, age 15, painted
by his Aunt Ernestine Lowag.

266

*John under the Christmas tree at age two. Painted by Aunt Ernestine, 1926.*

*Painting of John's childhood home by Aunt Ernestine Lohwag.*

*John's grandmother, Maria Gundel as a young girl.*

*John Szablya Sr. became an Honorary Citizen of the City of New York in 1939, when he organized the Hungarian Pavilion at New York World's Fair. He received all of his medals for promoting Hungarian art and artists, organizing exhibitions in many countries. He did this after his retirement from the Ganz factory at 55, where he became Director at age 32. After his retirement he became the President of the Society for Art in Industry. He quadrupled the export of folk art thereby helping rural women earn a good living. This was not a paid position.*

*Gisèle and I, June 1948. I am in my dream coat I received in Paris at the fashion show at Lucien Lelong, organized just for Mother and me because that day there was no scheduled show.*

*Marie, 14 years old, and I, age 16, go dancing before I got married.*

*My grandfather, István Bartha received this from his employees at Molnár and Moser
for his 70th birthday, August 20th, 1946. On this handpainted document the employees
drew all the great benefits my grandfather did for the druggist industry. The Istvan
Bartha Apartment House for retired pharmacists/druggists, a villa at the Lake Balaton
– a vacation home, a boat house on the Danube, a school for the druggist profession, his
many new products, scents, and excellent work in his field.*

*Wedding photo of my mother's cousin Jozsef Schmaltz and Ilona Csiky, who adopted my sister Marie at the time of the deportation of capitalists. He was an engineer therefore exempt.*

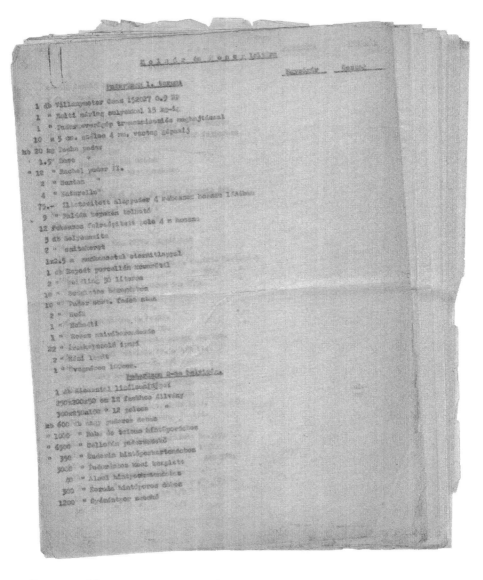

*Inventory of factory storage at nationalization. Received 1992 from employees.*

*Mother as a worker in 1951, assistant to an electrician, before moving to Törtel.*

*Mother selling her goods at the Cegléd market after we received permission to manufacture plastic handbags. Totally illegally we sold not only the plastic bags, but cosmetics manufactured by us secretly. 1951.*

# 28

By the time I returned from school, Mother was home, her old smiling self. I think she would have smiled no matter what happened to her in order to comfort those she loved.

"I'm back," Mother stated. "The policeman at headquarters was rather astonished when I told him that Father went to Basel to study methods of producing DDT which he then wanted to manufacture for the Hungarian state. After all, one had to live from something; the business was nationalized. He asked me how Father left and why we had spread the rumor that he went to Cegléd to visit his parents. I told him that we did not want people to gossip about his trip and that Father left with a valid passport. He seemed definitely annoyed. 'We forgot to revoke it,' he hissed between his teeth. He then snapped at me, 'He'll never come back, you just watch!' I asked him innocently, 'Do you think that he would leave me and the children?' He laughed sarcastically, 'We have seen things like that happen before, you know…'"

"That was all? When did you get back?"

"Pretty soon after that. I must tell you Mrs. Horvath thought she saw a ghost when I appeared at the door. She must have buried me alive when she heard what had happened this morning."

"Didn't you think that you would never come back? I did!" I hugged and held her tight and kissed her cheeks and eyes, wherever I could get hold of her. "I hope we'll never see them again."

"I wouldn't vouch for that," said Mother.

～

In the next couple of days we had more male help around than we thought we needed. It seemed that Father's departure stirred every man who knew us to offer his services. Alec came daily and Pista and Tommy at least called if they could not come in person. Uncle Charles and Uncle Stephen showed up every day at first and Uncle Feri, one of Father's college roommates, considered it his responsibility to take care of us in every possible way.

Suddenly Grandmother began to get better. A sixth sense made her realize that she was needed. She refused the morphine and as she slowly came out of its influence she changed back into a lovable person even if not completely her old self.

She helped to destroy our whole way of living before somebody else could do it for us. She did not seem to mind the loss of the car or anything else. She cheerfully helped Mother choose the upstairs to keep as our part of the house. The downstairs, the scene of our happy parties, was rented out to an architect, his wife, and step-daughter, my age, whose mother had been killed in a concentration camp. We had let the maids go immediately after the nationalization of our business. Now we were selling some of our things and packing away others into the cellar and the attic. Some were given to relatives to save them for us while they could make good use of them. Grandmother was relaxed and busy and so was Mother.

Our first move to follow Father was to offer up everything we still owned to the Government in exchange for passports. Several drugstores that were not under the trade name "Molnár & Moser" and therefore were not yet nationalized, all of our apartment houses, and the two houses we lived in, also the rights to our car, which we still owned in name, plus a certain amount of cash and an apartment they had asked for. A nice bundle of several million dollars. For weeks we lived in happy expectations. Other people received passports for single-family houses. We were convinced that we would get ours soon.

Spring filled the air and time came to have parties again. But where? Obviously we could not do them at our house. We had no place for it and it would attract the Communists' attention. Uncle Feri came up with the solution. The parties would be at his spacious apartment; he had two teenagers of his own and while we would supply the girls, he would invite the boys. We could bring food, he would serve drinks.

Life was fun again. Pista and I carried the creamy-frosted cakes over to Uncle Feri's house, while Marie and Elisabeth carried big boxes of sandwiches. We had to make several rounds to lug everything over. Alec and Tommy helped also. Uncle Feri made jokes and complimented us on our dresses. The one I wore was my favorite dress. The skirt was made of six yards of light blue muslin and when I danced it flew like the wings of a butterfly.

Uncle Feri pulled me aside.

"Helen, I have plans for you, I want you to meet a young colleague of mine today. His family has known yours about forty years but I don't think that you have ever met him. He has just received his Ph.D., he is an engineer at the Ganz Works, he plays the piano, tennis, he is well versed in art, he is tall, dark, and handsome, and I think that the two of you would hit it off quite well together. His name is John Szablya." He said this with a twinkle in his eye that seemed like matchmaking but I didn't mind; he was such a sweet man.

"I have heard the Szablya name often in connection with art. I've also heard what extraordinary people they are."

"Like I said, your families knew each other, but the name Szablya is only too well-known in art circles. His uncle was the director of the Art College and a well-known artist and interior decorator himself, both his aunts were famous artists, his mother a sculptress. His father was the director of Ganz Works, where John now works, and after he retired he became the director for the Society of Art in Industry. As such, he traveled widely to several European cities and countries, among them London, Berlin, Estonia, Lithuania, Latvia, Finland and many more where he exhibited and promoted Hungarian folk art and art works. In 1939, he was the co-chairman of the Hungarian Pavilion at the New York World's Fair. At that time he became an Honorary Citizen of the City of New York. John went with him on his trip to the United States. I like John very much. I think you will find him interesting," he said and he winked.

"He sounds fascinating. If he is half what you described him to be it will be fun talking with him. But how old is he? Will he be interested in a little girl like me?"

"Will he? Just leave that to me!" Uncle Feri laughed.

What I did not know was that I received a similar kind of introduction on his part when he talked to John about me. From the way John greeted me when we met it must have sounded something like "she is the most beautiful, charming, interesting, and intelligent girl in the company. She speaks several languages, dances like an angel, plays tennis, swims, and is her mother's greatest help around the house and in business matters. She interpreted for her father at business meetings in Paris and Switzerland. She writes poetry and business letters with equal ease and she is only fourteen. Just imagine what she will be like when she grows up! etc. etc." As a matter of fact, he was supposed to meet me at an earlier party which he could not make.

Thank God I did not know about that for a long time to come or I would have been scared to death that I might not live up to his expectations. As it was I was scared enough when we met in person. He was dark, tall (six foot five), and handsome with blue eyes and wavy hair.

Uncle Feri always thought of fun games to play. The game of the day was that the boys were separated from the girls into two different rooms, where a huge crystal vase full of tulips of the most varied kinds were presented to them and each had to choose one and pin it on. Then we met again in the spacious living room and had to find our partner for the party who chose the same flower we did. The only exception was John. He came later and he was older, so he had the privilege of looking around and picking a partner. Although we were not introduced yet, he must have liked my looks because he chose my flower and came over, "Apparently we have to entertain each other for the evening," he said and smiled. "Ah, John," Mother came running from the other room. "I have to introduce my daughters to you. This is Helen."

John turned to me, "So you are the one I always hear about! My godmother, who is your grandfather's sister, always talks about you. I even remember the day when you were born."

"I have heard your name too. It was always spoken with great respect," I said. Deep down I felt flattered that the star guest chose me when he did not even know yet who I was.

"How about a dance?" John bowed and I curtsied in fun.

It was different to dance with someone that tall. It felt like I had to reach up while he constantly seemed to stoop to hold his hand on my waist. The feeling disappeared rapidly as we waltzed around the room. Then all of a sudden I did not feel the ground under my feet anymore; I flew through the air and my legs joined my skirt in the twirl.

"That was fun!" I exclaimed when he put me down to the last beat of the music. His face beamed and everybody in the room clapped.

"Let's sit down for a while," he said. We settled in the corner on an elegant settee. I tried to concentrate very hard on what I would say. I did not want to seem like a fool confronted with such a brain. He was the perfect elegant figure I imagined according to the descriptions. His dark suit complemented his immaculate white shirt.

"You must like music," he said. "You followed me so well in the waltz."

"I love it. I go to the Opera as often as I can." I stopped here. I was not ready to tell him that I sang in the choir at school and that one of my secret ambitions was to become an opera singer because I knew it was folly.

"Which is your favorite opera?"

"Lucia di Lammermoore. I find the sextet and the grand aria, when she is overtaken by madness, enchanting, I could listen to it all day," I said with the exaggeration of a fourteen-year-old.

"Lucia di Lammermoore?" His eyes showed definite interest. "I thought you would say Madame Butterfly, or one of the Puccinis, or maybe one of the well-known Verdis. You are the first person I've met who mentioned something out of the ordinary."

"Did you think so little of me?" I teased him.

He smiled as he said, "No. I just judged by my own taste, I guess. My favorite is Aida. It must be because I first saw it in the Metropolitan in New York with an extremely good cast during the World Exhibition."

I did not betray that I knew his story already. "Tell me more about New York. It must be fascinating to go so far and see so many places. I have always wanted to travel."

"I enjoyed the trip very much. On our way to America we were allowed ashore in Gibraltar. We also stopped in Algiers for a while. Then America, oh, I can't tell you in only a few minutes what it was like, but I would like to tell you all I can if you want to hear it. How about another dance?"

We jitter-bugged our way through the room and grabbed other couples apart, danced a foursome, then threw them to different partners and grabbed another until everybody was with his or her sweetheart and we ended up in each other's arms. We laughed when we were back together again.

"Now how on earth did you do that?" I asked.

"Nothing to it. Everybody should dance with their own darling. Don't you agree?"

We had such a good time. Suddenly I became aware of jealous eyes when I looked at Pista, or Tommy, or even Alec. Even Alec? He was supposed to be my chaperon, my second cousin. I did not dwell on this long because John asked me for another dance.

This time we continued our conversation and John told me more about America.

"I saw a television set in America in the RCA building. The transmitter was on the Empire State Building, and we could see ourselves; it was quite ready to be put on the market."

"Was it green, like the one I saw demonstrated at an exhibition here not long ago?"

"Yes, it was. All early ones were. My mother and I really wanted to see Yellowstone Park, but that could not be, unfortunately. We got as far as Chicago and we were invited to the Ford's, you know, the automobile manufacturer, for lunch so there was no way to go to Yellowstone. Even if we could have made it that far in those days, one could only travel into the park by mule. Maybe next time."

"Will there be a next time?" I asked him with great interest. It was obvious that he liked music and travel, dancing and ... Uncle Feri was right about him. I wondered if he was right about the fact that he would be interested in someone as young as I. No, it could not be; I tried to quiet my imagination that, as always, ran way ahead of me.

"I wanted to go to America right after I had finished high school but the war broke out and there was no way. I intend to go as soon as I can but with today's conditions, who knows?"

"I want to go also. I've always wanted to study at the Technical University of Zurich and become a chemical engineer. I dreamed about being independent and owning a car, and other silly things like that." I ended abruptly because it seemed so pointless and because I had never told anyone so much about my dreams before.

He seemed pleased. "Why did you say 'and other silly things like that' so suddenly. Is it because they sound so impossible? I always liked things that were impossible. They pose a challenge. I want to conquer peaks that were not climbed yet."

"You, too?" I gazed into his dreamy, blue eyes. We were now standing on the balcony. Inside, the "one-two-three steps with each girl" craze was at its height and we wanted to talk.

I looked down and saw ruins across the street. The setting sun colored them pink. They reminded me of our lives. Our dreams were buried forever. Would we be able to forge others? This challenge seemed greater than any that our generation had faced before. We both seemed to be the type to cherish a challenge. I looked in his eyes again as he looked into mine. Nothing was said but we both felt that something happened out there on the balcony.

The party went on as always when in the wee hours of the morning, a tired group of us decided to play "spin-the-bottle."

The questions came one after another. "Who likes to lick out the bowl when Mother makes chocolate cake?" "Who was the last to be kissed?" "Who likes cheese?" The bottle pointed at Alec so he had his chance to ask the question, "Who will be Helen's husband?" He twirled the bottle and it hesitantly stopped and pointed at John. John laughed, jumped up, and spun the bottle. "All right, I'll be the first, but who will be my successor?" The bottle turned and decidedly pointed again at him. He laughed again, and all was brushed aside in the excitement of the game as more daring questions were asked and answered by blushes. Hardly anybody noticed when John went over to Mother and told her, "Baba, I'm sorry but the bottle predicted that I shall be your son-in-law." They both laughed. There were only ten years between them, the same as between John and myself.

# 29

"Hello, Sándor! What brings you here?" I was happy to see the handsome young man with whom I had had a few dances a year back while vacationing in the Mátra. He was an Army-man then, a drafted peasant boy, who enjoyed the luxuries of the resort hotel with his comrades. His movements were awkward but his smile was charming, his teeth glistened as he spoke. When he arrived today he was dressed very elegantly, in the latest style, with an expensive pair of sunglasses.

"I was walking past your house so I thought I'd stop. Is your mother home?"

"Yes, she'll be pleased to see you again." I led him up the stairs.

Mother made him sit down while I ran to the kitchen to get some goodies. When I came back they were talking seriously about something.

"That would be the only way. It is the decision of the passport department."

"What do you have to do with the passport department?" I asked when I heard his last words.

"I work there. I came to ask your mother a question.

My heart sank. So it was not my personal charms that made him look us up. My eyes ran down his expensive suit to his imported shoes.

"Go ahead. You can talk in front of Helen," Mother said.

"I suggested to your mother that you should agree to give us all the information you know about your friends and we will give you a passport."

"Information?" I asked.

"Yes, you know…any subversive activity, how they make their living, the jokes they tell. You know very well that some of them have no visible means of support yet they go on, they must be doing something illegal. They trust you, you then would get the passport you want."

"The passport," I repeated automatically.

Mother looked distressed. We were members of the class marked for extinction.

"What if we say no?" She looked worried as she asked the question.

"What if I decide I can't do it?"

"You will not get the passport."

"Despite the houses, stores, everything we offered?"

"We will get those anyway," Sándor laughed. "Well, Madam, I won't press you for an answer, it is for you to decide what you want to do. A few months of information can get you out of a possible hell. You can call me tomorrow. Say yes or no. Don't tell me any more. It was nice seeing you again."

"Will we never see Father again?" I burst into the room as soon as I showed Sándor to the door. "I don't remember what I said to him, he mentioned something about going out to dance again. I'm sure I did not tell him what I thought of that but he must have known it."

"If that is the price I'm afraid we won't." Mother still sat in the same place. She did not smile now. "One way or another we'll manage to see Father." Her voice had the ring of steel. "But never by betraying a trust. We have our integrity and that is not for sale."

"Mother, there are other ways to force you."

"They'll have to try them all, Helen," She looked me in the eyes as she said that, "we are free now. That is strange to say when you and I have finally realized that we are at the mercy of our enemies yet spiritually we are free. If we adhere to our principles, if we trust God, our enemies will have no power over us. Do you remember how I comforted you when you were little and you were afraid? 'If God is for us, who can be against us?' I did not invent that phrase. It is in the Bible. St. Paul wrote it to the Romans at the time Christians were persecuted. His source could have been Psalm 118 where the writer of this old passage cries out 'The Lord is with me, I will not be afraid; what can men do to me?' We are free, Helen, as long as we follow our conscience. There is no peace of mind in betrayal not even by gaining the whole world."

I thought of this when Sunday after church a whole crowd of us young people strolled along the quay of the Danube, bathed in sunlight. The gray stairs led down to the steel-gray water that had a little blue tint to it today. The Danube hardly ever shows the color of the Strauss waltz's famous "blue." Rumor has it that it only looks blue when one is in love. If the color of the Danube was any indication I was not really in love, yet it was delightful to laugh away the morning with my friends: Pista, Tommy, Alec, my girl friends, among them Bonzi. They were all here. As I listened to our conversation I realized that everything we said could have been reported to Sándor as "information" and in a month or two all of my friends and even their parents would have been in jail, concentration camp, or who knows. Mother was right. I could never again feel free if I had betrayed their trust. I knew she did the right thing when she called and said "No" to Sándor's unbelievable request. God would find a way to reunite our family. In the meantime, the sun felt good and the conversation was interesting. Pista was the center of attention,

"Do you remember after the siege, when the Hungarians put out the Ban War posters? The Communist Party protested and removed the posters from the walls everywhere. Now they want to show what great lovers of peace they are!"

"Yes," said Bonzi, "at school we learned that the Communist Party's main goal was peace. They were always instrumental in stopping the war. Ha!"

"Did you notice though when they did that? Always to the advantage of the Communist Party. Whenever it helped their cause, when people were tired of war and would have voted anyone into power in order to obtain peace. They did it in 1917 within Russia, then within the lines of the enemies of Russia and they..." Pista looked around but there were no other groups close by so he continued. "The Communists interpret peace according to one of the definitions in the dictionary: peace is the absence of all struggle. To them the struggle among classes is the most important one. Peace will not come until communism is everywhere in the world. Only classless society will bring real peace."

"I understand now why we have to keep fighting for peace," I exclaimed, "even though there is no war. At school I could not get my grade from P.E. until I ran through the obstacle course and threw the two training handgrenades."

"It is lucky that I am excused from P.E.," said Bonzi. "I don't think I could have managed to run through that thing. We only had time to practice once."

A twinkle in Tommy's eye warned us and we switched topics just as another group walked past us.

"Indeed that is an interesting equation," Alec said loud. "I will try and work something out with my study group at the university. Maybe we'll be able to discover something to further the fulfillment of the three-year plan."

"You should have been there yesterday, when our study group discussed Marx's book *The Capital*," Bonzi said. As soon as the group passed us she laughed and said, "You really should have been there. The arguments to contradict it and the examples brought up from real life to demonstrate the impossibility of living out a utopia were stimulating. One of us always stood guard and whenever a teacher approached we started to talk in the Communist jargon demonstrating the advantages of being the class marked for extermination."

"That reminds me of my aunt," Pista said. "You know they were landowners. At first she received one hundred acres of her original tract to work along with the others. Every year they burdened her with more and more taxes. She sold her jewels, her china, her books, finally the curtains and furniture. Then she was told to stop fighting by someone who respected her for all the trouble she went through trying to save the family's land for the time if and when her husband came home from Siberia. She was marked for extinction, and if she paid the amount she owed, the next day she would be taxed higher, then the next amount would be even higher until she would have to give up. She left her land without notifying anybody and sought anonymity in the tumult of the capital. She was looking for a job. Her husband was a former two-star general, now a prisoner of war. That gave her zero prospects to be allowed to have a job. Yet, she had to do something to survive and feed her daughter. Finally, she came up with the idea of starting her resume as so many good communists do: 'My father was a simple but honest proletarian, except she wrote 'My husband was a simple but honest soldier,' trusting her good luck that after reading 'simple but honest,' they would skip the next few words and jump to the qualifications. She was lucky and got a job. Her complaint against her boss is that he does not in the least know what he is doing. She is in charge and does everything. She is a beautiful woman and the slob is flattered by her presence. At first, he tried to be fresh with her but she stopped that in a hurry. He needed her talents, so he put a damper on it. As long as we deliver know-how that the Communists cannot acquire otherwise, we are safe.

"Just how long is that going to last?" asked Bonzi. Her father had escaped a long time ago. He lived in France. By now my father was in Paris too. He stayed at Gisèle's brother's apartment while Paul and his wife, Françoise, were still working in Hungary.

I wondered whether that landowner-lady was also asked to spy. I knew she would still have her land if she had agreed to do so. All of a sudden I looked at my friends and an icy fist closed around my heart. Were they asked? Could I trust them? Are they speaking as they are because they want to provoke my comments? I tried to forget my thoughts. I should not think that way about my very best friends. Yet the thought could not quite escape me.

Bonzi and I sat on the comfortable, wide window seat of her mother's apartment in the part of her apartment she was allowed to keep. The window looked out on busy Joseph Boulevard but most of the streetcars and people were hidden behind the green foliage of a huge tree in front of the window. We liked to sit there silently and watch the leaves move in the breeze. Quiet and isolation seemed to be the greatest pleasures since the siege. It was hard to think in the constant noisy presence of other people.

Before we had made ourselves comfortable in the niche of the window we checked on the co-tenants. There were two families living with them in the five-room apartment. One of them was a security policeman and his young wife, who was expecting. They were not home. The other was an old couple who were deaf. We could put our minds at ease when we talked, nobody would hear us.

"Do you have news from your father?" Bonzi asked.

"Just the usual, through the embassy mail. As far as authorities are concerned we are not on good terms. He deserted us. The court ruled that he had to send us $140 every month as child support and alimony, even though there was no divorce. If the money does not come in time, Mother is dragged to the police, 'How did the money come this month? Did he smuggle it in?' I don't know why but for some reason we seldom get the money in time. Is it because they want to question Mother every month, or Father is not sending it on time, I can't believe that. I just know that sometimes we don't get anything for two or three months then we get as many as twenty-two IKKA parcels at once. (IBUSZ Foreign Commercial Action, the only agency, run by the government, through which one is allowed to receive money from abroad, without paying customs and/or being harassed by the customs officers. For example some people received their cocoa and washpowder totally mixed together in normal parcels.) IKKA, having received the hard currency sent from abroad, converts it into an assortment of packages that contain coffee, cocoa, sardines, wine, rum, what have you, and hand us the parcels. We are allowed to sell these otherwise unavailable delicacies for whatever price we can get for them but they do not allow us to receive money straightforward."

"You mean that the government would delay some of the parcels on purpose so that they could harass your mother?"

"I am sure of it. They have to keep us in check. After all, we are the 'insects' of society. The other day Marie came home from school and yelled at Mother 'All of this communism came about because of you. Because you exploited the people.' I was flabbergasted, Mother cried. But what could we do? We did not dare to tell her. She is too young to remember the days before the siege, or understand what came after. She is a teenager, they have no heart. They think they know all the answers."

We both laughed. We too were teenagers but it certainly did not seem so. There was a generation gap between those who could and those who could not remember.

"How do you live when the parcels don't arrive?" asked Bonzi.

"We sell what we have: pictures, books, clothes, china, vases. Didn't you ever see the government's on consignment stores? They give you a down payment when you take your wares in to sell and they send you the balance when it is sold. They take a 30% cut."

"I saw them but I did not know what it was all about. My mother works as an accountant. We don't need much. Grandmother sews our clothes, makes preserves. My other grandmother sends us fruits and vegetables from the country, she grows them in her own backyard."

"Sewing is fashionable nowadays. We have already used up half our curtains for dresses and we constantly search for attic treasures. You know what I found yesterday? You'll love it. You can wear them any time you want to. I found a big box of Grandmother's old kid gloves, you know, the long kind: white ones and pink ones and I found hats…"

"Hats! I don't think many people wear hats since the siege."

"No, but they can always come back. Maybe we'll even be able to wear evening gowns some day. Or have a real, live ball."

"You dreamer," Bonzi laughed again. I liked her laugh because her dimples showed in her milk-white face and her brownish-red hair seemed to glow in the sunshine that stole into the room through the leaves of the tree.

I too, had to laugh. "Our stomachs are growling and here we are talking about balls. Were you able to get meat this week?"

"Once I found a line and stood at its end. I was not quite sure what they were selling but I thought that whatever it was it was better than nothing. I was lucky; I bought some pork, but I haven't seen eggs since two weeks ago."

"I couldn't get any milk the other day. As soon as I stepped in the door of the dairy, the clerk repeated the sentence she must have said a thousand times that day, 'We don't have anything made out of milk.'"

"What did she sell?"

"She had bread, then, that thing, you know, that we call 'zucchini-jam' that red-colored mess and alcohol-free beer."

"Why don't we have enough food in a country that is famous for its food? We had always grown our own."

"Ah, but then we had no co-operatives, government-owned lands, planned economy, or nutritional aid to our fellow Communist countries. Thanks to all these innovations we now are able to import Canadian flour," I said sarcastically. "What I can't understand is that Canadian flour is supposed to be the best in the world. Why does it act and taste like glue when you try to use it in food?"

"Because it wants to prove to us that capitalist grain is no good," we both had to laugh again even though we made fun of our own misery.

The doorbell rang, it was Tommy. Then soon after Alec and Pista arrived and finally John Szablya, whom for an unexplainable reason we all called "Szablya" among ourselves, instead of John. "I went to see you, Helen, but you weren't home and when I heard that you were here I walked over thinking myself real lucky to be able to be in the company of two charming young ladies instead of one." That sounded just like him; the real gentleman.

Since we first met, he came to see me every three weeks or so. That seemed about right. He kept in touch but I was sure that he had an older girl he was going with. I enjoyed his company whenever he came but I did not let myself have high hopes.

"Let's all go inside and talk. The policeman isn't home, thank God."

That was good news to everyone. The co-tenant situation had become so oppressive by then that it was hard to find a place where one could sit down and talk without being overheard. Was this why the Communists did not hurry with the rebuilding of houses or the building of new apartment houses in a city of 1.6 million that had gone through fifty-one days of heavy siege? If they had asked us to spy we could be sure that those in the service of the secret police would denounce anything they heard and would add figments of their imagination to flavor it just in order to get one more room from the shared apartments: the one who was in jail no longer needed his room. Besides, who could be sure about anybody? I looked carefully at every one of the people present. I remembered what Mother had said. Their faces mirrored inner peace of mind despite the fact that there was not one person in the room who would not have had a member of the family or a very close relative in jail, concentration camp, in Siberia, or outside the country where there was no hope to ever see them again. Bonzi and I were considered the lucky ones. At least our fathers were free and could even send us money. The peace that I saw on their faces was my only guarantee that they could be trusted.

"May I have a glass of water?" asked Tommy.

"Let me get it for you," Bonzi ran to the kitchen and came back with a glass of fresh, cold water. That was all she could offer. The kitchen was bare. They had no fridge and even if they had owned one nobody had enough money or opportunity to buy more than what was enough for a day.

Bonzi and her mother had two rooms. One was hers, the other was the living room and her mother's room at the same time. We now moved from her room to the living room and made ourselves comfortable in the overstuffed old fashioned armchairs.

"You know what?" Pista started. "We are going to get a new constitution on August 20th given to us by the Communist Party. I went to the library and studied the constitution of the USSR to prepare myself for the shock. You wouldn't believe what I found. So many things I don't even know where to begin."

"Start anywhere," Tommy suggested. We were all interested.

Heads bowed closer to each other. The policeman was not home but we did not want to be caught by surprise.

"Just the very beginning blew my mind! In the Soviet Union all power belongs to the people. Fine and dandy! But listen to the continuation: all natural resources, transportation, banks, agricultural holdings, means and tools of production belong to the government. Everything that would enable the people to exercise their power belongs to the government."

"Yet, we are not allowed to talk about 'state capitalism'," said Bonzi. "The other day I asked our history teacher and she hushed me up."

John came up with an anecdote. "That explains what happened in our factory. One of the workers was fired and while we were on our way to the streetcar he mumbled to himself: 'If the factory is mine and I am building the country for myself, how come I fired myself?' He wouldn't have dared to say it out loud. The other day an old cardcarrying member of the Communist Party asked a question during a session of the party-seminar where we are being 're-educated' to understand the Communist way of living. He thought he could afford it after having given his best years to the Party. His judgment was incorrect. He was arrested on his way home. Nobody has heard about him since. Not even his wife knows where he is."

"So we aren't the only ones who are not allowed to ask questions," I said.

"Definitely not. The Party is always right," said Alec.

A key turned noisily in the lock of the entrance door. In the resulting silence one could have heard a pin drop.

"Bonzi, are you home?" It was Bonzi's Grandmother. An audible sigh of relief cleared the tension. "Let me get the big pot, I want to make stew for tonight."

"You got meat somewhere?" Bonzi asked.

"I managed to find some horse meat and if I cook it with paprika it will taste just like 'gulyás.' Having fun kids?"

She rummaged around in the kitchen for a few minutes then all was quiet again.

Pista continued, "According to the constitution citizens of the USSR may possess personal belongings, a house, savings, and a small acreage (garden) without exploiting anyone's work."

"Exactly," Bonzi nodded, "like we had this apartment to ourselves and now we must share it with two other families. An apartment is a personal belonging, isn't it? We are even better off than my uncle, who owns a condominium but cannot live in it because there is a family with five children who got it right after the war. He was in the country at the time. He lives next door in a sublet. Yet, he has to pay taxes and upkeep from the rent they pay him and often, I should say always, he ends up in the red."

"Where does that leave the peasants who had just received their land from the Communists?" I asked.

"Don't worry," John answered. "They'll take care of them. Stalin, according to his own words, 'had to' kill off several million peasants to force them into co-operatives. Many peasants here are already joining the co-ops 'voluntarily' I thought of Grandpa in Cegléd, who on 'advice' 'voluntarily' gave up his forty acres."

"As to our savings," said Alec, "if we had any, the bank could devalue the money any minute the government felt like it. I know because my father works at the bank and told me that they have been ready for the devaluation of the forint many times. Then somehow free Western radio stations learned of the preparation and broadcast it in their Hungarian language news. The government, just to spite them, held back with the devaluation. When the government is the sole proprietor of everything, where can we find justice or recompense if we are cheated out of our life-savings?"

"Is this why everybody seems to live so well? They don't dare to save any money? The bars are always full, the dancing places swarm with people even when we are unable to buy food."

"Since we have this planned economy," John started to talk again, "factories have 200 to 300 purchasing agents, or buyers, while the sales force consists of only two salesmen. The salesmen have little to do. There is only one outlet for everything, no competition."

"That should be true in reverse also," Pista talked now as a law student. "What are all the buyers for?"

"Naturally," answered John with the same sarcasm that was in the voice of everyone when talking about our glorious government, "the buyers of the government-owned factories are trying to get the necessary raw materials from the equally government-owned mines. Let us say that our factory needed copper. Nearly impossible to get. There is only one government agency that sells the copper, but here you are in competition; many companies need this rare metal. Our buyer therefore goes to the other company and tries to talk to the salespeople there. He must be armed with, preferably, American-made goods. Then he talks to the secretary. While a 'self-respecting worker or employee,' as we are called in the Communist jargon, would never accept a tip or a bribe, a gift is quite a different proposition. If our buyer happens to have the right present, be it lipstick, nylon stockings, or a ball point pen, he will be the one to see the salespeople that day and probably the one to be allotted the copper. The fact that our factory is servicing the machines that make electricity to produce that copper, or anything else for that matter, would not make the slightest difference. Yet I can understand the secretary also. She could never live on her salary."

"Like you said, John, copper is a very important raw material for our economy," Bonzi started and walked towards the hall. We all tensed up at the change in her voice.

Now we heard the footsteps also. She poked her head out through the door.

"The fulfillment of the three-year plan must come first," Alec addressed himself to John, "did you say that you manufacture machines at the Ganz factory for the copper industry?"

"All clear," Bonzi pulled her head back into the room. "Whoever it was went past our entrance. I caught a glimpse of his passing shadow. On with your story, Pista."

"I am happy you brought up our planned economy because that is the next point in the constitution," continued Pista where he left off. "The country's economic life has to be conducted according to the governmental plan. Every citizen who is able to work is obliged to do so based on the principle: 'Whoever does not work, does not eat'."

"Does that include the people who are able to work but are unable to do so because they happen to be from a wrong descent, like their father happened to be a general, or a merchant?" asked Alec.

"Definitely. They are not worthy to live. Up to 1936 people of the wrong descent did not even have the right to vote in the USSR. After 1936 everybody who was eighteen could vote, yet every year there was a list of people who were not allowed to vote because of 'insanity' or because they 'could not be trusted'."

As they were speaking I realized that although we were still allowed to go to school we belonged to those who might end up not having the vote, the jobs, who would not be eligible to work and therefore forbidden to eat.

The sun went down and the room became dark and chilly.

"Now, listen to this," Pista became quite excited, "You know how we hear about communism, the wonderful stage of society when everybody works according to his talents and gets paid according to his needs. The Soviet Union did not reach that stage! Not even socialism, which they claim to be the stage when everybody works according to his ability and gets paid according to his work. That means that in more than thirty years they could not achieve what we had before the Communists came in. We worked and got paid according to the work performed. It just blows my mind! I can't believe that the whole world buys this. And they have veto power in the United Nations!"

Pista got himself so worked up he could not stop, "You know what? They think that their government is the ultimate voice in deciding everything and this is what they call 'the power belongs to the people'!?!"

"You know what else?" he continued. "There is no such thing as a conscientious objector. Everybody has to protect the communal property. General obligation to serve as a soldier is enforced by law."

"How about their voting system?" John poured more fuel on the already blazing fire of Pista's anger.

"You wouldn't believe it!"

"I certainly would," said John. "I heard that in Soviet 'elections' there is only one party, one candidate, which means no election but a plebiscite. As a matter of fact the Soviets write long articles every time they have a plebiscite about the misguided Western reporters who still talk about 'Soviet elections'."

"That is true!" Pista agreed. "They go through the most elaborate system of discussing candidates who can be nominated…now, listen to this…I had to read it twice to believe it. Nominations come from the members of the Communist trade unions, Communist professional unions, cooperatives and Communist unions, Communist youth organizations, and Communist deputies of factories and kolhozes. After I had read the thing twice I realized that of course it could not be any other way because they had no other organizations, they were all outlawed in the name of 'freedom of assembly'."

"That really floors me!" Alec felt the same way as Pista.

"I am not done yet. Anyway, they go through that most elaborate system of discussing the candidate but once he is nominated there is just one man to vote for. That's all."

"No, that's not all," added John. "There is no way to say 'no,' no matter how hard one tries. I talked to many people who were in Siberia as prisoners of war and nowadays I talk with engineers from the Soviet Union. Theoretically you can say 'no' but in reality, even though you have the right to go into the booth, if you do, you are a dead duck. You are expected to fold your ballot and put it into the box right in front of the committee who in turn check out your name from the list; another 'yes' vote: you have done your duty. It sounds ridiculous, but the same method was used by the German Nazis in Austria at the plebiscite after the Anschluss. Just a few days before the balloting plackards covered the houses in Vienna: 'Be proud when voting 'yes!' Do not go into the booth.' A distant uncle of mine went into the booth. Next day he was taken from his home; he disappeared without a trace. His wife does not even know today whether she is a widow or not."

"What are we going to do?" Bonzi whispered as she closed her eyes.

We did not even notice that somebody had switched on the lights. Pista was still going strong, "And then, they still had the gall to write about human rights! Just what kind of rights do they mean? The same kind they gave Cardinal Mindszenty during his trial? What did they do to the man? He did not even look like himself!? The great freedom-fighter stood there meekly admitting everything?!? I heard that he did not even remember what happened. He was still expecting the trial weeks after it had taken place."

"If we come to human rights, why can't we have our church affiliated schools? What rights did they have to take them away from us?" asked Bonzi.

"What right did they have to arrest priests on account of their sermons?"

Bonzi suddenly jumped up and looked out the door, "You guys, it's time to eat. Pista, didn't you say your mother expected you home at seven o'clock?"

We understood that the policeman had come home and started talking about the usual topics. Weather might be suspicious but studying was always in the interest of the Communist government.

"That was very interesting what you just said, Pista, about the Soviet Constitution. I can hardly wait for August 20th when we'll get our own. Let's all meet at Helen's house then. We can see the fireworks from there…" suggested Alec.

# 30

Autumn snuck up on us with its tradition of yellow, brown, and red leaves. It was time to go to school. Much had changed during the summer. Our ridiculous little principal who made sure last year that we were separated from our old teachers, the Sisters, proudly put in the yearbook that he managed to accomplish the feat with the help of five walls and thirty-three locks. He did not mention the constant traffic to the nuns through the side door that opened to a different street. Although he overlooked it, authorities apparently did not. He was removed from his post. Our teachers, the nuns, were taken during one night. They went singing. We had no idea where they took them but slowly rumors started to rise. "They were taken to prison." "They were deported to one of the Bishop's houses." "They were given passports after a while because, not one of them was a Hungarian citizen."

We all hoped that this last rumor was the truth. Yet I knew for certain that at least one of them was a Hungarian citizen. She had joined the order only recently. Where was she? What was she doing? We could not find out anything about our teachers although we knew of the whereabouts of many sisters whose orders had been disbanded.

Finally our nationalized school and two other private schools were merged into the Veres Pálné High School and thoroughly mixed in four parallel classes for each grade. We no longer knew our classmates and would not dare to trust them. With that new ingenious setup authorities also made it impossible for us to know which teacher sided with the Communists. It was no longer safe to discuss our views at study group time; we had to take everything at face value and regurgitate whatever we were told during class.

Another innovation was that except for Latin all foreign languages were banned. The only one allowed and made compulsory was Russian. The teachers were our former English, French, Italian, and German professors. Who cared about the tiny obstacle that none of them spoke a word of Russian apart from the expressions everybody picked up during the siege? The problem was solved in a simple and easy way: they started their Russian lessons three weeks before we did. Although I hated the Soviets, I was pleased to study the Russian language. I remembered that Father had always encouraged me to learn at least one Slavic language because it would be important when I took over the business; we were surrounded by Slavic countries. Our firm had already established a branch in Czechoslovakia prior to nationalization. Everybody in the country still had the feeling that Communism could not last much longer. "We can wait for the end even in a squatting position," was the whispered hope while everybody listened to the foreign radios. It seemed that the siege had disrupted our lives and the whole country, as one man, waited for its consequences to dissolve, to quiet down as the concentric waves caused by a thrown rock level out on the surface of the lake. Yet nothing happened that would have confirmed our hope. To the contrary.

Mother, as the first of the accused "criminals," would be tried by worker judges. The second was Grandfather, followed by fourteen of our employees. The hearings had started. Their crime: everything had belonged to the people originally. Whoever had a fortune must have taken it from them. For the time being none of them was locked up because there was no actual crime committed that the Communists could think of. The business was in Mother's name exactly because she knew nothing about it and our lawyers found it most advisable that way. There were times when the business changed owners within the family almost every week because of the change in different laws. Our other stores, operating under other names than Molnár & Moser, were also taken by now as were the apartment houses. Sándor, the security policeman, was right; the Communists did not need our generous offer. They had other ways to free us from our properties. We relied more and more on the parcels Father sent us.

Along with the trial came an order to take inventory of whatever we had, as one of the possible punishments could be complete confiscation of every personal belonging, Pista, being a law student, had had experience with that procedure and explained it to me in detail.

"I helped my uncle the other day with a 'total confiscation of property.' You know, he is a lawyer and he tried to save as much for the family as was humanly possible. As its name implies, this kind of confiscation involves everything you have, except a bed and chair for everybody, a table, a place to hang your clothes and then any kind of instrument or tool which is in connection with your profession. Typewriter, piano, sewing machine, carpentry tools are good examples. They are means to help you make a living. Children's clothes cannot be confiscated either because the government wants to win the good will of the younger generation. Actually, we could save from the government everything that belonged to the children."

His words resounded in my ear when, a few days later, two security policemen arrived to "list" all our belongings so we should not be able to sell them just in case the judgment would be "total confiscation."

When this took place Tommy was at our house. He too had experience with this kind of trouble when his aunt suffered the same fate. Mother and my grandparents sat with the two officers and talked things over.

Tommy motioned me into another room.

"Quick," he whispered. "Where do you keep your silver?"

"What?"

"Your silver. It's sterling, isn't it?"

My brain started clicking. I pulled him into the kitchen.

"Here!" I handed him a bag, then casually strolled back into the room where the policemen sat and out the other door, closing it tight behind me.

Pista's words rang clear in my memory. "They do not hurt the young generation. They want to make sure of their good will towards them."

I grabbed the huge oriental rug off the floor and dragged it into the back bathroom. I opened the window and managed to pull the carpet up to the windowsill. The bathroom window opened to a small back yard. I gave it a push. The rug fell two stories and landed with a heavy, soft thump.

By the time I shoved down the third carpet I was quite experienced. Then I ran back to the kitchen. Tommy's bag was filled with the cutlery, silver trays, platters.

"Take it down," I whispered. Then I looked around. I heard one of the policemen dictate: "One picture of a lady, valued at …

The pictures…

Tommy was back. I did not even ask him what he did with the silver.

"Quick, the pictures."

"Which are the most valuable ones?"

"Take this one with the hermit … it was done by one of Rembrandt's friends. Some claim that Rembrandt made a few of the strokes himself. And this one … this is Mother's favorite. We must save this one."

"Jewels! Do you have jewelry?" asked Tommy.

The door opened and Mother came out for a moment.

"One of the policemen must be on our side. He whispered to me: 'That's too many' when we opened Grandfather's closet. Take some of my clothes."

I ran to her closet and grabbed an armful.

"Give me the furs!" Tommy ordered. "Only the most expensive stuff. You must leave some or we'll get into trouble if they see that everything is missing."

We worked quicker than I ever thought possible.

Mother must have been right about the policeman. Was it her charm again that enchanted him? He made considerable noise before he opened the door; we had time to disappear.

Mother opened her own closet door and said, "And these are my clothes."

She nearly fainted when she saw that hardly anything was left in place. She quickly added, "This happens when one has three teenage daughters," and smiled her way through this obstacle as she had through many others.

The policeman smiled back. Did he have teenagers of his own? Or did he want to help a friendly "insect" to survive?

～

Then it happened again. Once more Mother was taken by the police. Our fright was no longer as intense although we were aware of the possibility that she might be put into jail, concentration camp or disappear forever. Slowly it became a way of life to have her gone now and then. The voice deep inside me gave me comfort: "There is nothing that you and I cannot solve together." I no longer despaired but every time Mother was gone icy fingers closed around my stomach and twisted it into knots. It was not so bad when she was home although I was constantly aware of my stomach and this awareness turned into pain every time I ate something besides mashed potatoes or cream of wheat. On days when Mother was taken, or when our house was searched I could not eat even that.

On that memorable day Mother came home from the police all smiles. She closed the door and whispered to the family, gathered around our dinner of boiled potatoes with lard.

"You know what happened today? When I got out from the police station the officer who was questioning me followed me and asked: 'Would you have an espresso coffee with me?' I did not think I should contradict him. When we sat down with the steaming coffee he leaned closer. I thought: 'No, not that.' But 'that' was not what he had in mind. He looked around then started to plead with me: 'I wasn't very bad to you, was I? Will you testify for me if anything, ever?... Well, you know what I mean?' I said: 'No, I don't know what you mean,' although I understood that he was talking about a possible change of power, a slight chance that Hungary might become free again. 'Please, don't pretend, I don't want to catch you, or tempt you. All I want you to do is be on my side if it ever comes to ... well, if somebody ever asks you whether I mistreated you.' I wanted to laugh straight in his face. I wanted to ask him where he got his information, or what he expected but I knew better. I just smiled and said 'Although I don't quite understand what you said, if anybody ever asked me about your behavior I will state the plain truth; I'll say that you behaved like a perfect gentleman. His face relaxed as he sat back in his chair. He ordered a cake and smiled as he asked me if I needed anything, if he could help me."

"I can't believe it," Grandmother said. "They too must think that this whole thing will soon be over and try to find friends among the 'enemy' in order to get protection if Hungary becomes free again." With a twinkle in her eye she continued, "I did not think they studied the Bible. I thought it was there that I read about the wisdom of making friends with one's worldly wealth to acquire true values."

"Then he went on with his ideas on how he could help our family," Mother continued. "He asked me how well off we were financially. I said that it was harder every day but that Father was sending us packages which seemed to arrive very sporadically. He then suggested that he could find you a job, Helen, at an import-export branch of the government, in sales. He said he was going to set up an interview with them. He suggested to use only one of your names, Helen Kovács, a very common name, instead of Helen Bartha-Kovács. He became rather excited when he heard that my daughter spoke several languages at this young age. 'We can use talents like hers.' Of course I said that you would have to finish highschool but he found that no problem." I was very excited at this news. The job would have suited me fine. I was prepared to take over our business, I knew commercial German, French, and English well and I was studying Russian as hard as I could. I did not think that Latin would come in handy. There would not be any business transactions with the Catholic Church, I was convinced about that.

The day of the interview came, while the day of Mother's trial by worker judges drew near. My heart throbbed in my throat as I entered the very official looking building and uttered the party secretary's name to the doorman. He was the highest official in the building. The Secretary, not the chairperson, or president is who really matters in the Communist Party.

"Do you have an appointment?" the man asked sternly.

After a brief phone call he ushered me in with a broad smile: "Comrade Szucs is expecting you." The transformation was miraculous. Doors opened silently. I was given the red carpet treatment.

When we were alone he shuffled around some papers on his desk. He avoided my eyes as he mumbled: "You will be called Helen Kovács. Don't tell anyone your real name." He nearly said, "They should not know that I patronize an 'insect'," but he didn't. His lean tall figure bent over his desk as he continued to rummage around his documents and avoid eye contact with me. "You know, you would be working with capitalists," while he said this I wondered why he was telling me this. Was I considered to be his ally just because I was young? Why did he trust me? Because he was doing me a favor and he expected another one in return? He went on and slowly the picture began to take shape. "We need these capitalists because they speak the languages and we do not. We need hard currency if we want to rebuild our country and successfully fulfill our three-year plan, the building of socialism in our country." He did not need to say anything more. I could have continued the well-known propaganda phrases myself, without his help and all of a sudden I heard myself say it out loud, "We have to enlist all forces to stand firm against a whole imperialist world that plants its spies within our very bosom. We must unite to ensure victory for the world proletariat." He suddenly lifted his head and looked straight at me with his steel-cold blue eyes that showed just the tiniest ray of joy. Then he concentrated on my attire. I was thoroughly "dressed-down" for the occasion. He approvingly nodded.

"You are all right. No wonder you were so highly recommended by the security police, you will do just right. Now, you must be on your guard," he said. "We are surrounded here by capitalists, or imperialists if you please. They, unfortunately for us, are in constant touch with the Western World because we need their knowledge. Until we can educate a generation of self-conscious young Communists, as you yourself might be soon, who, besides being class-conscious will also have the knowledge of foreign languages, technical knowledge, whatever is needed." He seemed to have completely forgotten that he was talking to a representative of the class of 'insects'. My one regurgitated sentence awoke his complete trust. "You must be on your guard," he warned me again. "Whenever you hear or see anything that is contrary to government policy or you are asked to write a letter that would in any way be suspicious you come to me. Straight to me."

"There goes my job," I thought while my heart sank but I went along with his ideas while I knew the answer I would send him tomorrow. "I want to finish highschool and go to university full time because I think I will help my country more if I devote my entire being to one job at a time. I want to follow Lenin's advice to young people: 'Study, study, study!'"

Right now I followed him to meet my would-be co-workers who were supposed to examine my knowledge of languages. I was highly recommended to them, then he left. After the door closed behind him I was looked at like a leper. Yet, everybody exchanged words with me. My name did not betray anything. I was one among the hundreds of thousands of Kovács residing in Hungary. I was a shy young girl who for some unknown reason talked many different languages remarkably well, yet she was highly recommended by the party secretary. Who was she? If I could only tell them. I knew they would accept me with open arms. I was one of them. Yet, how could I convince them? How could I warn them? These and similar thoughts crossed my mind while I was given a German trade magazine and translated it into French orally.

The woman smiled at me. Finally she caught me on something; "Can you take shorthand in French?" No. I could not do that. I grabbed at the opportunity to make myself incapable of doing the job. We talked each other out of having me there. I was relieved. I did not need to excuse myself from the job. They had done it for me, I could not blame them for their suspicion: I was asked to do exactly what they were afraid of.

John Szablya and I waltzed around the dancefloor of the Astoria, an international hotel close to our home. The orchestra played one of the favorites of the day "We'll have a beautiful evening once we get old…" The song pictured an old couple sitting by the fireplace hand in hand, thanking each other for the day they met and their happy lives together. John held me tight. Mother sat at one of the small tables with our lawyer and a glass of sweet vermouth. They talked business while she chaperoned me. Times had changed but we still were not allowed to go out alone with boys. Only after engagement …

I was thinking of the words of the song. Why be happy when we get old? What is wrong with right now? John's gleaming white teeth smiled at me and I closed my eyes. I imagined that I was at a big ball with him. One I had always dreamed about, where everybody wore a long gown and twirled around under a crystal chandelier that threw its glitter onto the mirror-lined walls.

I opened my eyes and I saw tables around us. Small tables surrounded by way too many people for their size drinking their "szimpla" expresso, or maybe a double one. Others sipped wine or vermouth. Everybody drank slowly. The price of one drink had to last all evening. That represented the cover charge.

Outside on the street a crowd was gathering around an American car. We had already paid our tribute to its beauty before we entered. John looked at every feature and noted the innovations since he had last seen one. It must have belonged to a diplomat. No tourists were brave enough or… they probably would not even be allowed to cross the border.

Mother was talking over the details of her trial under the disguise of flirting with the good old man. She was a beautiful single woman now. Nobody knew that she had not filed for divorce and did not consider herself to be eligible. She played her role well; the Communists looked at her approvingly. There is an "insect" that might be re-educated!

As I glanced out the window I saw a policeman approach the car. The crowd dispersed in a hurry.

"It is a beautiful car," remarked John. "A Ford. You know what I heard recently? Whether it is true or not it's a fitting story. I like to believe it really happened. An old English professor here, in Hungary, had one of the early model Fords still in running condition. He had it for the past thirty years. He wrote to the factory for some part that he needed and told them about his enthusiasm for the car. He received a brand new Ford in reply to his letter, along with the needed part."

"Is that so? You mean it would surprise them that somebody kept a car for so long, that the car still worked?"

"In America people change their cars often. They 'trade them in' on new ones all the time. They do not keep them after 100,000 miles."

"That sounds unbelievable. Why would you throw out a perfectly good car in working order?"

"Things are different in America than they are here."

"They must be. I would like to see it for myself some day."

It was safe to talk because we were dancing and moved around so quickly that no one couple could have made sense of what they overheard.

The music stopped. We sat beside Mother,

"The new accusation is that you sabotaged the three-year plan. That can mean at least three years in jail," I heard the lawyer say.

The icy fist twisted my stomach. I gulped down some vermouth.

"I could not have sabotaged something I did not even know about," Mother said very innocently.

"That's easy for you to say but how will you prove it?" the lawyer retorted.

"I won't. Just yesterday I received a message. It was very strange. Do you remember the apprentices with whom we used to play volleyball at the resort on the Danube we built for our employees, Helen?"

Mother looked around. The neighboring tables were empty. The music started again and the couples went to jitterbug. Despite all that Mother was whispering, "I got a message from the worker judge."

The lawyer squinted in surprise behind his thick glasses. "You got a message from the worker judges? What next? Do you know them?"

"I did not think so," said Mother. "But there was this apprentice in our store whose uncle is among the worker judges. He told our apprentice to tell me that nothing can harm me, nobody will bring judgment against me, because I am so charming and beautiful."

"What?" The lawyer's chin dropped. "I have never heard anything of the sort in my life yet. That is encouraging and of course completely possible because the worker judges' word is supreme. The real judge is there to give advice if requested but not to meddle in any way in the serious business of revenge. Because, my dear Baba, you must face it. This trial and whatever befalls you is an all-out revenge. Your charm might help but this would be the first case of mine where something like that would have been of any help. It's completely out of my experience. I really would not count on it if I were you. Let's try to prepare logical answers in case they will ask you questions."

The icy fist let go of my stomach, the voice that was audible again inside me kept up my hope.

"Let's have another dance?" John offered his arm and I took it with a smile.

~

A few days later when Mother was away, two other policemen walked into the house and started their usual search. They did not even bother to tell us what they were looking for. We took it for granted that it was the usual. Every six weeks they came to check whether Father had returned, or just to see if we had something to hide. We started to rely on them to find for us all that we had lost during the six weeks that had elapsed since their last visit. It was a thorough search. This time they concentrated on jewelry.

"What else do you have?" he gruffed at me.

What else? I brought out my jewelry box. He took my chains, bracelets, even the imitation jewelry from Paris. Those looked like real. He piled everything into a mound on the table.

"What do you have, old witch?" he yelled at Grandmother. I wanted to tell him that one did not talk like that to old ladies but I could not open my mouth. She brought out whatever she could think of but still the policeman was not satisfied.

"You must have some Napoleon coins," he scoffed.

"Why would you say that?" I asked finally because I realized that to keep "Napoleons," as these gold coins were nicknamed, was illegal.

"You know very well why. It is illegal and I happen to know that your Grandmother has some in her possession. We raided the house; there is no reason to lie about it. The old woman downstairs, in the lingerie shop, is a black marketeer. She already confessed. You were one of her clients."

I saw Grandmother relax, though her face turned white. The accusation was weighty, but the Napoleons were not in the house.

"Look, the woman told me that a friend of hers was in trouble," Grandmother started talking. "She talked about an old couple who were starving and sick but happened to have this gold piece. I agreed to give them money because I was always a pushover when somebody needed something. She promised to give me the coins today and I was going to find a legal way, through our lawyer, to hand them over to authorities. I do not have the coins."

"Anybody can say that. We'll see how true your story is at the trial. Now put all of these jewels into a bag and hand them over. You are lucky that we will not arrest you for the time being."

Grandmother's hands shook as she stuffed the jewels into the bag by the handful. Most of them were fine imitation jewelry. In times like these one did not keep the real stuff at a place where it was exposed to dangers like the one we were experiencing.

I remembered when Pista had talked about his aunt. When she had been warned to disappear from her own land because no matter what she did the penalty for her mere existence would become higher and higher until she would be taxed out of her land. We no longer had our business, or the apartment houses, or... What else did they want from us? I did not dare to think any farther.

# 31

Mother's trial was over—the day came and went. We had to go to school as on any other, ordinary day.

That icy fist, my constant companion, let go of my heart only when I saw her smile. Then nothing could be wrong. She was back home telling us what happened.

"It was just as that peculiar message had predicted. All sixteen of us who were accused of taking the wealth from the people were acquitted on the grounds that there was no crime committed. Even the one manager who confessed his guilt was pardoned because when asked what he was guilty of he answered that he did not know but if there was any lawbreaking he must have been in on it because Father discussed things with him. The worker judges made crude jokes, but they let him go, too. Thank God for that. He was a nice old man, rather scrupulous but very loyal."

"Then nobody was sentenced?"

"Nobody. Or I should say rather nobody to whom it would matter. You know that Father wrote us to blame everything on him. Being in Paris, he is no longer in a place where the Communists can hurt him. He alone was sentenced to a year and a half in prison and fined 300,000 forints."

When we were alone later that night, Mother's smile turned into a heavy frown. "I must talk to you," she said. "I feel terrible, absolutely awful about what I've done. I went straight to Father Vargha, my confessor, after the trial but I must tell you also. You are the only one of the children who would understand. Father Vargha said that what I did was the only sensible thing I could do and yet… Listen. When it came to this sentence the judge explained to me that the way for me to escape was to accuse Father of the same crime that they accused him of. I must say in front of the worker judges that if he had stolen money from the business, if he had sabotaged the three-year plan, then he did it without my knowledge, behind my back, and I too denounce him. I had to ask for his persecution, for his sentence. I, his wife, who loves him more than anything." She buried her face in her hands and shook her head: "Your father was right. We should have left Hungary. If only…"

I saw that Mother despaired, yet, in the tradition of survival, taught to me by both my parents, this seemed to be the only logical step to take. She would have betrayed us, the three girls and my grandparents, if she had gone to jail for false sentimentalism. All of us knew that the accusations were fabrications. What did she want? I went on and on with my arguments trying to console her, but she was hard to convince.

She finally said, "Look, that all may seem right but that is not the end. I had to file for divorce in order to prove that I meant business."

Although her words hit me in the heart I knew that they meant nothing concerning my parents' relationship. I wanted her to know that so I asked, "Did you really mean to do that?"

"Of course not. I vowed to remain true to your father 'until death do us part,' and that is still my intention."

"Then what is your problem? Don't you know that God is aware of your intentions? Can you imagine that He doesn't know when you pretend for the sake of survival? You make your separation from Father permanent in the eyes of the Communists, what does that mean to you, deep down? This is what it means to God. You just said that this is what Father Vargha also told you. You filed for divorce. So what? The procedure can go on for years. Maybe in the meantime..."

"You mean," Mother's eyes began to twinkle, "you mean we can outsmart them and leave?"

I took a deep breath of the lilac-scented fresh air. Stars twinkled in the sky but the street lights drowned out their feeble rays; we could see only a few of the hundreds of thousands that must have been in the sky on this velvety dark, lukewarm May evening.

Alec sighed. Again! What was the matter with him? We walked arm in arm under the bushes.

"Is something bothering you?" I asked.

He sighed again.

"Why do you keep sighing?"

"I can't tell you. I really shouldn't," he answered with an added sigh. Then he pulled me close. I jerked back automatically. We were taught not to let boys become too familiar. Our first kiss was to be saved for the "one and only." Besides...

"We must not lose Mother and Gábor..." I whispered into his ear, pretending to murmur secrets of love.

"They are right there. See, behind those bushes," he said in a very low voice, then continued normally. "I must have taken it for granted that I saw you every day. Now, when I think," he lowered his voice again, "that soon you may be gone..."

"That is not at all certain. You know as well as I do that so far we have had no success with our plans," I said keeping an eye on the bush behind which Mother was supposed to be. We slowly walked around it. She was sitting on a dark bench with a very good-looking, blond man. Her head touched his strong shoulders. They were whispering sweet nothings into each others' ear. At least it seemed so. Nobody but Alec and I knew what their meeting was about.

We stationed ourselves close to Mother, where we could see her, yet far enough to be able to screen the roads and bushes nearby. Mother and Gábor, the blond giant, should not be disturbed.

While we were watching, Alec absentmindedly played with the tiny blooms of a purple lilac. "Look, Helen, if your mother's talk with that pilot is successful, you may be gone in a week. What is going to become of me? I can't leave my family now. They need me. I am going to graduate in a few weeks. I'll be an engineer, I was promised a job at the Technical University. Yet, I would not dream of keeping you from going…"

I noticed a man standing underneath the lamp post.

"Tomorrow we'll have guests," I said in a loud voice. "Do you want to come and have fun with us?"

I saw Mother pull Gábor's face into her neck as if they kissed. Nobody could recognize him now. Good! She'd heard my warning, the code for "stranger near."

"I'm scared," I whispered. "What if Gábor is an agent and all he wants is to catch us?" I remembered the two times when I had been asked to spy. We had never seen him before this evening.

"Alec?" He must have sensed the question in my tone.

"I love you," he blurted out bluntly.

"*You* love *me*?" I asked while my thoughts ran over pictures of the past years. Yes, since that ominous first bouquet of lilacs at the time Gisèle was staying with us two years before in 1948. I recalled Alec's jealous look when I danced with John, the way he always tried to be wherever I was. He came every day to help us. He was always there when we needed him, that *was* love!

I looked at him in surprise as I said, "Yes, that *must* be love."

Alec pulled me close. It felt good to be in his secure and safe arms. Did I really want to escape and leave all this? The velvety softness of the night, the fragrance of the lilacs—the best things in life that were indeed free, as Mother always said. What was that strange contentedness in me? Could Alec be right? Was that love? How about Pista's freedom-fighting spirit and my matching sudden temperament? Our agreement on so many things? How about John, that premonition of mine about our perfect match? I brushed the thought aside. He was too old for me. Ten whole years older. Tommy's help and our common childhood? His trust in me? Was I in love with any of them? All of them? Could I be in love with more than one?

"Keep going or we'll lose Mother," Alec put his arm around my shoulders and pulled me back onto the path.

What an idyllic picture for any Communist to see! My single Mother walking with one of the "sons of the people" arm-in-arm, engaged in the sweetest love-talk, while Alec and I, as good young Communists should, accompanied them on their date. Alec and I, as second cousins, did not need chaperons and we were qualified to keep an eye on Mother.

"Mother, I am cold!" I said in a voice loud enough to be heard by the dating couple. The code meant that someone was approaching from the right. I saw them snuggle up close together as they sat on the bench in the dark shade of the bush, while Alec and I stationed ourselves under the street lamp to distract the attention of passers-by from Mother and Gábor. They were discussing the plans for a mock-hijacking: a way we planned to escape this time.

I drew closer to Alec. "Alec, how can we be sure this is love?"

"Can't you feel it in your blood? Don't torture me any longer! Day in and day out I must look at you and admire you from afar. Why can't I take you in my arms and kiss you?"

With that he did just as he said, because, I guess, he could not find any good reason why this should not be done. It was a gentle kiss, like the breeze that warmed us. It lasted only a few seconds, but its after-effect put us into the mood of spring. Pista and Tommy shared many memories of my childhood; John, although he seemed like a good match, was probably interested in someone older than me. But Alec! He kissed me! He kissed me! Who cared that we were about to part forever if our plans with the hijacking went through! Who thought of the disturbing fact that we were second cousins? Today the sky was full of stars, the lilacs' fragrance was overpowering, we were together, and we were in love!

～

We were back home, sitting around the dining room table with Grandmother, Grandfather, and Alec. The little ones were asleep. Mother explained:

"Gábor said that he would land on a field near the Lake Balaton. Some of the refugees would be on the plane already, one of the ladies volunteered to pull a toy pistol on Gábor and 'hijack the plane.' We would be waiting in the field. After the landing we'd board the plane and he'd take off, then fly towards the border. In twenty minutes, he could fly us to Graz, Austria. We have to consider the fighter planes that would be dispatched from Hungary and the Soviet zone in Austria as soon as they spot him flying in the wrong direction, so he wants to fly according to the flight plan as long as possible. He thinks we could escape the attention of the authorities until it is too late for them to react."

"How would we get to that field?" Grandmother inquired. She looked very tired. Somehow I had the feeling that she was not quite well.

"By car," Mother said. "Gábor's friend is organizing the trip to Keszthely."

"I don't think I like the idea of being shot at while flying in the air," said Grandfather.

"Well, we can take it or leave it," said Mother, "but I think it would be worth a try if it would buy our freedom."

Grandmother looked into the distance. It seemed that she did not see anything in the room. She did not answer,

I sat on her lap to cheer her up as we always did when we were little.

"Ouch," she moved her knee.

"Does it hurt, Grandmother?"

"Yes. In the last couple of days it hurt more than ever. Maybe it's the weather," she brushed it aside. I got up and put my arms around her.

"Dear Grandmother, don't you think we should try at least?" I asked.

"Yes," she said in resignation. "I guess so. You must try to reunite your family."

"But you are coming with us?!"

"Of course…" Again, that strange look.

None of us was satisfied with the plan but it was the only one we had.

❧

The plane-hijacking plot was aborted before it ever took off the ground. We were waiting for hours to be picked up at the designated place and finally gave up our vigil and went home. We heard later that half an hour after we left our post, the police came to arrest us. Luckily, we were not there anymore. The friendly pilot, Gábor, and many of the would-be refugees were arrested.

A few weeks after our attempt, we sat together at another meeting place for a different escape plan. Grandfather was pacing the floor with his characteristic limp leaning on his rubber-capped cane. Grandmother sat heavily in an armchair. A small bag she carried contained her medicines and insulin shots. She frowned and sighed occasionally.

Marie and Elisabeth played Monopoly in the corner of the room.

Alec was not with us. We had kissed our teary good-byes hours before.

I could hardly suppress the desire to look out the window into the darkening sky. Where are our guides? How is this night going to end for us? Will we sleep on the ship, built tightly into its very bottom, below the cargo? How can we even think of balancing a row boat, let alone sliding down into its hull so as not to be seen from the shore while two strong men handle the oars? How can we go unnoticed; the two huge bodies of my grandparents, both weighing over 250 pounds, three young girls, and Mother. That made six of us. This plan sounded just as incredible to me as that other one with the airplane. I shuddered at the sound of footsteps along the corridor. Mother lifted her head but she did not stop her sentence. She tried to behave as naturally as possible. The family whom we "visited" this afternoon did not know that they were accomplices to a "crime." They too would have risked arrest. For illegal border crossing, the penalty was two to three years in prison.

Nothing! The steps clicked down the stairs. Two hours had passed since the time when our guides should have arrived.

"Let's go home!" Grandmother demanded suddenly. "I can't stand it any longer." Then, realizing that she might have given away our secret she added, "My knee hurts very badly. We have to get home and start dinner. I am sorry to spoil your fun."

"Maybe we should leave," Mother was hesitant.

"Let's leave," I echoed Grandmother. I thought of Alec.

"Aren't we going somewhere?" Grandfather asked absentmindedly.

"Yes," said Mother. "We are going home."

It was a long wait. We had spent four hours at the house of our unsuspecting friends, chatting the time away. According to the custom of the day we were not offered anything to eat or drink. I doubt that they had anything in their kitchen.

Our hosts, still puzzled, ushered us to the door.

A few minutes later, as our streetcar passed our friends' door we saw a police car stop in front of the building. I thought I saw one of our guides in the vehicle.

"Thank you, God!" my prayer welled up in silence. I tugged at Mother's sleeves and she turned. Her face grew pale, but she said nothing.

# 32

"I won, I won, I won!" I jumped up and down with a joy that I could not understand. What I won was the competition writing a Russian article for the school's wall newspaper, a new tradition brought to us by the Communists because of a paper shortage. This way a whole class could read just one copy. My article was about the value of study and knowledge giving an example of Lenin's ideology on the subject. It was written in my halting, very newly-acquired Russian, but I had kept it simple and used Communist jargon. Yippee, I could fool them!

I, one of the chief "insects" in my class, won over the children of security policemen and real Communists who came to congratulate me. Agnes, the fat, little girl and her freckled, red-haired stepsister, Agi; Evi, the one whose father was an opportunist Communist using the Party for his own needs, and Mary, whose mother had died in a concentration camp during Nazi occupation.

For the reactionaries, this event was more than a triumph. It meant that we could outsmart them even in their own territory. Judy started humming the victory march from Aida and pretty soon they all joined in. Bonzi, with her ever-smiling face; Klára, the girl who sat beside me; Kathy, whose Father used to own a bookstore; tall and lean Elisabeth, an ex-princess; along with Niki, who was brought up by some nuns because her parents lived in the country, far from any high school.

I could hardly wait to tell the news to Alec. That night we stood in line in front of the Opera, the usual thing to do if one was a student. The fad of the times was to submerge oneself in the enjoyment of music, the only realm that could not be swamped by Communist propaganda.

It was a clear October night, the stars' brilliance faded in the glitter of the lights that adorned the Opera and the wide, glamorous, former Andrássy Avenue, now renamed after Stalin. The first frostbite of the autumn colored our cheeks red during the long wait. Yellow and brown leaves twirled around in the wind then fell on the clean-swept sidewalk. Until morning the dance of the leaves would go on. These messengers of fall would have ample time to remind us of the passage of time before they would end up in the dustbin, tossed there by one of the busy street sweepers' brooms.

Alec's peculiar half-smile showed that he was in a good mood and he raised his left eyebrow as he turned to Pista who stood not so far from us, "Are you coming with Bonzi?"

"I sure am, " he replied with a broad grin. "But I would not want her to come and stand in line in this kind of weather. Her kidneys are acting up again. I don't like it." His smile turned into a frown. "I wish they could do something about her problem. It all started when she had scarlet fever as a little girl. It's about time they found a cure for it."

The line was long already, although it was only ten o'clock in the evening. The ticket office did not open until ten the next morning but we were hoping that soon somebody would come out and hand us numbers so we could go home to sleep and come back the next day.

"Remember, last year we had to stand in line from about one o'clock after midnight until the ticket office opened at ten a.m. to get tickets," Alec reminisced.

"Lately our series tickets were cut back to only ten performances a year instead of the usual twenty in order to accommodate more people," I remarked.

"The rest of the tickets are sold in the factories." I heard John's voice behind me. Just as I thought, he was with an older girl, one I knew because she used to go to the same school I did. She was lovely and in high spirits. They must have had a great time together judging by her happy laughter. I felt my heart beat quicker although my mind told me that I was right in choosing Alec. He was nearer my age.

"In the factories?" I said, hoping that my voice would not betray me. I had to speak, I could not bear to stand by silently, watching that girl's triumph over me.

"Yes, Helen," John said with his entrancing smile. "They are selling tickets there in order to get the workers interested in going to the Opera. With the choice of plays nowadays, the job is quite easy."

"Have you been to a theatre lately?" I asked him.

"Yes. I have seen all that is worth seeing. Molière and Shakespeare. The rest..." John stopped short of finishing his sentence. A policeman walked past the line swinging his club, pretending not to pay any attention to the chattering lines of teenagers although his hawk eyes combed the lines with strict regularity. John's text changed according to the environment.

"They are very good musicals and dramas. I heard that one of them deals with an agricultural co-op. The boy is a tractor-driver and the girl is a manual laborer. They fall in love. The 'kulaks,' peasants bred in capitalism, want to stop the utilization of machines on the co-op in order to prove the superiority of their outdated methods. The tractor-driver, who is also the party secretary, withstands their attack and there is an especially intriguing duet in which the two lovebirds promise each other to be faithful to the three-year plan and over-fulfill their quotas, even in producing children for their country. The curtain falls before they even get a chance to kiss." John added that last sentence only when he saw that the policeman reached the other end of the line and all was clear. We burst into laughter.

The policeman was on his way back now. As a consequence John continued with the most serious face, "Yes, comrades, there are funny parts in it, too. It is indescribably funny how stupid the capitalist peasants, or 'kulaks,' are when they try to cling on to their miserable forty or fifty acres instead of breaking down the doors of the Communist Party in their impatience of their enthusiasm to offer everything up for use in the co-operatives. After all, many of them had received the land from the Communists, when it was distributed in 1945. Why not give it back? How can anyone be so land hungry?"

That was well put. It was funny but also the cruel truth. I thought of Grandpa in Cegléd, who by now had offered up the forty acres he had purchased when he was a young man. It was supposed to provide security for his family in his old age. His store was nationalized by now and he, at the age of seventy-three, worked with his two hands in his own ex-store under his former apprentice, Misi. He was still considered a "kulak." Just the other day, Little Grandma asked the policeman who took Grandpa to be "questioned" in the middle of the night why they still considered him a "kulak." The officer had no answer for her but his eyes showed sympathy. He was one of the better ones. He whispered, "I don't know, lady, I just obey orders." The fact that he called her "lady" and not "comrade" betrayed his compassion. Thank God that Misi was Grandpa's boss, I recalled the time when he had said that he liked Grandpa as his own father. Now he treated his old master better than most children treat their parents. I did not say anything.

The policeman continued his "inconspicuous" walk.

"How is your Grandmother?" John inquired.

"She is not at all well. She has cancer again. This time it's in her bones. It started in her knee, but last time she came back crying from the doctor. She is receiving X-ray treatments. Until now she was always told which part to expose to the rays, but that day when she asked how to sit some student nurse told her that it did not matter. She understood that the cancer had spread through her whole body. Since then, Grandmother has been slipping, and she is in bed most of the time."

"I should bring my parents up to visit her. It has been such a long time since they have seen each other," John commented. "My father tells me that it was during the First World War when he and your grandfather first met. Neither of them was able to fight on the front because my father had only one lung and your grandfather's eyesight was less than perfect. So the two of them got together and organized a hospital for the artists who were not officers. It was very important for artists to receive adequate care that would enable them to continue with their profession. Very often during the war simple enlisted men had their limbs amputated by poorly qualified surgeons when they could have been saved."

"Is that so?" I was amazed. "Of course, there was no penicillin and in the thick of the battle, who could blame those surgeons? It was better to stay alive and lose a limb, than to die."

"Anyway, that is where they met first. My mother, who was not married to my father yet, had a very good friend. She acted as the maid of honor at their wedding, where it turned out that the two good friends, the one of my mother and the one of my father—who was your grandfather, were brother and sister. My mother's friend then became my godmother."

Alec looked at me impatiently.

"What performance do you want to see?" he asked John in order to be noticed and to change the subject that left him out completely. The glamorous girl also seemed annoyed and she was glad to answer Alec:

"*La Traviata*. I love Verdi's catchy tunes. I heard that in his time, the grand arias were not released even to the lead singers until the late afternoon of the day of the first performance because otherwise the whole town whistled it before the curtains opened."

"I can believe that." Alec's eyes lit up. "We want to get some tickets for that performance also. The singers are excellent. Last week I tried to get tickets to it, but by the time the office opened all they had left were the most expensive seats."

John smiled at me. Did he notice also that the two were trying to make up for our involuntary intimacy? Was there some interest in him after all?

Puzzles, puzzles. The line started moving. The ticket window opened wide enough to hand out the numbers.

"Thank God. It's about time," Pista mumbled. "I thought my feet would freeze to the ground."

The brisk walk down the Andrássy (Stalin) Avenue felt good. On this same avenue in house 60, very inconspicuous in the row of gray houses, was the headquarters of the security police, the AVO. Many people breathed their last breath of fresh air on these very sidewalks. But we did not think of that. We were young, carefree, and happy that at least for today we had no worse worries than to get tickets to our favorite performance.

Alec by now had his degree in engineering and since the summer he had been working as an assistant professor at the Technical University of Budapest. When we reached the inside of our old house that was still locked by key from the outside world, he jerked me possessively into his arms and kissed me hard on the mouth. It felt good to be in his arms now and I was pleased about his jealousy. I must have meant something special to him. Yet, his kiss was that of a boy's. I am sure mine was not very passionate either. Was that what sex was all about? Was there more to it?

Christmas and New Year's passed. I saw Alec every day. John showed up occasionally. I still could not quite understand why he did not come more often. Alec and I were very close, we even kissed sparingly, but I knew that our relationship was not all it could have been.

On a gray day in February 1951, I was walking home from school, my overstuffed schoolbag bouncing against my legs at every step. Cold sleet fell around me as I left my friend Klára at the door of the apartment where she lived with her father and little sister. Klára seldom talked and seemed always in a hurry and no wonder. Her mother had died when Klára was only ten years old. Ever since then she had been mother to her little sister and housekeeper for her father.

"See you tomorrow," I called as she went into the house, but she did not answer.

I went on down the street, passing empty store buildings, where small, privately-owned shops had once flourished. Now all were closed and boarded up. The only employer was the state. There were no colors any more only the dull gray of defeat and despair. No smiles or laughter, either, and none of the courtesy we used to find in clerks. Only a few days before I had gone into one of the state stores looking for a pair of shoes, size nine. The clerk had stared at me and barked, "I haven't got any." "Could you please tell me whether you expect any soon or where I could get them?" "I dunno." She shrugged, turned, and left me to my fate.

Further down the street I saw a group of girls waiting for the bus. Most of them wore loose "kuli" style coats, fastened with a bow around the neck, the fad of the season. How I wanted to have one. Red or beige; those were the favorite colors. I sighed and turned away.

Another picture came to my mind as I hurried along the rainy street, chilled to my bones. Grandmother in her room. Thanks to free national medical care there was no oxygen available in the country for sick people. Luckily we found a friend who had a still unnationalized locksmith shop

313

and received oxygen for welding. He let us have a tank, Grandmother could hardly breathe anymore.

I prayed for her every day, when on my way to school. I stopped at University Church, arriving just in time for communion. Many of my friends did the same. In those welcome minutes of union with Christ, our bitterness welled up and was soothed for the day.

The thought of Grandmother made me recall the day when John Szablya had kept his promise and brought his parents along to see Grandmother. We cleaned and cooked and did our best to make them feel welcome. Mother had great respect for them and I heard so much good about them that I was scared to death to blunder in front of them. There was no reason to be afraid. Two lovely people emerged with completely white hair, benevolent blue eyes, and beauty beyond description. They were elegant in their simple black attire, but what made them beautiful? Their faces had wrinkles, they looked like ordinary people… finally I understood it! It was goodness, love and peace that made them different. A sort of inner joy radiated from their whole being. I thought of Mother's words when the security police asked us to spy. I knew that this was it! John's parents were completely free. There was nothing on their conscience that could have or would have bothered them. Two people, whose home was burnt during the siege, ignited by burning gasoline, their life savings eaten up by inflation, and yet they smiled as they tried to make a living from their pension.

I turned the corner and my heart started to throb in my throat. Will the black flag be out? Mother promised to put out this sign of death on the balcony as soon as Grandmother died. But what if she might not be home at the time? I thought gratefully of the two Franciscan sisters who had joined our household since their order was disbanded. They would do it. They took turns sitting with Grandmother. Grandfather would not leave her side, but he was not able to help much. Mother kept constantly busy; as if this busyness would keep her from falling apart! There was always something that had to be done in a feverish hurry. Was she afraid? We had never been without Grandmother before, but then, for years she had been confiding in *me*. Ever since Grandmother's first cancer surgery. No, the black flag was not out. Would there be hot soup on the table when I arrived home? I doubled my steps.

I remembered now the time when John's parents left that memorable day. It was one of the last clear moments in Grandmother's life. She looked at me with an impish smile: "They did not come to see me! They came to 'inspect' a certain girl!"

# 33

The warm April sunshine stroked my black veil. According to Hungarian custom, everybody was in stark black at the graveside of a relative, Joseph Tóth, the son of Aunt Majszi, Grandfather's sister.

I held Mother's hand tight as I watched the priest bless the coffin of my second-uncle. I thought of his miserable last months. A young man of thirty-five, or was it forty, eaten up by T.B., dying in a dark apartment. He was an officer in the war, and one night he was quartered in a peasant house. The woman did not tell him that her husband died of T.B. a few nights before in the same bed. Uncle Josef contracted the disease. There were no antibiotics yet at the time.

He married his wife, now a sobbing widow, during the war. When she was three months pregnant, they advanced in forced march towards Germany and she had lost her baby. A few months ago I saw her sneak her own food onto her husband's plate in hopes of keeping him alive. She took him to the doctor back and forth, carrying his wasting body in her arms up the stairs to the third floor, because the elevator had been out of order since the war.

Beside her stood Aunt Majszi, the mother of the dead officer. Her eyes burned feverishly. She had now lost two husbands and three children. Her only living relative was her daughter-in-law, shaking beside her under her veil. She was grasping John Szablya's arm, he was holding her. Of course, I just remembered, John was her godson, and the two were very fond of each other.

After the members of the mourning group all had a chance to pay their last tribute by throwing a fistful of earth on the lowered coffin. I felt someone squeeze my hand. It was John. He asked, "Grandmother?" I nodded. He squeezed my hand again. "When is the funeral?"

~

They were there at Grandmother's burial, John and his picture-book parents. I was happy that he was present. The church filled to the door and then overflowed. There were many to whom Grandmother had meant a lot. The employees, who were forbidden to see us, streamed to the church—old friends and beggars, whose lives had become bearable through Grandmother's good heart. Cleaning women and maids who worked for us. Relatives and doctors, and finally, family. As I watched the black-clad crowd, I hugged my sisters close to me. "What do they know about who she really was? Why do they say they are sorry? What did she mean to them?" I whispered to the two crying girls. "They'll never know what she meant to us!" A deep sob broke out from the very bottom of my soul.

Death.

How ironic of life that Grandmother, whose hand always shielded our eyes from disaster, should be the first to inflict that pain on three girls. She lay there, her face a yellowish color, her nose translucent, her eyes closed. All about her was peaceful. I felt I should be afraid. But why? She was still my Grandmother. I pretended that she was alive. I bent down as always and kissed her cheeks. They were ice cold but I knew that she was there, that she would be with us forever. For *her* earthly barriers no longer existed and pain was gone forever. There was peace on her face. A blunt pain around my heart told me that we would never be able to sit on her lap anymore or hear her voice. Her laughter would never again fill the air. I looked at her face that seemed to smile and tears poured from my eyes. I know I was crying for myself.

Grandfather and Mother sat together at the funeral. His shoulders shook occasionally. His cane rested between his legs as he sat in the pew. Mother's veil covered her face. That was the last trip for Grandmother into this church, where she lived half her life. Every day she would walk down to communion. Her work centered around the needs of the altar, the poor. As Mass continued, sobs broke out here and there. People I did not even know mourned for her. Did they too cry for themselves? That little part of them that will be put into the grave with Grandmother?

Death! Why didn't it seem as close during the siege as it did now? Will I ever be afraid of it again, knowing that Grandmother would be waiting for me?

I thought of how much she longed to see my wedding, at least the first wedding of her granddaughters! Now she was gone, yet I was sure she would be there when I pronounced my marriage vows.

Right after Mass the coffin was enclosed in more coffins. Mother and we three girls accompanied Grandmother on her last trip. We were taking her to Szolnok, to our family's burial grounds where Grandfather had built a small chapel when his son had died in 1933.

Grandfather's sister-in-law joined the four of us in the chapel with the priest and the cantor. The sunny weather was ruffled by a chilly breeze as the cantor intoned the "Dies irae," the customary hymn for funerals. I enjoyed listening to the tremendous words, the thunderous voice of God's wrath, that dissolved in the hope of resurrection through the grace given by God gratuitously to all, ending in a gentle supplication for eternal rest.

The trap door to the crypt opened and Grandmother was laid to eternal rest in the place prepared for her beside her son. Then it was all over.

When we came up from the cold cellar I heard for the first time the question that was posed by many in the coming months, as so many good, long-suffering people died one after another.

"Why do so many good people die?" asked Aunt Margaret, Grandfather's sister-in-law. "I must think of the times right before the first communism we had in 1919, then again before World War II. What is in store for us now?"

# 34

We didn't need to wait long for the answer.

Aunt Majszi, Grandfather's sister, called one spring-filled, sunny morning. She sounded puzzled. "I received an order, an eviction, or rather, deportation…"

We ran over to her apartment immediately and saw the papers. Tomorrow at 5 o'clock in the morning the security police would pick her up, together with her daughter-in-law. Whatever they could carry they were allowed to take along. Mother read it, so did Alec and I. Finally our lawyer arrived. He read every line carefully, then blinked a few times with his myopic eyes behind the thick glasses. "That is the first time I have seen one of these. I can't imagine what they mean. I'll be back." With that, he left.

I recalled Tommy's presence of mind when the security police inventoried our home. I asked, "Aunt Majszi, what is the most important thing that you will need, wherever they take you? Do you have a knapsack?"

Mary, her daughter-in-law, got out her late husband's army duffle-bag.

"Medicines," she mumbled and placed her mother-in-law's pills into one of the compartments. "Heavy shoes, warm clothes, lighter ones for the summer."

Alec and the co-tenants started hauling the furniture into the next room that was occupied by another family. "Who knows what will happen to the apartment. This paper only let them keep what they can take with them," Alec muttered.

I was astonished that I did not shake and that my stomach did not hurt. I was full of action and I felt every muscle and nerve in my body working against the enemy. "Outsmart them" something commanded inside me.

Aunt Majszi looked puzzled, yet the whole thing seemed to mean less to her than it did to the others. She had already lost everything that mattered: her husband, her sons. She still had her pension, nothing was said about that in the paper. However, nothing was said about where they were going either.

A shiver ran through me. Did that paper say deportation? Wasn't that the same word the Germans used when they … yes, they deported the Jews to Dachau … Auschwitz … I looked at my Aunt Majszi, at her old, pale, thin figure, her emotionless face, and at the healthy, good-looking blonde widow, her daughter-in-law. Gas chambers. No, it can't be. Why would they? I grabbed the sofa and shoved it so hard that Alec yelled at me, "Helen, not so fast, we have to open the other side of the door first." I had not even noticed what I had done. "I shouldn't," I told myself. "I can't start despairing now."

The telephone rang.

"For you!" Aunt Majszi handed the phone to Mother. Her face turned pale. She put down the receiver. "Two friends are being deported also. They asked for help in emptying their apartment." She looked around. "I think there are enough of you here. I will go over with Marie and Elisabeth to those other two friends. Maybe the janitor will look after Grandfather." She kissed Aunt Majszi and left.

I heard crying in the kitchen. I pushed the door open. The co-tenant's sister sat at the kitchen table. Her shoulders shook. "What's the matter?" I asked.

"My fiancé is being deported. The order came for his grandfather and all the family living with him. He was one of those. What am I going to do?" I grabbed her and pulled her off the chair, giving her a little shove towards the door. "Whatever you will do later, go now and be with him, help him for God's sake!" I yelled louder than I should have, having drained all of my excitement into this one shriek. My loudness surprised her. "You are right," she mumbled and ran out of the apartment.

Somebody from the apartment next door brought a big pot of beans.

"Come and eat, everybody! I bet none of you has had a bite since the morning." We looked at each other. We had not had anything to eat but we did not notice it. Now everybody gathered around the pot and she ladled out the food silently. I did not even know half the people who were there.

By seven o'clock in the evening the apartment was completely empty. "You can sleep with us," the co-tenants told Aunt Majszi and Mary. "You must be here when they come to pick you up. Everybody else must leave. They might appear suspicious to the police simply by their presence."

"But why?" Aunt Majszi's great dark-ringed eyes looked with a deep inner fear at something beyond the persons she addressed. "Why would they take *us*?"

The question hung in the air unanswered.

Our lawyer did not return, I kissed Aunt Majszi good-bye and left with Alec.

When we arrived home, we heard that mother was by now at the fifth place to help people move. Our next-door neighbors were among those deported. I always thought that they spied on us. Were the rumors false after all? Or did they run out of material? Where would the police take all these people?

We went to bed without knowing the answers. At four in the morning I woke up. I thought I heard steps, … no, that couldn't be … whoever would come would have to ring the doorbell two flights down. He couldn't just come

319

and walk around here. Then I heard the sounds of a car. The car stopped. Would the bell ring? I wanted to look out the window but somehow I felt that even if I moved I might invite disaster.

Then that too passed. It was morning and in the sunshine the shadows of the night disappeared. The footsteps were those of Grandfather, who heavily shuffled towards the bathroom. There was no trace of a car in the whole neighborhood, only the horses of the garbage collector trod the road. Children played in the park by the time I had to go to school.

The fear came back. Would my classmates be there? Do they deport teachers? Why not me?

School was there as usual. No news in the papers. Some people were being deported, but apparently it was nobody's business. All day silence. Dead silence hidden behind everyday sounds, smells, and tastes.

Three days later we knew more. Much more. The first notes, written on toilet paper, were thrown out of sealed box cars, the usual Soviet transportation convenience. "They are taking us towards the East, destination unknown." Only six years ago friends disappeared towards the West. Where are they taking them now?

Whispers circulated in town. There seemed to be no set pattern at first. One hundred families were deported because they were invited to a certain wedding. Hungary's ex-crown-prince, Otto Habsburg, got married and, foolishly enough, considering it a mere courtesy, he sent out wedding announcements to Hungary, knowing full well that none of the people could come. Were people responsible now for mail they had not even received yet? Among those deported were people of all faiths, including Jewish people, who, after having suffered during Nazi times, should be an obvious group to be exempt this time around. Lawyers shared this "honor" to be among the "chosen ones" with professors and policemen, bankers, and officers of the army, merchants and widows like Aunt Majszi. Who would be next was anyone's guess.

Father's good friends, Uncle Charles and Uncle Stephen, still joined us for dinner every Tuesday. We always tried to save something tasty for them like ham or smoked ox tongue from Cegléd. Little Grandma still found ways to surprise us with food packages. Love's expression often came through the stomach in Hungary.

About a week after deportations had started, we sat together with the two doctors. Uncle Stephen talked:

"I studied the history of the Soviet Union and the history of the Bolshevik Party and I discovered that Lenin was the first one to introduce deportations in 1922. Circumstances were very similar to ours. After the revolution there was a scarcity of apartments and there were 'insects' of all kinds in the big cities. Many still lived in desirable apartments, even though they had to share them with others. The best way to get rid of them and solve the problem of apartment shortage was to deport them into the homes of capitalist peasants, 'kulaks,' thereby inconveniencing both families."

"Yes. This is exactly what happened," said Mother. "Aunt Majszi's first letter tells us about the place, Hajdunánás, where they had taken them. She and her daughter-in-law were quartered into the house of a 'kulak.' They have one room that has an earthen floor and they have access to the outhouse and the kitchen. They have taken them towards the East, but they are still in Hungary. They were not taken to Siberia."

"If they follow the pattern set in the Soviet Union, they will remain in the country," said Uncle Stephen. "They are assigned a circle with a one-mile radius. They can move within that but not out of it."

"The younger ones are taken to work," I interjected. "My friend wrote that she is taken every day to work on an herb farm."

"But why do they deport some and not the others?" asked Mother,

"How do you know they will not deport all of us?" asked Uncle Charles. "Baba," he turned to Mother, "maybe you should finalize your divorce now."

"What difference would it make?" asked Mother.

"It could make a difference. A colleague of mine, a doctor, said that his wife received a deportation order, along with her parents with whom they shared an apartment. My colleague insisted that he would go with them into deportation if they took his wife. By the evening the order was reversed. The family was permitted to stay. Budapest needs doctors."

"I heard a rumor that one of my friends got married," I said.

"Could that have been the reason?"

I recalled the young men who had a Jewish wife in every town during Nazi times in order to save them from deportations.

It was Tuesday night. Tomorrow morning was one of those days ... Deportation orders came on Monday, Wednesday, and Friday. They were carried out the next day at 5 o'clock in the morning. Always at a time when one had to be wakened from sleep, completely confused, at the mercy of the arrestor.

Would our doorbell ring on Wednesday?

❧

It was the first week in June. We sat together again to discuss our future. Mother accepted a menial job, assistant helper to an electrician and left for work every day in her newly purchased coveralls. She wore her usual semi-high heeled shoes and got whistles wherever she went. However, she was one of the "daughters of the people" now, her identification card declared her to be a "worker."

We knew that this was not enough, Alec got me a job for the summer at the Technical University as a lab technician. Even two jobs would not make our family "irreplaceable." In order to avoid deportations one needed a certificate to indicate that one could not be substituted by anybody because one's absence would endanger the fulfillment of the five-year plan.

Mother was asking for a finalization of her divorce now with the help of Father's good friends, who testified that the couple had not lived together in the past two years. Six months was the officially required time. Desertion was a clear-cut case. That ensured a speedy procedure.

"Only medical doctors and engineers are 'irreplaceable' it seems," said Mother.

"Let's get married," I suggested.

"What?" Mother's bubbly laughter burst forth.

"Why not?" I asked. "Martha, a friend of mine saved her whole family by marrying an engineer."

Our lawyer blinked a few times and mumbled, "I've heard of such cases."

"That sounds like a musical," Mother laughed again.

"It sure does," said Uncle Charles who had come over to help us decide.

"How about John Szablya?" he suggested.

I thought of his white-haired parents and the laughing girl. "No," I said. "He wouldn't want to. He has to protect his parents." I did not say anything about the girl. "I'll ask Alec," I added. "He would be willing."

"Can you get married at sixteen?" Mother asked.

"I don't think that my friend was older," I said.

"With parental permission," said the lawyer.

"Granted," Mother laughed.

"I have others in mind also, if Alec is not willing, I can come up with a few young doctors," said Uncle Charles with a smile.

"I don't mean for you to really get married," Mother frowned.

"No, of course not. Why would I want to?" I replied. "I want to go to college first. But if I don't pretend to get married I will pretty soon be working in the rice fields or building roads."

Secretly I was excited and happy. What fun! To pretend that I was married! Nobody needed to find out. As a matter of fact no one should find out if I wasn't *really* married. I could hardly wait to talk to Alec about it.

"Listen, Baba, until your divorce comes through, I am sure Helen's husband could protect the whole household," the lawyer declared. "Now, let's see. It is Thursday today. I think the earliest day would be Tuesday when Helen could get married. The blood test takes 48 hours, and, let's face it, you still have to find someone. But don't fiddle around! Get on the ball! And fast!"

Suddenly I felt afraid. The date seemed too close. Or was it better that I had no time to think it over?

# 35

June 9, 1951. The warm breeze of early summer ruffled the thin, lace curtains on the window. As on every Saturday afternoon, boys kept ringing our doorbell. One of them played Chopin on the piano while we chatted with the others. The soft melody spread out the open balcony door towards the park across the street.

John Szablya was among the boys. Lately he came about once every three weeks. Now he sat and explained to my sister, "little" Elisabeth, a serious eleven-year-old, how the different bridges were built across the Danube.

"The Elisabeth Bridge was the most expensive one because just one span was used to cross the whole river…"

I was talking with Pista who was on leave from the army. He was called up as a member of the labor force. They would not trust a former landowner's son with a gun. His parents were also deported. Their espresso shop was abandoned.

"I just heard," Pista said, "that my parents' shop will be used as an apartment. Already eighty applications came in. I hope they will give it to the family with the four children. They live in a cellar and rats are running around in their only room. My parents' apartment was given to a high-ranking Communist official."

"So were all the other good apartments I've heard of," I replied. "Is it very bad in the army?"

"Much better than I thought," said Pista with his usual sarcasm. "At least the company is excellent. While we peel potatoes we discuss Rembrandt, Goethe, Steinbeck, Tolstoy. None but the best people are qualified to join the ranks of the labor force. Sometimes I even forget where I am. The only time I remember is when my stomach growls."

Pista looked much slimmer than he did before.

"I hope you don't mind, Helen, but I must go over to see Bonzi today."

"Of course not, Pista. You know that I know," we both laughed. His gold-rimmed glasses glittered in the sunshine as he left. I wondered when I was going to see him again.

Tommy had disappeared quite a while before. He never even said goodbye. I knew he was back in town occasionally. He sent messages with strangers saying that he could not come. We suspected that he was working for British Intelligence since he had graduated as a pharmacist and lived in Germany. He knew every blade of grass at the border. He grew up there. It was easy for him to find his way through the ever-thickening Iron Curtain.

I came back from the door. Mother waved at me frantically from my grandparents' bedroom door.

"Yes?" I went closer.

"John wants to talk to you, go in," she whispered.

John Szablya sat down in Grandmother's chair as I sat down in Grandfather's.

"Helen, I don't know how to start this, I am not very good at saying things like this. I mean I am not exactly used to it."

I looked at his embarrassed face, the big blue eyes that blinked now and his wavy brown hair. Drops of sweat appeared on his forehead. His long fingers were searching for mine but he did not quite dare to touch me.

"Whatever you say. You can say yes or no, or you can say that you only want to do it temporarily." Then with determination he blurted, "Would you marry me? I mean really marry. Ever since I first met you I knew, and I think, so did you. If you are not quite sure yet, I am willing to marry you in a civil ceremony first, to save you from deportation, but my intentions are serious. Would you marry me?"

My hands tore at the handkerchief I held in my hands. Yes, I remembered that first meeting and many others since. The laughing girl. I was determined to marry someone that very Tuesday, June 12, and I had already agreed on the terms with Alec. It would not change anything about our relationship. He was with us most of the time anyway. This was Saturday, only three days left. I did not want to let go of John. But Alec...

"When?" I asked.

"This is Saturday, two days for the blood test," the same logic all over again. "We could get married on Tuesday, Helen."

On Tuesday? Why does everything have to be done so quickly? How can I decide? I must have some time to think it over.

John continued, "My friend just saved his fiancée from deportation. He married her on the day before the order came. They were lucky they could pull it off. Don't wait until it's too late. You know, Helen, I was engaged once and when my engagement broke off I had decided that I would marry only if I found a girl about whom I felt, 'this girl, or nobody.' I felt that about you today, when we sat in the room, listening to Chopin, explaining to Elisabeth about the bridges. Yes, I felt that it's you or nobody. Will you marry me? Under any terms, depending on your decision."

"Look," I insisted, "I have to think this over. Would you give me twenty-four hours?"

"Gladly, I can't promise you a fortune, I can't give you anything you already do not possess, but I promise you that we would be very, very happy." He finally grabbed my hand.

"Stay for dinner," I said, and he accepted.

We set the table together. He tried to touch my hand whenever an opportunity presented itself.

We put out the everyday china and cutlery and served the usual boiled potatoes along with green peas, the vegetable of the season, and cream of wheat.

"A big glass for you because you are so tall," I joked. I felt embarrassed. We did not know what to say to the others.

As soon as he was gone my sisters both leaped into a huge embrace and nearly knocked me down.

"You will choose John, won't you?"

"He really wants *you*," Mother declared. "I think I acted very surprised at first. He also promised me that if you chose a civil ceremony he would not touch you until you decided to finalize your marriage. I don't know if you noticed but John followed me to the hall and asked me how I was. 'You are not so well, are you?' he asked. It sounded strange so I pulled him into Grandfather's room and asked what was the matter. He seemed embarrassed but he finally told me. I am afraid I acted rather strangely. I knew you already had an agreement with Alec. Besides, John had to protect his parents. However, if he wanted to protect us… I offered to marry him after I got the divorce because I still thought that he merely wanted to save the family. I offered him Marie. She is fourteen, she can get married with the permission of the attorney general and then we would have no problem. She surely would not want to marry him in real life. But John was adamant. He wanted you or none of us. He said that he did not only want to save the family, he wanted to have you forever. I could not believe my ears, although I secretly always hoped that something would come of the two of you."

My thoughts took so many shapes that they would have put the most colorful kaleidoscopes to shame. What was I to do? Lilac-filled evenings with Alec and that first kiss! Dancing with John. The shared worries and work with Alec. The first conversation and others that followed with John. I was going to work all summer with Alec but he was reluctant to get into a marriage so soon and also because we were second cousins. And he was right. John was not a second cousin and the two of us would have a good chance to have healthy children. Good stock. Since when did I care so much about children? I even surprised myself. John was an excellent provider; he had great potential, even in the Communist world. He made more money than his contemporaries and had better chances for promotion. Alec had bright ideas but would he be able to pursue them? Were they only dreams? Was the difference merely the three years? I recalled Uncle Feri's high praise of John, his colleague with a bright future. As his wife I would not only be protected, I would belong to the Hungarian scientific elite of 1951. Still an "insect" but an "irreplaceable" one.

Gradually I realized that John's question was a dream come true. He was the best one for me to marry. I would never be able to forgive myself if I did not try at least. I decided, "I will take John, for the time being. We'll get married by a notary and then I'll have a little more time to decide. We have to do that anyway according to Hungarian law and church weddings cannot take place without a civil ceremony first. To me the civil ceremony does not count and I know it does not mean anything to John either."

"Oh, goodie, goodie, goodie!" Marie and Elisabeth shouted and Mother hugged me. She said, "Good thinking! I think you made the right choice. However, we must tell everyone that you sneaked away to get married in a church. It will not be in the parish book because...well, nowadays, many people ask their parish priest not to make records of their marriage because of the Communists, who do not favor the Church's blessing on anyone."

"We'll tell that to everyone, except the Communists. Or maybe, knowing me, they would think that my marriage was serious only if I married in a church?" I felt happy now that I had made the decision and gathered my books to study for the finals next week. I was going to finish eleventh grade. Tomorrow was Sunday. The church bells were going to wake me up. There would be no more fear from the doorbell at five o'clock in the morning if ...if only Monday would pass uneventfully. Life was beautiful after all, and it *was* like a musical, only wilder.

# 36

Twenty-four hours later, on the dot, John arrived for the answer. Uncle Charles was there. He already knew about my decision, but John did not know that until I arrived home a few minutes later with Alec. We were at Mass and on the way home Alec tried to convince me that maybe we should not get married after all. I felt happy. I had made the right choice. I could hardly wait to tell him but I did not want him to know before I told John. We said good-bye on the street. He had to hurry home.

As soon as I came in the door, John jumped up. I grabbed his hand and pulled him into Grandfather's room.

"My answer is yes, but only a civil wedding for the time being."

John was radiant. He took me in his arms and kissed me—on my forehead. We stood by the window and watched the colors in the sky, the vivid pastels of the setting sun that barely hid behind the mountains of Buda. The fine sickle of the moon was crowned by a star today. I had never before seen a star sit right on the tip of the moon. The golden pink slowly slipped into the steel-blue of the evening. Seven years before I had looked at the same view when I felt myself stepping out of the shoes of a child and making my first steps as a grown-up. We held hands and the moments passed. John said sweet words to me. Then the magic broke.

Mother and Uncle Charles came in. "Aren't you going to let us in on your secret?" They both laughed. "We have to act quickly. The blood tests have to be done as soon as possible."

"I thought of that," said John. "I already talked with a friend of mine who will take them tomorrow morning and enter it in the books as if he had taken it on Sunday. This way we'll have the necessary forty-eight hours."

"Great! You will also need a TB X-ray test and a medical examination to get your license."

"I'll get your rings," Mother said. "I think Grandmother's ring would fit John just right and maybe I can find you one in the attic."

Monday I went to school and took the finals. There were more the next day and I knew I would not be able to attend because of the red tape connected with my marriage. I went to speak to my homeroom teacher.

"I won't be able to be here tomorrow for the history exam because I am getting married and I have to acquire some papers."

She was listening with only half an ear because she turned to me and said: "Your mother is getting married?"

"No, I am."

"What?"

I knew she was one of those who could be trusted. I mumbled something about the deportations. She understood.

"God bless you, my child. You are excused. Come for whatever you can."

Then she said loudly so everybody could hear, "Indeed, our great leader, Lenin, has said that, Helen. But, we should not neglect Stalin's comments on the subject because he was the one who developed Lenin's teachings even further."

I could hardly hide my laughter as we looked at each other. I was also relieved that I did not have to ask the same permission from a Communist teacher.

Blood was taken and we had our X-rays. Tuesday was more than halfway gone in excited preparation. I did not even have time to fix my hair but I was in the bathtub when John knocked frantically on the bathroom door.

"Helen, we must start all over. My father came to the factory door and hurried me along. The justice of the peace, an old friend of mine, will keep his office open until we get there. No matter how late. The X-rays are no good and the medical offices are only open for another hour."

"What happened to the X-rays?" I shouted while I pulled clothes on my half-wet body.

"Nothing happened to them. They look beautiful but they were not taken at the right place. We need the medical exam from our own district. So we have to start over."

"Is that free medical care? One government agency's work is not as good as the others? We had it taken in a hospital! That should be better than a clinic," I retorted as I pulled on my shirt. I was ready by now and we were on our way.

At the clinic a woman with a big party insignia questioned us.

"What do you want?"

"We want to get married and they said the X-rays are no good because…"

"Come back tomorrow," she cut off our explanation.

"But everything is all set for tonight. We want to get married tonight."

"Is it *that* urgent?" she asked taking a good look at my body, searching for a telltale protruding bulge.

"Yes," I smiled shyly.

As it turned out, she was the one who gave me the pelvic. She must have had the shock of her life when she found out that I was a virgin.

Whatever she thought, we had my papers. John caught the bus to run to his medical district to have the last sanction.

By the time he jumped on a bus to come back for me, he saw the members of the wedding party gathered in front of the office where the ceremony would take place. He waved goodbye to them as he held on to the bus with one hand and carried a huge bouquet of light pink roses in the other.

"Where are you going?" they yelled at him but the bus had already covered some distance and they did not hear his answer.

I waited impatiently for his arrival. A girl, who lived next door, noticed the comings and goings. She paced the sidewalk with me now. She was older than I was, yet as we were walking she remarked, "I would not get married for anything. I can't imagine leaving my parents' house yet."

I could not tell her that I would not leave my parents' house. As a matter of fact, not even Bonzi knew that I was getting married. I meant to keep it a secret.

Finally, John appeared in a taxi he managed to catch while traveling on the steps of the bus.

We sped through the June sunset towards the office of the justice of the peace, across the Chain Bridge, down the long avenue toward John's place.

"That is the most beautiful white-pink rose bouquet I have ever seen," I told John.

"It perfectly matches your dress," John commented. It was the same dress I wore often, especially designed for me, fitted, with a lily-line opening at the neck.

Mother and the girls followed us in another taxi.

Finally we arrived. John's parents, the best man, and the maid of honor were there, nobody else. I was excited and happy. I felt again that I had made a good choice. At least Alec's fear of our early marriage was dissolved. He looked relieved but not quite sure whether he liked my solution or not.

We entered the dirty office building and went into John's friend's office. The window opened onto a cobblestoned backyard. He closed the window.

"I don't want the dog's bark to disturb the ceremony," he said.

The dog's bark? In a moment we discovered what his real reason was. He talked about the school days when he and John were together. He, the upperclassman and John, the little freshman. How their friendship had developed. Then he touched on the times and our hope that should always lie in God. He talked about freedom and love for each other. He knew that we were not going to church from his office and he wanted to make the occasion special when we first said to each other, "I do." Along with most of our friends, he hoped that the two of us would stick together. We were lucky to have had the wedding after hours. It was eight o'clock in the evening, and nobody disturbed our celebration.

He sent us on our way with the blessing of his smile.

Mother invited everybody over for a snack. John and I went by taxi; the others took the bus. We stopped by a church and said a short private prayer. This way we would tell the truth when asked if we went to a church on our way home.

And as we were going up in the elevator, John kissed me.

A real kiss!

Mother opened boxes of sardines, a great delicacy sent by Father. She put some cottage cheese on the table, then biscuits, and somebody brought beer. That was the time when John realized that he had not even eaten breakfast.

Then, before he went home with his parents, John kissed me again. I got out my books and began studying for Wednesday's finals.

# 37

"Is it true, is it true, is it true?" Bonzi and two other friends greeted me with excitement the next day in school.

"Is what true?" I asked them, trying to sound casual.

"That you got married?"

"Oh, that. Yeah, it's true."

"Who to?" Bonzi shook me. "How can you say it so calmly?"

"To John," I muttered, annoyed because we had decided to keep it a secret, but everybody seemed to know it.

"To whom?"

I gave up. "To John Szablya."

"That's what I thought," said Bonzi.

By then the whole class jumped around with excitement. "Who is he?" "What is he doing?" "Are you coming back to school?" There was no end to their questions.

The deportations continued. Everyday we helped people destroy their own homes. John was moving over to our house. That also meant that his parents had to move to the country. If someone moved on his own initiative, he would not be deported because if a deportation order came and he did not reside under the address, he could not be taken. The goal to get them out of town was achieved. For those who could manage to move on their own, the advantage was that they could move freely and they lived at a place of their own choice. For John's parents that was a friend's house at Lake Balaton where they had always spent their summers. There was no bathroom in the house, only a well a hundred feet away and every drop of water had to be carried from there. John's parents were not young, but they wanted their son to be happy and they gave up their protection for his sake. Days and nights seemed to flow together in the constant moving of friends.

Our lawyer said one day to Mother, "I don't think John will be able to save your whole apartment. You still have four rooms. I would suggest that you and Grandfather move to the country, to as small a place as you can find. The girls should stay in the city."

331

"My cousin offered to adopt Marie," Mother said. "Should I go along with it? He is an engineer. Uncle Charles wants to adopt Elisabeth."

"Do it! Right now!"

The adoption procedure was simple. The girls changed names and Marie moved in with her new parents. Our family name slowly disappeared. On a nice, summer day, we three girls and John asked Uncle Charles to, please, marry Mother to save her from deportation, as a favor to his old friend, our father.

He said he felt honored and that he would have suggested it himself if it was not against his principle to steal his friend's wife, but if this was how we saw the situation he had nothing against it.

However, the divorce was not quite settled and in the meantime Mother and Grandfather had to leave Budapest because by now only one "insect" could be protected from deportation by one engineer or one doctor. "Your mother or your wife should be enough to cook your dinner," was the refrain.

John carried his certificate of "irreplaceability" in his pocket. His parents had left. A month later the government took their pension. No reason was given.

Mother and Grandfather found a place in a little village, Törtel, about twenty kilometers (or two hours by narrow gauge railroad) from Cegléd where Little Grandma lived. A former maid's parents took them in. It was a nice house, with electric light; Grandfather even had a sofa and a comfortable armchair. This way they were free to move, to come and go to Budapest whenever they could afford it.

Our lawyer found a nice South American couple, former Hungarians, who had returned to stay. They were idealistic Communists, thrown out from Argentina because of their association with the Party. They had enough money to separate two rooms from our apartment and build the dividing walls along with a second kitchen. It meant that my "husband" and I would have a separate two-room apartment. He could sleep in one room, while I slept in the other. John, as a member of the scientific elite, had the right to keep two rooms, one for his study, if he already possessed them. Before, he and his parents shared their apartment with four other families.

We were now completely alone.

"Let's go down to the Astoria for a dance," John said one night when we came home after work.

"But, we have no chaperon," I objected.

"Helen," John burst out laughing. "We are married, remember?"

"We are! You are right. We don't need a chaperon. Let's go." While my life was like an overstretched string on an instrument, John taught me to relax. Despite everything, life was beautiful in those moments.

The train chugged along at a crawling pace that fitted our moods perfectly. We had just failed again, for who knows how many times, to leave the country. Our depression was deeper than ever because this time we were expecting outside help. Yet nothing had happened during the whole, long weekend. I slept in the nest made by the arms of my husband. Now and then a stronger jerk woke me up and I looked around in the crowded railroad car. Mother and my sisters slept huddled together in a corner. I slid back to sleep. Whenever I awoke I thought of statistics and newspaper articles, headlines, and over-fulfillment of the five-year plan that made news. A week's crop of newspapers, the "Szabad Nép" (Free People), the official Communist paper, had to be reviewed by me that morning, at seven o'clock. Since I was one of the employees at the university, I was given the same responsibility as everyone else in the department. A sixteen-year-old high school student giving political commentary and explaining the news, editorializing from a Communist point of view to the omnipotent and omniscient party secretary, the head of department, and down the line, the whole laboratory where I worked. I was afraid to do it, scared of making a mistake. Having been an "insect," any one of my words could be misunderstood, even misinterpreted on purpose. However, the history and Marxism classes at school gave me confidence. If I could win the Russian article contest, I might muddle my way through a week's worth of newspapers without committing any disastrous mistake.

As the train clattered along I remembered how we had rattled in the opposite direction only a few days before with high hopes in our hearts. I thought then that I would never have to give the seminar I was preparing even while asleep now. The message arrived by word of mouth that Father was sending someone from Austria to help us across the border. Would the guide be there? How would we recognize him? I recalled as we clambered on board the train in Budapest and made it all the way to Szombathely, a town on the border. About thirty miles before we had reached our destination there was a routine inspection on the train. Our passports were in order. The little red identification booklets no longer betrayed our "insect" background. Mother's name was the only telltale sign, but she was listed as an electrician's assistant from Törtel. Perfect. The guard saluted. If she had been an "insect" at least she was on her way to being "re-educated."

When we got off in Szombathely, the place was swarming with policemen and policewomen.

"Police Convention" we read on posters on the walls. The women of the police force looked like starlets. Publicity and celebrations were everywhere.

We took a small room. "Now what?" None of us had ever heard of a police convention before. Were they strengthening the police protection of the border? Were all these policemen going to stay after the "Convention" was over? Would our guide be able to come across at all?

The next day the newspapers reinforced our suspicions. "John Kovats was sentenced for three years because he was captured trying to cross the border." "Mihaly Pataki got two years in prison for talking about a possible escape..." "Joseph Vargha and his wife were captured with their three children. They received two and a half years hard labor."

We looked at each other, questions in our eyes. There was nothing else to do but wait. We sat in the room for two solid days. Whenever we ventured outside, it seemed that the police force had multiplied by the hour. The promised guide never showed up.

Before we had decided to go back to Budapest, the convention was over. Yet, none of the police force gathered in town seemed to budge. They were still sitting around in the restaurants, talking, smoking, having fun. It was Sunday night and on Monday John and I had to be at work or suspicion would arise. We boarded the last train home to Budapest.

Was there a guide at all? Why didn't he come?

"Clatter-clatter-clatter," the train rattled as if in answer to my thoughts. "We over-fulfilled the five-year plan, the harvest was very good, the steel industry is catching up with generations of neglect and we are building new factories." While I was preparing for my seminar, I tried to remember the headlines, the most important articles from the newspaper we were supposed to read every day. Something inside me seemed to question why they did not build any new housing, or at least renovate the old buildings that were still in ruins. I woke up with a jerk. "No, I mustn't even think of that because my tongue might slip, I might ask it aloud and that would lead to disaster." A chill ran down my spine. I could not take chances now to think. I had to be careful.

"Are you cold, honey?" John asked.

"No, I am just trying to remember all the data." I was careful not to say "nonsense" where we might be overheard.

"Oh, your seminar. Don't worry. You'll do fine. Try to sleep some more. We have another hour to go. Then you can go straight to work from the train."

Yes, I thought sleepily as I dozed off in John's comforting arms, that is good! I still have some time to snuggle up to him.

❧

I made the dreaded seminar just in time. The numbers and statistics were all clear in my mind as I compared the different crops, the production of factories, the achievements of the work brigades, the headlines of the country. There was never a word about accidents, about problems. Everything was always glorious, except of course an occasional "sabotage," inevitably planned by the "insects" of society. The party secretary beamed at me approvingly. The head of the department looked through me with desperate boredom. I sympathized with him. Technicians fiddled around with their pencils, assistant professors gave me a little smile. I felt triumphant, I had fooled "them" again.

Alec looked at me as if he were seeing me for the first time. In a way it was true. Right after the meeting he came and sat beside me in the lab. While the others heard us, Alec explained something very scientific of which I didn't understand anything, but as soon as they had all disappeared he started to plead with me. "Helen, you can't do this to me! We can't go on like this."

"Like what?" I pretended I did not understand, while I acted as a living thermostat for one of the experiments. The university did not possess even one of those "fancy gadgets" the Americans had by the dozen in every household, or so we heard. My job was to keep the temperature of the molasses within ten degrees Fahrenheit, with the help of cold running tap water. While I did that we had ample time to talk. If someone came by we pretended to discuss our research and he explained to me some simple trigonometric equation that none of the Communists, placed to observe us, would have understood anyway.

"You must divorce John."

I thought of the mornings. Every day a light tap on the door woke me. It was John. Not once did he as much as forget to close the door.

We always slept till the last possible minute, then dressed and hurried away on the same streetcar. I got off at the Technical University. John continued on his way to the Ganz factory. I thought of the dances we went to at night. I recalled his warm embrace on the train.

"Alec, why didn't you think this over before? How could I divorce him now?" I rather liked the freedom marriage gave me.

Alec had got me my summer job as protection against deportation, even before the family decided on marriage as a shelter. For him, it was embarrassing that he asked for a job for his girlfriend and to everybody's amazement she married someone else. He went on, "I always thought I was too young to get married. I thought we needed time. But now, when I think of losing you forever, like this weekend, when you had left and I thought I would never see you again…I can't face it, I simply can't."

"Look at the molasses," I answered as I saw the party secretary approach our bench. "What do you think? Should we use a larger marble or a smaller one to get better results?"

Alec's face showed definite signs that he couldn't care less but he observed carefully, while he bent his head down far enough to touch my cheeks with his.

"You know, Helen," he said after a while, "when I was still going to the British Council to the square dances I used to borrow American magazines there. I read a short story about a boy and the girl next door. Now when I think back on it, I feel the same thing is happening to us. The boy goes away to college and when he returns the girl's wedding date is set. He realizes that he can't live without her and he talks to her about his feelings. The girl, who feels completely content about her well-thought-out marriage, decides to choose him instead of her fiancé. They become aware of the fact that they had always belonged together. Don't you feel that?"

I did not know. I felt confused. My brain said that I had made the right choice yet my heart yearned for the tender moments I had spent with Alec. I loved him as much as ever but I also loved John in a more mature way. If they just did not want to make me choose. Everything was fine as it was. I did not want to handle any more.

During our coffee break, Alec showed me the basement of the university. There were big, comfortable alcoves to hide in. The next thing I knew, he had his arms around me and we kissed.

On my way home I dragged my feet. I felt eighty years old. Tears ran down my cheeks until I could not even see the sunshine. When I stepped off the streetcar I turned into a confectioner's shop and bought myself an ice cream cone.

———

*Lucia di Lammermoor*, my favorite opera, sounded beautiful on the huge outdoor stage on Margaret Island. The music still rang in my ears as we walked away under the bright summer stars. John put his arm around my shoulders; the fragrance of the roses penetrated our senses.

"John," I pleaded. "Could I, please, ask you to do something for me?"

"Anything, you know, anything, but you must tell me what it is."

"Could I ask you not to kiss me for a while? Just for a week or two. Until I ask you to. I don't want my emotions to get into the way of thinking things over, I just…"

I looked at him. His eyes were sad in the dim light of the streetlamps.

"You know that I love you," he said. "But if that is what you want, I'll do it." He let go of me and we walked side by side. I felt awkward and I knew that he was disappointed. But what could I do? Alec kept asking me whether we kissed and I did not want to disappoint him either. Finally I had decided to ask both of them to lay off of me for a while.

They both complied with my wishes but they did not cease to besiege me with their words and try to outdo one another.

John waited with lemonade for my return from work every day. I loved lemons. There were none available in Hungary, but he managed to get it from an "acquaintance."

Alec's siege was more verbal than anything else. I was with him during the day and several evenings a week we played tennis. Every moment we spent together seemed like a line from a hit song, "It's easy to take happiness for granted but remember that to lose it is just as easy." When I felt content at his side it was a sweet hurt at the same time, because the good feeling was not mine to keep. These were stolen moments if I finalized my marriage. Yet, I could still decide to keep it forever, if only…

When I was with John I felt more and more irritated about the perfect match we would be. The more I wanted to write him off the more he tried to win me over to his side.

I played tennis with Alec and danced with John. We talked and talked and my tears kept rolling every time I was alone. Why did I want to decide in such a hurry? But how could I escape their constant pleas?

The janitor came up one day and announced that the police inquired whether we were really married. She told them that she was not watching through the keyhole but as far as she was concerned we were a nice couple. We thanked her and from then on we had to kiss a lot, in public.

Then one evening John and I went for a walk. We went past the Technical University and up the St. Gellért hill. The sun went down just as we reached the top and all the lights of the city came on as if touched by a magic wand. The Chain Bridge and the Parliament, the St. Stephen's Basilica and the Royal Castle's skeleton ruins were colored by the brush of the summer evening.

"Look," John whispered. "Isn't that beautiful? This is the time of the day I love, when the silhouettes of the city are etched against the pastel-colored sky and the lights are already on; tiny, twinkling glowworms in the ocean of darkness. I like to watch as the night steals away the brightness from the sky and turns it into a black dome."

"You, too?" I was shocked again by our likeness. His arm was around my waist.

I leaned my head against him. He bent down his head and breathed a kiss on my mouth. I wanted to let go of him but something inside made me hold him even tighter. I felt his lips part and his tongue was probing for mine. An ecstatic feeling breezed through my body. Then another one. I loved to be in his arms. *This* I had never felt before.

~

One weekend in the middle of the summer, John and I packed up all the good food, clothing, and necessities we could spare and find in the capital and made the rounds, visiting deported relatives and friends. We could make the trip in one weekend because all of them lived within only a few miles of each other, though in different villages.

Our first stop was at Little Grandma's house in Cegléd.

We had the treat of our lives with all the goodies Little Grandma could cook up. After dinner, in the light summer night we went out into the back yard, where the old swing still hung on the porch and waited for me to jump on it. John pushed me and I laughed just as when I was a child. I never wore a bra, but for some reason that night I especially wanted John to notice it. I kept slipping my sundress's straps down as I coyly kicked around on the swing. John caught me in his two strong arms and we kissed again.

~

The next day we traveled to Aunt Majszi. We found her in reasonably good spirits. We brought her wine and coffee. Her blood pressure was always very low and this seemed to help her. The coffee came from Father's parcels. On her pension she could not buy anything but the most necessary staple foods.

Mary, her daughter-in-law, told us about her work in the fields. The party secretary of the village admired her beauty and charm. She went out with him occasionally. Therefore their treatment was somewhat better than that of the others. I saw their little room, with the earthen floor, the outhouse, and the kitchen, where the irate peasant woman kept pushing Aunt Majszi's food off her wood-fired stove whenever she wanted to cook.

We parted in the silver lights of the moon, unbothered by artificial lights. It had a curious beauty if one could forget the inconveniences of being without electricity.

The black silver of the night accompanied us as we walked to the train station. Aunt Majszi and Mary were not allowed to come with us. It would have been out of their one-mile radius, the circle within which they were allowed to move.

The next family we visited in another village lived in a long barn with a dozen other families. They wondered about what they would do in the winter. They collected corn cobs because they heard that many people used them for fuel. They were also terrified of their job. "We are building crematoriums. You will see, Helen, they will burn us alive. It will be the same as with the gas chambers. Only we have to build it first. And hurry up doing it at that, if we want to eat and feed our children."

Their frightened eyes accompanied me to the next place, where our friends, a young couple with several children, had been deported along with the old Grandfather. They had one room to live in, bathe, and cook. No water in the house. Every time they would approach the outhouse, their landlord would menace them with murder. When they acquired water, they would bathe the children in about a gallon, think over carefully what else they could use it for, like washing clothes or dishes. Finally her husband, who kept his famous sense of humor, remarked, "If nothing else, we could still use it to make tea..!"

In the next village we visited one of John's best friends, who married his wife in deportation. He was happy to have her there with him. He got a slipped disc while building the railroad and lay in bed. His pain was excruciating, yet they would not let him go to the hospital. It was outside the one-mile limit.

How long would this go on? When would they let them go? Would they ever? Were we going to reach the same fate once we became replaceable? How long would it take? Was there hope for Hungary to become free again? Or were the deported people indeed building their own crematorium?

# 38

Our steps echoed through the dark, cool, wide corridors of the Technical University. Alec and I walked side by side during my last lunch break as a technician for the department. I gave up my job and announced to the party secretary that I had decided to pursue my studies and return to school full time because I had realized that this was the best way to serve my country and work towards the fulfillment of the five-year plan. He understood and was proud of me as he explained, "The Communist Party finds it very important for young people to complete their studies. We need all the knowledge we can get to outsmart the reactionary generation. Unfortunately, until we can bring up and educate our own scientists we will have to put up with these bourgeois relics (unknowingly he was talking about my parents and I guessed also John). In the name of the university I hope that we will be able to welcome you back here as one of the students after you have completed the last year of high school."

I made no comment although I was reasonably certain that I would have no such opportunity because of my "reactionary" background, which he seemed to ignore during his lecture.

Alec and I approached one of the alcoves where we kissed during the summer. He steered me in that direction and we leaned against the wide windowsill. "The last time," I thought as he put his arm against the wall right above my shoulder. I did not pull back. I still did not know whether I wanted to end everything or if I needed more thinking time. I wished I did not have to decide so soon.

"Helen, think it over," he begged me again. "Why don't you just move away to your godparents and live there until you decide. It is not easy. You are with me during the day, John waits for you evenings, we both try hard to get you. You could think much better in a neutral setting."

"You know that would be impossible. Even now the janitor was asked by the police whether we consummated our marriage. If I should move away we would be deported that instant. It is a tempting idea to be able to think undisturbed, but no… I'm sorry. I can't do it."

"I am afraid that we won't be able to keep up our relationship if I don't see you and how can we if you don't come to work anymore?" He raised his right eyebrow as was his custom when he was puzzled.

"Maybe it will be better," I thought but did not say anything. I put my head on his outstretched arm. It was steady. I felt his warmth and I thought of the many wonderful times when this man helped not only me but our whole family. Yet…

"Alec, you know as well as I do that we are second cousins. Will any good ever come out of our marriage? Think of our children. There is hope, of course, but the probability is that we would be much better off with someone else. Both of us."

"Don't you think that I have been thinking of that also? But I can't give you up. I even told it to Sophie, I told her everything about us and she was so understanding."

I pricked my ears. "Sophie?" I had heard him talk about her before. Good! Thank God he has someone. At least he will not be lonely. By then I knew that boys often started a flirtation by telling the new girl about their problems with their sweethearts.

"Sophie? Is she the girl whose mother is French?"

"Yes. Do you remember me talking about her?"

"You said that you met her and you speak French together. Is she pretty?"

"She is beautiful. Long, blond hair, blue eyes, fragile and…hey, we were not talking about her. We were discussing *our* relationship."

"We still have a few minutes left before we have to go back to work. Do you want to walk all the way around the path we took so many times discussing just the same question day after day?"

We walked on without a kiss. My eyes filled with tears as we passed the deep window seats. I stole a glance at him from time to time. I thought he too was crying. We reached the end of the circle. We stepped out of the building, and into the heat of the late August sun which shocked us back into reality.

The last days of August found John and me at Lake Balaton. The Feast of St. John was always a day for great celebrations in John's family. It was not only his father's and his name day but also his father's birthday.

John's parents had moved again, this time to their own lake cottage that had finally been vacated by the tenants. The house was built of bricks with a foundation of solid basalt rocks. Its glass-covered sun porch had a commanding view of the lake as far as the Badacsony Mountain and the shores on the opposite side. The house was surrounded by vineyards. Only an ox trail divided the building from the lake and to approach their home one had to walk through a thicket of green bushes. The dock was hidden from strangers by an abundant growth of reed. John's parents walked down the narrow planks leading to the dock every morning around five o'clock to try for a fresh fish breakfast. Then, even before we would wake, his father would pull up enough water to cook with and wash the dishes. We took baths in the lake and we washed our clothes there also. Women tied their laundry to the dock and when they came back a few hours later it was almost clean. The mud of the lake had the reputation of being a powerful cleansing agent. Boy Scouts used it as dishwashing detergent when they camped nearby. Ábrahámhegy was a small place, with barely a thousand inhabitants. It did not even have its own council but was attached to an adjacent community. However, there was a railroad station and a public beach, a general store and a tavern. A charming place to spend the summer. I loved the smell of the vineyards, the leisure time in the sun, the long swims we took, and walking on the dusty roads. These were fun weekends whenever we could make it but always too short.

John's mother tried to cook up a storm when we came. However, to find ingredients was all but impossible. Her love and ingenuity, her artist's creativity coupled with common sense about nutrition made her see food even where there was none. On John's name day she made us hamburgers out of walnuts. She had a big walnut tree in the yard and she collected and shelled them. When ground, the walnuts, prepared with the usual seasonings, not only tasted exactly like meat, they also contained the necessary protein. Mashed potatoes and green beans completed the menu. She walked miles to acquire the green beans that unfortunately tasted like thin wood because there was little rain that summer and they were all dried out on the stalk. At the end of the dinner came the surprise, chocolate cake with real whipped cream. She had hidden the cocoa we sent them from Father's parcels and used it all for this one surprise event. She beamed as she brought in her gift of love. Her white hair surrounded her happy face as a halo. John's father smiled quietly into his beard and his eyes lit up as he saw our astonished faces. We hugged them both. The sun shone through the glass windows of the sun porch and the water's blue turned into a soft yellow under the vapors of the hot summer day.

In the afternoon John invited me for a walk. We started out towards the three hills that edged up into the sky from the lake.

"Do you see the middle one? It's called Paphegytető," John said. "That is where I want to take you. The view is unbelievable. It is one of my favorite spots."

"Tell me about everything. I should like to know more about this region. We always went to the other side of the lake where we had to walk miles to reach deeper water. It wasn't as nice as it is here. Here we can swim right at the shore."

"I loved to come here when I was little," said John. "I used to put on my swimsuit in June and I never wore shoes, or anything else, until we had to go back to school in the fall. Sometimes, when the weather was nice we even stayed longer. I was so tanned I could have passed for a black person."

"I would have loved to see you. I never get that dark. I can't even stand the sun for very long, I get a headache. Once I got sunburnt and all my skin came off, but I was never really tanned."

"Do you see that house?" John pointed towards a smallish whitewashed house. "That is where one of my friends lived."

A peasant woman stepped out from the house as we approached it and started to hang out her laundry.

"Oh, Johnny, is that you? I haven't seen you for ages!" She started her sing-song as we approached. "Come on in and have a glass of our wine. It is as good as it used to be when you were a little boy. Remember, how you liked it always? Come on in!"

She led us inside and wiped the chair with her apron before we sat down.

"Don't say! You are married? You have rings on your fingers! When did you do that? Oh, but you are going to have such a wonderful husband, although he could get himself in quite a bit of mischief, he could! Father! Come bring the wine! Look who's here!"

Her husband, a stout, middle-sized man appeared with a slim bottle of wine and poured some for us after we shook hands.

"You sure are a big man now!" he proclaimed. "And you are married? Eh?" He did not say much, just lifted his glass, "To your health!" and we all drank.

"How is your son, Michael?" asked John.

"He lives in Budapest now, maybe he'll come home next week. We don't see him too often. But he has a good job in a factory and he has a girl. They'll get married after the wine harvest. I am real satisfied except for those…" For a minute she stopped, then John nodded his head to signal that everything was all right. She could go on, I was one of "us," not one of "them." "Those Communists, the devil should take them! They take all our grapes, the wine, everything. We have to let them have everything and buy back from the store what we need. Isn't that ridiculous? However," she turned her voice into a whisper, "we always manage to save some from our own vintage for our best friends. We are luckier than some people we know who live on the Great Plains. They grow wheat. They can't make their own flour, they need the services of the mill and this is how they lose even the very last of their crop."

"Woman, don't talk so much," the peasant admonished his wife. "I tell you, you will get into great trouble some day because of your tongue."

"You don't think that Johnny, here, or his sweet little wife…"

"I don't think anything," the peasant said sternly, "but I mean what I said."

Later as we were walking on in the afternoon sun, John pointed towards a little pine forest. "Look at our evergreens. There are a hundred different kinds of pines among them. The owner of that piece of land is very proud of it as most of the other trees around here are fruit trees."

I walked slowly because of the heat, but I enjoyed every minute of our walk. With every one of our steps the view of the lake grew. Then for a while we walked between bushes. Their shade provided a welcome coolness in the August heat. John put his arm around me. It felt so much easier to walk relying on his strong arm.

Then we were on top. Abruptly the whole lake appeared in its full splendor. The blue-yellow water's ripples, licking the hulls of tiny sailboats under blazing rays of the sun, breathed the peacefulness and stillness of the approaching autumn that hid behind the still green leaves.

"That is beautiful!" I whispered to John as I leaned my head against his shoulder.

He lifted me to the top of a rock. We were now eye-to-eye. Our nearly one-foot height difference disappeared.

"Helen, I know I promised. I don't want to break my word, but still… Would you, please, would you really marry me?"

I noticed once more the blueness of his eyes that matched the sky and the lake, I felt the softness of his wavy hair under my fingers, and my tears began to flow. Why, why did he have to ask? I never had a quiet moment. I was constantly thinking about it. Why did he have to bring it up? I kept asking this question, although I actually wished to be asked because I wanted to get it over with and settle it once and for all.

"Helen, did I spoil everything? Will you have nothing to do with me anymore? Did I lose even the hope?" Fear crept into his eyes. I remembered Alec's face and pleading. I looked at John again. He continued, "I only did it because I had decided a long time ago that when I wanted to ask a girl to marry me, I would do it right here. I had to. Can you understand?"

The sun shone warmly, its cutting heat disappeared. A slight breeze made me feel good all over. Something inside me said that there was no use to continue this game. I had to decide or lose my mind, and my mind said that it was John whom I should marry. I remembered his kiss on Mount St. Gellért. The one, when I knew that it was something I had never felt before. I remembered Alec's story he read in the American magazine. But I did not think it was true in our case. No, it could not be. Our feelings led us in opposite directions.

I looked at John, at his loving, pleading eyes. I felt his arms around my shoulders, "Yes," I said. "I will."

The next moment I was swimming in the air in John's arms. He scooped me up like a baby and twirled me around and around. I thought he'd never stop. "You will? You really mean it? You will be my wife?"

I felt as if a huge boulder rolled off my chest and freed me from months of aggravation, indecision, and tears, I felt like flying down the mountain in the form of a butterfly.

The sun began to go down as we sat and talked about our life together, the wedding, the children we would have. John thought that he would not mind how many except he wanted to have at least two girls. He was an only child and although he always wanted to have a sister he never had one.

The stars started to appear in the sky. We said goodbye to the most beautiful spot on earth. "Thank you for bringing me here. I love you," I whispered as we kissed. Little glowworms showed us the way through the thicket as the whole landscape disappeared into the black velvet of the night.

# 39

September came again. The first day of school. As I looked out the back window I saw the three trees in the otherwise barren stone square of the schoolyard slowly move their branches and drop their yellowed leaves. Their ballet produced a light show on my desk as the shadows of the leaves twisted and changed places with the sunshine.

"Girls, these forms will have to be signed by your parents and be back by tomorrow," I heard the teacher announce.

I put up my hand. "I live with my husband; my parents are not in town. Can he sign it?"

"Come and talk to me after class. I have no idea. It says that parents should sign it." She looked puzzled.

She was still answerless when I talked with her after class. "I would have to check with the principal. You know, we have a new one and I'm afraid," she turned her voice to a whisper, "she hates wedding rings. She is an old maid herself and announced at the faculty meeting that she does not want to see any married women in school where they don't belong."

"What am I going to do?" I whispered back. "I must finish school."

"I'll do what I can," she promised.

I ran back to class and borrowed socks from Bonzi. I noticed that my toenails were painted red, a definite bourgeois capitalistic remnant which had to be eliminated. I was glad I remembered.

I barely finished putting on the socks when I was called to the principal's office.

Her dyed golden-blond hair was piled up on top of her head in a crown of braids. She looked at me sternly with her ice-blue eyes. She was a small woman, forty to forty-five years old, I judged from her appearance and the hair-thin wrinkles around her eyes, deeper ones by her mouth.

"You cannot corrupt the other girls with stories from your bedroom. They undoubtedly will ask you questions and that will disrupt classes."

If I had not been so scared I would have burst out laughing. My classmates? Ask me questions? It seemed to me that every one of them knew more about life than I did, maybe with the possible exception of my closest friends. The principal obviously did not know me. It would have been ridiculous for them to ask me about sex. Not having had any brothers, I had not even seen a naked man. John and I were still not married in church and until then we did not consider ourselves married. But how could I tell her that? That would not only mean my dismissal from school, it would mean deportation, or maybe even prison and concentration camp for both of us. All of us? Grandfather, too? Why would I think of that! I was closely examining my socks. They stuck out like bumps from my sandals that were not meant to be worn with socks. At least I did not look bourgeois. Although my name, that was still my maiden name in school, would have betrayed me anyway. I did not say anything. How could I?

She was surprised. I did not look like the type she had expected. As a matter of fact there were three of us girls who were married and the other two had different reasons. One of them was pregnant.

"You see," she started another attack, "you don't know what to answer. I can't allow you to come to school."

"But," I interjected, "but last year…"

"That was last year," she silenced me with a short, dictatorial smile. "This year I am principal. You can no longer come to classes."

"Yes," I muttered.

On my way home I cried. What was I going to do? Bonzi came with me; she knew I needed her more than I needed her socks earlier. We sat together for a while before John came home.

"We'll do something," he said with determination. "I am going to that school and I'll tell her that she was darn right to let you go. Discipline is most important in school life."

"What?" I asked. "Are you out of your mind?"

"Just leave it to me! We must do something, and I think it will work. I will use Dale Carnegie's method on her."

"What?" I did not understand a word of what he said.

"She can't possibly know that method. You must finish high school. There are only public schools and without a high school diploma you are lost. Remember, we are 'insects'."

"I know it is important. That is why I am desperate."

"No wife of mine is desperate because of a little difficulty."

"You call this a 'little difficulty'? It's just about my whole life! I mean, I don't know if they will accept me at the university. With my background…but I hoped…I always wanted…"

"Come," John pulled me by the hand and we walked back to school.

We went straight up to the principal's office and after entering he kissed her hand.

She was so astonished she forgot to pull it back. Self-respecting Communists did not allow capitalistic greetings like that.

"You were so right to throw my wife out of school. I am an educator myself, although I am an engineer. I taught at a high school when I was practice teaching, and I would not have allowed something as disturbing as a married woman in my class, I am all for you."

Her eyes lit up. "Please, be seated," she motioned John and me towards the corner of the room, where we sat down on hard-backed, wooden chairs. "So you understand me?"

"I definitely do. It is of utmost importance to have the education of the young generation go undisturbed."

"Honestly, when Helen said that she was married, I did not think that she had such a responsible, mature man as a husband. I thought he would be a high school kid. I am glad to have made your acquaintance. That sheds different light on the whole situation."

"Comrade, I would like to ask you for help. I want my wife to be one of the strongholds of Communist society and therefore, knowing her intelligence, I find it very important for her not only to finish high school but also to go on to university."

"I am all for that," the principal melted under John's influence. "I will personally endorse her petition to become a special student. She should be able to come and visit any class she wishes, but she cannot be a regular student, I know you understand that."

"Thank you. I am sure that you will not regret your decision." John kissed her outstretched hand as they parted.

"I thank you, too," I said softly.

"Come in any time you feel you need help with a class."

As soon as we were out of seeing or hearing distance from the school, I hugged and kissed John. "You were great, great! How did you do it?"

"That is the Carnegie method I told you about. We have his book in Hungarian. I first heard about him during my trip to America. But, back to your principal! I agreed with her, then I asked her help, her version of the solution to the problem."

"She melted like butter," I said.

It had been an exhausting day. We had to celebrate. We turned into the confectioner's shop on the corner and bought ice cream cones.

As it turned out, Bonzi, too, had to become a special student because of her health. Her kidneys were in bad shape although I could not see anything special besides the puffiness of her face, and she did not feel pain.

We were free now all day. To study at home took much less time than to go through all the classes, even though we were seniors. As special students we only had to take the exams at the end of the year. There was no sense in preparing for them yet, especially since I was getting ready for my church wedding, the real thing.

"Bonzi, I want to tell you a secret," I whispered to her one day. "John and I are going to get married."

"Are you cuckoo or what? You mean to say that you weren't married all this time? That the principal kicked you out for something you did not even do? I mean… You haven't lived with John yet?" She blushed. "To think of the times when my mother and other mothers… Do you remember when they kept asking you when you would have a baby? Even Eva asked you."

"Remember what I answered?"

"I think you looked at John and asked him, 'When *are* we going to have a baby?' You know, maybe some of those mothers even thought that you can't have a baby."

I laughed. "I know. My mother was three months married when she became pregnant with me and already she was desperate. She had told me that she went to pray at St. Anthony's grave in Italy to become pregnant. She and Father had decided at the time that if they could not have any children they would buy a yacht and sail away all the money my grandfather made. What ideas!"

Bonzi laughed. "When are you," she turned her voice to a whisper, "getting married, and where?"

"Mind you, it is a secret. I only told you because you are my best friend. The wedding will be held at the Downtown Church after closing time, at 9 p.m., on Friday, in three weeks. The Communists should not know. They don't approve of church weddings. Besides they thought we were married all the time."

"You were, according to them," Bonzi corrected me.

"Of course. Anyway, we'll have a party afterwards for the closest friends only. The people who rented our downstairs volunteered their place for the party. You know the widow and the adopted daughter of the architect. He died a few months ago and Uncle Charles lives there now in one of the rooms in a sublet. He is planning to marry my mother next week."

"Oh, is he really? I didn't even know."

Oops, I thought, I nearly made a mistake. I nearly told her that we had asked him to marry our mother.

"Didn't I mention it to you? Of course, I did not. It was going to be a marriage of convenience and we were not going to announce it all over town. However, I thought as Mother wanted to move back to town, people would have to know about it. She would even have to kiss a lot in public. For us, the poor widow's room for sublet came in very handy. At least Uncle Charles could live in the house without having to actually share a room with Mother. Now, not a word of this to anybody."

~

I no longer lived alone with John. Grandfather, Mother, and my sisters moved back in with us in the two-room apartment. Officially they all lived in different places. The police demanded that everybody staying longer than twenty-four hours in a given place had to register at the police station. Failure to do so meant a prison sentence. Grandfather's registered residence was still in the small town of Törtel. Uncle Charles got him an official certificate from the district doctor that he was senile. This was true, but it was important to have a document stating his condition, in case he would tell someone that he had been in our home for longer than the past twenty-four hours. We also had to keep him within the house as much as possible. If he were seen too much, the whole family could have been in trouble. My sisters, who in name lived with their adoptive parents, often stayed in the attic. On the third floor of the house we had the laundry room and huge wardrobes in one of the spaces. We made that into a place to sleep. There was no heat there and of course it was not to be discovered. Although officially their addresses were different, finally the family was together again. Our largest available room where we could "receive" our guests was the master bathroom of our old house. Our two rooms were overflowing with furniture, mostly beds and wardrobes, tables and chairs. We were lucky because most of our furnishings had found good homes with friends. To get a bigger apartment would have been impossible. Besides, we were still in our own house though officially only John and I lived in the two rooms. We were not even eligible for more. Therefore we cheerfully invited our guests to sit on the edge of the bathtub, or on the bidet. There was a nice chest of drawers in the bathroom, where we used to be changed when we were babies. That could always be used as a table if needed. The closed lid of the toilet was one of the better seats. We had much fun in the bathroom and soon our friends got used to its intimacy. We could even lock the doors if it was necessary. In the summers we enjoyed free concerts from there. The windows opened onto the back corridor and the thick old walls of the house behind us provided excellent acoustics, reflecting the sounds of the orchestra in the park across the street.

The wedding date was set for October 12th. Mother was "married" on September 26, by the same justice of the peace friend who "married" John and me. She was a black bride as she was still in mourning for Grandmother. She wore a miniature black pearled hat with veil netting over her face and a black suit with a white blouse. After the ceremony, Uncle Charles went back to the hospital. Mother came home, tossed off her black veil, and resumed work on my wedding. Sometimes it seemed that she had to work hard all the time to keep her sanity. Yet, nobody could accuse her of being nervous, otherwise. Her smile beamed on everybody, always.

She especially enjoyed going shopping with me in preparation for my wedding. We combed the shops and walked arm-in-arm all over town in order to find private resources and seamstresses in dark alleys. She brought out her carefully saved pure silks that she had bought with Father in Italy, some of them even during their honeymoon, and laces from Brussels, and woolens from England. She gave me some of her slips, and linen, and we went to buy new things, too. She bought me a pair of gray flannel slacks, something Grandmother never tolerated and therefore Mother never wore. As a matter of fact, there was such a controversy over slacks for women that books were written on the subject and occasionally priests would not give communion to women in that kind of attire. But these were modern times and the storm over pants had subsided, giving way to much greater problems attacking the whole world.

I bought a new car coat made of corduroy and lined with red satin which looked very daring. "As an envied member of the scientific elite, because of your husband, you will be able to wear these," Mother said.

I enjoyed being looked at in the street so I had no objections when she wanted to buy something daring. Father provided the money from Canada where he had moved only recently from Paris. I did not need much else because we had too much of everything, anyway. What we needed most was a place to put our belongings.

A few times we ate lunch at the confectioner's that still had fine pastries, although the selection had shrunk to two or three kinds since the stores were nationalized.

We ran into difficulties with the most unlikely details. In the whole capital city of Budapest there was not a trace of starch and for John's shirt that matched the tails he had borrowed for the wedding, we needed potato starch. We went from one store to another and listened to the same reply, "Don't have any. Dunno where you can get it. Probably nowhere." Most of the clerks just shrugged their shoulders. Finally we found a place in a narrow little store in the backyard of a house where they had some left from the "good old days."

While we ran our errands we whispered the time and the day of the ceremony to several of our friends, always reminding them to be careful about whom they revealed the secret to. However, taking every possibility into account we had decided that if the Communists found out we would simply tell them that we got married in church only to yield to "family pressures." It was of no consequence to us. That was what they wanted to hear anyway.

Finally the day came. The organ of the Downtown Church, where both my parents and grandparents were married, triumphantly announced our arrival. John and I walked down the aisle together in borrowed but proper wedding clothes. I wore my mother's veil that was made of Brussels lace, all three and a half yards of it. My dress was also made of lace, a fitted bodice with a gathered, white skirt that started around my hips, first worn by a distant aunt at her engagement. John's tails fitted him perfectly; he borrowed them from his best man, who in turn wore those of his father. There was nobody else in the wedding party. Our families waited for us in the sanctuary. Yet, to my surprise, the whole ancient cathedral was packed with friends, relatives, teachers, classmates, and employees of our store, hundreds of people. We had planned a small, secret wedding, after the church closed its doors for the day. I could hardly believe it. Everybody had just whispered it to one trusted friend, and the whole thing snowballed. We thought we had planned our wedding to the last little detail, but this we had not planned.

The Bishop of Budapest, Imre Szabó, a friend of John's, performed the ceremony. He awaited us at the altar in golden vestments. We wanted to recite our vows by heart. I agreed with John that it was a good idea to know what one said. The Bishop was worried about it. He was afraid we might forget something. I knew that there was nothing I wanted more than to be his forever and his voice betrayed the same sentiments on his part. Our love had already withstood many trials. Our families stood by us, including Grandpa from Cegléd. Unfortunately, Little Grandma could not make it. I think she became too excited and did not feel up to making the trip.

As the ceremony went on everything seemed to disappear and nothing remained for me but John, I saw the Bishop as he talked about faith and love. "I give you these two virtues to accompany you through life. Remember the old couples on Castle Hill. When one of them died after having lived together all of their lives, the other one soon followed. It was quite predictable. Somehow I see you like that, bound together by immense love that permeates all your being. I believe that you will live a long and happy life together and will go together to your Maker as those old couples did."

There was nothing I wished more. I saw the twinkle in John's blue eyes as he kissed the bride. He was now really my husband.

The Bishop led us to the back of the church to save us from the push of the people who all wanted to wish us well.

Only a select few came to the party that followed and the excitement reached its peak. None of us girls had ever worn a long dress as we all grew up during the war. This was the first time for my seven chosen friends and my sisters, my bridesmaids at our home, to put on a long evening gown. Naturally nobody had any money to speak of, but all of the mothers had their own evening gowns in mothballs and for this evening they sewed and stitched, ironed and steamed, until their young daughters looked as they themselves did when they last wore these unheard-of fineries. They were all somewhat old-fashioned, but who cared! They carried the elegance and the romance of the parties from twenty years before. For them and for their daughters they meant luxury. What did it matter that the bridesmaids' gowns did not even match!

Soon the girls were all standing in a circle with their escorts and for a short moment they were recognized as my attendants. Then the dance began and the buffet was officially opened by the bishop who excused everybody from Friday fast except for himself. While everybody feasted on meat loaf and ham, sent by Little Grandma, he ate a can of sardines, which was also a delicacy, sent by Father through the government parcel agency, IKKA.

Wine that Grandpa brought from Cegléd was plentiful and soon the bridesmaids came one by one to check with me. "Do I see two of John's father? Am I already that drunk?"

I had to laugh as I answered, "No, keep drinking. There are two! One of them is his Uncle Feri. If they don't sit beside each other, I can't tell them apart either. My mother often talks to one of them thinking that he is the other. There are five years between them, but I guess, when one's hair is completely white and he wears a beard nowadays when nobody else does, at this age five years don't count much."

As the widow let us have back our rooms for this one evening to celebrate, it was just like "the good old times." I literally flew around in a waltz in John's arms, my feet lifted off the floor and my skirt swirled around us like a white cloud.

How I loved him! I felt that I was the happiest girl in the world.

*Civil wedding June 12, 1951.*

*Wedding October 12, 1951. Helen and John Szablya's wedding. Officiating is Bishop of Budapest Imre Szabó. In the background John's father, John Szablya Sr.*

*Wedding, October 12, 1951.*

*Graduation from high school, June 1952.*

355

"Uncle Charles," Dr. Károly Tarnai, was Father's best friend from grade 5 through medical school. He married Mother in 1951 to save her from deportation by the Communists. He adopted Elisabeth, my sister.

Mother's ID photo.

*One of my favorite photos: young, married, in my grandfather's Burberry coat he had bought before the war and it was remade for me at least 20 years later. It still was as good as new. I put one of my old leather belts on it. Our favorite dresses came from remakes of grandparents' clothing. 1952.*

*Having fun on John's and his father's Feast Day. Hungarians are said to cry as they are having fun. The gypsy is playing a sad song. John's Father and Mother, Uncle Ferenc Szablya Frischauf, the gypsy, and I.*

357

*John and I before leaving for the Opera. The dress I am wearing was sent to someone from Hollywood who first tried to sell it to the ballerinas of the Opera, but none of them could fit into the 21½ inch waist.*

*Going to the dentist ball in the same dress without the jacket. The dress was sold to my mother for the price of one yard of velvet because no one wanted it. Later, after our escape, my sister Elizabeth wore it.*

358

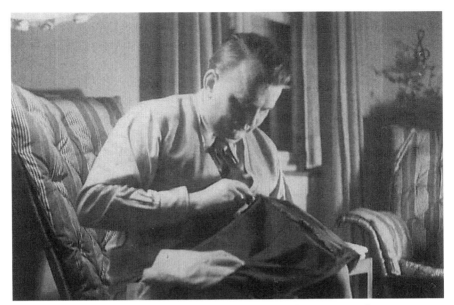

*My father in Winnipeg when he was an intern, mending his pants. His first year in Canada, 1952.*

*John, in Hungary 1954 – 55, works on a test. Description of test and photo appeared in Transactions of IEEE (then it was still AIEE) in 1959. John is the first one on the right of the photo.*

*Little Helen (Ilike) and I.*

*Ilike's baptism in our home, January, 1953. Godmother is my sister
Marie, godfather József Schmaltz Jr., who was also my godson. The
Schmaltz family, Marie's adoptive parents, are in the background with
their daughter, Ildikó. Officiating is Bishop of Budapest, Imre Szabó.*

*Ilike, 18 months old.*

*Baby Ilike makes a call.*

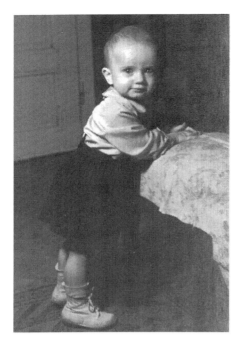

*Ilike the big girl starts walking.*

*Ilike with my mother in Károlyi Park, right in front of our (by then nationalized) Magyar utca house.*

*With John and Ilike on the day we learned that I was pregnant again.*

*Ilike with my mother and my grandfather..*

*Ilike (Little Helen) with John's parents.*

*Our daughter Ilike in the summer of 1956. We called this photo "Little Miss Sunshine." She is on the teeter-toter in the small park in front of our home in Óbuda, a district of Budapest, Bécsi u. 105.*

*Ilike in Hungary 1956.*

*Jancsi's baptism, June 1954. He, too, was baptized by Imre Szabó, Bishop of Budapest. His godmother is my sister Elisabeth and godfather is Miklós Jós, my first cousin. Aunt Mathilda, her husband Miklós Jós, and their two children Miklós – the godfather and Lajos, are also in the photo besides the usual family. The little girl in John's Uncle Feri's lap, right front, is the janitor's daughter, who just happened to be there playing with Ilike.*

*Little Jancsi and I.*

366

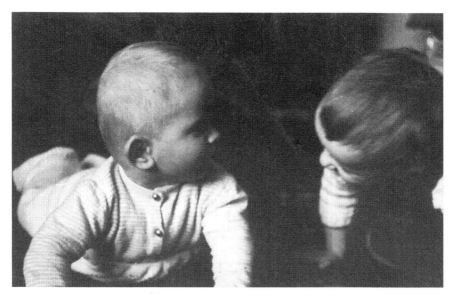

*Ilike and Jancsi playing in Óbuda. 1954.*

*Jancsi in my old crib in the yard in Óbuda.*

*Jancsi with light bulb. 1956.*

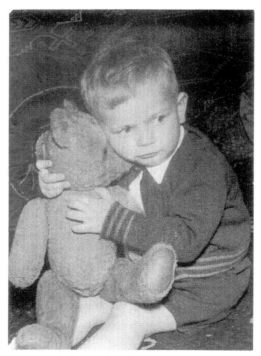

*Jancsi with favorite Teddy.*

*Family picture in Óbuda in the summer of 1956. I was five months pregnant with Lajoska.*

*Ilike and Jancsi with bread in Abrahamhegy. 1956.*

*Ilike and Jancsi at play
in the yard in Óbuda.
There are seventeen months
between them.*

*Ilike and Jancsi in the clothes
in which we escaped, in our last
home in Hungary, in Óbuda.*

*Hungarian Revolution, October 1956.*

*Parliament building today, behind the 1956 memorial monument with the flag of the Revolution with the hole in the middle, where the hammer and sickle were torn out.*

# 40

Then we were all alone in the room upstairs. The others were still dancing, living it up for this one time. A wedding was still a big event; my friends' first, and maybe only, chance to wear a long dress. In this strong, well-built house the sound insulation was perfect; as soon as we had closed the door behind us there was not a whisper of noise. John touched my dress with the slightest tremble in his hands. His face was all smiles as he helped me pull it over my head.

My first reaction was to stop him, but my anxiety dissolved in a smile when I realized, "It's all right now. He may help me with my dress."

I thought of the few times when I had felt his groping hands around my waist. They wandered in the direction of my breasts. I knew how hungry he must have been for my touch. Then one day, in our spacious bathroom, when nobody was around us, I pulled his hands to my breast and pressed on them hard as if to explain how much I too enjoyed feeling his warm touch. My face turned red from embarrassment and pleasure. Now we would be able to do that very act without embarrassment.

My white dress fell to the floor. A satin slip underneath covered my naked breasts and the white crocheted panty, the stockings, and the lace garters. John unwrapped me as if I were a long-awaited gift package, the ribbons falling off slowly under the impatient yet enjoying fingers of the birthday child who wants to prolong the anticipation of the present of his dreams. A little preview was all we had time for. I quickly dressed in my brown suit and we started out on foot, carrying our suitcases towards the Hotel Duna where we were going to spend the night.

In twenty minutes, we were in our large room with its big windows staring at the Danube's silvery blackness under the light of the full moon.

I slipped into my turquoise-ivory silk and lace cloud of a nightgown, while John changed into dark-gray striped silk pajamas. Why not seduce each other?

Before we got married Uncle Charles talked to both of us on how to make our honeymoon, especially the wedding night, a delightfully memorable experience for both of us. We followed his advice, although it must have taken John considerably more self-discipline than me to do it.

We stood by the window for a few minutes and while we experienced one another's skin through the silk, which is a sensuous adventure, we looked at the view, the lights on Castle Hill and the Hills of Buda. This was the only hotel on the quay of the Danube still standing after the siege. All the others were shot out of existence.

I looked into John's eyes and everything else seemed to disappear.

"Would you show me yourself?" he inquired.

I went into the bathroom and when I returned I was not wearing anything.

He embraced me with all his might. He too was naked. I had never seen anything as exciting, interesting, curious, and delightful in all my life. This was the first time I had actually looked at a person as a man. MY MAN! He was all mine. And I was all his.

We rolled around in bed and experimented with each other's bodies. He led my hand that was groping around shyly. I let him explore. The night went by in an amorous dream, yet we had not yet consummated our marriage. We simply enjoyed the complete possession of each other. Then, in the morning, when it was already full daylight, I could stand it no longer and I asked John that we become one. He complied with my wishes.

Uncle Charles was right. Although I let out a little scream, the desire cured the hurt. I was now a married woman, no longer a virgin.

While we got dressed and went down to have a feast of lunch, I felt constantly in my very intimate self that I was no longer a girl but a woman. I rejoiced in that feeling even as we left on our honeymoon and took off, for the first time in my life, in an airplane, to spend ten days in the beautiful ancient city of Pécs in southern Hungary.

⁓

Was it love that colored my spectacles pink? Or was life indeed as charming as it seemed to me in this small, ancient town of Pécs, set at the foot of the mountains? My eyes were used to the Great Plains around Cegléd and even the departed relatives all lived in the "puszta," the Hungarian prairies. Now I feasted on the colorful leaves of autumn and the warm, embracing sunshine, nature's gift for our honeymoon. Ten whole days lay ahead of us, free from the strain of everyday life.

Ours was a large, comfortable room with a bathroom; it used to be the royal suite. We enjoyed the warmth of the beds because other than that there was no heat in the room yet. Before mid-November, not even the luxury hotels were allowed to start the furnace. Our windows looked at an old Turkish mosque with its huge dome. It had housed a Catholic church for the last several centuries, since the Turks had left Hungary after their last desperate battles to hang on to their 250 years of occupation of the country.

We danced, ate, and made love. The hours flew and the days had that peculiar quality which happens only when one is very happy…they became timeless. Nights turned into days and days into nights as we enjoyed and loved each other, as we celebrated our oneness.

Golden days called us for long walks into the surrounding mountains. We hiked among vineyards and forests. Little brooks told us their tales as they hurried by and we strolled arm in arm. One day, around midday, we reached an old, worn gate, a half-circle arising from the ground, made out of bricks and plaster. We wandered through it and reached a sloping hillside. Down in the valley the view of the whole city unfolded as the noon bells started ringing all over town. The solemn bell of the cathedral led the others as they tuned in at different pitches, the tiny bells of the chapels, the middle-sized bongs of the many churches, and they all chimed in unison to the glory of God in thanksgiving for the victory over the Turks in 1456. Few people thought about the Turks nowadays when the noon bells rang out over Europe, but all must have felt at one time or other the magic of this peculiar music or else that custom would never have remained with us.

I remembered the times when similar sights moved me to tears. I thought of the almost helpless feeling that used to come over me, that made me want to do something, because of the beauty of what I had seen or experienced. I anticipated it again. Yet, it did not come. Instead, I felt a warm wholeness, the assurance that I was no longer wanting for anything and I suddenly realized that for the first time in my life I felt completely fulfilled.

# 41

One day when we returned from our long walk down the colorful slopes of the Mecsek, we found the heat on in our room. The temperature was caressingly warm. Without hesitation we threw off our clothes. Just then came a slight knock on the door.

"Who can that be?" John asked, annoyed.

"Excuse me," a frightened little voice spoke softly. "Would you mind terribly…I mean, I am sorry…but we will have to ask you to let us move your things into another room."

"Why?" John demanded as he opened the door, having thrown his dressing gown on while I had pulled the covers practically over my head.

The maid who stood there was obviously trying to find the proper words. She had to tilt her head back to look up at John.

"Chinese athletes arrived in town and we have to make room for them. We must give them the best rooms—this is why the heat is on, too. I am so confused," her voice broke. I thought she would cry in a minute. "You may come back after they leave. I am sorry…" "That's all right, we understand," said John. "After all, you didn't have anything to do with it."

The girl's smile showed her relief that this man turned out to be a friendly giant.

We helped her take our suitcases over to our new quarters, a small room with old-fashioned furniture and a view of the back yard. After all, a Communist country can give only the best to a fellow Communist country's athletes. Everybody would understand that, wouldn't they?

At least the room was heated, although it did not have its own bathroom. We made sure to bring with us our can of butter. Somebody gave it to us as a wedding present; it was from America and although it had a funny, salty taste, it didn't require refrigeration. That is what we used for our breakfast every day, with a couple of crescent rolls we bought fresh at the bakery.

Finally we were rid of the maid and shed our clothes again. We had to use the opportunity to bask in the heat conjured up to show our prosperity to the fellow Communists.

The gray light of dusk was just enough for us to see each other and to dream about old times and new as we sat in each other's embrace in the old bed.

"I've gotten an offer from the Technical University to teach. I think it would provide a great opportunity to couple my technical knowledge with theory. I have been working at the factory for four years now. What do you think?"

"I think it's great. I am impressed to have such a clever husband. How would that affect our lives? What would change? I mean, I am happy for you if it makes you happy..."

"The university presents a great challenge. There are new things to be learned and done every day, but I think I would miss being in close touch with what is going on in industry."

"Is there no way to do both?"

"I don't know," John said thoughtfully. "I can't be sure if they will let me go. You know, since we have the planned economy, an individual cannot decide for himself which job he wants to accept. I have to play it by ear. I asked around and it seems that they find me quite 'irreplaceable.' They must have meant it when they gave me that paper. Did you know, Helen, that when we started out in 1942 there were four hundred freshmen in electrical engineering? Guess how many finished in time."

I made a wild guess. "Two hundred?"

"Seven. The rest of them were either killed in the war or taken away by the Germans, 'evacuated' they called it; so they had lost at least a year. Other classes did not do much better either. This is why engineers are needed so badly in a country that was completely in ruins only six years ago."

I felt a rush of hope. "Then it will take quite a while for the Communists to bring up their own generation of engineers. Does that mean that we are safe for a while?"

"In the Soviet Union it took them about twenty years, but I don't know. We are trying awfully hard to learn from their example. As it stands now the university is working two shifts, day and night, to produce twice as many engineers in the allotted time. I was also asked to teach evenings."

I was not very happy about that. "Will that mean that you will not even be home in the evening?"

"Some days I won't. But let's not think about that now. Maybe I can work it out at the factory and switch to the university. You know, another good thing about changing would be that professors have forty-eight days of paid vacation."

"That I would love," I hugged John until he yelled. The room looked very romantic now with its dark-brown furniture that reminded me of Little Grandma and the past century. We heard foreign sounding voices on the corridor as the athletes' young steps hurried past our door. I felt grateful to them now because of the warmth, the only thing that had been missing from our dream of a honeymoon.

"I know so little about you when you were young. Tell me something."
I huddled closer to John. I liked listening to his voice in the darkening room.

"What should I tell you?"

"About your life, your dreams, your expectations."

"My mother always joked about throwing me out the window if I turned out to be a boy. Father claimed that he had rescued me from her fury. So when I was five years old I decided that I was going to give a very special birthday present to my mother. I whispered in her ear with great determination, 'Mother, if you want to, you may dress me as a girl from now on. I really don't mind. I know that you always wanted a little girl.' Mother laughed and put her arms around me. 'I would not exchange you for any girl in this whole world. I want my little boy just as you are.'"

I laughed softly, "I was always told that my father wanted a little boy, so I always tried to make up for that. Isn't it a coincidence that we met?"

"No, Helen, I don't think I would ever call our meeting a 'coincidence.' I think we were meant for each other," John said seriously.

"Go on, tell me more," I urged him. "I know that you went to America when you were fifteen and that you planned to go back but the war had prevented you from doing so."

"Is there anybody who was not prevented from doing something because of the war?" he asked in a choked voice. "We had many Jewish friends. There was a couple whom I especially liked. Mr. and Mrs. Krausz lived here, in Pécs. Mrs. Krausz went to school with my mother. The Krausz's were both very fat, but very sweet, the kind of people who would not hurt a fly. Everybody who knew them loved them. They owned a coal mine. After the first problems arose he got together with my father and sold the mine to us. As down payment, Father put up all the money he had, even mortgaged his share in a real estate property and the balance he paid in monthly installments, something he and his friend learned from Anglo-Saxon business practices. In those days it was unheard of in Hungary for a transaction of such magnitude. From this income our friends made a good living and could even help others, which they did generously. At the same time their property was no longer Jewish-owned, therefore it was exempt from confiscation. I became very much interested in the coal business. Both my parents and our childless friends wanted me to become a partner and take over as soon as I had finished my engineering studies. It was in a beautiful place, in the Carpathian Mountains, close to the Soviet Union.

"Hey, I didn't know I went to bed with the owner of a real mine!" We both laughed because, of course, mines were among the first things that were nationalized. Even if they had not been, John's parents were still alive.

"And how about me, making love to a million dollar baby?" John teased back.

"Isn't it nice to know that we couldn't possibly have married each other for our money?" I continued the joking.

"Of course that is not true," John went on in the same vein. "Everybody, but everybody knows that we can wait for the end of this communism even in a squatting position and then... Ah, you haven't thought of that, how I would use you and leave you after I had squeezed everything I could out of our relationship."

"We'll see about that. I don't think I'll let you. I'll do it first to you," I giggled.

It was quite dark now in the room.

"Go on, tell me more," I urged. "What became of the nice couple? After all, people are more important than mines."

"They were taken by the Nazis, they were separated; she died, he returned as a living skeleton after the war. His spirit unbroken, he started business again just to be nationalized by the Communists. He died heartbroken two months later."

The jokes died off in the dark and the spirit of these two benevolent people filled the room. They had helped until no one could help them, but now they were dead.

John's voice broke the silence. "Just before the siege began, our doctor and his family sought refuge in our house, right in the middle of Castle Hill, the stronghold of the German army. We lived in an apartment house. Constant air raids were the order of the day. We allowed them to stay but they could not go down to the shelter. I stayed with them because by that time I too belonged to those on the run. It was the fall of 1944. The university was 'evacuated.' I had decided to stay with my parents who were getting on in years. Father was forty-four years old when I was born and Mother, although she was thirteen years younger, had nearly died with a kidney infection in the summer of '44. At that time I did all the cooking, cleaning, and nursing. Father was brought up according to the customs of his days in the past century. He understood nothing about woman's work. Lucky that my mother had taught me everything, especially because she knew how hard it was for my father not to be able to fend for himself. Anyway, where was I?"

"Hiding with your Jewish friends."

"Oh, yes, the worst thing was that they had a dog. That blasted dog always barked at them and played with them. Every time someone suspicious came to the door, the three of them—the lady weighed about 300 pounds—and I hid in a closet. What we were all afraid of was that the dog would feel happy and playful and by doing so he would reveal our hiding place.

"Then one day came a ring at the door. Father pushes us into the closet and closes the door. We hear voices, they are German. I think of the German Nazi newspapers 'Der Völkischer Beobachter' that Father always keeps in the hall for show. I must admit, he has foresight. The boots sound harsh on the hardwood floor. 'Where are the Jews? I am supposed to find some here.' Then Father's most charming voice in perfect German, 'But my dear Captain, you don't think I would hide them here?' A second of silence, then the harsh voice, apparently having noticed my father's perfect accent and the Nazi newspapers, continues in a confidential tone, 'I am sorry if I inconvenience you, I can see that you obviously… I am only doing my duty.' I hear my father's calm voice again, 'How about some good German wine?' Apparently he agrees because soon comes the clinking of glasses. 'Heil Hitler!' he intones. 'Heil!' Father agrees. 'It is good to sit down a bit in a house that will accept a German soldier, I mean where I can find soul-brothers. Obviously you must be German.' 'My mother was,' Father agrees. 'We had a tiring but stimulating morning,' the voice says. Coarse laughter. 'We lined up Jews on the quay of the Danube. Just picked them out of the crowd. Then we used them for a shooting gallery. We shot them one by one. Pow, pow, pow! They fell backwards into the water like dolls filled with sawdust. That was fun!' 'How did you know that they were Jewish? Did you check?' 'Naw, if they looked Jewish, that was enough for us.' 'What if some other people got mixed in with them?' I can't believe Father's calmness while he listens to all that. I feel like breaking out of that closet, but that would only add another four trophies to the Germans' tally today. So I just listen. 'Oh, it doesn't matter if a few others…who cares?' I can see it in my mind as he shrugs it off. 'I am sorry, I must go now. I trust that you will tell me about any Jews you see around here. Here is my name and where you can find me.' I hear Father's voice now. 'S.A.?' 'Yes, I belong to that elite of the S.S. I was Hitler's personal bodyguard at one time. Heil Hitler!'

"I hear the door close. None of us dares to move until Father opens the closet door. 'That was a close one, but thank God, everything is all clear now. You were a good dog!' he says, patting the animal's head."

Why did the room feel so chilly all of a sudden? I snuggled even closer to John. He began to talk again.

"We kept them there as long as we could. Then somebody started to blackmail us. 'Beware of the three J-s!' said the anonymous typewritten message every day. We moved them over to another friend's in the middle of the night and the shooting. They made it safely. It was not the first time I have been startled by God's mysterious ways. They had barely left when a bomb fell on our house and then, as the siege proceeded, the whole house burned down."

"How did that happen?"

"The Germans stored barrels full of gasoline under our windows in big truckloads. An incendiary bomb started it. The flames leaped up to the second floor and set our curtains on fire along with the rest of the flammable materials. The whole house turned into a torch although it was built from reinforced concrete. I wanted to run back to save a few things but my parents held me tight. Everything we had in the apartment disintegrated but the fire still blazed on. The flaming gasoline poured into the air raid shelter. We evacuated the contents into the deep, ancient tunnels of the Royal Castle that had spread as an underground network beneath the whole hill since Turkish times. How lucky that we had this connection! By the time night fell the iron beams glowed red and white in the ceiling of the shelter. The heat was unbearable. I never thought that reinforced concrete would crumble in a fire. Whoever dared stood by the window and poured some of the drinking water and sand that we could find onto the burning gasoline that made its way into the shelter. Thank God we could fight it off and keep it out until its rage died down. We could do nothing more. When days later we came out of the bunker, the house was a pile of rubble. In one place I recognized a melted mass of our precious china, a family heirloom."

"You told me about the crucifix one day, the only thing you managed to find. *Our* crucifix now. I am so happy we have it."

"So am I. I can never forget the day when, much later, after the shooting had stopped, a friend of ours came and asked us why we were not looking for possible remnants of our things in the rubble. We told him about the melted china, the burning gas, the hopelessness of the situation. He started to push the dirt around with his feet as we were standing there, looking. 'I would still try,' he declared. 'Look!' he yelled and pulled out the corpus of the crucifix my mother had made for her wedding. My parents exchanged their wedding vows on that crucifix. That was the only thing, though, that we ever found. One day I dropped it. The bronze of the body of Jesus had become so brittle in the fire that its arm broke off. I scooped up the pieces and hid them. Later I took them to a jeweler whom my uncle recommended and he repaired it. He drilled holes into the two parts, connecting them by a sterling silver rod as thin as a toothpick. I had another cross made for the silver wedding anniversary of my parents; my uncle designed it and I surprised them in the morning. Their cross was in its place in their bedroom."

"Then they gave it to us when we got married to pronounce our marriage vows on it, even though that was the only thing they had saved from their apartment," I interjected.

"But then, I was their only son," John said, then continued. "Because our apartment burned we had to find a new place. After the siege, an aunt offered one of her rooms and we moved in with her. I went to the university as soon as it was reasonably safe to move. I wanted to see what was going on and finish my studies. At first I helped professors and janitors to shovel out the rubbish; ruins and manure, dead bodies, the usual remains of the war. Then we helped the Soviets to repair their tanks. We had to make technical drawings. Everything in 'chetyri exemplary!' four copies; we had no carbon paper. At first the occupying forces were a constant threat to all men who dared to move on the streets, but after we started our work on the tanks we received identification papers, stating that we had urgent and important work to do for the Soviets. That paper once saved me from being taken to Siberia. Classes had already begun in rooms without windows. The snow was falling in through holes and we sat in our winter coats. One day as I was nearing the university I was stopped by a 'patrol.'

"'Robot, robot,' he vehemently declared. There was no way to resist. All of us had to dig ditches. By the end of the day we dug our way out of the city and were put in a camp to sleep off our tiredness. The next day, early in the morning, when we all stood in line to be inspected, I waved to my best friend and whispered to him, 'Come!' I went up to the commandant and I began to talk very quickly, mixing in all the possible Russian words I knew, while waving my identification in hand and pointing at my friend also. As the identification was in Russian and he could read it, he showed me in sign language that we should follow him. He led us straight out of the camp and waved good-bye. 'It worked!' that was all I could think of. We started to run as fast as our legs could carry us straight up into the mountains. How I thanked my lucky stars that I knew all the forests near Budapest. Now I made good use of my knowledge of the region. Minutes later we saw, from the safety of our hiding place, that the rest of the men tried to work similar tricks, surrounding the guard, who angrily chased them back into line. Many of those people did not get home for several years. They were taken to Siberia. This was my closest call. From then on I was even more cautious every time I had to go in an open street where I was in plain sight of a patrol."

By now the room was dark and we no longer saw each other. I was not taken to Siberia because these two warm, tender arms protected me. If a man can give such tremendous love as my husband gave me day by day, how great can be the love of God who makes all of this happen! Yes, we were in the security of each others' arms; but for how long?

Outside, foreign voices and shuffling reminded us of the here and now.

# 42

Mother, John, and I were treading thick mud along the cemetery road. Through my tears I could hardly see Bonzi's coffin as it was pulled slowly towards her final resting place. Mother held my hand. She softly repeated the words of a Hungarian song that talked about fate's capriciousness as one girl was married while the other was taken to her grave. "I would never have thought…" she concluded.

"Neither did I," I sobbed as I recalled that unbelievable afternoon when I appeared at Bonzi's home to study with her, sitting in the comfortable over-stuffed armchairs, or gossiping in our accustomed place on the window seat. Her grandmother opened the door.

"Is Bonzi home?" I asked, expecting to meet her in a few seconds, even though the last time I had seen her was in the hospital. She was supposed to have come home the day before, and we were behind in our studies.

"Didn't you hear?" She looked at my red coat.

"What?"

"She died yesterday."

"What?" I did not comprehend. "She what?" I asked again "How? Why?" By that time I was crying. "It can't be, she said she would be home by today. We would study…" of course, this meant little when I realized that she was no longer alive.

Her grandmother put her arm around me. "Come in and sit down. I had no idea that you had not heard yet. Let me get you something to drink."

Her mother was inside. When she saw me she began to cry, "If only I had known. I would not have insisted that she come home early from your wedding party. She wanted to stay so badly. And I thought it would do her good to be in bed on time."

We cried on each other's shoulders for a while. I don't remember what I did or said. Whatever it was, it was genuine. Then all of a sudden we talked about socialized medicine. Apparently she had used up all her available hospital-stay days, but the doctor admitted her anyway for "research purposes." Was everything done for her? Was there malpractice? Her mother seemed to trust the doctor. He was an old acquaintance. Yet, without money his hands were tied. Did Bonzi die because of the lack of proper medical care? Or medicine? I thought of a friend's baby, born prematurely in the sixth month of her pregnancy. He weighed barely two pounds, yet there was no incubator available for him until his grandmother walked her feet off for a day, bribing several officials. He was still alive, but was that what socialized medicine was all about? Then realization struck us that no matter what we did there was no way to bring Bonzi back. Again we started to cry.

And now, here we were, accompanying her good-natured, smiling, twenty-year-old body to the murky, November earth. What a consolation it was to think that there was more to her than this "disposable" part. While we walked behind her coffin, I felt her presence as I never had before. I wished that all was over. I thought of our last visit in the hospital. She was in a good mood, drank a lot of berry tea, and was confident of being well in a few days. I thought of the many parties, the fun we had together, our intimate talks.

I knew that from now on John would have to take on her part in my life as he had already become both my father and my lover. He had no one but me and now my last "outside" companion had died.

The priest blessed the coffin and finally we threw on it the last fistfuls of earth. Her father was in exile in Paris. He would never see his daughter again. Both her grandmothers and her mother had to survive the pain associated with the death of one's child. I prayed that I should never have to know that agony. Bonzi's smile appeared in my mind as we left the cemetery. That is how I would always remember her.

The streets were dark by the time we reached home. I felt chilly. I could hardly wait to nestle against John's strong shoulders and be warmed by the heat of his body. When we finally reached our room and I could fulfill this desire, I started crying, "I don't know why, I feel so frightened." I buried my face in John's arms. "You are scared. There is a long stretch of life that we will have to cover together. Cry my sweetheart Helen, cry. It will go away. Together we can conquer anything. You'll see. God will lead us and we'll follow. Everything will be all right. You will see." He stroked my hair and talked and talked until I fell asleep in his arms.

I studied alone now. All day and part of the evenings, John was gone. The factory, as he had foreseen, did not let him switch jobs. The management was very "magnanimous" though and permitted him to take on a half job at the university. This resulted in his working sixty-four hours a week. He did receive adequate compensation for it but we hardly had any time together. Whatever time we did have for each other we enjoyed tremendously.

John was a member of the envied scientific elite. We had every possible convenience that existed in Hungary along with the accompanying pitfalls and dangers.

Research was done very efficiently. If one was successful, there were rewards. If one failed, there were demotions, transfers, and even prison. This method proved to be an incentive that worked.

We still did not have proper accommodations. We lived in our two-room apartment along with all the others: Grandfather, Mother, and my two sisters. We had beautiful furnishings left from our house, even a gas stove and a refrigerator. We went often to the opera, concerts, movies, and dressed according to the latest fashions, because we received parcels from Father, Gisèle, and other friends abroad. Through the factory, John had access to tickets. Whenever we went out, every eye was turned in our direction.

All this did not keep me from being constantly hungry, but then, so was everybody else in the country that used to be Europe's pantry.

Planned economy managed to take all of the food out of Hungary to a country ready for a Communist revolution as a "gift of the Soviet Union" while we received nothing in return from our glorious ally.

Every morning I had to do the marketing. One day I observed a vendor in the Market Hall where we always used to buy our supplies with Grandmother. He grabbed a potato out of the hand of a young woman. "No, you cannot just select one potato and buy it." The woman's eyes filled with tears, it is for my baby. I can't afford to buy more than one. I wanted to have a nice one." She left. There was nothing I could do; the vendor was the ruler of life and death. He had the food, we didn't. I never knew what I should wish for. If I did get food I had to carry it home in the several baskets and bags I had with me. If I did not, we went hungry.

In the grocery stores, all government owned, I had to stand in line three different times to buy the available food: at the counter where an irate employee would weigh out the thin slices of whatever there was, then at the cashier's stand, and finally at the place where it was wrapped and one could redeem it with the coupon marked "paid."

This was an ingenious method to keep the population busy. It normally took me all morning to do the daily shopping for our family. Eggs were bought by twos and I was lucky if I could get any. Housewives passed around recipes that called for no eggs. If someone wanted to buy more than the minimal amount, she was immediately suspected of "hoarding."

Potatoes, watermelons, and corn I detested. In the late August days I had to carry sometimes as much as fifty to sixty pounds in my bags, lugging them around on the streetcar simply because they were available and I did not dare risk leaving without them.

Then came the cooking. The merchandise I brought home did not even resemble the perfect foods we used to buy with Grandmother. One way of cheating the customers was to sell the merchandise without cleaning it. After a thorough washing and cleaning the weight of the vegetables would often be only half the original. All this in a country so proud of its produce! Recipes in cookbooks were a frustration for newcomers to the world of cooking. Every second ingredient was not available and had to be substituted by guessing. Yet, nothing could be thrown out.

In the winter, a good deal of time was required to build the fires in both rooms. This was an art in itself. To obtain fuel was not very easy. Even when we had the best available, it took a good part of an hour to coax the flames into life. Twice every day I had to build and watch the fire for about an hour until I could close the draft to keep the ceramic tile of the stove warm as long as possible.

The harsh rains of November turned into the soft snows of December. Suddenly it was Christmas Eve. Our first Christmas together! The more the Communists tried to diminish its significance, the dearer it became to our hearts.

John managed to get the whole day off on Christmas Eve. We set out in the morning with the fulfillment of fresh love-making and mixed with the shopping crowd downtown. There were many people but very little merchandise. The crowd was the result of that phenomenon. We went in and out of stores, asking the question, "Do you have any…?" then turned around and tried elsewhere. Even though it may sound like a futile exercise since all stores were government owned, it was not. By simply following this method for the past three weeks, I had managed to find a book John wanted very much, the second volume of some German mathematical tables. I had it safely hidden at home, John was still looking for something so we separated for a while and I went down the street feeling glorious. I was a married woman! My husband loved me! We were out together, Christmas shopping on the very first Christmas of our married lives! People went in and out of stores, I got pushed from one side to another, I looked into the bare store windows, but I was happy.

"Let's go get an espresso!" John suggested when he came back.

"What a wonderful idea! You really know how to live it up! It would never have occurred to me to do something that's fun while running errands."

John beamed as he steered me through one of the doors. The steam rose high from the espresso machine as we sat down at one of the tiny tables. They looked especially small when John tried to squeeze his knees under them. We ordered an espresso, a special treat in those coffeeless days. I hardly ever drank it because the price of coffee was prohibitive even though we had it

385

from Father's parcels. We always sold the coffee and kept only enough for Grandfather, Mother, and Aunt Majszi. They all had low blood pressure and coffee was supposed to be medicine for them.

The frosty air bit our cheeks to a rosy red. John's white teeth glistened as he drank the steaming hot coffee. He had a package that looked like a record. I hoped it was. The family's record player was in our room and we loved to listen to records while making love, then dozing off in the semi-darkness of the room under the warm feather beds.

The day went by like a beautiful dream. It was evening. The tree, as always, came into the house only on Christmas Eve. This year we all decorated it. Even Elisabeth was by now too old for a surprise tree. Besides, we could not afford to close down one of the rooms for an entire day. The whole family was together as was the custom in Hungary. At five o'clock in the afternoon all streetcars and buses made their last runs. By that time everybody had to be wherever he was going or had to walk. There were no private cars in those days and bicycles did not work very well in the snow. One Christmas the Communists arranged to have all the theaters and the Opera open and encouraged people to attend performances on that day in order to disrupt ancient customs, but they had failed miserably. Nobody showed up at the events and the Communists gave up in disgust. From then on they promoted Father Winter to take the place of the Christ Child with equally little success. At least that failure was easier to cover up as Father Christmas happened to arrive at the same time the baby Jesus did!

We lit the candles on the tree and sang Christmas carols. Tears rolled for those who could not be present or who were no longer with us, some of them for the first time. We remembered those in deportation. I shivered at the thought of their heating facilities, when I felt the warm glow of our own wood fire. I too could have been with those deported now if it had not been for John. Then, as the magic of the evening continued, we opened our presents. John did give me records! They were some of my favorites, The Afternoon of the Fawn by Debussy and Ceasar Franck's Symphony in D-Minor!

When we retired to our own room I had a surprise for John; a tiny Christmas tree, a replica of the big one, complete with candles. We lit them, sang, and prayed. It was our first, very own Christmas! We gave each other what we missed most, intimacy and privacy in our lives together.

# 43

On a sunny spring day I was returning from my morning errands, my bags loaded with treasures. I continued with my custom to go to church every morning to receive communion before I ran over to the dairy to pick up milk in my big can and the five pound loaf of bread. Some days I would buy yogurt and butter (when it was available), or some cottage cheese. As I walked along the Károlyi Palace, now a museum, I felt my heart beat quicker than usual and a dizzy spell sent me bumping into the wall. I put down my bags. What was this? I felt nauseated. Me? Nauseated? I could not remember when that happened to me last. I had problems with my stomach but I never felt that way before. It was always some kind of pain. But nausea?

A thought ran through my mind. I had to smile. Could it be? I remembered how I prayed every day to God to send us our first child whenever he judged that it was best for us. I wanted one, but I also enjoyed our life without responsibilities. Besides, everybody tried to impress on me the wisdom of waiting. I tried to lift the bags but somehow I couldn't manage. I wiped my forehead with the back of my hand.

"Helen, are you all right?"

"Oh, thank God, Eva!" It was one of my friends on her way to school.

"What is the matter?" she asked me again.

"I don't know," I grabbed her hand.

"You don't feel well," she said. Then, all of a sudden, she smiled.

Did she have the same thought? "Come on, let me take these bags! I'll help you get home! You shouldn't carry parcels when you…" She stopped short.

"Do you think?" I started.

"What else? When did you have your last period?" She laughed.

Something made me feel good all over, "So that's what it is. This is what it's like. Uncle Charles always said, 'if you feel something that you have never felt before, that's what it is, you are pregnant, my dear…'"

We giggled together as she carried my parcels all the way upstairs.

I could hardly wait to tell everyone.

It was all so exciting. John was ecstatic. Mother pouted jokingly, she said she had no intentions of becoming a grandmother at the age of thirty-eight.

Most doctors who knew John predicted a Cesarean because of the difference in our sizes.

———

Without Bonzi, studying was not half the fun it used to be. There was much to be done and little time left to do it. I had wasted most of my time by getting married and being happy; now I had to make up for it.

Senior matriculation was a hard test. The memory of it accompanied some people right into middle age in the form of nightmares. I was happy that I had a new life growing in me. The significance of the exam diminished considerably on account of it.

I found most of my subjects fascinating and would have liked to spend more time preparing for each thesis. First, I had to pass the finals for grade twelve. I got straight A's. Then came the written exams for senior matriculation. Two subjects a day. We handed in two copies of the papers and we received the benefit of the doubt. If the spelling, equations, etc. were correct on any of the copies, that one was taken into consideration.

Then came the orals. In one afternoon we had to answer questions in five subjects: physics, mathematics, literature, Russian, and Latin. There were 80 to 120 theses in each subject. We were supposed to be prepared to talk about any one of them for twenty minutes. We had no idea which topic we would get; we pulled it from a hat in front of the committee, formed by our own teachers and an outside president.

The many hours of study brought their reward. Whenever I drew a thesis I smiled involuntarily. "How could I have pulled the easiest one?"

All the teachers liked me and because of my "condition" they sent me out to take a break between questions. John was there so we could exchange excited kisses. He faithfully walked up and down the corridor supporting me with his presence. This was one good point of his job at the university. He could use one of his forty-eight days of vacation.

Then it was all over. I was free from studying until September when the university started.

It was a beautiful summer day when our graduation ceremony, affectionately called "The Wandering," took place. I recalled the day when the last "Wandering" sobbed its way through the convent four short years ago. Was that the time I really said goodbye to my carefree school days together with the seniors of 1948? This school was more a place of necessity. Yet it had its bittersweet memories as we cried as all students do when they "wander," singing the accustomed student melodies, adding their own versions, hiding meanings that provoke smiles from the understanding. We wove our way throughout the entire school.

John stood among the few parents who could get away from their work to watch us celebrate our last days in school.

Then we had our graduation dance. Even Alec came to celebrate. He was a good friend now. He asked me to dance and held me as carefully as one would hold an Easter egg.

"Are you all right?" he asked as he twirled me around.

"Of course I am all right," I laughed.

"I can't believe that you are really pregnant!" He laughed, too.

"There is nothing spectacular about it. People do become pregnant, you know."

We danced on the uneven cement of the schoolyard under the trees that were now dressed in their summer green. Apartment houses looked down on us from all around. The orchestra played the latest hits. We wore summer clothes, short, cotton dresses and sandals, the men were dressed in their everyday suits. We listened to the propaganda slogans in the disguise of a graduation speech delivered by our principal. We were celebrating as "people" should, at least according to the latest etiquette.

In the middle of the summer I was called to the Foreign Language Institute for an interview. They could have no quarrel with my grades although I happened to get a B in math in my senior matriculation papers. My origin was largely covered up by John's "irreplaceability."

"Why do you want to study English?"

"English is the language I know least. I should like to be of help in building the country. I think there is much to be learned from American technology and I could help my husband by translating for him even while I am having my baby."

"Why English? Don't you think that your husband would be much happier if you translated Russian technological literature for him?"

"I am sure he would like me to translate Russian also, but I speak Russian much better than I do English."

"Russian," was the verdict. "Who is next?"

I was happy that at least they did not accuse me of wanting to defect to the West because of my "erroneous" ways of wanting to study English. They knew that my father was in Canada and they must have suspected why I wanted English and not Russian.

The first days of September found me on a bench in Russian class.

"We will start from the very beginning," our Hungarian-born Russian teacher started and proceeded to write down the alphabet. I could have cried. I compared Lermontov and Pushkin for twenty minutes, without interruption, in Russian during my matriculation and now…"let's start with the alphabet," along with people who could hardly pronounce the letters.

Hungarian literature and history wasn't very much more educational either. I constantly had to remind myself to be patient. We'd get there eventually after the rest of the students caught up with the high school education I had received. Even after nationalization of my first school the one I had attended was among the very best in the nation.

I had all my assignments completed by the time I arrived home on the streetcar. The only course that presented some challenge was phonetics, and I enjoyed learning about the different Hungarian dialects. I had never realized that there were as many as sixteen. Now we had to study them all in detail. I quickly volunteered to give the report on the most difficult thesis.

I was less than enthusiastic though when I was asked to join the military "voluntarily."

"I am pregnant, you see," I muttered.

"That does not matter." Our recruiter smiled her nicest. "You'll have your baby and then you can come to boot camp. That won't happen before June anyway. Meanwhile you can attend the classes. Then, when you graduate you will be a lieutenant in the reserves. Won't that be something?"

"Yah," I mumbled without enthusiasm. By the next time she came around I made sure I had a doctor's excuse. Yet I knew that all the boys had to go through with it and that this was only a temporary excuse for me. Most of the other girls "volunteered."

After a few months of study a seminar was advertised, conversational Russian. A Russian-born teacher would talk with us. I showed up eagerly—and sat at the back of a classroom that was filled with a few hundred interested students. I listened intently but it was hard to understand him at first, especially from so far away. I hoped that in later years we would have more born Russians at a closer range. There were rumors that later we might add another language. I still had some hope to learn English.

I finished the first semester a day before my baby was born.

~

All the doctors I knew predicted that I would give birth on the 11th of January. Yet, John and I had decided that it would be on New Year's Day.

In August we were staying with John's parents in Ábrahámhegy at Lake Balaton. We hiked again to our mountain, the Paphegytető, where John had asked me to marry him. When we came back, we sat together in our room. I was mending stockings, a never-ending task as socks were not available in John's size at all. They had to be specially made for him and, therefore, were very precious. I mended them until they looked like the needlepoint handiwork of an artist. As I was busy weaving the needle in and out, I felt a slight tickle that I had already felt for the past few days. I was suspicious that it just might be the baby, yet I could never be sure that it was the real thing. As I sat there wondering, a sudden stronger push made me cry out for joy. "John, put your hand here, right here! This must be it! The baby moved!"

"Yes, it is, it must be! I felt it, too!" John jumped up and lifted me in his arms as carefully as he could manage. "This is it! It's the 15th of August. The baby will be born on New Year's Day."

❧

It was New Year's Eve. I again felt something that I had never felt before—a sure sign according to Uncle Charles. Around eleven o'clock in the morning I called John and told him that I thought I would have the baby soon.

"I knew it, I knew it. In the morning you said you had a stomachache twice while I was at home."

"What?"

"I have timed you ever since you were seven months pregnant. Whenever you said you had a pain in your stomach I looked at the watch."

I had to laugh. That was good old John! Why, he knew more about me than I myself did.

Still, there was nothing immediate I could do. I went to church that morning, as usual. It was especially exciting to know that I was in labor while I received communion. I was on a well-deserved vacation from the university, and I slept in. Churches had communion every half an hour until 12:30 p.m. to accommodate the many who sought the presence of Jesus in their disturbed lives.

I went shopping as usual, but today Mother came with me. She was awfully excited about her grandchild.

Uncle Charles thought that I should lie down because the baby was coming at least ten days earlier than the expected date. I assured him that I thought the baby was on time, but I didn't have anything better to do so I lay down.

John came home later and we listened together to the New Year's Eve radio program, which was hilarious except for the propaganda slogans and related paraphernalia to which we had become so accustomed that we did not even notice them.

"Which party should we go to?" John teased me.

"I think to all three," I joked back. "I wish I could go to the one with your colleagues and friends from the factory. I enjoy their company most. I feel like an adult among them. Although I would like to see the one that my sisters are having at Marie's adoptive parents' home. I wish I could wear a long gown like they will tonight. I have never worn one except for my bridal dress."

"That, too, will come," John squeezed my hand. He was very sympathetic.

"At least I will have a real baby tomorrow while all they will have will be hangovers!" I laughed. After all, what was a long dress compared to a new life? Yet, it seemed close to impossible that I would be a mother by tomorrow. I loved my little baby that stirred and moved in me for months now and yet, I did not know how it would all come about, what I would do with it, how I would take care of it. I never even worried. I believed that it would be instinctive. I thought of motherhood as a state of life. It was as natural as eating, drinking, or sleeping. Whatever else one did with one's life was beside the point.

I felt a pain coming again. Well, it was true all right! I was going to have a baby. Then suddenly water gushed forth from me. I thought gratefully of Mother who put a huge rubber sheet under me when I lay down. Now I understood the full meaning of her foresight.

I thought of last year's New Year's Eve as midnight neared. John and I went to the Opera to see the annual performance of Johann Strauss' *Die Fledermaus*, a funny, humorous, comedy-opera that was always specially improvised on New Year's Eve. The actors were allowed to say anything they pleased. After that we went to a party. Just before midnight we ran home, slipped into bed, and made love. Then we got up again and went back to the party amidst a joyous, mildly drunken crowd on the Grand Boulevard, blowing their whistles, parading in their funny hats.

Occasional pains brought me back into this year's mood. They were still irregular: five, ten, fifteen minutes apart.

"John, what will it be like? I have heard about giving birth but I cannot imagine it. Will it hurt very much? I think I don't even mind that any more if it just would be over. How long will this take?"

We were lying on our improvised "double bed." We were determined to sleep together from the very first day of our marriage, yet in Hungary the custom was to have separate beds standing side by side. Naturally, in the middle there were boards, a hole, a rather inconvenient solution. We saw a so-called "French bed" in an antique shop and we had dreamed about it ever since. It was a conventional American double bed, John had explained. What could we do to imitate it? After a brainstorming session our invention was born. We pushed two "divans" (Hollywood beds) side by side. One of them was higher, so we fixed wooden blocks to go under the shorter one. We tied their legs together and threw an oriental rug on the whole construction. It was one of those I had saved from the tax collectors some years back. The thick rug made the unevenness disappear and at the same time took care of the other problem, where to store the rug. Our dream was born, we had our double bed. Another oriental rug hung right behind our bed all the way from the ceiling to the ground. It was serving us well in keeping the room warm.

A third one covered the whole floor. A small lamp and the radio's light gave a warm glow to our love nest which contained all the treasures the family could save from our two houses. John walked over to the bar and opened its mirrored doors. He filled two little crystal glasses with chocolate liqueur, one of my favorites.

"It'll soon be midnight and we have to drink to the arrival of our first baby! To your health, Helen, and to all of us!"

"To yours, too!" I grabbed his hand because another pain was coming full force. Every time it came I felt it would never end. When it left me I thought I did not even have a pain. I was crazy to think that I was in labor. However, the remaining evidence of water, gushing forth with every pain, proved to me that I was indeed in labor.

The radio played the National Anthem. John held me tight in his arms. Then the music ended. "To your health!" I raised my glass and sipped the sweet, warming liquid.

"Let's call your sisters!"

We talked with Mother, Grandfather, with the whole family. Then we called the other party we had to miss tonight.

Denis, a father of three sons, answered the phone. "How frequent are the pains?" he inquired.

When John told him that they were about five, ten minutes apart, he exclaimed, "You should be on your way to the hospital. Can't you think for yourselves?"

Even though it seemed like an eternity, my pains would not get any more frequent or any worse. They would not stop either. I was feeling a little tired but I could not sleep from excitement. When I was just about to doze off another sharp pain would come. The radio went on with dance music, then that too was over.

Finally, around three o'clock in the morning Uncle Charles, who came home to check me, declared, "It will be a girl, because she was clever enough to have waited a few hours, thereby becoming a whole year younger. I think it might be a good idea to go to the hospital now."

John called the taxi company. "No taxis available anywhere," he said. He dialed the ambulance. I noticed that his fingers shook. "Ah, good. They can come, although they said they were very busy, too."

"Don't leave me," I grabbed his hand.

"I'll stay as long as they will let me. We won't ask," he said.

Mother and Elisabeth ran home just in time to see me embark into the ambulance. Elisabeth had time to hug me. She cried, yelling at John, "No, don't take her away! I won't let you take my sister!"

Mother laughed and tried to explain to her that everything was all right, I only traveled by ambulance because there were no taxis available, but nothing seemed to help her childlike fears.

The door of the ambulance slammed behind me as I climbed onto the stretcher. We were off.

I tried to be brave, but the pains were bad. Every time they came I felt like screaming but I did not want to. I lay there still, grinding my teeth, clawing my nails deep into my skin.

"Did you have any pains yet?" the doctor asked.

"About three since we had left home," I said as we passed the Grand Boulevard with its happy crowd and clinking streetcars that brought back last year's joyful memories again.

"That's good," she answered. "Crying out loud only wastes one's energy. You'd better save all of that for the time when you will have to push."

"When will that be?"

"Oh, you will know. You will feel like you have to go to the bathroom very badly."

The lamp of the car flashed its way through town as they rushed me to the Hospital on Uzsoki Street.

"Do you always use your flasher?" John asked.

"No, but today we have so many calls, we have to complete them as fast as we can."

"How many have you had already?

"You are the thirteenth."

"Did you ever have a baby born in the car?"

"Oh, yes," she smiled, "I had one even in the elevator between floors. But I prefer to get them to the delivery room. Here we are."

The big gray stone building loomed over us as we entered the gate and walked along the gray stone corridor. I felt a fist around my heart; I longed for relief. This gray hospital corridor was leading toward it.

"I'll say goodbye to you now," the doctor smiled again. "Have a nice delivery, and enjoy your baby." She squeezed my hand and quickly disappeared.

The nurse midwife greeted us as long-lost friends. Uncle Charles called ahead and learned that she was one of the midwives he used to work with when he was in Medical School.

She led us into a private room. She closed the door behind her. "You can stay together as long as I am on duty," she said when nobody could hear us any more. The room was just as gray as everything else in the hospital. Its stone floor and washable, oil-painted, grayish yellow walls would not have cheered up anybody. Yet this unexpected privacy filled me with peace. As I got dressed into the hospital uniform and lay down in the freshly made bed, I felt much better. John sat down beside me. We talked and prayed.

Nothing happened besides the rhythmic pains that began to drive me up a wall. Mother warned me of these "hopeless" pains as she had called them, while the cervix dilated but I felt that I had already had the required amount of them. I wanted to end it all. I did not care any more how it would end as long as the baby was normal and healthy.

The midwife came back and started to prepare me. If I thought I had had pains before, it was only because I did not know what they would be like after I had the enema. She sent me to the end of the hall to the only bathroom.

"I sure don't like this arrangement," she complained. "I am always afraid that one of the patients will give birth on the toilet. That bathroom should be right here, beside the delivery room."

The only thing comforting was that I thought the baby might come soon. After that ordeal the pains went back to normal. Would that baby never come? I despaired. I remembered that Uncle Charles said that running or walking helped. I started to go back and forth in my room. Then I ventured out onto the corridor. I passed the nursery. I looked at the babies. Many of them cried. I certainly did not like that noise. They were all red, wrinkled, angry little faces. There was one who looked bigger, smoother. A nurse stood right beside me. She picked out a puny little baby from the lot and pointed at it. "That will be about the size of your baby. You don't even look big enough to deliver."

I heard a yell from the end of the corridor. Then another one.

"One of the women is having a baby, I guess," the nurse said and hurried towards the sound. I followed her. Would I see something? As I went down the hall I saw several hospital-clad women talking or sitting in chairs along the wall. They all seemed to be in the same predicament that I was in. One of them moaned, "Is that your first? This is my sixth. I don't know how long I can wait. There are two babies being born in there at once. They have no more space in the delivery room. I have to wait until one of them gets out." I looked around. There were another four of us waiting. God help us if we would all deliver at once!

"It is my first," I answered her first question.

"Then you have a while to go yet. You are lucky, you will have the delivery room all to yourself. At any rate, I am happy that all these nurses here are midwives."

"They are?" I asked, astonished.

"Yes, oh, they are such a help during the delivery. You'll see for yourself. They tell you what to do. I myself would not even mind delivering without a doctor. Give me a good midwife any day! If it's a normal birth, that is."

A normal birth? Her words choked my throat again, I thought of the Cesarean. Would mine be a normal birth? What was a normal birth?

The moaning and screaming in the delivery room rose to a height then dissolved in the cry of a baby. A healthy, happy cry. I was shocked, how could I think of a cry as something happy?

The woman started to walk towards the delivery room. "Good, one of them will soon be able to give me a place there."

I went back to the room. John and I kissed, hugged, and prayed.

Then I ran around the room for a while.

"You have to leave now, Dr. Szablya, the supervisor will be coming soon." Our friendly midwife had returned. I clung to him as if I would never want to let him go. "I am afraid. Don't leave me."

He squeezed me reassuringly. "Everything will be all right, I will send in Uncle Charles and the doctor will be here any minute now. It is beginning to dawn."

"Visiting hours are twice a week, Thursdays and Sundays. You will be here for at least a week," she said. "Of course when the baby will be born, we'll let you know," she said to John. "But I am sorry, you really must leave now."

I stood at the staircase and waved to him as long as I could see his tall figure, waving back at me.

I was completely alone now, except for the kicks inside me. More and more the pain drowned out the assurance of even that tiny motion. Then suddenly I heard it. It came out of the darkness and the grayness of the hospital. It was that same voice that once, it now seemed ages ago, let me know that I was not alone. "There is nothing that you and I together could not solve. You will have a healthy, beautiful child. I am always with you." Peace flowed over me while I experienced the next powerful pain. Somehow it did not hurt so much, but it was not over. It continued late into the morning. My doctor appeared around eight and said he would be back later. I did not even dare to ask when to expect my little one to be born. All seven women who were expecting during the night went through the same routine by then. They screamed their babies into life, their cries having changed into the baby sounds that gained strength as time came for the morning feeding.

The midwives carried the babies to their respective mothers for nursing. The possibility of my giving birth now seemed so remote that I could have cried.

Around eleven o'clock a midwife had pity on me and showed me into the delivery room. She helped me on the delivery bed and explained that it took so much longer than it did for the others because it was my first baby. They all had several children and they were farther ahead in labor when they had arrived. There was nothing wrong with my child she assured me. To make me understand she brought in a new set of swaddling clothes and diapers. "For your baby," she explained.

I felt more comfortable after that, especially when Uncle Charles and my doctor appeared again. They checked me and then they chatted and joked around. Anger welled up in me. Why in the world don't they *do* something? I wanted to scream at them. Don't they care about me? Uncle Charles loved me, I knew that. Then, why doesn't he make my baby come? I remembered that somebody said I was supposed to push at one point. Oh, yes, it was Mother and the doctor in the ambulance. When was I to push? Someone pulled something on my legs.

"Sterile stockings," the friendly midwife explained. I remembered that Mother had said something about that. "Right before you will have your baby they'll put sterile stockings on you." So it is getting near. Not a minute too soon, I thought. Suddenly, I felt as if I would be coming up from a deep sleep. The midwife stood by me and counted my pulse. "You are doing fine," she said.

"It doesn't seem possible, does it?" Uncle Charles stood by my side. "Yet you are getting there."

One flowed into another; my whole existence dissolved into one big cramp. "I am going to die," I whispered when I saw Uncle Charles so close.

"No, you won't," he said with his familiar smile. "A few more pains like these and you will have a nice, healthy baby."

"A few more?" I couldn't believe my ears. "If I have just one more I am going to die."

"No, you won't," he repeated and walked away.

The midwife started to explain, "Pull up your legs now into a squatting position and hold your knees tight with both hands. When the pain comes, bear down. There, that's the girl!" She lifted my head as I pushed. "Very good!"

The pain vanished. I lay back exhausted. I was thankful for her advice. When I pushed, the pain left. Cooperating with the baby's efforts brought results.

Uncle Charles and my doctor came back. "I can see the head!" he declared after a few more pains.

I had nine months to prepare, but I still could not believe that I was becoming a mother at the age of eighteen.

"Let us know when the next pain comes. We'll make a little incision," the doctor said,

"Will it hurt? Here it comes!" I yelled.

"Did it hurt?" he asked.

"Did what hurt? You haven't done anything."

"I sure have. It's all done."

I felt another pain and another. I looked at the clock. It was 1:40 p.m. Suddenly the midwife threw a towel over my face and blew something onto it. I felt like falling down into a deep well while my body was torn apart. I arrived at the bottom and dreamed of my sister Elisabeth who was scolding me for something at the railroad station. Then I heard a baby crying. A healthy, sturdy cry. I looked at the clock right on the opposite wall. It was 1:42 p.m.

"Helen, you have a little girl," Uncle Charles spoke to me as I rose from my dream.

"I had a dream about Elisabeth," I started to tell him as his words did not quite seep in yet. "What? What did you say?" I finally realized that the cry came from my baby.

"You had a little girl. Look, look at her."

I saw a purple little creature with a squash-like head blinking her eyes, a toothless mouth, a near-bald head; she was the most beautiful creature I had ever seen.

"She is mine? My baby?"

"She weighs 7 pounds, 3 ounces."

"That big?" I thought of the midwife last night who predicted a six pounder. Will she have a surprise today! And it was not a Cesarean! And the pains? They were all gone. I had never felt better. I was as hungry as a wolf. And the baby's cry! That "disturbing noise!" How could I ever think of it other than what it seemed to me now? Why, this was heavenly music! It meant that she was alive and well and that my pains were over. They were done with, gone. Of course, I did not die. Maybe those pains never even existed.

I felt her soft little body on my stomach. She moved and cried. Her loud voice filled my whole being. I experienced what I knew must have been the greatest happiness in this world. A miracle happened through me. A child was born because of the love John and I had for one another.

I heard the talk, the jokes, and the doctor's asking for the needle to sew me up. Everything happened around me, but nothing counted anymore. I floated on a cloud of joy as I listened to the grandest symphony on earth, the cry of my own baby.

When she was all washed and prettied up, they gave her to me. I held her in my arms for the first time. A pink little bundle, sleeping quietly. Her tiny fingers made a fist. Her eyes were closed. For a few moments I didn't know what to do. Suddenly I realized that she was mine. I lifted one finger and touched her rosy little cheek.

# 44

"I want to hold her first!"

"Let me see her!"

"Wait everybody. I think Mother should have a first chance." I handed little Helen, our newborn daughter, to Mother when we brought her home from the hospital. We nicknamed little Helen "Ilike" from the Hungarian equivalent of her name, Ilona.

She held her close. "I never knew it was such a wonderful feeling to embrace one's grandchild. I heard it often enough but I had to experience it to know the joy."

Mother had the pleasure of holding our little Ilike first, but it was her father who gave her the first bath.

The baby bathtub was set up in the bathroom. Because of its spaciousness, the whole adoring family including John's parents were able to gather for the occasion. I had never seen a father bathe a baby, but John insisted.

"I learned. Don't you worry! Every time a friend had a baby I asked and they let me practice. I know how to give Ilike a bath."

He donned an apron. Ilike nearly disappeared in his two huge hands. They seemed to be made to make a baby comfortable. He did not drop her. He did not make her cry. Helen comfortably rested on his palm as he splashed lukewarm water over her tiny body. She loved warmth. I was told in the hospital that every time the heat went on she would stretch her head towards the radiator.

John turned her around and washed the other side, carefully cleaning every little crevice of her body. Then he lifted her onto the thick towel and patted her dry.

Our mothers clapped. They were enchanted. I was proud of him.

Ilike enjoyed it until she thought it was time to eat and then she signaled for me to satisfy her hunger.

My old crib was put up in our room right in front of the door that led into Mother's and Grandfather's room. On the other side of the door was Grandfather's bed. This way we had our privacy; whoever entered had to come in through the hallway.

We were determined to be very strict with our new baby according to the custom of those days. She was breastfed every three hours and in between she was not to be picked up. That was hard to enforce with the many grandparents and aunts around. Yet we wanted to keep our sanity and, therefore, remained steadfast in our decision.

During the night Grandfather often stood in front of our locked door, stamping his cane, "Feed that poor child," he would plead. "Bad parents," he would go on, not scolding us but expressing his solidarity with Ilike whom he adored. He would come in and sit beside her, watching her every move. The first few weeks were hard for everybody. John had to hold me down bodily to keep me from going to Ilike when she cried during the night. When the first trying nights were over, Ilike got used to sleeping through the night. Our doctor said that babies needed eight hours of uninterrupted sleep as much as we did and if we fed her more often than at two and a half hour intervals the old milk would still be in her stomach and spoil her appetite.

Ilike was a delightful baby. She smiled often and became excited if anyone as much as came near her crib. She would kick simultaneously with both legs, coo, and do her best in order to be picked up.

I was overflowing with milk. A very good friend of ours had her baby three weeks after Ilike was born. She did not have sufficient milk. I offered to give her some. This is how Ilike and her son, Adam, became milk brother and sister.

One evening I sat in our room, nursing Ilike, when John came home pale-faced. "Do you remember Mark? Somebody saw him yesterday morning, apparently headed for work, when a man stopped beside him and flashed his identification at him. He then was pushed into a car that sped away. Since then nobody has heard from him. His wife called him at work and he wasn't there. She is desperate."

Why did the room turn chilly? "He was such a good man! What did they want from him?"

"Who knows," John answered thinking hard. "His wife called all the police stations, all of them disclaimed knowing anything about him. The man who saw him last went to see his wife right after work. I doubt that we will see Mark again."

"What will they do with him?" Ilike's little fist slowly opened as her hunger subsided and her tiny fingers played with my breast. John's eyes followed her moves and rested on me. He must have liked what he had seen. "If ever I am in danger, I will call you and tell you on the phone that I will be late from work. Unless you know it's true it means that the factory is in trouble." After a little thought he added, "Of course if I am caught on the street, like Mark... Why would they arrest him? I still can't understand."

"Why did they arrest my second aunt in the mountains of northern Hungary, with the pretext that they knew she wanted to escape. She was two hundred miles off the direction in which she should have been walking if she had any intention of escaping. She was also charged with unlawful possession of a gun. She had an antique pistol hanging above the piano, you know, a front-loader. I don't know where she could have gotten ammunition to make it work or even if it would have worked if she had the bullets."

Ilike started to suck at my breast again as John settled beside me in a chair. Still enjoying the sight of our baby he started, "Did you know that I asked to marry my first fiancée in prison?"

"No, but I knew you had one. In prison? How? Why?"

"Her father was a general and he was in West Germany with Hungary's gold that was saved from the Soviet invasion. When the gold came home, he came back with it. He was tried and acquitted. But he was in jail when I asked Maria to marry me. As custom had it, I had to talk to her father also. I asked for permission to visit him in prison and with the help of the Bishop, I received a pass. In those days it was still possible to take food to prisoners, so I ended up taking him dinner every day. He was released later. But after that, very early one morning—as you well know all arrests happened early in the morning for shock value—a military cap appeared through the opalescent window of their hall door. It was the dreaded security police. The father was still in pajamas. 'Let me get dressed,' he pleaded. 'It won't be necessary. Hurry.' His wife threw him his overcoat. He slipped on his shoes. They pushed him out the door. The family hasn't seen him since. They went from one police station to another and begged to be told where he was. He was not at any of the prisons, nor at any of the known 'establishments.' To this day they have not heard of his whereabouts or what the charges were against him, if there were any at all."

"That is why I hate every minute when you are not with me. Every morning when you leave I am afraid that I will never see you again." I pressed Ilike to my breast so vehemently that she looked up in consternation.

"We never know, Helen. There is no one in this world who can guarantee our safety. You know as well as I do that the very basis of Marxism is the underlying dogma of dialectic materialism—change. When Communists change their attitudes and policies, they are true to themselves. For them life is made up of theses and antitheses and the battle of these will develop the new synthesis, the temporary 'truth,' which in turn becomes the new thesis and so on. This outlook can be applied to anything, starting with history and ending with everyday policies about our everyday lives. We have to face up to this."

"Translated into plain Hungarian, this means that we are at the mercy of the government and 'the end justifies the means'? Is that what you are trying to tell me?"

"Exactly. It means that any day you may never see me again. Yet, even then I would be grateful to God for the days He has given us together, that I had known the happiness of having you for my wife, Ilike for my daughter."

I was crying as I held up Ilike to burp her. I handed her to her father who gently patted her back with his hands that looked huge in comparison to her delicate features.

~

It was a cold but sunny March day when John appeared from the blue with a broad grin on his face. "Stalin is dead. He died last night at 9:50. We have the rest of the day off to mourn him. I ran home. I want to be the one to put out the black flag on the house."

We held hands and danced around the room. The fat blond janitor waddled up with the flag and John proudly put it out on our balcony. "Believe me, I have been waiting for this moment for years. There was never a time when people would have marched so enthusiastically as they will march to his statue on the day of his funeral, to 'mourn,' that is to celebrate our good luck."

"What will this mean, will any good come to us?" I asked as I looked searchingly at John.

"I don't know, Helen, but just to know that the tyrant is dead… Something good will have to come. You will see. Maybe the whole government will fall apart. Look at the French Revolution. The leaders were killing off each other. Could it happen again?"

The next months brought the answer. In quick succession Stalin's closest allies made their bid and died trying to get to power. Malenkov was the first successor with Molotov and Beria as first Vice Presidents and heads of the Ministry of Foreign Affairs and Ministry of the Interior, respectively.

It seemed that people wanted to forget Stalin with the greatest possible speed. Stalin who was called our Great Father and Teacher was still glorified in the newspapers a few days after his death. But in the new edition of the Soviet Encyclopedia that appeared only a week after Stalin's death, the word "Stalinist" (definition: Member of the Communist Party (Bolshevik) of the Soviet Union, a faithful disciple of Marxism-Leninism, unshakably devoted to the cause of Lenin-Stalin) was left out.

Stalin was buried beside Lenin, but his guidelines were thrown out in order to pacify the masses, at least temporarily. Soviet industry started the manufacture of consumer's goods and turned out washing machines and steel beds instead of industrial equipment. Malenkov wanted to please. People cried with happiness when it was broadcast from loudspeakers in rural railroad stations that peasants could now drink the milk of their own cow, keep some of their own products.

Beria, the executor of people, the head of the security police—disguised as Head of the Ministry of the Interior—fell into his own trap and was executed. Stalin's terror had to be banished forever.

On a sizzling July day, John and I, his parents, and our seven-month-old Ilike, whom we carried in a baby basket, took a long walk up the hills of Ábrahámhegy. We hiked to the hundred pine trees to gather branches for the kitchen stove and to pick berries. John's mother looked for mushrooms as well. She was an expert in transforming nature's gifts into tasty dishes. In order to stay alive she had to use her imagination. Since the time they had moved to Lake Balaton they had not received their pension from the Government despite the fact that John's father was forced into early retirement because he stood up for the workers in a dispute with management some twenty years before. The Government Retirement Office never gave him any reason for having taken his well-deserved livelihood. Since then John sent them part of his salary and they did the best they could to make money working at odd jobs available in the country.

As we descended through the multicolored blanket of the flowery fields and chased each other from berry bush to berry bush, filling our baskets, we reached the first houses of the settlement. A strong, friendly radio voice flowed out through the nearest window, talking about changes that had to be made in the Hungarian government, in our way of life. It sounded like a foreign broadcast. But it could not be! They would not have it on that loud! We stopped and listened. What was it? Soon the announcer came on and talked about a new Prime Minister of the country, Imre Nagy. We could not believe our ears. Some of private enterprise was to be seeping back into the economy. At least he said he would allow small industries, farmers could keep some of their own products and use them as they pleased, sell them on the market. Could it really be true?

We ran home to listen to the foreign broadcasts in the privacy of our own home. It was true! Was it the death of Stalin that slowly brought its results to Hungary, following the example of the Soviet Union? Who cared? The relief was unbelievable. We did not even dare to ask how long it would last. We only hoped that the thaw would continue.

Suddenly even the afternoons seemed brighter than before. Ilike was lying in her crib. John's father stood above her and whistled her favorite tune, Beethoven's violin concerto. She smiled and kicked with both feet to its rhythm. John's mother hummed a tune while she was preparing dinner. She did not want to be disturbed. There was but one thing for us to do. John clutched my hand into his. I always felt so small when he did that even though I had the largest hands in my family. We disappeared into our room that was barely big enough to hold our single bed and a chest of drawers.

He embraced me with his silky brown arms and I could feel his subtle thick lips caressing my mouth as he searched for my kisses.

A few minutes, or was it hours ago that we came back from our long, exhausting and exhilarating hike. We had heard words from the broadcast that might change our whole life for the better. We were still under their magic. Is there a more beautiful idea than an everlasting honeymoon? We vowed that ours would never end as we thought of the beauties of that afternoon. The vineyards were filled with golden sunshine and singing birds. Wildflowers covered the fields. The streams glistened and glittered as they flowed past us. Their chattering voice brought back remembrances of long-past centuries and memories of all the lovers who listened to their murmur and vowed to be true to each other.

Our feelings drove us to become one again in our love.

An hour of most ardent lovemaking followed. The skipping and jumping and the forceful feeling of our desire chased us to even wilder kisses. The blue of John's eyes became nearly invisible because it turned into pure black with a gleam in it that I had never seen before. His teeth cut deep into my flesh and I did not seem to feel it, while my nails clawed into his body and my breasts pressed against his in our desire to become more complete, to experience wholeness, to be fulfilled. The kisses multiplied and I hugged him closer and closer while our bodies started to tremble and push into each other to find the seeds of life. Our beings completely integrated. As we fulfilled each other, we also created something that was new.

We trembled like newborn babies and our sweat resembled the wetness of a new being when the climax came that shook us into stillness, into humble and grateful kisses, looking for each other's lips in our coming sleep. This time we felt it was also the beginning of a new life.

～

In September, Ilike refused to be nursed. I turned her head towards my breast and tried to pump milk into her mouth, but she made a face and spit out the milk. I was pregnant again. I never had my period between the two children. It was a warm summer evening when I came home with the news from the doctor.

John awaited me on the balcony with Ilike. He brought me a white-pink bouquet of roses in anticipation of the event, the same kind he bought for our civil wedding that now seemed a long time ago.

A warm breeze waved through the lace curtains. Across the street the orchestra started to tune up for the concert. I longed for the privacy of our own apartment when we could always be alone.

"John, I wish we could find an apartment for ourselves. It is impossible, but still…"

"I know, honey," he looked concerned. "We must think of something. Now there would be four of us in this one room, a shared kitchen, and a bathroom. Yet we are lucky because we only share with the family. Besides, the apartment is in my name. How can we leave it? If I leave, everybody else would lose this place.

"Listen," I turned my voice to a whisper. Next door to us lived the South American-Hungarian couple who remodeled our former apartment and thereby received two of the rooms. I did not want them to overhear us. "You know what I heard today? Mary and Laci got a divorce."

"No! They couldn't! They were so much in love. Why, if they divorced… who will stay married?" John exclaimed.

"Tchch! They divorced in order to get an apartment of their own."

"What did you say?"

"They divorced in order to get an apartment. He is entitled to two rooms if he can get it. Well, somebody died, Laci had moved in with them before the old man was dead and applied for the place, where he was already a resident. Naturally, he also paid the full price for the right to rent the apartment to the widow. Mary stayed with the parents. She had received the old apartment from her husband as settlement in the divorce. Now, Mary, as direct descendant, can and will transfer the title to the apartment to her parents in about six months. Then, after a year they will again get married."

John burst out laughing. "So this is your gentle way to let me know that you want a divorce, on the very day we find out that we are pregnant with our second child? But, this is not an impossibility. We *must* find a solution; you are right about that. Even if we have to get a divorce."

That started him laughing again. Ilike laughed right with him. Whenever she heard someone laugh she had to join in. She was a very happy baby. I liked to think that it had something to do with my decision to quit school and devote myself to motherhood, despite the mounting financial and governmental pressures.

❧

We were in the middle of the winter with no prospects for an apartment. We talked to one of our lawyer friends and decided that if nothing happened by the following week we would start divorce procedures.

In the meantime we had to travel to Lake Balaton to settle some official business about the house. That gave us a good excuse to visit John's parents who lived there year around.

I had never yet seen the Balaton in its winter beauty. It was a double treat for me as we walked out onto the whitely glistening smooth ice that sparkled with sunshine. A thick blanket of snow covered the landscape everywhere. The cold pinched our cheeks red as we walked on the immobile white water of the lake.

Slowly the dried-out cattails and reeds were left behind and we were on the open stretch of ice that covered the whole lake from here as far as our eyes could see. It was fun to tread the thick ice crust of the water with dry feet. In the summer we swam in this same place. John laughed and ran ahead, I followed right behind him and we slid across the mirror of ice.

"Let's draw a heart," John suggested. "Then in the summer we'll be able to swim in our love."

"Let's do that! Yes!" We started from one place and went in two directions to make a big heart with our initials in it and those of our children.

"How many children should we put into our heart?" I asked.

"As many as we'll have. You know that we had decided never to say that any one of them was the last one."

"Then let's just put 'children'."

"When this will melt, we and our love will forever live on in the waves of this lake. We'll swim in it this summer. Then our children will swim in it…"

"And their children and theirs," I laughed in answer to that amorous silliness. Yet I enjoyed it thoroughly.

The sunbeams reflected in millions of colors on the glittering snow and on the white sheet of ice under the baby-blue firmament.

There was not a cloud in the sky. As we reached shore we noticed the delicate designs of nature and technology, the branches of bushes and trees along with the telephone wires all covered by dainty layers of snow and ice and etched against the summery sky. Branches were bent under the weight of the snow. Snowflakes nestled in the crevices of the wrought-iron gates and on the crisscrossed wood of the fences.

The fruit trees were dressed in snow blossoms and brought back a frosty image of spring. As we walked upwards and finally reached the top of the hill, the whole lake opened up in front of our eyes as one uninterrupted white sheet of ice from shore to shore.

John put his arms around me and in his arms the winter disappeared, the snow and ice melted away. The warmth of his love poured into my body and from that warmth I sensed the movement of a tiny life within me.

～

Then one day it happened. John called from the factory. "Today I will be late."

"I love you," I answered.

"I know. I do, too. Forever." He put down the receiver.

MY GOD! Were these the last words we would ever say to each other? Will he ever come home? What can it be? What am I to do? I called our lawyer.

"Did he say anything specific?"

"No. A while ago, he said that if he'd call some day and say he would be late and I did not know any reason for it, it would mean that he was in danger."

"All right. I'll see what I can find out. I have some connections."

I called another friend, who lived close to the factory.

"I see an unusual number of people moving in and out. Nothing else. By 'unusual' I mean there are some people. Most of the time there is movement only in the morning and at night, when people go to and from work."

"Please let me know if you see something."

She promised.

Then there was nothing else to do but pray. I saw nightmares as I fed Ilike. I saw John being pushed into a car and taken. I saw him being beaten by the police. He was bleeding. I couldn't take it any longer.

I ran over to the other room. Grandfather was muttering, "What day is it?"

Not that again! Just like the time when my mother was taken to the police. Who cared what day it was?

"Where is Mother?" I asked.

"She was here a little while ago," Grandfather said. "I'll go in after a while to entertain Ilike."

"Why don't you go right now?" I suggested. That would take care of both of them.

I dashed to the kitchen. Mother was there. "Where were you a little while ago? I needed to talk with you. John might be in trouble." In my haste I forgot to even look around to see if there was anybody else there. Thank God the place was empty.

"How do you know?"

I told her what I knew.

"Now, listen. I have been to the police, you know, it must be about fifteen or maybe even twenty times by now. You'd think I know. Yet, it is impossible to guess what they might want. Not once did I know why they took me or where I was going to end up."

"I can't take it if something happens to John," I became hysterical.

"Nothing will happen to John. You must trust God. That is what I was just going to tell you. He brought me back every time. Didn't He? Even though I had no hope. I am an 'insect' and far from being 'irreplaceable'."

Mother's words gave me material for hope. After all John was not a general! Yet, he was a descendant of "insects." The doubt came back again.

The day moved on with the speed of a snail. Nightmares kept pursuing me. I saw all the pictures in my mind that I had ever seen about the Jewish concentration camps, about atrocities in police stations, everything I could think of.

I had no tangible proof, like a photo about Soviet treatment of prisoners, yet I knew. From the terrified silence of those who got away, from the complete numbness of their relatives. They never told about anything. Their physical shape spoke for itself. But what was most frightening was that a great number of them never returned; their relatives had never found out anything about them. They became nonpersons and in a week or two their wives claimed to have divorced them, their brother or sister suddenly became an only child. Who forced them into denying their own loved ones? I could never do that! Or would I, in order to save my child? I remembered when I told Mother that the best thing she could do for us was to divorce my father, how we asked Father's best friend to marry her and how he complied! I could have screamed, but I did not want to frighten Ilike. She smiled. She did not know what was happening.

I realized that I couldn't just stand around. There was work to be done. Imre Nagy's regime had brought with it the possibility of private small industries. Mother had started a small business, with money Father had sent, making plastic handbags with a drawstring. They were made in three colors: red, tan, and black. They sold like hotcakes because they were not mass-produced. Several relatives helped us with the work.

All that day, while I worked, I thought of John. I remembered when we were once talking about the German-Soviet treaty before the war. John told me that his mother had asked a high official of the German Embassy at a reception about this strange association. "How come the far left and the far right could make such an agreement?" The official answered that although it might sound strange, the two philosophies were very close to each other. The main difference was probably the nationalism of the Germans and the internationalism of the Soviets. Their basic principles and methods were very much alike. One had to think only of the fact that in the Parliament far right and far left sat beside each other; those on the extremes went full circle." When I had asked John about how the Americans could team up with an extreme dictatorship like the Soviets, he told me about his American experiences, then concluded, "Politicians make strange bedfellows. Sir Winston Churchill's idea was to bleed the Soviets and the Nazis to death, fighting each other, and then finish off whatever was left of them to give freedom to the whole world. Strangely enough that was the exact reverse of what I heard from the Soviet occupying forces. They claimed that they wanted to occupy all of Europe, then go on and conquer America. Why America? Why not the British? Why were the Americans called 'imperialists' by the Communists when it was Great Britain who 'owned' the world through her colonies? Churchill's plan sounded nice but somehow this had not happened. Whatever politics did, it certainly did not seem to work for my good."

Why did I think of all these things? Of course. The nightmares suddenly flooded me again. If the Germans did the things I had seen in pictures, the Soviets must be doing the same things if they were so close to each other in methods. That's what made me remember this whole mess.

I wished for some kind of news, but none came.

It was dark outside, but then John never came home before seven o'clock at night. I bathed Ilike. Mother came in and talked with me again. "He will come home, you will see." We prayed. Then I heard that voice again. "There is nothing that you and I together cannot solve." Peace flowed into my heart and the nightmares disappeared as I cried on Mother's shoulders.

It was eleven o'clock when I heard the well-known footsteps. They stopped at the door and John came in. I jumped out of bed and into his arms.

"It's over this time. I'm home. It seems I am still 'irreplaceable,' despite my mistake."

I did not want to hear what it was until I had my fill of the sheer ecstasy of having him in my arms. Then we sat down and he told me.

"I designed my first machine in the factory a long time ago. It takes many months to manufacture a mammoth like this one. I gave the specifications according to the modern way as taught at the university. I did not notice that half the specifications were given according to an old model. The design office drew the blueprints according to these specifications. Management did not notice. Neither did manufacturing. The machine was completed with this error in it. Then came the big day; the machine was to be tested. Within the first minutes after starting, the monster went up in flames. The fire was put out fast, yet the whole inside of the machine will have to be redone and the order will have to be delivered to the Soviet Union by the end of the month. According to Communist principles this could not have been an honest mistake. The factory swarmed with plain clothes policemen. Nobody was allowed to leave until they found out who caused the 'sabotage.' When the mishap occurred I phoned you immediately because I anticipated questioning. Thank God that we are still 'irreplaceable' and that for an 'insect' I am still young. When they considered all these facts they had decided to listen to the director who, being a good friend of both our fathers, called together a short meeting with the engineers and foremen. They had decided that it was possible to rebuild the machine in time by utilizing all half-ready parts of other machines and working around the clock. A miracle, if you think of the fact that it took them a year and a half to finish the original machine."

A miracle it was. A miracle of camaraderie and love, inspired help to a fellow human being.

# 45

The temperature went down to twenty degrees below zero. An unusual occurrence in Hungary. At least it did not last as long as in the winter of 1953-54. The dirty-gray snow characteristic of downtown was piled high on the dark gray streets. The sun hid behind charcoal-colored clouds as we set out on a house-hunting trip. John had a coworker, an unmarried woman, slightly crippled, who lived in one of the outlying districts, called Óbuda. Her father had died. She still owned their small house as it did not have six rooms (the maximum allowed by the Communists). She and her father had rebuilt it after the war. Because of these circumstances she was in the enviable position that she was allowed to decide for herself to whom she was going to rent the place.

"Helen, let's put ourselves into gear for this excursion," John recommended. "Let's do what I would have done if you had said 'No' on that memorable June evening."

"What was that?"

"I would have drunk an espresso with a double shot of rum at the Astoria."

"That sounds great. What does it do?"

"It puts you in a frame of mind that will help you see things in a better light."

"Is the apartment that bad?"

"I don't know, but in this kind of weather nothing can look too good. At least the drink will warm us up."

Fortified with the Hungarian equivalent of an Irish coffee we continued our trip to Óbuda. After a half-hour bus ride we arrived. A Roman amphitheater greeted us. No wonder they called this place Óbuda, which means Ancient Buda. Already in Roman times people lived here. I remembered that Grandfather's first pharmacy had been in this part of town. As we walked towards the house we passed a modern high school and a few stores. Then we arrived at Bécsi ut, the avenue that led straight to Vienna. A tavern with a small garden restaurant in the back was the first house on the corner. The next was Miss Jenny's house.

The avenue broke in front of it and widened into a small triangular park.

"Look, that would be a nice place for the children. There is a playground," I pointed.

Miss Jenny came to the gate with a pleasant enough smile. She must have wanted us as tenants.

"Come in, come in. I have been waiting for you," she said and led us to the door. "Step in. Let us go to the front room. Here, this is the largest room. The window looks onto the nice park. Next door to this room is the vegetable shop. You must have noticed when you came in that there was a store there. Oh, if only my poor Dad had not died. Although, I did not much approve of his second wife. Thank God, I am rid of her now. He left the house to me, not to her. She was a vulgar person. Let's not talk about her. The main thing is that I don't need to think about her anymore. Here is the next room. This one is smaller but it still has a nice window onto the yard.

"In the summer the children can play outside. Maybe you can make them a sandbox. Now, that is the hallway and the bathroom. Here is the problem; I do not want to share the bathroom and kitchen. Whoever comes here, I want them to build a new kitchen for themselves, beside the present bathroom and then a new bathroom for me on the other side of the kitchen. We would then have two complete apartments, and it wouldn't cost very much."

My head was spinning. We didn't have a penny. What was she talking about? But, the coffee-rum combination must have given me some courage because I remained silent. John talked with her as if we had all the money on earth.

"Do you have an estimate as to how much this would cost?"

"Not yet. But the man who had built this house will be here soon. He can do it himself. It would be ideal since he knows where everything is inside the walls."

A white-haired, stocky man of about sixty-five soon appeared. He listened to the plans, then sat down and made his calculations. In the meantime Miss Jenny showed us the rest of the house and our would-be neighbors.

"This is where my former maid lives with her daughter; an excellent playmate for your children. Now she is the janitor. She lives in the very end of the yard in that small house there. This is also where the laundry is. See, we have a big cauldron to boil the diapers and your linen. Then you can dry it in the attic. I have a very nice cleaning woman who lives about two houses down. I am sure she would not mind helping you too.

"Then these rooms are mine. The next two rooms could be yours. Right beside your two rooms is the vegetable store. The people are of Bulgarian origin. They have only the best merchandise, somewhat expensive but worth it. It's like old times…" She stopped short and looked at us with fright in her eyes; but when she saw that we agreed with her and did not shudder at her "old times," she went on more confidently. "Well, on this sun porch, behind the store, lives the only tenant I wish were not here. But then, he comes only sometimes. He has another apartment, where he lives with his wife. But they always get into trial separations, or whatever you want to call it and then he runs away and lives here for a few days." She turned her voice to a whisper, "I think he is also a Communist. He is a baker, or something. I wish he would leave. But, what can I do?"

In the meantime the contractor was ready with his estimate. "Twenty-four thousand forints, take or leave about five hundred."

Lucky that John was holding me by the arm, or I may have fainted! The effect of the coffee was fading. John did not bat an eyelash.

"That would include everything?"

"Yes," was the firm answer.

"That then would entitle us to rent the apartment as ordinary tenants."

"Well, not really," Miss Jenny was hesitant. "I do not want to get into that predicament. Then you would be able to trade the place with anybody without my consent."

"It seems to me that for this much money we should be able to do our own trading," John interjected.

"I only want it to be a sublet. I mean you should trust me to this extent if I trust you with renting you these rooms when, because of the circumstances, I am allowed to do with them as I please. After all, I am sure I can rent it to someone else."

Miss Jenny was getting annoyed. What was there to do? Did we want the place or not? We could not decide. We honestly didn't know.

"Let us think that over. We'll go home and try to raise the money. We'll talk this over with our parents, Miss Jenny."

She was not very pleased but she knew as well as we did that this kind of money was not readily available in Hungary in those days.

On our way home we were in a gloomy mood. The grayness of the city mirrored perfectly our state of mind. For a while we did not say a word. We took the streetcar for the forty-minute ride home.

Halfway across the Danube John asked, "What do you think?"

"I don't know, I really don't." I was freezing and by now all the coffee-inspired courage was gone from my body. "The first room is not too bad, but the second is pretty dark. That window is in one corner and it is not too big."

"Some light will come in from the hallway through the glass door." John was more optimistic.

"There is a stove in the big room, but in the little one there is none."

"Maybe we could put a stove into the hallway and heat the little room from there."

"She doesn't have hot running water at all, only the bath-stove in the bathroom. We would have to make a fire every time we wanted to take a bath and heat our water on the kitchen stove for the dishes. We don't even have a kitchen stove or a fridge," I panicked. All of a sudden it occurred to me that I would have to cook every meal by myself. I would be on my own.

"But we would be alone," John said it out loud.

I realized that this is what we wanted. Of course. Suddenly it seemed that no price would be too high to pay for that. We had never lived alone.

"That is true. Do you think we should?"

There was a daring glimmer in his eyes. "Let's try and see what we can do. At least we would not have to get a divorce," he winked at me as we climbed off the streetcar.

"You need an apartment," was Mother's reaction when we told her what we found. "There is no other way to get one, but I wish you would put the agreement on paper, sign a contract or something. I feel very insecure about this whole deal. True, nowadays one cannot terminate a sublet without the consent of the tenant, one cannot be evicted either, yet…twenty-four thousand forints is a thousand dollars. As far as I know none of us has it."

"How could we raise it?" I wondered.

"Your house," Mother said.

"What house?" I asked.

"The nationalized one, on Kossuth Lajos Street."

"What about it?"

"Half of that house belongs to you."

"I thought it all belonged to the state."

"It does, but that does not matter."

Of course! Why didn't I think of that before? I was too involved in wondering about the place, whether we really wanted it. We would have to sell part of my house on the black market. We had already sold several of our apartment houses to medical doctors, small business owners, the "rich" of our topsy-turvy times. They bought the nationalized apartment houses to invest their money in something "tangible." It was like Nazi times all over. Then Jews sold their property to Gentiles. Now we sold our property to people who believed that they would make a killing with real estate once times changed and apartment houses would be returned to their rightful owners. After the Nazi times all contracts made with Jews during the war were declared void and the buyers had to return their houses. However, Mother gave every one of our buyers a separate affidavit besides the contract, stating that she had received the best possible price for the house and that she would not sue to retrieve it. She considered the sale final. No wonder we got the best prices among all of our friends.

413

"You would not even have to sell your whole half, only one quarter of the house," Mother said.

"Let's do it then!" I thought of being alone with John. Completely alone. We wanted to trust Miss Jenny even though we had been warned. We wanted to believe because this seemed to be our only chance.

The building started, and our days were filled trying to find the necessary equipment for the kitchen. The underground network of house selling whispered through town that part of my house was available for sale.

We went in and out of stores trying to buy a stove. Finally we had to be content with a double-burner hotplate and a small separate oven. Mother found us an old icebox. Although we had to buy ice daily, at least we could keep the food cold.

We found a buyer for my quarter-house; the contract was sealed in perfect secrecy. How many years would we have had to spend in prison if the police had heard even an inkling of what we were doing! This transaction was an open act of counting on the downfall of the regime.

The police were still rummaging through our house every six weeks or so, trying to find Father among the linen and our shoes. Finally one day Uncle Charles was home when this happened. He started to yell at the policeman, "What are you doing with my wife's stuff? Do you think I would tolerate that the man who treated her so badly should return? Then hide him here? Just what do you think? Tell your commanding officer that I don't want any of that business anymore. Now get out of my house!"

I was shaking when I heard him yell at the police like that. I had only seen him angry one other time, when he had talked about his land the Communists took from him right after the war. How did he dare to attack the police in such a tone?

His yelling, however, produced unexpected results. The police gave up on Father altogether. Uncle Charles, a doctor, was "irreplaceable," like John.

Our little nest in Óbuda became more homelike every day. We hung curtains and started to move the furniture in as soon as the men were ready with the construction. Our kitchen was only three by four feet. There was hardly enough room to move after we put in the cupboard, a tiny table for just the three of us, the burner and underneath it the oven, then the sink.

Electricity was scarce. If I used the oven or the burners or if I ironed I had to turn off everything else except for one light bulb. If I forgot, the fuse on the pole went out and I had to call the Electric Company and thereby become a suspect to sabotaging the energy supply.

In the May sunshine the garden looked inviting with its lilac bushes and budding flowers. Finally a week before the baby was due we moved in. The first night, only John and I slept there as we still had quite a lot to do. Ilike was seventeen months old. She walked sturdily on her two little feet and her blue eyes followed every move we made. I could hardly wait to have her in our new home.

In the big room we stood Marie's and my old crib along one of the walls and across from them we had our fabricated "double bed" with its Persian rugs under, above, and behind it. We managed to put in two chests of drawers and a big armoire from Mother's bedroom. One of the chests of drawers had a built-in desk where I could write.

The other room we fixed up as our living room. An antique armoire, bookcases, the bar with its mirror and crystal interior, two lovely antique tables, a radio-record player combination, and John's bachelor sofa that could be opened into a slightly wider bed. This was where John's parents would spend their nights when they came to visit.

We had a little stove in the hallway, just as John had planned it, and we could heat the room from there. We could also bathe the children in the hallway because the bathroom was too small for our good-sized baby tub with its stand.

I was very impatient for my baby to be born. Only a few more days were left till the due date, and my obstetrician was about to leave for Korea with his wife. They had volunteered to work there because they wanted to travel, and in 1954 there was no other opportunity for a doctor and his wife to see the world but to fight in some faraway country for the spreading of Communism.

I took the sofa apart and put it back together after having thoroughly beat the dust from it in the back of the yard. Not even the lugging of the heavy pieces induced labor. I was disgusted with myself.

Finally three days before due date of May 25 I gave birth to our first son, Jancsi, named and nicknamed after his father and grandfather. He was even bigger than Ilike and his birth was a pleasant surprise. I only spent half an hour in the delivery room compared to the three I had had to go through with Ilike. She had to fight her way out, for him it was much easier. He was a sturdy little guy, always ready to eat. When John's mother saw him first she declared, "He looks just like your father, Helen." Finally it was time to bring him home. The taxi sped past the trees of the Városliget on this early summer morning towards our new little nest, the most precious place for us in this world.

Jancsi, lulled to sleep by the rhythmic swinging of the car, seemed to smile in his sleep.

"What is he going to be like when he grows up?" I wondered.

When we got out of the car, after ten days of absence, I was surprised by the beauty of the garden that had turned into its complete glory as a result of the warm May rains. Everything was green and the birds sang their love songs while preparing their nests for the new bird generation. We lived right in the middle of the garden now. The flowers were only steps away from the window that looked so gray and dark when I saw it first. Our own home, at last.

Ilike ran to meet us in her "big girlish" navy blue skirt and a sleeveless white pullover sweater. She could not take her eyes off the baby. She did not speak much yet, but she could express everything she wanted.

Jancsika opened his eyes and noisily demanded to be fed. I sat down, for the first time in our new home with our new baby and enjoyed his satisfaction as soon as he caught my breast. Unlike Ilike he was very greedy when it came to food. Ilike would suck a few times, then when the milk started to flow she would simply wait and swallow. Jancsi could not stop sucking for a minute. When the milk poured into his mouth he was still sucking full blast, just about choking himself with mother's milk.

Ilike stood beside him and watched him. She touched his face and pulled her hand across it. She put her fingers on his. She was amazed.

"Be careful with the baby!" I warned her.

"Baby!" she said and her eyes lit up. "Baby, baby!" She danced around happily. John joined in her dance. Then they came back and sat beside me, giving me and Jancsi a great hug from both sides.

The sun beamed in through the window and the birds continued their love songs.

Jancsi developed with every passing day. He spent much time in the yard in his baby carriage and smiled at everything that came near him. His favorite was Ilike who knew at the first sound of his cry what he wanted.

Then one day parts of his skin developed a rash. His skin slowly turned purple, then it started peeling. I made an appointment with the doctor but I did not think much of it. Every baby had rashes, I knew that much already.

That afternoon we went to see our old pediatrician. He used to be my doctor when I was a child and I still liked to rely on his judgment. After all, I was only nineteen. We climbed the stairs to the third floor with the baby in his basket, Ilike walking beside us.

The familiar look of the antique furniture in the doctor's waiting room made us feel at ease. We did not have to wait long. The doctor's slender figure appeared in the door. He asked us into his office. He joked around with Ilike and examined Jancsi carefully. His words, although he tried to lessen their impact, fell like stones.

"Jancsika has an illness called Leiner disease. Many children have it nowadays. It comes from protein deficiency in the mother during pregnancy and lactation. At least these are the latest findings." My head spun as he continued. "I would recommend that you bring him out to the children's hospital in Városliget tomorrow. I am the head of that hospital, as you know, and we'll do everything for him that we can. However, in order to help him we must hospitalize him."

Questions chased each other in my mind yet I dared not open my mouth. John asked, "How long does he have to be in the hospital?"

"I'm not sure yet. We have to bring this disease under control. We'll give him vitamins and mother's blood." He smoked his cigarette and seemed to be in deep thought. "Your father is in Canada, isn't he, Helen? You could write to him to send some ACTH, a cortisone product. This is the newest medical invention. I think we could try it on Jancsika."

He was no longer joking although Ilike tried to attract his attention and make him laugh.

When Uncle Charles heard what the diagnosis was, he abruptly left the dinner table and did not return. But what was wrong? What was that dreaded disease?

The next day we left Ilike with the neighbors and took Jancsi to the hospital which was at the other end of the city. The building was in the middle of a nicely kept garden. The babies were all in two fairly large rooms, in small hospital cribs.

"Make yourself comfortable," the nurse advised. "You may stay here with your baby if you want to. We welcome any help that we can get. I am alone with fifteen babies and some of them have to be fed every ten minutes. Yet, I am not allowed to feed two at a time because they might choke on their food. Here, put him in this bed. Here are his clothes. Only diapers and a small shirt. That will do. All of these children had Leiner disease," she spread out her arms. "In some hospitals all the children born there have it. Yet, I say they must be born with it. It certainly is not contagious."

Most of the other infants in the room were very, very thin, not even as big as Jancsi, who was only seven weeks old. Yet from the way they looked at me and formed coo-words with their mouths, I had to believe that they were several months old.

"What is wrong with him?" I pointed at a little bright brown-eyed fellow with skinny arms.

"He has a brain tumor. Not too bad or he wouldn't be so lively."

"And he had Leiner disease?"

"Yes."

"How about this other one? She does not look sick," I pointed at a curly blonde blue-eyed big baby. She looked about a year old.

"You are right. There is nothing wrong with her. She was very ill when she was only a few months old. Her mother brought her in and visited her daily until it was time for her to take the baby home. We haven't seen the mother since. We tried to find the parents but she registered the baby under a false name. Maybe she didn't have enough money to even feed the child. Or there was no place where she could have taken her." In the meantime the nurse was taking the temperatures of one baby after another. "Here, I'll show you something. You know they always say that you need to keep the thermometer in the rectum for three minutes. If you are watching the mercury, you'll see that it stops in about half that time. After that the change becomes negligible. We don't ever leave the thermometer in for more than a minute and a half." Even while she spoke she was changing and dressing the babies.

I nursed my little one. He stopped occasionally and looked up at me as if he wanted to ask a question. When I finished I said to the nurse, "I'll be back in about four hours, in time for the next feeding."

She looked concerned, "I don't know if that will be enough, every four hours." She put him on the scale to see how many ounces he had eaten. In Hungary it was the custom to weigh the babies before and after feeding to see if they had had enough.

"Hey, you are a good eater!" she addressed herself to Jancsi. "You sucked yourself full, eight ounces, I would say that was enough for you." She smiled at him and handed him back to me. "Take his temperature and change him. Put this ointment on him, but don't cover more than two-thirds of his body. His skin needs to breath." With that she was already feeding another baby.

The minute I finished with him I ran to the bus stop and was on my way home. Ilike awaited me at the iron gate, her two big blue eyes wide open. "Baby? Baby?" she inquired. I explained as much as I could and she and I hurried to buy food for the evening. I had an hour and a half at home. Then off I went to the hospital again to feed my son. I made the rough trip three times a day, twice the nurses fed him.

Whenever I mentioned Jancsi's illness to someone they became strangely silent. What was wrong?

I saw that every day his skin peeled off, all of it, after it had turned a hideous purple. One day he had a high fever. The specialist punctured his eardrums to relieve the inflamed pressure. I was in a daze as I went towards Mother's home when I made my discovery. Jancsi wasn't gaining any weight though he still ate well. His bowel movements turned a peculiar greenish-yellow and he had diarrhea. Where would all of this lead? I was deep in my thoughts while the streetcar neared my destination. Suddenly I remembered that I had not bought a ticket yet. I went to the conductor and asked for one. She hurled four-letter words at me while she gave me the ticket.

I wanted to cry but did not say anything. I didn't want to cheat her but was thinking so hard I had forgotten the world existed.

I was happy that I found Mother at home, "I don't know what is happening to my little one. They punctured his ears today and he is not getting any bigger. Every time I come close to the hospital I am afraid that they'll tell me he is dead."

Mother sat down with me and put her arm around my shoulders. "Don't worry, Helen. You will see that God will help you again. He always has. The Leiner disease is a grave illness; but if the baby survives until the time he is three months old, he will live and his rash will turn into a plain eczema or disappear. He has a good chance of survival. Most babies die because they lose so much weight. They actually lose pounds. Uncle Charles disappeared from dinner when he heard that Jancsi had the disease because a good friend of his, a professor of pediatrics, was not able to save his own grandchild before the war. He died in his grandfather's arms. However, Dr. Stühmer, your pediatrician, says that most cases are cured today."

"They gave him some of my blood, they said it would help. They took a big needle and stuck it in his head. Did you know that they give transfusions to infants through the veins on their head?"

"They gave the baby your blood?" Mother asked. "How are you going to be able to stand all this? Running back and forth between the hospital and home; taking care of Ilike, your husband and home, and nursing. You yourself weigh less than 110 pounds. Maybe I'd better talk to Dr. Stühmer about that." Mother was thinking of her daughter, but I was thinking of my son.

"I'd do anything to get him well again."

"It does not make much sense to make him well and lose you."

"There must be a better solution. You are worried. Why don't you call Dr. Stühmer?"

I lifted the phone and dialed.

His voice was as reassuring as always.

"What do you say? They punctured his ears? That is a normal complication of the Leiner disease. You see how his skin is peeling. Well, that same phenomenon occurs inside his ears, his bowels. I will see him this afternoon. Did the ACTH arrive yet?"

"Will he die?" A sob broke out of me.

"Helen! Where do you get that nonsense?"

"I just look at all those children in the hospital and I keep thinking that they, too, had the Leiner disease. What if mine will look like that soon? I'm afraid that one day they'll just tell me that he is dead when I come there to nurse him."

"Helen! Are you listening to me? Those babies all have other troubles as well. Leiner disease used to be fatal, but it no longer is. We do not know why vitamins and mother's blood help but they do. Did I ever tell you that your son may die?"

"No. You didn't." I quieted down somewhat.

"Well, he will not die. Do you have news about the ACTH?"

"Yes, it was mailed from Paris but we haven't gotten it yet."

"Call me immediately when it arrives. And in the meantime, no crying! Jancsi will get well. You'll see."

Jancsi's ears were punctured two more times. He received more of my blood. I went to the hospital to feed him three times a day and I prayed my way through those hectic weeks.

A pharmacist friend sent the ACTH from Paris within ten days. We started the cortisone treatment and Jancsi responded. He did not gain weight but he did not lose any either during that trying month he spent at the hospital.

One day as he was finishing nursing, he bumped his open mouth into my breast a few times and said in an audible way, "Mama!" I glowed with excitement. He was only two and a half months old. Maybe it did not happen, because he never repeated it, yet I remembered it clearly. While he said it he looked into my eyes as if he really meant it. A tight bond formed between us during those days. He recognized my voice; he knew when I lifted him from the crib.

Ilike and John came to visit Jancsi on a Sunday afternoon. We had a family reunion in the garden of the hospital.

A friendly young doctor came by and told us about her adventure with Jancsi. One night when she was on call at the hospital, the nurse ran in with a dripping wet Jancsi, straight from his bath, wrapped in a big towel. He was shaking from head to toe. His skin was purple. The nurse too was shaking. "What do I do with him? Look!"

"Well," the doctor answered to the inexperienced young nurse "he definitely looks cold to me." She took the baby and put him in bed with her, patting him dry, comforting him. "You see," she ended, "your son starts early. He slept with a woman that night."

She was a very attractive young woman. No wonder Jancsi liked it in her bed and quieted down.

"There wasn't much else I could have done but warm him with the heat of my own body. We have very little equipment. Socialized medicine provides 10 forints (30 cents) a day per child. From this we have to pay not only for their food and laundry but also for all medication and X-rays and whatever else is needed. We are seriously understaffed and under-equipped. Even in the winter we take the infants with pneumonia outside to get them some badly needed oxygen. We simply cannot get enough supplies on that budget."

"Of course we don't mind him sleeping with such a good-looking lady," John joked.

The doctor laughed. "Well, see you later. Good-bye, young lady," she said to Ilike.

Dr. Stühmer came by also as we enjoyed our family togetherness.

"I think you can take him home next week. He is three months old, which means that the Leiner disease is gone. Eczema will be the only remaining problem."

"When?" I became excited.

"Thursday. But you must find a doctor willing to give him his daily injections of ACTH."

I looked into Jancsi's little eyes and whispered to him. "We will find someone. You will see. I will not let you stay in the hospital just for that."

For the first time in my life I felt that I would do it even if the whole Red Army tried to stop me. I knew I would fight for my child tooth and nail. I looked up at John. I saw the same decision in his eyes. Ilike hugged Jancsi and repeated several times, "Baby Jaja Baby, home!"

# 46

We finally settled in with our little Jancsi. John's old Jewish family doctor, whom they hid during Nazi times, lived only two bus stops away and he knew our district doctor well. She agreed to come every day for the next ten days and give Jancsi his cortisone shot.

On a Tuesday morning as usual I went to communion at our parish church which was right beside the market. Our neighbors, Judy and Alex, had become our friends. Judy not only helped me clean, she also took care of the children every day while I did the marketing and made my ten-minute trip to church. I especially liked Tuesdays, devoted to St. Anthony, because the old ladies gathered in church and sang a lovely hymn right after Mass. In this district, at the morning Mass, there were only old ladies present besides me. Most young women were forced to work to keep their families alive, and I myself did not know how long I would be able to stay with my little ones. I took advantage of John's "irreplaceability" by daring to go to church every morning. Young people kept away from their own churches because they did not want to be reported at work. It was easy to lose one's job on account of attending Mass. Most people preferred to frequent churches that were big and anonymous. Those downtown churches were filled every evening at Mass. Communion was distributed before, during, and after Mass to satisfy the crowds desiring to partake in Christ's sacrifice on a daily basis.

I looked around as I knelt down that day. Could one of these old ladies be a spy for the police? Could their "innocent" gossip get me into trouble? What trouble? I heard myself retort. You are in enough trouble because of your father, your family background, and John's background. Don't kid yourself! You are an "insect"! God is the only one who has helped you! Why would you be afraid to associate with your only friend? I smiled as these thoughts came to my mind, and I stepped out into the blinding July sunshine.

In this part of town there were only a few apartment houses among the tiny, old, weather-beaten yet sturdy stone and brick cottages. Two blocks from the church my grandfather's first pharmacy still dispensed prescriptions. Every time I went past it I had to think of his stories about the old ladies who stopped for their heart medications in the morning on their way to the earliest Mass. They must have been the mothers of those I saw in church today. People of their generation were not mobile. Distances were great when one had to walk. The same house or apartment was occupied by one family for generations. If a daughter had the bad luck to marry someone only a mile away they cried at her wedding as they would have at her funeral. That was perhaps the last time they would see her.

I reached the market, only a short block away from the church. Women from surrounding small villages brought live chickens, eggs, whatever they could grow in their small garden, and sold it on the square. Buzzing chatter, the clinking of primitive scales and the colorful dialects gave me the impression that I was in Cegléd walking through the market square with Little Grandma. I spotted a woman with two well-fed chickens.

"How much for this chicken?"

The price she named was exorbitant.

"For this chicken?"

"Just look how fat she is! I myself fed her every day with good corn and look at her meaty breasts! I would not sell her if I did not need medicine for my children."

"She is plump. But I don't have that kind of money." I walked on. Finally I bought two eggs, a head of lettuce, and a bunch of carrots.

Then I boarded the streetcar. At this time of the day it was easy to get a seat. Morning's rush was over when people hung like clusters of grapes even on the stairs. At the second stop I got off and stood in line at the dairy. I received my quart and a half of milk for the day, my rations for the extra quality baby milk given to pregnant women and little children. Baby milk was pasteurized, whole milk. Whatever else the other stuff was they sold as "milk" I had no idea. The woman at the dairy handed me a bag.

"Here, you forgot this here last time when you came."

"Oh, thank you," I tried to show appreciation with my eyes. She smuggled me something special. Probably butter, the better kind that was rarely available. Then she added on the amount with my milk and I paid for it even though I did not know what the surprise package contained. I was filled with gratitude. I'll have to bring her a present some day, I thought.

I hurried as fast as I could. I was curious about what I had bought. On my way I stopped once more at the horsemeat shop and bought half a pound of sausage for dinner.

Ilike stood at the iron gate waiting for me in her old patched clothes. They were neat and clean but they were my old dresses, sweaters, whatever Mother had saved. To me it did not matter and Mother said, "She will outgrow them no matter how pretty or ragged they are and she will become a good person whether she has nice clothes or not." Her big blue eyes shone with happiness because I came home.

"Mama, mama," she said. She could hardly wait for me to open the door. Judy was inside with Jancsika, who slept soundly. Since he was healthy again, he was a happy young man, sucking himself full every four hours, laughing and sleeping through the rest of the time. Ilike still was his best interpreter. She always knew what he wanted. "Water," she would say very seriously and Jancsi would stop crying when he received the water.

Once inside I opened the package, it was butter.

"Let's go for a walk," I suggested to Ilike. She proudly watched me put Jancsika into the baby carriage. We went to the park across the street, and she sat on the teeter-totter. There was no other child in the park as most of the children were in nursery schools or daycare centers. I had to help her swing while Jancsika watched us.

The day wore on and I cooked lunch for the children; carrots and a potato. I mashed them through a sieve for Jancsika. That was our baby food. Ilike ate a slice of bread with butter, the hidden treasure, and I put a bit of jam on it.

Judy came over in the afternoon and together we tried out our latest acquisition which Father had sent from Canada through the IKKA agency. It was a brand new washing machine. Everybody who had one raved about it, and I was looking forward to having a helper with the diapers.

"Let's see. Here are the instructions."

"We must be very careful what we put into it," Judy warned. "A friend of mine put in her lace curtains. Nothing was left of them."

I peeked into the washing machine. The wheel that would turn the water was very small. Maybe three inches in diameter. No sharp edges. Now how could this hurt the clothes?

"Judy, are you sure?"

"Sure, I'm sure. Let's just try it with the diapers first."

"You know, I don't want to lose them. They are quite precious. I have only twenty-four of them. Granted, I got them free when I had my baby, a nice gift from the government as a reward for my having gone to the doctor regularly, yet they are all I have."

"I don't think it will hurt the diapers. Here is the boiling water from the stove," she said. "Where is the wash powder?"

"Here it is!" I handed her the small box of special detergent that Hungary was importing lately from East Germany. It did miracles with soiled clothes. Before that there were only the bar of soap, lye, and boiling the laundry.

Everything was set. We plugged in the machine, then started it for the first time.

"Swish!" The water whirled with such a speed that we immediately understood about the lace curtains. That tiny wheel had the power of a turbine. We dropped in clothes one by one until it looked like the machine was full, then quickly closed the lid.

"Now, we are set for three minutes!" I declared. "According to the instructions we should then wring out the clothes and rinse them."

"Let's fill the bathtub!" Judy suggested and we did.

The three minutes were up. We stopped the machine and started wringing the shirts and handkerchiefs, one by one. We dropped them into the bathtub and let them soak.

"Now, let's put in the second batch!" I said and started to drop in the diapers. If the other clothes did not fall apart, the diapers would hold up also. After the diapers we would have to change the water.

"Judy, is the next pot of water warm yet?"

"It's nearly boiling."

We both sat down and started knitting.

"Would you have believed it if someone had told you that it was possible to knit while you did the laundry?" Judy laughed in amazement as she said this.

"No, I certainly wouldn't have. Let's go, the three minutes are up."

We dropped the diapers into the bathtub, then drained the washing machine into a bucket and filled it with fresh water. We then wrung out the clothes from the bathtub and plopped them into the washing machine again to rinse them once more before the final wring.

Finally the laundry was ready to be taken to the back of the yard to be dried by the good old sun.

"We never finished washing that quickly!" Judy declared. "I can't believe my eyes. I simply can't believe it! Maybe some day I'll have a washing machine of my own. I hear it is nearly impossible to get one. That friend of mine whose lace curtains fell to pieces has one, but she stood in watch at the factory gates for weeks on end. They lived pretty close. Whenever the factory had a batch finished and she saw them being put on a truck, she would run after the truck and yell up to the men asking to which store they were going. After about a month's time she got to the right store in time to buy the last one of the machines."

"You can use ours in the meantime."

"Thank you, but we'll have to account for the electricity somehow. I can't let you pay for that and the hot water too. Right now let's celebrate! My husband got his salary today. I'll run over with a pitcher to the tavern next door and bring some draft beer."

A few minutes later we sat on the doorstep, enjoying the afternoon sun, listening to the accordion music from the tavern, sipping the rich foam of the beer.

Tuesday was a day when John came home early.

"Judy, can you baby-sit tonight?"

"Sure, why?"

"I'll ask John if he wants to go to see that new French film. There are finally other than Soviet films available though I still wish I could see at least one of those good Hollywood spectaculars or just any of the old American movies."

"This one is really funny with Fernandel playing the lead. Go, by all means. You deserve it. You had so much trouble all this year."

As soon as John came home we had our paprika potatoes with the horsemeat sausage, most of which was consumed by Ilike.

Then we walked along the romantic old streets with their tiny yards and small crooked houses towards the movie. The air was translucent. The setting sun colored the sky golden-red and then was covered by the blue of the night. We held each other tight. It was beautiful to be alive and healthy with two happy children, with all the conveniences of life and our own apartment.

Apparently others had noticed our happiness too. Now that our son was healthy again, Miss Jenny began to envy us for what she missed in her dour existence. She started to make trouble. Did she plot against us all these months? Was she using us and our money to remodel the house so she and her beloved janitor-maid would share the big house? Even if it were so, even if we wanted to leave, there was no place for us to go.

She summoned John one day.

"My electric bill is too high. I am sure that something went wrong during the construction and that you are using my electricity. I won't have that. I can't have it. I can't pay for your extravagances."

John promised that he would look into the matter. He asked an electrician from the factory who came and examined every one of the light bulbs and appliances. Everything was in perfect order.

After this matter was cleared up, we hoped that Miss Jenny would be satisfied. Her next complaint was, "Don't let your daughter stand at the gate. It gives people a bad impression about the house. Make her play where nobody can see her."

One complaint came after the other. There was nothing we could do. She drove me to my wit's end. I so desperately wanted to satisfy her every whim, but when we complied with one thing, she came up with something else. It became quite clear that she wanted to drive us out.

Finally winter came. With the cold we saw less of each other. By the time she came home from work we were inside for the day. My nerves were on edge whenever I as much as heard her name.

John's schedule was exhausting. We got up at 6:45 and he left by seven o'clock. Some days he would come home at seven in the evening. More often it was close to ten or even eleven at night. Then he would dictate the notes for his university lectures, and I would type them. We heated only one room. Ilike and Jancsika watched us with amazement and John walked up and down the room with a teddy bear while he dictated to entertain the children. There were times when we did this until two in the morning. We still had our desires and made love every day before we fell into a log-like sleep.

Private enterprise appeared on the university scene. The department would accept private consulting or designs from government agencies. These were projects that government-owned factories could not fit into their five-year plan or even their emergency contingencies, or they simply could not be handled by them because they involved extensive research. One-third of the money paid to the department for that work would go to the university's research fund, one-third to the department, and the last third to the staff involved in the work. We could always use the extra money, but it also meant more work if that were humanly possible.

We had more money than we had ever had since our marriage. John was working hard on his research; he published articles that I typed for him in triplicate without carbon paper, which was not available in Hungary at the time. For one of his articles he won the prestigious Zipernowsky medal from the Hungarian Institute of Electrical Engineers given to the best article of the year published in the field.

John's parents spent the coldest three months of the winter in our second room. Again there were six people in two rooms, but the rooms and especially the kitchen and the bathroom were much smaller than the ones at our old apartment. Although the children enjoyed the presence of the grandparents immensely, the crowding was close to unbearable at times, especially because there was no way out of the situation.

The food shortage was still the same, but this Christmas we were able to buy handpainted scarves, handkerchiefs, tablecloths, purses, and sweaters; individually made goods that did not bear the rubber-stamp of the government factory. The small private industries grew like mushrooms in the lukewarm benevolence of Imre Nagy's government. We could hardly believe it was true and worriedly asked ourselves now and again, "How long would this last?"

# 47

The answer came in March, 1955. Imre Nagy's government was toppled and Ernö Gerö took over the leadership of the country. We were back on the old Stalinist tracks. Most small businesses, though not nationalized, were unable to pay their taxes. The ones who survived the first wave did so on the verge of bankruptcy.

Mátyás Rákosi, Stalin's Hungarian counterpart, moved to the foreground again. Imre Nagy's "revisionist mistakes" had to be corrected according to the Communist Party.

"Why are they talking about Nagy's policies?" Uncle Charles exclaimed. "Nagy was simply an instrument in the hands of the Communists. His policies were the same Lenin employed in 1922 when he found it necessary to invent the New Economic Policy. He too gave permission for small industries to start again in order to reintroduce incentive into the economy. When everything started rolling, the businesses were taxed out of existence and the government gained much needed cash."

Mother bailed her business out with some of the money Father still sent every month. Her plastic purse clients supplied the constant flow of people she needed to sell the cocoa, coffee, rum, chocolate, and whatever came in the parcels from Father. By now it was possible to exchange these parcels through IKKA, the government parcel agency, for something bigger like a washing machine if she found a good customer who could pay cash. It was quite a complicated transaction but, at least, it was possible. The government would go to great lengths to procure hard currency.

Mother and the two of us often met at night in a tiny espresso confectionery close to our house. We sat together and discussed business deals when nobody was around or laughed over the children's antics if somebody came near. The manager knew us and respected our privacy. It was the perfect place to talk without interruption while sipping a "Giraffe" beer, Hungary's latest export product, or a dark, strong espresso coffee. Occasionally our lawyer joined us. Uncle Charles did not like to stay up late. He gave his opinion when asked, but he did not want to meddle in family affairs. Maybe because of that, he was truly a member of our family. We loved and respected each other.

"Look what I brought you." Mother's eyes shone with excitement when she arrived at our home on a lilac-scented May evening. "Just look at this!" She carefully opened a package that contained a purple maroon changeant velvet dream dress.

"Where did you get it?"

"I didn't get it yet. A friend of mine received it from her sister-in-law who is a starlet in Hollywood. She had two babies and now she can no longer fit into this beautiful dress. My friend had already offered it to all the ballerinas at the Opera, thinking that she could find the slimmest women there, but none of them could fit into it. If you can manage to put it on I'll buy it for you. She is willing to part with it for less than the price of the material, because nobody as yet can pull up the zipper."

I threw off my shabby old dress and stepped into the skirt. Yes, the zipper went all the way up. Then came the strapless top embroidered with thousands of glittery spangles. Perfect fit. The matching long velvet gloves covered my arms and the coat transformed it into an elegant evening outfit.

"Oh, Mother I have never seen anything that beautiful!" I jumped up and down and clapped my hands in excitement. "Thank you, thank you!" I couldn't even think straight I was so excited. "It's beautiful, it's perfect, it's lovely!"

I had always dreamed about my first evening dress but I never thought it would be that beautiful. It was only maxi length, just the style of the day. I thought of the Opera and the dances where I might be able to wear it. There were rumors that for the first time since the war there would be real balls in the fall in long evening gowns, organized by the universities as in the "good old days." Nobody really believed it. Now, if there should be such an opportunity, I would have the dress to wear!

"Look, I have something else here. This came from a friend of mine from Paris."

Mother pulled out of her big shopping bag a little beige coat for Ilike. "Look, Ilike, just the right thing for you for the winter. It is not warm enough but in the same parcel I received a quilted bed jacket. We'll make a lining from that. It will be just perfect."

Ilike slipped on the coat. It was a tiny bit big but just right for next fall when the lining would be in. She closed the buttons and twirled around in front of the mirror.

"Pretty, pretty," she said, laughing. Jancsi looked at her but then he found something much more entertaining. He tried to "steal" his grandmother's purse from her pocket. Grandmother laughed silently.

Jancsi was famous for the tricks he played on anybody who dared to stand beside his crib.

429

This time he was pleasantly surprised. Mother had put a candy bar in her pocket especially for him to find. He set out to bite into it, paper and all.

"No, no!" Mother protested. "First we take off the paper! Don't cry! It'll only be a minute." She quickly peeled off the wrapper and handed him the treasure. His eyes lit up and he pushed it into his mouth. He loved to eat.

John had been given a week's vacation and Mother had offered to take care of the children so we could go away by ourselves.

"I'd better be on good terms with them if I'm to baby-sit those two!

"When are you leaving?" Mother inquired.

"Right after Jancsi's first birthday, the 22nd of May, so we'll go on the 25th. We'll hike all the way across the Bükk Mountains," John answered.

Mother shrugged. "I don't think I would ever want to walk through those uninhabited hills. My idea of travel is to foreign countries, faraway places, by train, car, or plane."

"We would not mind that either," said John. "But for the time being I am not even allowed to travel to a scientific meeting. Right now I am grateful that the government allows us to have a peek at foreign magazines."

"You know what?" Mother interrupted. "Uncle Charles brought home a Sears catalogue from the University Hospital where he works. One of the doctors had received it from an American. We have to keep it a secret. When you come over I'll show you. Unbelievable things! Do you know that you can get a pair of men's shoes for five or six dollars? And I mean really good ones! You can't even find the likes in our stores. They look as good as the ones made-to-measure. Here they would cost a fortune! About a month's salary! And some people's salary does not even amount to that much!"

I nodded. "I know it. We have to plan ahead if we want to buy shoes for the children, and John gets top salaries from both his jobs plus whatever he makes on his extra work. That amounts to at least three times the salary of a skilled worker or grade school teacher."

"Well, I understand it," said Mother. "In America, people earn $300 and up per month. Father wrote that as soon as he had passed his test as a medical doctor he earned $1,100 the first month. And you can get shoes for five or six dollars?! Just look at these beautiful things they send over in parcels. How can they possibly afford to give them away? All these good materials. Even synthetics!"

"Let's put the children to bed so that we can sit down and relax a while," I suggested.

"I'll put them to bed. It's my turn," Grandmother insisted.

The three disappeared into the bedroom, while John and I went to the kitchen to see what we could hunt up. I certainly would not have dreamed of offering Mother some leftover mush, the only item in the icebox. There was no other food but we found some liqueur we had received in one of Father's parcels.

＊

The open cars of the storybook train chugged along their wooded tracks. John and I sat beside each other on the hard bench, holding hands. His eyes sparkled. This was our first time to go on a week-long hike to discover the beauties of our homeland.

Green fields, bushes and trees changed places as the narrow gauge train puffed farther up into the mountains. For the first time in my life I saw a big stretch of nothing but trees in their spring splendor. An occasional rock broke the continuous green of the foliage. May rains had performed their magic, turning the winter forest into a maze of green.

"Lillafüred! This is as far as we go," shouted the conductor.

"How come?" John wondered. "I thought the train went another five miles."

"Our summer schedule starts on June 1," the conductor announced as we got off with our knapsacks. That meant another five-mile walk besides the one we planned for the day. But the weather was nice and we could hardly wait to get going.

"Helen, let's look at the Lillafüred hotel before we go up the mountain. Uncle Feri designed its interior," John suggested.

"Yes, let's! I always wanted to see it. Mother said she spent lovely times there with Father."

The palace-like structure was reflected in the mirrored surface of the nearby lake. There was no life around the hotel yet. Guests would only arrive after the first. We were lucky that we had grandparents to baby-sit and that our children were not in school yet; we could take our holidays before the big rush. I liked the solitude of the green forest even if we had to forego some of the comforts.

John put his arm around me as we walked along the dusty highway. Our sturdy leather shoes grated against the rocks among the dust. Branches waved in the slight breeze. The sun's heat soon made us remove the outer layer of our clothes, our sweatsuits. Under them we wore shorts and short-sleeved shirts.

As we turned from the dusty highway into the green tunnel of the forest trail, the Valley of Szentlélek opened before our eyes. Between tall pines, that gave a dark frame to the softly green, sunlit mountains, the beautiful, empty road opened onto a magic forest.

John carried more weight than I did yet he had breath left to talk about things we dared not mention if other people were near.

"You know that this new professor is coming from Moscow, Dr. Benedikt. The university will have a Department for Special Electric Machines and according to my colleagues I am a natural to head it. But this man is Stalin's personal friend. I haven't a chance if I apply against him. All I can do is to transfer to that department if I want to remain in my chosen field."

"It is not fair. You should get that job. There is nobody in Hungary who would understand everything about the amplydin and the rototrol as you do."

"I know there isn't, and it is not fair. Yet, at least it makes me 'irreplaceable.' You know, Helen," John looked around; even here in the forest he was afraid of being overheard. I automatically followed his example. There was nobody close by; only a bird chirping merrily. He continued, "The other day I talked with my boss at the factory when everybody had already gone. He was the one who helped me when I was in trouble, the one who knows both our fathers. He was in Siberia as a prisoner of war. In the concentration camp he met with engineers who had been there since the big purge of engineers took place in the Soviet Union starting in 1927 when the Communists had raised their own young generation of engineers. The 'purged' engineers were still in prison camps in 1945. They received life sentences or sentences up to twenty-five years. They were the lucky ones. They survived. In Siberia they felt completely free after having been robbed of all their worldly possessions and finally even of their loved ones when they were jailed. They valued their ability to speak and think freely more than they did their lives. They believed that when everything is taken from someone, that person's freedom becomes complete. He has no fear left. The Communists, the government, lose power over these people who have nothing left to lose."

A sudden sob shook my body. "How can I relax even for a moment; how can I take anything for granted when I live in constant fear that I will lose you?" The tears streamed down my face.

"Helen, I am sorry, I didn't mean to upset you. I simply wanted to show you how lucky we are even though there are many unfair things happening to us."

"I know," I sobbed. "It's just that we are so happy that sometimes I think that even heaven can't be more beautiful than our lives. I love you so and the children…and when I think that someday just because they will have other engineers, they might dump you…"

"Helen, we must trust in God. You know that. He always helped us and He always will. It may happen any day that we lose each other.

"And yet we never will. We are one and will always remain together. If one of us had to go while the children are little, the other one will bring them up. We cannot let them down by becoming hysterical. But I certainly hope and trust that we will grow old together…"

"…And die in each other's arms as the Bishop predicted at our wedding." I finished his sentence.

"It would seem that even if the time comes to weed out the engineers, they will start with the older ones rather than with those who are more 'irreplaceable,' because of the load they carry or because they are the ones who know all the turbines in Hungary, as I do.

"To look at the bright side, I heard that this Dr. Benedikt has great influence with the government and may be able to get me over to the university full time. That would mean more time together and more outside work."

"Now you're talking! Maybe it would be worth being nice to him, even if he is taking your rightful place."

"Maybe he would even be able to make me exempt from military service. Quite a few friends of mine were called up for the summer months in order to become officers in the reserve. I have escaped it so far."

"How in the world did you do it? I am deathly afraid every time I see the mailman."

John looked around again as we wound our way through bushes. "Let's wait a minute to see if anybody is near us."

We walked in silence; only the song of the birds accompanied us. Small, colorful flowers waved their heads in the slight breeze and our shoes creaked on the pebbles as we approached a clearing. There was nobody around.

"Let's sit down for a few minutes here in the sun." John put his sweatshirt on a rock, and we sat beside each other.

"Listen, don't tell these things to anyone, not even to your mother. She might forget and mention it to one of her friends. It is extremely important that whatever we talk about should remain between us. Remember when I was called up to have my draft card filled out? Well, I was satisfactory from every point of view. They probably would have called me a long time ago; but when they concluded the interview, they asked, 'You don't have anybody abroad, do you?' to which I nonchalantly answered: 'No, not really, except for my father-in-law, whom I have never met.' 'Thank you,' they answered and I saw the sergeant write something across my card. No, I don't think that I will be called up."

As we walked on, I felt the muscles in the back of my legs tense against the steep trail. A healthy fatigue spread over me as we caught sight of a simple, low building with a rustic porch—the hostel, our goal for today. Cows grazed peacefully on the wide open field. A playful stream cut across the green velvet of the grass. I felt quite out of breath from the climb but the air was so fresh up here that breathing it felt like drinking nectar. Everything was crystal clear. The May rains had washed the whole landscape to a transparent sharpness.

Tantalizing aromas of a cooking dinner reached us as we came closer to the hostel. The hostess, a middle-aged plump woman in a dirndl, looked as if she had stepped out of a picture book.

"You must be our guests for today!" She greeted us at the door. "Dinner will be ready soon. Since we have only a few people staying with us, you can sleep in the same room. Usually men and women are separated. Let me show you to your bunks."

She opened the door of a small room with two bunk beds and a washstand. A table with two chairs completed the furnishings.

"Here, you can put down your gear. Over there is the outhouse." She pointed towards the edge of the forest.

We thanked her and quickly got rid of our burdens, then ran out onto the velvety field to stretch out in the grass. The cowbells played their peculiar music as the animals moved slowly from one spot to another. They bent their big heads to the stream and drank from it. The sun was slowly setting. We absorbed the peace and quiet, the beauty and stillness of nature. Neither of us wanted to break the magic.

Finally the dinner gong called. We entered the big dining hall with its long wooden tables. They were set with white tablecloths and simple dishes. Our hostess ladled stuffed green peppers into our plates. Food had never tasted so good!

The first sounds of the morning were those of the cowbells. I had heard about these sounds of awakening from stories of those who often hiked in the Alps. Now I understood their longing for it. My muscles pleasantly felt the workout they had had the day before, but I couldn't wait to get out again and see what wonders today held for us.

"Are you up?" I asked John.

He opened his eyes. "Do you hear what I hear? Let's go out there and look at those cows."

We jumped into our sweatsuits and stepped outside. The high altitude coolness of the morning air startled us. The storybook picture of last night was now flooded with the pale sunbeams of the early hours. The cowbells sang their morning greeting as the cows moved lazily through the sun-green field. They stayed close to the water. At the sight of the crystal clear, bubbling spring that turned into a stream running and bouncing from rock to rock, I became thirsty.

"Let's go down there and drink!" I ran back to the room and grabbed our thermos bottle.

"That must be the best water I have ever tasted!" I exclaimed.

I filled the thermos. The water flowed through a spout that had been erected by monks in the fourteenth century to make it easier for the occupants of the monastery and the pilgrims to fetch their water. An old iron gate brought back the magic of the days when the ruins closeby were inhabited by real people.

John went back to the house for our soap and we washed in the trough.

After a quick breakfast of bread, butter, jam, and tea, we asked our jovial hostess, "Could you sell us some bread?"

"I would if I could, but I haven't any. We bring all of our supplies up here on mule back, and today's mule has yet to arrive. Besides, we get barely enough for a day. This house belongs to the National Hotel Company, that is, the state. We cannot get more supplies than we need for one day. Sometimes, especially in the winter, this causes great problems. If I were you, I'd hike down to Mályinka, the closest village. It is only five miles away from here, about 2,000 feet down, no more of a climb than you had to make yesterday. They have a food store. You may be able to get some bread there."

"Well, we were going for a hike anyway. What do you say, Helen?"

"We have to get bread somehow if we want to eat at noon. What can we lose?"

"But let's go and see the view first!" John suggested.

The white rocks of the viewpoint contrasted with the blue sky and the dark green forests, accentuated by light green meadows as far as our eyes could see.

"Look, Helen, that is the path we'll take down to the village. And there, way down in the valley, right where the wheat fields start, there is Mályinka."

"We'll have to go all the way down there and back up just to get enough bread for our lunch? It hardly seems worth it. We'll have to spend all the energy that piece of bread can give us just in order to get it," I laughed.

"Isn't that beautiful?" John spread his arms wide towards the sky and the green sea of rolling hills below us.

"I have never seen anything like it. You know, I don't know where else in Hungary we could find a place where our eyes can roam forever and not see anything but greenery. No people, no houses, no anything, just beauty."

"There aren't many such places left, not only in Hungary but in Europe."

As we were walking down the valley, sometimes with John in the lead, at others me, we talked again about topics that were unsafe when we were around people. There was not a soul on the trail as far as we could see.

"John, although I hate even to talk about it, what happened to those engineers in the Soviet Union? And when were they liquidated? About ten years after the revolution in 1927?"

"Yes. It started in 1927, about the time when the first engineers of the new stock were ready to take over. At least that is what officials thought. Later on, especially during World War II, they bitterly regretted that they had finished off some of their excellent old engineers."

"Why have you never talked to me about these things before?"

"Some of them I did not know myself until recently. Others I did not want to speak about because I never knew when or why they would arrest us. If you did not know about things, you would not be able to talk about them."

435

"Didn't you trust me?"

"Of course I did. But I had to know you well. I had to be sure you would not say something inadvertently that would get both of us into trouble. Now after three years I know. I trust you as I trust myself. And yet what if we should be tortured? That is another thing I was told by many who were tortured, who were in Soviet concentration camps. Once 'they' get hold of you, you tell them everything. Only what you don't know will remain a secret. So, in a way, I gave you that freedom of not knowing by not telling you everything. I did not keep any secrets from you; I only wanted to protect you."

"John, I don't really know if I should thank you or feel hurt, but I know that you love me and that this is why you did what you did. I know all about the truth serums and hypnosis under the influence of which anyone might confess to anything, sign anything and not even remember it afterwards. This is what happened to Cardinal Mindszenty during his trial. But, what happened to those engineers who were sentenced for life, or twenty-five years?"

"They were condemned on two charges. The first were the 'wreckers.' Whatever shortages the drawn-out revolution and the consequent civil war produced were blamed on those engineers. It was their 'wrecking' that caused the shortage of power, the shortage of textiles, of railroad cars, metals and chemicals, and whatever else happened to be missing from the economy. A fellow named Meck suggested solving the locomotive shortage by doubling the loads the engines would pull. The government had him shot because they claimed that his proposal would wear out the roadbeds and rails and locomotives and freight cars so that in case of foreign intervention there would be no railroads available. Then, after his death, Comrade Kaganovich, the New People's Commissar of Railroads ordered exactly the same thing for which his predecessor had been shot. Since he was a Communist, his judgment could not be questioned. He even tripled the loads each engine had to pull and received the Order of Lenin for his 'discovery.' Older engineers protested against committing the same 'mistake' as Meck did. Now these older engineers were named 'limiters.' They became the second group to be condemned."

"Then…then there is really no way out of this diabolical, vicious circle."

"No, honey, there isn't. If my 'irreplaceability' runs out I'll be taken unless, of course, I can make myself a specialist in something else, keeping ahead of the new generation."

I felt a surge of hope. "You can do it. You know you can."

"I'll do my best, you can bet your life on that."

The way down was easy. Rocks rolled under our feet, and we could barely stop ourselves from running. The sun was warm but not hot yet as we descended quickly towards the village.

"Look at that nice spot there, Helen." John beckoned me towards a cluster of trees under which the grass spread like a soft new blanket. He sat down then stretched out on the ground. His arms were inviting. I sat on my knees right beside him and kissed his half-open mouth. Our teeth knocked, then my tongue searched his and we experimented with ever new ways to love.

The birds chirped and sang as we unbuttoned our shirts to feel each other's skin. His face was rosy-brown from yesterday's long walk in the sunshine. His blue eyes talked about enjoyment. I lost myself in his passion. The sun blinked at me through the dancing leaves. Its rays burst into fireworks through the foliage.

# 48

When we woke up the sun was right above us.

John jumped up. "It must be close to noon, we have to hurry to find our bread for today."

I stretched my limbs in the velvety grass, "I'd like to stay here forever," I declared. My whole being felt timeless. Who cared about the hour of the day?

John reached down for me and pulled me to my feet. Then he straightened his clothes and mine. "Let's go!"

The first houses of the village soon appeared from between the bushes.

A row of whitewashed houses with the customary church and steeple appeared. The bells started ringing. It was noon. The green wheat fields promised a good harvest; Hungarian wheat was well known throughout Europe. The bells were still ringing as we arrived at the first house and walked down the dusty main street to the store in the middle of the village.

"Closed for lunch, twelve o'clock to two," read the sign on the door.

"Now what do we do?" John asked as he peeked in through the glass door hoping to see someone inside. The store was completely deserted and the street quiet. Not a soul was in sight; only a few chickens scratched the dust, and sparrows hopped around. The heat was intense and we could feel our stomachs growl.

I had an idea. "Why don't we try to buy bread from the peasants? They must have some around the house. Don't they always bake their own bread? And isn't homemade, fresh peasant bread ever so good?" My mouth watered at the mere thought.

John knocked on the first door.

An old woman, dressed in blue cotton opened it. "Y-e-e-es? What can I do for you?" she asked in the characteristic dialect of Northern Hungary.

"We are tourists and just found out that the store is closed for two hours. We wanted to buy bread for our lunch. Could you, please, sell us some?"

The woman looked doubtful.

"I would love to sell you bread, if I had some. The store won't open till two o'clock, and I haven't bought our bread for today yet. I only have enough for lunch. We are just starting to eat. I can't possibly sell you any. Where do you live?"

"In Budapest."

She nodded. "That explains it. This is why you don't know. We can no longer keep our own wheat and grind our own flour. We hand everything over to the state. In our village there are only cooperatives and state farms. We get our bread from the store and only enough for the day. However, if you are from so far away…my son went to town and won't be here for lunch. You can have his share. I'll cut you two slices. That should keep you from starving before the store opens." She smiled at us and led us into the kitchen where she wiped off two kitchen stools with a dishtowel and bade us sit down. She took out the bread and divided it into three parts. We offered her some of our salami and cheese; our staple foods for excursions because they did not need refrigeration.

"Here have some fresh water, I just pulled it up from the well myself. It will cool you nicely after your long walk," she offered.

After lunch we walked around in the village and watched children lay in the yards while women hung out the wash. Finally two o'clock came and we could buy bread. Enough for a day; for our lunch tomorrow.

The climb back went much slower than the descent. We continued the talk we had started in the morning about everything we dared not discuss otherwise.

"Helen, have you read *Brave New World*?"

"*Brave New World*? What is that? I hope you are not referring to communism."

"No! It is a book written by Aldous Huxley. He takes the principles of Hitler and of Marxism and speculates about the scientific and technical possibilities and of what life could be like by the year 2000."

"That sounds like fun. Where could we get one?"

"Nowhere. We should not even talk about it. It was translated into Hungarian before the Communists took over. A friend of mine has a copy. Maybe we could borrow it. According to the Party we are not even supposed to know about its existence. It is like *1984* or *Animal Farm*."

"Now what are those?"

"Those are books written by George Orwell. They give a great picture of how Communists behave."

I grabbed at branches and pulled myself up the steep trail as I listened. He continued. "The other day we found one of those books at the factory in someone's drawer. He was lucky that we found it rather than one of the party members. We warned him. I'll try to bring it home some day but if they find it on me you may expect me to be jailed."

439

"Don't do it then. I take your word for it that they are interesting books. Remember what we have said before. We are already 'insects,' so we should not even think of things that could be used against us."

John pointed to a high-stemmed bluebell swaying in the grass. "Look! How beautiful!" We were again walking in a green tunnel. The only sound was that of the birds as we wound our way through the forest back up to the hostel.

"John, how long will I be able to stay home with the kids? Will I have to go to work?"

"I wish you would never have to. All children need their parents, yet everybody seems to be working nowadays. Nobody can make ends meet on one salary."

"We can still make it, but for how long? If we should have another baby, and we said we would, would we be able to feed three?"

"God has always provided everything we needed until now, but 'God helps those who help themselves.' I think you should become an electrical engineer. If you start university now, by the time you have to go to work you will have your degree. Maybe we could work together."

"I'll think about it. I don't know. What would become of the children if they should go to nursery school? So many of the young parents no longer dare to talk in the presence of their children." I looked around as we were nearing the hostel but I did not see anyone.

John followed my example before he continued. "A friend of mine said the other day that his three-year-old came home crying from the nursery school, 'Daddy, Daddy, please, sign up for the peace loan at work. If you don't, the Americans will come and drop an atomic bomb on us. Don't let them, Daddy, don't.'"

I stopped. "What a dirty trick to play on the parents. They have to sign up for the peace loan anyway. I mean they all 'volunteer' ten percent of their salaries if their jobs are precious to them. I haven't heard of anybody who has escaped it. Why tell such horror stories to the children?"

"This is why I want you to stay home with them as long as possible."

"Eva said the other day that the children get very good food at those nursery schools. They have meat every day and chocolate milk. They are even supplied with clean uniforms and diapers daily."

"The government makes these places available for children from the time they are about six weeks old. They want every mother to be able to work," John said. "Women are equal in everything. But why do they do it? Do you remember when the Germans claimed that Communists take children away from their parents? Everybody can plainly see that this is not true. It is the parents who are begging the Communists to take their children off their hands so they can feed them in the evening when the whole family arrives home just in time to collapse into bed."

"You know what?" I started whispering even though we were still between the bushes. "Zsuzsi complained to me the other day. Her children are now in grade school. The older one is in fourth grade. She cannot decide whether she should tell him something about her feelings against the regime, about the injustices that occur. She never dares to talk about anything in front of her children. Just the other day she and her husband discussed this problem at great lengths and they could not come to any conclusion. What is going to become of the next generation? What can we tell them?"

"I know of another case," John suddenly burst out laughing, "but this is different. A little girl who was always at home with her grandmother was only four when she heard two grown-ups tell each other a political joke. They did not pay any attention to her as she was playing in the corner. She abruptly turned and put her little index finger to her mouth, 'Tch! They are going to lock up all of us if you say things like that'."

I smiled but now I had something to tell, how teachers asked first graders if they had been given new white dresses in the spring. That way they could find out if a child had gone to first communion. And what their parents did on Sunday mornings, if they listened to a different radio station.

"Of course," said John, "that would betray them also. Hungary has only two official radio stations. If the parents tune in on something else it must be a western country. Then they take this information and put it on the parents' 'cadre cards.' Even if it's hearsay it can be used against them when, for some reason or another, they want to make them 'confess'."

Suddenly I felt chilly even though sweat was still pouring from my forehead. How were we going to bring up our children even if we could manage to feed them? Who would protect them from the pollution of their minds? My stomach started turning and aching, just as when Mother was taken to the police. How could I prevent the children from falling for false ideals?

We sat down near the stream and the cowbells' music soothed me. I began to pray. I thanked God for all the beauty that surrounded us, especially for our presence and love for each other. And I heard that voice again. "I am Love. You love me, your husband, and your children. I, who am Love, will guide you on your way. I have never lost anyone who trusted in me."

The noon sun painted the landscape golden. The bare rocks of the mountains enhanced the blue of the sky with its puffy white clouds. We were at the end of our trip. Our descent from the Bükk Mountains followed the path of a stream with small, playful waterfalls terraced over the slope. It led our way to a spot at the edge of the forest where a breathtaking green field opened up, strewn with the choicest wildflowers in all the colors of the rainbow.

"Let's stop here! I want to stay here forever."

"At least we could have lunch here," suggested John as he smiled at my enthusiasm. I seldom went on excursions while I was young, and everything, even a field with wildflowers, greeted me with the newness of things first-seen.

"Whatever you say. I think this is the most beautiful field in the world!"

"Could it be because we are in love?" I recognized the twinkle in John's eye and prepared for another fulfillment of happiness in the tall grass. I wanted it also. Everything was just right, and the field was our private room on the planet.

"John, thank you for teaching me to enjoy life."

"What do you mean?" He lifted his head.

"I mean that you showed me how to find the bright side of everything. To see the flowers and the grass, to enjoy my body and yours, our children, the tender moments, and not to dwell on fear, on what might happen. I know I still do it. Maybe I always will, but I try to think of the many good things I have. I give thanks to God, to you, and to all those who give me my special happiness, a peace that is inside of me."

"Thank you, Helen," his voice trembled with deep feeling. "That was beautifully said. You have learned all that from me? I feel that there are many, many beauties in life that I would have never known without you. Let's face it! When I first proposed to you, it was kind of a gamble. After all, you were but a child and it could have been a disaster to 'rob the cradle.' But my sixth sense gave me an inkling that we belonged together. I have never regretted popping the question on that Saturday afternoon. The more time we spend together, the more I love you and enjoy our life and love; every day I feel like I am experiencing you for the first time. Your personality is like a sparkling cavalcade. It is like when the fireworks go up and become red, green, and yellow stars up above; they scintillate then fall; but they are all one, a single unity. You are my all, my love!"

I couldn't answer him because his mouth covered mine and choked the words into me that they might be exchanged for a flow of uninhibited expressions of our feelings.

～

The setting sun painted red streaks in the sky that reflected on the yellow rocks of the mountain behind us when we arrived at the hostel in Bélapátfalva.

Another plump hostess greeted us merrily. "I am Bözsi, you must be Karl's friends whom he so highly recommended to me. My husband isn't here right now, but he will be back before dark. He went for supplies. You must excuse me. I am not finished cooking dinner yet. You are the only guests in the whole house today, but yesterday I had thirty-two tourists here. I had to wash all their sheets in the stream today. Quite some work! Can you help me to hang them out? Then I could get to dinner sooner." She wouldn't stop talking, a custom of people who seldom have a chance to meet with friends, even if the friends are just the friends-of-a-friend. Her roly-poly arms lifted the big basket of sheets as if they were feathers, and she hurried ahead to lead us to the clothes line.

"You wash everything in the stream? In cold water?" I asked.

"Where else?" She seemed undisturbed by the fact that she was operating a government-owned hostel and supposedly was responsible for keeping it clean.

"Well, of course. What else can you do if there are no other facilities," John said. "I heard that it was just recently that you decided on a life of seclusion in the mountains."

She laughed. "You could call it that, I guess." She went on hanging the sheets expertly and quickly. Our help seemed to be merely symbolic compared to her efficiency. The green of the trees and grass enhanced the vivid rosiness of her cheeks, the dark brown hair under the bright kerchief on her head. When she smiled she had dimples, and she smiled constantly.

"That is quite a story, and I'll tell you while I make 'tarhonya' for the soup."

"You are going to make 'tarhonya,' right now? Do you have time for that before dinner?"

"It'll only take a minute. I know most people think it has to be dried; but, come, I'll show you."

I watched her with fascination as she grabbed the empty basket, stacked it away in the kitchen, and started to knead a hard dough from flour, eggs, and water. Her strong hands did the job quickly and in no time at all she was grating the hard dough into tiny pearls to put into a good smelling vegetable soup that was already simmering on the stove.

"I prepared the soup ahead of time; it only needs the finishing touches."

"You are a magician," I declared.

"No, not really, but one has to be resourceful when one day we have no guests and on another we might end up with thirty-two.

"How could you get used to this kind of life after having lived in the city?"

"I wanted to be alone with my husband. When we got married, we did not have an apartment. We thought that we would be able to get one sooner or later because we both worked and our families were poor, hard-working people. Yet, after we moved in with my in-laws, there was no other place for us to sleep than on the couch in the dining room. That may not seem so bad, many couples sleep like that, I know, but my in-laws are very talkative people, friendly, always around, always trying to help. They were constantly on our backs." Her eyes dropped, she hesitated then went on. "A year after we were married, I was still a virgin. I wouldn't say that if it were not true, and I don't want to mention it in front of my husband, but I think you can understand our decision that this could not go on any longer.

"I certainly can."

She continued. "Then one day I heard from a friend, maybe it was Karl, a great tourist as you well know, that this hostel needed a caretaker couple. All I could think of was that finally we would be alone in the middle of a great forest. I did not even consider the work involved, only the fact that we would have a house of our own. No running water, no conveniences, and I would have to be the only servant for hoards of tourists with only my husband to help me. The hard winters with lots of snow and a frozen stream, yet still there were tourists. I could only think of one thing, we would have our privacy. We applied and we got the job. We made many mistakes at first. Yet, we were not fired. Was it our friendliness, or was it that they could not get anybody else? I really don't know. All I know is that we are alone."

"This kind of life must agree with you. You look great and you seem very happy," said John.

"Ah, here are our friends," a voice came from the back and Bözsi's husband, Frank, appeared. He was a thin man clothed in a gray sweatsuit, small in every respect but his happy grin. Life in the "wilderness" seemed to agree with him too, despite his frail looks.

"Hello, you must be Karl's friend," John shook hands with Frank.

"Dinner is ready," came Bözsi's voice as if she resented being ignored for even a moment. The fragrance of the soup, made from fresh ingredients, filled our nostrils as we sat down eagerly.

"See, I told you it wouldn't take long," she turned to me.

"I am amazed. I watched my grandma make it in Cegléd, but she always prepared it in the summer and dried it. If she needed it during the year, she had it ready to use as instant food. But I have never seen somebody make it and eat it within half an hour. I think I'll try it myself."

Bözsi laughed contentedly.

We ate ravenously in complete silence.

"Just like children," I said with a laugh. "We are all so hungry we can't even talk until we finish eating."

"One gets hungry working in the forest in this good clean air day after day," Frank mumbled into his soup.

"How could you get used to that after your job as an office clerk in the city? Karl said you never were the athletic type," John remarked.

"It is hard work until one gets used to it. But with my Bözsi anything is possible." He lifted his head and looked into her eyes. They smiled at each other. "We are alone here."

Since we had already heard the explanation, we too exchanged smiles.

～

We left early the next morning to make a detour in the forest before we had to get on the train to Eger.

"Helen, do you see the Palace of Szilvásvárad over there? That big, yellow building? That was remodeled according to the plans of Uncle Feri as was the hotel in Lillafüred."

"His works are everywhere, aren't they?"

"He was the most fashionable interior designer of the thirties and forties and his wife, Ernestine Lohwag, was a very famous portrait painter. My family and I used to live in a mansion with them in the Royal Palace District. It was a showplace to display his work. Our dining room was portrayed in art books."

"What was it like to be a child there?"

"Awful. The maids always covered up for me. I lived with two artistic couples. The house was spotless; elegant people came and went. Uncle Feri's wife was pregnant once but she had a miscarriage and could never have another baby. She became paralyzed from the waist down as soon as she neared her fortieth birthday. Luckily I am related to her only by marriage. This sickness was transferred through men in her family, but affected only the women. The four adults tried to bring me up, each according to his or her own taste. Actually Uncle Feri was the difficult one. He would never have approved of what I did one nice afternoon with my best friend, Thomas." John smiled like a mischievous little boy.

"What?"

"We played 'procession.' We tied a candle to the broomstick, lit it, and walked all over the house drawing a nice black line across the ceilings wherever we passed. If the maids had not saved me, I don't know what would have happened. But nobody told him. I can still remember when he remarked, 'If I did not know that it was impossible, I would say that John did this'."

"It's not much fun to grow up with that many adults around. I know I didn't have much of a childhood either," I said sympathetically, although I didn't think I would have approved of our Jancsi doing the same in our house.

"My best times were spent at Lake Balaton," John continued. "There I took off my shoes in the spring and did not put them back on until the fall when school started. When my uncle became the Director for the Academy of Art in Industry, he moved into the Director's quarters there and the mansion was

445

sold. We lived in an apartment near the Royal Palace, and I visited Aunt Tinti and Uncle Feri at least once a week. I liked to sit beside her and listen to her stories from old Vienna. We always spoke German around her; Hungarian is a difficult language to learn."

"The Palace of Szilvásvárad is exquisite even today. I love its simple elegance." I looked at every detail as we came closer to the building.

"Uncle Feri designed the Ambassador's room for the building of the League of Nations in Geneva also. I'll show you the picture at home. The same simple design characterizes all his works; maybe that is why they are not affected by time and fashion.

"He was a great artist, but he was also lazy. He only did his work when he had to. It was hard to make him stay with a certain job he started."

"Are all artists like that?"

"Many. When I think of it, maybe most of them are. At least they are somewhat eccentric."

We neared the village where we would board the train.

"I'm really sorry that I did not even have first cousins," John said. "I so wanted to share my childhood with someone as close as a sister or a brother. That is why I am happy that you have sisters. It is like having sisters of my own now. All I had before was second cousins, but I have about twenty of them."

"Twenty?"

"Yes. You know the famous innkeeper, restaurant owner, chef, Charles Gundel.

"How can anyone not know him?"

"Well, he was my father's cousin. They were pretty close, and the two of them as youngsters often made concoctions in the kitchen to the dismay of the real cook, but at least they ate everything they fixed. Maybe that is how he became a great chef. Anyway, he had thirteen children. And then I had a few on Mother's side."

John looked around, and so did I to see if there was anybody nearby. We were lucky; it was a weekday morning. The train was nearly empty. John lowered his voice. "One of the Gundel's was the manager of the Hotel Gellért. When the Soviets came in, they kept him in solitary for six weeks. They wanted to know what the Germans were speaking in his hotel; they demanded that he tell them where the microphones were hidden in the rooms. They did not believe that the guest's privacy was the prime concern of any hotel manager in Hungary as it is in most parts of the world. 'You must have had the rooms bugged. Either you tell us, or we shall regard you as an accomplice of the Germans.' They kept him in knee-deep water, sitting in a corner, water dropping onto his bald head, three to four drops a minute for a whole week. Finally they concluded that he must have been telling the truth and let him go."

"You mean that in the Soviet Union all hotels are bugged?"

"Apparently."

The conductor came to get our tickets. That was a good reminder that we were no longer in the forest, we must keep our thoughts to ourselves.

The train stopped at every village, but soon enough we arrived in Eger. We ended our excursion in a hostel where all they had to offer were bunk beds with straw mattresses. We shared our quarters with a whole school visiting there from the Great Plains. That was the first time these children had ever seen the mountains.

The old fort, churches, and buildings amply compensated us for our poor accommodations. Eger was one of the best known fortresses during the time when the Turks occupied Hungary. One thousand Hungarian soldiers and their families defended the city for more than a year against 100,000 Turks who finally left defeated. The "heroes of Eger" were famous all over Hungary. The women are still the idols of young Hungarian girls. They are said to have cut off their long braids, making them into torches, and then throwing them at the soldiers trying to climb the walls of the fortress.

"The children will be waiting for us," John said with anticipation.

"I never thought I would say this, but I miss them very much," I answered as the train ran into the night towards the little home hand carved by our love for each other."

# 49

The jasmine bush beside our wrought iron gate was in full bloom. John turned the key in the lock while I buried my head into the blossoms to absorb their delicate fragrance. As we crossed the street a breeze blew the scent of our favorite olive tree towards us.

We started up the mountain that stretched in a lazy slope on the other side of the street. We could oversee the whole district from here. There were only a few bushes, but they were low and did not obstruct the view. A small chapel in the middle of the hill was our goal today. We often took this hike after the children went to bed. When we left they eagerly stuffed dreams into their mouths with the help of their two fingers, a characteristic trait in our family. Once asleep nothing would wake them. Judy did not mind coming over with her book while we were away.

When we were a considerable distance from the street, John started talking. "Something very peculiar happened today. Nobody should know about the details. This is why I waited until we could be by ourselves. Do you remember Ede?"

"Sure. He and his wife are kind of sickly looking but very nice and kind."

"Her father came back from a concentration camp this week."

"You don't say! And he told about it?"

"Yes, but that is the secret part. His family has thought during all these ten years since 1945 that he was in Siberia."

"And he wasn't?"

"He was for a while. However, for about five years he has been in a concentration camp so close to home that his family members often walked past the walls. Yet he was not able even to send a message to them. His family did not even know there was a concentration camp nearby."

I felt sick at heart. "He couldn't find a messenger? Don't those guards have a heart? How terrible to think he was within reach for so long and still…"

"You know what else?" John went on. "When they let a few of the prisoners go free they were given documents from authorities that accounted for every day of those ten years as if they had never left Hungary. Documents complete with a supposed non-military job record. Both the Hungarian and Soviet governments steadily deny the existence of any forced labor camps so if there are no concentration camps nobody could be in them. Therefore…nobody was or is. If someone talks about things like that, it must be his 'imagination.' Besides, it is much better for him not to talk if he wants to keep his freedom. Not a word to anyone." John put a finger to his lips.

"I'll never mention it. So now there is something I wanted to discuss with you. Have you heard that people are typing religion books and books on child rearing? I was asked to help with it. Should I do it?"

"If they find out, you will be jailed. Yet, it is important that the young generation should know about religion." Then he added pensively, "Anybody entering our home has to come through an iron gate, locked by key. Nobody could take you by surprise."

I understood his answer so I said, "I really want to do it. To me freedom is very important. Besides I have yet to be personally threatened."

"Of course they don't always warn you. They might just take you. However, I think we could pull it off, and this is something worth the risk."

"John, do you think that things will get better? It seems to me that since Stalin's death a slow 'thaw' is taking place."

"I don't know, Helen, but I hear more and more criticism about the regime. By the way," he said shyly, pulling two pieces of paper from his breast pocket, "I got us some tickets to the Vidam Szinpad."

"Oh, thank you, thank you." I clapped my hands. "I just love their performances although I fear for the security of the actors."

"It has happened now and then that they were arrested after the show, yet they go on criticizing the government as much as is humanly possible."

I looked off toward the city getting ready for a sleepy weekday evening.

"I can't forget the skit about the ridiculous red tape that takes place every time someone wants to enter a factory. It took me at least three years to be able to see your office and the test facilities at the factory. Then I could go in only because I pretended to be one of the university students admitted to observe a factory in action. Anyway, in that funny skit the fat doorman chats with one of the women workers and promises her to bring her a recipe from his wife. But, when it comes to entering the factory, he sends her home for her I.D. card. The next person who wants to enter is dressed like a typical 'enemy of the people' and pulls a little toy tank after him. He has an aristocratic name that properly identifies him as an 'insect' but has an I.D. stating that he is a spy. The doorman admits him readily because all his papers are in order. I laugh every time I think about this joke that pokes fun at bureaucrats."

"Well, these are the skits the actors can get away with. If the joke is aimed at something that can be human error but does not state that it was a mistake of the Party, they can make fun of it."

We looked down onto our home from the tiny chapel then went in for a few moments of silent prayer.

On our way back I kept thinking of how lucky we were. "John, do you remember Paul, from Cegléd? He used to own a pharmacy there. He married a girl from Budapest. In the name of the five-year plan she had received a job in Cegléd, her husband in Budapest. Now they both live in Cegléd, and he commutes every day the seventy kilometers back and forth. Naturally, he cannot be allowed to work in their former pharmacy."

Night started falling, but from the mountainside we could still see everything that was going on around our house.

"They send people out to work all over the country," John said. "A former student of mine got his first job assignment in a very desolate part of the country, but he had to accept. One does not choose jobs in a planned economy. Especially not if one is an 'insect' or a descendent of one. The first day on the job he asked his colleague to take a picture of him in front of a fence. As they proceeded, a very angry guard with a sub-machine gun ran towards them. 'You cannot do that! You are not allowed to photograph military establishments!' 'Military establishments?' He was dumbfounded. 'All I see is a fence that belongs to a manufacturing plant with a huge sign! Candy Factory.'"

"Don't play the innocent, the soldier retorted. "Everybody knows this is a machine gun factory!"

"What? Even if everybody else knows, nobody has told me about it. I only arrived here yesterday."

'We'll see about that at the police station!' With these words he poked my student in the ribs with his sub-machine gun and took him to the police station where his pictures were developed. To his great luck the fence did not even show in any of the photos.

"We'll let you go this time. But remember, no more photographing on your job."

"If it weren't so scary, I'd laugh," I said, and we stopped talking because we were again close to inhabited streets.

The next day I started typing the forbidden religious handbooks. John was able to bring home carbon papers from the factory so I could make eight to ten copies at a time.

I happened to be typing one day when the doorbell rang. I quickly hid the sheets in the bathroom. This way if I needed to I could have flushed them all down the toilet, or burned them in the stove. I peeked out through the window. A man dressed in gray rags stood there. At least he was not a policeman, yet I was hesitant to open the door. I approached cautiously.

"Is John home?" the caricature of a man asked.

"No, he is working."

"I was a worker in the same factory, and I just came from jail," he whispered.
I opened the door. "What do you want?"

"I am hungry."

"I haven't much to eat here. I can give you some cream of wheat left over from yesterday. It may even be sour, I'm not sure."

"I don't mind. Whatever you have. Something you would give to a dog would be fine with me."

"I don't have a dog," I murmured, still puzzled as to what I should do with him. Once we were inside he said, "Who are you? Did John get married?"

"When did you last see him?" I asked. "We have two children. We married in 1951."

"I was jailed in 1951." The man smiled as if the whole thing would be of no concern to him. "I'll be put back in jail again. I can't help myself. I keep telling jokes."

"Is that why you were jailed?" I ushered him into our tiny kitchenette and started to heat the cream of wheat. Ilike was at nursery school, two blocks from home, where an old German lady offered language instruction for pre-schoolers. Jancsi was in the inside room. I felt a bit afraid of that man.

"Do you want to hear the joke?" He grinned.

I shrugged. "If it's funny, but I don't want to be jailed."

"If you don't blab on us, nobody will know," he said and then proceeded with the anecdote.

"It happened at an evening seminar the ideological schools held for workers in all factories since our 'glorious liberation'." When he said that, his voice became sarcastic. I nodded, urging him to go on; I knew what he meant.

"At this seminar the party-secretary-lecturer was asked by a certain Mr. Cohen, 'I just want to know where all the meat is,' meaning that there was none in the stores. The party-secretary promised to have an answer for him by the next time. The next time Mr. Cohen again proceeded with a question, 'I just want to know where all the sugar is.' Again he promised to have an answer by the next time. The following lecture was not even finished when Mr. Cohen demanded loudly, 'I just want to know where the coal is.' The same procedure, the next time there would be an answer. Finally, at the last lecture, someone else stood up and wanted to hear the answer to his question, 'I just want to know where Mr. Cohen is'."

I laughed so hard that tears streamed down my cheeks. Was the joke so funny, or was I crying because this bitter jest was the naked truth? Whoever asked a meaningful question disappeared.

"I have another one," he went on. "Stalin was looking for his pipe. Beria, the head of the secret police, was summoned to help him find it. He looked and looked; finally he departed and came back the next day to report, 'I have arrested one hundred people, but unfortunately the pipe is still lost.' The next day the same report with two hundred, then the third day with three hundred more arrests. Yet, no pipe. After all these days Stalin found his pipe under some papers on his desk and asked his faithful accomplice to his room. 'I am sorry for having caused all this trouble, I found the pipe.' Hearing this, Beria exclaimed 'Oh, no! Not now! Four hundred of the five hundred have already confessed to taking it!'"

Again I laughed hard. "No wonder they arrest you for these. You can tell them really well."

The gate screeched. We both froze. Hard steps came towards our apartment. I was certainly relieved when I saw John's face in the window of our little kitchen.

"Hi! Long time, no see," he greeted the man in rags. "Am I happy to be home for a moment! At least, I could see you."

"I just got out of jail." The man grinned again. I thought that he must be not quite with it to laugh all the time.

"Here, take this twenty forint bill. I can't spare any more but maybe it will help you survive. Try not to get back in," John suggested.

"But I always do. You know me. I have a few drinks, tell a few jokes and I'm back in jail. I don't want to work for the Reds. I won't keep my mouth shut."

He sat on the kitchen stool; his head leaned against the wall. He seemed content with the cereal he had just finished.

"Thank you for giving me a break. I'll be back."

He shook hands with John and started towards the door.

～

Hungary and other satellite countries had signed the Warsaw Pact with the "Great Soviet Union" in May of 1955. We were now guaranteed to be saved from any foreign invasion. Maybe even from ourselves? What did it mean exactly? We were told that the agreement was necessary to "protect" us from NATO forces. We would have liked to have some reason why this protection seemed necessary. Unfortunately, NATO did not even think of attacking us.

After our excursion in the Bükk we went often into the mountains closer to the capital city and left the children with their grandparents. The green quiet and privacy lured us even though it wasn't the same as in the Bükk where we saw nobody during our walks.

During the summer we traveled to Ábrahámhegy to be with John's parents for a few weeks. Sometimes I would stay for longer periods with the children and John would come for the weekends. They were lazy, beautiful days to enjoy our children, each other, the fresh air and the warm water of the lake. We picked fresh fruit, drank new wine and were spoiled by John's parents. The only thing that bothered me was the constant fear whenever John left.

Would I see him again? What if it was decided that they no longer needed him? Would I have to bring up my children alone as Mother had?

John was now working for the new department. The boss from Moscow had not come yet, but John was preparing everything for his arrival under the auspices of his old department. He had secret instructions that he could pick anybody for the jobs and that Dr. Benedikt could get the personnel John chose. What would the new boss be like?

We received an answer to our question when he arrived. Dr. Benedikt was a tall, sturdy man with white skin and hair, gold-rimmed glasses, benevolent blue eyes. He was rather like a Father Winter, a Communist Santa Claus! His wife was a roly-poly, brown, bespectacled short woman, a Czechoslovakian medical doctor. Their daughter, named Svetlana after Stalin's child, was slightly handicapped and walked with a cane, but her spirits were always high. She was a freshman in mechanical engineering.

"I want her to marry a Hungarian man," her father confided to John. "This is why I left my department in Moscow. I love Hungary. I would never have left if I had not been one of the revolutionaries in 1919. I fell in love with the ideals of communism. I escaped when the Communist regime toppled three months later. In Prague I married my wife, and I got my doctorate in Vienna. Then we moved to the Soviet Union. I still believe in the pure ideals of equality, and I wish that all the mistakes of the Party could be corrected according to the original thoughts."

John did not say a word. Who were we even to suggest that the Party made mistakes? Who was he that he could allow himself to make such statements even if he had once been Stalin's personal friend? After all, Stalin was dead. It was better just to let him speak and listen in silence.

Whoever he was, that big man, he had connections in the right places. He not only received a six-room apartment for the three of them but also a limousine with a chauffeur. When he had the sniffles, Comrade Gerö, the prime minister, personally asked about his health and welfare every day.

His wishes could not be contradicted. Everybody he wanted from industry to work in his department was made free to accept the job. Finally, John could go over to the university full-time and work half-time at the factory. It took him four years to accomplish this feat. Yet our dream of being together more could not materialize because of the excitement of establishing a new department and the design and building of a new laboratory with the latest equipment to the tune of several million forints. For Dr. Benedikt the best that was available had to be produced.

John noticed with surprise that even though this gentleman seemed almighty he would not so much as sign a document before John had signed it. What kind of consequences did he have to endure during his lifetime that he shied away from full responsibility?

"You think I should go and visit all the heads of departments? I want to do everything according to Hungarian customs. I haven't been home for so long I forgot." He listened carefully to everything John said and acted accordingly.

"You find the people for me, and I'll get them," he ordered.

John collected the cream of young Hungarian electrical engineers into the department, Communists and non-Communists alike. John even selected the man who would take second place of command in the department because he was the son of a worker and an assistant professor at the university. He knew that he could live with this man as his "boss."

After a few months the man invited him to have an espresso. "John," he began. "I know that you should be the one to get my position, but Dr. Benedikt said that nothing was to change in the present structure of the department. In practice you will still be second in command. Officially I have to be the one because of our backgrounds. I wanted you to know that I am aware of the situation and you have my full support. I also want to thank you for selecting me for the job."

John wanted to vacate his office for his colleague but he was stopped by Dr. Benedikt. "No, you stay where you are. I want you beside me all the time. The Deputy Head of Department can stay in the same room he has had. Everything will stay as it was before." He repeated the last sentence for emphasis.

At least John's "irreplaceability" was confirmed from both sources. We felt a bit more secure although it became quite clear that John would never become the head of department in this or any other institution. If Dr. Benedikt could not pull it off, nobody could.

John's work multiplied as the laboratory's building progressed but he had great fun planning it. We could hardly wait to see the finished product. Many nights he came home around eleven o'clock. The only change was that now, if he worked late, he was sent home by car. Soon the neighbors began to whisper and accused him of becoming a Communist. He traveled in one of the five thousand privately owned cars in a nation of ten million. Outside work became less, partly because of the intrigue of the Marxism-Leninism department and the Russian department at the university; they had no consulting jobs and envied the opportunities of the technical faculty.

On the first day of January we celebrated Ilike's third birthday. She beamed with happiness when my mother brought her five forints to spend as she wanted to. Ilike frequently accompanied me on my shopping trips and for months she had eyed a cutlery set for her dolls. She had all the pots and pans, cups and saucers, but no knives, forks or spoons. John and I accompanied her to the stationery store on the corner that also sold toys. She was dressed in the beige coat Mother had altered and lined with the quilted bed jacket. It was a perfect fit. She wore a new cap, mitten and scarf set, a gift from her godfather. It was hand-knitted by one of the many home industrialists, who were trying to supplement their husbands' income. She was the embodiment of happiness as she "ordered" the things she "needed" for her dolls with a smile that danced even in her huge blue eyes. She put both her hands in her pockets and rattled off, "I need spoons and knives and forks."

The woman who helped her knew her well and was delighted with her happiness.

"What else do you want? There is still money left from what you gave me," she prodded Ilike.

"There is?" She seemed to feel rich beyond imagination. "Let me see," she went on. She spoke like an adult, her grammar was perfect.

John lifted her so she could see the shelves more closely. She made careful choices and considered what her babies "needed."

John's parents were staying with us again as they did every winter. One day when Grandmother was breading chicken, she was called to the telephone. By the time she was back Ilike had finished the job perfectly. She imitated her grandmother and me in everything we did. We realized that if we wanted to have many children we had better let them do everything themselves as soon as they possibly could. We needed to free ourselves for more important tasks. Ilike was very self-sufficient. She also tried to mother Jancsi who was a rather independent little boy. He was very quiet; but the calmer he was, the more suspicious one had to be. One day our neighbor, Judy, while baby-sitting him found that he was unusually quiet. She found him in a corner sipping a quart size bottle of beer.

Another day we heard Ilike wail. "What is the matter?" We ran out of the house. She stood at the bottom of a step ladder, holding it with all her strength. Her one and one-half-year-old brother stood on top of it and smiled with a light bulb in his hand. "He'll fall, help!" yelled Ilike. Jancsi's huge grin betrayed that he was proud of himself for doing something Daddy would do. Jancsi was saved, and we praised Ilike for alerting us, yet secretly we were amused by our "big" son's antics. When he was so sick who would have thought he'd be this mischievous?

Since matters were under control and John's parents spent most of the winters with us, I thought again about John's suggestion that I should go to the university. One day he appeared with a physics book and suggested that I study for the entrance exams.

More and more people came home from concentration camps. Some were blinded, some had terminal kidney trouble. Others were dying from illnesses caused by cruel treatment, beatings and malnutrition. Miss Jenny, our landlady, was sick. We visited her at the hospital. We tried to be nice to her though she continued to vex us for even the smallest "offenses." In her hospital room on the next bed we saw a fat sixteen-year-old girl who was covered with hair. Miss Jenny was very kind this time because she had a secret and we were the only ones around she could whisper it to. "This girl was nine years old when she was marched off to Siberia, I don't know why. Maybe she was taken with her parents, but now she has none. I don't know if they will be able to ever straighten her out. She has hormone problems. She does not talk much." Miss Jenny's eyes glowed with excitement and we were happy that for once she did not bother us about where Judy hung the clothes or a flower that Ilike might have picked in her part of the garden.

The girl had big, sad eyes. She did not say anything. It was a wonder she could still speak Hungarian.

About the time I started studying for the entrance exam I knew I was pregnant again. This might bring complications but Judy said she would take care of the two little ones when the grandparents were not there, Ilike would go to nursery school. Now all I had to do was pass the entrance exam. John put down the children's names on the waiting list at the university nursery school which had an excellent name and was as apolitical as the Communists would tolerate.

"I suggest you try out for both the morning and evening classes," John said. "Sometimes 'insects' have a better chance for the evening school. Then, with a little luck, you might be able to transfer later to the morning section."

"I'd much rather go during the day. I don't want to be away from my family four nights a week for seven years. Morning courses are done in five."

"I know, but we have to try both. I don't think they would admit you to the morning section, because you are my wife. Children of university professors don't have a chance at all. 'Insects' are out of the question. Only perfect scores will do if you are not the descendant of a worker or a peasant." John said jokingly, "Now, if you were, the university would not only have to admit you, but would have to make sure that you passed and did not drop out. Remember how much tutoring I had to do? Sometimes I had to take the students one by one and get them through the exam if I did not want to be expelled."

"That is a mixed-up world!" I cried but I studied as much as I could to at least get the best possible grade even though I could not help being related to a university professor and being an "insect." I was still confident. If nothing else, Dr. Benedikt would certainly help!

Uncle Feri, Father's friend, the man at whose house John and I had met, invited us to a great event in his life. His only daughter was getting married to the son of a well-known Hungarian engineer and they were going to have the celebration of a lifetime. I put on my dress from Hollywood and became the center of attraction at the party. The silver-haired celebrity of the gathering, Dr. László Verebélÿ, father of the groom, insisted on my company. We sang to the music of the gypsy musicians until early in the morning while helping ourselves generously from the huge crystal bowl of champagne punch.

Midway through the party the father of the bride danced a traditional kerchief dance with his daughter and then "sold" the bride. Every guest had to dance with her and put money in a hat for the favor. This was a village custom and a new kind of fun. The party carried with it old-world splendor.

We met many of our friends of dancing school days and missed others who were either in deportation or in the Army Work Force, a service reserved for "dissenters."

"Did you hear that George was serving time in a mine?" asked Évi.

"No, why?"

"He escaped and was caught in Vienna."

"In Vienna?"

"He had the bad luck to go to the railroad station where the Soviets were patrolling. If it had been any of the other three, the English, the Americans, or the French, he would have been all right."

I sipped my champagne thoughtfully as I said, "I was in Vienna in '48. I remember how careful we were when we had to go to the Soviet sectors or when the Soviets were in charge of the sector that was controlled by all four powers. Can you believe that the Austrian State Treaty had finally been signed?"

"The Soviets did not sign as long as they could hold out," Géza interjected. We both looked at him. "What did you say?"

"The Soviets did not sign the Austrian State Treaty because according to previous agreements, in ninety days they would have had to leave Hungary and the rest of the Eastern European satellites. However with the Warsaw Pact now they have a counter balance. They still should have left, but I would not bet on it."

"If they left we would be free." A surge of happy thoughts flooded me. Wouldn't it be wonderful to be free again? Was it the champagne that brought back my yearning for freedom?

John and I danced a waltz while in the other room the "younger generation," that of my sisters, danced to the tune of long play records that were still precious possessions in Hungary. It was nice to be a part of both worlds: that of the serious, university professors and their venerable wives, and that of the swirling, whirling teenagers. For a moment I thought of Bonzi and wished that she were alive, dancing here with us, in Pista's arms. I hadn't heard anything from Pista for quite a while. His family had been deported, and he was serving in the Army Work Force.

"I hope Pista shows up some day. There are hardly any people left of those we used to dance with," John remarked at the very moment I thought of him.

Just then Alec and Sophie appeared from the other room. They were newlyweds and happiness was written all over their beaming faces. "Shall we exchange?" Alec asked. Sophie's slim figure nearly disappeared in John's arms as they galloped away to the sounds of a swing.

"How does married life agree with you?" I winked at Alec.

"Great, just great!" he declared. "We live with Sophie's mother. Her parents divorced when she was very young. There is plenty of room in their apartment. Not too far from the university. I am an associate professor now. Did you hear?"

"That's wonderful. Congratulations."

"Sophie is working too at least until we have a baby."

"Are you expecting?"

"Not yet. Are you?" He looked at me with suspicion.

"Yes, we are."

"You certainly don't show it. That dress! You look so slim it seems to me I could thread you into a needle." Alec laughed and pulled up his right eyebrow. Everything seemed now the same as when we had danced in these same rooms a few years, or was it an eternity ago, before the deportations had started?

I felt I had spent the past five years very profitably. I had two children with another one on its way and we were living in our own apartment, John was advancing in his career as much as an "insect" was allowed. We had access to everything imaginable in the world of this "Red Paradise": good company, drinks, good music, theater, clothes from parcels abroad, even a washing machine. Above all, our children were healthy in mind and body, and I was about to start the university if I passed the entrance exam. I had no doubts that I would.

# 50

White trees were shimmering through the orange air etched against the blue sky when we boarded the bus with both children to spend Sunday at Mother's. As soon as we entered the apartment we could smell the fragrant aroma of Mother's special chicken soup. She seldom engaged in elaborate cooking, but Uncle Charles, the doctor who had "married" her, liked to fiddle around in the kitchen and the two of them could come up with very good meals. Elisabeth, a budding beauty at fifteen, helped and grouched around as was her custom. She was like Grandfather in miniature. Whenever we asked her to do something for us, she did it right away while murmuring all the time about why she should not have to do it.

"Jancsika, come here to me," she called out to her godson as soon as she saw his head in the door and they disappeared into our former room which now belonged to my two sisters.

We helped Mother set the table in Grandfather's room. Uncle Charles had his separate sublet downstairs at the widow's apartment, but now he was here with us, his eyes twinkling with contentedness.

"The Queen," he said about Elisabeth, "is happy to have her most devoted subject with her. It's no problem to her to conquer Jancsika's heart." He stirred the soup and suggested a bit more paprika. "It is hot enough only if both your nose and eyes are running from its taste."

"You confine that to your own plate," Mother suggested. "Now let's get inside there. Everybody must be starved. Ilike, you sit beside me."

Marie also emerged from her book. She was a freshman in mechanical engineering at the university. The descent of her adoptive father must have satisfied the Admissions Office. She had also won the Rákosi prize at her senior matriculation; her grades were perfect. I could hardly believe my ears when I heard that because Marie had never been the studying type. We all contributed it to the good influence that her boyfriend and now fiancé exerted on her.

The soup satisfied all the expectations its vapors aroused in us.

"Oh, Helen," Grandfather turned to me. "You became such a beautiful young girl. Soon we can think of marrying you off."

"Grandfather," I laughed. "You just finished talking to my daughter, Ilike, your favorite great-grandchild."

"How about that?" Grandfather laughed too. "You could have fooled me! You look younger than your sisters sometimes!"

Uncle Charles put down his spoon and looked at John. "What do you think about the 20th Congress of the Communist Party in the Soviet Union?"

"After the experiences of Stalin's days, it was to be expected that they would condemn the 'personal cult.' What I think about the whole outlook is that the Soviets are not ready to attack the world yet. Khrushchev's ideas on 'coexistence' stem from that notion. Remember the well-publicized study during the last years of Stalin's life predicting that by 1974 the military might of the USSR would surpass that of the USA? This means that there is less urgency to promote 'world revolution,' instead Khrushchev was able to channel efforts to produce more consumer goods. This way he got some relief from internal pressures. There is an American saying I learned in 1939, together with its 'twisted version.' The Soviets will 'have their cake and eat it too'."

Uncle Charles nodded. "That is why Khrushchev declared at the Congress that peace was possible with the capitalistic nations. The Soviets would not gain anything today by an all-out fight with the West. They also believe that they can do much more harm within the United States and Western democracies by undermining every worthwhile movement there, by strikes, by slowly eating away their liberty and freedom. Why should they fight when they can get everything piecemeal? Election by election, island by island; in the meantime they can become strong and ready to fight if and when the time comes."

"Exactly," John agreed. "In the meantime we are all trained to 'fight for peace.' Of course, according to the Communists' dictionary, there can be no peace until the world has reached a completely classless society, because until then there will always be the fight between classes, against capitalism and imperialism."

"But why, why does the free world sit by and do nothing?" I asked in desperation. "I will never understand why the Americans did not insist upon free elections everywhere in Europe under the auspices of the United Nations. They had sole possession of the 'bomb' after the World War." I felt disgusted with the whole world. "Why do they wait until bad things happen to them? Why is the United Nations so helpless? Can't they enforce their decisions?"

"Why?" Uncle Charles looked at me with his calm, blue eyes. "Why? To me this seems like a nightmare. Americans live on their big island, isolated from the rest of the world. Until recently nobody could fly over and hurt their homeland. Even now, they are the only ones who possess that power. They are in no immediate need and they don't understand the long-range dangers and possibilities. The importance of foreign affairs is out of their experience. Stalin, the shrewd diplomat, lured President Roosevelt into signing away the East European countries to the Soviets. Churchill's ideas were ignored. Although the United Nations should have great influence, they are slow, indecisive, and almost never act firmly."

"How about the Austrian State Treaty?" I asked. "It was already signed in May. The Soviets should have left ninety days after that. Why are they still here?"

"Why?" Uncle Charles answered, leaving the issue up in the air.

The doorbell rang, Elisabeth blushed and ran to let Gene in. He was a young man from the neighborhood, the son of a lawyer. Although he was John's age he was still unmarried.

"Gene!" We both jumped up and hurried to greet him. "How nice of you to drop by. How is life treating you? Come have a glass of wine with us!"

"Your mother said you would be here today." Gene wiped his feet and took off his overcoat. He was as plump as when we last saw him. "I'm working at a factory my uncle used to own," he said while he made himself comfortable. "I even got a medal for being a 'model worker.' How do you like that? That was the factory I would have inherited, but…at least I am alive and not deported."

"We haven't seen you for awhile. Where were you?" John asked.

"I was in prison."

"Why?"

"Because I happened to watch the movie about the coronation of Queen Elisabeth. When I came out from the building of the British Council, we were all surrounded and taken."

"Because you watched a movie?" I repeated slowly. I remembered our talk with John about the religious handbooks I was typing and John's remark that they might take me anyway, without warning and for no apparent reason.

As if in answer to my thoughts Gene said, "I never dreamed they would take us away because of that, or I wouldn't have gone. After all, what is the Queen of England to me? I even said so at the prison, but my 'insect' descent hurt me. The son of the party-secretary was also arrested, but they let him go by evening. Maybe because he was not sixteen yet. I don't know, one never knows. There was no trial; they kept me for a year and a half."

"How did they treat you?" As soon as I asked the question I wanted to retract it. I did not want to embarrass him.

"Oh, much better than when I was a prisoner of war," Gene smiled. "One day in 1945 we were marched single file along the railroad tracks by the Soviets. I'll never forget the day; it was like today with sunshine and snow. We marched. All I could see was the head of the person in front of me when

I heard a shot from behind and then a soft 'thump.' I counted: 'One, two, three, four, five…' another shot, another 'thump.' I looked back while I counted to five again before I heard another 'thump.' On the snow there lay three bodies in fresh red blood. After the count of five, another one, then another. I took another glimpse back. There were only two marchers behind me, 'One, two, three, four, five' I murmured 'thump.' My muscles tensed. I had to be quicker than the guard who was shooting my friends, I had to fall before he pulled the trigger. My whole being concentrated as I counted the second five. After the thump I knew it was my turn. 'One, two, three, four, five' as I pronounced the 've' I threw myself onto the tracks and heard the bullet whistle a few inches above my head. I did not move. The soldier stepped over me and continued his deadly game. I was saved. I lay there for as long as I could hear them and then a little longer. When all was clear I looked around. Most of my fellow prisoners' heads were shot to smithereens. I rolled down the embankment, crawled into a culvert, and lay there till night."

"That sounds just like what the Nazis did to those Jews they caught at the quay of the Danube, remember, John? When you told me about how your father had saved Jews and about the German patrol which told of their fun in shooting Jews straight into the Danube."

Gene sighed.

"I don't know to this day why that Soviet guard did what he had done. Anyway, Helen, your question was how they treated me. A little bit better than that. Being a strong and healthy young man I was never in danger of death. However, many died around us. Especially old people. I knew an old general whose family I notified only yesterday. You knew him, John, it was your ex-fiancée's father who died in a prison hospital. I worked as an orderly there for a week. They never notified the families. Yesterday when I went to see them in the village, where they were deported, they said that they had not heard about his death. They asked me not to tell his wife, so I only spoke to the younger members of the family."

John looked very sad as he said, "He was taken in his pajamas one morning, and they have never heard from him since. Remember, Helen, when I told you about him?"

"That is a whole different world, I must tell you." Gene looked around, automatically.

"It's all right," we assured him.

Elisabeth and Marie had taken the little ones to the other room and we could hear their happy laughter that also provided us with additional protection from the neighbors. Through their noise nothing could be heard in the third room; on the other side we had no neighbors. The house met another house there which meant two thick firewalls side by side.

"Whether it's a forced labor camp, a concentration camp or a prison, it is ecumenical in all ways. The rabbis are thrown together with the Catholic priests and Protestant bishops rub elbows with militant atheists. Workers and capitalists share the cells, for 'sins' like viewing a movie, murdering a thousand people during the War, having written a history book, or having torn down Communist posters. We were all mixed together and we could discuss our views freely. After all, what else could they do to us? At least that is what we thought. Then we discovered that some of us were 'informers.' They would get privileges like bacon or cigarettes or work in the kitchen for tattling. Others adhered to their principles; they had the best chance for survival. There were many who prayed. We had a Bible hidden in parts so the guards were not able to confiscate it all at once. Day and night, people were taken to be questioned. Lights blazed at us, transforming the prison into eternal day. It was close to impossible to sleep. The stench of the latrines, the pain of malnutrition, the watery soup with its few beans and unrecognizable substances and the black hard bread were the daily realities of our existence."

We sat in complete silence.

"How long? How much longer can this go on?" Uncle Charles looked searchingly at us, the younger generation. "And, what can we do about it?"

For the first time since the war, in the spring of 1956, Hungary had formal balls again which were organized by the universities. We were invited to one by the Dentistry School of the Medical University, Uncle Charles' work place. The restaurant in the Városliget burst at its seams but there were reserved tables for the professors. We all squeezed around one table, dressed in evening gowns, old ones of course but as festive as ever, and John was in a real tuxedo. How many times had I imagined it? Yet, when it finally came true, it held none of my fantasies.

"When you are sixteen," I remembered my mother saying many years ago. I used to close my eyes and see girls in wide-skirted white dresses with boys in tails whirl across a glittering, shining floor, under huge crystal chandeliers to the melody of the Blue Danube Waltz. Everybody was beautiful in my dreams and ethereal. The halls of my dreams were not filled with cigarette smoke as dense as the London fog. The walls were not decorated with Communist slogans and the pictures of Lenin and Rákosi. There was plenty of space for everybody because there were many balls, not only a few, after eleven years of complete ban on this kind of entertainment.

It was a breakthrough to have balls at all and to be able to call them that. The noise level reached the point where we could no longer understand each other, so we left Mother and Uncle Charles and joined my sisters on the

463

over-crowded dance floor. When John took me in his arms, I closed my eyes and through the magic of dance I was transplanted into that ball of my dreams. If it had not been for the constant shoves from every side, I could have completely forgotten where I was.

"I would never have thought that I would reverse the normal process by becoming a debutante after I'd had two children..."

"And one on the way," John shouted in my ear. We both laughed. "It still feels good, doesn't it?" He pressed my hand.

Suddenly I could hardly wait to be at home with him, alone. Yet I did not think we should leave because it had taken quite a bit of doing to get the invitations, the tickets and the table.

"Do you know, John, that Évi and her group of friends who were invited to the Medical Ball at the Hotel Gellért rented a room there in order to be able to get in when the ball started?"

"It's beginning to get crowded here too," said John.

The band took a break and we went back to the table where my sisters and their boyfriends joined Mother and Uncle Charles. They drank champagne and ate.

Both my sisters looked beautiful in Mother's old evening gowns which had been altered for the occasion. Their eyes sparkled as they chattered with their boyfriends like two little birds.

"Cheers!" We toasted each other with the champagne and our eyes expressed many unsaid feelings as we strolled back to the dance floor.

We did not last beyond eleven o'clock. Balls were not for parents of young children and expecting ones at that. We decided to leave that fun to my sisters and search for ours in bed.

Our bicycles rolled merrily along the concrete highway. Whenever a car came, we got off and stood on the side to let it pass. We did not have many interruptions on our way to Tapolca, the county seat of Ábrahámhegy, at Lake Balaton. We had to go to the tax office there, and we used that excuse for a day off together. I was in the sixth month of my pregnancy and felt great. Mother always said that twenty-two was the best year to be pregnant. Maybe she was right. As we cycled side by side, John put his arm around my waist and swung me ahead; I felt like I was flying through the blue sky. The majestic slopes of the Badacsony were green with ripening vineyards. Whitewashed houses showed through the foliage. Huge basalt rocks displayed their wounds where quarrying had changed the color of their surfaces to dark gray and red.

"I used to work at that mine during the war," John said. "For a few months I lived here alone, my parents had to stay in Budapest. I took care of myself completely. I used to bicycle over every day. You see that red rock?" And he told me about the qualities and grades of the gravel quarried there.

We pedaled as fast as we could because we had to do the whole stretch and back in one day; twenty miles all told and, being city dwellers, we were not used to such long bike hikes, especially not when pregnant.

St. George Mountain's famous basalt pillars passed us by. Whitewashed houses met us then disappeared, blue wildflowers were blowing in the breeze. Finally, we arrived at our destination and took care of our official business.

"Let's go into the bookstore," John suggested. I gladly followed as bookstores were my favorite places. We found a book by Karinthy that we had not seen for at least a decade. Karinthy, an excellent humorist, made fun of other writers in this book by imitating their style.

"We can't take it with us on the bikes; we have no bag or knapsack."

"Would it be possible for you to forward it to our address in Budapest?"

"Yes, I'm sure we can do that," the clerk answered and took our address.

When we were out on the street again, I turned to John. "Can you believe that? They reissued the book even though it pokes fun at writers like the great Soviet poet Mayakovsky?"

"Since the signing of the Austrian State Treaty I can believe almost anything."

"Lately the National Theater started playing The Tragedy of Man again."

"I heard it is sold out for the next ten years," I laughed. "Put your name down at the factory. Maybe we'll have a chance. They play the whole piece without cuts. They even left in the Phalanster scene."

The Tragedy of Man was written by Imre Madach in 1859-60. It was an ambitious play that mirrored the history of man throughout the ages, starting in the Garden of Eden. Adam, Eve and Lucifer appeared in every scene as different characters; they went through slavery, feudalism, capitalism and revolutions. The Phalanster scene was a utopia which everybody in our times considered to be a prophecy on Communism. Like every other scene it ended in disaster. This is why it had not been produced in Hungary until now. From there the play portrayed space travel and the cooling of the earth with too many Eskimos and too few seals left. In the end Adam decided that if this was mankind's fate he would kill himself in order to prevent all this suffering. At this moment Eve whispered in his ear that she was with child. No matter what he did to himself, life would go on. At this point God's voice was heard from above, "O Man, strive on, strive on, have faith and trust."

We were rolling down on our bicycles to the Mill Pond. The walls of the surrounding houses rose steeply from the mirror of the water. The storybook picture took us back to medieval times. Goldfish played in the water right by our feet. In the distance the huge wheel of the mill completed the perfect idyll.

"There is the big cave! Remember last year when we visited its light blue waters? It was really scary when we rowed through the dark parts," I said, with my arm around John's waist.

"Of course I remember. I would like to take you to Aggtelek. There is a huge cave with beautiful formations of stalactites and stalagmites. It's the biggest one in the Carpathian Mountains. I heard that the Intourist government agency is going to have guided tours. Finally, we'd be allowed again to go close to a foreign country even if it is only another one behind the Iron Curtain. You know that the other exit of that famous cave is in Czechoslovakia and this is why people were not allowed to visit it for about a decade now."

"No, I didn't know that. But then, I guess I never thought about it much."

"Let's go there next time," John suggested as we started to walk up slowly in the direction of the church to turn back towards the highway and home.

"Let's! If it is true that we may, I would love to go there, to go anywhere."

"I have also heard that we are allowed to visit the Soviet Union. Actually, there is one place there that I would really like to see. The tours are very expensive but we might be able to swing it in a year or two."

"What is that one place?" I asked. We were now back on the highway and I started to get onto my bike.

"I want to see the Hermitage in Leningrad, the former St. Petersburg."

"Oh, I'd love to see that, too. Let's go!" I was ready to bicycle there this instant.

John laughed at my enthusiasm. "O.K., I'll try to put our names down for that too. But we have to remember our baby."

I kept forgetting I was pregnant. The sun was shining, the water in the distance was as blue as the sky that bent down to hug its shores.

When we were back home and the stars came up, we went down to the lake and swam out naked into the night, kissing and loving each other in the caress of the warm waves. The moon rose slowly and colored the reed a peculiar dark silver.

The following Sunday we bicycled over to Badacsony, a distance of about three miles, to go to church with our little daughter. Ilike sat through Mass like a young lady. She looked up to her dad, then back at me, then again at her dad and smiled. She did not say a word, just smiled. Such a treat! To be able to go to church with her parents! She was beautifully dressed and wore a tiny kerchief on her head. After Mass we went for a big excursion to the other side of the lake.

The boat blew its whistle and we started out with our bicycles loaded on deck. Ilike still enjoyed the adult treatment and looked at everything with curious eyes.

A sailor untied the boat, and it started puffing ahead across the several-mile stretch.

"It moves!" Ilike clapped her little hands. "Let's go to the railing!" she demanded. We held her so that she could watch the churning lake and the gulls following the ship, catching food thrown to them by the passengers and diving for it into the foaming water. "Bird," Ilike screamed with delight and tried to catch them. Luckily the seagulls, enormous compared to her size, kept their distance.

The ship neared the shore on the other side and a tall line of poplar trees appeared as if defending the coastline from intruders. Between those trees we continued our excursion with Ilike on her dad's bike in a specially made seat.

All day we visited relatives and friends on the other side of the lake, among them the Benedikts, who along with other fringe benefits had received a cottage from the government when they came back from Moscow.

The summer was golden and carefree. The "thaw" that had started after Stalin's death had continued. We saw more and more that our dread suspicions about existing conditions had been true.

We had always known about the Iron Curtain and had heard stories about people having exploded on mines or having been electrocuted on barbed wire fences while trying to escape, but now we read in the newspaper that the "technical Iron Curtain" would be removed. Hungary was going to show the West that nobody wanted to escape from our earthly paradise.

What we knew, but the world did not, was that there was no way to get close to the border. One day we happened to be at Mother's when Uncle Charles came home. He was unusually pale. "Come with me." He motioned us into Grandfather's room. "Today I had to identify a woman from her dental work. She was a patient of ours at the University Hospital a while back. She lived in a city near the border. It is better that I don't tell you any names. She lived there with her husband and she was pregnant. One day she was taken to the police. They accused her of trying to escape. She told them that she had no intentions of doing so. They did not believe her. For days on end this went on. Finally, she became so irritated in her condition that she screamed at them, 'Yes, you stupid fools, I want to leave here. I don't want to be treated this way. I should be damned if I would want to give birth in a country like this.' She then was beaten until they beat the child out of her, stillborn, and she too died. Now, months later, her husband found out, found her body, and the police have magnanimously permitted him to bury it. They could not find any trace of the child."

Under these conditions hardly anybody would want to go near the border. Besides, the area within some 30 miles of it was divided into sectors, each had a number and those living in a sector or authorized to stay in that sector had a special stamp stamped onto the last page of their certificates of identity, showing the number of the specific zone. Of course the sectors within six miles were never authorized for nonresidents and the so-called half-mile sectors were reserved for border guards and security forces only, and for some special people like a few foresters, civil engineers, etc.

Anyway, it was obvious that the government would be able to show off to the West that nobody would want to leave Hungary. It was also a nice gesture towards the new, neutral and independent Austrian government. How we all longed for the day when finally the Soviets would leave Hungary!

The children stayed in Ábrahámhegy with John's parents for two weeks and we enjoyed the privacy in our little home. On a delightful Sunday afternoon we went to the five o'clock Mass in the little chapel on the hill across the street. Coming down from there, I suddenly let out a cry. "Pista!" The man who took big steps in front of us as he hurried down the hill, turned. It was he! He ran back as soon as he recognized us. "Am I glad to see you!" "Oh, Pista," I gasped and we all hugged and kissed. "Come home with us. Look, see that little house? That's where we live now!"

"Hey, you are not in uniform anymore?" John asked.

"No, thank God, I'm back in Budapest and I have been re-admitted to the university. I am writing a book with one of my professors. I'm rather lucky, I would say."

I could see that he was bursting to tell us something. As soon as we were inside and well separated from others' ears, his eyes glowed with that old sparkle under his gold-rimmed glasses. "Have you watched the Literary Journal's crusade to make the Soviets leave Hungary?"

"No, we hardly ever read the Literary Journal. We did not know that it was worth exploring. Nowadays most papers serve the government," said John.

"Well, the writers are very, very clever. They argue that our Constitution and all the principles the Communists claim that they believe in should be kept to the letter. We should be better Communists and allow freedom of criticism, freedom of the press and of religion. But everything is said in such a way that only talented writers can express. No Communist can disclaim its validity. And you should come to their meetings! They are out of this world! I can hardly wait from one meeting to another."

"Pista, that is all so exciting!" I exclaimed.

"Do you think there will be some positive results?" John asked.

"If we could just make the Soviets leave, everything would turn out all right." Pista was so excited he could hardly contain himself. His optimism reached its peak. I had never seen him like that before. "It will work, it must work! Now or never! We are within our legal rights to demand that.

They cannot condemn us for wanting to become better Communists," he added sarcastically.

"Stay for dinner," I invited him.

"Thank you. I will. I am really happy to have found you again. I was going to look you up soon. I only got back to the capital about a month ago when I had left the Army Work Force. Apparently I must have given a good performance because they recommended that I go back to the university. What have you been up to?"

John told him about Dr. Benedikt. I too had news to share. I had been admitted to the evening school of the Technical University, and I was also going to attend morning classes because I was going to transfer to the morning as soon as possible.

"How about the children?" Pista asked.

"They will come with us every morning to the University Nursery School. Both of them were admitted. The youngest one will stay home with the neighbors as soon as it is born. Until then…" I started laughing. We all joked while I prepared our dinner of dumplings with eggs. We had four eggs and luckily most of our bread was left from the day, so we could share it with Pista. I even made salad from tomatoes and green peppers and we had grapes from Ábrahámhegy. Quite a feast!

"Come, Pista, let's go over next door to the tavern and fetch ourselves a little beer." John grabbed a pitcher, and the two went out into the warm evening to the tune of the accordion from the garden of the inn next door.

They were soon back and John poured me a glass of foam, my favorite part. It was nice to live so close to the source, I could always skim off the fresh bubbles before the others emptied the beer. I could never understand why they didn't care for the best part.

We sat there late into the night as we discussed possibilities and probabilities and planned for a future without the Soviets. Then Pista left. I'll never forget his glowing eyes as he said, "Finally we have hope."

---

It was the most beautiful weekend of the summer. We went to pick up the children who were overjoyed to see us again. They both wanted to put their little hands on my stomach to feel the baby kick. Then they wanted to tell us about everything they had done during the two marvelous weeks with their grandparents who gave themselves completely to their grandchildren during those days.

We enjoyed once more the golden blue water of the lake, the warm breeze, the invigorating walks, bike rides and swims. Sunday afternoon the whole family went to pick berries together. Ilike's dainty figure moved gracefully around the bushes as she picked out the juiciest fruits of the crop. She must have learned something during those two weeks. She ran ahead and then back to her grandmother, whose hand she held as if she never wanted to let go. Jancsi walked hand in hand with his grandfather, and tried to keep up with the older ones.

John's father loved to take long walks and listen to foreign radio stations. The magic of the voices coming from all over the world kept him well informed. To listen to his commentaries was a sheer delight even to the most learned person. Love radiated from his personality, from his subtle blue eyes. His beard and hair surrounded his face like a halo.

As we were coming down from the hills he explained to John, "Now or never! Pista was right. The Soviets are supposed to leave. As a matter of fact they should have left the country already. Any day now we'll be free. The English-speaking people will triumph in the end."

We listened patiently although we were a bit skeptical. True, he had predicted at the start of the Second World War that, though against great odds, the Allies would win. Maybe he would be right again.

Grandmother seemed to have a marvelous time teaching Ilike about the wonders of nature. I loved to see them together in deep conversation. She enjoyed children at the age when they begin to understand more about everything around them.

We had our last meal of the summer together. After the early dinner we boarded the train.

We stood at the window and waved to John's parents as long as we could see them, the sun-burned, white-haired, loving causes of my husband's existence who had given him up for me and for his new family. They smiled at our happiness and held hands as they waved back.

That evening we looked back onto Ábrahámhegy for as long as we could see it. We searched out all the places where we had ever been, and pointed them out to our children.

Something inside me whispered that we were seeing these landscapes for the last time. When the train took the turn around the bay and we faced a different view, we both broke into an unexplainable sob.

# 51

The alarm clock went off with its disagreeable buzz. I stretched into John's arms and kisses before I realized why we had to get up at this ungodly hour. It was the first day of school for me. My whole being was filled with excitement as I kissed the children awake and helped them overcome the grouchiness of the morning. I hurried through the bathroom routine in the ice-cold water that refreshed me from top to bottom yet I hated it with a passion. Then a quick breakfast of very weak tea with sugar and a slice of bread with butter and jam for the children. John was changing Jancsi while I combed Ilike's hair. We both worked, hardly exchanging words. Then we gave each other a big kiss and hugged the children before we walked them to the end station of the streetcar. We boarded in time to get good seats.

"I am so excited," I beamed at John. "Do you think…" I asked while I lifted Ilike on my lap. He didn't let me finish the sentence.

"Yes, I think you will do fine; you will be the star student of your graduating class." John carried Jancsi in his arms and let him stand on the seat once he sat down.

I laughed. "I'll be satisfied if I pass what with three children and all. Why do we believe that we can do it?"

"Because we have to if we want the best for our children," said John. There was a special glow in his eyes. We both hoped against hope.

Jancsi was preoccupied with all the sights as they appeared, then disappeared, through the windows of the streetcar. Ilike was more accustomed to them, but she was just as interested because she saw more in every picture due to her experience.

We transferred to the next streetcar and looked at our watches to see how much time it would take every morning to get our family over to the university. The second streetcar took us down the quay of the Danube all the way to our destination.

I caught myself explaining to the children the way my grandmother used to explain to my sisters and me. "Look at the Parliament on the other side of the Danube. It has two houses like the British Parliament." I stopped, partly because the Hungarian Parliament no longer had two houses, partly because I realized that not even Ilike would understand more of my jabbering than the fact that the Parliament was over there and that she should look at it.

It was a spectacular trip on a gorgeous morning. The colorful leaves were falling in the autumn sunshine, and the rocks of the St. Gellért Hill shone white among the multi-colored bushes. St. Gellért's statue towered over one end of the city, while at the other, the "goddess of liberty" stood on the mountain, guarded by the bronze statue of a Soviet soldier.

"It will take us at least thirty minutes to get here every morning," John declared when we finally arrived at the University Nursery School where we dropped off Ilike. She received her attractive uniform and we helped her get dressed. She had no problems of adjustment whatsoever. She waved good-bye to us in the most natural way. She had had experience with the German teaching nursery school last year.

Jancsi was a different matter. He, too, received a clean set of clothes in which we dressed him. When it came to parting he did not say anything, but his face took on a sad look and he stared deep into our eyes as if to say, "Will you really leave me here? Why? What have I done?" He grabbed me and clung to me as never before. I explained to him in a soft voice that we would be back to pick him up, and I stood him at the window where he could watch after us. He stayed there and looked with the same sad eyes as before.

"He will get used to it and he will love playing with the children," said John as we left him. My heart turned very heavy all of a sudden. What was I doing? Leaving him? Yet I knew that in order to be able to be more with them in the future I had to leave him now.

John kissed me goodbye at the classroom door. I stepped inside the busy beehive, loud with the sounds of healthy young boys and girls. Boys and girls? My own expression struck me. How could I say that? I was barely older than they were! I'd had my twenty-second birthday September, 1956. My classmates were the graduating class. So what made me think about these freshmen as "children"? Oh, but they were so young. Some of them looked as if they had never shaved before. Others were older-looking, yet, I felt a big kick inside of me that brought me to my senses. I was only twenty-two, but I was a parent, a mother of almost three children, I was constantly associating with women ten years my senior because of John's friends. It was only natural that I looked at my new classmates and thought of them not as adults but as, "soon Jancsi will look like this blonde-haired boy in the front row."

"Are you a student?" one of my classmates asked me.

"Yes, I am."

"My name is Gábor. Do you want to sit with me?"

"Sure." I was happy that someone finally addressed me. I was so astonished at their age and at the new, strange atmosphere that it had not occurred to me to introduce myself.

"My sister is pregnant, too," he said, "just let me know if you need help with something. I know she has problems sometimes," he laughed good-heartedly.

"Thank you," I whispered back as the professor walked in and everybody quieted down. He was a Communist, the one who had questioned me at the entrance exam. He started his lecture in math. I copied studiously what he said but pretty soon I lost him, I continued to copy; John would explain.

The next class was in the basement of the university. Descriptive Geometry. This man was a much better teacher, but his subject did not appeal to me.

Mechanics. Professor Muttnyánszky, the same man who had taught John, was an excellent lecturer. I understood everything he said. Even when the class was over, I wished he would have kept on talking.

Gábor was a very nice boy and did not grow tired of me. Others joined us and I noticed that nobody cared that I was pregnant, although I did not see others in the class who were expecting. Most of the girls wore simple blouses and skirts, the boys wore coarse suits.

At lunchtime John and I met at the faculty mess hall in the basement of the university. The long wooden tables were covered with linoleum. Everybody got an aluminum dish and lined up. The server slopped a ladleful of that day's food into the dish, then we could sit on the low benches wherever we pleased. Yet, we felt distinguished because this slop was somewhat better, though more expensive, then the stuff the students received.

"How did it go?" John asked as soon as we settled down.

"Quite well, except for math. I didn't understand the professor at all."

John chuckled. "Isn't it lucky for him that he is such a good Communist?" Then he turned his voice to a whisper as he said, "He is a lousy mathematician. When his recent book appeared, one of the reviewers wrote, 'Despite the several hundred basic mistakes...' He went on from there; it was a sarcastic criticism. Yet, he is the professor of math, head of the department. Good Communist," John repeated. "Maybe in the evening section you'll get a better math teacher. If not, I'll explain."

"I want you to explain. You know that I always understood you best of all. Even in high school."

"I will, of course I will." He kissed me again, then it was back to classes.

After the last one I joined him at the department. Dr. Benedikt had had a book published in Moscow. He wanted that book translated into German, and I volunteered to help John with it. I would translate and John would put it into the technical German language. I worked on that until John was ready to go home, and we could pick up the little ones.

Jancsi waited for us at the window in the same position where we had left him. It seemed that he had never budged from his watch. The teachers assured us that he did, but they said that he really missed us and spent a lot of time at his post.

Ilike enjoyed her stay at the nursery school tremendously. They had stories and games. She was allowed to swing and climb at the playground. She liked everything about daycare and chattered to Jancsi in the streetcar.

I fell asleep holding Jancsi in my lap. John held Ilike. When we finally reached home we all worked to get dinner on the table in record time because I had to be back by seven o'clock for the evening section's lectures. Four days a week that would go on until, if ever, I would be allowed to transfer to the morning section.

What a difference in the students! In the evening I was the youngest. There were several pregnant women and even middle-aged men who wanted to get their degrees while working at their jobs.

The teachers were good and more practical than their morning counterparts. These students all had industrial experience and wanted the subjects to satisfy their curiosity. I lacked their work experience, but was more at home among them. Our worries and problems were more alike.

I patiently listened to the same lectures over again, and once again enjoyed mechanics most.

By the time I got home after ten o'clock, I was happy to be able to drop into bed. John asked, "Should I explain the math to you?" "Not today, thank you," I murmured. I knew that next day I would have to scribble on without having quite understood the first lecture. I had no trouble falling into a deep sleep.

The next day the alarm rang at the same terrible hour. I buried my head into John's arms. I did not want to get up but made myself do it. The morning was hectic. I kissed the children's soft, warm sleepy red faces into the cruelty of the morning. They didn't feel like opening their eyes either.

Jancsika ate slowly. Somehow he didn't want to get going. I didn't blame him, and I felt guilty. His sad eyes staring after us at that window yesterday still haunted me.

"Where is the brush?" I screamed at Ilike. She looked back with astonished eyes, still blurred and fuzzy from sleep. She seemed to ask, "How should I know?" while she pulled on her sweater.

I threw my clothes on and found the brush right beside me under my nightgown.

The tea burned my mouth. John helped and soothed over the problems. He was the one who could keep his head in this helter-skelter; he had one goal in mind and it had to be accomplished for the good of the family. He made himself wake up properly and did everything in his power to get us to the streetcar in time.

Finally we got into a routine at home and at school as well. I experimented with teachers and went to selected classes from both sections. I hoped to be able to transfer by the end of the semester. Judy came over every second day to cook and clean. John caught me at times when I was awake to help me with math. His colleagues in the department were also very helpful after classes.

Jancsi still looked at us with the same sad expression when we left him, but he did not complain or make any fuss. We wished he were older and in the nursery school with Ilike; it looked like a much happier place.

In about a month's time we got so well accustomed to our new way of life that we decided to have a small party on a Saturday, the day following our wedding anniversary. We invited a few of our most intimate friends to celebrate with us. We bought two pounds of sugar wafers, the fashionable delicacy of those days which we served with strong espresso coffee that Father had sent us in his customary packages.

The discussion was spirited, though we tried to keep our voices down. One joke followed another. Most were connected with our common wish that the Soviets leave Hungary.

Others talked about the dreaded Stalin times.

"Did you hear this one?" asked Pista. Since he had re-discovered us he often came and told us about the latest developments at the Writer's Association or the Petőfi Club, a recent organization of intellectuals for freedom. When he saw our interest, he settled back and took a sip of his coffee. "Stalin asked Truman in Potsdam, 'Tell me, what is so great in your democracy that we cannot match?' Truman thought a minute and then said, 'May I give you an example. In America anybody can come to the White House lawn and yell at the top of his lungs, "Down with Truman, he is a murderer, long live Stalin" and nothing will happen to him.' 'What is so big about that?' replied Stalin. 'Anybody can come up to the Kremlin and yell, "Down with Truman, he is a murderer, long live Stalin." Nothing will happen to him either.'"

We all rolled with laughter in the small room as we sat around the plate of sugar wafers and sipped espresso coffee.

"What do you think about the exhuming of Lászlo Rajk's body?" somebody asked abruptly.

"How come you did not get used to the constant rewriting of history by now?" Pista asked, happy to be able to comment on one of his pet topics. "Just like in the book, 1984. Do you remember when Rajk was executed on October 15, 1949?"

"How can I forget?" John answered. "I was working at the factory. We were all absorbed in what we were doing, minding our own business when the party-secretary walked in and looked around searchingly in the room. He proceeded slowly, then went into the next room. A worker followed him with a tall stepladder. The party-secretary motioned towards the wall. The worker put down the ladder, climbed up and removed one of the pictures. When they left, I dared to look up and saw that Rajk's picture was missing. Only days before that we applauded his praise-worthy acts and greeted him as one of the heroes of Communism. Now he was a traitor, a non-person."

"His wife was pregnant at the time," I added. "She was a classmate of my mother in grade school. She was an orphan. An aunt brought her up. Most of the children did not care for her; but Mother was always nice to everyone, and they became friends. After her husband was executed she was taken to the Soviet Union where she gave birth. Now she has been brought back to be celebrated as the widow of the hero. How can we be sure about anything in a world like that?"

"Listen, you may not believe it, but Imre Nagy, our fallen ex-prime minister, was reinstated into the Party this very morning. Just be patient for a while, and our time will come. The Soviets will have to leave. You'll see." Pista beamed his optimistic smile while he stuffed a sugar wafer in his mouth. "Then we'll end this non-person nonsense."

John smiled, but his face betrayed skepticism. The others were divided in their outlooks, but they all hoped for the same, neutral independence for Hungary.

The lovely sunshine was marred by the chilly breeze on the morning of October 23, 1956, when we took the children to nursery school. It was a Tuesday, everything went as usual...until the nine o'clock lecture started. Just before the math professor opened his mouth a third year student appeared for an announcement. The lecturer waved at him to go ahead. Had he known what the announcement was he might have acted differently.

"Fellow students, at universities and in the factories across the country these sixteen points are being read today. We, the people of Hungary, have come to the conclusion that we must present our demands to the leaders of the country. We can no longer tolerate the Stalinist terrors that partially remain with us. We must work together for freedom."

He received a standing ovation. He waved showing that he wanted to go on. Finally the applause died down, and he continued to state our demands. First and foremost, the Soviet troops should leave Hungary and free elections should be held as soon as they left. The one party system should be abolished. He spoke about basic human rights: freedom of the press, of assembly and of religion. He pointed out the necessity of accurate accounting about the war reparations and many important changes that should be introduced in our everyday lives: economic, financial, educational and cultural. The sixteen points also demanded radical changes in the condition of workers, peasants and retired people.

Several times he was interrupted by wild applause. Each time he waved his arms indicating he had more to say. My cheeks burned with excitement.

"We are planning a march to the statue of General Bem for this afternoon to show our solidarity with the Polish people. Independence and neutrality is the desire of all Poles and Hungarians…"

An excited voice interrupted from the back of the classroom. "Remember those who gave their lives in the Poznan uprising last June?"

"You are right," the speaker went on, "and is there anyone who could better symbolize our solidarity with Poland than General Bem, a born Pole, one of the greatest figures of our own war of independence in 1848 against the Habsburgs? Make red, white and green rosettes with the coat-of-arms of those times and let the hammer and sickle never be seen again as the symbol of Hungary. Make many rosettes and give one to everybody you meet today. Hungary must stand united and so must the Poles, the Koreans, and the Vietnamese. Our quest transcends boundaries."

Applause continued even after he had left the room. We made rosettes of paper which we colored red, white and green, the colors of our national flag. In the middle we drew the traditional Hungarian coat-of-arms. The room was noisy with heated discussion of the events. In minutes we all had rosettes. Someone handed one to our Communist professor who, after a few unsuccessful tries, gave up his attempts to lecture. He was rather puzzled at what had happened, and did not dare to refuse the tiny paper bow. He put it on his lapel and left us to our fate.

"Gábor," I turned to my faithful classmate and companion, "can it really be true? Are we going to become free? Will the Soviets leave?"

He grinned from ear to ear. "They'll have to. Our demands are legitimate. The whole world will understand."

I thought of Father and the many other Hungarians I knew who had escaped to different parts of the world. Could they help us in any way?

"A committee went to the Ministry of the Interior to ask permission to demonstrate peacefully at the statue of General Bem." The rumor blew through the class of one hundred and fifty students.

"Will they allow it?"

"Why would they grant our demands?"

"Just demands, but who can make them do it?"

The class was like a disturbed beehive.

477

I could hardly wait to see John at lunchtime. By then most of the students had decided to assemble in the yard of the university. Quite a force, five thousand young men and women with one set goal in their minds, a demonstration at the statue of General Bem. The next step after that, who knew?

"John, do you know exactly what is going on?"

"It looks as if Pista's predictions may come true," he answered. "Dr. Benedikt asked me about this demonstration. He looked me in the eyes and searched for an answer. 'Is everything really that bad?' I answered him honestly, 'Yes,' and I even went further, 'and I would suggest that if you consider yourself a Hungarian, join us. Come with us to demonstrate'."

"What did he say? What did he do?"

"It looks now as if both he and the party-secretary are coming to the demonstration. Permission has been given."

A tremendous roar came from outside. We heard fragments of voices; the sounds became louder and louder along the corridor. Finally the message reached us. "The Government revoked the permission."

Several students yelled, "We'll go anyway!"

A strong voice overruled them. "We'll do no such thing. They shouldn't have anything to say against us. This is not a revolution. We'll demonstrate for our cause peacefully. Let's send another delegation."

"You go with them," we heard several voices.

In half an hour the demonstration was on again. The Communists did not dare oppose the growing crowd. They came in swarms from the other universities and from the factories; young people, who had been brought up by the Communists themselves. The oldest university students were ten years old when the Soviets occupied the country.

"Isn't it lucky for us that 'they' taught us how to hate and how to fight?" A classmate of mine giggled as she said that.

A young, excited assistant professor joined John and me. "Am I glad I came home from Moscow in time for this." He had returned in September, having finished his graduate studies. "I know very well what the problems are. It is the same in the Soviet Union. I saw very few people smile there in my long stay of three years. They go about their business in a constant gray, crabby mood except for the exhilarating times when they drown themselves in vodka, which is every time they can put their hands on some." He didn't wait for a reply but ran ahead to join a group of young students. He seemed to be their leader.

"He is the head resident at a dorm. They must be his 'sons.' I always thought he was an idealistic Communist. It's interesting to see him so excited about the demonstration," John said.

The crowd struck up an old Kossuth song as people pushed towards the university gates.

"Helen, let's pick up the children and take them over to Mother's house before we go to the statue of General Bem. We can catch up with the demonstrators if we go by streetcar."

Of course, I thought, we had to get them. We ran all the way to collect Ilike. We pinned a rosette on her and gave some to the teachers too. As we went over to get Jancsi, we handed one to every passerby. They proudly pinned them on their coats.

When we arrived at the nursery school, Jancsi was standing at the window as usual. Would this be his last time to have to cope with being left? Would anything change? We pinned a rosette on him too. He beamed up at us; I gave him a big hug. "We came early today. Isn't that nice? We'll go to Grandmother's house." "Grandmother's house," Jancsika repeated with joy.

On the streetcar an old lady accepted a rosette with a smile.

"What is happening?" she asked.

"We want to be free. The Soviets should leave! We have drawn up our demands, sixteen points we want the government to grant us," John answered.

Her face lit up. "Will I live long enough to see that?" She closed her eyes, her face took on a dreamy expression. "Wouldn't it be wonderful?" Then she opened her eyes again. "But I can't believe it. It is too good to be true. It would be so terrible to be disappointed again. So many times in my life…" she stopped. "We must hope. More power to you! We must work for the future," she said, looking at the children.

I practically burst into Mother's home. "Look," I showed her my rosette. "It's happening, it's finally happening."

"Is it true?" she asked in a worried tone. "How can it be? There are two hundred million of them and only ten million of us. How can any good come from that?" She had to fend off the children who nearly knocked her off her feet.

"We are not fighting. The whole world will be on our side, you'll see," I explained as my cheeks began to burn. "The Communists taught us their techniques, and now we are using them. We demand in the name of communism that they should exercise self criticism and grant us our rightful demands. The Soviets should have left a long time ago according to international agreements! Yet they are still here. They should account for what they take! We want more than one political party! I myself learned at school that the Constitution assures us freedom of expression and religion, but… Anyway, they will have to do something when they see that the whole country is standing up to be counted as one. The whole world must understand! Here is the chance to make the whole Soviet Union fall into its tiny, nationalistic pieces. If Hungary wins its independence, the other oppressed countries will follow."

Mother smiled at my tirade and shook her head.

"Just watch what you are doing. Remember, we're 'insects.' We'll have to take the consequences of these events; we'll be the scapegoats."

"But I don't want to go on living like this." I stopped when I said that. Was it true? Yes, pregnant and already being the mother of two, in a happy marriage, I said that, I realized I'd rather die than go on living and bringing up my children at the mercy of the government.

# 52

Having deposited the children at Mother's, we hurried towards the quay of the Danube. We wanted to approach the statue of General Bem from the Pest side and hoped that we could save time by going along the shorter route by streetcar. However, as we saw no streetcars around, we started to walk as fast as we could. Soon we noticed people streaming across the Margaret Bridge towards Pest.

"The Parliament!" John exclaimed. "They must be going to the Parliament! Let's hurry."

We would have to pass the Parliament building anyway to reach the Margaret Bridge, but we never made it there. John was right; while we were still blocks away from the Parliament, we could hear the sounds of old Kossuth songs from the days of the 1848 revolution. The square in front of the building was huge, big enough to accommodate at least a hundred thousand people, or more. Excited talk, gesticulating people, happy faces betrayed the anticipation of the crowd.

"They recited poems at the Bem Statue," I overheard one couple as we passed them. We did not want to stop to ask what else they knew; we wanted to get where the action was. I thought of the poem that started the 1848 uprising, the one every child learned in grade school, "The National Song"! I was sure that they had repeated its refrain several times today not only at the Bem statue but all over the country. Its words were as appropriate today as they were when Petőfi, Hungary's most famous poet, wrote them.

> *Magyars rise! Your country calls you!*
> *Now or never. Time enthralls you.*
> *Shall we live as slaves or freemen?*
> *These the questions. Choose between them!*
> *By the God of every Magyar*
> *Do we swear.*
> *Do we swear the tyrant's handcuffs*
> *Not to bear!*

We reached the thick of the crowd and pushed ahead. The Parliament building was dazzling in its old-fashioned beauty, but the view was spoiled by the flags bearing the Communist Hungarian coat of arms with the hammer and sickle. I turned my head when I saw them and stared instead at the people. Where did they come from so suddenly? Most of them were young, the new generation brought up according to Communist dogma.

Among the groups of students I saw typical Hungarian workers in their work clothes. They apparently had left the machines to take part in the demonstration. There were fewer peasants, only some who had come to town on business. The sixteen points were just now being read in the cooperatives and the villages. They would probably join us soon. There were old ladies with kerchiefs on their head, office workers in their customary raincoats and young couples arm in arm. Some older children who were tall enough to see, along with the adults, stretched their necks and stood on their tiptoes. I didn't see any little ones. I suppose their parents had realized as we had that it would be dangerous for them in this crowd. Everybody talked and gesticulated until finally with the strength of a tidal wave one sentence seemed to emerge.

"Imre Nagy! Imre Nagy! We want Imre Nagy!" The crowd chanted and the whole square echoed from the voices of the close to a quarter million people who had managed to squeeze into the space for half as many. Some started climbing the lampposts while others could not push their way out of the surrounding streets. John looked at me.

"Are you all right?"

"Oh, yes." I didn't notice anything in my excitement.

"Helen, we'll soon have to go. I'm worried. I don't want them to push you."

"Let's just stay a little longer. Do you think Imre Nagy will come and talk?"

"Someone else is talking now," John reported. He could see well above everybody's head. It paid to be six foot five.

"Look, look, Helen," he shouted with excitement. "Look at the flags!"

I saw different flags fly above the heads of the people: Korean, Chinese, North Vietnamese, and especially Polish. The international students, studying in Hungary, all came under their national flags to show their solidarity with our cause.

A red, white and green flag appeared… then another… and another. There were no traditional (Kossuth) coats of arms on them but no hammer and sickle either. A huge hole was in the middle of every one of them in less than five minutes after people had noticed the first such symbol of dissent. Pocket knives and scissors cut and tore at the emblems of communism as if to remove them from the flesh of our suffering country.

I cried and laughed at the same time.

"Imre Nagy, Imre Nagy, we want Imre Nagy!"

He finally appeared on one of the balconies of the Parliament and said a few words to the crowd. Naturally we could not hear him. It was enough to know that he was talking.

"Helen, we must go. The crowd is getting too tight for comfort. Remember, you are going to have a baby within a month." John took my hand and pulled me towards the street that seemed the safest. "Come, we must take the children home." I obeyed with reluctance.

What a glorious feeling! We would be free! Even the baby sent happy Morse codes through his kicking.

But to Mother I shouted the news, "Imre Nagy was speaking, we are gaining ground. We always said that this could not go on for long. Now it is happening, and you don't believe it can be done?"

"I wish," Mother said with mixed feelings. Some hope still must have surged in her because her cheeks colored as she asked, "You really believe in this?"

"I do, I do!" I jumped up and down, unlikely as it may seem considering my condition. "Oh, I'm so excited. Finally those good days I have dreamed about since I was a little child will come and we'll be able to talk and think and do what we want. Oh, Mother!" I hugged her, and then I hugged Grandfather and the children.

"And you won't have to go to nursery school any more," I told Jancsi, whose eyes lit up.

"No more, no more," he repeated after me. "Ilike, no more nursery school!" he yelled to his sister.

Ilike looked from one to another. Her father hugged her and finally she understood that something joyous was taking place although she was not so enthusiastic about leaving nursery school.

"Helen, we must go!" John urged me as the city enveloped into the darkness of the night, and we heard sounds of a crowd approaching. "What is happening? Look, we must get home before the buses and streetcars stop running! It is awfully far to walk from here. We couldn't do it with the children."

Once on the street we found out what the sounds were all about. The crowd at the Parliament had apparently decided to march over to the Radio Station. Hungary had only two official radio stations, both government-owned and machine gun protected. Everything was taped that went on the air. A committee now entered the building to negotiate about broadcasting the sixteen points. People flooded the two-lane street in front of the baroque building of the Radio Station. As we jumped onto the bus the crowd surrounded us, "Where are you going? Join us! Come to the Radio Station."

"I would," the bus driver replied, "but I am on duty. I have to take this bus to the depot. I'll join you later." Several people got off the bus and went with the demonstrators.

"I would love to go with you," John told them, "but we have to take our children home first."

Later on we learned that this bus was the last one that went to Óbuda.

"Do you think 'they' will broadcast our demands?" I asked John.

"I hope so," John said.

"Goddamn those Soviets," an old man in worn clothes spoke to himself. "They better leave now, or else…"

I let my thoughts wander on these words. What 'else' could we possibly do? From Pista I knew that no revolution was being organized, that the dissenters had no guns, only their pens and ideas. Besides, Mother was perfectly right about the overwhelming Soviet force present. At the time I did not know yet that Ernő Gerő's government, the Communist government still in power, had asked the Soviet Armed Forces to intervene, to help put down a non-existent revolution.

When we arrived home I started to undress the children, while we switched on the radio. No trace of the sixteen points, no reports about the demonstration right in front of the Radio Station. We switched to the BBC in London. Music. The house began to shake. Was it an earthquake? It couldn't have been because the rambling went on and on, and it sounded like an endless rattle of engines.

The phone rang; I peeked out through the window.

"Tanks," I screamed. "John, tanks are going towards the city!" John first peeked then ran outside while he shouted back to me. "It's all right. They are Hungarian tanks with their turrets backwards. That means they are friendly. At least they are not ordered to shoot instantly."

"Watch yourself!" I shouted after him while I answered the phone.

It was Mother. "I don't have any time to talk but I wanted you to know. Pista was here. He ran over from the Radio Station and wanted me to alert all our friends, whoever you can think of. You can help me. The Committee did not get a chance to broadcast the points. They were probably arrested. Instead a sub-machine gun volley was fired into the crowd packed tightly in that narrow street. It seemed that besides the two guards at the gate, security policemen were shooting from the rooftops. The crowd reciprocated by throwing bricks at the two guards, then snatched their machine guns and started shooting back. Then a few, including Pista, ran to the armory close by. The Hungarian soldiers guarding the armory understood the situation and handed out ammunition and guns, anything the people wanted. The crowd dispersed as fast as it could, yet there were quite a few casualties, including the two guards who met their death within a minute after they had fired their first shot."

"Mother, don't hang up," I interrupted her. "There are Hungarian tanks rolling into Budapest from the direction of Vienna. If you wait a minute… anyway they have their turrets backwards. John ran out to talk with them if he could."

"Do what you can, I have to keep calling," Mother said.

Apparently she no longer worried about being an "insect," having to accept the responsibilities for the consequences, about the overwhelming power of the Soviets, about being overheard on the telephone. She was helping the cause.

John came back. "Many people of the neighborhood are outside shouting up to the soldiers in the tanks, 'Don't shoot! We want the Soviets to leave! We, the people, the students, workers and peasants are in the streets. Don't shoot your brothers!' They are yelling back at us, smiling, 'Don't worry, we know where to shoot.' Helen, the revolution is on! And the Army is on our side!"

# 53

"The night of October 23, 1956!" We, the young people, had grabbed the opportunity to act and had taken our fate into our own hands. This was our revolution! The generation brought up by the Communists had turned against them. I jumped out of bed to switch on the radio. I wished someone would call. Everybody was still asleep. I heard no shooting. I peeked out the window. No tanks and not a soul outside. Everything looked as usual. The two little cribs standing side by side with our two children, dreaming their dreams. What is their life going to be like? What is in store for the generation that comes after ours? The baby kicked inside my womb.

I tiptoed out into the other room and called Mother.

"Do you have any news?" I inquired.

"Do you remember the big bronze statue in the Városliget?" she asked.

There were, in fact, many statues in the Városliget, the place where we used to go skating, but…my heart started beating faster. Since the days when the Communists had come into power we talked very carefully even on the phone, I realized that there was only one statue she could have meant. A large parish church, the Regnum Marianum, was torn down by the Communists to make room for a hideous, giant statue of Stalin.

"It was pulled down yesterday by the students and they hammered it to pieces. I have a piece of it."

"That's great," I declared calmly, though my heart was pounding. I could hardly keep from screaming, "Other news?" I must not betray myself. Maybe someone was listening.

"Shooting all night in the city. Not in our street, but we can still hear it. People go about their business as usual despite the shots."

"Complete quiet here."

"We have Soviet tanks in front of us."

That did not sound very good.

"Are they shooting?"

"No, I don't know where the shooting is coming from; I hear it only now and then."

"Call me if you have news." I heard Ilike climbing out of her crib. I hurried in to stop her from waking up her little brother.

John was stretching and yawning in bed. I gave him the news. Ilike listened and looked at John and me. "Are we going to nursery school today?" She sensed that something was different.

"No, not today. I don't think it would be very safe to go to the university."

"I have to go to my jobs to see what is going on," said John.

"Please, avoid the places where there is fighting."

"I'll call the factory and the university before I go."

"John, remember, during the siege we had no telephone. Yet now all the phones seem to be working. How come?"

"Don't talk about the devil..." He jumped out of bed and dressed.

I put on one of my two maternity dresses and boiled water for our customary weak tea (one bag to a whole kettle) and the barley coffee for the children which they drank with milk and sugar. I wasn't going to risk going to classes today. Besides, I seriously doubted that there would be classes.

Just then the radio announced that dastardly revolutionary troops were fighting all over the city and the Gerö (communist) government had asked the Soviet troops to come to the aid of the Hungarian people in accordance with the Warsaw Pact. The Minister of the Interior ordered a curfew until one o'clock p.m.

"The bastards!" I had never heard John curse before.

Shots could be heard from outside.

"Let's roll down the shutters. I think we'd better stay in the inside room. We'll have more protection if shooting comes from the street," John suggested.

The children were very quiet, but Jancsi was on the verge of crying.

"Come, I'll give you some bread with jam." I coaxed them to come to the kitchen; that was the room farthest from the street.

As I fixed their meal it struck me that as usual we had no more than one day's supply of bread, sugar, and flour in the house. We had a good supply of preserves, which every housewife in Hungary made herself, some staple foods like beans and dried peas but not much else. Authorities had stopped housewives from "hoarding" food (stocking up for three or four days), by executing a few of them. They were accused by the press of "causing famine" by building up unneeded stockpiles of food in their homes. Most of those shot were "insects" anyway, no great loss to society. The rest of the women had learned their lesson. What an ingenious method to keep people from revolting! What were we going to eat if this situation kept on for days or weeks? It would take only a short time to starve the population into submission.

The radio repeated again the promise of amnesty to all the fighters who would put down their arms by one o'clock p.m. Imre Nagy succeeds Ernö Gerö as prime minister. He speaks to the nation. But the fights still go on. Zoltán Tildy, the first President of the Republic after World War Two, also goes on the air. Fighting continues. We listen to the British Broadcasting Corporation, to Radio Free Europe, to the Voice of America, to the local radio station. Shots outside.

Finally, I call Mother. There, too, shooting, more than here. She does not know any more, either. She says everybody seems to side with the revolution; young and old, even most of the Communists agree that the Soviets should leave. Hungary, for the first time since I can remember seems united in this one cause, "Soviets, go home!"

I couldn't stand the idleness. We kept the radio on and I started mending the children's clothes while I watched them play quietly. John read a book to them; I did not want him to go out. I was afraid. I needed his presence. Who is fighting and where? I thought of Pista. I remembered the assistant professor who had just returned from Moscow, an idealistic Communist. As the leader of his dorm, he, too, must have been fighting. I thought of my classmates, past and present. How many of them were still alive?

The conflicting news over the radio made one thing clear. Something held back our prime minister. The way he talked was not what was expected of him. Gerö, the ousted prime minister, was still the head of the Party; he held the job of First Party Secretary. Could Imre Nagy act freely while he was under the control of this man? If we were truly granted our demands, why did the fighting go on? Why didn't Imre Nagy do something besides becoming prime minister? Why his ambivalence?

Mother called. Pista's friend was there. She fed him. He was dead tired. He said that fights were very heavy around the Grand Boulevard, the Kilian Barracks.

Good old Pista! I knew I would hear from him and that he would be in the thick of the fighting.

Amnesty was announced again and again over the radio for all freedom fighters who surrendered, including those who belonged to the Armed Forces. Hurray! That meant that the Armed Forces were on our side.

When night came, we were still cooped up in the small room, mending clothes and listening to the radio. We couldn't make heads or tails out of the whole garbled mess. The curfew was extended and darkness swallowed the daylight. We listened until exhaustion claimed us. We did not go back to our bedroom. We dragged the cribs over to the small room and made our bed on the sofa. As we dozed off we could hear shots here and there from the distance. My grandmother's menacing "tomorrow" re-entered our lives. We prayed and I thought again as I did so often when I was a little girl, "Maybe there is no tomorrow for us." Yet, a deep, happy peace surrounded me; I knew I was in God's hands.

October 25. We woke up to the crackling of gunfire and immediately switched on the radio. The same garbled nonsense as yesterday. From the foreign radio stations we learned that the fights were still going on, the Soviets were not about to leave, and that Imre Nagy seemingly was a puppet in Gerö's hands just as we thought from what we had heard over the radio yesterday. Whatever Imre Nagy said could not be his ideas.

"Helen, we don't have an air raid shelter in this house. I'll go over to Judy's house. It has a cellar we might use. Also I'll try to get some bread or whatever I can. Obviously nobody is working at the university; the students are too busy fighting."

"Be careful!" I begged him as he dressed quickly.

He was back soon. "There is a bakery on the corner and I could get bread from them. I learned that if we cannot go out on the streets it is possible to climb across the fences of backyards and get there. Judy was more than happy to have us for the day. So we'll wait until the fire is distant and we'll run over. It's only two houses away."

We dressed the children silently, packed food and the most important items. I took my mending with me. It proved to be an excellent tranquilizer.

As soon as we reached our gate we yelled at the children, "Hurry! Run as fast as you can!" It did not take us a minute to reach Judy's house and we all ran down to the cellar.

Jancsika shouted up to Judy's dog on the second floor—a huge German Shepherd—whom he dearly loved, "Villám!" The dog barked back at him.

"Not now, Jancsika, you can't play with him now. You have to stay inside!" Judy pulled him back from the door just as we heard a round of machine-gun fire.

We became very quiet. The shooting went on for a while. Then we listened to the radio Judy brought down from her apartment. The same news, the fighting goes on.

Late afternoon a neighbor, a thirtyish, blond, white-faced accountant, stumbled in the door. He was a young father. "You wouldn't believe what I have just come from. I can't believe that it was really happening. I can't." Tears trickled down his face.

"What's the matter? Is your family all right?"

"Yes, but I...I didn't think I would survive. Only a few hours ago, I didn't mean to fight. Yet...I couldn't stand it any longer. I had to know what was happening." He combed back his hair with trembling fingers. "I went out and started walking towards Pest. I thought I'd look around very carefully.

Whenever I heard shots, I jumped into a doorway or behind a wall. I found myself at the Parliament. Women and children were coming with flowers in their hands. Like the waves of the sea they came from the surrounding streets. Unarmed demonstrators: only a few men, mostly women and children. A little girl…just like mine, a year and a half, walking, marching." He buried his face in his hands. "They were singing, carrying signs that read 'Soviets, go home!'…flags. But most of them just carried flowers. Then a volley of submachine-gun fire. The little girl on the ground, in a pool of blood, the flowers scattered around her. Her mother sobbing over the dead body, a flood of blood… Something screamed in me. A Soviet soldier beside a tank, who previously smiled at the signs demanding that the Soviets should leave, pushed his own gun in my hand and pointed at the rooftops, 'Shoot those bastards! We have to protect the children!' I automatically pressed the trigger. On the roof of a house one man fell, only to be replaced by another. They were our own security police. I don't know what happened to me. I went wild and shot like a blood-thirsty savage until I ran out of ammunition. The Russian beside me worked his submachine gun. He threw me more ammo. I haven't done any shooting since my boot camp days, but it all came back. The Russian was right; we had to defend the children. Finally the crowd began to push towards the Parliament. A door opened on the side and someone pulled us in. People streamed inside the building's protective thick walls while ambulances shrieked and doctors and hospital personnel ran back and forth with stretchers. They, too, were shot. A white-coated figure ran doubled over towards the bushes and fell. That was the last thing I saw. Everything was over for me; I was inside the building. After a while the guns stopped. The security police had had their fill of innocent blood."

"What is going on here?" I heard myself say. "Why doesn't the world do something? What good is the United Nations if they cannot act at a time like this? Can't everybody see what is happening? We, all the nations under oppression, want out, want to be free. All of Hungary, even the Communists, demand that the Soviets leave. The Russians themselves seem to understand if what we heard was true. It was a Russian soldier who handed you the gun?"

"Yes," the young man said. "I did not mean to fight until I saw that pretty little girl torn to pieces by a machine gun! She looked just like mine. Flowers in her hand…" he kept repeating. "But I saw more. Much more. I saw people in the streets who got hold of security policemen and clobbered them to death, hanged them, tore them to pieces. A few were spared because the crowd realized that violence only breeds more violence. However, after that scene in front of the Parliament I could understand them, I could understand the rage that would lead people to claw the security policemen to pieces."

"I heard rumors about big fighting going on near the Kilián Barracks." His misery was so deep that for a moment he could not speak. Then he went on. "A certain Colonel Pál Maléter was sent there with his troops and tanks to attack the revolutionaries. When he saw what was going on, he joined them. Now the government is trying in vain to fight him. I heard that he has twelve hundred people with him—a few soldiers, mostly students, workers, some ex-party members, and youngsters trained in paramilitary techniques at schools. On one corner the whole building is torn to pieces although its walls are three feet thick. Yet, they don't give up."

The radio interrupted his tale by asking the freedom fighters again to stop fighting.

"I saw barricades being built by children six to eight years of age," he continued. "At least they did not look any older. I realized that I was in the thick of the fighting and desperately tried to get out. I saw someone with a Molotov cocktail. I recognized it right away, a bottle filled with kerosene and a rag stuffed into it through the cork. I pulled into a doorway and watched him. I noticed how young his face looked. Above the big coat I saw his determined features, those of a sixteen-year-old boy. Suddenly a tank appeared at the turn of the street with turret forward: enemy. A teenaged girl materialized from nowhere and started to parade in front of the tank, attracting attention. The tank turned slowly towards her, aiming. In a split second the boy ignited his bomb and threw it into the opening of the tank. A burning human torch tried to climb out and was shot by some teenagers. The tank burned inside; the huge monster became completely disarmed and useless. The freedom fighters disappeared. I could hardly believe my eyes." He wiped his forehead with his sleeve.

The radio came on again with new messages. Comrade Gerö was relieved from his post of First Party Secretary to be succeeded by János Kádár, who himself had suffered much in a Communist prison. Rumor had it that security policemen had urinated in his mouth while he was tortured.

We all hugged and kissed and screamed. Imre Nagy spoke, then some writers. We felt that this last news meant something good. Yet, it was still not full victory.

We scanned the radio stations. Suddenly a new voice came on the air, "Radio Free Miskolc." This station claimed that we were being betrayed and that we should not stop fighting. What was going on?

# 54

The next few days did not bring answers. Conflicting news arrived with every passing hour. No matter what changes took place in the government; the Soviet presence still compelled the freedom fighters to go on with their attacks. Soon the radio announced martial law, anyone caught with arms in hand would be executed on the spot. That did not sound like a free government. Free radio stations from abroad and also from some parts of Hungary talked about an increasing, rather than a decreasing, Soviet presence and that fighting was stronger than ever. Yet around our neighborhood there was hardly any shooting. We moved back to our small room, keeping away from the street; but we did not have to stay in the cellar all the time. The air was pregnant with expectations; I listened to the radio and mended the children's clothing when there was nothing else to do.

Finally, on the 28th of October, the United Nations Security Council gathered to discuss the matter of Hungary. Judy and her husband, Joe, ran over to celebrate. We cried while toasting each other with what remained of the liqueur Father had sent. Our happiness was even greater when, in the afternoon, the prime minister, Imre Nagy, declared that a new police force would be organized and that the dreaded security police (AVO) would be disbanded. That sounded much more like our original demands.

The next day, Imre Nagy came on the air and revealed the cause of his previous ambivalence. He too had been a prisoner of pro-Soviet elements; everything was dictated to him so that he had been unable to execute his own ideas. As a result of the ongoing revolution, he was now accorded complete power. He was forming a new government; and as soon as the Minister of Defense was named, he would start negotiations with the Soviets on immediate withdrawal of their troops. The AVO no longer existed.

We cried and kissed and decided to go over to my mother's in Pest to see what was happening. Judy agreed to watch the children.

Our first stop was at Dr. Imre Éber's home. He was the family doctor of John's family, the one whom they had saved from the Nazis in 1944. We asked him to recommend an obstetrician who would be closer than our own in case the baby came at a time when it was impossible to go to my doctor on the other side of the city.

"I know Dr. Mecseky well," Dr. Éber said. He called him at once. "He works in St. Margaret Hospital, only a ten-minute walk away from your home. He would be glad to deliver your baby. He would like to see you now if you could visit him."

Dr. Mecseky was a good-humored and kind middle-aged man. I trusted him immediately.

"I'm happy you did not wait until an emergency was at hand. This way we can get acquainted. With the curfew and no public transportation, I don't see how you could run over to Uzsoki utca. On foot it would take at least two hours even if you were not in labor. With the third child that would be a very unwise proposition. Yes, I'm happy that you came."

I was happy, too. As a matter of fact I felt like flying through the clean, crisp, sun-filled air all the way to Mother's house. The only thing that prevented me from flying was the heavy weight of my body.

"What will we do without diapers?" John wondered as we started out towards the Margaret Bridge, avoiding the quay of the Danube, because there we would have been exposed to potential danger.

"I used to swim across to Margaret Island here, after the war," John reminisced.

"You did? It is not allowed now."

"I don't know if it was allowed then either. I think it is partly because of pollution," said John. "Yes, the water is pretty dirty nowadays, but then… Nobody had an opportunity to take a bath, as you well remember. I used to enjoy the fresh water and I felt clean afterwards."

I spotted an infant and children's wear shop. "Look, John, there's a line. They must be selling something. I hope it's diapers."

"We don't have our rations for the diapers yet," John reminded me.

"Rations, well, you can't get those until you are a month away from your predicted date of birth," I lamented. "However, we could pay for the diapers and cash in the coupon for other clothes for the children later."

John began to laugh. "What are we talking about? We no longer have the old system, remember? We are free. Who needs rations?"

We approached the line. "What are you waiting for?"

"Apparently the store is open and there are some things for sale inside."

"Would you please ask if they have any diapers?" I approached a woman standing closest to the door.

"No, they don't," she sighed. She looked as pregnant as I was.

"What are we going to do?" I asked her.

"I heard that everything was used up for bandages, for the wounded," an old woman said from the back.

"Well then, I don't think we should stand around here. John, let's go and see what is happening in town."

We hurried towards the bridge. Mother's place was also at least an hour away and we had to return home while there was still daylight. Evening darkness brought with it the curfew of the revolution. Would there be a curfew today? Who knew what to expect?

The bridge was full of Soviet tanks that were parked along the curb. They did not bother anyone. The streetcars and buses were not operating. Pedestrians streamed from one side of the Danube to the other and the Russian soldiers climbed out from their tanks. They enjoyed the sunshine. Today nobody was in a fighting mood. After all, the Soviets were finally going to leave and the Russian soldiers had no quarrels with that. One of them stood patiently and listened to the translation of a request by the people for the Soviets to leave Hungary. Another one explained that he had listened to the Ukrainian broadcast of Radio Free Europe, and he understood perfectly what our revolution was all about. He was for it. Others were simply lazing around.

We enjoyed the breeze over the Danube, that good old river which once more had swallowed the blood of Hungarian freedom fighters and washed the shores clean. Yet the Danube's color did not change, it was still the bluish-gray it always had been.

No matter how friendly the soldiers seemed, and even though the tanks were unarmed, I did not feel secure around them and tried to double my steps. Once we had arrived on the Pest side the picture became quite different. On every corner a tank stood, turret aimed straight at the pedestrians. Big piles of bricks and ruins greeted us in front of every house: debris, rails of the streetcars torn out from the pavement, the remnants of barricades. There was a shot in one of the side streets.

"Run!" I heard John's voice. The main thoroughfares seemed safe but here and there we heard occasional shots.

The breeze brought sounds of singing and the voices of chanting people. We went towards the voices. A group of peacefully marching people approached on one of the main avenues as we crossed it.

"Remember the shooting at the women and children with the flowers?" John whispered, "Let's go!"

I was curious, but he was full of concern. He pulled me away from every place where something was going on.

All shop windows were broken, yet the merchandise was untouched. Signs were put in the windows, "We want to protect the purity of our revolution. We are not criminals. Do not touch the merchandise!"

In another place we saw a collection basket for the victims of the revolution. People were putting money into it. There was quite a heap. Yet nobody watched it, and not a soul took anything out.

A passerby remarked as he noticed us staring at the sign. "Yesterday I saw someone who tried to take a pair of shoes from one of the stores. He was severely beaten on the spot. Our revolution does not condone stealing," he added with pride.

"Look, John, there is a poster of the Smallholder's Party! They are back again!"

"Another one of the Social Democratic Party!" John pointed.

Someone handed us a leaflet. It was one of the first newspapers of the revolution, with the demands of the last couple of days in print.

Another shot from a nearby street made us speed up.

"Are you out of your minds?" Mother greeted us. "How did you get over here?"

"We walked," I smiled quietly.

"You walked? What if the baby had been born on the way? What if you had gotten into the fighting? What if…?"

Pista appeared from behind Mother.

"See what you did, you woke him up now," Mother said.

"I was up already. I have to go back to the Kilián Barracks. The fights are still going on there."

"The fights? Haven't you stopped fighting yet?" John asked. We were happy to see Pista alive.

"Not until the Soviets get out." He looked very serious. "But actually the fights are dying down."

"The Russian soldiers on the bridge are quite ready to leave," I reported.

"They are, eh?" Pista smiled. "Good for them, because they'll have to do it anyway, one way or another. It is just to their advantage if they go on their own. I've been in the Kilián Barracks ever since the revolution started. John, you know Iván, the assistant professor who just came back from Moscow, a 'fortress of communism,' one of the firsts of the 'new generation' of engineers? Well, he fought with me all the time. We were sitting together, firing through one of the windows. He told me that no matter how much he was for communism he wanted those 'bastards,' that was the word he used, to leave us, the Hungarians, alone. He wanted communism but only on the basis of free elections."

As always, Mother's house was filled with a collection of diverse people. Another person I did not expect to meet there was our old cleaning woman, who also used to work for us in the store when she was a young girl. She was very poor. Although a perfect subject for the Communists, she was never for them. "Oh, Helen, how good to see you! Why did you come out of the house? A pregnant woman should never go into dangerous places. Remember when I told you how I had a piece of shrapnel in my lungs during the siege and gave birth to a girl who died because I could not nurse her? You shouldn't, no, you shouldn't."

"Look, there is hardly any shooting outside. Practically none where we live, at least not today. I hadn't realized that fighting continued in Pest. Anyway, Mariska, I just could not take it any longer at home. I had to see what was happening. I am so excited."

"So is my husband," Mariska said. "He is a worker but he can't stand the Communists. He said it was a good thing that the revolution had started. But don't mind me, I talk too much. You know, the children at school? Now, yours aren't as old yet, but mine, I really had a problem explaining things to them. They said that the teacher told them that all people are equal. Then, one day a boy's father was taken by the secret police. Right away everybody shied away from him. The teacher explained that his father was no good. My son would come home and ask, 'How come he was no good if everybody is equal? Will there be a day when my father will be declared 'no good'? Oh, Helen, you are lucky that your children are so small."

"Helen, remember my friend, Lisa, the wife of the dean?" Mother asked.

"Sure, I remember. I used to play with her children. How could I forget? That was the only time that I was around a campfire; we roasted bacon over it and she made shish kabobs."

"Well, she just told me today, now, that Imre Nagy had taken over the government, and the breeze of freedom is in the air. A few years ago something extremely peculiar happened to her. It all came up because we were discussing the atrocities against security policemen. I'm afraid they get killed wherever they are caught."

"And they deserve it, too," Mariska interrupted Mother. "I'll go to the kitchen and fix you something to eat. Just talk with your mother now since you have walked so far just to be with her. You'll need your strength to get back home. What a daring thing to do!" She shook her head in consternation as she bustled out the door.

"Anyway, Helen," Mother continued, "Lisa said that she used to host a weekly bridge party. All were wives of heads of departments or deans. They had known each other for twenty years or so, since the days when their husbands were assistant professors. One day after the bridge party she found a small notebook. In the book all kinds of information was jotted down about all four of them; the jokes they told, the gossip about other faculty members. Every word was printed. These words could have put them into grave danger. She was wondering what to do with the notebook because she had no clue as to who had left it, and she did not want to embarrass anybody. She felt like burning it. That moment the doorbell rang and a security policeman stepped inside as soon as she had opened the door. 'Madam, you have found a notebook. Please, hand it to me. You are to continue your weekly card games with your jokes and gossips as if nothing has happened. We need this information and we cannot let our source dry up. Remember, you will be in serious trouble if there is the slightest leak.' The security policeman vanished. The whole thing seemed to her like a nightmare. She didn't know what else to do; she followed the instructions of the policeman."

I gasped and remembered the time when we had been asked to spy. "No one can be trusted anymore. Those ladies had known each other for decades. I would never have thought… yet, one can't even guess how they blackmailed that woman into doing it."

I heard someone coming. It was Elisabeth with her beau, Balázs. A few months before she had confided in me that she had a long talk with a very wonderful man and fell in love with him. She was sixteen and happy. She was excited. "Mother, down at the corner there is a truck that has canned milk and all sorts of goodies, cheese, and cereal. It says CARE on the side of the truck. Let's all go down."

"Let's," John agreed. We were very low on food by then. The truck indeed stood there. We received some staples we hadn't seen for years. By the time we got back we were as hungry as wolves. Mariska had fixed a good soup and we all dug in.

"I'm dead tired," declared Uncle Charles when he arrived home. He brought a big bag of flour and some rice. "A truck stood on the corner of the Museum Boulevard opposite to a burnt-out Soviet tank. Peasants brought food from the country to keep the revolution alive. They realized quickly that there wouldn't be any food in the capital city. They did not want the population to be starved into submission." He looked extremely worn, with big black circles around his eyes. "I decided to come home for a break. We have been operating practically nonstop since the beginning of the revolution. I wish we could save more of the wounded. I hate to see so many young people die, so very young, in their early teens. Mothers by the hundreds are looking for their children. Their faces become relieved when they don't find their sons and daughters among the wounded, but they start to worry again when they walk past the graves and the yet unburied dead bodies."

I looked out the window as he spoke. The park opposite Mother's home was full of fresh graves. It looked like the end of the Second World War all over again. Where once green grass stretched across the block, now small crosses stood: Tina, 14 years; Christopher, 16; Boy, age 11. Freedom fighters with weapons they could hardly carry but which nevertheless they had raised against those who had taught them how to fire a gun. Among the crosses children were laughing and playing, the next generation which was going to grow up free because of the sacrifices of many.

55

On our way home we saw the Soviet tanks leave the Margaret Bridge. The huge monsters moved very slowly among the pedestrians with turrets backwards.

On October 30th, Cardinal Mindszenty, the head of the Hungarian bishops, was freed from his prison along with many other prisoners. The officer who freed him was John's schoolmate from high school. Mindszenty's release meant that the government was definitely our government and that it was free. Mindszenty, our primate, had been jailed for so long by both the Nazis and the Communists that he had become a symbol of Hungarian freedom. The following day he arrived in Budapest and promised to make a major speech in a few days after he had some time to orient himself. He had spent the past eight years sealed from the outside world in a prison.

In the following days our dreams became reality. Pál Maléter, the hero of the Kilián Barracks, became Minister of Defense and Chief of Staff, and he started negotiations with the occupying forces. At one point the Hungarian Air Force was determined to bomb Soviet tanks if they did not immediately leave the country.

On November 1, Imre Nagy finally proclaimed Hungary neutral, and announced the country's withdrawal from the Warsaw Pact. He also asked the United Nations to put the Hungarian issue on its list of priorities. New parties were being organized, and their free newspapers appeared; Népakarat (People's Will) was the newspaper of the Free Hungarian Trade Unions; Szabad Szó (Free Word) was the Petöfi Party's newspaper. The latter party was called The National Peasant Party before the one-party system took over in 1948. The Communists too started to reorganize under the name Hungarian Socialist Workers' Party.

Pista called. "Soviet tanks are surrounding Hungarian airfields. I don't like it. They claim that they want to protect the 'evacuation' of the Soviets. Nobody would bother them if they wanted to evacuate. I don't like it."

"Pista, take care! Our country needs men like you. Don't be too aggressive," John warned him. It was delightful to be able to talk over the telephone without having to fear repercussions.

On the evening of November 1, All Saints' Day, small lights burned in every Hungarian window in remembrance of the heroes who had died for our freedom. The solidarity of the country was demonstrated in this one simple act. Every window blinked the light of hope into the dense darkness of the years our homeland had spent imprisoned. The chains were cut, but they were still dangling from our hands and feet. The Soviets were still a menacing presence, although we were assured that they must leave. Two thousand young people had paid for this with their lives.

John went to see what was going on in his department and also at the factory. He found his coworkers busy emptying the party-secretary's files. The infamous "cadre cards" were now discovered—complete files about every individual. Whatever got onto this card on the basis of hearsay, evidence, a mistaken phone call, or the words of a letter one wrote to one's own mother, could be used against that person if the time came to make him or her a "non-person."

John found his. "His father probably played a leading political role during the days of the Horthy regime," he read out loud. "That is complete nonsense," he addressed himself to Dr. Benedikt.

"That is not true?" His white face blushed under his snow-white hair. He looked worried and puzzled. His ideal, communism, showed another shortcoming, the infallible "cadre card," on the basis of which he did his firing and hiring, turned out to carry false information.

"My father had often talked with Governor Horthy. They walked along the same route on his way to work. But my father's belief was that politicians are crooks, and he would never have accepted a political office on principle."

"Why haven't you told me that before?" he asked.

"You didn't ask me. Who would have thought such a thing! I mean, do you go around denying things that never have happened to you? I was not accused with it outright," John said indignantly.

Dr. Benedikt's silence indicated that he was considering what he had just heard. He suddenly burst out, "Then those people were crooks who made the 'cadre cards'!"

"I guess that is one of the things we are trying to tell the world!" John laughed. There was nothing else to do about it anymore. He cheerfully burned his card along with the others that were in a big pile in the middle of the office.

Everything started happening all at once. The country rose up as one man and democratic organizations, in the form of revolutionary councils and free trade unions, organized. People did what was expected of them without being asked. What a time to be pregnant! Nobody let me do anything. They did not even let John out of the house. When we talked about this with Pista, he voiced the opinion of the freedom fighters. "We need the next generation and they need parents," he addressed his words to John. "You stay home with your children. I won't even let you come near the fights!" The oldest ones fighting seemed to be twenty-five or so; Pista was a veteran among them, being close to twenty-seven. The very generation that had received free education from the regime, all that was supposed to be pleasing to young people, were the backbone of freedom fighters. They were the only ones who dared to trust in the impossible. The generation of our parents helped in everything but they knew from experience that a small Hungary in the sea of Germanic and Slavonic nations cannot expect freedom unless the whole world rallied behind us. Our parents had never known this to happen. We, the generation caught in between, strongly hoped that this one time the world would see the great opportunities hidden behind the uprising of a small country. If enough support were given to the Hungarians, all the other small nations would arise and break the whole Communist world to pieces. The very young did not even consider these thoughts. They fought the Soviet tank that was right in front of them. Their enemy was the one they could touch. They knew that life was not worth living if they had to go on living as before, surrounded by lies and at the mercy of the government. Who had taught them what they knew? Where did their gut feelings come from? When does a nation decide that something can no longer be tolerated?

There were many thoughts to be mulled over while we listened to the radio and became an information center to friends, some of whom were busy making the news.

The revolution had its own art even before it broke out. A very talented young man, Tibor Tollas, was imprisoned for several years in Vác. He and his friends wrote their poems mentally and repeated them until they were burned into their brains. Now they were handed around on leaflets. I was most impressed by the one that talked of an incident, when all the windows in the prison were walled up with tin, shutting out their last palm-sized view of the sky.

New poems were born as a result of the first fights in the uprising. One that captured my heart was "Red Blood on the Streets of Pest." The "streets of Pest," was a living concept for all Hungarians. Many happy songs had been written about these streets. Because of this connotation, "Red blood" on these streets cried about the rape of our freedom.

We tried to go to church one day without knowing exactly when the priest would say Mass. We had a hard time finding him. Finally, we discovered him in the backyard, slaughtering a hog. He was dressed like a farmer; his sleeves were rolled up. "I want to distribute the meat among my neighbors. They haven't had any meat since the revolution started," he explained. Two or three other men were helping him with the chores. A friendly fire was lit.

To our question about Mass he answered, "Yes, I will have Mass a few hours from now; but since you have walked so far, let me give you at least communion. Who knows, nowadays..." he muttered the last words. "Let me change into something more suitable. I'll be with you in church in a few minutes," he said as he threw another piece of wood on the fire.

He was a well-liked man and was understanding with children, old people, and families. It was like him to think not only of the spiritual but also of the physical needs of his people and not to stop at mere thinking. His prayers were always translated into action.

As we were walking home an old lady came up to me and said, "Woman, don't go home! You won't be able to go back to the hospital if they start shooting. Besides, there is curfew. You should stay at the hospital."

I assured her that I did not come from the hospital. I was not in labor and that the shooting was over, but she just shook her head as she reluctantly let us go on.

In the afternoon Pista came over. He had so much to say that the words poured forth from him non-stop. "We found an underground prison. There was this knocking coming from somewhere. We went around listening for the sounds, but the only thing we could figure was that it came from under the blacktop. We grabbed picks and ripped out the pavement. The knocking became louder. We worked as fast as we could. More people came to aid us. We worked feverishly to win the race against death for those wretched souls. But the knocks slowly died down. We lost this battle against time.

Other prisons were easier to open because we knew where they were. An old man, one of the first prisoners to emerge was surrounded by several of us.

'Who are you? What was your crime? How long have you been here?'

"'I think it has been five years, right after my thirtieth birthday...' he started. 'I actually don't know why I was jailed, I guess I was an 'insect' of some kind...' I suddenly realized that this sixtyish-looking ghost of a man was only thirty-five and that his crime was not much more than what I, too, had committed. I happened to be born into a condemned class. I did not hear the rest of his reply. I left him to the care of the assembled women and went to help free the next batch."

"Then it must be true what I heard in the factory from one of the workers," John said. "He said that he was called upon, a few months before the revolution, to fix a meat-grinding machine in the basement of one of these police stations."

"That was the way they made 'non-persons' out of living human beings." John's revelation was no news to Pista. "That's how they disposed of the remains. No dead bodies—no proof. Ingenious! No wonder people skinned those policemen alive when they found them. Except I saw an incident when a woman screamed at the crowd, 'Don't do it! Violence only breeds violence! Don't let the vicious circle begin again. We must forgive!'"

"Did the crowd listen to her?" I asked.

"That one time they did. That one miserable rat of a policeman disappeared as fast as his legs could carry him, but I don't think he could get very far unless he shed his uniform. It is hard to forgive when one's own people are bleeding to death because of these few leeches."

"It sounds so awful, so terrible, how can anyone…?" I started but suddenly remembered the Nazis. There was no difference. None whatsoever. Only, maybe these Communists were more thorough and more ecumenical. They wanted to annihilate everybody who was against them regardless of race, creed, or national origin.

"It bothers me quite a bit," John started again, "that it is so hard to keep a crowd from killing, from tearing apart those who are their enemies. Freedom is much more a responsibility than a right. We'll have to live with the consequences of our actions as much as those security policemen. Will that mutual killing never end? Will mankind never grow up?"

"Maybe it's the animal instinct in us," Pista said thoughtfully.

I went to the kitchen and started cooking rice for dinner. Since the first trucks had arrived in Budapest from the country and from abroad we had had more food than in any of the preceding years. I had bought a goose from one of the peasants and cut up some of its meat to eat with the rice. The tantalizing smell brought the children after me.

"Will Uncle Pista stay for dinner?" Ilike inquired.

"I certainly hope so; come, help me set the table and listen to him talk."

"I don't understand what he says, but I'll keep Jancsika quiet." Ilike led her little brother back into the room to set the table there. In the kitchen there wasn't enough room for the five of us.

I heard Pista's voice. "So many political parties have sprung up in only a few days! It is good to see them reappear, but we have to remember that one party has to be in the majority if we do not want to slip back into the hands of the Communists again."

"The country was really united during the revolution," said John. "We have to guard that unity in order to keep our independence."

"Definitely," Pista agreed.

Suddenly we became aware of a festive moment on the radio. Cardinal Mindszenty's long-awaited talk was announced.

"Come, Helen, sit down; the food can wait. You have to be here for this," John shouted with great excitement in his voice. I switched off the oven so the rice would not burn with the precious meat in it. Then I joined the others around the radio in the corner. When I heard our Primate's voice I remembered his glowing eyes that could ignite deep emotions in the crowds he used to address. He was now addressing the whole nation, the whole world. He said that he did not need to apologize for anything. He had never stated anything publicly or privately for which he should be ashamed now. "I stand with my conviction physically and spiritually intact, just as I was eight years ago, although imprisonment has left its mark on me." He thanked the free world and press for their continued support of the Hungarian nation. He recalled the history of Hungary, the easternmost defendant of Western Civilization. He expressed hope that our nation had no enemies because the whole world was headed towards the end of nationalism and the emergence of only one human family. He said that we should live in peace with all nations, the great United States as well as the Soviet Union. He hoped that the Soviets would not misuse their power, and noted the radio announcements that said their forces were still growing in the country. He asked whether the leaders of the Russian empire realized that Hungarians would respect the Russian people much more if they would not try to oppress them. He then appealed to people to get back to work as soon as possible to prevent famine. He pointed out the importance of having as few parties and party leaders as possible in order to keep our freedom intact through unity. He warned, "Private revenge has to be avoided and eliminated." He himself did not accuse anyone. He finally spoke up for democratic achievements and religious freedom.

"He took the words right out of my mouth," Pista exalted when the Primate ended his speech. "Weren't we just talking about that? Tell me!" He looked around triumphantly. "You will live in a beautiful world," he said to Jancsika and pulled him onto his lap. Jancsika looked at the glowing eyes behind the gold-rimmed glasses and smiled. He did not quite understand why he should have such a glorious life but he was all for it. He liked to ride on Uncle Pista's knees.

"This is our revolution!" Pista continued with the same enthusiasm. "Did you hear on the radio this afternoon that Ferenc Nagy, the Prime Minister of 1948 who had defected to the West, wanted to come back to Hungary with others who had escaped previously but were not allowed in? As a matter of fact, he was advised to leave even the territory of Austria. We do not want any interference from abroad! This is the revolution of the youth of Hungary! The workers, peasants, and students, we who were brought up by the Communists, want to show them that their system has failed miserably!" Jancsika fidgeted around for a while in Pista's lap. When he realized that he couldn't catch Pista's attention, he jumped off and headed for his toys.

"But how, Pista, how? Don't we need all the help we can get?" I heard John ask while I went back to the kitchen to look after our food. Ilike followed me.

"If there is justice in the world, if there is an ounce of good will left in people, they must see what is happening. Help will come. They did decide in the United Nations that Hungary should be free, and I trust that they will stick to their decision. Otherwise what is the United Nations for?"

John was older than Pista; he was thirty-two. He had lived through many trying times he could remember well, many days and weeks, months and years, even decades when the good will of people was swallowed up by the will of extremist regimes. He must have thought of the Soviet veto in the United Nations Security Council and of the simple rule of numbers and machine guns when he said, "Pista, let's be sensible. The Suez Canal crisis is going on right now. The eternal problem of the Middle East! Oil. Oil is more important for Americans and Soviets and in fact for the whole Western world than Hungary's freedom. Ideals are beautiful, but oil is reality. If there would be a world war, it would not be over the freedom of ten million freedom fighters. It should not be that way; I don't argue your point. I'm just not as idealistic as you are. I want to believe, but my past experiences make me shudder."

"Look," Pista retorted. "What would happen to the country if everybody felt the way you do?"

"Pista, listen. If fighting would go on right in our district, I would probably get into it myself. I am for the revolution, but it seems too beautiful to come true. Freedom for our long-suffering nation! I'm scared because of this coincidence with the Suez Canal problem."

"I trust President Eisenhower," Pista chuckled as he continued. "Do you remember the pun about his name when he became President of the United States? How everybody predicted that he would show Stalin...Stalin's name meaning 'steel' and his the 'beater of iron'?"

"Well, we have yet to see him in this role." John was still skeptical. "Besides, the Presidential elections will take place in three days. He has other things on his mind now than the Hungarians. He certainly would not want to be credited with the outbreak of the Third World War."

"But, what are we talking about? The United Nations decision was that the Soviets should leave the country. Pál Maléter is discussing it with the Soviet commanders. Everything seems to be going according to our demands... We are neutral, we got out of the Warsaw Pact, the Communist Hungarian UN representatives were recalled, others are being sent..."

"And our airports are surrounded by Soviet tanks to assure the safe departure of Soviet citizens..." John concluded Pista's optimistic reports on the one point that worried us all. "How will all this end? This is my question."

"Oh, John, if we don't have our optimism, what do we have?"

Pista frowned. "I won't go on living under Communists."

"Don't misunderstand me. I enjoy tremendously our sudden freedom. It has already lasted almost four days, but I want it to last forever. Above all, I want it for my children. They should never know what it is like to grow up the way we did."

"They never should," I joined in while I brought in the steaming risotto, rice with goose meat and whatever vegetables I could find, mostly carrots. "We were always trying to escape from Hungary while there was a possibility, but today I would not leave for anything. With a beautiful and free future as a possibility, who would want to? Even though we have our Canadian visas," my hand flew to my mouth and I looked around, afraid that someone might have overheard me. Then I started laughing. "You see, the power of habit, we don't need to be afraid anymore." Pista looked interested, so I continued. "Three years ago we received our Canadian immigrant visas not long after Father flew over to make his permanent home there. The British Consulate sent them out by one of their chauffeurs because a week before we received ours somebody was arrested for having been notified through the mail about his visa. They did not want to get us into the same kind of predicament. We then carefully removed bricks in a certain wall and put the documents behind them. There we could always have found them if we needed them, yet they could not get us into trouble."

"That's amazing." Pista even stopped eating while he listened. "People were arrested because of mail they received? How can anyone be responsible for something that was mailed to him? I mean you could just mail something to someone and get him arrested on the charges that he solicited that mail from you. Think of the many people imprisoned because of careless relatives who had written them something from abroad?"

"I am convinced that very often we did not get letters from Father, and he did not get ours. But that was simply a matter of not delivering it. Maybe they have them somewhere, and I guess they could be used against us if they found it necessary some day. John's father received a letter from his Uncle Feri last year. The envelope contained a woman's letter to her sister in a completely different part of the country. On the outside there was no sign showing that the letter had been opened. Another time we found a piece of paper with Russian letters on it right inside the intact envelope."

"Censorship within the country! That just figures! I'm so mad I could fight a buzz saw!" Pista was fuming as he shoveled the food into his mouth.

"Calm down, we have won the revolution so far. Nobody is fighting. The next victory has to come in the election booths. Imre Nagy promised general elections soon," I said as I wiped Jancsika's mouth over his vehement protests. Ilike started to remove the plates as I put up the water on the stove for the dishes. I started the espresso machine; soon the aroma of the fresh-roasted coffee filled our little room. We always had coffee on hand from Father, but we only used it for special occasions. It came in the form of green coffee beans. Every true coffee lover in Hungary roasted the beans himself and ground it in the presence of the whole company to show them that it was indeed in its prime.

As we were sipping the strong, dark liquid we wove plans for a free future despite our worries. Our dreams reinforced each other's plans, and we managed to see everything through rose-colored glasses of hope.

# 56

"Cannon fire!" I jumped out of bed. It was still dark.

"No, don't worry! They found an AVO house, I'll bet, and there is a shoot-out," John said in an uncertain voice.

I wanted to believe him but I repeated, "This is cannon fire about five miles away. You can't fool someone who grew up listening to it during the siege."

John did not answer. He switched on the radio. It was 4:20. We heard the Hungarian National Anthem. We realized that we were in grave trouble. Then Prime Minister Imre Nagy came on the air. "Today at daybreak Soviet troops attacked our capital with the obvious intent of overthrowing the legal democratic Hungarian government. Our troops are in combat. The government is in its place." This was repeated in English, Russian, Hungarian, and French for the whole world to hear and understand.

John and I listened, huddled together, holding onto each other in complete terror.

There was an announcement that Imre Nagy had notified the UN.

And another that the UN Security Council had received the Hungarian appeal.

"They'll have to do something. They will! You'll see!" I whispered only half-believing my own words spoken against a background of cannon fire.

The Hungarian government then asked the Soviet soldiers not to shoot at the Hungarian people who were very sympathetic with the Russians and wanted them to remain their friends.

The Hungarian Writers' Association came on the air with a message to all writers, scientists, and intellectuals of the world and begged for their intervention on behalf of Hungary. "You know the facts, there is no need to give you a special report! Help Hungary! Help the Hungarian writers, scientists, workers, peasants, and our intelligentsia! Help! Help! Help!"

The Hungarian Anthem was played again.

Then the whole sequence started over; Imre Nagy's talk, the Writers' Association's message.

A bulletin announced that Pál Maléter, who had gone to negotiate with the Soviets, was missing. The Chief of Staff of our Army was kidnapped.

We listened, petrified.

Then a final SOS! SOS! SOS! At 7:25 a.m., Radio Free Kossuth went off the air.

"It's all over!" John whispered as he held me tight in his protective arms. My teeth chattered. The children started whimpering as they saw our fright. The cannon fire sounded much louder.

Our short-lived freedom was now in the hands of the free world; in the hands of its leaders…we had done what we could.

# 57

The phone rang. I jumped up and ran into the small room to answer it. It was Mother and she sounded worried.

"Are you all right? I can hear cannons. I wanted to know that you were safe. Thank God that the telephone is still working."

"We are all right, but what is going on there? Oh, Mother, what is going to happen?" I did not yet think of controlling what I spoke over the telephone, I couldn't care now. Mother's voice sounded calm and collected as if it were a simple social call and her silent signal reached my senses. We were back where we started. From now on we would have to look behind our backs again, and talk over the phone, thinking of the invisible third party. I started to cry.

"Your nerves must be shattered," Mother said calmly. "No wonder, being pregnant under these conditions. Do you have any diapers yet?"

How could she think of a thing like that in the middle of all our troubles? Something inside me whispered that she was only covering up and that I should keep the conversation going.

"No, of course I don't have any diapers. You know that we get the rations only in the last month of pregnancy when we have made our third official visit to the doctor and after we have gone through all the possible health checks including X-rays. No store has been open during my last month," I answered hoping that she would come up with the real meaning of her phone call.

"Did you see Pista?"

"Yes, he dined with us yesterday. He was in a good mood."

"You may see him later today," Mother said. "If you do, tell him that he could pick up some diapers for you the next time he is around downtown."

I scribbled down the message. It was obvious that Pista was fighting and Mother had to convey this coded message to him. Whatever it meant, it was a clever one.

As I hung up the phone, the full impact of the phone call hit me.

"John, John, everything is not lost! Something is going on! I got a coded message to deliver to Pista." I skipped back into the room electrified by my new knowledge and handed him the message I had written down.

"What's he up to now?" John looked at the words, puzzled. "We do need diapers, don't we?"

"That's a fact." I laughed in excitement and anticipation. Apparently there was still hope, only now it seemed even more challenging. I heard that voice inside me again. "Abraham hoped against hope and he became the father of all nations. Remember? There is nothing that you and I together cannot do. One way or another, I will set you free."

Again the phone. This time it was Dr. Benedikt. "I can't believe what is going on, John. You know how much I rely on your judgment. I just had to talk with you. I hear shooting. The Soviet troops have come to put down this revolt. At least that is what I think. Then a young man comes by and tells me that down on the square Russian troops are shooting at the newly arrived Mongolian troops, all under the same red star of the Soviet Army. Not one Hungarian took part in that deadly shoot-out. What is happening?"

"I can't possibly tell you what is happening in every instance, but I have some overall impressions. The Russian troops stationed in Hungary knew very well what the revolution was about. Hungarians have been learning Russian for the last couple of years in every school. They were perfectly capable of translating the sixteen points. Many Soviet soldiers who understand what is going on fight for the revolution."

"You must be right. That young man also told me that the Mongolian-looking Soviet troops pointed at the Danube and asked, 'Suez Canal?' Then, when they heard the first shots their faces became angry and they yelled, 'Americans!' They proceeded to shoot the alleged 'Americans,' their own Russian troops. What do you think will happen?"

"I honestly don't know, Dr. Benedikt. Take care and don't become involved in the shooting. If it comes close go to the air raid shelter. Don't speak Russian with your family!"

While John was speaking, I turned on Radio Free Europe. Our own radio station was silent. Here and there along the radio dial free stations came on the air and disappeared again, bothered by crackling noises. Radio Free Europe was loud and clear. Unfortunately there was not much they could say. The United Nations was negotiating, throngs of people were demonstrating in front of Soviet embassies all around the world. "Freedom for Hungary!" was their motto. President Eisenhower's message was that he could not do anything until he had been re-elected.

Pista showed up that afternoon just as Mother had predicted. He was dirty and tired. He carried a gun. We slipped him inside the kitchen and gave him the message. His characteristic broad smile reappeared on his tired face. "Hurray! This means that the film the Hungarians made about the revolution is at the American Embassy or is safe with Western authorities. The first place the Soviets attacked after the airports was the movie studio, Hunnia, because the Communists knew about the film. But it's safe now, it's safe! At least the whole world will now have a complete account of what has really happened here. Our fight for freedom was not in vain!"

"Let me fix you something to eat," I suggested, and the two men went inside. Jancsika ran to greet his beloved Uncle Pista and seemed very interested in his gun.

"No, no, that is not for you." Pista put it on top of the bookshelf, out of reach of the children. "Let me clean up a little," he said and went to the bathroom.

"Wait, I have some hot water." I brought him the big pot. "I just finished washing the dishes and I have some left. Would you have time for a bath?"

"No," Pista laughed. "I must go back. We have to stop the tanks from coming into the city. They are still far away but we have a plan. We'll do what worked someplace else already. We'll spill liquid soap across the highway. I heard it's a scream to see the tanks turn round in circles helplessly. Another troop maneuvered so close to some tanks that they were able to push iron bars between the wheels. That stopped them in a hurry! We also managed to 'buy' a few tanks and machine guns from the Russians for vodka, food, or jewels. Some of them even decided to stay with us and fight until their last breath. They did not want to go back to the Soviet Union." Pista's eyes shone feverishly as he said these last words.

Jancsika and Ilike were standing in front of the bookshelf, eyeing Pista's gun. Ilike was whispering to her brother. Outside the shooting was still audible, still several miles away.

Pista came back, only half washed, his hair combed back, his tired eyes glowing with excitement.

"I will never give up," he declared while he wolfed down the food.

"Keep us posted," were the last words we told him when he finally took up his gun and went out the door.

The only sounds that moved me from the radio in the next days were the childrens plaintive, "Mommy, I'm hungry!" Then I would go to the kitchen and fix whatever I found there. John went out every day to fetch us bread from the corner bakery. We still had preserves. I don't exactly know what else we ate or what we did to keep the children occupied. We read them stories or rolled a ball across the room. Ilike dressed and fed her dollies with the new set of tiny knives and forks she had received for her previous birthday. That time seemed ages ago.

I was thinking of our future because John suggested that he would help me with my math as long as we didn't have anything else to do. Something inside me revolted. "I'm not going back to the university. I do not want to return to the way we used to live. There must be a change! I must be me! I can no longer do what I am told, think what I am told, speak what I am expected to.

"I won't, I won't, I won't!" I screamed.

John looked at me surprised. "What won't you do?"

I broke down in a sob. "I can't take living the way we did. Constant fears, lies, always having to leave the children, practically handing them to the Communists to bring them up as they please and then, kissing their hands for giving them enough nutrition in exchange for their souls. I want my children back! I want to bring them up!"

"Helen, quiet down honey!" John stroked my hair. "It has been too much, I know. Believe me we have always done our best for the children. We always will."

Ilike stopped feeding her dolls and looked at me. She was not used to outbreaks like that. Jancsika ran over and hugged my knees. The baby kicked from the inside. They rallied to stop my tears. For them I wanted to do everything but I did not feel strong enough to go on.

Then I suddenly stopped crying. "Look," I said with determination, "we have to leave the country."

"Leave the country?" John repeated my idea. "I have thought about it ever since we heard Imre Nagy on November 4, when the Soviets came back. The Austrians had sealed their border during the four days of freedom because they figured that only security policemen wanted to escape at that time. I am sure that they are more lenient now. However, shooting is still going on all over the country. How can we get to the border, two hundred miles away? And you are pregnant!"

"And it had seemed such a perfect time to become pregnant when our baby was conceived. Never did everything work so much in our favor," I reminisced. "How I hate to be pregnant now."

The doorbell rang. It was Judy.

"Look what I found!" She was ecstatic. "A Red Cross mini-bus is stationed down the road close to St. Margaret Hospital. They are giving away these goodies. This orange stuff is American cheese. They have big round boxes full of this. Come on, let's all go and get some."

"Cheese," Ilike jumped up and down. Then she turned to her dollies. "We'll have cheese for dinner."

John went with Judy and returned with cheese, coffee, and canned milk. "That's not all I brought," he said with a secretive smile. "I brought good news. The driver of the Volkswagen bus said that he would try to give us a ride across the border when he leaves. So far nobody has stopped him. Maybe we could go with him. I told him you were pregnant but it did not seem to bother him."

"He said that? We could? I want to talk to him too!"

John and I went back there, and the fiftyish-looking man, dressed in a long gray army coat assured me that he would try to do what he could to get us out of the country.

"Oh, God, just don't let me give birth now, not before we leave," I prayed as I went about my duties, cleaning, cooking, and playing with the children.

In the evening we went to Mass. During the service a young man with a gun ran into the church and whispered something to the priest. When the young man left, Father turned to the congregation. "Calmly leave the church now and hurry home. The young man warned us that soon there will be shooting around here."

We hurried down the back street, hidden from the mountain-side which was occupied by Soviet forces. As we crossed one of the side streets a tank ran straight at us. It slowed down after its driver assured himself that we were not fighters. We doubled our steps and arrived home just in time to run over to Judy's with the kids.

Judy's pointed face was pale and her hands trembled as she let us in.

"John, if you have to come for bread in the morning, climb through the fences. Don't ever go on the street before curfew is over. You know that the mountainside is occupied by the Soviets. The man next door with those nice three children went out this morning at three o'clock to line up for bread. Curfew was supposed to last until seven o'clock. He was shot and died on the spot. Those stupid fools on the hill shoot at everything that moves."

We didn't dare tell her about our latest experience with the Soviet tank. We didn't want her to become hysterical. Instead we asked, "Was that the man you were always talking about? The tailor?"

"The same one." Judy's tears flowed down her face. We heard sub-machine guns.

Jancsika played with Judy's big dog, Villám, who refused to stay upstairs today. He followed us to the cellar. He wanted his playmate and would not leave his side. It occurred to me again that Jancsika would have to go to the nursery school he hated so much if the revolution would be a failure.

"Eat something." Judy pushed a piece of bread and some American cheese into my hand. "You have to eat for two now!" She tried to distract me, but with little success.

In about an hour's time the shooting died down and we were able to return home before curfew.

We barely got in the door when the doorbell rang. The man from the Red Cross mini-bus stood at the gate. "I must run. I came by to tell you that we were thrown out of the country. I can't take you. We are being escorted to the border by Soviet military."

As he left, he took our dreams with him. Bitterness welled up within me when I realized that all we had left now was "hope against hope."

When the fighting resumed, we again slept in our back room close to the radio.

The official Hungarian radio station began broadcasting again around ten o'clock at night on November 4, but now it was the mouthpiece of the Communists, János Kádár had become the puppet prime minister. Although he had been a member of Imre Nagy's cabinet, he betrayed the cause of the revolution on November 1 and started separate negotiations with the Soviets. They were the ones who put him into power on November 4. Imre Nagy sought refuge at the Yugoslavian Embassy, while Cardinal Mindszenty received asylum at the American one. At least they were safe.

The United Nations negotiated.

President Eisenhower was re-elected.

The Mongolian-Soviet soldiers were fighting the Hungarian Army, the freedom fighters, and some of their own Russian army-buddies who were for our cause.

Every day we kept asking ourselves the same questions. Can't the free world do something? There are so many of our compatriots outside of Hungary who are willing and able to interpret our desires! Anna Kéthly, a member of Imre Nagy's cabinet, was outside the country, en route to the United Nations. They surely must believe her! Is the whole world, especially the United States, our greatest hope, so disastrously unaware? Don't they know that the Soviets are not ready for an all-out world war? That their whole Communist empire would crumble if individual nations could see that a fight for freedom had reached its goal? Was helped by the free world?

And the fighting went on. We heard occasional short wave broadcasts by the freedom fighters, some in English. They begged the United Nations and later the United States for help. In desperation they even asked for paratroopers. That was the first time I heard anybody ask for more than a firm stand in the United Nations.

Their voices traveled along the wavelengths and were caught by radio stations abroad. We heard them reconfirm the messages. Then, even the last broadcasting static was silenced.

Yet, the fighting went on. Small victories were earned through the blood of many.

A young boy in an ill-fitting huge soldier's coat, toting a gun, headed towards our house and rang the doorbell.

"Are you Mrs. Szablya?" he asked as I hurried towards the gate.

"Yes," I answered as I let him in.

"Pista gave me your address. He said I should tell you everything if ever…"

"Where is he?" I cut him short.

"He is dead."

"No! Not Pista!" I hugged the boy on impulse and at my touch a big sob broke out of him.

"We stopped the tanks. Several times…" He sobbed as I led him into the room.

"Sit down. Tell me everything!" My tears ran uncontrolled.

"We did the liquid soap trick, we used Molotov cocktails. Today he was exhausted…we heard more tanks…but he had to go on…he saw the tank go up in flames. The next minute he was dead."

"The last thing he saw was victory," John remarked as his voice also choked. "Lord," he continued in a muffled voice, "may eternal light shine upon him."

Suddenly I saw Pista through my tears, his glowing eyes and the determination in his voice when he said as we last parted, "I will never give up."

# 58

"My water broke!" I shook John frantically. He opened his eyes halfway. Then with a sudden realization of what was happening, he jumped out of bed. It was past midnight. We still slept in our back room because of occasional gunfire in the district. Our house stood completely exposed to the hillside now occupied by the Soviets. There was curfew from seven in the evening until seven in the morning.

John ran to the phone and dialed. The phone was still in working order despite the general strike in the country. When we became certain that the cause of the revolution was lost, by whispered agreement the country came to a complete halt except for the vital industries and utilities. They worked better than ever. Each day miners brought only enough coal for survival. If the revolution was dead, we were going to act dead.

Dr. Mecseky answered the phone. I thanked God that we went to see him in the first days of the revolution. Would I be able to even get to the hospital that was ten minutes from where we lived? I was scared.

John laughed.

"What are you laughing about?" I was indignant.

"Dr. Mecseky says that you should try to hold it back." I couldn't help laughing myself. "Wishful thinking," I added a bit relieved. "Tell him I have no pains yet."

When John put down the receiver, he turned to me. "Dr. Mecseky said that if the baby started coming, I should call him. He would give us instructions over the telephone."

"Over the telephone?" I wasn't quite sure that I liked the idea.

John dialed again.

"Whom are you calling now?"

"The ambulance."

That call did not bring a solution to our problem either. "They said that they will not come because they are an excellent target, they are white. Besides, the Soviets shoot at every ambulance on principle."

"What are we going to do now?" I felt a fist tighten around my throat.

"Pray!" suggested John, and we did. While we uttered our words of frightened supplications, that voice reminded me again, "Remember, there is nothing you and I together cannot accomplish. I gave you your husband to stand by you." I felt thankful for having a strong man by my side and it was reassuring to hear the two little ones' quiet breathing.

Far away I heard shots.

Then we drifted into sleep.

I woke up again around three-thirty a.m. Everything was quiet. John slept. I felt the first mild cramps. "Lord, help us make it through the night," I whispered. I crawled down from the sofa that was much too narrow for us in my present condition and checked the children. Jancsika was still in diapers during the night, and he was soaked through. I changed him and thought of the fact that we still did not have our new diapers. There were only six diapers in the house. I put two clean ones on him. I then soaked the two wet ones in a pail.

Somebody would have to wash them first thing in the morning. I shook with the cold outside of our only heated room. In the bathroom I could see my breath, although the night before we had a nice wood fire in the hot water furnace. We all had taken a hot bath. Then while it was still warm there, I had scrubbed the tub and the sink and had put everything in perfect order. Somehow I always had that urge to clean before I gave birth. At least, that's what I thought as I hurried back to the warm bed. Was it my nerves that made me shake or only the cold?

I remembered how much quicker my second childbirth had been than the first. Would this one be even shorter? The pains came closer together. "Help me, Lord!" I kept praying. There were still three more hours until curfew was over. I thought of the man who was killed because he tried to bring bread for his children. The hillside across the street that I used to like so much with its green grass and bushes now brought terror in my heart. Soviet troops camped there, and we had no cover from their sharp binoculars.

"Love and faith!" I thought of the words of the Bishop when he married us. I wanted to love everybody and live in peace with all people, yet what I believed in was more important for me than life itself. That is what the revolution had proved beyond the shadow of a doubt. "I want to bring up my children in freedom!" This thought was followed closely by a question. "What if they die because of the fighting?"

My thoughts turned into a wild kaleidoscope of colors and ideas. Then they formed an olive tree, like the one outside the house. Its silvery leaves were turning in the wind. The peacetime of summer was gone. It was November. The leaves turned into piercing, cruel swords. A sharp pain woke me. "Not yet, Lord, not yet!" I begged.

"She died of pneumonia!" The words of a friend stabbed at my heart. She was talking about her baby who had died during the revolution at the hospital.

517

There were no windows; they had broken during the fights. And now a baby was on its way on that fateful November 15, 1956. Two weeks too early.

Diapers! What will we do without diapers?

I dozed off again.

Another sharp pain. The slits in the closed shutters on the windows let in more light now. I looked at the clock. It was five a.m. The pains came closer together. John woke now and then and inquired.

Finally it was dawn. John got dressed and climbed across the fences to Judy's house. By the time they came back along the same route, it was close to seven o'clock. I was quietly biting my fist. As soon as we saw the first people move on the street, we started out on foot to the hospital. By that time the pains seemed to melt into each other, I tried to run as fast as I could and I saw John eye every one of the doors of apartments houses where he could push me in and yell for help in case of a sudden emergency. My nails clawed into his palm. I remembered that running made the baby come quicker. But I knew that if I didn't hurry, I'd never make it to our destination. After ten minutes of agonizing fear and pain we arrived at the hospital. The nurse handed us a form.

"Fill this out!" she commanded.

"But…" John started.

"No 'buts,' we need the forms." She started questioning me.

"How far apart are the pains?"

"They don't stop at all."

"What did you say? Leave those forms!" Now she panicked as she pushed me towards the delivery room. Its windows were broken; there had been shooting during the night. I didn't feel the November cold; I was so glad to be in the hands of a midwife. The doctor was not there. He lived twenty minutes farther away from the hospital than we did.

The midwife was on the phone. "Yes, that is right. I've been on duty for the last forty-eight hours. They are shooting where you are? Well, don't come then, but try to find a replacement. You have a phone, for goodness sakes! I have three women here giving birth at the same time. Do what you can!" She sounded desperate.

While I was giving birth she alternately coached all three of us on what to do and what not to do.

"Go home," she told John, "as fast as your legs can carry you because your baby and your wife will both be naked until you get back. We have been cut off from our laundry for the past three weeks. We have no bed linen, no diapers. I suggest you also bring your own food."

I thought of the woman whose baby died of pneumonia in the hospital and I looked at the broken windows. Did I see well? Three workmen stood there repairing the broken panes. Thank God that would be taken care of! Then I thought of our six diapers. Now we would have to supply the diapers also. How would John manage?

Our doctor finally arrived just in time to catch the baby's head. His vigorous cry made me feel glorious.

Another life was born to replace the many who had died for freedom.

John must have been running. He appeared with the linen, clothes, and diapers. His grin from ear to ear showed how pleased he was with his healthy, eight-pound baby boy. We called him Lajos after my father and grandfather. We had decided on names long before our children were born because in Hungary the first name the mother uttered at birth was immediately put down in the register and it was very hard to change it afterwards.

According to Hungarian medical practice, the mother of the baby had to stay in bed for five days, preferably on her back with a sandbag on her stomach. It was a helpless feeling, especially at night when we heard the shooting and never knew whether something would fly in through the window. Even if it were only broken glass...at least we could see the hillside from my ward. In the ward next door there was no view of the rockets that were only flares most of the time. We knew that there was nothing to be afraid of because we saw the colored flames in the sky, they only heard the sound. They would wail and moan and scream every time they heard a "cannon shot."

The evenings were dark and unfriendly. A doctor who came in for duty that night said, "I was at the worst fights in the Soviet Union around the Dnepr River when Hitler's luck turned, and the Hungarian Army was surrounded by the Soviets. I tell you, I was more afraid coming to work tonight than I was then."

While I lay there I studied chemistry. My inevitable fate seemed to be to have to go back to the university.

John and Judy faithfully brought food and some of our diapers every few hours. Six diapers and two children in them! They had to be washed and dried constantly, starting with cold water in a kitchen where one's breath froze.

Then came the day when I was finally allowed to go home. On that day I got up for the first time after five days of lying flat on my back. I shook with weakness, but I was happy to show the children their little brother. In the first half hour Ilike wanted to feed him chocolate, and Jancsika threw blocks into his basket to entertain him. They could hardly wait to establish contact with the little Lajoska they had known so well through his kicking in "mommy's tummy."

The first night at home was an unbelievable relief. Lajoska didn't wake us until the morning. He behaved just as miraculously day after day.

Mother and my sisters came over. They oohed and aahed over Lajoska. They squeezed him and declared that he was definitely the cutest baby they had ever seen. They brought with them damask napkins for diapers that did not absorb water as well as the diapers did, but they proved to be lifesavers.

John already worked at both his jobs, but only the minimal amount, observing the general strike without offending his Communist bosses. We kept in mind our "insect" status. We remembered that we might have to live with our actions for the rest of our lives; especially now that Lajoska was born.

The day after I came home John went to the university and returned with a huge bundle of white material. "It is from the party-secretary," John answered my unasked question. "He gave me this today at the department. He said, 'I heard that your baby was born and got to thinking that you probably did not have your diapers yet. My wife did not cut up this material for our second child because we had enough diapers left over from the first. You are welcome to it until you get your own rations. Then you can return your share of diaper material to us. We can wait a while."

"That was very nice of him." I fingered the material with delight. No more damask napkins! No more freezing diaper washes for John who insisted on doing it himself, so I could stay in bed during the night.

"You remember him. He was the one who was the deputy chairman of the department, whose job I was doing in all practicality, the one..."

"...Who invited you to have a coffee with him and confessed..."

"The same one. I guess that besides wanting to help, he also wanted to reassure me that he had no hard feelings against me in particular."

"That is an advantage," I said with relief. I felt good about this man even though his presence at the department meant that the Communists were back in power.

Day in and day out Radio Free Europe broadcast coded messages from refugees who made it successfully to freedom. From the code words I understood that many of my classmates had escaped. Day and night I thought of how we too could get to the border. The usual dangers of the Iron Curtain; the minefields, electric barbed wire fences, watchtowers and bloodhounds were removed at the time the Austrian State Treaty was signed. We had a chance now that would never return. Yet, I had in my arms an obstacle that was dearer to me than my own life.

∼

Lajos was one week old when Mother called at night. She talked in code. Father sent somebody to pick us up. "But how?" The question tore at my heart. "How can we do it?"

The next day John went over to Mother's in order to discuss details. Both my sisters and their fiancées were there. Elisabeth had announced the she would marry Balázs although she was only sixteen.

The decision about our departure was made. Waiting at home was difficult with the many chores to be performed.

Elisabeth and Balázs decided they would help us with the children. Marie and Dennis already had made arrangements to start out on the same day with friends on another route. We were going to leave early the next morning. My heart beat in my throat when I heard this. "Tomorrow?" was all I could utter. Why did everything have to come so quickly? I let my eyes wander around our little home that was so dear to us. But when I looked into John's eyes, everything else seemed to disappear except my worry for the children.

"What are we going to do with the children? How will we go? Will we have to walk?" I had too many questions.

"I don't know. Our guide will bring a truck to Mother's. Somebody is going to pick us up with a car and drive us over to Mother's house as soon as the curfew is over."

"Can we take something?"

"Only what we can carry. We have to carry our children also. Thank God that Elisabeth and Balázs are coming with us."

"What should we take?"

"Diapers, clothes for the children, some medicines, maybe a souvenir or two. But nothing suspicious. We cannot take our documents, birth certificates, or diplomas. That would make it too obvious that we want to escape."

I felt as if I were giving birth again; I stood in front of a hurdle that had to be overcome. I trusted that it would be. We would have to give birth to our children again. Only this time it would be the difficult birth into freedom. Would we survive it? I did not want to be separated from my family. Prison would mean separation, but prison could be anybody's fate, any day, as living conditions were under the Soviets. What else could go wrong? I was afraid. That inside voice calmed me. "This might be your answer to 'hope against hope'."

"Hope is greatest when there is no reasonable hope, isn't it?" I asked John.

He was surprised. "What made you say that? I think you are right. There was no logical reason why the revolution should have won, yet 'hope against hope' produced a unity in our nation that was unheard of in the history of Hungary, except at times of great revolutions." Then he added, "Exactly as you said, at times of 'hope against hope'."

"What are we talking about? We should be packing, not philosophizing," I suddenly remembered.

"Helen, there is one thing I should like to do before we leave," John said. "We don't know what is going to happen to us. Let's baptize Lajos. I'll run over and get Judy before curfew time. She could be the godmother."

"Let's," my eyes were full of tears as I held his marble-round head in my palm. It fit so perfectly! How fragile such a baby was! I could kill him by simply squeezing too hard. What would happen to him on our way?

Judy came in a few minutes. Tears ran down her face as she held the little bundle under the water that John poured from a glass.

"Lajos Pista, I baptize you in the name of the Father and the Son and the Holy Spirit."

# 59

Judy stayed way past curfew time and helped us pack a knapsack and a suitcase. She left only after she had given a last kiss to her new godson.

We fell into bed for a short night's rest. We were up again at five o'clock. John and I held hands as we walked through our apartment for the last time. As we said goodbye to everything we owned, we recalled the personal memories attached to the antique furniture, some of which dated back to the days of my grandmother's grandmother, as well as the many books and records we had given to each other or had inherited from our parents. "Let's take this tiny book, *Daphnis and Chloe*. It will always remind me of the days when you used to read it to me while I was nursing Jancsi," I said. We added the thin paperback to our luggage. The children's diary/notebooks were also in the suitcase. I had some of my poems in a small leather-bound calendar from the days I had spent in Switzerland. The treasures of both our families; the pictures, the china, the crystal, and the silver, entrusted to us by our parents, would stay here. We hoped that it would be our parents who would empty the apartment. There, in the kitchen, was the twin basin ceramic sink we had managed to get in a store and which John had somehow carried home on the streetcar to provide us with this luxury. Then it was all over; we made our rounds. There was no way back. We woke the children and concentrated all our attention at the only gems that mattered, their eyes that shone at us with the usual glow. These eyes would not have to see what we had. Our children would grow up in a free world.

We were barely ready with breakfast when the car arrived.

"No looking back." John smiled at me encouragingly. "What matters comes with us. The only important things are our children and their well-being. From now on our home is where we are together."

I kissed him. The children must have felt something in the air because they too hugged us closely.

Lajoska was sound asleep in his basket. He didn't need to say good-bye to a home he had never come to know.

The car wound its way through abandoned streets. The city was just wakening. The church and the little espresso shop where we used to meet with Mother passed us by quietly. I would never again go to the dairy, to the bakery, to the horsemeat store. The market was empty today. Because of the curfew people just started to move around after seven a.m.

The next district was closer to downtown. Its houses resembled the state they were in after the fifty-one-day siege, but only when we crossed the bridge into Pest did the full impact of the fighting show. "The streets of Pest," I thought of the revolutionary poem about the red blood spilled over them and also the happy melodies written about them. I looked at their wounded surface, frozen brick rivers flowing from tumbled-down walls, like the spilled blood of the many who now rested in the thousands of graves that popped up everywhere where there was no blacktop. In these graves a nation's dreams were buried.

We arrived. Mother greeted us with "mignons," the chocolaty, creamy, nut and whipped cream, fruit and marzipan-filled delicacies. Where did she get hold of such things right after the revolution? Mother never ceased to amaze me. As I silently munched on a sweet I could hardly swallow I thought of the love she had given us all her life. In so many intricate ways she showed her dedication to her children.

"I can't go with you," she declared in a very simple tone of voice. "When I thought of leaving today, I realized that your grandfather would starve to death without me. He does not even let his own sister come near him. He will not take food from anyone but me. I cannot walk out on him."

I didn't know what to say. What she said was true.

I understood but I did not want to leave her, "When will we see you?" When would I experience Mother's all-pervasive love again? The kind of love that produced mignons for her children at a time like this.

"We'll get a passport; don't worry," she said.

I had heard those words before, in 1949, when Father had to escape. I had already experienced the impossibility of seeing Father again, once the Iron Curtain came between us. I did not answer. Although I was being unreasonable I felt that Mother had betrayed me and all of us who were leaving. As if she guessed my thoughts, she said, "You must go, Helen. You are young. The children's future is more important than anything else. We'll survive somehow. We always have. We have most of our lives behind us. You go!"

I understood that from now on I was the "Mother" who had to carry on the legacy of love in our family.

When the truck came I held Mother in my arms as if never to let go of her. Grandfather did not really understand what was going on. We always came and left, today was no different. He cheerfully said good-bye. Uncle Charles had tears in his eyes as he put his hand on Lajoska's head as if in a blessing. "Bring him up to be a good Canadian citizen!" he said.

Marie and Dennis had already left that morning. Elisabeth and Balázs were coming with us in the big pick-up that our guide brought to the house.

Lajoska and I were allowed to sit in the driver's cabin because of Lajoska's age, he was ten days old. The rest of the family sat in the back. Their only protection against the freezing rain was a canvas held up by a broomstick.

The truck drove around town as it picked up more and more people. Where did they all find places in the back? I wondered as I said goodbye to the well-known places, in ruins again. The only things I wished never to have to see again were the Soviet tanks on every corner, the guards with the machine guns, and the infamous red star which marked all their paraphernalia.

We slowly wound our way out of the city and onto the highway that led to Vienna.

From the talk between our guide and the truck drivers I understood that the two truck drivers had been sent to pick up another government owned truck at the border that was used by refugees to get to their destination. The Austrians did not let anyone bring guns or vehicles into their country because they feared international repercussions. The driver had permission to take one additional person with him to assist him. He now had forty "helpers."

The truck's rhythmic bouncing lulled both Lajoska and me to sleep. A sudden jerk woke me up. To my great shock an officer stood in the middle of the highway and waved at us. He wanted to see our papers. When the driver showed them to him he laughed in his face. "You mean that," and he pointed at the truckload of people, "is some help? Ingenious, but no," he muttered. Then, with a bored expression, he waved at us. "Come on, turn back, and no more of that nonsense."

I couldn't believe what was happening. This captain here, instead of asking for everybody's papers, or arresting us, or whatever was the custom, practically laughed us off the road.

As the truck made a U-turn and started back towards the capital, I grasped what was happening. The truck was now traveling against a river of people, carting, carrying, and pushing their belongings towards the Western border. I had seen that picture before. When was it? I closed my eyes and suddenly I knew. I was carried back in my half dream to another time in my life when we had driven against such a flood of people. Then too they were escaping the Soviets. It was in 1944, when we came back to endure the siege in our own home town. This time it was different. We were one of those fleeing.

I looked back and saw the officer stop every one of the desperate creatures pointing them into the opposite direction. "Come on, get out of here, go home!" I imagined his half-kind, half-bored words. He did not arrest anybody. Even if he wanted to, it would have been foolish. Two soldiers against hundreds of would-be refugees.

Our truck went in the wrong direction only until we found the first side road. We then turned west again and continued our way towards the border. We were now on dirt roads. After a few miles the truck was in mud up to its axle.

The driver cursed his bad luck while he got out and ordered all men off the truck into the windy, freezing rain. "Now! You are going to push!" He jumped back into the front seat and started the engine. The guide stayed outside and gave orders, "One, two, three, push!" A big jerk and the truck was freed from its predicament.

We were on our way again. We had no road map. Road maps were considered military secrets by the Communists and therefore unavailable for the public. We had to rely on directions we could get from passersby, mostly children.

The sky slowly darkened around four o'clock in the afternoon and changed the gray of the sleet into an all-out blackness.

I heard the guide inquire from a little boy, "Where is the next roadblock? How far are we from the border?" The little boy pointed at some lights far away, "Those lights are in Austria!" My heart started beating faster, and my mouth became very dry as I swallowed. Would we make it? Then I heard the little boy say, "There is a Soviet tank not far from here, about three miles from the border." Our guide thanked him yet he continued in the same direction. "I don't believe what that little kid said. I was around Mosonszentjános only a couple of days ago. There were no tanks in this area."

I didn't know what to say or think because at that very moment we nearly ran into that tank which stood exactly in our way, turret forward.

A Mongolian-looking colonel stood beside a young, blond soldier who addressed us in Russian. He looked at the truck driver's papers. The driver asked me to interpret and tried to negotiate. I thought of the many deals made with Soviet soldiers. For gold or a watch or vodka they might do anything. I had heard that they might even sell a tank for any of these luxuries. I was thinking of what we, our truckload of people, would be able to offer them.

The colonel disappeared and the young soldier sat in the driver's cab, right beside me. "The colonel went in to radio to the police station in the next town. They'll come and get you. Why in the world are you all running away?" He was obviously one of the new Soviet troops brought in especially to crush the Hungarian revolution. I just smiled at him while he continued.

"I have a baby and a wife at home. I'll show you a picture," he took out a black and white photo of a one and a half-year-old child on a swing. The child smiled the same way he did.

The soldier's blond hair shone from the rain and his blue eyes showed his disbelief of what he saw as he looked at the bundle in my lap. He asked me, "How old is your baby?" "Ten days," I said. "Ten days? Shouldn't you be home with him? Why don't you just go home, so I can go home too?"

How could I explain to him in "twenty-five words or less," WHY? I myself, longed for a place I could call my home but remembered that "home" for us was no longer a place but a concept; home was where we were together.

The Mongolian was back. He barked a few syllables at the Russian who translated his Mongolian words. "They'll come and get you. You know, you are lucky that you are in a truck. If you had walked, we would have had to make you sit on the ground. You would have had to sit there until the morning. Whoever stood up would have been shot."

"Why?" Now it was my turn to ask.

He laughed. "How else can two people keep more than forty captives?"

I didn't know the answer; I never tried to keep anyone captive or even thought about the problem.

He continued. "That's very elementary. After all, I want to be home with my family again. Wouldn't you? I heard that many guards were attacked by some of your people who keep trying to run away."

About an hour later the Hungarian police arrived. One of them jumped into the driver's cab while others stepped on the back of the truck. Our guide joined the people in the rear.

As we left the Soviet tank, the truck bumped along between plowed fields which were as muddy as the road. We were driving away from the lights of the Promised Land, Austria. Then suddenly the truck stopped again.

There was commotion in the back that lasted for minutes. I thought of the Russian soldier who had told me about would-be refugees attacking guards. What was taking place there in the back? I listened but I only heard muffled voices. The Hungarian policeman beside me did not budge. He lit a cigarette. I saw people scramble down from the truck. I desperately wanted to talk to John, but I did not see him or any of the members of my family.

Then we started out again with a jerk. Our next stop was in front of the police headquarters in Magyaróvár, the city where I had spent a few interesting months in 1944 and where I had met Tommy for the first time. Where could he be now?

We were taken off the truck, and I saw John again. He hugged me and whispered in my ear, "Most of the people left; they jumped off the truck. There was an agreement. We decided not to go with them. What could we do with the children in the middle of plowed, muddy fields, miles from the border in this miserable weather? I didn't think you would want to…" He looked at me questioningly.

"No. You did well."

We were under arrest. We had feared this all our lives, and now it was happening to us. The Hungarian police were not unfriendly, but they too were under the supervision of the Soviets. I remembered with relief that the Soviets liked babies.

Sure enough, we were told to go into the only heated room in the whole station. All families with children were put into this black hole of a room. There were five beds in it for more than that many families. An off-duty solider had one bed which he surrendered to us when he saw me with the little one. He disappeared among our profuse "thank yous."

Lajoska started to cry. All day he had slumbered in the driver's cab where it was warm and he was comfortably rocked. He decided now that it was time to eat. I nursed him and looked around in the dark. A tiny light burned at one end of the room and gave this prison the atmosphere that our air raid shelter had had during the fifty-one-day siege of Budapest.

At first I could not tell the many dark shadows apart; but during the long night, I started to distinguish people by their voices.

A woman in the corner was talking. "We were approaching the border, walking one behind the other, when guards appeared. My youngest son, a good runner, tore away and ran across to Austria. The guards caught up with us and captured my husband, me, and the three other children. What am I to do?" She wrung her hands.

The father added, "I'm a miner, a well-paid worker, but I will not live under the Soviets any longer. My son yelled back from across the border, 'You come after me, I won't go home.' The Austrian guard shouted to us as the Hungarians led us away, 'I'll take care of him until you get here.' But what will happen to us? What is the penalty for illegal border crossing?"

"We have to find our son!" the woman sobbed.

"I am thirsty!" Jancsika complained with the matter of factness of one who was used to being well cared for.

"There is no water in the building!" a voice came from the other end of the room. "That is why only this room is warm. All the pipes are frozen and the central heating is out also. This is the only room that has a wood stove."

I saw through the darkness that Balázs sat on a chair and Elisabeth settled on his lap.

I thought about how I could give Jancsika something to drink. A thought occurred to me, my own milk! "Give me a glass," I said to John. He handed me our aluminum tumbler. I pumped milk into it with my hands. When the cup was half full I handed it to Jancsi. He gulped it down and was satisfied. The voice inside me whispered, "See, you and I can solve every problem." I was wondering how we were going to solve this next imminent problem, how we would get out of prison and out of the country. I listened to another woman's story.

"I was walking through a swamp with my husband and our two children. We were given a hand-drawn map and tried to find our way in the dark. I started to sink. It was a terrible feeling. The ground had no bottom. A slow but constant power kept pulling me down, down, down…" Her voice became hysterical. "My husband wanted to help, but he too got caught. There was nothing left for us but to scream and hold our toddlers above our heads to at least save them. The border guards heard our screams and ran to help. Thank God, they were Hungarians. I would never have thought I would scream to be captured. Now we are in jail. What is to become of us? Is there no way out?"

She spoke the questions that burned in every one of the black shadows in that room during that night and at many other police stations along the Hungarian border.

# 60

We didn't get much sleep that night. A Soviet officer came in with an interpreter and questioned all of us. We had to be processed before the morning. What was the hurry? Lajoska wanted to nurse every hour on the hour. For him, day had just started after the long sleep in the truck. The miner's wife whose son had run over to Austria offered her help. "Give me the baby, I'll rock him so that you will be able to get some sleep. I can't even close my eyes for worry. Where is my baby? He's eleven, but he'll always be my baby!"

I gratefully handed Lajos to her and she managed to keep him quiet for a while.

Morning brought the explanation for the policemen's hurry to get rid of us. During the night one hundred and twenty families were housed inside the police station in addition to many single people. From early dawn more arrested refugees had been streaming in from the border. They were standing in line to get into the building. They were "stored" on the frozen ground all night, just as the Russian soldier had explained to me when he had captured us.

Families with many children were loaded onto the first bus. The policeman frowned at my sister and her fiancée, "Who is he?"

"My fiancée," Elisabeth answered.

"What does that mean? Are you married, or aren't you?"

"No."

"Then he can't go with you."

"But we are engaged."

"That does not count," he gruffed.

John intervened. "We need them both to carry the children." He lifted Jancsika and handed him to Elisabeth while Balázs took Ilike in his arms.

"Hmmm," the policeman muttered something under his breath and passed us by. We boarded the same bus. A sergeant jumped on board to accompany us to our unknown destination.

The bus ran between the fields as snowflakes danced in the air. The morning was quite agreeable except for the fact that we were prisoners.

Without warning the bus stopped with a jerk.

"Flat tire!" declared the driver.

The Hungarian policeman got off and inspected the bus with the driver. Then he returned to us. "You are law-abiding citizens, and you know very well what your duty is in a case like this. I am now going to get help with that tire. I expect to find you right here where I left you in an hour and a half, it will take me at least that long to find someone who can fix a flat." He opened the door of the bus to leave. Suddenly he turned around and with a big smile and a wink said practically to himself, "Of course, I cannot be held responsible for whatever you do while I am away."

He was barely out of sight when everybody got off the bus and started out towards the border on foot. At this point the border was at least twenty miles away. We hoped to find guides in the next village, Öttevény.

As we were walking along the highway with our fellow would-be refugees, that picture of the flow of refugees in the fall of 1944 appeared to me again. This time I was one of the crowd that walked, carrying all they possessed. To an outsider we must have seemed like a sorry lot, but deep down we represented humanity in all its glory and perfection. We were driven by an ideal. Our outside shells no longer mattered. Not even the children fussed. We were totally free from all financial worries; we had nothing. Nothing but a tremendous trust in God and in other people's help, even that of the guards. This last supposition was truly "hope against hope."

A passenger car drove by and offered the children and me a ride. He took us right to the railroad station, then returned and picked up the next group until he had hauled everybody to the station. The attendant at the station made chicory coffee for us in a large pot. He poured milk into it and watched us feast on our breakfast while he called ahead to the next railroad station in coded language to find out where the Soviets were asking for I.D. He found that it would be all right for us to travel to Horvátkimle, a small village. This would save us at least five miles of walking.

We boarded the next train. In Horvatkimle we went into a pub to inquire about possible ways to escape. Naturally, it had to be done very subtly. The days of the revolution were over.

An old man in drab, gray clothes sat at one of the rickety tables, sipping a glass of wine. He said more to himself than to any of us in particular. "The guides were all rounded up last night. The police took them. I can't imagine who squealed on them."

"Aren't there any around anymore?" the miner's wife asked. Obviously she was most eager to go straight back to the border and try again.

"Nope," the old man snapped.

"Is there no way out?" she tried harder.

"Yep, there is. Through a swamp."

531

"Do you know someone who knows that swamp?" she inquired, while I thought of the story last night about the parents' sinking with their babes above their heads.

"Nope."

"How do you know there is a road?"

"I used to go into that swamp quite often," he said pensively, then added, "It was about fifteen years ago, when I did it last."

"I must get to Austria," the unfortunate mother wailed and told her story to the man.

"Well, I can tell you which way I used to go, but I won't go with you."

"John, let's go back to Budapest. This is not for us," I pleaded.

"I'm afraid we'll have to," John answered. "There doesn't seem to be a way to get out of here. At the next station there is a Soviet roadblock. We would have to walk with the children all fifteen miles from here through muddy, plowed fields."

"Only to end up in the arms of the border guards again? At least, we are not in jail now."

"The police have our names," John worried.

"But look at all the others they have arrested with us! They can't hold the whole country in prisons! There aren't enough jails for all of us!"

With heavy hearts we boarded the train towards Budapest. Elisabeth and Balázs had decided to come with us. We had no money to bribe the guards and we were in no mood to threaten them with kitchen knives, even if that had proven successful in the face of guards with submachine guns and pistols.

The train crawled the next eighteen miles in an hour and finally came to a complete halt in Győr. The conductor announced, "We will not go any farther tonight. Curfew time is near and I would suggest that you find yourselves a place to stay before dark."

We got off the train and stood at the railroad station wondering what to do.

"No hotels have been open since the revolution," Balázs remarked.

"We don't know anybody in this town," said John.

We stepped out of the railroad station and saw a Red Cross sign on the building across the street

"Red Cross." I pointed to the large sign and in silent agreement we walked towards the old building.

We crossed the street and opened the door. We found ourselves in a gray hallway. A policeman sat at a wooden table and asked questions of a young couple while he scribbled down the answers. Well, that seemed to be all right. After all, everyone had to be registered wherever they stayed for longer than twenty-four hours.

Red Cross ladies greeted us and as one of them led us away from the desk she whispered to me in an unguarded moment, "You are under arrest. The police have occupied the building. They won't let us take off the Red Cross. We can give you anything you need, but they won't let you go out." To avoid suspicion she added in a louder voice, "Definitely, we can get you something for the baby. How cute he is! Yes, we have something for diaper rash."

"Let's leave before he takes our names!" John suggested and we started out towards the door. It was already locked.

"I'm sorry, but you can't leave!" the Hungarian policeman said in a firm voice.

"Why not? We only want to go outside and see the sights. We'll be back before long," John argued.

"No," he said sternly.

"Come, I'll show you to your room," the Red Cross lady offered.

She led us to nice, clean beds. Soon afterwards someone with a Red Cross armband came around and asked whether we needed medication.

The policeman himself went down to the cellar after curfew time when he could not expect any more "clients" and cooked us a big pot of chicory coffee. He poured milk into it and we were all welcome to our fill. I couldn't remember whether we had eaten or what it was if we did during the past forty-eight hours. All I could think of was the fact that we were now arrested for the second time. This time it happened in Győr, thirty miles from the Austrian-Hungarian border in a Red Cross building occupied by the Hungarian police. I guessed that the charges would be, "attempted illegal border crossing."

That night six hundred people were arrested in this one place alone.

❧

In the morning a Red Cross lady boarded the bus with us and announced that we would be taken to the International Red Cross building in Budapest and then released to go home.

Just before the bus started moving an armed policeman stepped on the bus and pushed the lady off. "Yes, yes, I will take them to the Red Cross building!" he yelled at her.

I saw the fright in Elisabeth's eyes as she looked at me, pleading for consolation. What could I offer her that would calm her? Balázs held her hand. I heard that voice again. "There is nothing that you and I cannot solve together." I thought with comfort about the fact that Elisabeth too had her strong man, given to her by someone who cared for even the smallest one of us.

It was amazing how well the children behaved. They felt that something vibrated in the air, that their parents needed their help to preserve their sanity. They too were afraid, and their fright was different from a child's fear in a dark room. It was the fear of an adult when confronted with the unsolvable.

I nursed Lajoska. I changed his diapers; John told stories to the children; Elisabeth sang little songs with them. The familiar landscape ran past our windows as the bus swallowed the miles towards the capital city.

When we were finally back in our hometown, the bus did not turn towards the International Red Cross building. It headed straight towards Deák Ferenc tér, the dreaded headquarters of the security police, the AVO.

"Men, off the bus!" the policeman ordered. "Women and children can go home."

I gave John a quick hug before we were separated. I saw Elisabeth clinging to Balázs. In less than a minute they were inside the modern building. We could see them through the swinging glass doors that were guarded by security policemen with submachine guns.

"We are not going home!" the women shrieked. "We cannot carry the luggage as well as the children." We huddled close in a circle outside the police building in the cold.

To each other we whispered, "We won't let our husbands be taken to Siberia!"

"I heard that whole city blocks had been surrounded by the Soviets and that all male pedestrians were taken captive."

"That is correct!"

By the time an armed guard came to watch us we had decided to rescue our husbands one way or another.

I had some toilet paper with me. I wrote a message on it for Mother and another one to Uncle Feri. He lived very close to this police station. He was at that time still the Chairman of the Revolutionary Committee of the Technical University. "Please, take these for me," I whispered to a pedestrian, a total stranger, who grabbed the papers and disappeared.

Elisabeth's nerves were beginning to give out. She was shaking. I held her hand in mine and looked her straight in the eye as I had often when she was younger and needed my reassurance. She was again the "little one" to me. Besides, she was still only sixteen. "Everything will be all right. You'll see that everything will turn out as is best for all of us. Trust in God, there is nothing that He and we cannot achieve together!" For the first time the voice inside me was heard by another human being. "Yes!" she whispered and nodded her head.

My mind started working. "I have to go to the bathroom!" I said to the guard.

"You still can't go into the building!"

"What should I do then?"

"Go to that apartment building for all I care!" He was gruff as he was resentful that he had to watch a bunch of women outside in the cold.

I ran across the street. Once in the house I rang the bell of the first apartment.

"Please, let me make a phone call! It's a matter of life and death!"

The old lady looked at me and her eyes betrayed that she understood that I was in trouble. Would she let me use the phone? Under Communists rule she was responsible for every phone call made from her apartment.

"Oh, go ahead!" she said.

Ever since the revolution, people showed tremendous solidarity and unity.

I dialed the number of Uncle Feri. "Lord, let him answer the phone!" I prayed.

"Hello, is that you, Helen? I heard you had your baby!" his friendly voice greeted me.

"Yes, yes, but that is not why I called. As a matter of fact we are at the police station, Deák Ferenc tér. We were captured at the Red Cross building in Győr..." I told him in a few words about our ordeal.

"I'm glad you called me. As Chairman of the Revolutionary Committee I am now negotiating with the Justice Department about the kidnapping of pedestrians from the streets. They are taken to Siberia, I need proof, an actual example, and yours is a good one. You were kidnapped from the Red Cross building! I'll be down there in fifteen minutes. Let me make a few phone calls first."

"Hurry!" I put down the receiver and thanked the lady.

Uncle Feri arrived in less than fifteen minutes. We could still see our men inside the building.

Uncle Feri was a huge man. His two hundred and fifty pounds loomed tall over the guard with the submachine gun. He ignored the guard as he pushed his way through the swinging glass doors right inside the police station. The women and children followed his lead. The guard must have been too surprised to act.

Uncle Feri marched straight up to the highest-ranking official he could spot and started to present his case in a thundering voice. "You have kidnapped these people from the Red Cross building."

"Red Cross? What are you talking about?"

We all reinforced his statement. "Yes! That's where we were arrested!" "Thirty miles from the border!" "We'll definitely thank the International Red Cross for that!" Forty different voices shouted their accusations at random.

"Quiet!" He waved his arms with a puzzled face.

"We were kidnapped!" Somebody raised his voice from the crowd.

"Could someone tell me slowly what you all are screaming about?" the officer asked.

"These people here were captured at the Red Cross building in Győr, thirty miles from the border. What do you want with them?" Uncle Feri demanded.

"Want with them?" The policeman seemed to wonder himself what he should do with us. "I received a busload full of people, most of them women and children. Ever since then I have been trying to figure out what has happened. Kidnapped, eh???"

Memories of the revolution were still fresh. Only a year ago we would have been put in jail without trial, without even a chance to argue. He certainly would not have tried for hours to figure out how and why he got us.

"It is a crime to try to leave the country," the officer stated.

"Thirty miles from the border, when they were ordered off a train traveling towards Budapest?" Uncle Feri inquired.

The officer pondered these words and finally gave up. He pulled out a sheet of paper and handed it to the men. "Put down your names!" he ordered, "then get lost!"

We complied with his wishes and walked out through the dreaded swinging door into the crisp, cold night air, straight into Mother's arms.

"I came as soon as I got your toilet paper letter," Mother whispered as Elisabeth and I hugged her.

"Mother, there is no way, absolutely no way left to leave this country!" I sobbed.

# 61

The gray morning perfectly matched my mood. It was early when I nursed Lajoska. The children were still asleep when I left them in Mother's care and went with John to explore what was happening at the university.

The streetcars were already in service along the short route between Mother's house and the Technical University, but their yellow carriages passed between dark ruins, leftover barricades and menacing Soviet tanks on practically every corner.

"Just like after the siege," I whispered to John, hanging onto one of the straps in the crowded streetcar.

A man ran after the moving vehicle and jumped onto the stairs, joining the others who had no place inside. Just like before. Would there be no change in our lives?

We passed the nursery schools; first Ilike's, then the street that led to Jancsika's. "I don't want him there anymore!" my heart screamed. My head replied, "You tried and you couldn't leave the country. What do you want?" My mind worked overtime as I saw pictures of frozen babies, sinking parents. I shook my head. I was now back in Budapest and we were on our way to re-establish our lives. Nobody should notice that we even wanted to leave.

When we entered the department, Dr. Benedikt was just giving instructions to the secretary. He turned when he heard John's greeting and gave us a relieved smile.

"Come with me!" he beckoned and led us into the next room. The party-secretary was there with one of the assistants.

"Let's go!" He waved us on.

We were now in his room. He closed the door, looked around to double-check that we were alone then locked it.

"Come on over here!" he called us to the farthest corner of his room. He turned his voice to a whisper. "You know what nonsense people are talking about you?" As we did not answer, he continued. "They said that you tried to escape and were captured." He looked at us and said, "I told them that this was impossible. You just had a little baby. I am so glad that you are here. It isn't true, is it?" Then he went on answering his own question.

"How could it be?" He looked at John, then at me, waiting for us to deny the ridiculous charges. He seemed happy and proud that he had defended us and that he was right.

"Uncle Otto," John started. When they were alone, he was used to addressing him in this familiar way. "It is true. We did try to escape and we were captured. And this is not all. I tell you and you alone, that we would try again if we had the slightest possibility."

Dr. Benedikt looked searchingly into John's face. "It would be worth it? You are really convinced? Again I ask you, is it that bad?"

"Yes, Uncle Otto, it is that bad."

Unexpectedly Dr. Benedikt's eyes filled with tears and he hugged John. "God bless you, son. I hope you can make it."

Contrary to the radio announcements, lectures did not start at the university. As a matter of fact, if more than two young people gathered in any place, a Soviet guard would appear and chase them apart.

As there was nothing else left for me to do and the public transportation was not yet in service to our own home in Óbuda, I returned to Mother's. John continued on his way to show himself at the factory and also at our own home to make sure everybody knew that we were still around; we did not escape.

All day I thought of our meeting with Dr. Benedikt and of John's words. "We would try again if we had the slightest possibility," and those of Dr. Benedikt, "I hope you can make it." Did he know something we didn't? What was in store for us if we stayed? Again "hope against hope" haunted me, and my eyes filled with tears as I nursed Lajoska. "I'm just too tired," I thought, "I must rest a while." But the children kept me busy until John came home at night.

"At the factory nobody noticed that I was gone. They thought I was at the university. The only one who turned as white as the wall when she saw me was Miss Jenny. 'You're here?' she asked. A sixth sense urged me to go to our apartment right away. I am glad I went before Miss Jenny got home. The whole place was in an upheaval. Every piece of furniture was pushed out of its place, drawers pulled out, clothes turned over. Nothing was missing except the bills for the remodeling of the house."

"She took our proof that we put money into her house." Now it was my turn to become pale. "I never thought that she hated us that much, that she would sink that low."

"She still can't throw us out," John stated calmly. "According to the laws, a sublet can be terminated only by the tenant because of the apartment shortage."

I did not answer. I imagined our love nest torn to pieces.

"I am happy that you did not come with me. At least you did not see our home in its present state."

"What are we going to do?"

"We'll go back, clean up the place, and pretend that nothing happened. Maybe she will return the papers."

Hope against hope! I thought again. Yet I knew that we could go back and start over if we had to. Only now I was very tired, and I had no fighting spirit left for Miss Jenny.

Another day passed while we listened to the messages broadcast by Radio Free Europe and to the talk of Mother's customers who streamed to her home now, not so much to buy bags as to exchange the latest news.

This is how I learned that one of my classmates was in jail because they had seen her tear down Communist posters during the revolution. Many people were arrested because their faces were recognized in pictures of the uprising published by the free press. I listened intently to learn anything new about the border conditions, about ways to get near the Promised Land, Austria.

An inconspicuous middle-aged man arrived around noon the next day. He handed an envelope to Mother. She tore open the envelope and screamed, "They have arrived! Where did you get this letter?" "From your daughter, in Vienna."

"You came from there?"

"Yes, I am a chauffeur."

"What does the letter say?" I asked Mother.

Mutely, she handed it to me. I read it aloud. "We have arrived safely. Tell anyone who wants to come that if they get to Sopron they should go to the same people who helped us across. The sooner they get there, the better." The next paragraph hit me in the heart. "Vienna, the free world, is really as beautiful as you have always described it to me. Everything you said is true." My own sister had believed the Communist propaganda she had heard at school, at least to the extent that she would doubt her mother's and my words; what we talked about was out of her experience.

Sopron. This was something new for me to think about. One hundred miles from here. The obstacles started thirty miles from the border. How could we cross those last thirty miles? My mind worked while I took care of the children.

The following day John's parents arrived from Lake Balaton. His mother could hardly conceal her surprise that she found us still in Hungary. "You did not leave?"

When she heard the story of our ordeal, she was happy to see us alive and well. She did not know how to divide her time between the newest arrival and the two older ones, especially Ilike who was now a perfect conversation partner for a loving grandmother.

At dinnertime we all sat around the big dining room table in Grandfather's room along with Uncle Charles. It was almost like old times. As always, politics and the future of the country were discussed.

Marie's letter was, naturally, the greatest event of the day.

"How could we possibly reach Sopron?" I asked the question that had bothered me ever since I read the letter.

"That's a good question!" said Uncle Charles. "Sopron is in border zone '2.' It seems a practical impossibility when in Győr, thirty-three miles from the closest point on the border, people are taken off the train. You could not walk that far."

"Thirty miles, carrying three children… There must be another way," John lamented.

"There is a university in Sopron, isn't there?" Grandfather suddenly interjected. He did not remember recent events but old memories were crystal clear in his mind. "Don't you teach at the university?" he asked John.

"Yes, I teach electrical engineering, but they only have forestry and mining divisions at that university."

"Don't they need a professor of electrical engineering?" Grandfather pursued the issue.

"They do, as a matter of fact," John became pensive.

"Could we go there?" I asked with excitement.

"Let me think; I'll investigate," John said.

My heart started beating faster. Was there another opportunity for us in Grandfather's casual remark?

Balázs and Elisabeth sat side by side. They were preparing for their civil wedding ceremony. They too wanted to leave the country again, but they did not want to take the chance of being separated because, according to the Soviets, there was no such thing as "being engaged." Elisabeth was going to become the third in our family to enter into marriage because of a political situation.

When I married at age sixteen because of the Soviet deportations, Mother had vowed to keep at least Elisabeth a little girl as long as she could. She did not want to lose her baby at an early age. It seemed that Mother simply could not win. The Soviets forced Elisabeth into an early marriage in a different way. Nevertheless, the young couple was excited, happy, and in love.

Uncle Charles worried about her. To him she was like the child he never had. He had taken care of her need for a father ever since she was eleven years old. Now she would belong to that tall, dark, bespectacled, handsome young man at whom she looked with such admiration. Even if Uncle Charles worried, he had to admit that Elisabeth made the right choice. They were a good-looking couple who seemed like a perfect match for each other. Balazs was a civil engineer with a good-paying job.

I had motherly feelings towards my little sister. She was more than five years younger. To me she was always *my* baby. Now she was getting married. What if they were not able to leave after all?

Suddenly, I heard myself ask a question. "What is going to happen to our country?"

John's father answered. "What always happened after Hungary's big revolutions, every time we wanted to get rid of our oppressors. When the uprising was crushed, the nation started working like an ant colony to make up for our vanquished ideals by taking everything from the enemy in material goods, by making the country economically strong."

"For some reason we always hoped that a strong economy would bring freedom with it one way or another," Uncle Charles agreed. "I'm sure we'll pull through even though we have to start rebuilding from ruins once again."

"I wish we could get out of here somehow." Elisabeth took the words out of my mouth. I did not feel like starting to scramble again. Somehow I felt that after twenty-two years, the span of my whole life, I deserved peace of mind and the freedom to bring up my family without all the man-made pressures of different extremisms.

The next few days went fast. We were bathed in the warmth of our parents' love while we poured out the same onto our children who played happily under their grandparents' eyes, not noticing the gnawing doubts in our hearts. Should we leave or stay?

Saturday, Elisabeth's wedding day, finally arrived. We went together to the office of the notary where the ceremony took place. The drabness of the day was only cheered by the happy sound of their "I dos." They knew their love was meant to last for a lifetime even if they had to wait until after the church ceremonies for the consummation of their marriage. According to the Communist state they were now married. The next ceremony would have to be in "secret," as ours had been.

I held her close to me as I kissed goodbye to my "baby" and greeted the emerging young woman. Balázs's glasses sparkled in the sunshine and the expression on his face showed that he felt in highest heaven. They chattered all the way home. When evening came, Balázs left with his parents and Elisabeth helped me with the dishes.

That day nobody talked about escape.

When John returned from the university on Monday, he waved some sheets of paper in his hand.

"Helen, if you are done with Lajoska, would you translate these papers?"

As always in the past couple of days, I was so preoccupied with my thoughts that he had to ask me twice before I understood. I was not thrilled at having to do anything with the Russian language for understandable reasons, but I could never say no to John. As soon as I finished with Lajoska I looked at the papers.

Why did he not yell the news into my ear? How could he keep quiet while I was dragging out the minutes to stay away from those papers? The document looked official. It was an order to go and take over the department of electrical engineering at the Sopron Forestry University, located right at the border of Austria, in the town where Marie had found the guides who might lead us to freedom also.

"How could you? How could you keep so quiet?" I attacked him with my kisses.

"I wanted to surprise you," he calmly smiled.

"Are these real?"

"Not exactly, but just about. You know I have access to all these orders. I made myself one. If it were completely official I would not ask you to translate it into Russian. Then we could get the zone number 2 into our passports which we cannot as it stands now. But to make it sound more feasible, I put in the explanation that because lectures had already begun, we had to leave immediately and that an apartment has been secured for us. Naturally, lectures have not started, but no self-respecting Communist could deny it because the radio affirms it in every newscast."

"True. But what if they inquire?"

"I was told at the university that people in Sopron would understand the situation and would accept us. Apparently they are a nice bunch. But I don't think we need to worry. I have all the official stamps from the department at my disposal. And…what is most important is that Soviet soldiers would be able to read the Russian translation. They tear up documents mostly because they cannot read them and get frustrated by them."

"You're not kidding," I reinforced his statement. "In our grammar book one of the example sentences in Russian says just that. 'The guard looked at their documents and tore them to pieces.' It is common practice."

"That is why I thought of making out the orders in six copies. I'll have one in every pocket. Then if they tear one apart, we can present the next one to a higher official and repeat this procedure until finally someone will read it."

"Excellent, excellent, you think of everything, don't you?"

I started to translate right away and by the next day we had our "official" documents.

"I'll accompany you to the border," John's mother said. "This time I want to make sure you get across. Besides, I couldn't sit around here and wait until I got news. It might take days, especially if the railroad strike goes through."

～

By the evening all my bravery and joy disappeared to give way to doubts and fears. I cried in John's arms. "What if we get caught again? Maybe out in the open, the way the Soviet soldier described it for me? Sit on the ground all night with the children? What if they get sick or crippled for life? What if they die, freeze to death? Oh John, I can't, I don't want to…I'm afraid."

"What are our alternatives?" John asked calmly.

"To go through life without freedom. To think, speak, and do as we are told. To sell our children's souls for their material well being, to make them go to Communist nursery schools, to…I don't know what else…to be at the mercy of the government… Oh, John, I don't know what to do."

"You know that if you don't want to go, I will never force you. But I don't think you could live with yourself if you didn't give it a fair chance."

"I'm such a coward," I sobbed.

"No, you are not." John stroked my hair as he tried to quiet me. "Would you call a soldier brave who would run into the thick of the fighting like a fool and get killed before accomplishing anything because he didn't realize the dangers? Real bravery is when you know exactly what you are up against, you conquer your fears, prepare, and then go ahead and do it."

"It is?" My voice became a bit steadier.

"Helen, listen to me." John pulled up my chin and looked straight into my teary eyes. "Think of the Holy Family and their flight into Egypt. They too had to escape with a little baby. Pray to them when you feel low. If anybody can understand us, they surely can. We'll try it once more. If we are captured again, then it's God's will that we stay."

John's words again triggered that voice inside me. "There is nothing that you and I won't be able to do together."

# 62

The next day Grandpa arrived from Cegléd, just in time to say goodbye to us and to see for the first and maybe last time his little namesake, his great-grandchild, Lajos. His big stature loomed over the baby, and the tiny head got lost in Grandpa's big, callused palm as he stroked the fluffy hair.

Elisabeth and Balázs promised to follow us as soon as they could, probably within twenty-four hours. This time they wanted to try it on their own.

Grandfather, whose idea had helped us find the way to Sopron, said his usual cheery parting words. He did not realize that we were leaving forever.

Our mothers and Uncle Charles were on the verge of kicking us out of the house. They felt that for us the best solution would be to leave.

The only one whose face became clouded was John's father who was seventy-six years old at the time of our departure. He did not think that we would see each other again. John was his only son and the grandchildren were his only descendants. Throughout these last days he had watched them with the hunger of a man who had only a few days left with those who mattered most to him. For a moment he and I were alone in our huge bathroom. I can never forget his sky-blue eyes glowing from above his white beard, tears trickling down his cheeks. "I will never see you again." I loved him very much and hugged him close. I decided then in that curious setting for our expression of love that we would see each other soon if I could arrange it in any way.

~

The station was so crowded that we could not get a place on the morning train. We were sure to be there early for the afternoon one. John's mother boarded the railroad car with us while Ilike and Mother went to shop for a toy. They returned with a doll rattle and a bottle for the doll Ilike would get in Vienna if she behaved properly on the way. Mother also bought us a pocketknife because we realized that we had forgotten to bring some kind of cutting tool with us. Knowing the Hungarian railroad system, especially under the present conditions, it could take us days to travel to the border, a distance of about a hundred miles.

I hugged Mother once more and whispered to her, "Come as soon as you can!" She squeezed my arm in reply.

Just then Ilike chattered in a loud voice, "Grandmother, the last time when we escaped…" The blood froze in me until I heard laughter along the whole railroad car. That convinced me that most passengers had the same intent we had. Even the conductor jokingly exclaimed: "All aboard for Győr, Hegyeshalom…Vienna."

Everyone laughed again out of sheer nervousness, especially because they knew that this train never went all the way to Vienna and because the frightening obstacle, the Iron Curtain, lay between the last two cities he had mentioned.

Mother ran along beside the train. I held her hand for a few steps. Then she blew kisses. As the train gained speed, her figure disappeared in the distance. The last thing I saw of her through my tears was a big white scarf she waved up and down.

We had a knapsack with life's necessities and a suitcase with a change of clothes and a few little treasures.

In Győr, thirty-three miles from the border, the train stopped. We were back in the place where we had been captured in the Red Cross building.

"This time I have a few addresses. One of them is the friend of Uncle Charles. Let's try him first."

Curfew time was near. John, his mother, and I grabbed the hands of the children as we hurried along the curving streets. We arrived in front of an old apartment house. We rang the bell. At the mention of Uncle Charles' name the door opened wide. They had just started their dinner. Food was scarce in Hungary at the time, yet they made a place for the six of us and shared their dinner. We also pulled out our supplies and listened with interest to what they had to say about the border conditions.

Since we had last been there, a whole support system had developed to counteract the constantly strengthening military reinforcements and help the would-be refugees. Railroad men and members of the Hungarian military and police were working together. Most border guards did not shoot at people, only into the air if they had to. Nobody devised the ingenious methods, yet everybody understood somehow what was expected of him or her and simply did it.

In the meantime three children of the family who hosted us, about five years older than ours, distracted Ilike and Jancsika from our talk by helping them clean their shoes. I thought of this as a useless occupation in view of the mud we would have to tread the next day until I overheard their conversation. They were talking about Santa Claus! Suddenly it dawned on me that it was December 5, the day when Hungarian children put their shoes in the windows for good old St. Nicholas to fill them by the morning of the 6th with all kinds of delicacies. Would ours be disappointed? Curfew was on and all the stores closed.

The Saint must have thought even of the refugees. In the morning the shoes were filled to the brim, without our intervention.

We, the parents, had received our presents also; that wonderful couple called all the railroad stations on the way up to Sopron and asked in code language where the Soviets stopped the train. Their gift to us was the most important information we needed for our trip.

As we left their home rested and our hunger satisfied through their kindness, I knew I would never forget what they had done for us, the strangers who came in from the night.

# 63

It was early afternoon again by the time the train pulled out of the railroad station in Győr. This milk run would stop at every second tree, or so we joked as the children settled down for their afternoon nap. We had a small compartment for ourselves this time. Ilike dozed off clutching the doll rattle in her little fist. Jancsika's head rested in his grandmother's lap, while Lajoska stretched and yawned in his basket on the opposite seat.

We couldn't sleep but we did not know what to say either. There was so much on our minds but nothing that we would want overheard. My thoughts ran back and forth between those we had left behind and those we hoped to see.

What would Father be like? I hadn't seen him for so long! I conjured up all the pictures in my mind I could remember. I thought of the many signs of love he had shown through supplying us with everything he could think of. He had even sent us a guide…

Then another train of thought cut into this one. When would I see Mother again? I thought of the Communists' promise. "In ten years we would give you a passport." But why would they keep this promise when they never kept any others?

Would all the "insects" like Mother have to suffer the consequences of the revolution as she had feared?

The train rattled along and stopped every now and then. Time seemed to crawl with the speed of a snail.

Finally the dark-gray clouds broke up only to show the sun on its way down in the western sky. Trees fenced in the horizon. The sky above us was still an angry black, while behind the trees blue firmament underlined the pink sunset that slowly changed into flaming red, giving a strong, shining, golden, red, or pink outline to the scattered black clouds above the trees.

The curtain of darkness finally shut out all the orange in the sky, and the first stars showed on the velvety black background.

Lajoska started to whimper. It was time to nurse him again. I lifted him out of the basket and felt that he was wet.

"Put on the light," I asked John.

He fumbled around for a while; then I heard him mutter, "These lights don't work. No matter which way I turn the switch, they won't go on."

"Let's go to another carriage where we can see," I suggested.

"The children are so well settled, why don't we wait?" John's mother said.

"We have a flashlight." John opened the knapsack and groped around. When he found it he flipped it on. The compartment now resembled our air-raid shelter of Budapest's fifty-one-day siege and the cellar of Judy's house, where we had spent several hours of the revolution when the shooting was near. Our moods matched the dark surrounding. The fear of those days returned. Yet John's mother was right. If the children were calm, nothing else mattered. Darkness made it easier for us to utter our silent prayers.

"Nagycenk!" We heard the conductor's voice. That was the station where, according to our information, the first Soviet guards would ask for our I.D.'s.

We saw nothing in the dark night. The building of the railroad station had a few feeble lights. Slamming of doors, then nothing. After a few minutes we heard sounds, then more sounds, screaming, sobs, pushing. We peeked out the window. A Soviet soldier was pulling a woman off the stairs, "I am going to see my grandchildren!" she shouted in Hungarian.

"No number '2,' no go!" the Soviet soldier explained in the simplest Russian he could conjure up, yet the woman didn't seem to understand.

"Look, look!" she screamed at him holding a photo in her hand. "These are my grandchildren."

"No number '2,' off the train!" he shouted back and the woman gave up.

From everywhere I heard the same sentence. "No number '2,' no go! Off the train!"

Would our papers work?

The slamming of compartment doors came closer and closer.

Finally it was our door. "Help us, Lord!" I couldn't think of anything else. My blood froze as the door opened and there in the rays of a flashlight I saw a Hungarian uniform.

"Good evening! Where are you going, please?"

"To Sopron," John replied.

The young solider sounded startled. "To Sopron?"

John handed him the papers. It was dark. The soldier had to read the document with his flashlight.

He read through it once, then twice. He looked probingly at all of us, separately. He had a twinkle in his eyes. Or was it the flashlight?

He saluted and said to John, "Thank you, professor. What a nice baby!"

He shut the door.

"Were the papers checked here?" Another voice sounded from the corridor. Our soldier's voice was loud and clear! "Yes, I just cleared them."

The train started moving slowly while we sat motionless for a few minutes before allowing ourselves to relax. We passed the moaning, groaning, restless crowd that had been taken off the train by the Soviets.

This time the voice inside me had the same twinkle as the one I had noticed in the soldier's eyes. "There is *something* good about a dark compartment, isn't there?"

John spoke my thoughts. "I suppose the Soviet soldiers did not dare to come into this carriage because of the light failure. Who knows whether we would have escaped this checkpoint if we had moved?"

I thought of the Soviet soldier's tale about refugees who carried knives to kill their captors. No wonder they sent Hungarians into the darkness!

～

"Sopron! This is as far as we go!" I heard the conductor.

"Let's wait a few minutes," John looked out the window. "We are at the end of the train, practically out in the fields. I don't want to go near the railroad station. Why don't we get off on the other side of the tracks and walk straight into the street?"

"Good idea!" said John's mother.

We dressed the children and divided the little luggage we had between us. This part of the railroad station was deserted as we stepped across the tracks to reach the street. We did not know the town at all but we had the address memorized. We did not see any pedestrians; curfew time was close.

In front of the depot we noticed an old man and a young boy chatting beside a donkey cart. We approached them with our question.

"I don't know where that street is." The old man pushed his cap to the top of his head and scratched his forehead.

"Grandfather," the young boy interjected, "that must be one of those streets they just renamed."

"Golly, you're right," the old man said. He turned to John. "Who are you looking for? I have lived in this town all my life. Maybe I know them, and I could get you there even if I don't know the street you want to find."

When we mentioned the name, the old man's wrinkles danced for joy. "He is a good friend of mine. Of course I'll take you there."

As we settled onto the donkey cart with our luggage, I thought of the Holy Family who had escaped on a donkey. Donkey carts were very, very scarce in Hungary. How did this one get here and from where? Why at this hour of the evening? Was this a sign for us?

The donkey's hooves clacked along the ancient streets, on the wobbly cobblestones. Then the cart stopped in front of a lovely old house. We had arrived at the given address. Would they still have their connections at the border? Marie had left on the 26th of November. Today it was the 6th of December, 1956.

# 64

"Helen, John!" somebody yelled from behind the corpulent, middle-aged woman who opened the door for us. Having heard our names, she pulled us in quickly and closed the door behind us.

The person who shouted our names was Éva, a friend of ours whom I definitely did not expect to find here.

"Where have you been?" she asked not knowing whether to cry or laugh. "Your mother sent the three of us after you today. She wanted us to help you carry the children. We want to escape, too. She said that you had left yesterday. We did not see you here when the train arrived and thought that you had been captured again." She threw herself at me and started crying. "What happened? Were you on that train this afternoon? How did you escape the Soviet raid?" Her questions poured forth so quickly I did not know which one to answer first.

I looked around the tiny apartment, one of the many that were conjured up in the lovely old home. We obviously had interrupted a card game but nobody seemed to care.

Éva kept talking while her husband, Illés, and another man were silent.

"We were on the train from Győr this afternoon. When I heard the Soviets coming I hid in the washroom and hoped that they would not find me. They shook the door but I yelled at them that they had already checked my papers and that I was sick. Illés and our friend, Tibor, kept moving through the coaches, always a bit ahead of the patrol. Finally they came to a dark carriage where only Hungarian soldiers dared to go in. They simply said that their papers had already been checked. The Hungarian soldier believed them."

"We traveled in that dark railroad car," John said and told them our adventures.

Lajoska began to whimper. Our hostess hurried to his basket and lifted him up, trying to lull him back to sleep.

"It's all right, I said quickly. "I don't mind if he cries."

"We can't let him cry," she said with fear in her voice. "There are no children living in this apartment house. You know that you should have gone straight to the police to register if you were going to stay here. I am sure you did not do that. If any of our neighbors complain, we would all be found out."

I felt my heart stop. "How can we keep the children that quiet?" I wondered. "I don't know, but we'll have to," she said.

I nursed Lajos which stopped him from making noise. John's mother distracted Ilike and Jancsika while John and the others made plans.

Soon Mr. Viktor, the landlady's husband, came home. He was as tiny and slim as she was big. His bald head reflected the light from the only bulb that hung above the table where the cards were still strewn around as the players had dropped them when we came in.

"I will go tomorrow and investigate," Mr. Viktor said. "The guides are still around who took your sister across, but I would suggest that you walk from here to Fertőrákos. That village lies right beside Lake Fertő. My friends are fishermen on that lake. I don't know if they will want you to walk or if they'll choose to row you across the border. We'll see..." he muttered the last words to himself. "I will walk through the forest and observe which way the tanks are stationed. I have the zone number '2' in my I.D. After all, I do live here." He was only mildly excited about his scouting trip. He had done it quite often in the last month and knew the ins and outs of helping those who trusted him. On the other hand, every one of them brought new problems.

The next day arrived slowly. The one room and big kitchen apartment now housed twelve people instead of the usual two. John and I spent the night on a narrow sofa, sleeping with all our clothes on. When I dozed off I saw the hostess and our friends around the card table, playing with unusual fervor. When I woke up they were already playing again. Scarred nerves made both eating and sleeping difficult. We jumped at every sound.

We were busy all day keeping the children from raising their voices. We made up games and told stories while we turned numb with the fear of the unknown. We prayed silently and watched each other's faces, trying to guess unspoken thoughts. The air became stuffy. Outside the rain poured, I thought of our host who walked through the forest to prepare our way. Whenever the children opened their mouths to cry, we would hold their mouths and noses shut, while slowly letting out the air. When they would begin to turn red we would let go of them so they could take a deep breath. A microsecond later our hands were back on their mouths and noses, slowly letting out the air once more. In the meantime we explained to them very softly what we were doing. They learned to "cry quietly" during the two days we spent with our hosts.

Relief came on the evening of December 7, when just before curfew time, the old gentleman arrived back safely on the bus. Everything was settled. The next day he would lead us to our guides in Fertőrákos.

65

The day crept on. It was December 8, the Feast of the Immaculate Conception. The bells rang every hour to mark the beginning of Mass.

At noon the clouds parted, and the sun shone through them just as the bells started ringing. This was when we slipped out from the house, one couple after another. We did not want to arouse suspicion by leaving together.

This was as far as John's mother accompanied us. She swallowed her tears as she said, "I'll wait for word that you arrived safely in Austria. Our host promised that he would stay at the guide's house until he hears that you had arrived safely. Then I can be sure and I can take the message to everybody at home."

She looked at her only son and his family for the last time.

Tears rolled down her cheeks as she kissed us all good-bye.

The old man was first in line. If he stopped at the corner and wiped his bald head with a handkerchief we knew that everything was clear. If he twirled his cane he signaled danger. We had other code signals for "duck right," "left," etc. Our host stopped now and then and looked back to make sure that everybody was still following.

Ilike walked with Éva and her husband. They looked like a nice family, in search of mushrooms in the forest.

John and I followed with Jancsika walking by our side and Lajoska in the basket. I carried a knapsack with six diapers and medicines. We left our suitcase behind. John's knapsack was empty. That would be Jancsika's traveling place after his little legs grew tired.

The sun was warm as our strong hiking boots slipped around in the mud, the result of two days of pouring rain.

After about a mile and a half Jancsika was ready to take his place in the knapsack. There was fear in his eyes but he did not say anything. He trustingly swallowed the sleeping pills we gave him. The dosage had been discussed with our family doctor. Lajoska had already gotten his share and was sound asleep.

It was extremely important to keep the children quiet. Many sounds or movements could be taken by the guards to be a squirrel, deer, or a bird whooshing through the bushes; but a baby's whimper was a human voice. Where there was a baby, the parents would have to be near.

We walked on for three long hours which seemed like that many days.

Suddenly two men in black leather jackets jumped out from the bushes. We froze. Leather jackets were the symbols for the security police. Were we captured once again?

"Hi," one of the young men addressed us. "Who are you and where are you going?"

I noticed that he was smoking a cigarette.

"Do you need guides to the border?" The other man did not want to waste time.

"No, thank you," John gave a relieved smile. The two were guides waiting for would-be refugees. Apparently they must have done pretty well if they could afford to buy themselves leather jackets.

"Good luck." They waved after us and returned to their vantage point in the underbrush.

The next pair who scared us were our own guides. Both were middle-aged family men, dressed in coarse but well-kept trousers and jackets, characteristic of village tradesmen.

As we cut through the vineyards, Ilike began to cry. We were close enough that I could hear her voice. "My doll rattle; I lost it! Grandmother's present!" My heart twisted because at her words Mother's face appeared in my mind. The picture flashed of Mother's going hand-in-hand with Ilike to buy that little toy. I felt I had to find it for her as much as for myself. I looked hard in the graying evening. We were about twenty feet behind them. As I strained my eyes, I saw the yellow and blue colored tiny ball with the handle half buried by the sand under a vine stalk.

"Here, Ilike, here it is!" I handed it to her. She stopped crying immediately and looked trustingly up into my eyes. "Thank you, Mommy."

Not far from there we saw a house among the vineyards. It belonged to one of our guides. They chose that place for our rest because it was outside the village. Nobody would see us there. We now had walked seven miles.

We entered the house. This would be the last time we would eat and drink on Hungarian soil.

"Make yourselves comfortable." The guide pointed to chairs in his kitchen while his wife in a wide skirt and kerchief busied herself with preparing refreshments for us. Their children looked wide-eyed at ours for a moment or so, then they invited them to sit on the floor and join in their game.

I sat down to nurse Lajoska.

"I am going to the pub," the other guide declared, "to arrange everything with the guards." He left immediately while his partner stayed and explained.

"These guards will go on duty in about an hour. They patrol a certain stretch of the border. We know every inch of it. Naturally, the soldiers cannot tell us where they would or would not be at a certain moment. All they can reveal to us is the time and place of the changing of the guards. At that moment all the guards and also possible supervisors would have to be where the change takes place. From this information we would know exactly the safest place and time for our crossing. They would not be able to return there sooner than fifteen minutes after the changing of the guards took place. There is another important part to their 'duties' once they start dealing with us. Have you heard of the 'no-man's-land'?" Then he went on answering his own question. "Of course you have heard of the soft, raked strip of land between Austria and Hungary. Its purpose is to show footprints. When the border guards find the footprints they have to report it and an obstacle would be constructed there to prevent future escapes on that point. Now, the guards we deal with rake the footprints off the 'no-man's-land.' This makes it possible for us to use the route again and again." He finished with visible satisfaction.

While he was talking the sky became darker as the setting sun disappeared behind the horizon. It was a perfect night for our escape. No moon. Only brilliant, rain-washed stars spangled the cloudless sky. They emitted just enough light to see but not enough to be seen.

"Everything is in order," the guide reported when he came back from the pub. "We have to cross the border on the lakeshore, on that ox trail," he explained, turning to his partner, "between six and six fifteen." It was almost five thirty p.m.

Then he addressed us. "If lighting rockets go up, freeze. You are invisible if you don't move."

I saw Éva's hands tremble. Ilike looked at her, then at me.

"You will get your dolly if you're a good girl all the way to Vienna," I told her again. She nodded her head.

We gave the baby and Jancsi another dose of sleeping pills.

"Let's hurry, we should be on our way if we want to reach that spot in time," our recently returned guard urged.

Lajoska did not want to stop nursing. "Just a few more minutes," I begged, "I am afraid he will cry if I stop now."

Jancsika reluctantly climbed back into the knapsack and John lifted him on his shoulders. Ilike obediently reached for Éva's hand. I finally persuaded Lajos to stop nursing and tucked him quickly into his basket. John grabbed it. I put on my knapsack. We stepped out of the house and looked up at the shining stars.

"Let's hurry," our guide murmured. "We have to make two and a half miles in forty-five minutes. The road is a muddy ox trail."

I grabbed John's hand. We looked at each other. "Let us look back once more," John suggested, "then never again. Our home is where we are together."

We looked back at the dark landscape, eerie in the clear starlight. Ahead of us were the lights of Austria. Would we reach the "Promised Land" tonight?

I shuddered when I looked at the lights. They brought back the memories of our first capture.

As we walked on the muddy trail, I suddenly felt myself slipping. I wanted to pull my leg back but it would not come upwards, only down. Very slowly, inch by inch I slid. I could not stop. What was it? I had never felt like that before. I tried to pull myself up but could not. I felt my coat catch on something. The strong arms of our guide pulled me up to my feet.

"Watch where you are going," John whispered.

"What was it?" I wanted to ask as I looked down and my blood curdled when I saw what had happened. We had walked along the edge of a terrace in a vineyard. One of the stones was missing and I had stepped into the hole. I had started sliding down the twenty-foot retaining wall while underneath vine-stalks pointed at me like a bamboo trap waiting for the enemy or some wild beast. Had I fallen into them I would no longer be alive. The barbed wire fence above the embankment caught my coat as I was sliding and our guards had come to the rescue. The chills ran down my spine, but we had no time to reflect. Every step was an effort in the mud, and we had to run to beat the clock.

Jancsi's drugged head hung limply over the opening of the knapsack. Ilike was still running on her own two feet. Lajoska was whimpering. "Oh no, dear Lord, please, no!" I prayed. I pulled my feet from the mud as fast as I could to catch up with him to see what was wrong, but nobody would stop.

"We have to run; you can check him in Austria," said the guide.

By now we were walking on the shore of Lake Fertő. Another man joined us with two guides. Would-be refugees came from all directions. Our group grew. The man with the two guides was extremely upset because of the whimpering baby. How could he cry despite the six baby sleeping pills? The question haunted me.

I fell. My coat, the one I had worn when I went to Paris in 1948, felt so heavy that I wanted to throw it away. I wanted to be free to run.

Ilike was carried by one man, then another, even by strangers. Lajoska was taken from John by one of the guides. He stopped crying. Maybe the sleeping pills had worked after all. I gathered all my strength.

It was so dark that I lost sight of Ilike, even of John although I knew he could not be very far ahead of me.

I kept looking for John and the children. I kept asking the guide who walked beside me, holding me up, if he knew where they were. We had decided that if any of us were captured, the rest would go back. We were not going to be separated.

To each of my questions he answered, "They are ahead of us!"

"Our home is where we are together." I remembered John's words.

"Do you see those pear trees?" The guide pointed. "Two hundred feet beyond those is the border."

Why did he have to say that? We were so close to the border last time! Would we make it now? I prayed to the Holy Family and suddenly felt their presence.

I remembered what I had said to Mother when they brought us back last time. "There is no way left for us to escape!" We were now trying the impossible again. Indeed we had only "hope against hope." The border seemed so far away and every step was an effort.

Every minute a lighting rocket could break our hiding place of darkness.

I fell again and again.

Then we were beyond the pear trees.

I thought of all that we would leave behind: Mother, Grandfather, Little Grandma, and Grandpa, our friends, our homes, and the country that was our own. It hurt as I cut the umbilical cord between Hungary and me. I remembered Uncle Charles' words. "Where there is no memory, there is no pain."

I felt something soft under my feet. The realization hit me in the chest; "no-man's-land"!

I walked over the mud as quickly as I could.

In the faint light of the stars I saw John's outstretched arms as he waited for me in the darkness, half crying, half laughing. I fell into his embrace and looked up. Through my tears I saw the Austrian flag.

Kiküldetési rendelvénykivonat a Szállodaipari Vállalat részére.    Sorszám: 208941

A kiküldött neve:
A kiküldött állása, beosztása:
A kiküldetés helye:

A küldetés tartama: 195____ hó ____ tól 195____ hó ____ ig.
Útirendelvény kelte: 195____ hó ____ n.

osztályvezető

Bp. Műszaki Egyetem    KIKÜLDETÉSI RENDELVÉNY    Sorszám: 208941
hatóság, hivatal, szervezet megnevezése        szervek és közületek részére.    Rendeletszám:
    Utasítom    dr. Szablya János    -t, hogy 195 6. dec.    hó 5. n
    perctor induló személy (gyors) vonattal (autóbusszal, repülőgéppel) utazzék    Sopron
városba (községbe), majd a kiküldetés céljának megfelelően
        városlakba, községeikbe és működését azonnal (megérkezését követő nap 8 órakor) kezdje meg.
A kiküldetés célja:    Szolgálati hely elfoglalása

A következő tárgyakat vigye magával:

        összesen ____ kg súlyban.
Kiküldetésben    együtt utazik
Kiküldetését 195____ hó ____ n fejezze be és munkahelyén 195____ hó ____ n ____ órakor jelentkezzék.
Egyidejűleg    (    Fű útielőleg felvételét engedélyezem.
A kőliség ____ tércét, ____ vállalatot ____ arányban terheli.
Az igénybevett gépkocsi ____ tulajdonát képezi.
    Budapest    1956. évi ____.    hó 4. n

    P. H.

    _____    Benedek
    vüolú        aláírásvezető

A kiküldetés utasítás szerinti teljesítését, valamint a felszámítás    Kifizetendő: házipénztár MNB ____
közigazgatási (rendelet) szempontjából való helyességet    ____ címen, szla terhére ____    Ft ____ f
igazolom.    azaz ____    Ft ____ f
    Visszafizetendő házipénztár útján
        ____ címen, szla javára ____    Ft ____ f
    azaz ____    Ft ____ f
    Az útiszámlát felülvizsgálta:    Utalványozta:
    _____ 195____ hó ____ n.    195____ hó ____ n.    195____ hó ____ n.

Utazási számlajárandóságom érvényesített, ki-írandó összegét    Feljegyezve:
hiánytalanul felvettem.    Az útiszámla nyilvántartás ____ lap ____ t. a.
    _____ 195____ hó ____ n.    Az útielőleg nyilvántartás ____ lap ____ t. a.
    Szálmajelzőkönyv (könyvelés) ____ old ____ t. a.
    kiküldött aláírása

    Sorsz.: 208941        Sorsz.: 208941
hatóság, hivatal, ki-álló megnevezése        hatóság, hivatal, a szerv megnevezése
    NYUGTA        ÚTIELŐLEG-NYUGTA
____ Ft ____ f, azaz ____        ____ Ft ____ f, azaz ____
    ____ Ft ____ fillérről,        ____ Ft ____ fillérről,
mely összeg, mint fenti sorszámú kiküldetési rendelettel kiállított    mely összeget útielőleg fejében felvettem.
útielőleg, érfütmény        ____ 195____ hó ____ n.
    t. e. bevételezített.    Utalványozom:
    _____ 195____ hó ____ n.        kiadást utalom
    ____ 195____ hó ____ n.
    P. H.
0068—14 r. sz. — Nyomtatványellátó 280        MONSZ 0050-51        Közlekedési Nyomda

BUDAPESTI MŰSZAKI EGYETEM
KÜLÖNLEGES VILLAMOSGÉPEK TANSZÉK
Budapest, XI., Budafoki út 4—6. K.mf. 58.
Telefon: 258-955/481. mellék

Budapest, 1956. december 4.
Ügyintéző:
Számunk: 118/956
Hiv. számunk:
Tárgy:

Megbizom SZABLYA JÁNOS adjunktust, hogy a Soprpni Müszaki Egyetemen az Elektrotechnikai tanszék vezetését, a nyugatra szökött tanszékvezető helyett, vegye át. Lakása uj szolgálati helyén biztositva van. Utasitom, hogy az oktatási munka folyamatosságának biztositása miatt helyét azonnal foglalja el. Egyuttal jelenlegi beosztása alól felmentem.

A Rektor megbizásából:

Benedikt

/ tanszékvezető /

BUDAPESTI MŰSZAKI EGYETEM

Поручаю адъюнкту Янош Сабля что он принимает руководство электротехнической кафедры политехникума Шопрона вместо заведующего кафедрой, который прыгал на запад. Там он получает квартиру. Поручаю его, что он сейчас занимает его место чтобы обеспечивать непрерывность учебной работы.

18787. Dózsa-nyomda. 956 II. 3000. (5)

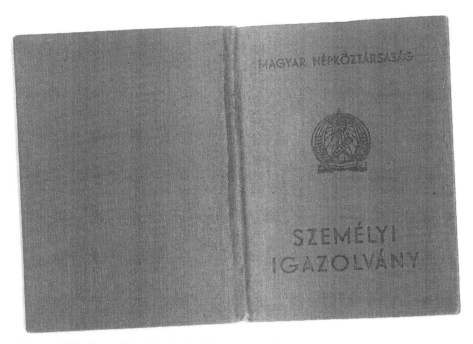

*Personal I.D. front. These IDs had to be carried on the person at all times. If you were seen even in your own yard, or on a beach and you did not have it with you, you would be arrested.*

*The district number where you lived was indicated. Border district was One. Five miles from the border was Two. If you went near the border and did not have the number, you were arrested. If you stayed anywhere over 24 hours, you had to register with the police department, or you were arrested.*

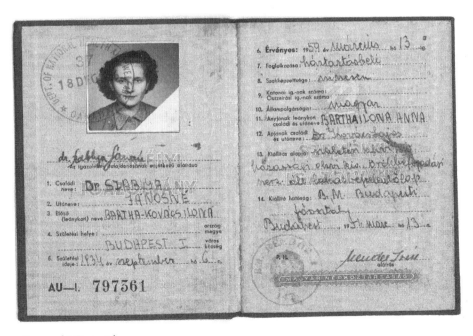

*Personal I.D. inside.*

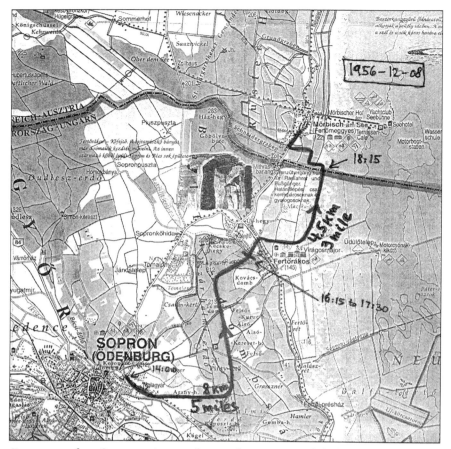

*Escape route from Sopron to Austria, drawn when we revisited the border in 1992.*

*On the Promenade deck of the Empress of Britain, Canadian Pacific ship that brought the Sopron Forestry University and other refugees, along with 500 other immigrants to Canada. This is what our family looked like when we arrived into freedom. In this photo Louis was six weeks old. This photo was taken after an 8 day crossing of the Atlantic in a winter storm. The waves splashed over the 24,000 ton ship, which was five stories high. We started our English-interpreting careers here. We made all 500 refugees' visas during the storm, while everyone but the nursing mothers were seasick. Luckily, I was one of them. 1957.*

**SMALLEST HUNGARIAN** is Louis Szablya, 4-month-old son of faculty couple. Here he naps on serving table ledge during dinner given by Hungarians for Canadians. The dinner included swan-shaped pastries baked by students.

*Louis Szablya, the youngest Hungarian refugee of 1956, in LIFE magazine's article about the Hungarian Forestry University's escape and resettlement in Vancouver B.C. Canada. Issue: May 13, 1957.*

*Elizabeth, Grandfather, and Mother, after we had left the country.*

# Epilogue

What happened to the characters in the story? Where are they today?

Elisabeth and Balázs were married shortly after we left Hungary. They got out of Hungary, via Ethiopia, in 1965 (a story by itself ). They live now in Toronto with their three children, nine grandchildren, and a great-granddaughter.

Marie and Dennis were married in Winnipeg in January 1957, shortly after we got reunited with Father. They also live in Toronto, have two children and five grandchildren.

Shortly after her forty-fifth birthday, Mother and Grandfather received passports and arrived in Winnipeg in August 1959, to be reunited with Father after ten years of separation. She died in 1962 in a fast killing sarcoma and was preceded in death by Grandfather by only a few months.

John's parents received passports in 1960 and arrived in Vancouver in time to celebrate his father's 80th birthday. Both are buried in the city of which they became so fond. He died in 1965, she in 1976, but not before she learned about the birth of her first great-grandchild.

Grandpa died in 1958. After his death, Little Grandma came to visit Father in Winnipeg twice, spending more than a year each time. She visited us in Pullman twice and we visited her in Winnipeg. When she died late in 1979 she had two great-great-grandchildren.

Uncle Charles stayed in Hungary. After his retirement, he was just about to visit Father and us when he died of a heart attack the day he was supposed to pick up his airplane ticket.

Father lived in Winnipeg, surrounded by friends and was going strong. He was one of the very few family doctors left who still made house calls until he was 87. He visited us frequently. He died in 2005 at age 98, the same year my husband died.

Uncle Paul ended up at the university in Winnipeg as professor of international law. He and Father spent their Sundays together, the old friendship was un-shattered until Uncle Paul's death.

Alec and Sophie live in West Germany where he was director of research at one of the world's largest chemical conglomerates. We had much fun together when we visited them in 1974. They are now retired.

Winnipeg became the home of Éva and her husband who had carried little Helen (Ilike) across the border, and of one of our guides who had helped us. My old teachers, the Sisters, had left for Austria in 1949 where some died while others were still alive. We spent three weeks with them after our escape at the Convent of the Sacred Heart in Pressbaum, near Vienna, and again for ten days, with six of our seven children, in 1974.

Elsie, our old governess, still lived in Vienna until her death and took care of the same mentally disabled girl who since then also died.

After our arrival in Vienna in 1956 we got in touch with the Canadian Embassy and joined the Forestry University of Sopron, the same outfit to whom John had issued our fake papers. Dean, faculty, students, secretaries and mechanics, some five hundred in all, crossed into Austria and John and I became their interpreters on the long trip to Vancouver, B.C. We stopped for a few weeks in Winnipeg where Marie's wedding took place. In Vancouver, the University of British Columbia had an opening in John's specialty and by May 1, 1957 he was working as assistant professor of electrical engineering. The Sopron University became associated with the University of British Columbia and all five years of students graduated there. We made many lifelong friends among them and still go to their exquisite Homecoming Balls.

After six and a half years at The University of British Columbia, John was invited to work at Washington State University in Pullman where he was a professor for 19 years. He then retired and joined a consulting company, Ebasco in Bellevue WA, across Lake Washington from Seattle. The University of Washington immediately asked him to teach, so he continued teaching and still had his appointment at age 81, when he died. He was a Fellow of IEEE. He became a member of the Hungarian Academy of Sciences in 2002.

In Vancouver B.C. I started a business, Centennial Agencies. I imported goods the newcomer Hungarians wanted and needed. I graduated in Sales and Marketing Management, which was then brand new. When we moved to Pullman, I decided to slowly get another degree in Foreign Languages and Literatures, as I already spoke, translated and interpreted in six languages. I challenged many of the courses. I got my degree and became a grandmother the same year, in 1976. I was also a freelance writer, journalist, author and columnist with more than 700 articles published, many of them award winners. I was President of the Washington Press Association in 1987-88.

With my daughter-in-law, Marcey, we researched, wrote, and along with son Janos, produced the oral history drama *Hungary Remembered* for the 30th anniversary of the Revolution, in 1986. We won the George Washington (gold) Honor Medal from the Freedoms Foundation at Valley Forge and the Gold Árpád Medal from the Árpád Academy in Cleveland.

John and I chose not to visit Hungary until it became free, but instead to talk and write about freedom and both left and right extremisms. Based on our activities, when Hungary became free we started doing trade consulting (translating ways of thinking) and finally, I became the first Honorary Consul of the Republic of Hungary on the West Coast, and the first woman Hon. Consul in the USA for Hungary. My territory includes Washington, Oregon, and Idaho. 2009 to 2011, I have been the President of the Consular Association of Washington. My books include: *56-os Cserkészcsapat*, *The Fall of the Red Star*, *A vörös csillag lehull* and *Mind Twisters* (translation and editing) besides *Hungary Remembered*, written and produced both in English and in Hungarian.

Five days before my husband's death we received the Hungarian Presidential Order of Merit for both our lives' work.

All our children graduated from university, married and had children. The total count: seven children, sixteen grandchildren and two great-grandchildren.

Helen (Ilike) married Barry Meiners in 1973. Together they received Rockefeller Fellowships at the University of Iowa's Center for New Performing Arts as members of the Iowa Theater Lab. They went on to form their own company, Eclectic Union, through which they created original theater pieces and toured the country. In 1979 they moved to Baltimore to create a play based on 7,000 pages of oral histories through the Baltimore Neighborhood Heritage Project funded by the National Endowment for the Humanities. "Baltimore Voices" became a national model. They divorced in 1989. In 1983 Helen changed professions and has had a successful 30 year career in communications in Maryland and Washington, DC. She was twice named one of the "Top 100 Women of Maryland." In 1994 Helen married Baltimore lawyer Chuck Dann.

Anna, Helen's daughter, my oldest granddaughter married Brazilian Fred Pompermayer Morini in 2006. They have a daughter, Ava Dora, our great-granddaughter. Alex Meiners, Helen's son, married Korean-American Kim Bubar in 2012 with his father, Barry, officiating at the ceremony. They live in Los Angeles, CA.

János (Jancsika) married Marcey Painter in 1977. They divorced after 33 years of marriage. Janos broke into the entertainment industry in Hollywood and has worked in theater, television, radio and film. János has co-produced two Broadway shows; spent a third of his career managing some of the top theaters in the United States; and generating 11 Tony Awards for those with whom he worked. János has joined with Charla Brand in a domestic partnership and together live in the Reno-Tahoe area where he continues to work in the entertainment industry. János has three children: Genevieve, Janos Stacey, and Elizabeth. Janos married Brianna Prentice-Crain in 2009 and gave me a great-grandson, János the 5th who is affectionately called Miles. Genevieve wed Persian Amin Tehrani in New York in 2013.

Louis (Lajoska) became an Electrical Engineer working for Washington Water Power Company (now Avista Utilities) in Spokane, WA. He has worked in the energy field for energy marketers, investment and commercial banks, energy solutions companies, and as a consultant. His current focus is in the Smart Grid and is well published. He married Kathleen Fowles, my faithful helper with this autobiography, in 1978. She graduated with honors in Organizational Communications in 1994. In 2004, she became a licensed physical therapist assistant. They have three grown children: Nadine, who graduated from Johns Hopkins SAIS with high honors in 2010, Steve, who is the Lead Power System Trader for one of the largest electric utilities in the U.S., and Mary, who is an elementary school music teacher and Orff certified, as is her husband, Jeff Gleason whom she married in a beautiful ceremony in Denver, CO in 2012.

Stephen, the first Canadian-born child, is an electrical engineer with an MBA, now Director of Facilities at Seattle University. He is widely published in his field. His wife, Kristy Tenwick Szablya, is the director of admission at a private school that provides special education services. They have two grown children, both graduated, Maria and Adam. The entire family spends most of their spare hours working on sustainable solutions to humanitarian problems worldwide.

Alexandra, Canadian by birth, my first proofreader, married Navaal Ramdin from Trinidad. They became acquainted while we lived there on a sabbatical in 1980-81. Alex graduated in psychology and was a pharmaceutical rep until she decided to stay home with their children, Shivana and Rohan. Navaal was a Boeing engineer until his untimely death of a heart attack at age fifty-two. Alex will finish her master's degree in psychology at Seattle University in 2013.

Rita, the first American-born, also my proofreader, is a Scientist with Pacific Northwest National Laboratories (PNNL), acting as Project Manager in several Asian countries establishing radiation protection systems at international seaports. She married Karl Pool in 1984. Karl is an Analytical Chemist and is a Project Manager for Analytical Services at PNNL. They live in Kennewick, WA. Their daughter, Krystal, graduated in Biology from Carroll College and son, Aaron, graduates in May from Washington State

*John and I surrounded by our seven children, their spouses, and our grandchildren, August, 2004. (In the color version of this photo it is easier to see that families are grouped by color!)*

University (WSU) with a degree in Mathematics. He and Amy Martell, also a senior at WSU (Psychology), will wed in August 2013.

Dominique (Niki) McKay graduated from Seattle University at the age of 20 with a double major. She began her career in the corporate offices of Nordstrom but quickly moved into the world of Events and Production. Niki worked with a team that performed, directed, and produced a Children's Summer Program for 1000s of children. In 2007, she launched Blue Danube Productions and has built it into a successful production company in Seattle, WA, which has won numerous regional and national industry awards. Niki lives with Dave Jungck, a visual artist and digital animator, and her two children, John (18) and Michelle (16).

All in all, I hear the inside voice within me, "See, there is nothing you and I together cannot achieve."

# The History of Hungary in a Nutshell

Hungary is a small country in the middle of Europe whose freedom-loving people have a history of tears and suffering and whose constitution developed in a remarkably similar way to those of the Anglo-Saxons.

The Hungarians arrived at their present country of the Carpathian Basin over a thousand years ago after having lived as nomads for all their previously known existence. They settled the country. A hundred years later they adopted the prevailing form of medieval government and became a kingdom.

Their Golden Carta dates only six years after the Magna Carta, and the two documents contain similar provisions and were preceded by similar events. The two thousand miles which separate Britain and Hungary made it impossible for an exchange of ideas to have taken place between the two countries.

Less than twenty years later (1241), the Hungarians were virtually wiped out by the forces of Genghis Khan; only the latter's death prevented the Tartar army from staying more than two years.

In the next hundred years Hungary rose to splendor. By the middle of the fourteenth century it expanded to hold all the territories between the Baltic and Mediterranean Seas.

Yet glory did not last long; the empire soon collapsed. To protect themselves from the cruel governments that followed, the Hungarians established their two chamber parliament at about the same time as Great Britain.

The greatest tragedy in Hungarian history was the two hundred and fifty-year-long Turkish occupation of the country which began with the wiping out of the Hungarian army in 1526 near the southern city of Mohács.

When the country was finally liberated from the occupation, the Habsburgs of Austria took over the country. Their reign triggered many wars of independence, all of them, unfortunately, without significant results.

The establishment of the United States of America drew many Hungarians to the "land of promise." Many fought in the War of Independence, and many others in the Civil War. Many became well-known citizens. By the 1920s, Cleveland, Ohio, became the second largest Hungarian-speaking city after Budapest, the capital of Hungary. Many prominent Hungarians made the United States their home.

In 1867, the Austro-Hungarian Monarchy was born. After World War I, Hungary lost two-thirds of its territory to its former enemies. Many Hungarians were forced to live under foreign rule.

Then came World War II and Hungary, against her will, was forced into the war. After the war it lost further square miles, but hopes were high that, at last, freedom and peace would come to her battle-scarred soil.

For three years there was a remarkable upsurge, but in 1948 the pressure by the Soviet Union broke that trend, erased all laws that were related to civil rights, and for the next few years Stalinism lashed out.

# *Historical Background*

**1914 – 1918**

**First World War** – Hungary was on the losing side. After World War I Hungary lost two-thirds of her territory in the Peace Treaty of Trianon (June 4, 1920). The northern part of Hungary became part of Czechoslovakia. The eastern parts and Transylvania became Romania. The southern part became part of Yugoslavia. The northeastern part went to Ukraine, which then was part of the Soviet Union. Some parts in the west went to Austria. A few square miles were annexed to Poland and Italy.

**1919**

Hungary had ninety days of communism under the leadership of Béla Kún.

**1920 – 1944**

Governor Horthy ruled instead of the king who was in exile. Up until 1941 there was freedom and democracy in Hungary.

**1933**

**March** – Roosevelt and Hitler became heads of state.

**1938**

The annexation of Austria by Hitler.

The Munich Conference; peace was saved for a while.

**1939**

Hitler occupied Czechoslovakia.

New York World Fair opened in May.

**September 1** – Germany attacked Poland, and World War II broke out.

**1941**

Count Teleki, Prime Minister of Hungary, committed suicide in protest of Hungary's involvement in World War II on Hitler's side.

**June 22** – Germany attacked the Soviet Union. Hungary was forced to enter the war on the side of Hitler. This way the country escaped immediate occupation by the Germans.

**December 7** – Pearl Harbor.

**1942**

**September** – Budapest was bombed by the Soviets.

**November** – Stalingrad.

**1944**

**March 19** – The German Army occupied Hungary.

**June 6** – D-Day.

**October 15** – Hungary tried to get out of the war; the Germans ousted Governor Horthy and his government and established their own puppet government of Szálasy.

**December** – Battle of the Bulge.

**December 24** – Budapest was surrounded by Soviet troops.

**1945**

**December 24 to February 11** – the siege of Budapest. The surrounded German troops had to fight until they all perished. They were left as a sacrifice and under direct orders from Hitler were not allowed to surrender. The promised reinforcements never came.

The capital of one and a half million people lived for those fifty-one days without water, food, electricity, and telephone service while under constant sniping by both sides. The city was saved by a snowfall which served as both food and water and the cold weather prevented the outbreak of major epidemics. The dead and wounded horses were at a premium as they made good food. All the bridges were blown up by the Germans.

**February** – Yalta Conference between Roosevelt, Churchill and Stalin. Decision for UN.

**March 15** – All land, over one hundred acres, was taken from the landowners and distributed among the peasants.

**April 4** – All of Hungary was "liberated" by the Soviet Army.

**July 17 to August 2** – Potsdam Conference between Truman, Stalin, Churchill and then Atlee who succeeded Churchill as Prime Minister.

**August 6** – First atom bomb.

**August 9** – Second atom bomb.

**September 2** – Japan surrendered.

**1945**

**November** – Elections in Hungary. Small Landowners Party received 57.7% of the votes. The Communists had 17%. Nemzeti Parasztpárt was collaborating with the Communists and received 8% of the votes.

**1946**

**March 7** – The Communists forced the Social Democrats and the Nemzeti Parasztpárt into the Leftist Block within the Coalition government and annihilated all opposition.

**August 1** – With the introduction of the forint, the Hungarian inflation was stopped by the government. The new currency, one forint ($ .10) was worth $6 \times 10^{33}$ pengős (the old money).

**1947**

**February 10** – The Paris Peace Treaty was signed consolidating Hungary's occupation by the Soviets. The country became part of the Soviet block.

**August 1** – The Three-Year Plan went into effect. Prime Minister Ferenc Nagy abdicated and left the country. A new government was formed under the leadership of Lajos Dinnyés.

**August 31** – Elections in Hungary. The Communists received only 22% of the popular vote though much cheating was going on all over the country. Good party members were transported by trucks in order to cast their votes with absentee ballots in different cities. Again a Coalition government was formed. Banks and heavy industry were nationalized.

**1948**

**February 13** – A friendship, cooperation and mutual aid pact was signed between the Soviet Union and Hungary.

**March 25** – All factories and businesses with over 100 employees were nationalized.

**June** – The Communist Party officially merged with the Social Democrats in order to enable the Communists to take over power. Most of the Social Democrats were against that merger. The Hungarian Worker's Party was officially formed. This was the name of the Communist Party from then on.

**1950**

**January 1** – The first Five-Year Plan started.

**1951**

**Spring and summer** – Deportations of the "reactionary" elements (insects) of society to the country.

**1953**

**March 5** – Joseph Stalin died.

**July** – Imre Nagy became Prime Minister.

**1955**

    **March** – Imre Nagy ceased being Prime Minister and was ousted from the Communist Party.

    **May 14** – Warsaw Pact between the Soviet block countries was signed as a countermeasure to the NATO Alliance.

    **July 27** – Austrian State Treaty was signed.

**1956**

    **February 14 – 25** – XX Party Congress in the Soviet Union.

    **October 23** – Hungarian Revolution started.

    **October 28** – The UN Security Council discussed the situation in Hungary.

    **October 29** – The Soviet troops started to evacuate and the AVO was dispersed.

    **October 30** – Hungary reached the state of freedom.

    **November 2** – Imre Nagy declared Hungary's neutrality and asked the UN and the four major powers for protection of that neutrality. Hungary withdrew from the Warsaw Pact.

    **November 4** – Soviet troops again attacked Hungary. End of the four days of freedom.

The Honorable Helen M. (Ilona) Szablya is the Honorary Consul General of Hungary for the States of Washington, Oregon, and Idaho based in Seattle.

Born and raised in Budapest, Hungary, she is an award-winning author, columnist, translator, lecturer, and former publisher of Hungary International, a newsletter for Americans about business in Hungary. She has two university degrees, speaks six languages, and lived in five countries under seven different political systems. The number of her English language publications exceeds 700 articles and five books, many of which have won awards,

Helen was President of the Washington Press Association (WPA) and received its highest award, that of the "Communicator of Achievement." The National Federation of Press Women (NFPW) awarded her with a National First Prize for Editorials and the First Affiliate Presidents Award in 1988. Helen was project director and co-author of *Hungary Remembered*, an oral history drama/lecture series – a project commemorating the 30th anniversary of the Hungarian Uprising of 1956 (with a major grant from the Washington Commission for the Humanities). It was featured on world wide wire services in 42 languages. It won two international awards and the George Washington Honor Medal from the Freedoms Foundation. Helen was an "Inquiring Mind" lecturer for the Washington Commission for the Humanities about freedom related topics.

Her book *The Fall of the Red Star* is about an illegal boy scout troop during the 1956 uprising. It won first prizes from the WPA and the NFPW. The book, translated by Helen, was published in Hungarian by Holnap Kiadó under the title *A vörös csillag lehull*, with a grant from the Ministry of National Heritage (Hungary). Both versions were exhibited at the Frankfurt Book Fair, when Hungary was the honored guest.

Helen is listed with Marquis Who's Who in America and several other biographies.

Helen Szablya and her late husband, John, who was Professor Emeritus of Washington State University, Fellow of the Institute of Electrical and Electronics Engineers (IEEE), Registered Professional Engineer in seven states and two Canadian provinces, outside Member of the Hungarian Academy of Sciences, and author of over 140 technical publications, have been living in the Seattle WA area. The couple has presented many hundreds of lectures on Hungary. They coauthored papers in the areas of energy affecting human culture and on translating/interpreting. The Szablya's have seven children, 16 grandchildren and two great-grandchildren. The family was named "Hungarian Family of the Year" by the Hungarian Congress in 1981, in Cleveland, OH.

Five days before John's death the couple received the Order of Merit from the President of the Republic of Hungary for their lives' work, October 2005. In 2011, Helen was awarded the Spirit of Liberty Award from the Ethnic Heritage Council.